The Lesser Terror

Col. General V. S. Abakumov, Minister of State Security, 1946.

THE LESSER TERROR

Soviet State Security, 1939–1953

Michael Parrish

Westport, Connecticut
London

Library of Congress Cataloging-in-Publication Data

Parrish, Michael.
   The lesser terror : Soviet state security, 1939–1953 / Michael
Parrish.
      p. cm.
   Includes bibliographical references and index.
   ISBN 0–275–95113–8 (alk. paper)
   1. Soviet Union—Politics and government—1936–1953. 2. Political
purges—Soviet Union—History.   3. Secret service—Soviet Union—
History.   I. Title.
DK267.P326   1996
947.084′2—dc20   94–38565

British Library Cataloguing in Publication Data is available.

Library of Congress Catalog Card Number: 94–38565
ISBN: 0–275–95113–8

First published in 1996

Praeger Publishers, 88 Post Road West, Westport, CT 06881
An imprint of Greenwood Publishing Group, Inc.

Printed in the United States of America

The paper used in this book complies with the
Permanent Paper Standard issued by the National
Information Standards Organization (Z39.48–1984).

10 9 8 7 6 5 4 3 2 1

Pour Cecile Gul,
Meudon, France, avec mon estime et de tout mon Coeur.
Heureux sont ceux qui la connaissent.

Anyone who studies history and still expects human beings to be rational is truly an optimist.

–Thomas Sowell

It is characteristic of all movements and crusades that the psychopathic element rises to the top.

–Robert Linder

Truth will come to light; murder cannot be hid long.

–Shakespeare, *The Merchant of Venice*

Contents

Photo essay follows chapter 6.

Foreword

Historians will be debating the nature of Stalin's regime for decades to come. Has any state ever wreaked such violence on itself? Human history has seen plenty of conquering empires, and—as people in the Baltic states and Eastern Europe can attest—Stalin's Soviet Union was one of them. But what made his long rule so remarkable and so baffling was that its greatest violence was directed against its own people. There are few instances of such a massive self-inflicted genocide.

The main engine of that genocide was the Soviet secret police. It was born within weeks of the October Revolution, has been through a variety of reorganizations and name-changes over the years, and still exists, in less lethal form, today. It will be a long time before we really know this organization's secrets. However, penetrating its veil became markedly easier with the arrival of Gorbachev's *glasnost* in the late 1980s and in the 1990s with the partial opening of archives and the profusion of memoirs published in Russia and abroad.

Michael Parrish has made good use of this trove of material in writing this book. Working with the far more scanty array of sources then available—mainly such things as announcements of police promotions and retirements appearing in the highly censored Soviet press—Robert Conquest did a similar job of looking at the internal bureaucracy of the terror machine in his *Inside Stalin's Secret Police*. That book concentrated on the NKVD, as the force was then known, at the time of the Great Purge of the late 1930s. In this volume, Parrish carries the genealogy further, tracing the rise and fall of groups and individuals in the police bureaucracy from just before World War II until just after Stalin's death.

Because of the vast amount of blood that was shed during the 1930s, we often think of the next decade as a slightly less repressive time in the Soviet Union—or at least as a time when the country fought, and then recovered from, a terrible war. But this book is a reminder of how the police state continued unabated during those years. Under Stalin's direction, the NKVD shot generals who had lost battles, sped up prisoner executions in areas the Germans were about to capture, and deported whole ethnic groups that had supposedly collaborated, or might collaborate, with the Nazis. Parrish quotes one retired officer who says that the secret police arrested some two million people—enough to form 250 divisions to fight the Germans—during the war years alone. After the war there were further mass arrests of the "Vlasov army" of ex-POWs who had fought with the Germans, more than a million starving Red Army soldiers who were released from German prison camps only to be sent immediately to Soviet ones, participants in imaginary conspiracies in Leningrad and among Kremlin doctors, and, in Stalin's last years, of people whose main crime was to be Jewish. (Anyone whose main crime was to be socialist, in the democratic sense of the word, had already been shot years earlier.)

As Stalin put his stamp on the country, the people who quickly rose to the top of the secret police were those who shared his ruthlessness and measured their accomplishments by the numbers of people arrested, conspiracies discovered, confessions extracted. To fill these quotas, as this volume documents in abundant detail, they eventually turned on each other, finding enough illusory conspiracies to justify the arrest of more than 20,000 members of the secret police itself after Beriia's takeover. Arthur Koestler said it best in *Darkness at Noon*: "Bravo!" The monarchist officer taps in code on his prison cell wall when he learns that a high-ranking Bolshevik has just been thrown in the next cell. "The wolves devour each other."

We will never be able to calculate with complete accuracy how many other people the wolves devoured. It is hard to know even where to begin counting. For example, should we lay the blame for part of the staggering World War II Soviet death toll at Stalin's door because of his obstinate rejection of so many clear warnings of the German attack? This strange blind spot was the flip side of his paranoia about everything else. Even putting aside those deaths, how many other people died as a result of Stalin's orders? A confidential study of such matters was prepared at Khrushchev's orders seven years after Stalin's death—using documents many of which have since been destroyed. The Old Bolshevik and *gulag* veteran Olga Shatunovskaya, a member of the Party commission that did the study, says that between 1935 and the beginning of the war in 1941 more than 19 million people were arrested; seven million of those arrested were executed outright. Recent statements by Russian security officials and by the historian General Dmitri Volkogonov about the death and arrest toll are consistent with the Shatunovskaya's numbers.

Since the NKVD released few prisoners after interrogation, we must assume that almost all of the 12 million people arrested but not shot were sent to the *gulag*. Untold millions, perhaps most of them, died there. If there is still anyone who doubts that huge numbers of prisoners died, I would like him or her to join me for a walk through some of the *gulag* graveyards I have seen, from those in Arctic Kolyma where bones have been bleached white by sun and snow, to that of the great transit camp at Krasnoyarsk where today you can reach down and pick up one dirt-yellowed skull after another, each with a bullet hole through it.

And, beyond these deaths at the height of the terror, we must also count those who perished before 1935—at the hands of the secret police or in the great collectivization famine—plus the many victims of the various secret police operations mentioned in this book, almost all of which took place after 1941. What a waste of human life, and of effort and riches that could have gone into building a country instead into sending people to their deaths and inspiring fear and passivity in the survivors. Russia is still struggling to recover from the Stalin era today, and will be for many years to come.

Adam Hochschild
San Francisco, CA

Preface

Oscar Wilde claimed that there was no greater tragedy in life than having all your wishes come true. This may have been the case with Stalin in 1945, when he stood at the apex of power presiding over an empire extending from the Adriatic and Baltic to the Pacific Ocean. The Great Patriotic War, won primarily by the sacrifice of millions of Soviet people despite Stalin's military and political blunders, had left the country in ruins, but at the same time with an unrealistic sense of power bordering on arrogance which proved to be a contributing factor to the ignominious collapse of the Soviet system 45 years later. The victory of the Great Patriotic War was pyrrhic indeed. At the end of the war, Stalin, who had crushed all his domestic and foreign enemies, was proclaimed, at least in the USSR, the Greatest Leader in the history of the world. Despite this, not all was well with the aging dictator, whose physical decline had only increased his ever-present sense of isolation and paranoia. The fact that Stalin was also haunted by the specter of his own immortality could also be seen by his sparing of the academician L.S. Shtern, the Soviet Union's leading gerontologist, from among the Jewish intellectuals sentenced to death in 1952. The years 1945–1953 are perhaps the least known in the Soviet history.

In 1993, Russia's chief archivist, R.A. Pikhoia, stated "...the Russian historians do not know post-war history. We lived in the epoch, but had no idea of what was really going on. Even specialists in this period did not know much....Beriia is considered the arch villain, and yet after the war, he was neither Minister of State Security nor Minister of Internal Affairs, and in fact the organs of state were ordered to compile compromising material against him...."

The foreign policy during this period was marked by caution outside the Soviet sphere, even withdrawal from the most exposed areas, and oppression in the satellites. As John Lukacs has pointed out, Stalin's real interest was security and not revolution, territory, or ideology. One notable exception to this policy was Stalin's approval, despite his better judgement, of Kim il-sung's proposed blitzkrieg to invade South Korea in April 1950. During the post-war years, despite the Sisyphean problems faced by the Soviet Union, the domestic policy was marked by confusion and inertia. As we are learning now, the pre-war economy, a great deal of it of the Ptomkin Village variety, also failed to recover from the devastations of the war. Meanwhile, Stalin was surrounded by acolytes whose loyalty was only matched by lack of scruples and whose zealous fealty was reinforced by the ever-present fear of arrest. Yet Stalin found pleasure in sowing discord among them, thus spending in intrigues the time and energy which should have gone to tackling the enormous social and economic problems facing the Soviet Union. As early as 1933, O.E. Mandel'shtam, a mere poet, had accurately described Stalin's minions as a "...rabble of thin-necked leaders—fawning half-men for him to play with, they whinny, purr or whine as he prates and points a finger." In pre-Glasnost days, Western social scientists, who in Arthur Laffer's words preferred complicated errors to simple truth, claimed that Stalin ran (mismanaged would be a better characterization) his empire in a collegial mode, similar to the academic departments where the writers toiled. An "embattled" Stalin was portrayed as perhaps an overly stern chairman who had to referee between "radicals" and "moderates" who had their own ideas and agendas. These theories were perhaps also inspired by the fact that academic politics, as the late Charlie Halleck put it, are even more amoral and vicious than those practiced by professional politicians. Unfortunately, under Stalin there was no tenure and the losers would end up in Lubianka dungeons. Under the academic model, Zhadnov was the "auteur" of the "anti-cosmopolitan" campaigns, and Khrushchev the force behind the "Doctors' Plot" rather than mere agents of a policy decided by Stalin. Although this analogy may hold true for the post-Stalin period, it has little relation to reality under Stalin. People with alleged independent power bases, such as Malenkov and Zhukov, would be sent to exile, while others, such as A.A. Kuznetsov, N.I. Voznesenskii and the mighty Abakumov, would be arrested without a hitch and no protest. Glasnost literature and biographies of such men as O.V. Kuussinen (Politburo member 1952–1953, and 1957–1964) should lay to rest the notion that the leading organs of government and Party in the Soviet Union after 1938 were collegial bodies. The true picture that has emerged shows a group of spineless courtiers vying for favors and jockeying for power under a capricious and omnipotent master who never let them forget who the chief capo was, and who reinforced this fact by such acts as sending their wives to the Gulag. The sight of these men trembling before the weakened master in the first week of the war, and even as he lay dying, confirms the essential correctness of Stalin's judgement in choosing his henchmen—nonentities who were nothing more than the extension of his will, trusted to carry out his wishes no matter what the cost. At best, they were no more than scriptwriters in movies produced and directed by Stalin. The historian Iu.S. Aksenov (*Voprosy istorii KPSS*, November 1990) presents evidence that during 1946–1950, the Politburo officially met only 50 times and most of the agenda was taken up with the minutiae of personnel and organizational questions and not with substantive issues. Every meeting of the Politburo in 1949, at the time when the Soviet Union was facing serious domestic and international problems, was dedicated solely to the "Leningrad Affair." Some of the Western diplomats, such as Averell Harriman, and military officials who came into contact with Molotov, Voroshilov, Merkulov, and other high Soviet functionaries had the clear impression that these men were mere courtiers and "jasagers." The requirement for serving in Stalin's inner circle was to be a short nonentity.

Volkogonov is right when he states that . . . for Stalin, the Politburo was nothing more than a convenient assembly which gave legal force to his will. Acting on the age-old concept of dictators, he had liquidated all his comrades who had known his weaknesses and his failings, and in their place he had put new "comrades-in-arms" who owed their promotions to him...and vying with each other to invent some new epithet with which to praise the "Leader." Frequently, during night-long carousals at his dinner table, Stalin would have ideas and make plans which he would share with his fellow drinkers. Next morning, it would only remain for Malenkov to formulate the "wise decision" as an order of the Politburo. Lenin had translated the dictatorship of the proletariat into the dictatorship of the Party, and Stalin went further by making the dictatorship of the Party into that of one man.

It is extraordinary that despite such keen observers as Harriman, as well as the existence of operative intelligence organizations, both Truman and Churchill felt in 1945 that Stalin was constrained and even cornered by the military leadership, the Politburo, and was perhaps no more than a first among equals. The truth, as Malenkov said, is that the Politburo ceased to function in the 1940s. Stalin remained the one who defined all crucial directions of domestic and foreign policy.

There were of course factions and infighting, but this was based mainly on personal rather than ideological or policy differences (comrade did not mean friend, merely colleague) and, except at the very end, was usually orchestrated by Stalin, whose modus operandi, be it in the inner sanctums of the Politburo, in the Battle of Berlin, or in the far away Nagorno-Karabakh, was to divide and conquer. What the inner circle could not afford to forget was not what had happened to those who had opposed Stalin, but to such men as Chubar, Eikhe, Kosarev, Kosior, Postyshev, and Rudzutak, all bonafide Stalinists who nevertheless were sent to the wall. The manner in which Stalin treated Malenkov, Marshal Zhukov and Admiral N.G. Kuznetsov during the post-war years offers an example of how he, and he alone, continued to make the critical decisions about who ruled the Soviet Union and ran the Communist Party. Stalin failed to see through only Khrushchev, whose clownish behavior concealed smoldering resentment, and even more unlikely, a touch of decency.

Medical science may one day explain Stalin's bizarre behavior, which even included dabbling in such arcane subjects as linguistics, where his previous efforts had included ordering the Leningrad philologist D.V. Bubrikh to invent a brand new language for the Karelians. In all fairness, Stalin's amateur writings in this area ring with Gibbonesque lucidity compared to what passes as scholarship in a field supposedly devoted to the study of how man communicates.

As Walter Laqueur has pointed out . . . historians have on the whole been less shocked by foolishness, cruelty, lack of compassion, missed opportunities and various tragedies than sociologists and students of political science, simply because historians have been preoccupied with what actually happened rather than with what should have happened.

The Bolshevik legacy of terror was perfected under Stalin and became the hallmark of his rule, including during the post-war period, while other facets of the revolution were allowed to atrophy. Under Stalin's successors, the legacy became a playground for hacks, "facilitators," and opportunists. As Kafka put it...every revolution evaporates, leaving behind only the slime of a new bureaucracy.

After the war, the population of the Gulag, stable since 1939, was increased by deportees and Axis and returning Soviet POWs. In 1948, Stalin began talking about "new enemies." The Minister of State Security, Abakumov, and Kruglov, the Minister of the Interior, were more than willing to indulge Stalin's paranoid fantasies and came up with proposals to set up special camps. We now know a great deal about the "Great Terror" that played such an important part in the consolidation of Stalin's power, but less about the "lesser terror" used in the following years to maintain the totalitarian system. During the period 1939–1953, terror was just as pervasive as it had been during the previous three years, but it was less publicized, claimed fewer victims among those in the top leadership, and had a larger percentage of victims who were either foreigners or minority nationalities of the USSR.

The chief instrument of terror during the post-war period was the Ministry of State Security (MGB), officially headed by V.S. Abakumov from October 1946. Abakumov correctly gauged Stalin's anti-Semitism and his fear of Bonapartism as the main concerns of the security organs. His stewardship was marked with persecution of the Jews and the military. He was also involved in the power struggles among different Party factions inspired, and at this time led, by Stalin, which culminated in the "Leningrad Affair."

This book is also a biography of Abakumov, the longest-serving of Stalin's secret police chiefs, but in examining his role in the Soviet security apparatus, we need to go back to the pre-war period, when he began his rise in the NKVD, to touch on the various operations that were carried out during his ascendancy; and to examine what role, if any, he played in them. Finally, his downfall and its aftermath, which brought the security organs from the realm of lawlessness to a more controlled instrument of socialist "legality" under Khrushchev and his successors, are considered. This study is not intended to be the definitive history of Soviet state security during the latter part of Stalin's rule but should provide a framework for further research. It is mainly a history of massive crimes committed by the Soviet state during 1939–1953, usually initiated by Stalin and always carried out with his approval and consent. Our view of Stalin as the ultimate monster (Genghis Khan with a telephone, in the apt words of Sir Fitzroy MacLean) must be tempered by the fact that millions made the ultimate sacrifice on the field of battle to keep him and the Soviet system in power. Public opinion polls conducted as recently as 1993 show him to be more popular than the "liberator" M.S. Gorbachev. Besides being a catalog of crimes committed by the Soviet state during 1939–1953, usually against its own citizens, this book is also about victimizers and victims (sometimes the same people), the *dramatis personae* in the nightmare that was the Soviet Union under Stalin. This analysis is definitely not about espionage. Those who still are searching for the fifth (or is it the sixth?) mole or curious about which atomic scientists gave away which secrets to which agent, questions that I find profoundly marginal, will not find the answers here.

I start where Robert Conquest's *Inside Stalin's Secret Police: NKVD Politics 1936–1939* left off and cover some of the same ground for the period after Beriia's appointment. The study makes heavy use of Glasnost publications; Soviet Party documents, particularly those published in *Izvestiia TsK KPSS*, the Central Archives of the Ministry of Defense, the archives of the Military Collegium of the USSR Supreme Court, and the collection of documents edited by N.I. Bugai (Chief, Department on Repressed Ethnic Groups, Russian Ministry for Nationalities and Regional Policy); in *Iosif Stalin-Lavrentiiu Berii: "Ikh Nado Deportirovat"*, the most important source currently available on the deportation and pacification campaigns and the Gulag, and two volumes of NKVD-MVD archives (*Osobaia papka*) published in 1994 by the State Archives of the Russian Federation.

In matters of style—by ignoring its recommendations in toto—I am indebted to the *Guidelines for Bias-Free Writing* (Bloomington, Indiana; 1995), the neo-Stalinist tome on politically correct writing.

The views expressed in this book reflect my own sentiments as a confirmed "Novembrist."

Acknowledgments

My deepest thanks go to Robert Conquest for his support. Conquest's *The Great Terror*, one of the seminal books of the twentieth century, and his other writings, so refreshingly different from what passes as academic history in the United States, which usually are of the "scholar-squirrel" variety, were the inspiration for the present volume. We do have, of course, our disagreements, not over the nature of the Stalinist system, nor on the philosophy of writing history expounded so brilliantly by him in his 1993 Jefferson lecture, but on the nature of America's response to the Soviet phenomenon. Here I feel more comfortable with the views of another astute observer, Robert Nisbit, who sees the American history of the twentieth century as a relentless march, with occasional pauses, toward socialism at home and adventurism abroad. After all, the architects of the Great Society also gave us the Vietnam War. Over the years the Wilsonian urge to intervene, once a liberal orthodoxy, has been taken over like other unsound leftist ideas by many conservatives. Their advocacy of Pax Americana, at times buttressed by Conquest's writings, contradicts their historical roots and former spiritual inclinations.

Terry Reynolds was responsible for assembling and typing the numerous versions of the manuscript. Without her superb work, as well as patience and understanding, the book would not have seen the light of day. I have been most fortunate in having Terry as a colleague and collaborator for over ten years.

Others whose help was essential include Inna Caron, Elena Cherniavskaya, Nilufar Egamberdieva, Kelly Faddis, Irena Goloschokin, Manana Khartishvili, Jay Marmé, Alla Smyslova, Tamara Vishkina, William Wood, Roman and Sonia Zlotin, and Cynthia Mahigian Moorhead, who was responsible for the final formatting. Special thanks goes to Nouné Seghpossian of Erevan, Armenia, whose friendship has been a source of joy and inspiration.

Once again, I would like to express my appreciation to various departments of the Indiana University Library, including Murlin Croucher, the Slavic Subject specialist; Julie Anderson of the Document Delivery Service; Rhonda Stone of the Interlibrary Loan Department; and their assistants. Their help was indispensable. This study was supported by a grant from the Indiana University Office of Research and the University Graduate School.

My deepest appreciation also to S.D. Miakushov of Russia, A.A. Maslov of the Ukraine, and V.I. Gavrilenko of Kazakhstan for sharing their personal archives. Mr. Maslov, a former student of the late academician A.M. Samsonov, is a leading specialist on the losses of the Red Army during the war. The Russian Federation Counterintelligence Service and Mr. D. Mikheev, Vice Council in the Russian Embassy in Washington, were most helpful in providing specific information about the careers of Abakumov and V.M. Bochkov.

Chapter 1

Beriia Takes Over

On December 12, 1938, L.P. Beriia, former First Secretary of the Communist Party of Georgia during 1931–1938, and before that Head of Georgia OGPU and Head and Deputy Head of Transcaucasus OGPU, was *officially* appointed Commissar of NKVD, replacing N.I. Ezhov, who had officially held the position since September 26, 1936 (from January 17, 1937, with the rank of Commissar General of State Security), and who had led the "Great Terror."[1] Ezhov had been officially removed from his position on December 8, 1938. Beriia had first been appointed as Deputy Commissar NKVD in July, as first Deputy Commissar on August 22, and as head of GUGB/NKVD (the Main Administration of the State Security, which in the future would function at times as a separate entity under the rubrics NKGB, MGB, and KGB) on September 29. Despite the official announcement, the latest documents (*Voenno Istoricheskii Zhurnal* [*VIZH*], 2/1993) show that Beriia had been the head of NKVD since November 25, 1938, even before Ezhov was officially removed. The text of the order signed by Stalin and Molotov sanctioning Ezhov's dismissal (*Istoricheskii Arkhiv*, 1/1992) also bears the same date.

There are a number of theories for Beriia's transfer from Georgia to Moscow. Roi Medvedev claims that Kaganovich proposed Beriia as Ezhov's Deputy, and Khrushchev adds in his memoirs that Stalin actually contacted Ezhov about a new assistant and recommended Beriia only after Ezhov could not come up with a name, an explanation which seems rather unlikely. Beriia's assistant, Merkulov, as quoted by Amy Knight, claimed that Beriia was surprised and disappointed at his appointment as Ezhov's Deputy, an opinion seconded by Khrushchev, but Beriia certainly had the credentials for his new position. He had served as head of Georgia OGPU and Deputy Head Transcaucasus OGPU (December 1926–March 1931) and head of the entire Transcaucasus OGPU (March 1931–November 1931) before being appointed as the First Party Secretary in Georgia.

Robert Conquest, in *Inside Stalin's Secret Police*, argues that Beriia's first appointment as the Deputy Commissar of NKVD was not necessarily a blow to

Ezhov, but an attempt by Stalin to weigh his options and decide on which satrap would be more useful to carry out his agenda. Stalin was to repeat the same pattern in 1952–1953 even when operating with diminished mental powers. He used both S.D. Igant'ev, the secret police chief, and one of his deputies, M.D. Riumin, but at the time he worked with Riumin alone, thus undermining Igant'ev's authority. This, in fact, may have inadvertently saved Igant'ev's neck after the dictator's death.

In his heyday, criticism of Ezhov was tantamount to suicide, as was discovered by a few brave souls. On June 25, 1937, three days after the opening of a Central Committee meeting, G.N. Kaminskii, Commissar of Public Health, spoke against the terror. A committed Stalinist who had certified that V.V. Kuibyshev and G.K. Ordzhonikidze (a personal friend) had died of natural causes, he apparently had come to the conclusion that the terror had gone too far. According to his surviving daughter, S.G. Kaminskaia (reported in the collection *Oni ne molchali*), he was supported by 12 to 15 people, including I.A. Piatintskii (shot October 30, 1939), M.S. Chudov (shot 1937), M.M. Khataevich (shot February 23, 1939), B.P. Sheboldaev (shot December 16, 1937), and P.P. Liubchenko (suicide with his wife August 29, 1937). Stalin's reaction was swift. He not only defended the terror, but accused Kaminskii of being a counterrevolutionary. Kaminskii was arrested on the same day by M.P. Frinovskii, but was not officially replaced in his post until August 2, 1937, by N.F. Boldyrev, who lasted until September 8, 1939. On February 9, 1938, Kaminskii faced the Military Collegium, whose members included V.V. Ul'rikh, D.Ia. Kandybin, and Zarianov, and was accused of being a part of an "anti-Soviet, diversionary-terrorist, rightist" organization, condemned to death, and shot a day later at age 42. He was rehabilitated on March 2, 1955. In the July 1953 meeting of the Central Committee, Khrushchev tried to blame Beriia for Kaminskii's repression, and this gave rise to another myth, that Kaminskii spoke against Beriia in the February 1939 meeting of the Central Committee, when, in fact, he had been dead for a year (the date February 9, 1939, given in *Who Was Who in the Soviet Union* is a year off).

It is true that as the First Party Secretary in Azerbaidzhan in 1920, Kaminskii and his friend Ordzhonikidze had had run-ins with M.D.A. Bagirov, head of Azerbaidzhan Cheka, and his deputy (at that time, Beriia) that resulted in the latter's arrest as a suspected Mussavat spy. In this power struggle, Stalin backed Bagirov and Beriia and Kaminskii left Caucasus in 1922. At the 16 Party Congress, Kaminskii personally accused Beriia of having driven A.A. Khandzhian, First Secretary of the Armenian Party, to suicide as well as causing the untimely death of S. Lakoba, the head of the Abkhaz government. Obviously there was no love lost between Kaminskii and Beriia, but it was Stalin who decided the fate of Kaminskii, who was shot six months before Beriia's appointment as Deputy Commissar NKVD. On July 7, 1937, Ezhov personally arrested I.(OSIP)A. Piatintskii (Tarshis), one of those who had supported Kaminskii. Despite 220 hours of interrogation by the investigator A.I. Langfang (survivor of Ezhov years, Lt. General, 1945), Piatintskii refused to confess. His letter to the Politburo on February 23, 1938, published in the collection *Oni ne Molchali*, shows a man of courage who has trouble understanding why he has ended up in prison. Piatintskii survived Ezhov, and even though he had been right about the terror, he was shot in October 1939 under Beriia at the time when Ezhov was also under arrest. Piatintskii had once said that he only served the working class and not personalities—a statement that was certainly grounds for arrest under Stalin. Piatintskii's wife, who tried to save her husband, was also arrested in 1938. Their son, I.I. Piatintskii, had already been under arrest since 1937.

On April 8, 1938 (other dates given include April 9, 1938 and even as late as September 21, 1938), Ezhov received the additional title of Commissar of Water Transport in addition to the NKVD portfolio and was also practically in charge of GRU. Whether this new appointment to a not-insignificant position was actually a demotion is debatable. Most likely this was part of Stalin's Machiavellian machinations. In his new job, Ezhov was faced with two Deputy Commissars who were not his men. Z.A. Shashkov had been a Deputy Commissar of Water Transport since February 20, 1938. On August 25, 1938, he was joined by Regiment Commissar S.P. Ignat'ev, a graduate of Lenin Military Political Academy. The two men would be watching Ezhov. The fact that they both survived and prospered is a clear indication that their loyalties were elsewhere.

In October, Igant'ev was also appointed as chief political officer and Deputy Commissar of the Navy, now headed by Ezhov's former First Deputy, Frinovskii. For his efforts in March 1939, Igant'ev would be elected as a candidate member to the Central Committee. On April 4, 1939, probably after Ezhov's arrest, Shashkov was promoted to Commissar of River Transport, although he had to wait until 1952 to make it to the Central Committee.

A minor mystery in Ezhov's downfall was that on May 29, 1938, he also received an additional appointment as the acting head of the GRU, whose previous leader, Ia.K. Berzin, had been arrested on November 28, 1937. Ezhov's appointment to this position, which also involved foreign intelligence, adds weight to Conquest's argument that Stalin was still not committed to Ezhov's complete removal from the scene. On the other hand, it is also plausible that Stalin also wanted Ezhov engaged and guessing before the final blow. Regardless, Ezhov was not officially removed from the GRU until the end of 1938.

Ezhov tried to counter the threat to his position by organizing a pathetically fabricated assassination attempt on his own life, helped by Commissar of State Security 3 Rank N.G. Nikolaev-Zhurid, head of GUGB/NKVD counterintelligence. Ezhov also came up with the trial balloon of renaming Moscow "Stalinodar," but his brilliant suggestion was vetoed by Stalin. On October 4, 1938, Ezhov was forced to accept as Deputy Commissar (for economics) G.V. Filaretov, joining Beriia. The role played by Filaretov (who was later purged) in Ezhov's fall is not clear. Overall, 1938 was a bad year for the "Iron Commissar." His decline and fall also led his wife, E.S. Gladun-Khaiutin, a former actress from Odessa, to commit suicide. After Ezhov's arrest, his adopted daughter, born in 1931, was sent to a special orphanage and eventually was exiled in Magadan. She and Iagoda's son may have survived Stalin. Ezhov's daughter later changed her name and may very well still be living. By the summer of 1938 even the ultra-Stalinists such as A.A. Zhdanov and A.A. Andreev, who had been important cogs in the terror campaign, were alarmed about the rampant chaos in the country caused by repressions, and by late summer and early fall they were joined by L.M. Kaganovich and A.I. Mikoian, two other Stalinist stalwarts.

The arrest of Corps Commissar I.P. Petukhov, once Voroshilov's secretary, on July 4, 1938, could not have made the latter well disposed toward Ezhov, who was creating other powerful enemies on all fronts.

V.D. Uspenskii in *Tainyi Sovetnik Vozhdia* relates how in 1937 the NKVD in Rostov, under V.P. Grigor'ev,arrested the Party leadership in Veshenskii raion (the bailiwick of writer M.A. Sholokhov), including the Party Secretary, L.K. Lugovoi, and prepared a case against Sholokhov, who immediately went to Moscow and contacted Stalin. The result was a meeting of the Politburo in which the two sides confronted each other. The performance of the NKVD officials, L.I. Kogan and P.M. Shchevalev, who tried to blame Grigor'ev was not satisfactory. Ezhov did not help matters when he admitted that he was ignorant of what had happened. He admitted that a mistake had been made and called Sholokhov a friend, but the damage had already been done. Ezhov's cause was also not helped by the August 1938 defection of G.S. Liushkov, head of NKVD in the Far East, to the Japanese, followed by the suicide of I.I. Il'itskii, another close colleague, and by Ezhov's alleged rudeness to Molotov. Despite gathering clouds, Ezhov was at the grandstands on Red Square with Stalin and other functionaries at the May Day celebrations in 1938.

The first crack to appear in Ezhov's armor was the appointment of Beriia as the Deputy Commissar of NKVD in July 1938, probably without Ezhov's consent. By late October, Stalin had apparently decided that Ezhov was a liability when he arranged for a Central Committee Communist Party of the Soviet Union (CC CPSU) Committee made up of Molotov, Beriia, Vyshinskii, and Malenkov to investigate NKVD. There are also claims (by B.A. Starkov) that this committee was headed by L.Z. Mekhlis, another man who had closely worked with Ezhov. In the fall of 1938, five resolutions were passed by the Central Committee on the structure operations and investigative procedures of NKVD (dated from September 13 and 23, October 14, November 17, and December 1). They were all aimed at Ezhov, as were two other related resolutions dating from November 17 and December 8, one suggesting ground rules for arrest and investigation, the other about recruiting "honest" people to do Chekist work. Sudoplatov claims that when Beriia first came on board, Stalin ordered that all of Ezhov's directives also be countersigned by Beriia.

There was another ominous event when on October 25, 1938, Beriia ordered the arrest of the wife of M.I. Kalinin, the head of the Soviet state, an act that must have been sanctioned by Stalin, who was thus signaling to his satraps that a new man was about to take over the machinery of terror. The text of a telegram signed by Stalin and Molotov, dated November 17, 1938 (*Istoricheskii arkhiv*, 1/1992), and sent to NKVD and prosecutorial officials as well as Party leaders, in which the Party and the government tried to dissociate themselves from the Great Terror, shows clearly that Ezhov was about to get the same treatment that had been previously meted out to Iagoda.

On August 18, 1938, when Stalin and his high command gathered for the air show at Tushino, it was Beriia, and not Ezhov, who was part of the inner circle, the latter conspicuous by his absence. There is also a secondhand report by the Bulgarian prisoner Blagoi Popov that Ezhov met in October with Molotov, Beriia, Mikoian, and Tevosian (Deputy Commissar of Heavy Industry); in the meeting he presented evidence and confessions implicating Tevosian in subversive activities. Despite Ezhov's persuasive arguments, he could not make the charges stick and Tevosian was not arrested. By mid-November Beriia, who had begun to assume full responsibility by September-October, was in the driver's seat.[2]

B.A. Starkov suggests that Stalin had originally proposed Malenkov as the candidate to replace Ezhov, but the majority of the Politburo preferred Beriia. Even if such a meeting took place, it could have been only a charade. The "search and screen" process used in the West to hire kindred and politically correct spirits and exclude those who might rock the boat in moribund organizations was not a stratagem favored by Stalin (although at times, he would go through the motions), who was not about to be outvoted by his hand-picked toadies in a matter as critical as the head of NKVD. Stalin could not have come up with a better candidate had he access to a headhunting firm. Beriia was Stalin's candidate to replace Ezhov.[3]

Another account of events given by A.G. Malenkov, son of G.M. Malenkov, first in an article (*Zhurnalist*, February 1991) and later expanded into a short biography, claims that his father began to feel uneasy about the purge in 1937 and in May of that year counseled patience in the Moscow city Party conference. For this he was criticized by the local secretary, Khrushchev, who allegedly owed his position to Ezhov and, in fact, it took Stalin's intervention to prevent Malenkov from being arrested. This, of course, did not keep him from launching purge campaigns in Belorussia, Armenia, Iaroslavl, Tula, Kazan, Saratov, Omsk, and Tambov which claimed many lives and careers. In the Central Committee meeting in January 14, 1938, Malenkov spoke about mistakes made in expelling Party members and measures that had to be taken for their readmission. Malenkov also began to realizethat although Ezhov enjoyed Stalin's complete trust, perhaps the dictator was beginning to feel uneasy about the extent of Ezhov's power and even potential threat. A more likely explanation would be that Stalin orchestrated the whole affair and was the actual author of Malenkov's report. According to A.G. Malenkov, his father risked everything in August 1938 by writing to Stalin through Poskrebyshev (an ally of Ezhov) that NKVD was exterminating thousands of loyal Communists. Stalin then met with Malenkov, who repeated his charges. Stalin wrote, "I agree," on Malenkov's letter and forwarded it to members of the Politburo. Stalin then asked Malenkov whether he had a candidate for the position of the NKVD First Deputy Commissar, and Malenkov in turn consulted one V.A. Donskii, who recommended Beriia. Stalin, however, asked for additional names, and six more were submitted. Stalin chose Beriia.[4] The relationship between Beriia and Malenkov, who on occasion walked arm-in-arm, is always interesting with the two public servants using, but never quite trusting, each other, a perfect example of the bureaucratic state at work. The latest version of Ezhov's fall comes from P.A. Sudoplatov, who in his memoirs,

published in 1994, claims that according to Beriia associates S.S. Mamulov and
B.A. Liudvigov, with whom he was imprisoned, Beriia was involved in a conspiracy
to remove Ezhov by having the NKVD heads in Iarosval and Kazakhstan write to
Stalin in October 1938 that Ezhov planned to arrest the Soviet leadership on the eve
of the November celebration of the Revolution.

On September 23, 1938, Ezhov wrote a pathetic letter to the Politburo and Stalin
(*Istoricheskii Arkhiv*, 1/1992) in which he defended his record but also admitted to
some mistakes such as Liushkov's defection and the temporary disappearance of
A.I. Uspenskii, head of NKVD in Ukraine. At the same time, Ezhov swore eternal
allegiance to the Central Committee and Comrade Stalin. In February 1939, after
he had been replaced by Beriia, Ezhov, now desperate, wrote to Stalin again through
the doorkeeper Poskrebyshev accusing Malenkov of being an "enemy of the people."
This was followed by a meeting of the Politburo in which Stalin sent both men to
another room so they could await his decision. When Ezhov left the room, he was
arrested by Beriia. The last time that the "Iron Commissar" was seen in public with
other dignitaries was on January 21, 1939, when he was sitting next to Stalin during
the memorial meeting of the fifteenth anniversary of Lenin's death. At the 18 Party
Congress held during March 10–21, 1939, Ezhov was not listed as a delegate, a
most extraordinary thing for an alternate member of the Politburo. It is most likely
that Ezhov was arrested on the same date as his First Deputy M.P. Frinovskii (April
6, 1939) although other dates such as April 4, April 10, or even as late as June 10,
1939, have also been suggested. Sudoplatov claims that Ezhov was arrested in
March 1939 in Malenkov's office. Even today, the last year of Ezhov's life remains
a mystery and there is disagreement about the exact date of his execution. There are
claims, including one by his fellow prisoner, microbiologist P.F. Dorovskii, that he
was kept in the Sukhanov prison, at times a private preserve of Beriia. A.K. Sul'ianov
in *Arestovat' v Kremle* writes about Ezhov after his arrest and claims that he was
severely tortured and confessed to everything but cites no sources. Roi Medvedev
in *Let History Judge* states that according to Shabalkin, an old Bolshevik and Party
official in the Far East who survived the Gulag, Ezhov told fellow prisoner D.A.
Bulatov that he had planned to seize power and get rid of Stalin. Sudoplatov, who
incorrectly lists 1941 as the date of Ezhov's death, states that Ezhov was personally
interrogated by Beriia and B.Z. Kobulov, and Ezhov went to execution singing the
Internationale. In all probability, Ezhov was put to death on February 2 or 3, 1940
(although dates as late as April 1, 1940, and even 1941 are also given), after a
perfunctory appearance before the Military Collegium with Uk'rikh pronouncing
the sentence on his former collaborator. The charge against Ezhov was supposedly
"groundless repression of the Soviet people."

Ezhov's fate, however, had already been decided. In the indictment filed early
in 1940 against the writer I.E. Babel' (*Literaturnaia Gazeta*, No. 18, 1988), under
arrest since May 16, 1939, one of the charges was his involvement in anti-Soviet
activities with E.S. Gladun-Khaiutin, wife of the "enemy of the people" Ezhov. In
Ezhov's safe, incriminating material was found about members of the Politburo,
even allegations about Stalin's involvement with the Tsarist secret police. The

problem with the junior Malenkov's story is that other sources agree that Beriia's appointment as the First Deputy Commissar was made in July 1938, a month before the senior Malenkov allegedly wrote his letter. Also, it seems doubtful that Stalin would appoint Beriia on the advice of a nonentity such as Donskii. The fact is that Stalin had known Beriia intimately at least since 1930 and was familiar with the man's flawed past. With his record of unparalleled opportunism, complete lack of moral scruples, and hidden secrets, Beriia had the perfect resumé for the new police chief.

In *Moi Otets*, his rambling apologia for his father, S.L. Beriia is usually reticent about the circumstances which led Stalin to appoint Beriia as Head of the NKVD, but nevertheless he claims that his father did not want the job, despite his background, and twice turned down the Politburo's (Stalin's) offer preferring economic work to police work. He further adds that in February 1941, when NKVD was divided into NKVD and NKGB, Beriia unsuccessfully proposed to Stalin that his Deputy, S.N. Kruglov, be appointed Head of the former, a change that was finally made in January 1946. In view of Beriia's penchant for empire-building and power-grabbing, such claims should be treated with healthy skepticism.

Stalin's greatest asset was his uncanny ability to pick for high office men who did not dream of treason, a dictator's nightmare. Few would have a man's wife killed, as Stalin did Poskrebyshev's, and continue to have him as the closest confidant. There would never be a Brutus in Stalin's court. Stalin was also aware of bad blood between Ezhov and Beriia. In July 1938 or perhaps even earlier, Ezhov had ordered S.A. Goglidze, head of NKVD in Transcaucasus, to arrest Beriia. Goglidze, one of the few top-ranking members of the Iagoda regime to survive into the Ezhov era, took a major risk by informing the fellow Georgian and thus guaranteeing his eternal gratitude and friendship. Beriia then contacted Stalin, and perhaps with assistance from Kaganovich, who also was beginning to feel ill at ease with Ezhov, persuaded Stalin to countermand the order. Iu.B. Borev, however, claims in *Staliniada*, that it was Malenkov who warned Beriia of imminent arrest and arranged for him to come to Moscow and meet Stalin, who then countermanded Ezhov's order. Beriia's son states that Ezhov tried but failed, despite torture, to force Kudriatsev, the Second Secretary of the Party in Georgia, to testify that Beriia was a Trotskist. Ezhov's intrigues against Beriia are also touched upon in books by Suren Gazarian and M. V. Rosliakov and the article by G. Bezirgani (*Kommunist Gruzii*, 11/1990). Rostliakov's account is based on testimony of NKVD investigator A.A. Rusetskii, who survived. Rusetskii, however, dates Ezhov's attempts to compromise Beriia somewhat earlier to the spring of 1938. During his interrogation on August 7, 1953, Goglidze contradicted this by claiming that Ezhov and Beriia always enjoyed cordial relations, and, in fact, Ezhov reminded him to strengthen Beriia's personal security. Goglidze, under arrest, however, had every reason not to pose as Beriia's savior and, in fact, ended up denouncing the former master during their trial.[5] Dr. Johnson, who was right, as always, observed that nothing concentrates the mind more wonderfully than the prospect of hanging. Had Goglidze carried out Ezhov's order, history would have looked at Beriia as another honest revolutionary who fell victim to Stalinist repression.

Beriia's troubles with the organs went back to November 1922, when M.S. Kedrov, GPU representative to Azerbaidzhan, ordered Beriia arrested, who at that time was deputy head of the local GPU as well as the Secret Political Department. Beriia was finally released by the order of S.M. Kirov, then commissar of the Independent 11 Army, but he remembered Kedrov's part. According to Beriia's son, S.F. Redens, Beriia's predecessor as head of the Georgia GPU and Stalin's brother-in-law, also intended to prosecute Beriia, who was, however, saved by the intervention of Ordzhonikidze. The dissolute Redens was shot in 1941, probably, when Beriia settled the score. One of the most important documents in regard to Beriia's arrest was the testimony of N.F. Safronov dating from August 17, 1953, and published in 1992 in *Geroi i Antigeroi Otechestva.* Safronov, in 1920 attached to the prosecutor's office in Azerbaidzhan, testified about the way documents incriminating Beriia were destroyed and about the role played by M.P. Frinovskii, at that time head of the local Cheka. In response to Safronov's inquiry, Frinovskii sarcastically told him that Beriia's file had been sent to the Museum of Revolution. The fact that Frinovskii ended up being Ezhov's closest associate also is proof that the latter was also aware of Beriia's checkered past.

The period of transition from Ezhov to Beriia did not, however, mean a respite in terror. In Belorussia, for instance, the NKVD Head, the soon-to-be-purged A.A. Nasedkin, was carrying out mass atrocities. In one day (November 21, 1938), at the very end of Ezhov's reign, NKVD shot 292 senior government and Party officials, including 26 People's Commissars and Deputy Commissars. These included E.I. Kviring and V.I.Mezhlauk of the Gosplan; M.L. Rukhimovich (defense industry); R.I. Eikhe, M.I. Kalmanovich, and N.N. Demchenko (all in agriculture); M.I. Pakhomov (water transport); I.E. Liubimov (light industry); A.V. Bakulin (transport); I.A. Khalepskii (communications); and A.D. Bruskin (machine construction).[6] On August 3, 1938, B.S. Stomoniakov, Deputy Commissar of Foreign Affairs, was arrested. (He was put to death or died in camp in 1941.)[7] It is difficult to know whether to credit these crimes to the outgoing Ezhov or the incoming Beriia. In November 1938, Beriia was involved in the torture of Marshal V.K. Bliukher and shortly after personally arrested A.V. Kosarev, the disgraced head of the Komsomols who had once mocked him.[8] According to Soviet documents (*VIZH*, 2/1993), Beriia arranged that Bliukher, arrested on October 22, 1938, was put in the same cell as the Commissar of State Security 3 Rank, D.M. Dmitriev. A veteran provocateur whose career went back to the early 1930s and the "Menshevik" case and later the "investigation" of Kirov's murder, Dmitriev had been appointed head of NKVD in Sverdlovsk on July 15, 1936, and on May 22, 1938, head of the NKVD highway department. He had been arrested on June 28, 1938. Despite doing his job as provocateur, Dmitriev was shot on March 7, 1939. Accounts in 1956–1957 of Captain of State Security P.A. Zimin, head of Lefortovo prison; his deputy, Iu.I. Khar'kovets; Rozenblium, head of the medical services; and others indicate that Beriia, B.Z. Kobulov, and B.V. Rodos were present at the interrogations and Bliukher, who was accused of espionage and selling out in the Far East, was savagely tortured and finally died during interrogation on November 9, 1938. According to the 1963 testimony of former NKVD official V.Ia. Golovlev, Beriia called Stalin, who ordered him to the Kremlin. After returning, he relayed to Merkulov, Golovlev, Captain of State Security A.N. Mironov, and investigator V.V. Ivanov (a future Major General) Stalin's order that Bliukher's remains be taken to Butyrsk Prison and cremated.

Beriia also continued the policy of repressing the families of the victims. In the case of Bliukher, his wife was shot. His brother, Air Force Captain P.K. Bliukher, was sent to camps, where he perished in 1943. The Marshal's young son, V.V. Bliukher, somehow survived, to become a General in his own right in the 1980s. In December 1939, A.M. Larina (Bukharin's young widow) was transferred from the Astrakhan prison to NKVD's Lubianka prison and was summoned to the office of the Commissar of NKVD expecting to see Ezhov and finding instead Beriia and B.Z.Kobulov. Larina had met Beriia twice before, first in August 1928 during a visit with her father to Georgia. Beriia was obviously smitten with the pubescent beauty of Larina, at that time 15 years old. During her interrogation, Beriia was conciliatory, although she tried his patience with her defiant attitude, Despite a busy schedule, Beriia continued to supervise some interrogations including that of Mirzoian Party Secretary in the Kazakh SSR and M.P. Shreider, head of the militia.

The overwhelming majority of members and candidate members of the Central Committee elected in the 17 Party Congress held in February 1934 had been arrested and shot during the Ezhov years, but a number who had survived inside or outside prison were executed after Beriia took over. These included P.A. Alekseev, E.G. Evdokimov (1940), A.V. Kosarev (February 23, 1939), S.V. Kosior (February 29, 1939), L.I. Mirzoian (February, 1939), P.P. Postyshev (February 26, 1939), V.Ia. Chubar (February 26, 1939), A.I. Egorov (1939), M.M. Kul'kov (February 27, 1939), B.P. Pozern (February 25, 1939), P.I. Smorodin (February 25, 1939), A.I. Ugarov (1939), and N.A. Filatov. G.Ia. Sokol'nikov (Brilliant) was murdered in prison (May 21, 1939), M.M. Kaganovich was forced to commit suicide (February 1941), and S.A. Lozovskii was shot during the post-war years (August 1952).[9] Purged government and Party officials were not alone in their suffering under Beriia. The brilliant poet B.K. Lishitz was put to death on May 15, 1939—a fate he shared with another distinguished poet and translator, V.O. Stenich.

Unlike earlier victims, these men did not become part of the Stalinist demonology, but simply became non-persons. Stalin was philosophical about the whole matter: "Who remembers the Boiars who were put to death by Ivan the Terrible?" he is supposed to have said. These remarks parallel Hitler's assertion about the Armenian genocides of World War I. It is extraordinary that during the period 1905–1912 in Russia the Tsarist regime executed only slightly more than 6,000 people, a number exceeded on some weeks during the Great Purge.

Beriia's first job was a complete overhaul of the security apparatus with the purge of the Ezhovite high command, which was almost as thorough as Ezhov's getting rid of Iagoda's people after his appointment. Already Beriia had placed his moles in several important positions. Since September 15, 1938, B.Z. Kobulov had been the head of the Secret-Political branch of NKVD's 1 Department. On December

17, 1938, he became deputy head of GUGB/NKVD and head of the NKVD investigation department, and on September 4, 1939 head of the NKVD Main Economic Administration. On September 25, 1939, V.N. Merkulov, a fellow student of Beriia in the Baku Technical School back in 1918, was appointed Deputy Head GUGB/NKVD and took over the 3rd department (counterintelligence) on October 26, 1938. On December 16, 1938, Merkulov became the First Deputy Commissar NKVD as well as head of GUGB/NKVD. In October 1938, S.R. Mil'shtein was appointed as head of the NKVD Transportation Department. Soon all of Ezhov's deputies except V.V. Chernyshev were removed.

In late summer or fall of 1938 Stalin showed his utter cynicism by appointing Ezhov's First Deputy, the brutal M.P. Frinovskii, a man who quite possibly had not been in a boat in his life, as Commissar of Navy. The date for Frinovskii's appointment has been variously given as August, September, or even as late as November 5, 1938 (September 8 is the most probable date). The official history of the Navy, *Boevoi Put' Sovetskogo Voenno-Morskogo Flota* (Moscow, 1988), states that Frinovskii replaced Army Commissar 1 Rank P.A. Smirnov as Commissar of the Navy on November 5, 1938. The problem here is that Smirnov, who had been the head of the Red Army Political Administration after Gamarnik's suicide and head of the Navy since December 30, 1937, had been under arrest since June 30, 1938 (he was shot on February 23, 1939). It is, however, possible that there was no one in charge of the Navy during July–November 1938. On October 25, 1938, there was more bad news for Frinovskii, when S.P. Igant'ev was appointed as the Chief Political Commissar and Deputy Commissar of the Navy. The former position had been vacant since the arrest of the obscure Corps Commissar M.R. Shaposhnikov (rumored to be a relative of Marshal B.M. Shaposhnikov) on April 21, 1938 (M.R. Shaposhnikov was sentenced and shot on August 22, 1938, and rehabilitated on July 21, 1956). Igant'ev, already Deputy Commissar of Water Transport under Ezhov, now was in the position of watching over the two main executioners of the Great Terror. In March 1939, after Frinovskii's removal and arrest, Igant'ev was replaced by the more professional I.V. Rogov, who stayed in this position until 1946. Igant'ev, however, also remained with the Navy, reaching the rank of Rear Admiral and serving as the Commissar of the Caspian Military Flotilla from July 1942 until January 1947. In March 1939, N.G. Kuznetsov was called from the Far East to join the Naval Soviet, and during the 18 Party Congress held on March 10, 1939, Molotov pointedly asked Kuznetsov rather than Frinovskii to report on naval matters. Soon Frinovskii and P.I. Smirnov-Svetlovskii (not to be confused with the fallen P.A. Smirnov), First Deputy Commissar of the Navy, were dragged away and Kuznetsov was appointed as Head of the Navy. Smirnov-Svetlovskii, caught in the cross fire, was arrested on March 26, 1939; tried on March 16, 1940; and shot the day after. According to Kuznetsov, during meetings of the naval high command, Frinovskii deferred to other members. Frinovskii was removed shortly after and arrested on either April 6 or 26, 1939.[10] In February 1939, Beriia approved the execution of 413 Party, military, and government leaders, including a number of NKVD functionaries associated with Ezhov. Among them were former Deputy Commissar S.B. Zhukovskii, former Head of NKVD in Kirgizia

V.N. Chvertakov, former Head of Gulag and Commissar of Communications M.D. Berman, and the latter's brother B.D. Berman, former Head of NKVD in Belorussia. This group also included L.M. Zakovskii, former Head of NKVD in Leningrad after Kirov's murder and later a Deputy Commissar of NKVD. Zakovskii, born G.E. Shtubis in 1894 in Libau and author of a manual on torture, was a Bolshevik version of Baron Ungern von Shternberg. He had once claimed that, if necessary, he could have made Karl Marx confess that he was an agent of Bismarck.

The killing of Ezhov's high command continued during 1939–1940, claiming, among others, A.P. Radizviloskii (January 1, 1940), I.I. Shapiro (January 2, 1940), D.M. Dmitriev (March 3, 1939), N.N. Fedorov (February 4, 1940), N.G. Nikolaev-Zhurid, Z.M. Ushakov (February 4, 1940), M.A. Trilisser (1940), L.I. Kogan (1939), M.A. Listengrut (1940), E.A. Evgen'ev-Sheptitskii (March 2, 1939), A.A. Nasedkin (1939), A.M. Minaev-Tsikhanovskii (February 25, 1939), I.I. Pliner (1939), and I.Ia. Dagin (1940). Komdiv N.K. Kruchinkin, the former Commander of the Border Troops apparently was not killed until 1941. On February 2, 1940, M.A. Trilisser, a major figure from the Iagoda regime who has somehow survived the Ezhov era by working in the Comintern, was put to death. Most of the NKVD provisional leaders under Ezhov were also purged (Goglidze was a notable exception). Some of the better known were A.I. Uspenskii (Ukraine), A.A. Nasedkin (Belorussia), M.G. Raev (Azerbaidzhan), V.V. Khvorostian (Armenia), D.Z. Apresian (Uzbek SSR), I.P. Lotsmanov (Kirgiz SSR), N.A. Zagvozdin (Tadzhik SSR), and G.F. Gorbach (Far East).

The case of A.I. Uspenskii, the last head of NKVD in Ukraine under Ezhov, however, poses some problems. According to Khrushchev's memoirs, Stalin personally ordered the execution of Uspenskii, who had managed toescape briefly to Siberia. Another document (*Istoricheskii Arkhiv*, 1/1992) claims that Uspenskii was appointed as head of the NKVD in Western Siberia and was not actually shot until 1941. The total number of purged Chekists is estimated to be nearly 20,000. Robert Conquest in *Inside Stalin's Secret Police* stated that of the 122 top leaders (department, branch, provincial, and major city heads) only 21 survived. Of 634 officials holding the "State Security" rank who had received citations under Ezhov only 43 were to serve under Beriia.

Beriia, like his boss, was a man with a long memory and even tried to settle scores with those Chekists who had not been part of Ezhov's group. The old Bolshevik I.P. Pavlunovskii may have been the first head of the Cheka Special Department. In Siberia, he had been instrumental in the defeat of Baron Ungern von Shternberg, one of the most unsavory characters on either side during the Civil War. He had also carried out Trotskii's order to execute Admiral Kolchak. In the late 1920s, he had been the head of Transcaucasus OGPU, where Beriia served as his Deputy as well as the head of Georgia Branch. The two did not get along and Pavlunovskii finally left Caucasus in February 1930 and was not employed again by the secret police. In March 1931, Beriia took over the Transcaucasus OGPU. Pavlunovskii somehow survived the Ezhov years, perhaps in prison, but Beriia had him shot on February 10, 1941. There were also other witnesses from the past whose continued existence might prove embarrassing. One such example were the four members of the Ural Soviet that had organized the murder of Tsar Nicholas and his family. A.G. Beloborodov, Chairman of the Soviet, and his deputy V.N. Tolmachev (both men would later head NKVD/RFSFR, a rival organization to the Cheka which finally absorbed it in December 1930) had already been shot under Ezhov. Surviving in prisons were two others, G.I. Safarov and F.I. Goloshchekin (Party Secretary in Ekaterinburg). Beriia had the two men shot, Goloshchekin on October 28, 1941, in the massacre of senior military officers in Kuibyshev.

Another personal enemy with whom Beriia was to settle old scores was B.E. Kalmykov, Party Secretary in Kabardo-Balkar, who was tortured by Beriia, Kobulov, and Rodos before being shot on February 27, 1940. Kalmykov had been a friend of Ordzhonokidze. In the summer of 1939, Beriia shifted his attention to Uzbek SSR where thousands of Party officials, including the leaders A. Ikramov and V. Khodzhaev, had been exterminated under Ezhov. On June 3, 1939, he ordered the arrest of A. Pizhurin, assistant to the First Party Secretary and a member of the Supreme Soviet. When the 2 Party Secretary V. Chimburov protested to Stalin, he in turn, was arrested in January 1940. Both Pizhurin and Chimburov survived the Gulag and in 1956 provided critical evidence against their investigator, B.V. Rodos. On May 5, 1941, Beriia ordered the arrest of K.K. Ordzhonikidze, the last surviving brother of his old enemy, S.K. Ordzhonikidze. K.K. Ordzonikidze was to spend 12 years in prison.

Under Beriia, the Gulag high command suffered particularly heavy losses. Executed (some without a trial) were M.D. Berman (March 7, 1939), I.I. Pliner (1939), L.I. Kogan (1939), Z.B. Katsnel'son (1939), and S.G. Firin. Between April 7 and April 9, 1939, the military tribunal of Moscow District NKVD Internal Troops took up the cases of a group of high-ranking Gulag officials: N.I. Izrailev, G.V. Astrov-Shirpanov, Iu.P. Brill' (Solomnovich), V.Z. Matveev, I.G. Ginsburg, A.P. Ermakov, A.L. Sylin-Etin, A.V. Polinosov, L.M. Abramson, Iu.K. Maksimovich, and M.F. Goskin. Israilev, Brill', Ginzburg, Ermakov, Sulin-Etin, Polisonov, Abramson, Maksimovich, and Goskin were sentenced to death, the rest to prison terms. On August 16, 1939, the USSR Military Collegium changed the death sentences of Abramson, Izrailev, and Polisinov and reduced the prison terms of Astrov-Shirpanov and V.Z. Matveev. On August 31, 1939, the USSR Supreme Court changed the death sentences of Ginsburg and Ermakov to 25 years in prison. On August 6, 1955, the USSR Military Colegium set the sentences aside and freed the survivors.

In Frinovskii's case, he was tried by the Military Collegium on March 4, 1940, and shot four days later, to be followed by his wife and his son, a university student in Moscow.[11] Besides being Ezhov's closest compatriot, as mentioned, Frinovskii, as the head of Azerbaidzhan Cheka in 1920, was privy to some of Beriia's darkest secrets. He simply could not have been allowed to survive.

There were also attempts to rein in those in lower ranks who had been running rampant under Ezhov. On February 3, 1939, Beriia, for instance, ordered the arrest of one N.K. Sakharchuk, an investigator in Moscow NKVD, for use of torture. On

January 31, 1939, 30 investigators attached to the NKVD Moscow-Kiev railway security were arrested for having used "illegal" methods, and on February 5, 1939, the same fate fell on the members of the Special Department of Baltic Fleet. In an article written on March 15, 1939, Beriia set out his views about the crucial role of NKVD in protecting the Soviet Union from enemies that were surrounding her.[12] Beriia's campaign for a complete overhaul of the security organs and a purge of former executioners reportedly cost the jobs, and most probably the lives, of over 20,000 officials. There are also claims that after Beriia's appointment, 200,000 prisoners arrested by the previous regime were released.

In his takeover of NKVD, Beriia was helped by his own "Caucasian" mafia, men whom he had known in the 1920s and 1930s when he was consolidating his power base in the Caucasus. They included Georgians such as Tsanava, Rapava, and Goglide; Armenians such as Merkulov, Dekanozov, and the Kobulov brothers; and Azeris such as M.A.D. Bagirov. Over the years, Beriia's preference for the Caucasians, who included the head of his Chancellery S.S. Mamulov and his chief bodyguard R.S. Sarkisov, (both Armenians) his adjutant and his alleged procurer S.N. Nadaria, a Mingrelian, aroused Stalin's suspicion despite the fact that many of the individuals involved had Russified names. Beriia felt particularly comfortable with fellow Mingrelians, an ethnic minority in western Georgia and Abkhazia, with a strong sense of identity and last names that usually end in the letter *A*. Beriia's Mingrelian entourage included Gagua, Tsanava, Rapava, Shariia, Sadzhaia, and Bziava. The loyalty went both ways. During the "Mingrelian Affair," none of the arrested Mingrelians turned against Beriia despite torture, and I can think of only one, L.F. Tsanava, with whom Beriia had a falling out. The loyalty to Beriia was not dissimilar to the SS's sentiment about Himmler.

Besides Merkulov and B.Z. Kobulov at the central apparatus, by 1939 Beriia had also managed to place a number of his Caucasian cohorts as head of provincial NKVDs. These included A.Z. Kobulov (B.Z.'s brother) (Ukraine), L.F. Tsanava (Belorussia), A.N. Rapava (Georgia, replacing S.A. Goglidze, transfered to Leningrad), S.F. Emel'ianov (Azerbaidzhan), A.N. Sadzhaia (Uzbek SSR), S.N. Burdakov (Kazakh SSR), A.V. Kharchenko (Tadzhik SSR), Z.V. Nikolaev (Altai), I.F. Nikishov (Khabarovsk), M.M. Gvishiani (Far East), I.V. Ivanov (Sverdlovsk), K.F. Firsanov (Orel), and G.T. Karanadze (Crimea). In other areas, Beriia, however, had to make do with survivors from the Ezhov regime. This was not always easy and at times Beriia had to try out different individuals before finding the right man; for example, in Moscow V.A. Kurustkii, and V.(?) Korovin were appointed before being removed (and in all probability shot) and Beriia finally decided on the drunken V.P. Zhuravlev in March 1939. Some of Beriia's colleagues also held dark secrets. There were serious questions about Dekanozov's sexual proclivities and Sh.P. Tsereteli had been a former officer in the old army and in the Georgian Legion and Sumbatov-Topuridze a Menshevik, facts about which Stalin could not have been ignorant.

There were not, however, enough men with "Caucasian" background to run the entire security apparatus and Beriia was forced to retain a number of people who had served under Ezhov. These included some technical experts such as the indispensable V.M. Blokhin, head of the NKVD execution squads since Iagoda's days, who was to continue to do yeoman's work during the remainder of Stalin's reign. Komkor N.A. Frankel, who had headed the construction of the White Sea canal, was the sole survivor of Ezhov's Gulag high command and eventually took over the NKVD railroad construction which employed slave labor.

Another technician that Beriia decided to keep was K.A. Pavlov, Head of the Dal'stroi Slave Labor Organization since December 1, 1937 when he replaced the founder, E. Berzin, who was purged. In July 1945, Pavlov would become one of nine police officers to receive the rank of Col. General. In 1956, he committed suicide. Pavlov's chief executioner, the illiterate sadist, S. Garanin, was, however, shot as a Japanese spy.

Also surviving into the Beriia era were some "investigation technicians" from the Operation Department, including V.G. Nasedkin, N.I. Sinegrubov, A.N. Mironov, N.N. Selivanovskii (a future Deputy Minister MGB under Abakumov), N.V. Surkov, Ia. S. Vizel', G.E. Ionov, B.P. Obruchnikov, Ia.N. Matusov (interrogator of Tukhachevskii Iakir and A.M. Larina), L.F. Raikhman, A.Ia. Sverdlov, and, most importantly, L.E. Vlodzimirskii, the future head of the yet-to-be-formed Department of Investigation of Especially Important Cases.[13] Sinegrubov and Obruchnikov had, respectively, received on July 22, 1937 the Order of the Red Star and the Order of the Mark of Honor for their "investigative" efforts. By February 1941, Obruchnikov was a deputy Commissar of NKVD, and somewhat later Sinegrubov became the head of the NKVD Transportation Department. Obruchnikov continued to be associated with Beriia, but Sinegrubov faded. Luck seems to have played a part in the purge of secret police functionaries since equally gifted investigators such as V.S. Agas and L.V. Kogan were sent to the wall.

The most prominent survivors of Ezhov's regime included V.S. Abakumov, V.V. Chernyshev, G.G. Sokolov (head of border troops and a Deputy Commissar of NKVD from March 1939), P.V. Fedotov (identified as the alleged head of the Secret Political Department in April 1939, a position also claimed to have been held by B.Z. Kobulov, Abakumov's sponsor) and K.A. Pavlov (head of Dalstroyi camp organizations), the latter's replacement I.F. Nikishov and V.P. Zhuravlev, head of NKVD in Moscow. Besides these men and his own mafia, Beriia took on or perhaps was persuaded to add two other individuals whose roots were elsewhere. S.N. Kruglov had worked with the CC CPSU in the 1930s, and in 1938, and perhaps after Beriia's appointment, was appointed as the liaison between the Central Committee and NKVD. On February 29, 1939, he was appointed as Deputy Commissar NKVD for cadres. In his conversation with F.I. Chuev, Molotov claims that while on Party business in Georgia, Kruglov wrote a report critical of Beriia, the First Party Secretary (1931–1938). This report surely must have been known to the doorkeeper Poskrebyshev, and probably to Stalin, and maybe even to Beriia, and must have played a part in Kruglov's appointment as Beriia's deputy, particularly in such a sensitive position as the head of the cadres. Keeping everyone off balance was the hallmark of Stalin's management style, and it seems that most Deputy Commissars/Ministers were appointed primarily to watch over their bosses. I.A. Serov's background was in the military, and as late as 1938, he was a student in the Frunze Academy. In September 1939, Serov was appointed as the NKVD head in Ukraine. There is even a possibility that both Kruglov and Serov had served in Stalin's personal secretariat. This would explain their rapid rise. They were both cold, cynical bureaucrats, unlike the more animated thugs who formed Beriia's own entourage, even though the six-feet-six-inches-tall Kruglov also enjoyed taking part in interrogations. Many years later, both were to betray and survive Beriia.

Along with these appointments, Beriia was busy positioning his men in the Party apparatus. At the 18 Party Congress held in March 1939, Beriia and Merkulov were elected as full members of the Central Committee and Dekanozov, Goglidze, Gvishiani, B.Z. Kobulov, Nikishov, and V.P. Zhuravlev as candidate members. Sadzhaia and Tsanava were appointed to the Party Control Commission.[14] Nikishov, although a Slav, was almost a member of Beriia's Caucasus mafia, having served as head of the Border Troops in Azerbaidzhan from 1936 to March 1938 before taking a similar position in Leningrad and finally moving to the head of Khabarovsk NKVD. In December 1939, he took over the Dalstroyi. V.P. Zhurvalev had been the head of NKVD in Kuibyshev, but later served with the Commissariat of Railways. In March 1939, he had been appointed as head of NKVD in Moscow. In February 1941 he was, however, expelled from the Central Committee because of drunkenness. It seems also that Beriia made both personnel and some organizational changes in NKVD—the latter a subject that needs further study. Under Beriia, the Investigation Department, put at first under B.Z. Kobulov, finally became the "Department for Investigation of Especially Important Cases" and was taken over February 1941 by Kobulov's Deputy, L.E. Vlodzimirskii. Kobulov may also have served briefly as head of the "Secret Political Department," but the job eventually went to P.V. Fedotov, another survivor of the Ezhov era. It seems that in April 1940, he was replaced by N.D. Gorlinskii when Fedotov was moved to the Main Counterintelligence Department. Beriia did not keep A.P. Radzivilovskii, the last head of the Economics Department under Ezhov, but he managed to survive without holding a position and testified in 1956 on how Ezhov and Frinovskii fabricated the case against Tukhachesvskii and his colleagues. *Istoricheskii arkhiv* (1/1992), however, claims that Radzivilovskii was repressed in 1940. In 1939, the Operations Department was probably headed by A.N. Mironov or V.N. Gul'st.

At the time of his takeover, Beriia was particularly troubled by the state of the Foreign Department, which handled intelligence. The purges had decimated both the leadership and the agents of NKVD as well as GRU, which was also run by Ezhov from May 29, 1938 to December 1938. An additional problem was the possibility (proved by Alexander Orlov, Ignace Reiss, Walter Krivitsky, and M.A. Shteinberg) that agents defected rather than returning to the Soviet Union to face an uncertain future or worse. Under Beriia, the last head (and the least-known) of the Foreign Department, Z.I. Passov, and his Deputy, the better-known M.A. Shpigelglas, were removed, arrested, and later shot. Contrary to all the other writers, A.I. Vaksberg claims that Shpigelgals, whose real name was S.M. Shpigelglas, survived and served as an undercover agent in the Jewish Anti-Fascist Committee (JAC) during the war. The very junior P.A. Sudoplatov became the acting head, despite his former sponsor, the fallen Shpigelglas, for less than a month before he also came under a cloud. Beriia finally decided on V.G. Dekanozov, an old crony with no experience in intelligence, who was appointed as head of this department. Beriia, however, appointed a committee made up of A. Garanin, V.A. Liagin, A. Liunenko, and P.M. Fitin to assist Dekanozov; and Fitin also served as his deputy. With Stalin's approval, Sudoplatov was also appointed as deputy head with the specific task of eliminating Trotskii. In April 1939, Fitin, a former agriculture journalist, replaced Dekanozov and held on to this position until 1946. Liagin, a trained engineer, born in 1908 and a Party member only since 1939, after spending time as an agent in San Francisco, returned to the USSR in 1940 and was appointed Fitin's deputy. Working behind the enemy lines in Nikolaev, he was arrested and murdered by the Gestapo at the end of 1942. On November 5, 1944, he became a posthumous Hero of the Soviet Union. Until Beriia's arrival, with the exception of A.Kh. Artuzov (1934–1937), the department had been headed by Jews. This would not happen again.

On February 25, 1941, when the NKVD was temporarily divided into NKVD and NKGB, Beriia had as his first Deputy Commissar of the NKVD, S.N. Kruglov, who was joined by V.A. Abakumov, V.V. Chernyshev, I.I. Maslennikov, B.P. Obruchnikov, and G.G. Sokolov (none of them part of his Caucasus mafia). On March 22 and 28, 1941, L.B. Safraz'ian and A.P. Zaveniagin were also appointed as NKVD Deputy Commissars. Over at NKGB, headed by Merkulov since February 3, 1941, I.E. Serov was appointed as First Deputy Commissar on February 25 and joined by B.Z. Kobulov and M.V. Gribov as Deputy Commissars on the same date. In the beginning of the war with Beriia at the height of his power and presiding over a once again unified NKVD, he had in addition to his Deputy Commissars (now joined by the demoted Merkulov) the department heads P.M. Fitin (Foreign), P.V. Fedotov (Main Counterintelligence), B.Z. Kobulov (replaced during the war by Vlodzimirskii) (Investigation of Especially Important Cases), I.M. Tkachenko and possibly P.Ia. Meshik (Economics), N.I. Sinegrubov (Transportation), A.G. Galkin (Militia), G.G. Sokolov and A.N. Apollonov (Border and Internal Troops), V.G. Nasedkin (Gulag), N.D. Gorlinskii (Secret-Political), I.F. Nikishov (Dalstroyi slave labor organization), and P.A. Sudoplatov (Terror-Sabotage)—men who incidentally were all Slavs. This was significant since it shows that the "Caucasian" mafia, although holding a number of high positions in the provincial NKVD, was not omnipotent in the central apparatus. Stalin had not reached the pinnacle in order to allow the existence of independent power bases.

V.S. Abakumov in many ways remains the most enigmatic of Stalin's police chiefs. To my knowledge, Abakumov's picture did not appear in the Soviet press until 1990 (*Nedelia*, 44/1990). The picture, incidentally, differs from those that were published in 1991 in K.A. Stoliarov's *Golgofa*. The photograph, not a portrait, was taken during the post-war period in Germany and showed Abakumov during his campaign for a seat in the Supreme Soviet. In contemporary newsreels, we may be able to get a glimpse of Abakumov during the meeting of the Supreme Soviet sitting next to his erstwhile enemy Marshal Zhukov. The secrecy surrounding Abakumov seems somewhat unreasonable since a picture of his predecessor V.N. Merkulov had appeared, at least in the Soviet press, in July 1945 when he became the first purely police officer to receive the rank of Army General. There was also a question of his background since it was assumed by some that his name indicated "Caucasian" nationality. The usually reliable *Who Was Who in the Soviet Union* had him born in 1894 and joining the Cheka forces during the Civil War and serving on the Southeast Front. None of this turned out to be true.

The name Abakumov, arguably the second most powerful man in the USSR for nearly five years, has yet to appear in *The USSR: A Record of Events*, the comprehensive chronicle of Glasnost since 1989, or in *Encyclopedia of Russian History* (1994). Every line of the entry for Abakumov in *A Biographical Dictionary of the Soviet Union 1917–1988* (1989) and *The Biographical Dictionary of the Former Soviet Union* (1992) contains errors, including the date of birth and removal from office as well as the claim that Abakumov personally shot Wallenberg and was freed by Beriia after Stalin's death, only to be re-arrested after Beriia's fall. The claim about Abakumov's release by Beriia is also repeated by Andrew and Gordievsky in their history of the KGB. The fact is that from the day of his arrest on July 12, 1951, until his execution on December 24, 1954, Abakumov never left the confines of various prisons. There are also rumors that the archives of Reinhard Gehlen's "Fremde Heere Ost" contain some tantalizing information about Abakumov. The fact that there Abakumov is identified quite incorrectly as a Georgian compatriot of Beriia and Stalin should deflate this claim.[15]   After his trial and execution in December 1954, Abakumov, a man of mystery under Stalin, became a semi-nonperson (Khrushchev occasionally spoke of the Beriia/Abakumov machine) and during the Brezhnev era was completely erased from the pages of Soviet history. The massive eight-volume *Soviet Military Encyclopedia* does not mention Abakumov once and devotes about 30 lines (Vol. 2: p. 564) to SMERSH, the war-time counterintelligence organization headed by him. The first volume of the second edition of the same encyclopedia, published as recently as 1990, also has no listing for him, nor is he present in the *Bol'shoi Entsiklopedicheskii Slovar'* published in 1991. In interviews covering over 600 pages with F.I. Chuev, Molotov fails to mention Abakumov, a man who had arrested and sent his wife to exile. Unlike his predecessors Iagoda, Ezhov, Beriia, and Merkulov (in an ill-fitting uniform on May 1, 1946), Abakumov never appeared on the Red Square reviewing stand with other Soviet dignitaries.

The numerous military memoirs published under Khrushchev and his successors universally fail to mention Abakumov, as do the books about the so-called military Chekists. Khrushchev mentions Abakumov in his self-serving memoirs, but only as a mere appendage of Beriia. This is repeated as fact by such Western specialists as Robert McNeal (*Stalin: Man and Ruler*, p. 295). In Conquest's *Great Terror*, Abakumov is mentioned but once. *Victims of Soviet Terror*, a book published as recently as 1993 in the West, makes no mention of Abakumov at all. Abakumov, Zhukov's erstwhile enemy, is also never mentioned in the unexpurgated memoirs of the Marshal published in 1990. F.D. Volkov in *Vzlet i Padenie Stalina* (Moscow:

1992) simply puts Beriia in charge of the secret police for the last 13 years of Stalin's rule and slates Abakumov with Beriia's Caucasian inner circle, which simply is wrong. Even the eminent historian Roi Medvedev, with supposed access to inside information, claims in his biography of Khrushchev that Abakumov was arrested at the same time as Beriia, when in fact he had already been in prison for nearly two years. In her biography of Beriia published in 1993, Amy Knight devotes little space to the complex relations between Beriia and Abakumov, but at least she retreats from her former position that Abakumov was Beriia's protegé.

Actually Viktor Semenovich Abakumov was born in Moscow in 1908 to a Russian family. His father was an unskilled laborer (stoker), his mother a hospital worker and laundress. Abakumov's formal education ended at age 13 when he graduated from a local school (Col. of Judiciary A. Liskin, who interrogated Abakumov in 1951, even questions this). Later, he joined the Red Army and served with the 2 Special Task Moscow Brigade. Demobilized in December 1923, he was unemployed for a period before joining the Komsomols. In January 1930, he became a candidate member of the Party. For the next two years, he was employed by the Commissariat of Supplies and in the "Press" factory. He was also a member of the secretariat and head of the Military Section of the Moscow raion Komsomols. In the beginning of 1932, Abakumov was recommended by the Party to join the NKVD and was assigned to the Gulag and later possibly to the Investigation Department even though his name does not appear as an investigator in any of the better known cases. In his memoirs, *NKVD Iznutri*, written in 1973 and published in 1995, the late P.M. Shreider (arrested in May 1938 as Deputy Head NKVD Kazakh SSR) states that in 1933, when he was employed in the NKVD Economic Department, he was informed by M.A. Deich, the Deputy Head, about a new employee, one Abakumov, who was supposed to have been the adopted son of the unstable N.I. Podvoiskii (1880–1948), former member of the Petrograd Revolutionary Committee and one of the rare old Bolsheviks that Stalin had allowed to survive. Abakumov, however, turned out to be a compulsive womanizer which Shreider felt made him unfit to be a chekist and arranged for his dismissal from the Economics Department only to see him assigned to the GULAG. Abakumov apparently had friends in the higher echelons of NKVD.

Abakumov, however, was kept by Beriia even though evidence has yet to be produced that the two knew each other before Beriia arrived at NKVD in the summer of 1938. As late as 1939, Abakumov was a mere operative agent in the Secret Political Department, now headed by B.Z. Kobulov, one of Beriia's closest associates. It was through Kobulov that Abakumov started his meteoric rise. Sudoplatov claims that in 1938, Abakumov was the investigator in the case against Ia.A. Serebrianskii, who had been the head of special operations for more than ten years in the 1930s. Serebrianskii was condemned to death, but was not shot.

In his memoirs *Special Tasks* (p. 114), Sudoplatov also names Abakumov as the investigator in the case of P. Zubov, even though on page 112, he had already blamed Kobulov, Sergienko, and Rodos for the same act. Zubov was a senior agent who had served as conduit with President Benes of Czechoslovakia but organized an anti-German military coup in 1938 in Serbia. As a result, he was arrested by Stalin's direct order. Zubov, who was tortured by B.V. Rodos, survived, and despite injuries suffered in prison, worked along with Serebrianskii under Sudoplatov during the war.

In 1939, Abakumov was appointed as head of NKVD Rostov, where he must have performed well, probably purging the Ezhov operatives and was elected in March 1939 as a delegate to the 18th Party Congress. Whom did Abakumov replace in Rostov? During 1937–1938, the NKVD in Rostov, as elsewhere, had waged a campaign of terror, led there by V.P. Grigor'ev, whose persecution of Sholokhov's friends (already discussed) may have contributed to Ezhov's downfall. It is, however, also possible that Grigor'ev had already been replaced and Abakumov replaced an interim appointee. In Rostov, Abakumov also became involved in "Affair Fokin." Stalin had been extremely annoyed that Trotskii had been allowed to leave the Soviet Union with his personal archives. Ezhov, whose inability to liquidate Trotskii may have contributed to his eventual downfall, blamed several Chekists for this lapse, including P.P. Budanov (Iagoda's secretary), S.G. Volynskii (identified as possible head of NKVD/GUGB 3rd Branch), and F.P. Fokin (head of militia in Rostov). Abakumov personally interrogated Fokin, who had survived Ezhov's downfall in prison, and Fokin was shot in due course. Abakumov must have performed well in Rostov but probably could not equal the record of Beriia's man in Belorussia. L.F. Tsanava managed to arrest 27,000 people within a short time after his appointment, including some of the operatives of his two bloody predecessors, B.D. Berman and A.A. Nasedkin.[16] In *Moi Otets*, Beriia's son puts a completely different spin on Abakumov's tenure in Rostov. Under him, 60% of the political prisoners were released, and he was even accused of excessive leniency. Apparently, these humane qualities prompted Beriia to transfer him to Moscow. Abakumov's duties after his return to Moscow, however, are not clear. Sudoplatov claims that, after his recall, Abakumov was put in charge of investigations, but during this period this responsibility has also been identified with B.Z. Kobulov, L.E. Vlodzimirskii, and even V.T. Sergienko. What is extraordinary about Abakumov's rise is that he neither was a member of Beriia's Caucasus mafia nor came from an independent power base as had Serov and Kruglov. Information provided by the Russian Federation Counterintelligence Service to the author dates Abakumov's appointment as a Deputy Commissar of the NKVD from February 26, 1941.

Before we continue with Abakumov's career, we need to examine the complex relationship between Stalin and Beriia. The talk about a "Beriia Machine" running the security apparatus from 1938 assumes Stalin's complete trust of Beriia, which runs directly against Stalin's psychology. Stalin, who knew something about history, was determined not to have a Fouchet on his hands. Although he obviously respected Beriia's ability as well as his personal company, he was not about to put his trust in a man with a history of opportunism, even a suspected mussavat. A.I. Mikoian was correct when he stated in the July 1953 meeting of the Central Committee that Stalin's division of Beriia's empire (in February 1941 and then again in April 1943) showed a lack of trust. At times, Stalin encouraged, or at least tolerated, criticism of Beriia.

According to Iu.B. Borev in *Staliniada*, when A.A. Fadeev returned from Georgia after attending the Rustaveli jubilee, he told Stalin that the celebration was more about Beriia than the poet. This resulted in Stalin dressing down Beriia, who later on three occasions tried to have Fadeev arrested, only to be stopped by Stalin. Beriia then tried to have Fadeev replaced as Head of the Writers Union by writer and scenarist P.A. Pavlenko (1899–1951), a suggestion that was pointedly ignored by Stalin. P.K. Ponomarenko, the Party leader in Belorussia, was another man that Beriia repeatedly tried to compromise. Instead, Stalin would appoint Ponomarenko to the Party Presidium. Even during the Khrushchev years, Ponomarenko would display a bust of Stalin in his office. When Beriia vetoed Admiral Isakov's decision to send a naval officer to London, Isakov went directly to Stalin, who overruled Beriia. Beriia later complained to Isakov that they could have settled the matter between themselves. On more than one occasion, Beriia suggested to Stalin that Erenburg, who had most of his colleagues in the NKVD custody, should also be arrested. Stalin ignored this. Events of recent years prove the essential correctness of Stalin's position in not trusting Beriia or, for that matter, any other Georgian politician. In *Twenty Letters to a Friend*, Madame Alliluyeva, for understandable reasons, makes the following extraordinary remarks:

Beriia was more treacherous, more practiced in perfidy and cunning, more insolent and single-minded than my father. In a word, he was a stronger character. My father had his weaker sides. He was capable of self-doubt. He was cruder and more direct than Beriia, and not so suspicious. He was simpler and could be led up the garden path by someone with Beriia's craftiness. Beriia was aware of my father's weakness.[17]

Alliluyeva, as well as others, has also spoken of Beriia's excessive flattery of Stalin, as if he were alone in what was the foremost requirement for survival in Stalin's court.

Alliluyeva goes on to blame Beriia for Kirov's murder even though Beriia was thousands of miles away and evidence points to a Stalin/Iagoda complicity. Khrushchev and Marshal Zhukov also speak of the Beriia/Abakumov combine as if it were a separate entity operating on its own rather than a willing and subservient tool of Stalin's tyranny. Stalin himself encouraged this mythology when in 1940 he told aircraft designer A.S. Iakovlev, "Ezhov—a scoundrel, in 1938 he killed many innocent people and for this we had him shot." At another time, Stalin would refer to Ezhov as a "double-dealing secret agent of imperialism." It is interesting to note that while most of Ezhov's henchmen were exterminated, his colleagues in the Party and government such as Molotov, Voroshilov, Malenkov, Kaganovich, Shkriiatov, Mekhlis, Poskrebyshev, and Shchadnenko—who also under Stalin had played major parts in the Great Terror—all survived. At the Central Committee meeting in July 1953 after Beriia's fall, Khrushchev chimed in with remarks very much like those made by Svetlana Alliluyeva. After denouncing Beriia as being the devil incarnate, he added that Beriia securely hooked his dirty paws into the soul of comrade Stalin; he knew how to force his opinion on comrade Stalin. He found ways to raise doubts while examining one question or another; he found ways to cast a bad light on certain comrades. For a time, Beriia was able to turn Stalin against one worker or another. His main qualities were his gall and impudence. These self-serving remarks about Stalin, the ultimate manipulator, being manipulated just do not ring true. Stalin did not need prompting from Beriia, or for that matter anyone else, to wage terror.

On the crucial question of executions, there is little doubt that at above a certain level they could only be carried out with Stalin's approval. Can anyone believe for one moment that Beriia or Abakumov on his own could have arrested Poskebryshev's wife and kept her in prison for three years and then shot her without approval from Stalin? Soviet documents released in recent years about Trotskii's assassination, the Soviet Generals returning from German captivity, and the "Leningrad Affair" show how Stalin "micromanaged" the terror, providing guidelines and hints for his executioners.

Svetlana Alliluyeva has an understanding of the modern bureaucratic state in both its Stalinist and welfare state manifestations, if not of her own father's psychology when she further writes, "Who had contrived all these stratagems? Not he. It was the system of which he himself was a prisoner and in which he was stifling from loneliness, emptiness and lack of human companionship."[18] The sad fact is that the quality of friendship and loyalty is as alien to a modern bureaucrat as is efficiency. All that matters are power, empire-building, and turf.

Lenin, a more objective observer who was not above using Stalin when it was called for, was on the mark when he called Stalin a man without sentiments, and, in fact, Stalin's life is proof positive of Swift's claim that loyalty is the high mark of a civilized man. The only occasion in which Stalin acted out of character was his reluctance to execute the former Bolshevik members of the Fourth State Duma, but even here there was a caveat. Former members A.E. Badaev (1883–1957), F.N. Samoilov (1882–1952), and M.K. Muranov (1873–1959) were spared, although except for Badaev they were forced into retirement by 1940 (one former member, R.V. Malinovskii, had already been shot in 1918 when he was exposed as a Tsarist spy, and another member, N.G. Shagov, also died in 1918). The best known of the group, G.I. Petrovskii (1878–1959), candidate member of the Politburo (1926–1939), after whom Ekaterinoslav had been renamed Dnepropetrovsk, would be removed from all positions in 1939 and allowed to rot away as Deputy Director of the USSR Revolution Museum, under the aforementioned Samoiov, but several members of his family were shot. There was also softness towards poets as indicated by the fact that Pasternak and Akhmatova, although targeted, were allowed to survive.

Stalin has also been compared to Ivan the Terrible, but the fact remains that the old despot at times was overcome by a sense of guilt over his monstrous crimes. Not an iota of evidence exists that shows Stalin to have felt a tinge of conscience over the sufferings for which he, and he alone, was responsible. Volkogonov is on the mark when he states that Stalin despised pity, sympathy, and mercy, and all that mattered to him was naked power. Stalin also once told Iagoda that he preferred obedience through fear rather than conviction because the latter was subject to change. If the protagonist in *What Is to Be Done?* is right in saying that "a man with a desperate admiration of goodness can't be but a somber monster," then surely a man who is indifferent to evil must be even more monstrous. Stalin was such a man, and the key to his personality can best be found in his unbridled admiration for S.G. Nechaev (also a favorite of Lenin), the merciless nineteenth century Russian revolutionary for whom violence and cruelty were the central facts of life. Nechaev, who called blood and violence the "midwife of history," frequently discussed with fellow revolutionary P.N. Tkachev the number of people from the old society who needed to be destroyed in order to create a happy future. Cruelty and envy formed the core of Stalin's character indicated on numerous documents by the use of his favorite acronym, VMN (highest measure of punishment), against the names of thousands of victims. Shakespeare's Richard III, deformed, vindictive, power-mad, with an unbounded confidence in his own judgement, personified Stalin. At times he was Nero-like in his childish ideas, tyrannical principles, and lunatic actions. Stalin's cruelty was congenital and the seminary training proved invaluable in teaching him that doctrine could be used to justify anything. Hitler, for one, was simply bowled over by Stalin's elegant phraseology justifying the rape of the Baltics. Marxism-Leninism provided Stalin with the necessary excuse that social engineering could create paradise on earth. On his way up, Stalin would slap backs; in the pinnacle of power, he only knew how to stab them. He also, Al Capone-like, believed that hearts and minds would follow twisted arms. Stalin sought power for the sake of power, and once he achieved absolute power, he used others as toys. As Gore Vidal, in an extraordinary admission for an American liberal, has said, to learn the simple fact that men seek power in order to wield it one must wade through a sea of evasions such as history as sociology, leaders as teachers, bland benevolence as a motive force when, finally, power is an end to itself.

Stalin exemplified Oswald Spengler's Faustian man, totally unrestrained by principles or ideals. He was also the personification of the utopian left, as well as the greatest mass murderer ever. There are of course other theories, one blaming Stalin's father for the terror since he supposedly beat the young Josef in his formative years. This, of course, does not answer why Lenin, who had a happy childhood, was equally fond of terror. We get these theories, as well as others (such as blaming Auschwitz on Hitler's toilet training) courtesy of something called "psychohistory," and example of science fiction and humbug that thrives in academia.

To paint Beriia simply as Stalin's "alter-Iago" simply does not ring true in view of historical facts. It is extraordinary that even today the name of Beriia continues to be used as the generic for terror during the last 14 years of Stalin's rule. Stalin used Beriia just as he had used Iagoda and Ezhov and was to use Abakumov and Riumin. It is true that on occasions when his own survival was at stake, Beriia would play up to Stalin's worst instincts. A case in point was in 1944 when Beriia, aware of Stalin's dissatisfaction over NKVD's failure to forestall the German subversive efforts in the Caucasus, suggested additional nationalities for deportation, but Stalin needed little prodding from Beriia. By every standard, Stalin was a bigger monster than the reptilian Beriia, who at least showed consistent loyalty to his friends—

a concept totally alien to Stalin. Beriia rarely sacrificed any of his own henchmen in the manner which was routine for Stalin. In fact, Beriia only purged two of his senior operatives, Rukhadze and Tsanava, after they had doublecrossed him. Beriia, within reason, also tried to protect his Jewish operatives during the post-war anti-Semitic campaigns and made sure that the Jewish nuclear scientists who were working for him were left unharmed. After Stalin's death, Beriia reinstated his Jewish colleagues, who had been shunned and even imprisoned during Stalin's last years. In July 1946, for economic reasons, Beriia recommended that 100,000 invalid prisoners, incapable of "useful" work, be released. On the surface, Stalin agreed, only to add a proviso that negated this sensible suggestion. The family life of the philanderer Beriia was a paragon of stability compared to the cruel soap opera of Stalin's relations with those closest to him. So far as Beriia's alleged craftiness, we only need to see how he was outmaneuvered by the Khrushchev/Malenkov combine after Stalin's death.

Abakumov, who was a major force in the post-war anti-Semitic campaigns, also protected his Jewish colleagues such as Raikhman, Broverman, and Shvartsman. In fact, according to Army General P.I. Ivashutin, who was in a position to know, Abakumov was always considerate to those who worked for him. Since 1953, except for the stagnation period when discussion of Stalin's crimes became taboo, Beriia and, to a lesser extent, Abakumov have served as convenient scapegoats for Stalin's crimes. It is extraordinary that when the Soviets finally admitted their responsibility for Katyn, Gorbachev's official statement did not mention Stalin and pretended that Beriia was the instigator rather than the executioner of a policy ordered by Stalin. The fact that terror came to an end with Stalin's death also points out that he, and he alone, was the moving force behind it.

The glasnost literature has many examples of how Stalin pulled the strings of terror (some referred to in this book). Stalin had almost daily contacts with the hanging judge Ul'rikh who passed out the death sentences. Stalin would replace Beriia's name with B.Z. Kobulov on the document sanctioning the killing of the Polish POWs. On other occasions, for reasons that had nothing to do with charity, he would commute the death sentences of G.N. Kupriianov (Party Secretary in Karelia) and gerontologist L.S. Shtern. Sometimes Stalin's "micromanagement" would take bizarre turns. Archives of the Ministry of Defense indicate that on August 18, 1943, among the many documents that crossed Stalin's desk was a report by Commander of the Red Army Armor, Col. General of Tank Troops, Ia.N. Fedorenko, and his Political Commissar, Lt. General of Tank Troops N.I. Biriukov, about the fate of the little known Maj. General of Tank Troops A.A. Kotliarov (also listed as Kotliar). Kotliarov, Commander of the obscure 58 Tank Division, 30 Army (commanded at the time by K.K. Rokossovskii), had committed suicide on November 20, 1941, after the decimation of his unit. Stalin immediately took an interest in the matter, ordering the alteration of records so Kotliarov was listed as killed in action and then ordering that his name be stricken off the ranks of the Red Army. Nothing ever escaped Stalin's attention. In his memoirs (*VIZH*, November 1993), Col. General I.S. Glebov relates the circumstances that led to the demotion of Army General

A.I.Antonov from Chief of Staff to the first Deputy Chief of Staff in March 1946. Stalin inquired why Antonov had received the Order of Victory, which was only given to Marshals, and asked S.M. Shtemenko, Stalin's handmaiden in the military, to poll the Marshals whether Antonov should be promoted. The vote was unanimous, except for that of I.S. Konev, who raised the point that Antonov had never commanded a Front (or for that matter even an army or a corps), and the matter was shelved. We can only wonder about the source of inspiration for Konev's blackball. Antonov in due course was replaced by A.M. Vasilevskii, a Marshal. In June 1950, Shtemenko replaced Vasilevskii. Another case, involving Maj. General of Aviation I.N. Rukhle, will be discussed in Chapter 4. Stalin found out that the inscription on the memorial, in Kiev, to the fallen Army General N.F. Vatutin was in Ukrainian and angrily ordered Khrushchev to change it. The collection *Staliniada* by Iu.B. Borev contains hundreds of examples that show Stalin to be the champion busybody of all time with interest in every facet of Soviet society, with the goal of punishing the wrongdoers.

Stalin also showed his doubts about Beriia by protecting two old Chekists who had compromising material about Beriia. M.S. Kedrov, an old colleague of Dzerzhinskii and a Party member since 1901, had served in 1921 as GPU representative in Azerbaidzhan and had suggested Beriia's removal. He also knew of an order by Kirov in 1919 to arrest Beriia as an "agent provocateur." Kedrov had left the Cheka to work with Gosplan RSFSR and the USSR Supreme Court, but in 1939 his son and fellow Chekist, Senior Lt. of State Security I.M. Kedrov, and Lt. of State Security V.P. Golubev wrote to the Central Committee about lawlessness in NKVD. Arrest was immediate and the younger Kedrov, along with Golubev and the latter's mother, N.V. Batorina, was shot without trial on January 25, 1940. Kedrov's wife, R.M. Kedrova, who also had been arrested, was not released until 1955. M.S. Kedrov was arrested on April 16, 1939, and even though he was cleared by the Military Collegium, he was not released. His letters to Politburo member A.A. Andreev went unanswered. Beriia used the confusion of the early days of the war and had Kedrov shot in Saratov on October 28, 1941.[19] Recent documents published in A.I. Vaksberg's *Neraskrytye tainy* show how shortly after the war, Merkulov worked closely with Ul'rikh and I.T. Goliakov (Chairman of the USSR Supreme Court) to reverse the decision clearing Kedrov. Another Chekist who also was aware of Beriia's checkered past was Ia. D. Berezin, who had served from 1918 to 1921 as secretary of Moscow Cheka and from 1922 until 1924 as head of GPU/ OGPU administration. Berezin was also a colleague and friend of M.S. Kedrov.[20] He managed to escape Beriia's clutches, and his survival would have been unthinkable without intervention by Stalin. Today there are rumors that Stalin was considering replacing Beriia with the national hero aviator V.P. Chkalov, and, in fact, according to Chkalov's son, this forced the NKVD to arrange Chkalov's accidental death.

Another writer, V.D. Uspenskii, claims that Chkalov, rather than Beriia, was Stalin's original candidate to replace Ezhov. The circumstances of Chkalov's death on December 15, 1938, three days after Beriia was officially appointed as head of the NKVD, appear suspicious. The prototype of fighter I–180 that Chkalov was testing had been left unprotected overnight in –24° cold, but this kind of carelessness was the hallmark of how the Soviet system in which only one man, Stalin, was indispensable, operated. Stalin ordered the arrest of D.L. Tomashevich—the designer, Ushachev—the director of GAZ–157 Aviation Factory where the plane had been built, and Beliakin—the head of GKAP (State Committee on the Aviation Industry).[21] We do not necessarily have to accept far-fetched theories about Beriia's replacement to note that Beriia's *total* control of the security organizations lasted for a relatively brief period. Only from December 1938 to February 1941, from July 1941 to April 1943, and from March 1953 to June 1953 was Beriia in complete charge. In 1946 at the height of Beriia's power, Molotov had no problem getting rid of Dekanozov, Beriia's mole in the foreign service, on such an insignificant account as moral turpitude. (Dekanozov allegedly shared Beriia's predilection for Nabokovian nymphets.[22]) At the Yalta conference Roosevelt asked about a man sitting opposite Gromyko, and Stalin answered, "That is Beriia, our Himmler."[23] In April 1972, Congressman Cornelius Gallagher would call his bete noire J. Edgar Hoover "the American Beriia." Thanks primarily to Khrushchev, Beriia's name had become the generic for ultimate evil. This kind of name calling, however, avoids the central issue that Beriia, Himmler, and Hoover did not operate in a vacuum. They existed primarily to carry out the orders of Stalin, Hitler, FDR, and LBJ.

Stalin recognized Beriia's talents and rewarded him for his efforts. In 1939, Beriia, elected to the Central Committee in 1934 and one of the few who survived the Great Purge, was elected to the Politburo as a candidate member along with N.M. Shvernik, joining in that august body full members Stalin, Andreev, Molotov, Kaganovich, Voroshilov, Kalinin, Khrushchev (also elected in 1939), Mikoian, and Zhdanov. It would take Beriia nearly six years to become a full member of the Politburo, an honor that had come to Khrushchev in one year.

There continues to be increasing evidence of Stalin bypassing Beriia at times and dealing directly with Merkulov, Abakumov, Kruglov and, later, Riumin and S.D. Ignat'ev. On June 20, 1941, Stalin met alone with Merkulov and P.M. Fitin, head of NKGB Foreign Department, who warned him of the imminent German attack.[24] P.A. Sudoplatov, who organized Trotskii's murder and was in charge of terrorist operations, also at times reported directly to Stalin. There were times when Stalin even dealt directly with the local leaders, as in January 1948, when, according to his daughter, he ordered L.F. Tsanava, head of MGB Belorussia, to organize the murder of actor S.M. Mikhoels.[25]

On February 3, 1941, the police and security apparatus was divided between NKVD and NKGB with Beriia holding on to NKVD and Merkulov heading the NKGB. The division of his empire could not have been a pleasant occasion for Beriia, but Stalin softened the blow on January 30, 1941, by giving him the rank of "Commissar General of the State Security," held previously only by Iagoda and Ezhov. He also appointed Beriia's confidant, V.N. Merkulov, as Commissar of the new NKGB. Beriia probably welcomed the outbreak of the war since on July 20, 1941, the two Commissariats were combined under him and once again called NKVD. Beriia held on to this portfolio until April 14, 1943, when the NKVD was divided again. Early in 1941 also, the GUGB/NKVD 3rd (Special) Branch was replaced when the 3 Department of the Commissariat of Defense was formed. The main responsibility of this organization continued to be watching over the military under the rubric of "counterintelligence," and this was the organization later called SMERSH with which Abakumov was later associated.

Abakumov's prominence could also be seen through his advancement in rank. On April 27, 1940, Abakumov was one of 634 NKVD functionaries who were awarded various citations. He received the Order of the Red Banner. Here Abakumov was listed as one of the 25 or so Senior Majors of State Security (a rank equivalent to Colonel in the Red Army). In July 1945, the rank of General was given to purely police officers and Abakumov was one of seven Colonel Generals. He was the only Senior Major of State Security from the 1940 list to achieve this rank, and, in fact, only seven of that group even achieved the next-lower rank of Lt. General.

Sometime in 1940, Abakumov was called from Rostov and was appointed on February 25, 1941, as one of Beriia's deputies, but he was not yet the head of the Special Branch and his exact duties remain unclear. The GUGB/NKVD Special (OO) (Upravlenie Osobykh Otdelov) 3rd Branch served as NKVD's watchdog over the military and once in the early 1920s was headed by no less a personage than Iagoda. It had gone through a turbulent period in the 'twenties and 'thirties while being led by G.I. Bokii, M.I. Gai, I.M. Leplevskii, A.K. Zalpeter, and perhaps G.E. Prokof'ev, who were all purged. In April 1937, Gai, in prison, had provided testimony about the existence of a "military conspiracy" which was used as the springboard by his successor Leplevskii, working under Ezhov and Frinovskii to launch the campaign that doomed Tukhachevskii and his colleagues. For much of 1936, the Department was headed by S.G. Volynskii, Commissar of State Security 3rd Rank (April 3, 1937); A.M. Mineav-Tskhanovskii was appointed as its deputy head on April 7, 1937, and its acting head on July 11, 1937. He was arrested on November 6, 1938, and shot on February 2, 1939. He has never been rehabilitated. The Branch also provided brutal investigators such as V.S. Agas, A.A. Avseevich, A.N. Mironov, N.N. Selivanovskii, I.D. Surovitskikh, Z.M. Ushakov (deputy head), L.I. Reikhman, M.A. Listengurt, Z.V. Nikolaev, and E.L. Karpeiskii, who worked over the unfortunate military officers and imprisoned NKVD colleagues such as M.I. Gai, G.E. Prokof'ev, and Z.I. Volovich to produce the needed confessions. Some of the investigators such as Ushakov and Agas fell with Ezhov, the latter allegedly for having compromising material about Beriia, while others such as Avseevich (who retired as a Lt. General) and Selivanovskii (also a Lt. General and a Deputy Minister of MGB in 1946) survived to testify to the Central Committee in December 1962.

The department was finally taken over sometime in May 1938, and possibly even after Beriia's arrival, by Kombrig N.N. Fedorov. Soviet documents indicate that in July 1938, Fedorov worked closely with Frinovskii in the case against I.F. Fed'ko, the First Deputy Commissar of Defense from January 25, 1938, until his arrest on July 7, 1938 (Fed'ko actually was not shot until February 26, 1939, after Beriia's takeover).[26] Glasnost literature cites examples of the close cooperation of this department, with L.Z. Mekhlis and Voroshilov in waging a campaign of terror against the military. For instance, after the arrest of Kombrig K.I. Sokolov-Strakhov, head of the Military History Section of the General Staff, as an "enemy of the people," his Deputy, V.D. Ivanov (a future Army General), wrote a letter of protest to the Special Branch, which was immediately forwarded to Mekhlis. On March 30, 1939, Komkor M.O. Stepanov, head of the Chemical Department of the Red Army, wrote to Voroshilov expressing concern that 40–45% of the chemical officers in military districts and 60–65% in corps and divisions had been arrested. Voroshilov simply forwarded the letter to the Special Branch. Arrest followed.[27] Soviet documents indicate Fedorov's ordering the arrest of the aforementioned Komkor M.O. Stepanov in early April 1939, and yet Fedorov himself had been under arrest since November 1938. Volkogonov cites a telegram dating from July 27, 1938, from Mekhlis to E.A. Shchadenko in which he suggests that Fedorov look into the connections between M.F. Lukin, Chief of Staff of the Siberian Military District, and enemies of the people. Mekhlis claimed that Fedorov should have enough material about Lukin. The fact that Fedorov could not or perhaps preferred not to make a case against Lukin, who was also later subject to an investigation by Abakumov after Lukin's return from German captivity, did not obviously help Fedorov. A later memo (*VIZH*, June 1992) from Mekhlis, dating from November 18, 1938, refers to Fedorov as former head of the "Special Branch" and as "an enemy of the people" to boot.

The most detailed information about Fedorov (born in 1900) indicates that from July 20, 1937, he was head of NKVD in Odessa and from February 2, 1938, in a similar position in Kiev and from May 28, 1938, head of the "Special Branch." He was arrested on November 11, 1938, and shot on February 2, 1940. He has never been rehabilitated. On June 9, 1938, Commissar of State Security 3 Rank N.G. Nikolaev-Zhurid, a close confidant of Ezhov who since November 26, 1937, had served as the head of two branches in GUGB/NKVD (2nd and 5th), was appointed head of the 3rd Branch. He also received the additional title of deputy head of the NKVD 1 Department. It seems that he was still in office when Beriia arrived, but not for long. He was arrested in December 1938 and eventually shot on the same date as Fedorov. He has never been rehabilitated. On October 26, 1938, Merkulov, already deputy head GUGB/NKVD, also became the head of 3rd (Special) Branch in this organization and held this position for a short time until he became first Deputy Commissar of NKVD and replaced Beriia as head of GUGB/NKVD.

It is easy to confuse the "Special Branch" with the Main NKVD (counter-intelligence) Department, which deserves separate coverage. In 1940, Senior Major of State Security V.M. Bochkov had been identified as head of the "Special Branch."[28] Bochkov had graduated from the Frunze Academy in 1938 and had been immediately appointed Head of the NKVD Prisons. He was appointed Head of the Special Branch in December 1938 and served until 1940, when he was transferred to the North Fleet, probably as Head of the Special Branch before being appointed as the USSR Prosecutor General. After Stalin's death, Bochkov claimed that all these appointments, for which he was not qualified, were made against his will and, in fact, he read about his appointment as Prosecutor General in the local newspaper in August or September 1940. In fact, Bochkov, however, had been appointed as Prosecutor General of USSR in July 8, 1940 (replacing M.I. Pankrat'ev who had replaced Vyshinskii on May 31, 1939), and he stayed in that office until November 13, 1943. Information provided to the author by the Federal Counterintelligence Service dates Bochkov's appointment as Head of the Special Branch of GUGB/ NKVD from December 1938 until August 23, 1940. There was tension between Bochkov and his operatives and the military. Documents cited in the collection *Oni ne Molchali* show one such case when members of the Special Branch attached to the 11 Army did not attend a meeting of the Military Soviet called by Col. General of Tank Troops D.G. Pavlov, Commander of the Belorussian Special Military District. As a result, Pavlov banned the attendance of head of the Special Branch Captain of State Security Kokshaev, who in turn complained to Bochkov and he to Mekhlis to set Pavlov right. In the summer of 1940, Kombrig, later Army General and Hero of the Soviet Union; D.D. Leliushenko, Commander of the 39 Tank Brigade in the Moscow Military District; and his Commissar, Solov'ev, complained to the district command about the illegal behavior of the operatives of the Special Branch. On July 29, 1940, A.I. Zaporozhets repeated these complaints to Mekhlis. The military's dissatisfaction may have contributed to moving the Special Branch from GUGB/ NKVD to the Commissariat of Defense in February 1941 even though as we learn later that this was merely a cosmetic change and was reversed shortly after the German invasion.

Bochkov received the rank of Commissar of State Security 3rd Rank on March 14, 1941, and Lt. General of Judiciary in 1945. His brief career as Commissar of the Northwest Front in the beginning of the war will be discussed later. During his tenure as prosecutor general, Bochkov worked hand-in-hand with NKVD, particularly in the Baltics. Later, he organized the arrest of children of the purged officials such as A.I. Ikramov, former First Secretary of the Uzbek Party. He was removed for mishandling the "Youth Terrorism Organization" case.[29] Conquest states that Bochkov served as head of SMERSH on the Northwest Front. In fact, he served for only a few days as the political commissar of this front in fall 1941 with disastrous results for the Chief of Staff, Lt. General P.S. Klenov, who was arrested and shot.[30] In 1950, Bochkov was the deputy head of the Volga-Don Canal project, and in 1954 he was head of the Kingir labor camps.[31] Besides Bochkov, Mekhlis was also involved in Klenov's purge since he had been instrumental in the removal of Army Commissar 2 Rank V.N. Borisov, who had first been sent from Moscow as a representative of the Supreme Command to the Northwest Front. Despite his record, Bochkov, who died in 1980, remained in good standing and is mentioned favorably in *Sovetskaia Prokuratura* (Moscow, 1982).

Bochkov was replaced on August 23, 1940 by A.N. Mikheev. According to recent documents (*VIZH*, 3/1994), by March 1941, shortly after the Branch was transferred to the Commissariat of Defense, Major of State Security (at times also identified with the rank of Brigade Commissar) A.N. Mikheev continued as its head. At least one of Mikheev's deputies was F.Ia. Tutushkin (Lt. General, July 1945), who on July 8, 1941 reported to Stalin on the losses suffered by the Northwest Front. Transferring the responsibilities of the 3rd (Special) Branch from GUGB/ NKVD to the Commissariat of Defense was purely cosmetic, and in all probability its offices remained in the NKVD rather than the Commissariat of Defense Building. Mikheev, who reported to Timoshenko and against whom he would intrigue, if anything was even worse than Bochkov, who had been under Merkulov/Beriia. The 3 (Special) Department remained Stalin's watchdog of the military and a nest of provocation. The shadowy Mikheev, born in 1911 and a graduate of the Kuibyshev Engineering Academy, had joined counterintelligence only in 1939 and had first served as Head of the Special Branch in the Orel Military District.

During 1940–1941, Mikheev has also been indentified as Head of the Special Branch of the Ukraine Special Military District, where he was involved in anti-nationalist campaigns in the recently occupied territories. This contradicts that he was Head of the entire Department since August 1940, but then he could have been on a special assignment in the Ukraine. Mikheev received the Order of the Red Star on April 27, 1940, when a large number of awards were given to the security personnel—mostly for contributions to Katyn. On July 4, 1941, Mikheev helped Mekhlis in the arrest of the doomed leadership of the West Front. A set of recently released documents (*VIZH*, 2/1994 and 3/1994) show the sinister role played by Mikheev and his Deputy Captain of State Security A.N. Klykov (born in 1896, but otherwise unknown). The documents date from mid-July 1941 and are addressed to Timoshenko and Beriia. Klykov's long and detailed report accused Marshal S.M. Budennyi (whose second wife was lingering in camps) of nothing short of treason by dredging up old charges made by purged colleagues under duress. Klykov clearly fails to do his homework, referring to I.R. Apanasenko as a member of a "military conspiracy" atthe time when the latter was actually commanding the Far East Front. At the time of this report, Budennyi was Commander of the Southwest Theater desperately trying to stop the German tide. Mikheev's targets were Army Commissar 1 Rank E.A. Shchadenko, Deputy Commissar of Defense and Head of the Red Army Personnel Department since November 1937 and a major figure in the military purges; Army Commissar 1 Rank A.I. Zaporozhets, Commissar of South Front from June 21, 1941, and before that head of the Red Army Political Administration (he had replaced Mekhlis in this position in September 1940, but in turn was replaced by Mekhlis in the beginning of the war); Col. General M.P. Kirponos, Commander of the Southwest Front; Lt. General M.P. Kovalev, Commander of the Transbaikal Military District; and Lt. General I.S. Konev, Commander of the 19 Army and before that Commander of the North Caucasus Military District. None of the accused were, however, arrested.

A different fate, however, awaited Col. General G.M. Shtern, Commander of the Far East Front. In March 1941, Mikheev, signing as a mere Major of State Security, made similar charges against Shtern. Timoshenko's response (*VIZH*, 3/1994) here was more positive. Shtern was arrested on June 18, 1941, and was one of the victims of the mass killings of senior officers on October 28, 1941. On July 16, 1941, Mikheev went even after bigger fish. Directed to Malenkov at the Central Committee, two reports from Mikheev (*VIZH*, 12/1993) implicated Timoshenko, the Commissar of Defense, and in considerable detail Marshal G.I. Kulik, Deputy Commissar of Defense and head of the Main Artillery Administration. The report on Kulik, which will be covered in more detail in Chapter 7, also implied that Mikheev had been involved in other arrests. This report understandably was not sent to Timoshenko. When all the documents are released, I have little doubt that they will indicate that Mikheev was involved in most of the arrests of other senior military officers during March–June 1941. Mikheev's charges against the military men bordering on treason were made at a time when they were holding vital positions in a desperate war. The fact that the targets included such stalwart Stalinists as Budennyi, Kulik, Shchadenko, Timoshenko, and Zaporozhets, and the charges were made by a 30-year-old Chekist of a very recent vintage, is a clear indication of the power enjoyed by his office and the rogue character of the 3rd Department, from whose forays no one was safe. Although at this time the 3rd Department was a part of the Commissariat of Defense, it was nothing less than Stalin and Beriia's private watchdog agency in the military, sowing discord among those designated to defend the very existence of the USSR. Under Abakumov, Mikheev's successor, who was to receive the additional rank of Deputy Commissar of Defense, the reports went directly to Stalin.

Except for Shtern, none of the officials targeted was, however, arrested as a result of these reports sent to Timoshenko and Beriia. Documents about the circumstances under which other repressed officers, such as Proskurov and Smushkevich, were arrested have yet to be released. In Shtern's case, his position as head of PVO since February 1941, for which he was not really qualified, was undermined when in March 1941 a German Ju–52 transport plane managed to land in Moscow without being detected by Soviet anti-aircraft forces. Contrast this with the fact that no heads rolled when on May 28, 1987 (Border Troops Day), a German teenager, Mattias Rust, landed his "Stealth" Cessna in Red Square.

On July 24, 1941, when the 3rd Department of the Commissariat of Defense once again became part of the NKVD, Mikheev was promoted to the rank of "Commissar of State Security 3rd Rank" and was transferred to the Southwest Front to serve under Kirponos, a man whom he had just tried to compromise, which of course made perfect sense in the Stalinist state. On July 31, 1941 Abakumov was appointed Head of the 3 Department. Adding to the confusion, however, is a Soviet document from July 11, 1941, addressed to the head of 3rd Department NKVD, Senior Major State Security A.M. Belianov (Deputy Head of this office at the time of Katyn).[32] Mikheev and his Deputy Brigade Commissar (also identified as Major of State Security) N.A. Iarunchikov, incidentally, died on September 21, 1941, during the breakout from the Kiev pocket near Shumeiskovo where the Commander of the Front, Col. General M.P. Kirponos, and most of his staff met a similar fate. Mikheev reportedly committed suicide after both of his legs were blown away by an enemy shell. He is buried in Kiev. His biography by Iu.I. Semenov, published in 1979, says nothing about his unsavory acts, but a great deal about his heroic death.

There are indications that Timoshenko, the Commissar of Defense since May 1940, as well as G.K. Zhukov, the Chief of Staff from January 1941, and as usual L.Z. Mekhlis, Head of the Political Administration of the Red Army, worked closely with the 3rd Department. Soviet documents show how Timoshenko and Zhukov worked together in April 1941 to get rid of P.V. Rychagov, Commander of the Air

Force.[33] On July 7, 1941 (other sources give a later date), it was Mikheev as Head of the 3rd Department who, ordered by Mekhlis, arrested Army General D.G. Pavlov, Commander of the West Front, and his colleagues near Dovsk.[34] In this matter, Mekhlis had no legal authority but was representing Stalin and was merely repeating what he and Frinovskii had done in the summer of 1938 to the High Command in the Far East. This time Mekhlis was officially appointed Political Commissar of the West Front, replacing A. Ia. Fominykh. Mekhlis held the position officially from July 3 until July 12 (other Soviet documents indicate July 15 or later)—long enough to arrest and send Pavlov and his colleagues to face Ul'rikh. Also as we will see later, such operations as the mass execution of senior military officers in October 1941 was organized primarily by the NKVD proper and not by the Special Department. Under Stalin, as well as Hitler, in matters of intelligence, security, and terror, confusion was the rule rather than the exception.

K.A. Stoliarov in *Golgofa* incorrectly places Abakumov as head of the GUGB/NKVD Special Branch in 1940. Abakumov's appointment as head of the Special Department is also disputed by A.I. Romanov in *Nights Are Longest Here*. He claims that the first head of the 3rd Department, during the war, and, in fact, also the first head of SMERSH, was V.V. Chernyshev, the only survivor among Ezhov's Deputy Commissars. According to Romanov, Chernyshev was later replaced by Abakumov and became his first deputy. Soviet documents do not confirm this.

In his speech to the 18th Party Congress in March 1939, Stalin denounced those who did not understand the role of the "punitive and intelligence organs" in the building of socialism and those who "indulged in idle chatter to the effect that the secret service in the Soviet state was all trivialities and nonsense." Stalin further explained that "underestimation of the secret service" had arisen, "owing to the imperfections and inadequacy of some of the general theses of the Marxist doctrine on the state." Stalin also added that although the purge was necessary, beneficial, and unavoidable, it was accompanied by "serious mistakes," adding that such mass purges would not be needed in the future. Zhdanov, Stalin's present mouthpiece, whose record in Leningrad after Kirov's murder was second to none, chimed in along the same lines, claiming that massive purges were against the Party rules. This was the charade of a step backward and, in fact, the machinery of terror remained intact.[35]

Back in 1934, before he learned to become politically correct, M.A. Sholokhov had questioned Stalin about the use of torture. Stalin's laconic answer was perhaps not among friends. On January 20, 1939, Stalin sent a telegram in code to the local Party and NKVD leaders stating that the Central Committee of the Party approved of the methods of physical pressure practiced by the NKVD since 1937 since they were "correct" methods. Parallel with this, however, was the setting up of a commission by CC CPSU (P.A. Shariia, Stalin and Beriia's ghost writer, was a member) to eliminate "acts outside of socialist legality admitted by N.I. Ezhov," but this was merely window dressing. The suggestion that terror declined considerably under Beriia seems illusionary at best. There would be no Thermidor here since Ezhov's fall did not translate into a decline of Stalin, the Robespierre of the Bolshevik

Revolution. In a series of articles in 1991 in *Istoriia SSSR* and *Sotsiologicheskie Issledovaniia*, statistician V.N. Zemskov presented documents that showed that between 1921 and February 1, 1954, nearly 3.8 million were arrested, 2.9 million of them by the security organs. In 1937, 6.9% of those arrested were sent to the Gulag; in 1938, 50.2%; and in 1939 and 1940, under Beriia, 40.6% and 45.5%, respectively. According to two other Russian writers, I. Ivashov and E. Emelin (*Krasnaia Zvezda*, August 4, 1990), between the outbreak of war and July 1, 1944, 1.8 million additional individuals were put under protective custody. Without citing his sources, in *Moi Otets*, Beriia's son claims that by March 1, 1940, his father had freed 28.7% of the 1,668,000 political prisoners in the Gulag, and that during the war 750,000 prisoners wre evacuated, with 420,000 of them released to join the Army. All in all, from 1941 to 1945, 970,000 former prisoners served in the military ranks (157,000 in 1942–1943 alone). Among them were Heroes of the Soviet Union S.T. Breusov, A.I. Otstavnov, I.Ia Serzhantov, and the most famous of them all, A.M. Matrosov.

The winter 1938–1939, the first after Beriia's appointment, was particularly deadly for the Gulag prisoners with thousands of deaths due to cold, starvation, and disease, as movingly related by various memoirs of the literary historian L.E. Razgon, himself an inmate. There was also mass execution in camps of those who could in any way be identified as former supporters of Trotskii and his ideas. The next two winters were not much better. Memoirs of surviving Polish prisoners such as Janek Leja show that in some labor camps the death rate was over 90% amongthe new prisoners. J. Arch Getty, G.T. Rittersporn, and V.N. Zemskov (*American Historical Review*, October 1993), minimalists so far as Stalin's crimes go, first state that the Central Committee called off the purge in 1938, only to add accurately a bit later that the terror did not subside in the 1940s, and in some respects even intensified.

So far as the military was concerned, in 1936, 3,816 individuals were tried by the Military Collegiums, 8,681 in 1937, and 8,360 in 1938. In 1939 under Beriia, the number decreased only to 7,826. In 1940 the number shot up to 38,527, presumably as the result of the Winter War, and included the POWs repatriated by the Finns. In the beginning of 1939, there were over 350,000 kept in *regular prisons*, but at the end of the year the number was reduced to 186,000, only to jump to 434,000 by the end of 1940. Between 1940 and 1948, except in one year, the prison population remained between 200,000 and 300,000. Only in 1943 did the need for cannon fodder cause an emptying of prisons and the population was reduced to 150,000. Soviet documents show that the prison and Gulag population increased from 1.7 to 2.5 million during 1935–1938. It declined only to 2.4 million by 1941, after three years of Beriia's stewardship. On the official day of Beriia's appointment (December 12, 1938), Stalin and Molotov confirmed the execution of 3,176 people.[36] In March 1939, Chairman of the USSR Military Collegium V.V. Ul'rikh wrote to Stalin that from February 21 to March 14, 1939, his court had disposed of 436 cases and 413 of the defendants were sentenced to death.[37] Victims included L.I. Mirzoian, First Party Secretary in Kazakhstan; Marshal A. I. Egorov; Komandarm 1st Rank I.F. Fed'ko; Komkors G. D. Khakhan'ian and S.A. Turovskii; Corps. Commissar A.P. Prokof'ev; Politburo members and candidate members P.P. Postyshev, S.V.

Kosior, and V.I. Chubar; and former Komsomols Heads A.V. Kosarev and P.I. Smorodin, who had been arrested by the previous regime. The architect of collectivization, Ia.A. Iakovelev, was put to death on March 14, 1939, a fate shared by his Chief Executioner M.M. Khataevich, who had been under arrest since 1937.

Senior military officers who were arrested under Ezhov, but who were executed or died under Beriia, included Marshal of the Soviet Union A.I. Egorov, former Chief of Staff of the Red Army and later Commander of the Transcaucasus Military District, arrested in April 1938, sentenced to death on February 2, 1939, and shot or died under torture a day later; rehabilitated on March 14, 1956. The case of Marshal Egorov was an anomaly since his wife, G.A. Egorova, had already been shot on August 28, 1938. Under Stalinist justice, the family usually follows rather than precedes the victim to the wall. Army Commander 1 Rank I.F. Fed'ko, former 1 Deputy Commissar of Defense, was arrested on July 7, 1938, sentenced to death on February 26, 1939 and shot on the same day, rehabilitated on May 26, 1956. Army Commissar 1 Rank P.A. Smirnov, former Commissar of the Navy, was arrested on June 30, 1938, condemned to death on February 2, 1939, shot a day later, and rehabilitated on May 16, 1956. Komkor G.D. Khakhan'ian, former Commissar of the Far East Red Banner Army was arrested on February 1, 1938, condemned to death on February 2, 1939, and shot the next day, and rehabilitated on April 11, 1956. Flagman 1 Rank K.I. Dushenov, former Commander of the North Fleet, arrested on May 22, 1938, sentenced to death on February 3, 1940 and shot the next day, rehabilitated on April 29, 1955. Komkor M.P. Mager, Commissar of the Leningrad Military District, was first arrested on September 10, 1938 and finally shot on October 16, 1941; his case will be discussed later in some detail. Komkor G.D. Bazilevich, secretary of the Red Army Committee for Defense, was arrested on November 23, 1938, sentenced to death on March 2, 1939, and was rehabilitated on July 27, 1955. Komkor G.I. Bondar', Deputy Commissar Defense Industry, was arrested on August 25, 1938, sentenced to death on March 10, 1939, and rehabilitated on June 25, 1939. Komdiv K.Kh. Suprun, Assistant Commander of the Transbaikal Front, was sentenced to death on February 26, 1940, and shot the next day, and rehabilitated on July 28, 1956. Komdiv A.S. Tarasov, Chief of Staff Transbaikal Military District, was sentenced to death on May 20, 1940, and rehabilitated on November 26, 1955.

In addition, a number of officers already in prison received additional sentences under Beriia. Komdiv Ia.I. Ziuz'-Iakovenko, former Commander of 2 Rifle Corps, received an additional 20 years (15 in prison plus 5 in exile) on November 8, 1939, later died in prison, and was rehabilitated on February 2, 1956. Komdiv V.I. Malofeev, former Commander of 1 Rifle Corps Leningrad Military District, received an additional 20 years on November 15, 1939, later died in prison, and was rehabilitated on September 17, 1957. Komkor Ia.Z. Pokus, Deputy Commander of the Far East Red Banner Army, was arrested on February 22, 1938, released on February 18, 1940, re-arrested on October 3, 1940, sentenced to 10 plus 5 years on July 16, 1941, died in camps, and was rehabilitated on April 11, 1956. Komkor S.A. Pugachev, head of the Military-Transport Academy, was arrested on October 10, 1938, sentenced to 10 plus 5 years on October 26, 1939, died in camps on March 23, 1943, and was rehabilitated on June 30, 1956.´ Komkor V.N. Sokolov, Chief Inspector Defense Committee, Commissariat of Defense, was arrested on November 14, 1938, sentenced to death on April 14, 1939, and shot the next day, and rehabilitated on June 30, 1956. Komkor M.O. Stepanov, head of the chemical department of the Red Army, was arrested on December 9, 1938, sentenced to 20 plus 5 years on May 31, 1939, died in camp in 1945, and was rehabilitated on June 30, 1956. Komdiv S.V. Nikitin, former Commander of the 11 Rifle Corps Leningrad Military District, received an additional 15 years on August 20, 1939, died in prison on June 16, 1941, and was rehabilitated on June 16, 1956. Komdiv K.P. Ushakov, Commander of the 9 Cavalry Division, received an additional 20-year sentence on July 20, 1939, died in camps in 1943, and was rehabilitated on March 14, 1956. Komdiv I.F. Sharskov, head of the Odessa Artillery School, received an additional 15 years on May 8, 1939, died in camps in 1942, and was rehabilitated on August 11, 1956. Komdiv G.I. Kassin, Commander of the 45 Rifle Corps, arrested on August 5, 1938, was sentenced to death on April 14, 1939, and was rehabilitated on October 20, 1956. Komdiv I.F. Maksimov, head of the 7th Department of the General Staff, was arrested on October 15, 1938, sentenced to death on April 15, 1939, and rehabilitated on May 30, 1956. Komdiv A.K. Malyshev, Chief of Staff, Central Asia Military District, was arrested on August 23, 1938, and sentenced to death on February 8, 1939; the sentence was carried out on March 19, 1939. He was rehabilitated on March 19, 1957.

Corps Commissar K.G. Sidorov, Commissar of the North Caucasus Military District, was arrested on May 25, 1938, sentenced to death on February 2, 1939, shot on June 25, 1939, and rehabilitated on June 25, 1955. Corps Commissar I.P. Petukhov, Commissar for Special Assignments in the Commissariat of Defense (Voroshilov's secretary), was arrested on July 4, 1938, and released on February 14, 1939, re-arrested on March 12, 1939, and sentenced to 5 years on April 20, 1939. He died in camps in 1942 and was rehabilitated on December 11, 1954. According to Soviet documents (*Voprosy istorii,* No. 6, 1991), on January 19, 1939 Voroshilov inquired from Beriia about Petukhov. The inquiry may have led to his temporary release.

Corps Commissar A.M. Bitte, the former head of the political section of the Transbaikal Military District who had been arrested under Ezhov, was condemned to death on November 10, 1939. Corps Commissar M.Ia. Apse, the commissar of Transcaucasus Military District and already under arrest, was sentenced to 25 plus 5 years on August 3, 1939, and died in camps in 1942; he was rehabilitated on October 27, 1956. Corps Commissar A.P. Prokof'ev, Commissar of the Special Corps in Mongolia, was arrested January 25, 1938, sentenced to death on May 9, 1939, and rehabilitated on July 28, 1956. Corps Indendant A.I. Zhil'tsov was arrested on December 8, 1938, and sentenced to 20 plus 5 years on May 8, 1939, and died in prison in 1941 and was rehabilitated on May 19, 1956. Division Commissar R.L. Balychenko, Commissar of Volga Military District, was arrested on November 10, 1938, sentenced to 10 plus 5 years on May 14, 1939, and died on May 31, 1943 in camps. He was rehabilitated on February 19, 1959. Division Jurist A.S. Grodke,

Deputy Commissar of Justice, was arrested on November 3, 1938, and was shot on June 9, 1941; he was rehabilitated on February 22, 1956. Brigade Jurist P.S. Voiteko, Military Prosecutor of the Black Sea Fleet since 1933, was arrested on February 9, 1938, was sentenced on February 28, 1940, to 15 years, and was rehabilitated on July 13, 1957. Voiteko's case, as related in the collection *Oni ne Molchali*, is particularly poignant since he was one military prosecutor who decided to stand up to the NKVD and with disastrous results.

Division Commissar I.G. Indirkson, Senior Instructor in the Red Army Political Administration, was arrested april 26, 1938, sentenced to death on February 22, 1939 and shot a day later. He was rehabilitated on February 8, 1957. Division Commissar I.I. Zil'berg, attached to the GRU, was arrested on September 19, 1938, sentenced to death april 14, 1939 and rehabilitated June 27, 1957. Division Quartermaster A.M. Sokolov, Assistant Commander of the Central Asia Military District for Materials, was arrested June 23, 1938 and sentenced to 15 plus 5 years on March 8, 1939. He died in exile April 29, 1953 and was rehabilitated March 28, 1957. Two Division Commissars arrested after Beriia's takeover were D.Ia. Egorov, Head of the Economics Branch in the Civil Aviation Department of GOSPLAN, arrested March 26, 1939, sentenced to death February 1, 1940, and rehabilitated on May 30, 1957, and I.S. Mal'tsev, Head of the Political Section of the 12 Rifle Division, arrested and sentenced to death in 1939.

Political and government leaders also continued to fall under Beriia. Ia.A. Iakovlev (Elshtein), who as Commissar of Agriculture during 1929–1934 had carried out the collectivization, was shot on March 14, 1939. Ezhov had served as Iakovlev's Deputy during 1929–1930 in his first major government job, which proved to be an excellent training ground when he took over the NKVD in September 1936. Other prominent men who were to die in the early years of Beriia's regime included B.A. Breslev', M.M. Landa, A.M. Liubovich, M.M. Mairov, Ia.A. Piatnitskii, M.L. Rukhimovich, G.Ia. Sokol'nikov (Brilliant; originally sentenced to 10 years in 1937), B.S. Stomoniakov, M.I. Frumkin, M.M. Khataevich, A.V. Kosarev, A.I. Bekzhadian, and I.I. Khodorovskii. The condemned were shot or died under torture (in the case of Marshal Egorov) during February 22–26, 1939. The death of the Komsomol leader A.V. Kosarev, who had once badmouthed Beriia, had been put squarely on the latter's shoulder, and yet Beriia's son, in his conversations with R.Sh. Chilachava, heatedly denies this. According to him, Kosarev's fate was determined in the Central Committee meeting on November 22, 1938, three days before Beriia's appointment as the head of NKVD. Documentary evidence in the collection *Oni ne Molchali* and in *Ogonek* (February 14, 1988), however, shows a different scenario. In fact it was in the 7 Komsomol Plenum which met by Stalin's order on November 19, 1938, that sealed the fate of Kosarev and his colleagues. It was announced (*Pravda*, November 23, 1938) that during this meeting the work of the leadership was denounced by the two provocateurs, N.A. Mikhailov and O. Mishkova, working hand-in-hand with Stalin's henchman M.F. Shkiriatov. Kosarev, S.Ia. Bogacheva, and V.F. Pinkin were arrested on November 28 to be followed by 77 of the 93 participants in the Plenum.

Mikhailov was put in charge of Komsomols and eventually was Minister of Culture under Stalin's successors after serving as a member of the court that tried Beriia and his colleagues in 1953. The former leadership were now in the hands of Beriia and his interrogators, B.Z. Kobulov, Rodos, Shvartsman, Makarov, and Arshatskaia with expected results. Among those arrested, only Pilkin somehow managed to survive and returned from camps to be rehabilitated on October 28, 1954. Here he was joined by A. Milchakov, another survivor from the Komsomol Central Committee. Kosarev, a former cheerleader for the terror, was shot on February 23, 1939. He was rehabilitated in 1954 and readmitted to the Party in 1989.

Besides Kosarev, all the former secretaries of the Komsomol Central Committee (O. Ryvkin, L.A. Shatskin, E. Tseitlin, etc.) became victims during the Great Purge. G.I. Lomov was shot on December 30, 1938; A.S. Bubnov on January 12, 1940; L.A. Shatskin on October 1, 1940; N.P. Glebov-Avilov on 1942; Ia.R. Berzin on April 12, 1941; and R.I. Berzin on September 11, 1939. Bela Kun died or was killed in Saratov prison in the early 1940s, although a date as early as November 30, 1939 is also given for his demise. K.B. Radek (Sobel'son) was sentenced to 10 years on January 30, 1937, and was murdered, possibly by a fellow inmate, on May 19, 1939.

Under Ezhov, who besides the NKVD had also taken over the GRU (May 29, 1938–December 1938), the Soviet foreign intelligence had been decimated through purges and Soviet-inspired assassinations. Although few potential victims were left, the repression continued under Beriia. His major victims included S.Ia. Efron and N.A. Klepinin-L'vov, employed by the NKVD since 1933, who had worked in France as Soviet agents. Klepinin was arrested in July 1939 and Efron two months later (*Literaturnai Gazeta*, 47, 1990). The case was handled by A.A. Esaulov (Maj. General, July 1945), head of the Investigation Department in GUGB/NKVD, and the Chief Military Prosecutor N.P. Afanas'ev. With the war raging, the USSR Military Collegium with Judges A.A. Cheptsov (encountered elsewhere in this book), Bukanov and Uspenskii had no trouble meeting on July 6, 1941. On the dock, Efron and Klepinin were joined by E.E. Litauer, Count P.N. Tolstoi, and one N.V. Afanasov, an employee of the Kaluga Canal who had served in the White armies as a junior officer. Despite their denials, Klepinin and Efron were convicted of espionage and were shot on July 28 and October 16, 1941, respectively. A tragic footnote to this affair was the fate of Efron's wife, the playwright, poet, and translator M.I. Tsvetaeva (born 1892), who had left the Soviet Union in 1922 only to return with Efron in 1939 to see her husband arrested. She committed suicide in Elabuga on August 31, 1941. Efron's daughter, A.S. Efron, was arrested on August 27, 1939, and was roughly treated by the woman investigator S.M. Orchatskaia, and on July 2, 1940, was sentenced to 8 years as a French spy. She was released on August 1947 and returned to Riazan, where she was re-arrested on February 22, 1949. She survived and saw her father rehabilitated on February 19, 1955. She also helped edit and publish her mother's poetry in 1965. Her brother, G.S. Efron, volunteered for service and was killed in action during the war. Most of the surviving former leaders of Comintern such as V.G. Knorin and I.A. Piatintskii were also put to death in 1939, the latter on October 30.

The show trials, however, were stopped only to be revived after the war, and only in the satellites. Under the assembly line justice which replaced the show trials, broken prisoners were dragged to face Ul'rikh to be sentenced to death decreed by Stalin and usually shot on the same day. Ul'rikh routinely reported the executions to Stalin. On its own within two years, the Beriia regime would arrest men such as the candidate member of Politburo R. I. Eikhe (arrested in summer 1939 and shot on February 1940), the writer I.E. Babel' (arrested May 16, 1939, shot January 27, 1940), and the impresario V.E. Meierkhol'd (Meyerhold) (arrested June 20, 1939, shot February 2, 1940). Meierkhol'd was followed by his wife, Z. Raikh, who was found murdered. In his memoirs, engineer D.M. Panin, arrested in July 1940, relates that he shared a cell in Lefortovo Prison with one of her murderers, a professional thief named Varnakov.The Meyerhold's apartment was allegedly given to V. Matardze, a former mistress of Beriia, and her husband; she lived there between her own two terms of imprisonment, but was expelled from the apartment as a pensioner during the Gorbachev years. B.K. Lifshitz, a poet and the distinguished translator of both French and Georgian literature, was also shot in 1939, although he may have been arrested during the Ezhov regime. I.K. Luppol, who played a major part in the purge of the USSR Academy of Sciences for which he became an academician in 1939, was arrested in 1940 and perished on May 26, 1943. The Menshevik chronicler of the Bolshevik Revolution, N.N. Sukhanov-Gimmer, in Siberian exile since 1920, was executed on August 27, 1939 by the personal order of Stalin. A leading Polish Communist writer, Bruno Jasienski, who had immigrated to the Soviet Union in 1929, was also shot or died in camps in 1941.

One of the most famous Soviet journalists, and possibly an NKVD operative on the side, was M.E. Kol'tsov (Fridliand), known best for his reports from Spain during the Civil War. He was arested on December 17, 1938, and was executed on February 2, 1942, although other dates such as February 1940 or April 1942 are also given. Kol'tsov's commonlaw German wife, Mariia von Osten (Gressgener), who had tempted fate by returning to the Soviet Union, was condemned to death by an NKVD troika on August 8, 1942 and shot the same day. Former Military Prosecutor, B.A. Viktorov, implicates Abakumov in Kol'tsov's arrest but gives no sources. Academician N.I. Vavilov, Russia's outstanding geneticist, first denounced to NKVD by fellow scientist G. Shlykov as a "rightist and a saboteur" in March 1938 and at loggerheads with T.D. Lysenko, Stalin's favorite scientist, was arrested on July 25 or August 6, 1940 and sentenced to 15 years. Vavilov died of hunger in prison on January 26, 1943.[38] In his conversations with R.Sh. Chilachava, Beriia's son claims that his father actually saved Vavilov from execution and tried to place him in a laboratory environment before the latter actually died of dysentery. Vavilov's fate did not keep Stalin from appointing his brother, the physicist S.I. Vavilov, as president of the Soviet Academy of Sciences in 1945.

The families of the arrested were also victimized. The fate of Postyshev's family is a case in point. His wife and older son were shot and the young son, L.P. Postyshev, a naval aviator, was sent to camps until after Stalin's death. Bukharin's first wife, N.A. Lukina, was shot in March 1940 and his third wife, A.M. Lorina, barely survived, perhaps because of an administrative error. Even though the German invasion had vindicated Richard Sorge, whose warnings Stalin had chosen to ignore, the NKVD arrested the spy's wife in September 1942 and had her sentenced to a 5-year exile where she died in Krasnoiarsk on May 28, 1943. In the winter of 1938, the physicist L.D. Landau (Nobel Laureate, 1962) was arrested as a German spy and only released a year later after the direct intervention of the academician P.L. Kapitza. In January 1940, M.M. Kaganovich (Lazar's brother), Commissar of the Aviation Industry, was removed and accused of being a German spy. He avoided arrest only by committing suicide. There are rumors that another brother, Iu.M. Kaganovich, disappeared during the 1930s, but A.I. Vaksberg disputes this, claiming that the individual in question served with the Commissariat of Foreign Trade as a trade representative in Mongolia and died of natural causes in the early 1950s. Vaksberg also puts to rest the rumors that Kaganovich's sister Rakhil (also called Roza), who actually died in Kharkov in 1925, was Stalin's last wife. In April 1941, a Leningrad NKVD "troika" sentenced Komkor S.N. Bogomiakov to death on a charge of having sabotaged the Far East fortified zones even though the alleged crimes had taken place two years before his arrival at Khabarovsk.[39]

On March 30, 1939, Komkor M.O. Stepanov, head of the Chemical Department of the Red Army, wrote to Voroshilov that between 40%–45% of his officers in Military Districts and 60-65% in Corps and Divisions had been arrested. Voroshilov forwarded the letter to the Special Department, and Stepanov was arrested. On July 20, 1939, Komdiv S.V. Nikitin, former Commander of the 11 Rifle Corps, was sentenced to 10 years for membership in a "military conspiracy." Komdiv L.M. Gordon, Commandant of the Kronshtadt Fortress, was arrested in 1939. Even those who had been freed from prison were not safe. In 1939 Kombrig Ia.P. Dzenit, Commander of the 86 Rifle Division, was arrested but was released in 1940 and was appointed senior lecturer in the Academy of the General Staff. On July 26, 1939, the Commander of the North Fleet and Deputy to the Supreme Soviet K.I. Dushenov, was arrested. He wrote to Molotov and complained about torture in Lefortovo, where he was being interrogated. The 267-page letter had an effect opposite to the intended effect since Dushanov was sentenced to death in February 1940.

There was also the extraordinary case of Komkor M.P. Mager (already mentioned), Chief of Staff Leningrad Military District and a Party member since 1915. Marger was first arrested on September 10, 1938. Shortly after his arrest, he confessed, naming 37 fellow "conspirators," only to retract the confession in February 1939. The newly appointed (from August 1939) Chief Military Prosecutor and the future (1943) Lt. General of Judiciary, P.F. Gavrilov, felt that Mager had been a victim of provocation and ordered his release. Mager was finally released in January 1940 and in March was re-admitted to the Party. On the same day that Gavrilov reported the matter to Beriia, he received a call from Stalin questioning Mager's release and suggesting that it was politically necessary to exile him to Siberia, a decision which Gavrilov argued against. Stalin also added that the decision to release Mager must be approved by the Central Committee. Over the phone Gavrilov also heard Stalin discussing the matter with Beriia speaking in Georgian. Stalin and

Beriia now found in V.M. Bochkov, head of the Special Branch, a man willing to carry out the order in regard to Mager, who was re-arrested in March 1941, a decision that was approved by Timoshenko. On May 15, 1941, Mager wrote to Stalin professing innocence. On June 6, 1941, Poskrebyshev sent a list of charges against Mager to the Central Committee, and on July 20, 1941, the Military Collegium sentenced him to death. For his efforts, Gavrilov was replaced in 1941 by V.I. Nosov. Incidentally, Gavrilov and another military prosecutor, A.A. Cheptsov, whom we shall meet later, are extreme rarities—men serving the Stalinist state who nevertheless tried in vain to introduce an element of justice to the proceedings.[40] In a period when the Soviet state was facing major international crisis, Stalin would take time to micromanage the terror, which says a great deal about his character and priorities.

Other senior officers arrested after Beriia's appointment include the aforementioned Komndarm 1 Rank M.P. Frinovskii, former Commissar of the Navy, and Fleet Flagman 2 Rank P.I. Smirnov-Svetlovskii, Deputy Commissar of the Navy, arrested on May 26, 1939, condemned to death on March 16, 1940, shot the next day, and rehabilitated on June 23, 1956. Flagman 2 Rank G.V. Vasile'v, Commander of Submarines in the Black Sea, was sentenced to 20 years on June 4, 1939 and rehabilitated on April 20, 1957. Komdiv A.G. Orlov, head of the foreign languages Department in the Dzerzhinskii Artillery Academy, was arrested on June 31, 1939, sentenced to death on January 24, 1940, shot the next day, and rehabilitated on May 21, 1955. *VIZH* (1/1993) contains a report dated May 25, 1940 from Timoshenko to Ul'rikh that in 1939, 19,000 military personnel were sentenced by the military courts. Another report dated November 11, 1941, from Prosecutor General G.N. Safonov to the Central Committee, states that in the beginning of the war there were 18,000 arbitrarily arrested military personnel who could not be released in time to join combat units.

According to the testimony of NKVD investigator, N.F. Adamov, in April 1939, Beriia ordered the formation of a top secret group made up of Kobulov, Vlodzimirskii, Arenkin, Meshik, Rodos, and Shvartsman. Based in Sukhanov Prison, this group was Beriia's private army of terror. One of its first acts was the arrest of I.A.Makhanov, Head of the Artillery Testing Department in a Kharkov factory. His forced confession provided Beriia with the needed ammunition to later compromise the main artillery administration.

On August 20, 1940, Beriia seemed to have accomplished his greatest success when his operatives organized the assassination of Trotskii, the most non grata of personas in Stalin's Russia, but as we now know through P.A. Sudoplatov, who organized the operation, that he reported to Stalin and not to Beriia, but the latter must have received some credit for providing the manpower. The Beriia team was also not kind to Soviet diplomats. The Ezhov-Vyshinslii machine had already claimed such outstanding diplomats (and in some cases leading Armenian Bolsheviks) as A.A. Bekzadian (1879–1938), D.V. Bogomolov (1890–1937), L.M. Karakhan (1889–1937), I.Kh.Davtian (1888–1938), S. Pastukhov, L.N. Stark (Riabovskii) (1889–1943), K.K. Iurenev (Krotovskii) (1888–1938), B.S. Stomoniakov (1882–1941),

N.N. Krestinskii (1883–1938), Ia.S. Ganteskii, Kh.G. Rakovskii (1873–1941), L.M. Khinchuk (1869–1944), B.S. Mel'nikov, A.Ia. Arosev, L.Ia. Gaikis, and V.A. Antonov-Ovseenko (1884–1939). In May 1939, there was also a new massive purge of the Commissariat of Foreign Affairs that claimed many victims and allowed Beriia to place his mole, V.G. Dekanozov, as Deputy Commissar of Foreign Affairs. Those with particularly strong anti-Fascist credentials such as M.I. Rozenberg, who had served as Soviet Ambassador to Spain since August 1936, were singled out. Also arrested was B.E. Skvirskii, the Soviet Ambassador to Afghanistan, who died or was shot in prison in 1941, a fate shared by A.S. Chernykh, Ambassador to Iran (1935–1939); I.L. Lorents, Ambassador to Austria (1935–1938); S.P. Natsarenus, Ambassador to Turkey (1921–1922); A.N. Vasil'ev, Ambassador to Mongolia (1923–1925); A.Ia. Okhtin (Iurov), Ambassador to Mongolia (1927–1933); S.A. Bessonov, former ambassador to Germany; and successive Heads of Protocol Florinskii and N. Barkov; as well as some low-ranking officials such as E.A. Gnedin (author of important memoirs), Shcheglov (Head of Information Bureau, released in 1953), Grishfel'd and Mironov (Pines). There was also the strange case of S.I. Kavtaradze (1885–1971), former Ambassador to Turkey and the Deputy USSR Prosecutor. Kavtaradze had known Stalin in his youth, but in 1927 he had been expelled from the Party as a Trotskyist. Beriia had him arrested, but Stalin later ordered his release. Kavtaradze, who was readmitted to the Party in 1940, served as the Deputy Commissar of Foreign Affairs (1943–1945) and the Ambassador to Rumania (1945–1952). The purge in the Foreign Service was organized by Molotov, Vyshinskii, Beriia, Dekanozov, and A.Z. (brother of B.Z.) Kobulov. The investigations were handled in the typically brutal manner by Captain of State Security I.L. Pinzur.

A.I. Vaksberg, in *Stalin Against the Jews*, states that Stalin had planned to launch a major trial involving the diplomats, but abandoned the plan because of the change in international situations and finally because of the outbreak of war. The man designated to be the chief witness during the trial was E.A. Gnedin, son of A.L. Gel'fand (Parvus), and former press attache at the Soviet Embassy in Berlin. Under arrest since 1939, he was sentenced to 10 years on July 9, 1941. Gnedin survived and was rehabilitated on August 13, 1955. Vaksberg's account, however, lists diplomats such as K.K. Iurenev, former Ambassador to Germany (1937), and Ia.Kh. Davtian, former Ambassador to Poland (1934–1937) as potential victims of the proposed trial even though the men had already been shot under Ezhov.

F.F. Roskol'nikov (Il'in), hero of the Civil War and onetime husband of L.M. Reisner, had served during 1930–1938 as Soviet Ambassador to Estonia, Denmark, and Bulgaria. His refusal to return to the Soviets caused the Military Collegium on July 17, 1939, to condemn him for "desertion" and drove him to write his famous open letter of July 26, 1939, denouncing Stalin, causing a sensation in the West. Raskol'nikov died on September 12, 1939, in a hospital in Nice under circumstances that some have found suspicious. Sudoplatov, who was in a position to know, however, has nothing to say about this. Ambassador to Germany A.F. Merekalov was recalled in April 1939, removed, but managed to survive and died in 1983. He was replaced in September 1939 by A.A. Shkvartsev (a mere professor, in Molotov's words), who was in turn replaced by the Beriia operative Dekanozov in November 1940, and his fate remains unclear. In September, the same fate came to Luganets-Orelskii, the representative to China. Sudoplatov (*Special Tasks*, p. 412) claims that he saw documents from the Central Committee in which Beriia was accused of having organized the killing of Luganets-Orelskii and his wife. The new Soviet envoy in China was A.S. Paniushkin, more of a policeman than a diplomat. He eventually headed the KGB Foreign Department for 13 years (1953–1965), longer than anyone else. Beriia and A.Z. Kobulov also did their best to implicate M.M. Litvinov, the recently sacked Commissar of Foreign Affairs, but gave up in October 1939 since Stalin still had uses for Litvinov. Most of Litvinov's colleagues, however, were arrested. Replacing the fallen diplomats were men such as A.A. Gromyko, Ia.A. Malik, K.V. Novikov, F.T. Gusev, B.F. Podtserob, K.A. Umanskii, A.S. Paniushkin, and rare survivors such as I.M. Maiskii, S.A. Lozovskii, and A.M. Kollontai, who, led by Molotov and later Vyshinskii, formed the foot soldiers of Stalin's foreign policy.

There were also non-Soviet victims.[41] Foreign Communists residing in the USSR continued to suffer under Beriia as they had under Ezhov. For instance, in 1939 the Bulgarian Communist Blagoi Popov, a fellow defendant of Georgi Dimitrov at the 1933 Reischtag fire trial, was arrested. Dimitrov's efforts to help Popov and other arrestedBulgarians came to nothing and Popov was not released until after Stalin's death.[42] After Franco's victory, a number of Spanish Communists and Republicans had sought refuge in the USSR. By 1940, most were sent to camps.[43] There was also the question of cooperation between the NKVD and the Gestapo during the years between the signing of the Hitler-Stalin friendship treaty and the start of the war, when many German and Austrian Communists were returned to the Nazis. The study by Hans Schafranek, *Die Betrogenen*, lists many cases of Austrian citizens residing in the USSR who were handed over to the German authorities. In the collection, *Staliniada*, Iu.B. Borev also claims that Hitler offered to release and repatriate the imprisoned leader of the German Communist Party Ernst Thälmann (1886–1944) to the Soviet Union, but he was turned down by Stalin. Thälmann was murdered in Dachau in 1944.

Parallel with the terror campaigns, there were attempts to release some of the victims of the Great Terror, particularly those in the military. Unfortunately, most of the victims were beyond help since reviving the dead was perhaps the only power that had yet to be claimed for Stalin's genius.

According to documents in the collection *Oni ne Molchali*, as a result of the rehabilitation commission in the beginning of 1940, 4,661 individuals expelled in 1937, 6,333 in 1938, and 184 were readmitted to the Red Army in 1939. In addition, the pending cases for 2,416 individuals were dropped. By May 1, 1940, a total of 12,461 individuals, most of them in the junior ranks, were restored. There was a peculiarly Stalinist touch in regard to the released or re-admitted senior officers. Although the rank of General had been introduced to the Red Army, most of these officers continued to hold archaic ranks of "Kombrig," "Komdiv," and "Komkor," along with some other officers who lacked higher education or were politically suspect. In the beginning of the war, the Red Army, the army of the classless society, had at least eight ranks above Colonel. The rank of Kombrig, Komdiv, and Komkor in this period was as if the officers were still wearing prison stripes. Occasionally, when such an officer distinguished himself or was actually killed in action, the rank of General was bestowed. Case in point: L.G. Petrovskii (son of G.I. Petrovskii), Commander of the 21 Army, West Front, who had been in prison from May 1938 until December 1940 received the rank of Komkor on his release. On July 31, 1941, this was changed to "Lt. General." On August 17 near Zlobin, he was fatally wounded during the breakout from encirclement. Komdiv E.Ia. Magon, Commander of the 45 Rifle Corps, 13 Army, West Front, who also had been imprisoned in the 1930s, was promoted to Maj. General after he was killed in action in August 1941. Among the better known survivors were the future Marshal of the Soviet Union K.K. Rokossovskki; future Marshal of Tank Troops S.I. Bogdanov; future Army General I.I. Gusakovskii; future Col. Generals V.A. Iushkevich and V.D. Tsvetaev; future Lt. Generals L.G. Petrovskii, K.P. Podlas, M.G. Efremov, and A.I. Zygin; Komdivs E.Ia Magon and A.A. Trubnikov; Kombrigs S.P. Zybin and Ia.P. Dzenit; Corps Commissar Ia.V. Volkov (Commissar of the Pacific Fleet 1937–1938); and Brigade Commissar I.A. Kuzin, head of the political section in the North Caucasus Military District. Corps Commissar I.P. Petukhov, Assistant Head of the Special Task Department, was arrested on July 4, 1938 and freed on February 14, 1939. Several of these previous victims such as Petrovskii, Magon, Podlas, Zybin and Zygin, later fell in battle. Of course, not all surviving officers were released. Corps Engineer Ia.M. Fishman, who had been the head of the Red Army Chemical Department since 1925, was arrested on June 5, 1937, but somehow was not shot. On May 29, 1940, he was sentenced to 10 years and released in 1947, only to be re-arrested in April 1949 and not freed until after Stalin's death. Even better known was Komkor A.I. Todorskii, the former head of the Zhukovskii Air Academy, who survived 16 years in prison to become a major force in the rehabilitation of repressed officers during the Khrushchev years, as well as a biographer of Tukhachevskii.

Lesser known military personalities who served their sentences included Komdivs Ia.Ia. Alksnis, department head in the General Staff Academy, whose cousin Ia.I. Alksnis, the head of the Air Force, had been shot on July 29, 1938; M.F. Bukshtynovich, Commander of the 7 Motorized/Mechanized Corps, V.K. Vasentsovich, Chief of Staff of the Red Banner Far East Army; M.P. Karpov, Commander of the 17 Rifle Division, department head in the Military-Electrical Academy; F.P. Kaufel'dt, head of Border and Internal Troops, Far East District; F.G. Sokolov, department head in Commissariat of Defense; V.N. Chernyshev, Commander of the Air Force in the Central Asia Military District and others.

Meanwhile, the game of musical chairs also continued. On March 7 and 8, 1941, four Army Commanders, 42 Corps Commanders, and 117 Division Commanders were newly appointed. None of these attempts could fill the gaps created by the Great Purge in the senior ranks, and rapid and undeserving promotions were made to fill the vacant positions. Captain F.I. Matykin, a Battalion Commander in 1938, was made a "Komdiv" and commander of a division. Captain I.N. Neskubo jumped from head of a regimental school to command a division. Major K.M. Gusev, Commander of a squadron, also became a "Komdiv" and was put in charge of the Air Force in the Belorussian Military District. Senior Lieutenant I.I. Kopets was promoted to Colonel and was appointed as Deputy Commander of Air Force in the Leningrad Military District.

Also released from prison were a number of scientists and designers. Arresting scientists with military skills antedated the Great Terror. In 1929, the veteran N.P. Polikarpov, who had copied French and British designs (an activity in which the Soviets excelled) as well as designing his own planes, was arrested. While in prison, he designed the L–5 fighter, which became the mainstay of the Soviet Air Force for many years. In 1930, designer D.P. Grigorovich was also arrested but was released three years later, as was Polikarpov. In the early 1930s, the OGPU arrested ship and submarine designers A.A. Asafov, S.A. Bazilievskii, A.N. Garsoev, E.E. Kriuger, B.M. Malinin, N.P. Papkovich, and others, but most were released within two to three years. The Great Terror claimed numerous victims among military designers. Those who did not survive included G.E. Langemark (inventor of Katiusha rocket), K.A. Kalinin (designer of flying wing, shot on October 22, 1938), V. Bekauri (radar), V. Zaslavskii (armor), I.T. Kleimenov (Director of the Jet Propulsion Research Institute [RNII]), Iu. V. Kondratiuk (writer of theoretical essays on rocketry), M. Leitenzon (space travel), L.V. Kurchevskii (recoilless gun), and Smirnov (tank). Aircraft designer V.N. Riutin (older brother of M.N. Riutin), who served as an assistant to A.N. Tupolev, was shot despite a personal plea to Stalin by Krupskaia. Stalin's feelings at this time toward Lenin's widow were similar to Henry VIII's vis–á–vis Cardinal Wolsey. The meddlesome woman, however, died on February 27, 1939 and so another reminder on Stalin's nonexistent conscience was conveniently removed.

Those who were arrested but survived were academicians L.D. Landau (Nobel Prize in Physics, 1962), L. Zil'berg and P. Zdorovskii, A.I. Berg (father of Soviet radar), and V.P. Glushko (designer of rocket and jet engines).[44] A leading ship designer, P.I. Serdiuk, was arrested in 1937 but was not convicted until 1940. He was released in 1944. The physicist P.L. Kapitsa, naive and somewhat arrogant, who had failed to show proper respect, was also on Beriia's hit list. A desperate Kapitsa wrote to Stalin in December 1945 complaining about Beriia's behavior. Stalin's cryptic reply is quoted in R.Z. Sagdeev's autobiography: "I have received all of your letters. They are very instructive. I hope one day we can meet and talk about them." On August 17, 1946, Kapitsa was removed from all of his positions and was put under de facto house arrest, but was otherwise unharmed. As usual, it was Stalin and not his satraps who decided the fate of important people.

In addition to the scientists mentioned, there was a group of nearly 100 men who were arrested and put to work in prisons in a bizarre organization called OKB EKU GPU/NKVD (Special Construction Bureau, Economic Division GPU/NKVD) popularly known as "Tupolev Sharaga" and named after aircraft designer A.N. Tupolev. Tupolev, who along with N.E. Zhukovskii had organized the Center for Aerodynamic Research (TsAGI) under the Soviets, had known Stalin, who shared his interest in long-distance flights for many years. In the 1930s, Stalin would use record-breaking flights by Soviet airmen to divert the attention of the populace from the mass terror that was taking place. In mid–September 1935, Tupolev met with Stalin, Molotov, Voroshilov, and test flyer S. Levanevskii, who was critical of the Tupolev–designed single engine AN-25, which as it turned out was reliable. On July 20, 1936, V.P. Chklaov and his crew flew an AN-25 from Moscow to the mouth of Amur. On June 20, 1937, Chkalov and his crew flew an An–25 from Moscow via the North Pole, to Vancouver, Washington, and Chklaov was hailed as the Russian Lindbergh. On July 14, 1937, another Soviet pilot, the future Col. General of Aviation M.M. Gromov, a man with possible NKVD connections, flew 6,300 miles from Moscow, again via the North Pole, to San Jacinto, California, breaking the world's long-distance flight record. Meanwhile Tupolev's critic, Levanevskii, embarked on August 12, 1937, with a five-man crew on an arctic flight in a multi-engine DB–A plane designed by V. Bolkovitinov never to be seen again. Despite the enormous success of Tupolev's design, he was arrested on October 21, 1937. After Tupolev's arrest, Ezhov had allegedly said, "We could have thousands of Tupolevs."

According to A.K. Sul'ianov, investigation began on January 7, 1938, and on January 4, 1939, the NKVD investigator Senior Lt. of State Security Esipenko submitted his report, which stated that Tupolev, according to the testimony of prisoners Nekrasov and Val'ter, had organized a terrorist group in service of the fascists. Esipenko also managed to collect incriminating testimony from 22 of Tupolev's colleagues, including A.E. Fradkin, A.V. Nedashkevich, G.A. Ozerov (later author of a book on the Tupolev "Bureau"), B.S. Miasishchev, V.M. Minker, K.V. Osipov, A.A. Cheremukhin, A.M. Iniushin, and K.A. Pogosskii. Tupolev, in turn, on October 28, 1937, shortly after his own arrest, had confessed to belonging to an "anti-Soviet" group and named fellow designers Petliakov, Pogosskii, Ozerov, Nedashkevich, Petrov, Sukhoi, Nekrasov, and others leading to their arrests. (On January 30, 1940, Tupolev retracted his confession.) In February 1939, Tupolev, imprisoned in Butyrka Prison, met with Beriia and agreed to work under NKVD auspices with fellow designers who were also in prison and form "brigades" to build planes to Beriia's specifications. Despite this, on May 28, 1940, he was sentenced to 15 years by the Military Collegium. Only after the start of the war were Tupolev and his colleagues released. *Voennyi Vestnik* (January 1990) also records a strained conversation between Beriia and another imprisoned designer, R.L. Bartini, who had been arrested in January 1938 after the crash of his Stal–7 plane. Bartini (of nobility, born Roberto Cros di Bartini) was among the founding members of the Italian Communist Party in 1921. In 1923 after Mussolini came to power and started the crackdown on Communists, Bartini emigrated to the Soviet Union. From 1924, he worked as a designer, and in December 1930 he headed his own design team. He was a pioneer student of helicopters and jet aircraft before his arrest. After Bartini's arrest, a member of his team, V.G. Ermolaev, had redesigned the plane as a potential bomber. In August 1939 it set a long-distance flight record of over 5,000 miles. Stalin inquired about the designer, and although Voroshilov and the future Maj. General of Aviation G.N. Zakharov recommended Bartini's release, he took no action. Instead, Beriia met with Bartini and suggested that he could be released if he designed another successful plane. Bartini was eventually released and received the Lenin Prize in 1967. He died in 1974.

The role played by the NKVD in the development of weapons going back to Special Bureau 39 in 1929 needs further study. The Medvedev brothers, in their biography of Khrushchev, go as far as to claim that artillery designers A.A. Blagonravov and Iu.P. Pobedonostsev and the tank designer Zh.Ia. Kotin (chief designer of the T–34) did their work under the sponsorship of NKVD. Recent research by J.N. Westwood on Soviet naval construction also points out the interest displayed by the organs in the design and building of ships.

The entire Tupolev enterprise was run by V.A. Kravchenko (Maj. General, July 1945) who in 1941 was appointed Deputy Head Gulag. He was assisted by another Gulag veteran, N.A. Frenkel'. Cooperation between the scientific community and NKVD was a fact of life in the Soviet Union and no less a personality than the saintly Andrei Sakharov worked hand-in-hand with Lt. General A.P. Zaveniagin (Deputy Commissar/Minister NKVD/MVD, and at times in charge of the Gulag during 1941–1950) during the development of the hydrogen bomb. The "Tupolev sharaga" was indeed a distinguished group, which included six members or future members of the USSR Academy of Sciences: S.P. Korolev, Iu. A. Krutkov, A.I. Nekrasov, B.S. Stechkin, Iu. B. Rumer, and A.N. Tupolev. Besides Tuploev, well-known designers included V.M. Petliakov (designer of the PE–2 attack bomber), V.M. Miasishchev (designer of TB planes), A.A. Arkhangel'skii (designer of the Maksim Gor'kii Bomber), and B.S. Vakhmistrov (pioneer in the "piggy-back" composite concept). Some, but not all, of these prisoners were released before the war.

Other prisoner-scientists included A.I. Putilov, R.L. Bartini, V.A. Chizhevskii, A.S. Markov, I.G. Neman, D.L. Tomashevich (designer of the I–180 fighter in which Chkalov crashed), M.M. Kachkachian, and A. Nevdachin. Tupolev, Miasishchev, A.M. Cheremukhin, and G.A. Ozerov were freed in August 1941. Others were freed in Omsk in the fall of 1942, and the remainder were kept until the end of the war. The fate of S.P. Korolev, the Soviet Union's greatest rocket scientist, was typical. Korolev was arrested on June 27, 1938 after being denounced by his colleague, L.G. Kostikov (academicians in the USSR and elsewhere are not above this sort of thing). He was sentenced to 10 years and assigned to the Tupolev group and continued there after it was transferred to Omsk. According to Iu.B. Borev in *Staliniada*, in 1943, Korolev, who was working on an experimental "flying wing" aircraft was brought over by Molotov to meet with Stalin and was given three minutes to present his report. Stalin asked him about the speed of the plane and when Korolev mentioned 360 kilometers an hour, he dismissed the designer as a fool since German planes were already flying at 500–600 kilometers. During 1943–1944, Korolev was transferred by NKVD to Kazan, where he continued to do rocket research. Korolev was officially released on July 27,1944, but the charges were not actually dropped until 1957, after he had been named Hero of Socialist Labor and had won the Lenin Prize. V.M. Petliakov had been released earlier. When he was killed in an air accident on January 12, 1942, Stalin ordered arrests of a number of people who had supposedly caused the death of a "talented constructor and patriot."[45] According to the military prosecutor B.A. Viktorov, the provocateur A.G. Kostikov, who had denounced his colleagues, later was in trouble himself (*Nauka i zhizn'*, No. 12, 1988). On February 18, 1944, GKO removed Kostikov, now a Major General, from his position as director of RNII (Jet Propulsion Research Institute), where he had replaced the purged Kleimenov. Kostikov's fall resulted from unsatisfactory progress in the development of jet aircraft, but the military prosecutors also took an interest in his intrigues against other scientists, whom he had accused of sabotage. On March 16, 1944, the prosecutors turned the matter over to NKGB. On February 28, 1945, Merkulov dismissed the matter, calling Kostikov innocent of malicious intent and a needed specialist. Under Stalin the real saboteurs obviously enjoyed immunity.

In his conversations with F.I. Chuev, Molotov defends the arrest of specialists such as Tupolev and Korolev and their confinement to work in a "controlled environment." He compares Tupolev unfavorably with another designer, S.V. Il'iushin (once Molotov's son-in-law). Tupolev was a "bourgeois type" who was not a "Soviet man" and allegedly had connections with intellectuals hostile to Soviet power. Despite all of this, even Molotov has to admit that Tupolev was a superior designer who made great contributions to Soviet aviation. The coming of the war, as will be seen, gave Beriia additional opportunities to expand his empire by becoming the overseer of the defense industry. Another area which became a monopoly of the NKVD was airfield construction. This labor intensive enterprise was logically put under the NKVD which had unlimited access to slaves. L.B. Safraz'ian, head of military construction in the Commissariat of Defense since October 21, 1938, was appointed on March 22, 1941 Deputy Commissar of NKVD and would supervise airfield construction during the war. During the entire period covered in this book, NKVD also continued to run its vast economic empire (mining, etc.) with slave labor, its brutality tempered only by inefficiency. Stalin, however, thought so highly of Beriia's efforts that in 1943 he awarded him, still a civilian, with the title of Hero of Socialist Labor and in May 1944 appointed him as Deputy Chairman of the GKO. In *Moi Otets*, S.L. Beriia goes into some detail about the arrested specialists. He claims that Tupolev, Korolev, Miasishchev, and Mints, among others, told him that they owed their freedom to his father. He further claims that these men were originally arrested by the order of the Central Committee and not by NKVD. He also states that when his father was in charge, no military specialists were arrested. Even under Ezhov, important military figures could not be arrested without the approval of Stalin and Voroshilov. S.L. Beriia and Sudoplatov were the foremost proponents of the theory that the Party, not the organs, were behind the repressions, and that the worst crimes took place under men such as Ezhov or Igant'iev who were essentially Party functionaries and not professional Chekists. Abakumov, although a Chekist, also took his orders only from the Party, or more accurately, from Stalin.

After September 1939, the focus of terror on a massive scale was transferred to the newly occupied territories in Poland, Belorussia, and West Ukraine under the leadership of I.A. Serov, L.F. Tsanava, and N.A. Krimian. The Hitler-Stalin treaty of September 28, 1939, had brought under Soviet control 77,500 square miles of territory and 13 million people, many of whom were of doubtful loyalty. At times there was cooperation between NKVD and Gestapo against common enemies such as Polish nationalists as well as the forced return of German anti-Fascists. In late January 1940, many German and Austrian refugees from the Nazis were collected from camps and transferred to the Gestapo. Among them was Franz Koritschoner, one of the founders of the Austrian Communist Party, later murdered in German captivity.[46] The latter tradition was going to be repeated a half-century later when Herr. Erich Honecker, formerly of the German Democratic Republic, was unceremoniously returned to his now united homeland to face an uncertain future.

During the Soviet occupation, between one and two million people were deported and thousands were executed under a regime so harsh that many preferred the German occupation, which was yet to get into high gear for the "Final Solution."[47] Volkogonov cites a report from V. V. Chernyshev, Deputy Commissar NKVD, to Beriia that from September 1939 until the outbreak of the war, nearly half-a-million individuals were deported from the former Polish areas that had been incorporated into the USSR. This figure does not include those deported from the Baltic region and Moldavia. According to M.F. Bugai (*Ukrainskyi Istorychnyi Zhurnal*, October 1990), three separate operations organized by NKVD dating from December 29, 1939, March 2, 1940, and April 10, 1940, sent thousands of Polish officials, landowners, and policemen from the newly occupied areas to Siberia, Komi ASSR, and Kazakhstan. All in all, Bugai claims that a larger number (1.2 million) of Poles were deported during the Soviet occupation, but some were released after the outbreak of the war. The historian V.S. Parasadanova, in two major articles (*Novaia i Noveishaia Istorria*, May 1988 and February 1989), also sheds considerable light on the extent of deportations from the occupied territories. She states that 312,800 families and 1,173,170 individuals were put under Soviet custody in occupied areas of western Ukraine and Belorussia.

Two documents from Beriia to Stalin, dated May 1, 1944 and June 17, 1945 and included in Bugai's *Iosif Stalin—Lavrentiiu Beriia* (pp. 33 and 217), however, state that as of August 1941, 389,382 individuals from captured Polish territories were under custody in the USSR in camps, POW camps (25,314), resettlement camps, prisons, and exile. After the amnesty of August 12, 1941, all but 341 were released. Among the released Poles and their families, 119,855 were evacuated in 1942 to Iran, mostly to join the Anders Army. Between 1941 and 1943, 11,516 had died (mostly of hunger) and 36,510 had joined the pro-Soviet Berling Army. By June 1945, according to Beriia, there were still 50,094 Poles in custody, but most of these had been arrested after the occupation of Poland and, according to Beriia, included Poles who had served with the German forces. Nothing in these reports mentions the fate of the Polish officers murdered at Katyn and elsewhere in the spring of 1940.

On October 11, 1940, mass deportation began in the Baltic states under I.A. Serov and was repeated during June 13–14, 1941, just before the German invasion. Soviet records indicate that during 1940–1941 and 1944–1952, 175,000 Estonians, 170,000 Latvians and 320,000 Lithuanians were arrested, many of whom were to die in camps.[48] In January 1953, the population of the Gulag still included the following survivors from this period: over 14,000 from the Baltic, 9,700 from Moldavia, and over 5,500 from the former Polish areas of Ukraine and Belorussia.

The experience gained here was applied during the war to deport entire nationalities. For instance, I.M. Tkachenko, who organized the deportations from Lithuania, did the same for the Karachis in 1944 when he was the NKVD chief in Stavropol.

In the early days of the war, terror reigned everywhere. Abarinov includes the report of one junior Lt. Kompaneets, head of the 3rd Department of the 42 NKVD Escort Battalion, dated June 26, 1941, to Senior Major of State Security A.M. Belianov, Head (more likely Deputy Head) of the NKVD 3 Department, that because of confusion and enemy air attack, near the village of Cherven the Battalion shot 209 political prisoners who were being evacuated from the Minsk prison.

The collection of documents *Skrytaia Pravda Voiny: 1941 God* contains reports about the extent of terror in the early days of the war, including a request on July 5, 1941, by Rumiantsev, Military Prosecutor of the West Front, to V.I. Nosov, Chief Military Prosecutor, to arrest Sargeant of State Security Primyshev, head of Vitbesk prison, who on his own had begun to carry out illegal executions of the prisoners. Rumiantsev's attempt to stop the executions was opposed by Motavkin, head of NKVD Vitbesk, and by Ptushkin, deputy head of NKVD in Belorussia. In another report, Major of State Security A.M. Leont'ev, head of security for Mozhaisk sector, informed N.A. Bulganin, Commissar of the West Front, that during a three-day period in mid–October his "interceptor battalions" had arrested 23,064 Red Army troops as deserters. For this kind of diligence, Leont'ev was later appointed head of the NKVD Office for Security of Front Armies and received the rank of Lt. General in July 1945.

In June and July 1941, during the Soviet retreat, the NKVD rear guard managed to murder nearly 100,000 prisoners.[49] Major massacres took place in Lvov (1,500), Stanyslavl (2,500), Zolochiv (800), Chortkov (800), and Dobromyl (500). On June 26, 1941 in Sambir, 1,200 inmates were killed when the NKVD dynamited the prisons. In Galicia, there were at least 10,000 executions, mostly in Rovno, Lutsk, and Volynia (5,000). In some areas, the mass killings gave the German occupiers and their local allies the necessary excuse to mount pogroms even though Jews had also been victimized during the Soviet occupation. A case in point was in L'vov, when three days after the start of the war, in response to an unsuccessful attempt to free the 12,000 political prisoners held in Brygidki Prison, the NKVD killed them all. On July 2, the occupying Germans and their Ukrainian allies launched "AktionPetliura," in which thousands of Jews were massacred.[50] According to Soviet sources (*Novaia i Noveishaia Istoriia*, 5/1990), during the evacuation of L'vov, NKVD murdered 1,834 prisoners and attributed their deaths to "bombing by the German-Fascist air force during the evacuation." It is estimated that in the first six months of the war, the NKVD rear security arrested 600,000 alleged deserters and had over 10,000 shot, some after drumhead court martials, some out-of-hand, and frequently in the presence of other troops. On November 17, 1941, Beriia, through NKVD courts, ordered the execution of all prisoners under the death sentence: 4,905 individuals were shot in eight days.

On occasion, the regular NKVD and militia, aware of Hitler's Commissar Order, would beat a hasty retreat. A case in point happened in the city of Kalinin in mid–October 1941. Soviet documents published in *Skrytaia Pravda Voiny: 1941 God* contain the text of a report by Jurist 2nd Rank Berezovskii, Military Prosecutor of 30 Army, dating from October 16, 1941 which indicated that the militia and the local NKVD, headed by Major of State Security V.S. Tokarev (more about him later), acting solely on Tokarev's initiation had deserted the city. Tokarev had held his position in April 1940, when Polish prisoners from the Oshtakov prison (many former policemen) were shot in the local prison. He probably expected, with good reason, similar treatment from the new invaders.

As a Deputy Commissar of NKVD for a part of this period, Abakumov could not have remained uninvolved. A recent Western source, *La Terreur en URSS durant les Années Trente*, refers to him as the "Gauleiter" of occupied territories, but this remains unsubstantiated. The detailed history of Latvia between the two wars, *Latvijas Vesture 1920–1940*, makes a passing reference to Abakumov's helping Serov in the last wave of the deportation a week before the start of the war, but gives no details.[51] During 1940–1941, the security organs, however, were involved in three well-documented mass repressions: the massacre of Polish POW officers in Katyn and elsewhere in spring 1940, the executions of 157 political prisoners in Orel on August 1941, and the execution of 25 senior military officers and some of their wives in Kuibyshev and Saratov on October 28, 1941. These, as well as the massive deportations of various nationalities, will be discussed in the next two chapters.

NOTES

1. Considerable material was published about Beriia during the Glasnost period. Besides Conquest's book, *Inside Stalin's Secret Police*, important sources include *Beriia, Konets Kar'ery; Izvestiia TsK KPPS* (1 and 2, 1991); a series of articles in 1989, 1990, and 1991 in *Voenno Istoricheskii Zhurnal* (VIZH); *Sotsiologiskie issledovaniia* (March 1988); *Kievskii novostii* (November and December 1992); *Kommunist Gruzii* (November 1990); *Kommunist* (March 1991) D.A. Volkogonov, *Triumf i tragediia*; Uri Ra'anan, *Inside the Apparat*; Arkady Vaksberg, *Stalin's Prosecutor; Sovershenno sekretno* (June 1989, June 1990); and Amy Knight, *Beriia, Stalin's First Lieutenant.*

2. D.A. Volkogonov, *Triumf i tragediia*, book 1, part 2, p. 246 and *Kommunist Gruzii* (November 1990), pp. 93-95.

3. Robert Conquest, *Inside Stalin's Secret Police*, p. 79.

4. A.G. Malenkov, "Skhvatka s Ezhovym," *Zhurnalist* (February 1991) and A.G. Malenkov, *O Moem Ottse Georgii Malenkov*, p. 32-33.

5. For Goglidze's relations with Beriia, see *VIZH* (July 1989 and October 1991); *Beriia: Konets Kar'ery, Nedelia* (44/1990); *Zvezda* (January-February 1989).

6. *Istoriia SSSR* (February 1991).

7. Jonathan Haslam, *The Soviet Union and the Threat from the East:1933-1941*, p. 121.

8. V.V. Dushen'kin, *Ot Soldata do Marshala*; N.D. Kondrat'ev, *Marshal Bliukher; VIZH* (January 1990); and *Aleksandr Kosarev.*

9. *Izvestiia TsK KPPS* (December 1989).

10. Robert Conquest, *Inside*; N.G. Kuznetsov, *Nakanune; Boevoi Put' Sovetskogo Voenno-Morskogo Flota*; *Izvestiia TsK KPPS*; *Kommunist Vooruzhennykh Sil* (16/1989); and *Knizhnoe Obozrenie* (December 8, 1989).

11. *Krizhnoe obozrenie* (December 8, 1989).

12. *Beriia: Konets Kar'ery,* p. 392.

13. Robert Conquest, *Inside*, p. 104.

14. Ibid., p. 93.

15. E.H. Cookridge, *Gehlen, Spy of the Century*, p. 80.

16. The most important Russian source on Abakumov to appear so far is K.A. Stoliarov's *Golgofa* (Moscow: 1991). The book's first part is devoted to Abakumov and the rest to the career of Army General N.A. Shchelokov, Minister of Interior, who committed suicide with his wife in December 1981. Stoliarov's account is mainly about Abakumov's career after he became Head of MGB and about the events after his arrest, and finally about his trial. It is less-detailed about Abakumov's early career. There are also differences between this account and those of other Russian writers. Information about Abakumov also can be found in an article by V. Kutuzov in *Leningradskoe delo*; D.A. Volkogonov, *Triumf i tragediia*; A.I. Romanov, *Nights Are Longest Here*; Peter Deriabin, *The Secret World; Beriia: Konets Kar'ery*; *Druzhba narodov* (4/1988); *Izvestiia TSK KPSS* (3/1989); *Nedelia* (Issue 44, 1980); *Sovetskaia Militsiia* (4/1991), etc.

17. Svetlana Alliluyeva, *Twenty Letters to a Friend*, p. 195.

18. Ibid., p. 196.

19. For Kedrov and his career, see M.I. Sboichakov, *Mikhail Sergeevich Kedrov*; I.V. Viktorov, *Podpolishchik, Voin, Chekist; Voennye Kontraazvedchiki; Izvestiia TsK KPSS* (3/1989); *VIZH* (11/1963); and A.K. Sul'ianov, *Arestovat' v Kremle*.

20. *Beriia: Konets Kar'ery*, p. 201.

21. *VIZH* (5/1991); V.D. Uspenskii, *Tainyi Sovetnik Vozhdia*, p. 403.

22. E. Gnedin, *Katastrofa i Vtoroe Rozhdenie*; *VIZH* (5/1989 and 6/1989).

23. *Beriia: Konets K ar'ery*, p. 221.

24. *Pravda* (May 8, 1989), p. 4.

25. Svetlana Alliluyeva, *Twenty Letters to a Friend*, p. 164.

26. For the careers of Gai, Lepevskii, Zalpeter, and N.N. Fedorov, see Michael Parrish, *Soviet Security and Intelligence Organizations 1917-1990*. For Fedorov, see also *VIZH* (3/1993), p. 27.

27. *Kommunist* (7/1990), p. 71.

28. Ibid., p. 73; and *VIZH* (1/1993), p. 96.

29. For Bochkov, see Anton Antonov-Ovseenko, *The Time of Stalin, Sovetskaia prokuratura*; and *VIZH* (4-5/1992).

30. Robert Conquest, *Stalin, Breaker of Nations*, p. 242; and *VIZH* (4-5, 1992).

31. *Kommunist* (Issue 17, 1990).

32. *Izvestiia TsK KPPS* (7/1990), p. 201; V.K. Abarinov, *Katynskii Labirint*, p. 44; Iu.I. Semenov, *Komissary Gosbezopasnosti,* pp. 8-9.

33. D.A. Volkogonov, *Triumf*, book 2, part 1, p. 73.

34. For Mikheev, see Iu.I. Semenov, *Komissar Gosbezopasnosti*; and I.F. Stadniuk, *Voina*.

35. Michel Heller, "Stalin and the Detectives," *Survey* (1/1975), p. 166.

36. *Sotsial'no-politicheski nauki* (7/1990), p. 91.

37. *Kommunist* (1/1990).

38. George Gamow, *My World Line*, p. 101; and *Moscow News* (Issue 46, 1987).

39. *Kommunist* (Issue 17, 1990), p. 72.

40. Ibid., p. 73.

41. For purges in the Commissariat of Foreign Affairs, see E.A. Gnedin, *Katasrofa i Vtoroe Rozhdenie.*

42. Blagoi Popov, *Ot protsesa v Laiptsig do Lagerite v Sibir.*

43. Karlo Stajner, *7000 Days in Siberia*, p. 88.

44. For victimized scientists, see *For Human Rights*. Also, E.K. Moshkin, *Razvite Otechestvennogo Raketnogo Dvigatelstroeniia*, and *Soviet Encyclopedia of Space Flight.*

45. For scientists and designers in prison, see A. Sharagin, *Tupolevskaia Sharga*; A.P. Romanov, *Korolev*; V.S. Gubarev, *Konstruktory; Beriia: Konets Kar'ery*; V.D. Uspenskii, *Tainyi Sovetnik Vozhdia*; and *Nauka i Zhizn'* (October 1988).

46. Stajner, op. cit., pp. 79, 95.

47. Jan Gross, *Revolution from Abroad*, p. 178.

48. *Beriia: Konets Kar'ery*, p. 48; and *Voprosy Istorii* (1/1991), pp. 33-49.

49. V.K. Abarinov, *Katynskii Labirint*, p. 44; and Gross, op. cit., p. 22.

50. Gerald Reitlinger, *House Built on Sand*, p. 166.

51. P.F. deVillemarest, *GRU, Le Plus Secret des Services Sovietiques, 1918-1988*, p. 132; Edgars Andersons, *Latvijas Vesture, 1920-1940*, Vol. 2, p. 522.

Chapter 2

Mass Killings of Polish POW Officers

Although the Stalinist state was markedly inefficient in providing its citizens with the basic necessities of life, it was the epitome of proficiency when it came to mass murder. Students of Hitler's "Final Solution" and its model, the Turkish massacre of the Armenians have noticed the necessity of the bureaucratic machinery when the modern state embarks on physical extermination of a large number of individuals. In fact, every facet of the Nazi regime was involved in carrying out Hitler's order to make Europe "Judenfrei." The liquidation of 14,700 helpless Polish POW officers, including one woman (the aviatrix Janina Lewandowska, murdered in Katyn), and 11,000 other prisoners held by the NKVD in Western Ukraine and Belorussia in the spring of 1940 in the Soviet Union was the "Final Solution" on a smaller scale. In a handwritten memo registered on March 9, 1965, but probably written on an earlier date, A.N. Shelepin, member of CC CPSU administrative organs in charge of secret police and a former Chairman of KGB (from December 25, 1958 to November 13, 1961), suggesting to Khrushchev the destruction of records related to Katyn, mention is made of 21,857 individual files relating to the victims.

As complex an operation as the mass killing of the Poles required the full cooperation of almost every department in NKVD's vast bureaucracy even though as Stalinist crimes went, Katyn was not such a major event: after all, nearly a million people had been "legally" executed during Stalin's rule—compared to about 6,000 during 1905–1912 at the height of Tsarist oppression—most of them probably for non-political crimes.[1] In all probability, the number of those killed by the NKVD rearguard during the retreat from western borders in the summer of 1941 is considerably higher than the number of Polish officers murdered in the spring of 1940. Merkulov called Katyn a mistake, but as E.A. Robinson put it, there are mistakes too monstrous for remorse and Katyn was such a case—magnified by 50 years of Soviet mendacity and denial in view of inconvertible evidence to the contrary.

In its attempts to embarrass M.S. Gorbachev (who may yet end up in Mexican exile), on October 14, 1992, the Russian government released documents that showed that the order to exterminate the former Polish citizens, including the officers held in camps, was approved by the Politburo on March 5, 1940, and was signed by Stalin. Besides Stalin, the document was signed by three other full members of the Politburo: Molotov, Voroshilov, and Mikoian. Kalinin and Kaganovich were not present, but had indicated that they were in favor of the measure. Three other full members (Andreev, Khrushchev, and Zhdanov) were not recorded, although according to Beriia's son, Zhdanov was a strong supporter. There is also a possibility that documents implicating at least Khrushchev were later destroyed. Beriia and Shvernik, as candidate members, were not eligible to vote. The approval came in response to a request of the same date by Beriia to dispose of certain categories of Polish prisoners including 295 Generals and 2,080 majors and captains. The list includes two groups: 14,736 prisoners in camps and 18,632 individuals kept in prison in Western Ukraine and Belorussia. In 1940, the Politburo was of course a mere rubber stamp, and the decision was made by Stalin, who alone was responsible for the death of the prisoners who formed only a percentage of those victimized during the introduction of socialism to occupied territories. To give the operation a legal pretence, a troika with Beriia as a self-named member was set up to "try" the prisoners. As Soviet documents show, Stalin for unknown reasons crossed out Beriia's name and replaced it with that of B.Z. Kobulov. Merkulov and Bashtakov also were members. Along with the order to exterminate the Poles, the Politburo also approved Beriia's plans to remodel Lenin's tomb.

The genesis of Katyn was the Red Army's "liberation march" in September 1939 into Western Belorussia and Ukraine. The Polish government, busy with fighting the German invaders, ordered its armed forces not to resist the Red Army. As a result, the invaders were faced with thousands of unarmed troops, who posed logistical as well as political problems. One deeply concerned individual was Senior Major of State Security L.F. Tsanava, head of NKVD in Belorussia since December 1938, who complained bitterly to Moscow about the lack of "screening" of Polish troops. All and all, over 130,000 officers and troops of the Polish Army were under Soviet jurisdiction. On September 21, 1939, Marshal G.I. Kulik, commanding the invading "Army Group," citing logistical problems proposed that Belorussians and Ukrainian prisoners of the former Polish Army be allowed to go home. Two days later, Voroshilov, Commissar of Defense, and B.M. Shaposhnikov approved this basically sensible and humane decision. A day later, L.Z. Mekhlis, the Head of Political Administration of the Red Army, as always a fire-eater, registered his complaints and Stalin reversed the decision on September 26, 1939. Voroshilov repealed the original order.

Meanwhile, Beriia had been busy. On September 19, 1939, Beriia established the NKVD Office of the POWs (NKVD document 0309) under Captain (later Major) of State Security P.K. Soprunenko and his Commissar, S.V. Nikhoroshov. The new office reported to Komdiv V.V. Chernyshev, Deputy Commissar of NKVD (for militia) since July 1937 and the only member of Ezhov's high command who had continued to serve under Beriia. On September 22, Chernyshev reported to Shaposhnikov the establishment of ten camps with capacity of 10,000 each, including those at Kozel'sk, Oshtakov, and Starobel'sk. The ten camps, however, could not handle so many prisoners, and on October 4, Voroshilov and Shaposhnikov convinced Stalin of the soundness of Kulik's original proposal. Prisoners from areas incorporated into the USSR, as well as those of Czech nationality who served in the Polish Armed Forces, were allowed to return home. The order, however, contained a couple of more sinister provisions, one that captive soldiers from the German part of Poland would be handed over to NKVD, which in turn repatriated them by force and against the wishes of many of the Jewish prisoners. Intelligence and counter-intelligence personnel, gendarmes, and prison officials would also be handed over to NKVD. On October 3, 1939, Beriia issued an order in which all captive officers were assigned to Starobel'sk, all gendarmes and policemen to Oshtakov, and all petty officers and privates to Kozel'sk and Putivl camps.

By December 1, 1939 there were nearly 4,300 prisoners of Kozel'sk in the Kalinin Oblast. The transfers were to be completed by October 8, 1939. Besides petty officers, Kozel'sk contained many professionals who had been called up from reserves after the outbreak of war. On the same date, the Oshtakov camp contained nearly 6,000 prisoners, the overwhelming majority former policemen. Tishkov, head of the 1 Section of the NKVD POW office, wrote in a report that most of the prisoners in Oshtakov were not professional policemen, but drafted workers and peasants too old or unfit to serve in the regular Armed Forces, and also that most officers were reservists. Tishkov's suggestion that most of the prisoners be released was rejected by the NKVD high command. The third camp, at Starobel'sk in Kharkov, contained 4,000 inmates, mostly senior officers, but also a good number of professionals, intellectuals, and government officials as well as the chief Rabbi of the Polish Army. Most of the officers were from L'vov. Polish prisoners not assigned to these camps were assigned to various NKVD slave labor projects, some ultimately working with repatriated Red Army prisoners captured by the Finns during the Winter War.

On November 24, Soprunenko wrote to Beriia stating that under the ruling of the Supreme Soviet many of the POWs were Soviet citizens and could not legally be held as POWs, adding that the prisoners were demanding to be sent home. Soprunenko proposed that POWs be granted the status of "enrolled civilians" allowed to stay where they were employed. Beriia rejected Soprunenko's suggestion and instead demanded that order be restored to camps. Soprunenko's proposals are interesting since he must have been aware of Beriia's directive of October 8, ordering that the camps be searched for potential agents as well for those hostile to the Soviet Union, including members of nationalist organizations and even Zionists. On October 31, Major of State Security V.S. Zarubin arrived in Kozel'sk to carry out this task. The investigators at Oshtakov camp arrived on December 4, 1939, headed by Lt. of State Security S.E. Belolipetskii (Maj. General, July 1945). He was accompanied by investigators N.F. Bykov, A.M. Marisov, N.K. Kleshchev, M.S. Galafeev, V.A. Maklakov, A. Kiselev, A.Z. Fediunin, V.I. Senkin, P.N. Volchenkov, and two men from the NKVD Economics Department, Kholichev and Logunkov.

Belolipetskii had been Beriia's original candidate to head the entire investigation, but he seems to have worked only at Oshtakov. In Starobel'sk, the investigators arriving in October were headed by Captain of the State Security (B.P.?) Trofimov (Maj. General, July 1945) head of the 3 section in Gulag. The POW Department as well as the local camp Commandants received strict orders to cooperate with the investigators. On December 31, 1939, Beriia issued an order (NKVD document 5866/5) not only to Soprunenko, but also to the heads of NKVD in Smolensk, Kalinin, and Kharkov oblasts, where the camps were located, to assist the NKVD investigators. The involvement of the local NKVD was to be a bad omen for the prisoners. On January 28, 1940, another step was taken to seal the fate of the doomed prisoners when the Chairman of the Military Collegium of the USSR Supreme Court, V.V.Ul'rikh, and the acting Chief Military Prosecutor, N.P. Afanas'ev (the Poles were to become his specialty), ruled that cases of POWs came under the jurisdiction of NKVD courts. By February 10, 1940, the investigators had sent their reports via Suprenenko to the NKVD "1 Special Section" headed by L.F. Bashtakov and his Deputy, A.Ia. Gertovskii, who acted as a clearinghouse for the "court" that made the final decision. The court was actually none other than V.N. Merkulov, First Deputy Commissar of NKVD, assisted by Bashtakov, with possible assistance from B.Z. Kobulov. Merkulov and Bashtakov granted exemptions for a handful of individuals, including some recommended by P.V. Fedotov and P.A. Sudoplatov, which in some cases proved to be too late. Soprunenko continued his pitiful attempts by writing to Beriia on February 20, 1940, suggesting that some of the prisoners, including the disabled, incurably sick, and intellectuals against whom there was no evidence, be released. Once the final decision was made, Soprunenko and his camp officials fully cooperated in carrying out the mass murder.

The first executions probably took place in early March, when Merkulov ordered the transfer of a small group of officers identified as troublemakers from the Kozel'sk camp to the jurisdiction of NKVD in Smolensk. On March 16, the prisoners were prevented from receiving or sending out mail—to be resumed in September. During April–May 1940, according to the NKVD/POW Department, 14,587 prisoners from the camps had been transferred to the jurisdiction of the local NKVD departments (reports by the same department in 1941 and 1945 upped this figure to 15,131). The transfer, however, required the cooperation of the NKVD Transportation Department, which moved the prisoners to execution sites, as well as the NKVD escort troops, which provided the security. By May 20, 1940, the operation was complete and on June 6, NKVD officially confirmed this. The POW Department also destroyed all of the camp records. On June 9, 1940, Chernyshev reported that the camps were ready to house new prisoners from the Baltic region. Poles from Lithuania were now housed in the evacuated Kozel'sk camp. Soprunenko, however, had learned his lessons. Writing to Beriia on March 4 and 27, 1941, he stated that most of the new prisoners were counter-revolutionaries and 1,527 were members of "punitive bodies" and confirmed enemies of Soviet power. Suprenenko suggested that in view of the information available, these prisoners should be indicted and handed over to the "Special Court." Beriia, however, ordered on April 8, 1941, that the 4,000 prisoners be transferred to Murmansk and put to building an airfield at Ponoi (NKVD document 000358), a fate only slightly less deadly than ending up in the Katyn woods.[2]

Not all those destined for elimination ended up in Katyn. Prisoners from Kozel'sk camp were to be moved and executed in the Katyn wood near Smolensk using the local NKVD executioners, while prisoners from the Oshtakov camp were to be shot 100 at a time in the Kalinin prison with the executioners coming from Moscow. To prevent future exposure, German-made revolvers and bullets were used. The weapons either dated back to the 1920s when the Soviet Union imported arms from Germany or came from captured Polish stocks. Of the three camps housing the Polish officers, the fate of the nearly 4,500 from Kozel'sk is best known since their remains were found in Katyn. Abarinov claims that the NKVD headquarters ordered the liquidation of camps on February 12, 1940, which is possible even though the official decision of the Politburo was not made until March 5, 1940. Abarinov's meticulous research in the archives of the NKVD Escort Battalion (commanded until January 1941 by Col. T. Mezhov) and through personal interviews shows that between April 8 and May 12, the prisoners in this camp, escorted by the 136 Battalion, were taken by train and later by bus to execution sites. There is some dispute about who actually carried out the killings, the escort troops who were not above doing such things, or for that matter, the local executioners from Smolensk NKVD. Abarinov, for one, absolves I.I. Stel'makh, head of NKVD Prison in Smolensk. Stel'makh does not appear on the list of those who received awards for Katyn on April 27, 1940, nor does E.I. Kupriianov, Head of NKVD Smolensk, although their boss, L.F. Tsanava, was honored with the Order of Lenin. Kupriianov's fate is not clear.

Kupriianov's name is missing from the 1945 list of NKVD generals. The 129 NKVD Escort Regiment Troops provided the escort to transfer the nearly 7,000 prisoners in Oshtakov to the NKVD headquarters in Kalinin. According to Tokarev, head of NKVD in Kalinin, Blokhin, head of the execution squads coming from Moscow, assisted by (M.S.?) Krivenko and one Semianikov, decided that 250 killings a night would be an ideal number. Using German Walther revolvers, they disposed of the prisoners in soundproof rooms during April 1940. The victims were buried near the village of Mednoye, a site used by NKVD for mass burials. For his efforts, Blokhin received the Order of the Red Banner on April 27, 1940. The problem withTokarev's account is that he, supposedly an innocent bystander, also received the Order of the Mark of Honor on the same date. Less is known about the executioners of nearly 4,000 Polish officers from the Starobel'sk camp. The 68 NKVD Escort Regiment accompanied the victims to the execution site near Piatikhatki village about five miles from the center of the city and another favorite NKVD graveyard. Some of the prisoners were probably shot at the NKVD Headquarters in Kharkov and buried at the same site. The sources for the preceding allegations are witness testimonies that appeared in *Moscow News* (No. 24, 1990) and in the collection *Katynskaia Drama* (1991), but none of the documents released so far, nor the books by Abarinov and Tucholski, directly implicates the leadership of NKVD in Kharkov, whose names also do not appear in the list of those who were decorated on April 27, 1940. It is possible that the NKVD from Sumy, Poltava and even Voroshilovgrad had a hand in eliminating the Starobel'sk camp. On June 15, 1990, Maj. General N. Gibadulov, the head of KGB in Kharkov, reported the existence of Ministry of Defense documents stating that the Polish victims from the Starobel'sk camp were buried near Kharkov, adding that the NKVD records for that period had been destroyed. The exhumation planned for July 1990 did not take place until July 25, 1991. By August 9, 169 bodies were identified, including those of two women. Some were obviously Polish, but this was only a small percentage of the victims, and the fate of the inmates of Starobel'sk has yet to be clarified.

Besides Beriia, Commissar of State Security 1 Rank V.N. Merkulov (Order of Lenin, April 1940; Army General July 1945) and Commissar of State Security 2 Rank B.Z. Kobulov (Order of Red Banner, April 1940; Col. General July 1945), the chief organizers in this bureaucracy of annihilation, were Maj. of State Security L.F. Bashtakov (Order of Red Star, April 1940; Maj. General, July, 1945) in March 1940, head of NKGB 2 Department and later head of the dreaded 1 NKVD Special Section; his Deputy Captain of State Security A. Ia. Gertsovskii (Order of Mark of Honor, April 1940; Maj. General July 1945) and his assistants, Captain of State Security A.M. Kalinin (Order of Red Banner, April 1940), Lt. of State Security Sakarov, head of the 1 Branch Special Section, and Lt. of State Security Makov, head of the 4 Branch of this section. Working in close cooperation with this unit which came from Moscow was the NKVD Department for POWs headed by P.K. Soprunenko (Maj. General, July 1945); his deputies Lts. of State Security I.I. Khokhlov, I.M. Polukhin, and M.A. Slutskii; Commissar of the Department, Regiment Commissar S.V. Nekhoroshev; heads of the 2 Branch Senior Lt. of State Security Makliarskii and Major of Quartermasters Denisov; and the latter's assistant Lt. Pis'mennyi. Other participants from this department (mostly interrogators) included N.A. Vorob'ev, D.I. Lisovskii, N.T. Pronin, I.I. Senkevich, N.I. Romanov, I.M. Bashlykov, M. Ia. Seifullin, M.E. Goberman (the liaison between Soprunenko and Bashtakov), and F.V. Surzhikov. Involved in organizing escort and security for the operations were Komkor (Army General, July 1944) I.I. Maslennikov, Deputy Commissar NKVD; Komdiv (Col. General, July 1945) V.V. Chernyshev (to whom the POW Department was also subordinated); Deputy Commissar NKVD for Militia; Komdiv (later Lt. General) V.M. Sharapov, head NKVD Cavalry; and his Deputy Kombrig (later Lt. General) M.S. Krivenko and Kombrig (later Lt. General) I.S. Liubyi of the NKVD Railroad Troops. The GUGB/NKVD 2 Department (counterintelligence) was represented by its head Commissar of State Security, 3 Rank P.V. Fedotov (Order of Mark of Honor, April, 1940; Lt. General, July 1945), who was ably assisted by G.S. Zhukov (Lt. General, July 1945), head of the Central and East Europe Section and Major of State Security L.F. Raikhman (Medal for Bravery, April 1940; Lt. General, July 1945), head of the Polish branch. The movement of victims required involvement by the NKVD Transportation Department, headed since October 1938 by an old crony of Beriia, S.R. Mil'shtein (Order of Red Banner, April 1940; Lt. General, July 1945), and it was assumed that he had provided the transportation for the operation. Recent Russian documents, however, show that the NKVD Transportation Department was headed by Major of State Security L.G. Nikol'skii and his Deputy Major of State Security K.S. Zil'berman, the latter a Volga German and a fellow student of Beriia in the Baku Technical School during World War I. Also involved was Senior Major of State Security T.N. Kornienko, of the 3 (Special) Branch GUGB/NKVD. Since some of the prisoners (usually non-officers) were to be deported to camps, prisons and the Gulag was represented by its deputy head, Captain of State Security P.S. Safonov (Order of Red Star, April 1940); head of the 2nd Branch, Lt. of State Security G.M. Granovskii; and a Junior Lieutenant of State Security named Iatsevich, also of the 2nd Branch; and sometimes later by Corps Commissar (future Lt. General of Engineering-Technical Services) N.A. Frenkel', head of Gulag's Railroad Building Department, as well as Majorof State Security P.N. Zuev, head of NKVD prisons (Order of Mark of Honor, April, 1940) and P.S. Safonov, deputy head of Gulag (Order of Red Star, April 1940). P.I. Mal'tsev (Medal for Bravery, Maj. General, July 1945) was another labor camp official who was involved, but his exact role is not known.

The NKVD 1 (Foreign) Department at this time was headed by Senior Major of State Security P.M. Fitin (Lt. General, July 1945), and his Deputy, head of the "Special Section" P.A. Sudoplatov (Lt. General, July 1945). Sudoplatov's agents would comb the camps to recruit potential agents and saboteurs. The head of the investigation team in the Kozel'sk camp was V.S. Zarubin, a close friend of Sudoplatov whose career is extensively covered in his memoirs. According to Sudoplatov, who is extremely circumspect in his memoirs about Katyn, Zarubin had no idea why "selections" were taking place in camps and what fate was to befall the prisoners.

The local NKVD organizations probably provided facilities and additional killers. In Belorussia, the NKVD Commissar was Commissar of State Security 3 Rank L.F. Tsanava (Order of Lenin, April 1940; Lt. General, 1945); assisted by his Deputy, M.I. Reshetnikov, and the head of NKVD in Smolensk since 1939 Captain of State Security, E.I. Kupriianov. In Ukraine, there were I.A. Serov, the NKVD head since September 1939, and his Deputy, Captain of State Security (Major General, July 1945) N.T. Ratushnyi. Also involved was head of NKVD in Kalinin V.S. Tokarev (Order of Mark of Honor, April 1940; Maj. General, July 1945). V.M. Blokhin (Maj. General, July 1945), who probably carried out the actual killings of the inmates of the Oshtakov camp in the Kalinin prison, received the Order of Red Banner. One of his assistants, Maj. of State Security N.I. Sinegrubov, received the Order of Mark of Honor and in 1941 was promoted and became the head of NKVD Transportation Department replacing L.G. Nikol'skii.

Besides those officials from the NKVD Central apparatus and the provincial NKVD leaders (Tsanava and Serov), a number of local NKVD leaders were also involved in this affair. They may have provided security and escort, carried out the actual killings, or helped the executioners sent from Moscow. Others outside central Russia were involved in "re-settlement" of those POWs who had been spared but were moved to camps farther north and east. Besides the already mentioned Tokarev (Kalinin) and Kupriianov (Smolensk) the following have been implicated in the Soviet documents: P.P. Kondakov (Vologda) (Order of Red Star, April 27, 1940; Maj. General, July 1945), Veshchenikin (Sumy), Bukhtiarov (Poltava), Cherevatenko (Voroshilovgrad); V.V. Gubin (Order of Mark of Honor, April 27, 1940; Maj. General, July 1945) (Gor'kii), A.S. Blinov (Order of the Mark of Honor, April 27, 1940; Lt.

General, July 1945) (Ivanovo); and N.D. Gorlinskii (Order of Red Banner April 27, 1940; Lt. General, July 1945) (Kiev). Until the release of further documents, we have to assume that the major contributors to the Starobel'sk killings were the NKVD branches in Sumy and Voroshilovgrad. Then there were the commanders of camps, which fall into two groups—those where the prisoners were kept and others outside the central USSR to which those who had been spared were to be transferred. The camp Commanders were Major of State Security Borisovets (Ostashkov), who actually outranked Soprunenko, Senior Lt. of State Security Korolev (Kozel'sk), and Captain of State Security Berezhkov (Starobel'sk). These men, besides running the camps, provided support for the investigators who were making the "selections." Tucholski's book contains numerous communications from Soprunenko and his assistants to Borisovets and Korolev (but none to Berezhkov) listing the names of prisoners who should be put at the disposal of NKVD in Kalinin and Smolensk, respectively. Other camp Commanders involved who received a copy of Beriia's directive of December 27, 1939, to Soprunenko include Mateev and Filippov (Vologda), Kadyshev (Iukhov), Smirnov (Putivl'), Sokolov (Kozel'shchany), Sorokin (Bogorodskii raion near Gor'kii) and Kii (Iuzha near Ivanovo). None of the camp Commanders seem to have received high decorations.

A number of individuals implicated in Katyn continued to be involved in Polish affairs. As will be discussed later, Beriia, Merkulov, Bashtakov, Raikhman, and Zhukov later all played parts in the case against Alter and Erlich, the two Polish Bund leaders.

What role the 3rd (Special) Branch played in the killing is not completely clear. Copies of Beriia's directive to Soprunenko on December 27, 1939 (Tucholski, p.578), which laid the foundation for the whole operation, were sent to 24 individuals, including a number of minor camp Commanders. Three people listed as stationed in Minsk were Tsanava, his Deputy M.I. Reshetnikov, and V.M. Bochkov, head of the Special Branch. What Bochkov was doing in Minsk is not clear, and his name does not appear in other documents, but we can be sure that his office was atleast aware of the fate that was being prepared for the Poles. Another important document involving the Special Branch (Tucholski, pp. 581 and 582) dating from December 23, 1939, is from Major of State Security P.A. Osetrov (Order of Red Star, April 27, 1940) to V.V.Chernyshev, Deputy Commissar of NKVD, in which he discusses the result of investigations of 364 officers in the Uikhov camp and the transfer of most of them to the Kozel'sk and Ostashkov camps. Osetrov, at this time, has been identified as Deputy Head of the Special Branch. Later, he would serve in the NKVD Economics Department in post-war Germany and in Beriia's Atomic Trust. Other Soviet documents further indicate the involvement of Major of State Security A.M. Belianov, also identified as deputy head Special Branch GUGB/NKVD, and at the local level Major of State Security P.G. Begma (Order of Red Banner, April 1940) head of Special Branch Belorussian Military District, and Col. M.E. Rostomashvili (Order of Mark of Honor, April 1940), who fulfilled a similar function with the Kharkov Military District.[3] The general responsibilities of the Special Branch were listed in paragraph 9 of a directive issued by Beriia on September 19, 1939, in which their representatives in camps were subordinated to the Military District superiors as well as to the provincial heads of NKVD.[4]

Abakumov's name is conspicuous by its absence. What is intriguing is the official list of 634 individuals associated with NKVD who on April 27, 1940 received various awards such as Orders of Lenin, Red Star, and Red Banner. Many of these were given for participation in Katyn. Abakumov was one of 11 Senior Majors of State Security to receive the Order of Red Banner. This was not necessarily for involvement in Katyn, since the list also included S.N. Burdakov, Head of NKVD in Kazakh SSR; A.S. Zodelava, Head of NKVD in North Ossetia; N.D. Mel'nikov, Head of the Foreign Department in the Far East; M.M. Gvishiani, Head of NKVD Maritime Territory; and P.T. Kurin, Head of NKVD in Chita, who could not possibly have been involved in Katyn. Another individual, Captain of State Security I.L. Pinzur, also received the Medal for Bravery on this date, but this was for his role in the investigation of foreign service officials.

The date in 1940 when Abakumov was recalled from Rostov has yet to be established. Nor do we know his exact responsibilities when he arrived in Moscow, although he was most likely with the Investigation Department. It is quite possible that he received the Order of Red Banner for his accomplishments in Rostov. The admirable research done by Soviet investigators such as Abarinov and Lebedeva is hampered by the fact that, for understandable reasons, they had to work from the bottom to the top. Only documents from the center, as yet unavailable, could shed light on the direct responsibility and actions of various departments and individuals, but as Abarinov hints, the existence of massive files on Stalin's crimes may be only a pipedream.

In November 1940, although not officially acknowledged, Merkulov accompanied Molotov to Berlin, where he met with Himmler and probably dropped a hint or two about Katyn. In view of what was to happen later, this was obviously a mistake, but it made sense at the time since the Germans also had been conducting mini-Katyns against the Polish intelligentsia in their occupied territories. The local German Commander, Col. General Johannes Blaskowitz, found the lawlessness detrimental to troop morale and complained to Hitler. On May 29, 1940, as the Katyn operation was winding down, Hitler sacked Blaskowitz, who never returned to the East. Under "Governor General" Hans Frank, there would be no protests and occupied Poland became not only the crucible of European Jewry, but a place where all opposition to German rule was brutally crushed. In April 1943 after the discovery of mass graves in Katyn, the Goebbels propaganda machine blamed the "Jewish Commissars" even though only four of those involved (A. Ia. Gertovskii, L.F. Raikhman, M.A. Slutskii, and N.A. Frenkel') and possibly M.E. Goberman, happened to be Jews, and Frenkel' was not one of the main actors. There were also Jews among the Katyn victims, even though the endemic anti-Semitism in pre-war Poland excluded them from higher military ranks.

The German motive for exposing Katyn was, of course, not humanitarian. In all probability, they already knew about the crime but chose spring 1943 for a number of reasons. There was the probability that the Red Army would re-occupy the area in the near future. Ewa Thompson has also suggested in *World War II and Soviet People* that the Germans were hoping that Katyn would divert attention from their "Aktion" against the Warsaw Ghetto planned for the same time. The main goal was, of course, to create trouble between the Polish government in exile, the Western allies, and the Soviet Union. They succeeded. Stalin used the 1943 events to break off diplomatic relations with the Polish government in exile, which in turn caused the Home Army's ill-advised uprising in August 1944, which was put down with utmost savagery by the Wehrmacht, the SS, and their East European mercenaries with results that were equally welcome to Hitler and Stalin.

In September 1943 after the recapture of Smolensk, the Soviets established a committee chaired by Lt. General of Medical Services N.N. Burdenko, since 1941 the Chief Surgeon of the Red Army. Other members included N. Voropaev, Chief Pathologist of the Red Army, and "Comrade Count" A.N. Tolstoi, a writer—despite his name—of modest talents who embodied "political correctness." After forensic tests, examination of documents, and interrogation of local inhabitants, the committee issued *The Truth about Katyn: Report of the Special Committee Responsible for Investigating the Circumstances of the Killing of the Polish Officers, Prisoners of the German Fascist Invaders in the Katyn Woods*, which claimed that the POWs employed by their Soviet captors in road construction in the border areas were overrun in the early days of the war by the German Army and were later murdered in 1941. The report contradicted the German-sponsored report issued in May 1943 by a group of international forensic experts chaired by the Swiss Professor François Neville of the International Red Cross, which had set the date of death correctly as spring 1940, when the POWs were under Soviet jurisdiction. The report by the Burdenko Committee, however, provided the false framework for the Soviet version of Katyn for almost 50 years. For his efforts, here and later at Nuremberg, Burdenko was promoted to Col. General in 1944, but before his death in November 1946, he told his son and a colleague, Prof. Olshanskii of the Voronezh University (who later defected), that Katyn was the work of our "friends at NKVD."[5]

Unless future release of Russian documents proves the contrary, we must assume that Abakumov did not play a central role in the massacre of Polish officers in spring 1940. He, however, became involved with Katyn after the war when Stalin set up a top-secret "Government Commission on the Nuremberg Trial" chaired by A. Ia. Vyshinskii. The members included K.P. Gorshenin, Prosecutor General of the USSR (a position once also held by Vyshinskii), who was to serve as Minister of Justice under Khrushchev; I.T. Goliakov, Chairman of the USSR Supreme Court; N.M. Rychkov, Commissar of Justice (both Goliakov and Rychkov had served on the Military Collegium of the USSR Supreme Court under Ul'rikh in the 1930s); V.N. Merkulov, Commissar of NKGB; V.S. Abakumov, Head of SMERSH and Deputy Commissar of NKVD and Defense; and possibly B.Z. Kobulov, First Deputy Commissar of NKGB. The main job of this commission was to prevent disclosure of anything embarrassing to the Stalin regime such as the secret protocols of the non-aggression pact with Nazi Germany. To ensure this, the Commission dispatched M.T. Likhachev, soon to become the Deputy Head of the MGB Department of

Investigation of Especially Important Cases, to Nuremberg. Likhachev played an important part in the entire Nuremberg trials. According to retired Colonel of Judiciary A. Liskin (*Shchit i Mech,* 53/1993), there was tension within the Soviet prosecution team, and Likhachev drove Colonel of Judiciary N.D. Zoria, former Prosecutor in the 3 Army, to suicide. Rudenko and Gorshenin kept Stalin appraised. On their first report, Stalin wrote, "Neither fish nor fowl," and changes had to be made.

What was extraordinary about the Commission was the fact that most of the members, as well as one of the Soviet judges, Ul'rikh's former colleague I.I. Nikitchenko, were as guilty as those who were about to be tried by the international tribunal. The Commission was also to prepare evidence blaming the Germans for Katyn. In a meeting held on March 21, 1946, and attended by Vyshinskii, Abakumov, Merkulov, Gorshenin, Rychkov and the recorder I. Lavrov, the following assignments were made:

1. Abakumov was assigned to find Bulgarian witnesses. This basically involved tracking down one Dr. Markov, a Bulgarian pathologist, who had been a member of the international team organized by the Germans in Katyn in April 1943 and made the report that blamed the Soviets. Markov was easily persuaded to retract his original testimony, which he claimed had been made under force.

2. Merkulov was assigned to find three to five Soviet witnesses and two medical experts to support the Soviet version of Katyn.

3. Polish witnesses to support the Soviet version were to be selected. This task was assigned to Gorshenin, to be assisted by two Chekists, P.S. Safonov (deputy head of Gulag in 1940), and K.S. Savitskii (once a member of the Special Department in the Georgia NKVD, shot in 1955 in Tbilisi as a Beriia accomplice). Because of Savonov and Savitskii, Abakumov may have also been involved in this phase of the operation.

4. Merkulov was also assigned to prepare "authentic" papers and documents as well as autopsy results to confirm that the prisoners had been shot by the Germans. Merkulov was further assigned separately to find a German witness to back the Soviet version. Merkulov's central role made complete sense since he had organized the whole affair.

5. Vyshinskii was assigned to make a documentary film about Katyn.

Abakumov and Merkulov, however, were called to different duties while others labored on.[6] The final version of the fabrication was prepared by L.R. Sheinin, Assistant Soviet Prosecutor at Nuremberg; L.F. Raikhman; and one A.N. Trainin. Sheinin, a member of the Soviet Writers' Union and the Jewish Anti-Fascist Committee, had served as Vyshinskii's Deputy when he had helped fabricate the "Leningrad Opposition Center." Raikhman, of course, had been the head of NKVD Polish Office and knew as much as anyone about Katyn. The Soviet account of Katyn presented by Deputy Prosecutor Iu. Pokrovskii based its allegation on the report by the Burdenko Committee. As was the normal practice under Stalin in Nuremberg, the Soviet Judges worked closely with the Soviet prosecutors, who in turn received their instructions from the fabricators back in Moscow. According to this version, the Katyn executions had been carried out in August and September 1941 by the Wehrmacht 537 Construction Battalion commanded by one Lt. Colonel Friedrich Ahrends. The falsifiers, however, had not done their homework. German documents showed irrefutably that Ahrends had not arrived in Smolensk until the latter half of November. Nor did the official diary of the 537 Battalion show any activities related to mass killings.[7] The Soviet version was also supported by B.V. Bazilevskii, a former professor of astronomy at the Smolensk Teachers College, who had served for a time during the German occupation as the Deputy Mayor in Smolensk under the shadowy figure of B.G. Men'shagin (more about him later). Bazilevskii, who had already testified before the Burdenko Commission, claimed that Men'shagin had told him in September 1941 that the Germans had shot the Poles. Despite the splendid efforts of all involved, the International Tribunal, to its credit, refused to blame Katyn on the Nazis.

The Polish officers were, of course, not the only POWs who were victimized. According to former camp inmates, during 1941–1942 there were mini-Katyns which claimed the deported officers of the Estonian and Latvian Armies as victims.[8] These have yet to be officially acknowledged.

Why Katyn? Social scientists continue to make futile searches to find rational reasons behind irrational acts such as Katyn and the "Final Solution." It has been suggested half-heartedly by such Russian writers as N. Lebedeva that Katyn was Stalin's revenge for the humiliating defeats suffered by the Red Army at the hands of Poles in the summer of 1920, but the fact remains that Stalin used these setbacks to score points against military and political opponents. As usual, Stalin's motives are less complicated. The murdered Polish officers were considered potential enemies, and in 1940 there was no room in the Soviet Union for real, potential, or imaginary enemies of Stalin, particularly if they were defenseless. Stalin had the Poles murdered for the same reason that Genghis Khan and Tamerlane would put the inhabitants of captured cities to the sword—a concept that those who believe in the "progressive" nature of history find difficult to accept. It could also be argued that the crimes were a small price to pay for creating the perfect society through state intervention and social engineering—an illusion which continues to mesmerize the Left everywhere. When on November 14, 1941, the Polish Ambassador Stanislaw Kot inquired about the missing Poles, Stalin pretended to make a phone call and then changed the subject. In his meeting with Generals Anders and Sikorski in December 1941, he expressed concern about the Poles, suggesting that they may have escaped to Manchuria (also repeated by Merkulov in his meetings with the Poles) or had yet to be reported by negligent camp Commanders. Stalin could have given Stanislawski acting lessons. Sikorski, for one, refused to believe that the Soviets could have murdered 15,000 people in cold blood. He was, of course, not alone in being fooled by Stalin's playacting; at times, Churchill, Roosevelt, and Truman were also deceived.

Not all the Polish POWs in Soviet captivity were, of course, murdered. The survivors provided the nucleus for the Armies of Anders and Berling with one fighting on the Allied and the other on the Soviet side. Anders, who somehow survived the fate of his fellow Poles, was released from Lubianka on Aug. 12, 1941. The security organs were deeply involved in the armies' formation, and the main actors besides Beriia included Major of State Security G.S. Zhukov, Commissar State Security 3 Rank P.V. Fedotov (head of NKVD 2 Department, Counterintelligence), and Maj. General of Tank Troops A.P. Panfilov, head of GRU.[9] In a report to Stalin on May 1, 1944 (*IstoriiaSSSR*, 2/1991), Beriia stated that in 1942, 76,100 Poles had opted to join the Anders Army and 43,775 family members had left for Iran. Some 36,510 Poles had joined the Berling Army, and during 1941–1943, 11,516 Poles had died while under Soviet jurisdiction. There was no need for Beriia to tell Stalin about the large number of Poles who were still missing. Beriia's figures did not tell the whole story. It is estimated that between September 1939 and July 1941 nearly 1.7 million individuals, including thousands of children, were deported from the occupied former Polish areas, and nearly 75,000 died in captivity.[10]

It is of interest that in the first Soviet admission of culpability for Katyn on April 13, 1990, Gorbachev failed to mention Stalin's name, blaming the whole affair on Beriia and his assistants. This was the last chapter in a cover-up going back 50 years which continued after Stalin's death kept up by Khrushchev, Shelepin, Brezhnev, Andropov, Chernenko, Gromyko, and perhaps even Gorbachev.

In his conversations with R.Sh. Chilachava, as well as in his book, Beriia's son claims that his father felt that Katyn was a major mistake, and the decision to kill the Poles had been made by Stalin with encouragement from Zhdanov and Voroshilov, the latter because of the Red Army's defeat by the Poles in 1920. They were opposed by Beriia who argued that the Polish officers were potential allies in case of a war with Germany. As a result, Beriia also had his first disagreement with Stalin. S.L. Beriia states that his father's misgiving about Katyn caused Zhdanov to threaten him with dismissal as Head of NKVD. The younger Beriia also makes the astonishing claim that documents yet to be released will prove his father's innocence. Zhdanov's attitude is of some interest. It was not too long ago that more than one Western political scientist, using "scientific" methods, concluded that Zhdanov was a moderating influence on Stalin. Beriia's actions in 1939–1940 do not show a lack of enthusiasm for Katyn. He obviously had overcome whatever private reservations he might have had once he knew Stalin's feelings about the matter. Beriia would no sooner oppose Stalin in regard to the Poles, than Himmler would stand up to Hitler in regard to the Final Solution, even though he may have at times felt squeamish about the task in hand. Still, Stalin replacing Beriia's name with Kobulov on the execution order has to be adequately explained. The junior Beriia also states with more justification that his father was responsible for saving 600 Polish officers, including General Anders.

Following the release of documents on October 15, 1992, there was considerable discussion in Russia and the West about who knew what and when and the role played by the Party leadership in Katyn.[11] The controversy is, however, purely academic. It would be the height of credulity to believe that anyone in a position of power in the Soviet Union after 1940, or for that matter in Communist Poland, would not have known or at least suspected who were the real perpetrators. So far as the role of the Party is concerned, it would have been unthinkable for the spineless Politburo members who had stood by while Stalin was killing their colleagues to come to the defense of the Poles. In 1940, the Politburo existed only to rubber stamp the decisions of Stalin, who also wanted for his own reasons to see others dirty their hands. The role played by the Party and the government after Stalin's death in covering up Katyn, understandable perhaps in Cold War terms, is another shameful chapter in the history of the Soviet Union.

The Poles under Anders were to fight with exemplary bravery at Monte Cassino, Arnhem, and elsewhere. The Berling Poles, who fought along with the Red Army, formed the nucleus of the post—war Polish Armed Forces.

NOTES

1. The most significant source for Katyn is a set of Soviet documents released by the Polish government: *Dokumentov arkhiva Prezidenta Rossiiskoi Federatsii na Katynskomu Delu*, reprinted in *Voennye Arkhivy Rossii* and in *Dokumenty Katynia Decyzia*. An English translation edited by W. Materski, *Katyn: Documents and Materials from the Soviet Archives*, was published by the Institute of Political Studies, Polish Academy of Sciences, in 1993. There was also a flood of publications on Katyn during Glasnost, with most coming from Poland. Some are listed in the Bibliography, among them the bizarre account by Romuald Swiatek, *The Katyn Forest*. Swiatek, a former Gulag prisoner, supports the 1944 fabricated Soviet version. Most of the Polish publications are about the victims rather than the victimizers. For a bibliography of Polish publications on Katyn, see *Wojskowy Przeglad Historyczny* (4/ 1989). Such Polish newspapers as *Trybuna* and *Zycie Warszawy* have also had extensive coverage of Katyn. The most important Soviet sources are V.K. Abarinov, *Katynskii Labirint*, and the article by N. Lebedeva in *International Affairs*. Other writings by Abarinov and Lebedeva appear in *Raduga* (8 and 12/1989), *Moscow News* (Issues 21 and 32, 1989 and 3, 12, and 16, 1990) and *Literaturnaia Gazeta* (May 11, 1988). The English edition of Abarinov's book, *The Murders of Katyn*, includes additional information and an index, albeit a poor one. Also, Franz-Anton Kadell, *Die Katun Lüge*; Hendrik van Bergh *Die Wahrheit Über Katyn*; Arkady Vaksberg, *Stalin's Prosecutor*; *France Soir* (August 31, 1990), and *Liberation* (September 4, 1990). German publications with articles about Katyn, particularly in 1990, include *Neue Zürcher Zeitung, Die Welt, Die Zeit Süddeutsche Zeitung, Neues Deutschland, Frankfurter Allgemeine Zeitung, Frankfurter Rundschau, Rheinischer Merkur*, and *Der Spiegel*. Other sources used include the author's *Soviet Security and Intelligence Organizations 1917–1990*; *International Affairs*; *RFE/RL Research Report* (August 6, 1991); and two articles by Nicholas Bethell, *Mail on Sunday* (June 17, 1990) and the *Observer* (October 6, 1991); *The Times* (October 23, 1992); *Gorizont* (5/1990); N.V. Novikov, *Vospominaniia Diplomata; VIZH* (11 and 12, 1990); *The Times* (October 23, 1992); *New Times* (Issue 16, 1990 and 44 and 45, 1992); *Ekho Planety* (6/1989); *RFE/RL Research Reports* (November 6, 1992); *Report on the USSR* (10/1989); *Izvestiia* (October 15, 1992); and *Komsomolskaia Pravda* (October 15, 1992); *Nol Gvardiia* (12/1990); and *Orlovskii Pravda* (June 22, 1990).

2. *New York Times* (October 23, 1992) and *Dokumentov Arkhiva Prezidenta Rossiiskoi Federatsii po Katynskomu Delu*.

3. V.K. Abarinov, *Katynskii Labirint*, p. 107.

4. *Beriia: Konets Kar'ery*, p. 177.

5. For Burdenko, see S.M. Bagdasar'ian, *Nikolai Nilovich Burdenko*; M.B. Mirskii,

Glavnyi Khirug; M. Giller, *Vo Imia Zhizni*; and Yakov Rapoport, *The Doctors' Plot of 1953*; and Salomon Slowes, *The Road to Katyn*.

6. *Beriia: Konets Kar'ery*, p. 183. See also Arkady Vaksberg, *Stalin's Prosecutor*; Allen Paul, *Katyn. the Untold Story*; and *New Times* (Issue 16, 1990).

7. *Katvnskii Labirint*, p. 57 and pp. 142–63; and *Sovershenno Sekretno* (6/1989 and 6/1990). See also Kadell: *Die Katyn Lüge*.

8. Karlo Stajner, *7000 Days in Siberia*, p. 139.

9. For the fate of surviving Poles, see *Novaia i Noveishaia Istoriia* (2/1989, 1/1993 and 2/1993), which includes documents, as well as commentary by V.S. Parasadanova.

10. Alick Dowling, *Janek: A Story of Survival*, p. 115.

11. Vera Tolz, "The Katyn Documents and the CPSU Hearings," *RFE/RL Research Report* (November 6, 1992), pp. 27–33.

Chapter 3

The Orel Massacres, the Killings of Senior Military Officers, and War-Time Deportations

A second major operation of NKVD, which has been documented, is the massacre of 157 political prisoners in the Medvedev forest near Orel on September 11, 1941. Because of rapid German advance (although Orel was not actually to fall until October 3, 1941), Beriia wrote to the State Defense Committee (Stalin) and proposed that because of the military situation between Germany and USSR 170 political prisoners (actually 161, since some had already died and others had been released) be killed. Usually, the NKVD rearguard routinely massacred the prisoners before the advancing Germans, but in this case because the group included a number of important individuals, Beriia sought Stalin's sanction. When approval was received the next day, the matter was turned over to the Military Collegium of the USSR Supreme Court, whose members were V.V. Ul'rikh, D. Ia. Kandybin, and V.V. Bukanov. On September 8, 1941, the court simply resentenced the prisoners to death for "espionage-diversion" activities. This was extraordinary indeed since the prisoners had somehow managed to commit their new crimes while being held in prison. On September 11, 1941, 157 of the prisoners were executed in the Medvedev forest and four others, E.P. Semenov, G.K. Shneider, L.V. Korkhonen, and E.A. Lysova-Mukhotdinova, were shot in the Orel prison. The victims ranged from those in their mid-seventies to two individuals, E.P. Semenov and A.S. Myl'nikov, both born in 1922.

The prominent victims included Kh. G. Rakovskii (age 68), the old Bulgarian revolutionary sentenced to 12 years in 1938 at the Bukharin trial; and O.D. Kameneva (age 68), widow of L.B. Kamenev and sister of Trotskii. The older son of the Kamenevs, Air Force officer A.L. Kamenev, age 33, had been shot on July 15, 1939. The younger son, Iu.L. Kamenev, was shot on January 30, 1938 at the age of 17. Only Kamenev's illegitimate son, V.I. Glebov born in 1929, survived despite imprisonment. His mother was also shot in 1937. Glebov, who today lives as an historian in Novosibirsk, was interviewed by Adam Hochschild in *The Unquiet Ghost*. Other victims included the old SR assassin M.A. Spiridonova who had been out of politics since the Revolution, but nevertheless was arrested in 1937 for plotting to assassinate Voroshilov; V.N. Iakovleva (age 56), a well-known former left Communist and former RSFSR Commissar of Finance; Dr. D.D. Pletnev (age 69), the alleged "murderer" of Gor'kii; and the "saboteurs" K.B. Arnol'd (age 47), and M.S. Stroilov (age 42). The last three had been sentenced to 10 and 8 years on January 30, 1937, as part of the Piatakov-Radek group, the economist A.Iu. Aikhenvald'; and P.G. Petrovskii (age 43), the younger son of the old revolutionary G.I. Petrovskii. On August 8, 1941, L.G. Petrovskii's older son, Lt. General Petrovskii, Commander of the 63 Corps who also had been imprisoned in the 1930s, died a hero's death not far from where his brother was to be murdered. Altogether, P.G. Petrovskii, a former candidate member of the Politburo, lost two sons and a son-in-law, but he survived in obscurity as the Deputy Director of the Revolution Museum. Well-known victims were V.D. Kasparov, a member of the opposition in the 1920s; a "Red Professor," A.Iu. Aikhenval'd; V.V. Karpenko, Professor at Kiev University; S.A. Bessanov, former Ambassador to Germany; S.A. Ezhov, brother of N.I. Ezhov; three veterans of the Left SR Party absorbed by the Bolsheviks, A.A. Izmailovich, V.A. Chaikin, and I.A. Mairov, who was the husband of fellow victim, M.A. Spiridonova. Mairov was a former Commissar of RSFSR Agriculture.

The presence of a good number of women should also put to rest the myth that Stalin usually spared them. Among the victims there were many with German and Oriental names, whom I have not been able to trace.[1] A.I. Vaksberg claims that N.K. Antipov, former member of the Central Committee, Commissar of Post and Telegraph and Chairman of the Committee on Soviet Control, who had been condemned to death on July 28, 1938, was also among the victims, but his name does not appear on the official list.[2] Claim has also been made that the wives of purged military leaders Ia.B. Gamarnik, A.I. Kork, and I.P. Uborevich were also in this group. If this was the case, they must have been listed under their maiden names. Anton Antonov-Ovseenko also states that historian A.A. Svanidze (brother of Stalin's first wife) was also shot at Orel. Actually, Svanidze was shot or died in camps on November 14, 1942. Incidentally, the exact location of the execution site has yet to be established. Claims that the prisoners were shot to prevent their falling into enemy hands is also incorrect since it was another month before the Germans entered Orel. Anton Antonov-Ovseenko further claims that the statistician D.V. Osinskii, the father of the Soviet auto industry whose 1933 report about the sad state of Soviet agriculture had aroused Stalin's ire, was among the victims of the Orel massacre, but his name does not appear on the official list either. The released documents make it clear that besides Beriia, Ul'rikh and his court, the executioners included B.Z. Kobulov, another of Beriia's Deputy Commissars; L.F. Bashtakov, Head of 1 NKVD "Special Section"; M.I. Nikol'skii (Maj. General in 1945), Head of NKVD prisons from August 1940, when he had replaced Major of State Security P.N. Zuev; and K.F. Firsanov (Police Maj. General in 1945), NKVD Head for Orel oblast. Local support for the operation was provided by S.D. Iakovlev, Head of Orel prison and the local NKVD investigators K.A. Chernousov, K.A. Sliunniaev, and G.I. Terbkov. In 1991 the USSR Military Prosecutor began an investigation of Bashtakov (who is still living) for complicity in Spiridonova's murder. In none of the Soviet accounts or documents is Abakumov mentioned. During the war, killing of civilian prisoners continued. Disappearing from the Saratov prison were Iu.M. Stenkov, former editor of *Izvestiia*; D.B. Riaznov, first Director of the Marx-Engels Institute; and N.K. Luppol, first Director of the Institute of World Literature.[3] Bela Kun and academician N.I. Vavilov also met their end in the Saratov prison.

On October 28, 1941, near Kuibyshev and Saratov and by the order of L.P. Beriia, 25 individuals were shot. The executions of these men and women, most of whom were senior military officers, were carried out without even perfunctory trials. Enough documents had been released in the late 1993 and 1994 issues of *VIZH* to indicate that the officers arrested in 1941 were primarily victims of the intrigues of the 3 Department (counterintelligence) of the Commissariat of Defense, headed between spring 1941 and July 1941 by A.N. Mikheev, who did not survive to see the results of his handiwork. At the time of executions in October, the 3 Department, now probably part of NKVD, was headed by Abakumov, even though his name does not appear on any documents released so far. The arrested officers had been moved from Moscow during the night between October 15 and 16, 1941, when the NKVD Central Office was moved to Kuibyshev in view of the German threat. The complete list of the executed individuals can be found in Sul'ianov's *Arestovat' v Kremle* (p. 189) in a directive dated October 18, 1941, ten days before the execution, from Beriia to Senior Lt. of State Security D.E. Semenikhin, who carried out the sentences. Semenikhin had served with the Gulag in the mid-1930s and received the Order of Red Star on November 28, 1936. As a probable member of Blokhin's execution squads, he had survived Ezhov's fall. The executed officers included two former Commanders in Chief of the Air Force, Lt. Generals of Aviation Ia. V. Smushkevich and P.V. Rychagov; the former Commander of the Baltic Military District (and also a former Commander of the Air Force) Col. General A.D. Loktionov; the former Commander of PVO (anti-aircraft forces) Col. General G.M. Shtern; the 2nd Deputy Commander of the Main Artillery Administration and former Commissar of the same department, Maj. General of Artillery G.K. Savchenko; the former Head of the 5th (Intelligence) Department of the Commissariat of Defense Lt. General of Aviation I.I. Proskurov; the Head of the Infantry/Artillery Department in the Main Artillery Administration S.O. Sklizkov; the Head of Air Force Command/ Navigation Academy Lt. General of Aviation F.K. Arzhenukhin; the former Chief of Staff of the Air Force Maj. General of Aviation P.S. Volodin; the former Head of the Materials Section, Main Artillery Administration and Adjutant to Marshal G.I. Kulik, Maj. General of Technical Services M.M. Kaiukov; the former Deputy Head of the Air Force Weapons Department I.F. Sakrier; and the designer of artillery equipment Ia. G. Taubin. The interrogation of those associated with the Main Artillery Administration was organized by Captain of State Security (Maj. General, July 1945) A.A. Esaulov, Deputy Head of NKGB Investigation Department, and the senior Lieutenant of State Security A.G. Khvat. The testimony was also later used against Marshal G.I. Kulik.

Then there was F.I. Goloshchekin, former Party Secretary in Ekaterinburg and one of the four members of the Ural Soviet who had organized the murder of the

Tsar and his family. P.A. Bulatov had been a department head in CC CPSU at the same time as Ezhov and, for a time, his neighbor. Later he had served as Party Secretary at Omsk. He had refused to confess after his arrest even after being interrogated by Ezhov. Bulatov's life in prison, including a meeting with Ezhov, is discussed by Roi Medvedev in *Let History Judge*. The 63-year-old Chekist M.S. Kedrov, an old nemesis of Beriia, has been discussed elsewhere in this book. The positions held by I.I. Zasosov, M.N. Sobornov, A.I. Fibikh, S.G. Vainshtein, Z.P. Rozova-Egorova, I.L. Belakhov, Kh.I. Slezberg, E.V. Dunaevskii, and D.A. Rozov have not been revealed.

There were also three women in the group—Z.P. Rozova-Egorova, M.P. Nesterenko, and A.I. Fibikh, respectively married to fellow victims D.A. Rozov, P.V. Rychagov, and G.K. Savchenko. Nesterenko, a well-known aviator, was a Major in the Air Force. Five of the victims, including Vainshtein, Belakhov, Slezberg, and Kedrov were shot in Saratov; the rest in Kuibyshev. Sul'ianov cites an April 12, 1942 document by Merkulov ordering the confiscation of their property. Only two of the arrested senior military officers, former Commissar of the Defense Industry B.L. Vannikov and former Army Chief of Staff General K.A. Meretskov, for reasons unknown, were spared. Also released were a few individuals associated with the defense industry, including V.P. Balandin, First Deputy Commissar of the Aviation Industry, factory Directors I.A. Barsukov, F.K. Charskii, and S.K. Medvedev; and Director of the Construction Bureau I. Gesse. The victims in Kuibyshev included three men who had commanded the Air Force before the war, two of the four men who had received the rank of Colonel General in June 1940 (Loktionov and Shtern), the two senior Jewish military officers in the Red Army (Shtern and Smushkevich), four Heroes of the Soviet Union (Proskurov, Rychagov, Shtern, and Smushkevich, who had received the title twice); three (Loktionov, Smushkevich and Shtern, as well as Merestkov) were members or candidate members of CPSU Central Committee, and five (Smushkevich, Proskurov, Loktionov, Shtern and again Meretskov) had been Deputies to the Supreme Soviet.[4] The case of ultra-Stalinist Loktionov was particularly puzzling. The Central Asia Military District during his brief command in 1937 had boasted the highest percentage of arrested officers. Loktionov's removal from the command of the Baltic Military District in March 1941 and his arrest three months later were perhaps caused by his running afoul of Zhdanov, Vyshinskii, or Dekanozov, Stalin's proconsuls in the Baltic. Loktionov was savagely beatn by Vlodzimirskii, Rodos, and investigator V.G. Ivanov, but refused to confess. Proskurov was the former head of the GRU, a jinxed office. Except for its first head, S.I. Aralov (1880–1969), whose life reads like a John Le Carré novel, all its subsequent leaders, O.A. Stigga, A.M. Nikonov, Ia.K. Berzin, I.S. Unshlikht, S.P. Uritskii, and N.I. Ezhov, had gone to the wall. Only Proskurov's successor, F.I. Golikov, who was willing to feed Stalin's fantasies about Hitler's benign intentions, survived and prospered. The wives and children of Smushkevich, Shtern, Proskurov, Volodin, and Sklizkov were all sent to camps.

Who besides Stalin and Beriia were responsible for this atrocity? The Khrushchev memoirs, which are often guilty of making reckless charges, blame it on the Beriia/Abakumov machine, but Soviet documents do not list Abakumov in the chain of command. Also writing in the early days of Glasnost in *Krasnaia Zvezda* (September 30, 1989), the writer V. Kutuzov blamed Abakumov for the massacre. Writing a year later in *Leningradskoe Delo* about the same subject, he completely omits this accusation. There are other problems with Kutuzov's articles which will be discussed later. Also, in his memoirs, Lt. General of Judiciary B.A. Viktorov makes a passing remark about Abakumov's involvement in this affair without giving any sources. As was previously discussed, the former head of the 3 Department, Mikheev, was involved in the case against G.M. Shtern, and there is little doubt that once all the documents are released, he will be implicated in the arrest of other senior military officers from March 1941 until his transfer to the Southwest Front shortly after the war. In his report to Malenkov about Kulik and Timoshenko (*VIZH* 12/1993), Mikheev indicated that he was involved in the arrest of two of Kulik's colleagues, Maj. General of Technical Services M.M. Kaiukov and Maj. General of Artillery G.K. Savchenko, who were among the victims of the October 28 massacre. Mikheev was, however, dead by the time of the executions. Those definitely involved besides Beriia were L.E. Vlodzimirskii (Head of the Department for Investigation of Especially Important Cases), Merkulov, Senior Maj. of State Security L.F. Bashtakov (who seems to have been everywhere), Majors of State Security B.V. Rodos and L.L. Shvartsman, and NKVD functionaries and investigators V.M. Tikhonov, V.G. Ivanov, N.A. Kuleshov, A.A. Zozulov, Z.G. Genkin, A.N. Marusov, Ia. M. Raitses, I.I. Rodovanskii, A.I. Zimenkov, and two individuals identified as Sorokin and Smenikhin. During Beriia's trial, when questioned by a court member, N.A. Mikhailov, Merkulov accepted the responsibility for ordering the arrests, following Beriia's order. Abakumov is not mentioned in the testimony of Shvartsman or Rodos during their secret trial in 1955. The two survivors, Vannikov and Meretskov, also do not mention Abakumov, although Meretskov apparently met with Merkulov before he was freed.

For several years, Vannikov, formerly Director of industrial factories in Tula and Perm, had been associated with the turbulent Soviet defense industry. The Commissariat of the Defense Industry was founded on December 6, 1936, and was at first headed by M.L. Rukhimovich, a former revolutionary from Kharkov who later was attached to various economic enterprises such as the Donetz Coal Trust. Serving under Rukhimovich were Deputy Commissars M.M. Kaganovich, I.F. Tevosian, G.I. Bondar', and R.A. Muklevich, representing the Navy (the latter two fell victim to purges and Tevosian had a close call). On October 15, 1937, M.M. Kaganovich replaced Rukhimovich, who was soon arrested (shot early in 1939 during the Beriia regime), and Vannikov was appointed Deputy Commissar on December 21, 1937. On January 11, 1939, the Commissariat was divided into the Commissariat of Armaments and the Commissariat of Aviation Industry, which were, respectively, taken over by Vannikov and M.M. Kaganovich. Vannikov was facing some formidable problems in trying to improve the state of weaponry in the Red Army, and his work was hampered by the interference of the Deputy Commissar of Defense Marshal G.I. Kulik, at this time Stalin's favorite hardware specialist. The interrogators of Vannikov, Meretskov, and others included B.V. Rodos, L.L. Shvartsman, L.E. Vlodzimirski, I.I. Matevosov (Maj. General, July 1945), A.A. Zozulov, G. Sorokin, Semenov, and even Beriia and Merkulov. Although they are silent in their memoirs, it seems likely that Vannikov and Merestkov implicated others under torture. Vannikov, for instance, had every reason to finger Kulik with whom he had clashed, and Meretskov may have provided adverse testimony against D.G. Pavlov, the fallen Commander of the West Front with whom he had served in Spain. According to A.I. Vaksberg in *Neraskrytye Tainy*, after Vannikov's interrogation on June 28 by Matevosov, Merkulov suggested the arrests of Marshal Kulik and Generals Kaiukov, Sklizkov, Arzhenukhin, Sakrier, I.A. Gerasimenko, I.A. Barsukov (Vannikov's Deputy), and Vetoshkin to Beriia. Arzhenukhin was shot on October 28 and Gerasimenko in February 1942, but Barsukov and Vetoshkin were later released. Stalin, however, vetoed Kulik's arrest. Among those arrested as a result of interrogations were Maj. Generals of Tank Troops I.G. Lazarev and P.V. Kotov, Maj. Generals of Artillery V.I. Khokhlov and Vetoshkin, and other high-ranking officials involved in the defense industry such as F.K. Charskii, S.K. Medvedev, I. Gesse, I.A. Mirzakhanov, Vertsev, Shelkov, Batov, Zhezlov, Gul'iants, and Ioffe. Most were later released after Vannikov's own freedom, but the date for Batov, Zhelzov, and Ioffe needs to be cleared. Mirzokhanov was re-arrested in 1952 and not released until after Stalin's death.

Vannikov returned to service in July 1941 as Deputy Commissar of Armaments under the 33-year-old D.F. Ustinov, a man over ten years his junior (officially Ustinov's appointment dates from June 9, 1941), before becoming the Commissar for Munitions in February 1942. In *Moi Otets*, Beriia's son claims that his father picked Ustinov and defended his appointment despite the latter's junior rank. Other defense industry specialists who owed their jobs to Beriia included V.A. Malyshev (Commissar of the Tank Industry), M.G. Pervukhin (Commissar of the Chemical Industry), M.Z. Saburov (Chairman of Gosplan), and I.F. Tevosian (Commissar of the Ferrous Metallurgy). There was no doubt about Ustinov's loyalty. Stalin's calendar for June 28, 1941 (*VIZH*, 6/1994), shows a meeting with Ustinov which indicates that Stalin was privy to the shake-up in the defense industry. Having the dubious honor of becoming in 1976 one of the four "civilian" Marshals of the Soviet Union (the others Beriia, Bulganin, and Brezhnev), in 1976 Ustinov also became a full member of the Politburo and Secretary of the Central Committee as well as Minister of Defense; in the latter role he became the Soviet version of Robert McNamara trying to translate his success as a defense industry czar into fighting the Afghan guerrillas with results not dissimilar to those precipitated by McNamara's disastrous policies in Vietnam. As late as 1985, he would denounce Khrushchev for having exposed Stalin's crimes, of which he had been a direct beneficiary. In 1978, in a speech commemorating the 60th anniversary of the Red Army, 5,000 officers and veterans would cheer Ustinov's remarks in praise of Stalin. Ustinov and aircraft designer A.S. Iakovlev were good examples of able men who were willing to work the Stalinist system to their advantage even if it meant climbing over the bodies of colleagues. On November 18, 1944, Vannikov received the complicated rank of

"Col. General of Artillery Engineering Service." His hour of glory came during the post-war period as the head of the "First Main Administration." Under the Council of People's Commissars, the group organized the production of nuclear energy and atomic bombs. Winner of six Orders of Lenin and three times Hero of Socialist Labor, Vannikov, who died on February 22, 1962, is buried on the Kremlin wall.

Meretskov, after serving as Assistant Commander of the Northwest and Karelian Fronts and Commander of the 7 Army, in December 1941 took over the Volkhov Front. After the fiasco of the 2 Assault Army in May 1942, he was demoted to Commander of the 33 Army. From June 1942, his career was again on the rise as Commander of the Volkhov, Karelian, and eventually 1 Far East Fronts during the campaign against Japan. In October 1944, he was promoted to Marshal of the Soviet Union. Despite these achievements, Meretskov's health never quite recovered from the ministrations of Merkulov and company.

In *Moi Otets*, S.L. Beriia claims with some justification that his father rescued Vannikov, but he then adds that the arrests of senior officers in the summer of 1941 were ordered by a commission, chaired by Zhdanov and whose membership included Voroshilov. He states that the officers were tried and sentenced by the Military Collegium, when, in fact, there were no judicial proceedings, not even the usual perfunctory window-dressing. It is, however, true that Vannikov was arrested on June 4, 1941 before Beriia's takeover of the Commissariat of the Defense Industry. Iu.B. Borev adds in *Staliniada* that, after his release, Vannikov was taken to the Kremlin where he met with Molotov, Malenkov, and Stalin who told him that Vannikov had been right. Despite this apology, Vannikov did not get back his old job.

It is important to note that the victims were not all arrested at the same time. Loktionov was arrested sometime in June 1941, Smushkevich in early June while recuperating in a hospital, Shtern on June 18, Meretskov on June 24 or 26, and Vannikov on June 4. It seems inevitable that the Special Department under Mikheev was involved in these arrests, but in reality the actual arrests were probably carried out by a group designated as "NKVD 1 Special Section," the ad hoc organization which carried out really sensitive operations. Headed by L.F. Bashtakov, this group, whose history remains obscure, was also implicated in Katyn and in the Orel massacres. Peter Deriabin refers to this organization as the "Special Bureau No. 1," which organized terror campaigns and worked until 1953 directly under the Commissar/Minister NKGB/MGB and, in fact, organized the partisan war behind the German lines. He claims that the organization was headed by P.A. Sudoplatov (rather than Bashtakov).[5] My own impression is that Deriabin is confusing the "1 Special Section" with the "Executive Action" Department (headed by Sudoplatov), to which it may have been subordinated. In Sudoplatov's memoirs, which read like a Who's Who in NKVD, Bashtakov's name does not appear at all. The "1 Special Section" does not seem to have operated in the post-war years.

Besides the well-documented case of the officers who were executed on October 28, there are hints that there were other arrests. For instance, there was the case of Army Military Jurist N.S. Rozovskii, Chief Military prosecutor of the Red Army, who was arrested on June 16, 1941. Rozovskii, who had been in this position at some unspecified time between 1935 and 1939, must have played a major role during the Great Purge. Rozovskii later died in prison; the date is unknown. His only partial rehabilitation on December 6, 1956, clearly indicates a checkered past. Maj. General S.M. Mishchenko, an instructor in the Frunze Academy, was arrested on April 21, 1941, and shot on October 10, 1941. On May 31, 1941, Hero of the Soviet Union Lt. General of Aviation P.I. Pumpur, commander of the Moscow Military District Air Force was arrested. Pumpur was shot in February or March 1942 probably without a trial. On June 18, 1941, Rear Admiral K.I. Samoilov, head of Leningrad naval defense, was taken into custody. Someone had discovered that Samoilov had been arrested before, back in 1918, by the Kronshdat Cheka after an explosion in the fort. With his additional responsibilities for the defense industry, it was logical for Beriia to serve in the GKO (State Defense Committee) and as its Deputy Chairman until May 1944. On February 18, 1942, he established the Special Department for Military Production and, with the resources available to him, launched a major campaign to address the shortage of munitions, particularly artillery shells, which had plagued the Red Army. As Edwin Bacon points out in *The Gulag at War*, slave labor made major contributions to this effort.

Beriia's taking over of the defense industry at the end of June 1941 proved to be ominous for a number of other officials and designers. (Conditions improved later when Malenkov took over some of the Beriia's responsibilities in this area.) Among those arrested as an "agent of German intelligence" was V.P. Balandin, First Deputy Commissar of Aviation Industry, but his boss Shakhurin persuaded Stalin to release him. A day later, Stalin called Shakhurin and told him to put Balandin in charge of a factory, since "we badly need engines."[6] Shakhurin himself was considerably less unfortunate when he was arrested after the war. G.I. Kulik, who had been in charge of weaponry before the war, however, had been too closely associated with Stalin to be arrested at this time. Instead Merkulov, under Beriia's order, and undoubtedly with Stalin's approval, kidnapped Kulik's wife, who was then murdered in secret while her husband was serving at the front. Around this time, a number of scientists, including N.V. Kovalev, A.I. Mal'tsev, and K.A. Fliaksberger, were arrested in Leningrad. Cytologist G.D. Levitskii, correspondent member of the USSR Academy of Science, was first arrested in January 1933, but was freed from exile because of his scientific work. He was arrested again in 1937 and released after serving a term in prison. He was again arrested on June 28, 1941, along with other colleagues from Leningrad, evacuated to the Urals, and finally shot in Zlatoustovsk prison.[7] After the start of the war, government and military officials were, of course, not alone as targets of persecution. The absurdist writers A.I. Vvedenskii (1904–1941) and D.I. Kharms (1905–1942) had first been arrested in 1931, but later exiled, confining their activities to writing children's stories. Kharms was re-arrested on August 23, 1941, and died or was killed in prison on February 2, 1942. Vvedenskii was arrested early in the war in Ukraine and probably was murdered during the Soviet retreat. Writer A.P. Kamenskii, a former émigré, met a similar fate on December 1, 1941. In 1943, the tubercular landscape artist A.V. Shchipitsyi was overheard telling a politically incorrect joke. He was dragged away and shot. In late October and early November 1941, there were a number of executions in Saratov and Tambov prisons with the most prominent victim being the aforementioned M.S. Kedrov.

It is significant that according to Stalin's calendar for the first week of the war (*VIZH*, 6/1994), he met with Beriia 15 times, more than with anyone else, and many were long meetings. He also met five times with Merkulov (sometimes without Beriia being present), and four times with Mekhlis. For Stalin, maintaining internal security was just as important as fighting the invaders, who had now given him an additional excuse to tighten his grip. The minutes of these meetings have yet to be released and perhaps do not even exist, but we can be reasonably sure they brought death and suffering to thousands of people.

The massacres of October claimed the largest number of victims of Soviet officials during the war, but the campaign to terrorize the military started from the very beginning and continued throughout the war. The Special Department and, later, SMERSH under Abakumov played a significant part. The reason for the campaign was obvious. In June 1941, the Red Army was not quite ready for the war, but it was superior in quantity and quality to the enemy, and it was of course led by the Greatest Military Leader of All Time. Yet it continued to suffer defeat after ignominious defeat in the hands of an enemy who was fighting on several fronts. The only explanation for the setbacks was the existence in the Red Army of saboteurs, spies, Trotskiites, and assorted "enemies of the people." Considerable research in this area by historians, including Volkogonov and A.F. Vasil'ev (*Voprosy Istorii*, 4/ 1994), shows that it was the failure of Soviet political and military leadership, and above all, Stalin, that led to the catastrophe. Also, according to Iu.B. Borev in *Staliniada*, Stalin depended on a Jewish psychic, V. Messing, to map out military strategy. It is interesting that along with *sturm und drang* policies, Stalin allegedly was contemplating sending peace feelers to the enemy. Volkogonov, quoting Marshal K.S. Moskalenko, states that according to Beriia's testimony, Stalin, Beriia, and Molotov met in July 1941 with the Bulgarian Ambassador, Ivan Stamenev (at this time, Bulgaria was neutral), to use his good offices to arrange for what was nothing short of a second Brest Litovsk. Nothing came of these overtures since Stamenev refused to get involved. Sudoplatov, who claims that he had recruited Stamenev as a Soviet agent back in 1934, denies that such a meeting ever took place. The peace feelers were a disinformation campaign organized by him to confuse the Germans, and, in fact, Stalin was so sensitive about this issue that he forbade any direct contact between high-ranking Soviet officials such as Beriia and Stamenev, who was supposed to spread the word among the diplomatic corps in Moscow and back in Bulgaria.

Despite the vigilance, the performance of the Red Army during the war was marked by incompetence, total disregard of losses, and the universal primacy of political over military considerations. Hitler once told Field Marshal Reichenau, "losses can never be too high; they sow the seeds of future greatness," but compared to Stalin, Hitler was a conservationist when it came to the lives of soldiers. In fact, after the enormous losses suffered by the German airborne troops at Crete, Hitler vowed to use them only as an elite infantry. Stalin, in contrast, always added to his war-time operation orders that the mission be carried out regardless of casualties. The indifference to suffering was the hallmark of the Stalinist state in war and in peace, and this despite the fact that Stalin had once remarked that there is nothing more valuable in the world than the man himself. During the war, however, his orders were followed by, "This task must be carried out regardless of losses." The enormity of the setbacks suffered by the Red Army during the first two years of the war can best be seen through documents that have been released during the Glasnost years. A sample of these in the collection *Nashe Otechestvo* and elsewhere shows that in the beginning of the war, the Red Army had more than 22,000 tanks, including 1,861 T–34s and KVs—superior to anything that the Germans had. In fact, these tanks could knock out the enemy from a distance of 1,500 meters whereas the German tanks could do so only from 500 meters. 1,475 of the T–34s and KVs were deployed on the western military districts where the greatest defeats were suffered. Even the older Soviet tanks, T–26s and BT–7s, were superior to most of the German armor in speed or armament. Against this massive force, the Germans deployed 3,582 tanks (of the total of 5,639 that were available)—1,634 of these tanks were the newer mark T–IIIs and T–IVs, 1,700 were mark T–IIs (armed with only a 20-milimeter cannon) and T–1s (armed only with a machine gun) and the rest mostly Czech T–38 tanks. In artillery, the Red Army also enjoyed a clear superiority. In the Kiev Special Military District (Southwest Front), the Red Army enjoyed a 1.2 superiority in manpower, 1.4 in artillery, 3.5 in heavy and medium tanks, 5 in light tanks, and 2.5 in aircraft.

In comparing the careers of Hitler and Stalin, there is no doubt that both men were responsible for the death of millions of people. Most of Hitler's major crimes were committed when Germany was at war, his victims mostly non-German and included only a handful of fellow Nazis. Stalin's crimes, on the other hand, were committed both at war and in peace, his victims mostly citizens of the USSR and included thousands of fellow Communists. At the start of World War II, the population of the Gulag was more than ten times higher than that of Hitler's concentration camps. Zensl Elsinger, who spent time in both the Gulag and German concentration camps, had stated, "Stalin, das ist Hitler plus Asien." There was also a number of plots (mostly ineffectual) against Hitler during his rule-none against Stalin.

There is also little doubt that the Red Army carried out the major share of combat during World War II. Until the middle of 1944, the German Army deployed 63–77% of its forces on the Eastern Front; the number was reduced to 57% after the opening of the Second Front, but a high percentage of armor remained in the east. On D-Day, the Western Allies faced 56 under-strength German divisions and a non-existent Luftwaffe, the Red Army 157, and potent air opposition. The Russian summer offensive in Belorussia, launched two weeks after the Normandy landing, dwarfed anything that was happening in the West. Of the German losses 73.5% were suffered in fighting the Red Army, whose own losses perhaps can never be established with certainty, but could have been as high as seven times those suffered by the Germans.

It is now officially admitted that the Red Army lost 8,668,400 killed in action during the Great Patriotic War (the number does not include nearly four million who died in German captivity)—more than twice the losses suffered by the Wehrmacht. John Erickson's latest research puts the Soviet losses during the war at a staggering 49 million, a major influence on the post-war behavior of Stalin who tried to bluff his way by putting up a show of strength. The most extensive Russian study of the subject, *Grif Sekretnosti Sniat*, states that during the war the Soviet Armed Forces lost 11,285,000 combatants, including 421 Generals and Admirals. Between December 1941 and June 1944, more than a million soldiers lost their lives in vain on the "quiet" West Front, which was commanded by such "modern" Commanders as Zhukov, Konev, and Sokolovskii. These men were sacrificed in senseless attacks against vastly outnumbered but well-entrenched German forces led by brilliant Commanders such as Walter Model (a distant relative of Lenin, no less) who had no trouble switching from blitzkrieg to meatgrinder tactics. A search in Soviet archives (*Novaia i noveishaia istoriia*, 1/1994) by Army General M.A. Gareev indicates that the Red Army in late 1943 to early 1944 enjoyed at times almost a ten-to-one superiority to the enemy on the West Front and yet the Soviet commanders repeatedly failed to defeat the vastly outnumbered Wehrmacht. Recent relevations (*Journal of Slavic Military Studies*, September 1994) also provide evidence of the enormous significance of Western aid to the Soviet Union during the war.

During almost the entire war, the Red Army was superior to the Wehrmacht in both quantity and quality of most weapons as well as in number of troops and yet suffered enormous defeats in the first two years of the war. It took the Russians nearly three years to drive the Germans out of areas that the latter had occupied in the first 14 months of the war, and this against an enemy that was fighting on several fronts and had its home base under constant bombardment after 1943. Even as late as May 1944, the Germans were a mere 290 miles from Moscow. Charles DeGaulle, no stranger to matters of military strategy, stated that the most remarkable fact about the campaign on the Eastern Front was not the ultimate Soviet victory, but the depth of the German advance. One of the favorite pastimes of Maj. General Henning von Treskow, Chief of Staff of the Army Group Center, when he was not plotting to kill Hitler, was playing war games in which the German Commander would be in charge of the Soviet forces with disastrous results for the Wehrmacht. Stalin's preference for offensive action and the Red Army's penchant for costly and unimaginative frontal assaults were matched by superb improvisation by the Wehrmacht. Although Stalin ran the war, he did so from a safe distance and only once, on August 5, 1943, actually met with a local Commander when he visited the Kalinin Front, then commanded by A.I. Eremenko. The ensuing Dukhovshchina-Smolensk operation failed. In the final analysis, the war on the Eastern Front was won by the bravery and resiliency of the common Soviet soldier fighting for reasons that beggar logic, by the USSR's enormous natural resources, and assistance from Western Allies, and not by Stalin and his Generals. Only in the summer 1945 campaign against the dispirited Kwantung Army, did the Soviet high command show flashes of brilliance reminiscent of the early days of the German blitzkrieg. This was particularly true in the case of the

Transbaikal Front, much of it due to the superb staff work of its Chief of Staff, the future Marshal M.V. Zakharov.

At the end of June 1941, the Special Department under A.N. Mikheev, with help from L.Z. Mekhlis, arrested the leadership of the West Front, including Army General D.G. Pavlov; his Chief of Staff, Maj. General V.E. Klimovskikh; Chief of Signals, Maj. General of Signal Troops A.T. Grigor'ev; Chief of Artillery Lt. General of Artillery N.A. Klich; Commander of the 4 Army, Maj. General A.A. Korobkov; Deputy Commander of the Air Force, Maj. General of Aviation A.I. Taiurskii; and Commander of the 14 Mechanized Corps, Maj. General S.I. Oborin.

Recently published documents (*VIZH*, 4/1994) indicate that on June 30, Stalin ordered Zhukov to recall D.G. Pavlov to Moscow, and on the same date, the GKO removed him from command. On July 1, the head of NKGB in Gomel, D.S. Gusev (living in 1993), received a call from Mekhlis ordering him to help the counterintelligence people from Moscow (Mikheev, etc.) to arrest Pavlov when he arrived in Dovsk from Gomel. Pavlov's car was stopped, and he was told that there was an urgent message for him supposedly from Mekhlis in Smolensk. When Pavlov went to the local post office to receive the call, he was arrested.

On July 4, the first interrogations of Pavlov were conducted by Deputy Head of Special Branch of West Front, Koval'skii, assisted by Goiko, who held the similar position with the 10 Army, and investigator Cherkashin. There was also a tense meeting between Mekhlis and Pavlov, whose case was not helped by the confessions extracted from K.A. Meretskov, who had served with him in Spain and was now also under arrest. On July 21, a 12–page indictment was sent to Abakumov, who was the Deputy Commissar of NKVD in charge of the case. The charges went back to 1936 and service in Spain, and Pavlov was identified as a full-fledged member of various military conspiracies as well as for the setbacks of the West Front.

On July 6, 1941, Mekhlis sent a telegram to Stalin also signed by Timoshenko and the newly appointed Political Commissar of the Front, P.K. Ponomarenko, asking for approval to arrest Klimovskikh, Klich, Korobkov, Chernykh, and Oborin. In his confusion, Mekhlis failed to mention the name of Grigor'ev, head of the signals, and also made a Freudian slip by requesting the arrest of Deputy Commander in Chief of the Air Force "Todorskii," confusing him with the actual officer involved, Taiurskii. Mekhlis was obviously thinking of Komkor A.I. Todorskii, the former head of the Zhukovskii Air Academy, whom he had helped purge back in 1937. Besides the senior Commanders, approval was requested for the arrest of I.S. Lazarenko, Commander of the 42 Rifle Division (who survived after being sentenced to death); Dorofeev, head of the Front's Topography Section; Kirsanov, head of Staffing and Replacement; Iurev, Air Force Inspector for Combat Readiness; Sheinkin, head of Military Stores; Berkovich, Assistant Commander of Armor; Dykman, Commander of 8 Disciplinary Battalion; his Deputy Krol; Beliavskii, head of Minsk Military Pharmacy; Ovchinnikov, head of Veterinary Services and Commander of an Artillery Regiment Sbirannik. Stalin replied immediately, giving his approval.

Spared, however, was the Commissar of the West Front, A.Ia. Fominykh, a hardened Stalinist who while attached to the Red Army Personnel Office in the

1930s had played a significant part in the purges. Fominykh was first replaced briefly by Mekhlis and then by P.K. Ponomarenko, who in turn was replaced by D.A. Lestev and after his death on November 18, 1941, as a result of an enemy air attack, by I.S. Khokhlov and N.A. Bulganin. Fominykh now became the Commissar for Rear in the Southwest Front, where he was briefly associated inNovember 1941 with A.A. Vlasov and then in the same position with the 124 Rifle Division, a major comedown; although he later made a partial recovery, he never became a major player. This was the same treatment that was meted out to Corps Commissar P.A. Dibrova, the Political Commissar of the neighboring and equally defeated Northwest Front. Stalin certainly was more considerate of the Political Commissars who under the Soviet system of command should have been held equally guilty of the military setbacks.

Korobkov, Pavlov, and Klimovskikh were accused of having exhibited cowardice, Grigor'ev and Klich of dereliction of duty.[8] Working hand-in-hand with Mekhlis and the Special Department was the Military Prosecutor of the USSR, the future Lt. General of Judiciary (1943) V.I. Nosov.

The arrests were quite arbitrary. According to Stalin's order, there had to be one front Commander, one front Chief of Staff, one Chief of Communications, one Chief of Artillery, and one Army Commander. Stalin could have just as easily ordered the arrest of the leaders of the Northwest Front (the Baltic Military District), who had performed just as poorly as their neighbors on the West Front. It had been decided that an Army Commander should be among those arrested, and Korobkov was the only one who could be found. The Commanders of the neighboring 3 Army (V.I. Kuznetsov) and 10 Army (K.D. Golubev) were caught in the confusion behind the enemy lines, and thus were spared. Since the Soviet Air Force had been wiped out (mostly on the ground) in the first few days of the war (by October 4, only 4% of the aircraft from June 1941 pre-war Air Force remained), a suitable scapegoat had to be found. The Commander of the Air Force on the West Front, Maj. General of Aviation I.I. Kopets (a mere Senior Lieutenant in 1938), thwarted Stalin's plans and a sure court-martial by committing suicide on the third day of the war. Because of this, his Deputy, Maj. General of Aviation A.I. Taiurskii, was dragged away. The defendants faced the Military Collegium of the USSR, chaired by Ul'rikh and assisted by his colleagues the military jurists A.A. Orlov and D.Ia. Kandybin. Justice or mercy in this court would have been unthinkable. Ul'rikh sent the draft of sentences through Poskrebyshev to Stalin; Stalin approved them, although he was irritated by the usually laconic Ul'rikh's flowery description of a "military conspiracy" and ordered Poskrebyshev to tell Ul'rikh to "cut out the nonsense." There would be no appeal from the sentences. Pavlov, Klich, Klimovskikh, Grigor'ev, Korobkov, Taiurskii, and Oborin were deprived of military rank and property and except for Klich were all condemned to death and shot the same day on July 22, 1941. The executions were organized and reported by the Junior Lt. of State Security Sashenkov of the 5 Branch of the NKVD Special Section headed by Bashtakov. On October 1, 1942, the military tribunal of NKVD in Gor'kii sentenced Pavlov's parents, wife, son, and mother-in-law to 5 years. Partial texts of court hearings as published in 1993 in *Palachi i Zhertvy* show that Pavlov continued to defend himself against

Ul'rikh's absurd charges. For some unexplained reason, Klich was not executed at this time. He was shipped to Kolima only to be executed on September 17, 1941. Although there is general agreement that the leadership of the West Front were shot, rumors have persisted for years that they were spared, and more than one individual has claimed seeing Pavlov alive after 1941. The executed Generals were rehabilitated by two military collegium rulings on November 5, 1956 and July 31, 1957.

In the movie *Voina*, based on the novel of the same title by I.F. Stadniuk and first published in 1974, there is a scene in which Pavlov is being personally questioned by Beriia. This can be dismissed as artistic license. At this stage of the war, Beriia was too busy to waste time on the already doomed Pavlov, and in fact Stadniuk is the first Soviet source that correctly identifies Mikheev as the arresting officer.

The West Front, however, was due for another wholesale shake-up in 1944, but this time in a more orderly fashion. In spring 1944 Stalin appointed a committee chaired by Malenkov and heavy with Party representatives and including N.S. Shimanov (Political Commissar of the Air Force), S.M. Shtemenko, F.F. Kuznetsov (head of GRU), and A.S. Shcherbakov (head of Red Army Political Administration) to look into the inability of this Front to break through the enemy lines despite superior forces and suffering enormous losses. As a result, on April 12, 1944, Stalin issued an order (*Novaia i Noveishaia Istoriia*, 1/1994) in which the Commander of the Front, Army General V.D. Sokolovskii; his Chief of Staff Lt. General A.P. Pokrovskii; General of Artillery I.P. Kamera, Chief of Front's Artillery; the Head of Intelligence, Colonel Il'nitskii; and the Commander of the 33 Army V.N. Gordov were all sacked and the West Front was divided into the 2 and 3 Belorussian Fronts. This time, however, there would be no bloodletting, and despite their records, all the individuals involved received other appointments, and in the case of Bulganin and Pokrovskii to positions of equal importance. Bad leadership, however, continued to dog the Soviet high command. I.E. Petrov and L.Z. Mekhlis, respectively the Commander and the Commissar of the 2 Belorussian Front were soon at loggerheads, and in May Petrov was replaced by G.F. Zakharov, who in turn was replaced by K.K. Rokossovskii in November.

In the beginning of the war at the Northwest Front, the Commander F.I. Kuznetsov was replaced on July 4 by Commander of the 8 Army P.P. Sobennikov. Both Mekhlis and Bochkov were sent there to shore up the command, and Bochkov may have served for a few days in mid-July as the Commissar of the Front, an unusual distinction for a police officer. The Chief of Staff, P.S. Klenov, was replaced by N.F. Vatutin, who may have even actually commanded the Front for a few days. Klenov was subsequently shot. Mekhlis also had Army Commissar 2 Rank V.N. Borisov, the Stavka's former representative, arrested (he got 5 years). In a report to Stalin dated July 11, 1941 (*VIZH*, 4/1994), Mekhlis and his assistant Listkov, a CC CPSU functionary, stated that Borisov had hidden his service in the White Army, his arrest by the Cheka, and the fact that his father was a priest, and on his own initiative had returned to Moscow from the assignment on the Northwest Front.

In the case of the Commissars of the Front, Corps Commissar P.A. Dibrova was removed and demoted, whereas Corps Commissar V.N. Bogatkin was left in place. Maj. General I.S. Kosobutskii, Commander of 41 Rifle Corps, was sentenced to 10 years and Maj. General N.M. Glavotskii, Commander of the 118 Rifle Division, was sentenced to death. The Commander of the Air Force, Maj. General of Aviation A.P. Ionov, was removed in the beginning of July and his fate remains unclear. As elsewhere, the Commissars got off relatively easy.

In August 1941, Mekhlis showed up at the headquarters of the 34 Army, which was engaged in bitter fighting with the German 10 Corps, 16 Army which resulted in the loss of Staraia Russa in mid-August The performance of Maj. General V.Ia. Kachanov, the Commander of the Army (*VIZH* 4/1994); his support of his subordinates; and perhaps his reluctance to launch a counterattack caused his removal on August 12, 1941. He and his Artillery Commander, Maj. General of Artillery V.S. Goncharev, were both arrested and shot. Kachanov's replacement, Maj. General P.F. Alfer'ev, launched a desperate counterattack, forcing the German high command to divert Manstein's 56 Panzer Corps from its march to Leningrad. The 34 Army was surrounded and decimated by August 23, but valuable time may have been bought. The motive behind the killing of the leadership of the West Front was to find scapegoats for Stalin's failures. Despite popular beliefs to the contrary, there had been little bloodletting after the Winter War. A few (none above the rank of Colonel) officers were court-martialed, although many deserved to be. The reason for leniency was that the Red Army could not afford another massive purge at this critical time; also the Winter War was regarded, at least in propaganda terms, as a victory. In 1940, after the purges of the 1930s and the gathering of war clouds in Europe, Stalin was not in a position to launch a massive bloodletting among the military. He replaced Voroshilov as Commissar of Defense with Timoshenko; Smushkevich, the head of the Air Force whose planes had bombed the Soviet Embassy in Helsinki in their first night attack and, in general, had turned out a dismal performance, was removed and demoted. Matters were different in the summer of 1941 since the defeats were on such a massive scale. Once the military situation stabilized, the Stalin propaganda machine came up with a new myth. The setbacks of 1941 and 1942 were part of the grand strategy to lure the enemy into the interior where the advantages were on the side of the Red Army. Stalin was the new Alexander I. Under this assumption, Pavlov should have been decorated instead of shot. If terror was the cornerstone of the Stalinist rule, mendacity was the glue that held it all together.

Stalin's arbitrary policies continued throughout the war with Commanders being removed, imprisoned, or shot on flimsy pretenses, while at other times incompetence deserving of a court-martial would be tolerated. In the beginning of the war, the Northwest Front under F.I. Kuznetsov did not fare any better than the West Front under D.G. Pavlov, but Stalin kept faith in the obviously untalented Kuznetsov, employing him until 1943 as Commander of various armies and fronts. In September 1942, the Commander of 37 Army, North Group of Transcaucasus, Front Maj. General P.M. Kozlov simply lost control of his troops, allowing the enemy to capture Nal'chik and threaten the entire Soviet position in the north Caucasus. Only desperate measures prevented a collapse, but Kozlov was allowed to continue to command the 37 Army until May 1943.

It is doubtful despite access to archives that we will ever have a complete list of senior officers who were repressed under Stalin or the circumstances of their downfall. A case in point is Lt. General of Aviation K.M. Gusev, Commander of the Air Force in the Far East in 1941. Gusev, a very senior commander, was repressed, but even today the date and reasons remain unclear. He simply disappeared from among the living, although it is doubtful considering his rank, without Stalin's approval. Although the figures are subject to change, we can be sure that between June 1940, when the rank of General was introduced in the Red Army, and March 1953 at least one former Marshal of the Soviet Union (G.I. Kulik), one Chief Marshal of Aviation (A.A. Novikov), two Marshals of Aviation (S.A. Khudiakov, G.A. Vorozheikin), one Marshal of Artillery (N.D. Iakovlev), two Army Generals (K.A. Meretskov, D.G. Pavlov), three Colonel Generals (V.N. Gordov, G.M. Shtern, A.D. Loktionov), one Colonel General of Artillery (I.I. Volkotrubenko), one Admiral (L.M. Galler), six Vice and Rear Admirals, 20 Lieutenant Generals, and 73 Major Generals were arrested. There were also a number of Komdivs and Kombrigs (ranks above Colonel that were kept until Oct 1942) who were "repressed." A conservative estimate would be that at least 100 Soviet Generals were "repressed" during 1939–1953, one-fourth of the number of Generals killed during the war, with some groups being singled out. For example on December 29, 1940, 20 former officers from the Baltic countries were given the rank of General in the Red Army (three Lt. Generals, the rest Maj. Generals). These include 12 attached to ground forces, five to artillery, two to rear services, and one to engineers. Most of them were to come to bad ends. The Generals that were arrested during the war include:

· Maj. General I. I. Alekseev, former Commander of 6 Rifle Corps Southwest Front, was captured in September 1941, escaped in October 1941, was arrested December 14, 1941, and was released in December 1945.

· Maj. General K.Ia. Arkhipchikov, Military Commissar of Latvia (1940), was sentenced on February 21, 1942, by the Military Tribunal of the Northwest Front to loss of rank and 10 plus 5 years. He was in prison as late as 1946.

· Maj. General G.A. Armaderov, son of a Tsarist General and Captain in the old Army, Senior Instructor in the Cavalry Department of Frunze Academy. Arrested on November 28, 1941, he was accused by Abakumov of criticizing the Soviet government and belonging to a military conspiracy in the academy. Sentenced to 25 years (October 19, 1951), he was released after Stalin's death.

· Lt. General B. I. Arushanian, former Chief of Staff of 12 and 56 Armies, was arrested, released, and restored to command.

· Lt. General of Aviation F.K. Arzhenukhin, Commander of Air Force Command/ Navigation Academy, was shot October 28, 1941.

· Maj. General S.A. Baidalinov, Commander 83 Alpine Division, Central Asia Military District, was expelled from the Army and arrested July 12, 1941.

· V.P. Balandin, First Deputy Commissar Aviation Industry, was arrested at the beginning of the war. He was later released.

· Maj. General of Engineering/Technical Services, I.A. Barsukov, Deputy Commissar of Armaments, was arrested at the beginning of the war and was later released.

· Maj. General of Aviation A.P. Beliaev, Deputy Chief of Staff Air Force as a Colonel (October 1941), was head of the Soviet Air Force mission to the U.S. (1943). Arrested and accused of corruption, he was Solzhenitsyn's fellow prisoner in Kaluga Gate camp (September 1945).

· Rear Admiral V.P. Bogolepov, Chief of Staff and Acting Commander of Ladoga Flotilla (July 24, 1941–August 8, 1941), was arrested and imprisoned, but released later.

· Army Commissar 2 Rank V.N. Borisov, Deputy Head Red Army Main Political Administration and representative of the Supreme Command at the Northwest Front, was accused by Mekhlis of having served in the White Armies and concealed his arrest by the Cheka in 1919–1920 (July 11, 1941). He was sentenced to 5 years by the Military Collegium.

· Maj. General G.A. Burichenkov, former Deputy Commander Central Asia Military District, was arrested August 29, 1943. He was accused by Abakumov of having given information to the police about the Vladivostok underground organization after his arrest in 1912! Sentenced to 15 years in prison (March 27,1952), he was released after Stalin's death.

· Maj. General F.S. Burlachko, former head of the Mobilization Department, Frunze Academy, was arrested November 22, 1941. Accused by Abakumov of having criticized the purges and joining an anti-Soviet conspiracy in the academy, he died in the psychiatric ward of Kazan prison in 1949.

· Maj. General A.F. Bychkovskii, formerly attached to the General Staff was arrested on May 26, 1943. He was accused by Abakumov of having approved of German efforts to dissolve the collective farms in Ukraine and of contributing to the failure of the 31 Army's offensive in August 1942.

· Maj. General I.K. Chernius, Chief of Staff 29 Territorial Corps in Lithuania (September 1940), was arrested in early 1941. His fate is unknown.

· Maj. General of Aviation S.A. Chernykh, Hero of the Soviet Union, Commander 9 Mixed Air Division, West Front, was shot July 27, 1941.

· Kombrig A.S. Chichkanov, Commander of 189 Rifle Division, was captured in August 1941, escaped, but did not return to the Soviet side, and was arrested on March 17, 1943. Abakumov accused him of panic, abandoning his troops, destroying his Party membership card and uniform, hiding for 17 months in enemy territory, and contacting German intelligence.

· Maj. General I.F. Dashichev, former Commander of 9 Rifle Corps in Crimea, was arrested and sentenced to 4 years (early 1942) then released. He was again arrested on July 4, 1942, accused by Abakumov of making anti-Soviet and anti-Semitic remarks.

· Maj. General A.N. De-Lazari, Military Historian, attached to the Voroshilov Chemical Defense Academy, was arrested (June 25, 1941 by the order of the 3 Department) then moved from Butyrka prison to Saratov (October 18, 1941). Sentenced to 10 years by an NKVD troika for spying for Italy (February 13, 1942, at the age of 62), he was nevertheless shot (February 23, 1942). He was rehabilitated April 28, 1956.

· Maj. General G.S. D'iakov, Deputy Head of the General Tactics Department in Frunze Academy, was arrested April 10, 1942, accused by Abakumov of anti-Soviet agitation and membership in a military conspiracy in the academy. Officially expelled from the Red Army (October 26, 1946), he died in March 1951 in Butyrka prison.

· Maj. General D.G. Egorov, Commander of 14 Rifle Corps, South Front, was sentenced to 5 years, released, and demoted to command of 469 Rifle Regiment. He was killed in action in May 1942 during the Kharkov Operation as Commander of the 150 Rifle Division.

· Maj. General A.N. Ermakov, Commander 2 Rifle Corps, 13 Army, West Front, was court-martialed January 29, 1942, but was later released.

· Maj. General A.A. Filatov, Commander 12 Guard Rifle Division, was arrested April 30, 1945, as part of a campaign to compromise Marshal Zhukov.

· Maj. General S.C. Galaktionov, Commander 30 Alpine Division, 48 Rifle Corps, Independent Coastal Army, was accused of having surrendered the town of Bel'tsy without authorization. Arrested by personal order of Stalin (July 16, 1941), he was sentenced to death by the Military Tribunal of the South Front (August 8, 1941), and shot in the Pervomaisk cemetery. Stricken from the ranks of the Red Army (September 25, 1941), he was later rehabilitated (May 29, 1961).

· Maj. General N.I. Gapich, Commander of the Red Army Signals Troops, was dismissed July 23, 1941 and arrested August 8, 1941. He later was released, but not restored to command. He was accused by Abakumov of a dubious past (service with Kolchak) and poor leadership of signal troops at the start of the war.

· Maj. General of Artillery P.A. Gel'vikh, former Senior Instructor in the Artillery Academy and member of the artillery Committee of the Main Artillery Administration, was arrested January 27, 1944. He was accused by Abakumov of a dubious past and of working for German Intelligence. The indictment was finally prepared by the MGB 3 Department and approved by Lt. General L.F. Tsanava, Deputy Minister MGB (February 12, 1952). Sentenced at the age of 80 to 15 years in prison (March 27, 1952), he made a request for pardon that was denied by the Supreme Soviet (July 8, 1952). Amnestied July 23, 1953, he died in 1958.

· Maj. General of Artillery I.A. Gerasimenko, Department Head in the Main Artillery Administration was arrested (July 5, 1941), sentenced to death by NKVD troika (February 1942), and rehabilitated (July 23, 1955).

· Military Engineer 1 Rank A.A. Giunner, former head 2 Branch in Main Artillery Administration, was arrested September 18, 1941. He was accused by Abakumov of contacts with German intelligence, theft of secret documents, and anti-Soviet and defeatist statements to cellmates.

· Maj. General A.A. Glazkov, instructor in the Frunze Academy, was expelled from the Army and arrested (November 28, 1941).

· Maj. General N.M. Glovatskii, Commander 118 Rifle Division, 41 Corps, 11 Army, Northwest (Leningrad?) Front, was condemned to death by the Military Collegium of the USSR (July 26, 1941) for surrendering Pskov.

· Maj. General of Tank Troops N.D. Gol'tsev, Commander of Armor, 18 Army South Front, was Commander of an "operative group," arrested for giving up the town of Kakhovki without authorization in order to help the surrounded 296 Rifle Division. Sentenced to death for betraying the country and shot February 13, 1942, he was rehabilitated in 1955.

· Maj. General V.S. Golushkevich, Chief of Operations Section West Front, was transferred to the Southwest Front and arrested on July 19, 1942, as part of the campaign against G.K. Zhukov. Abakumov accused him of contact with the military conspirators in the Frunze Academy. Sentenced to 10 years (March 27, 1952), he was released July 19, 1952, and rehabilitated July 28, 1953. Golushkevich died in 1964.

· Maj. General of Artillery V.S. Goncharev, Commander of Artillery 34 Army Northwest Front, was arrested and ordered shot in the presence of other officers by L.Z. Mekhlis (September 12, 1941).

· Maj. General of Signal Troops A.T. Grigor'ev, Commander Signals West Front, was court-martialed and shot in July 1941. He was rehabilitated November 5, 1956.

· Lt. General of Aviation K.M. Gusev, Commander of Air Force Far East Front, was arrested and shot in 1941(?).

· Kombrig N.F. Gus'kov, former Head of Artillery, 58 Reserve Army, was arrested February 16, 1942. He was accused by Abakumov of criticizing the Soviet government and praising German equipment.

· Maj. General of Artillery I.V. Iodishus, Commander Artillery 179 Rifle Division Baltic Military District, was arrested in 1942 and sentenced. His fate is unknown.

· Maj. General of Aviation A.P. Ionov, Commander of Air Force Northwest Front, disappeared in 1941.

· Maj. General G.S. Isserson, a leading military theoretician, was arrested and sentenced to 10 years in March 1942.

· Maj. General of Aviation P.P. Iusupov, Deputy Chief of Staff Air Force, was arrested on June 28, 1941.

· Lt. General F.S. Ivanov, former Commander 8 and 42 Armies, Leningrad Front, and former Head of Leningrad Garrison and Commander of Internal Defense, was arrested on February 22, 1942 and released in December 1945.

· Maj. General K.M. Kachanov, Soviet Senior Military Adviser in China (September 1939–February 1941), Commander of 34 Army Northwest Front (August 1941), was arrested by the command of L.Z. Mekhlis (September 12, 1941), who ordered a military court to sentence him to death (September 26, 1941).

· Maj. General of Technical Services M.M. Kaiukov, former Deputy Department Head in the Commissariat of Defense and Adjutant of Marshal Kulik, was shot October 28, 1941.

· Lt. General S.A. Kalinin, formerly of the 24 Army and the Kharkov Military District, was arrested June 24, 1944. He was later released but not returned to command. He was accused by Abakumov of anti-Soviet agitation and pro-Kulak views.

· Maj. General A.A. Kazekamp, attached to the high command course in the General Staff Academy, Chief of Staff 180 Rifle Division, was arrested July 30, 1941 and died in prison October 3, 1942.

· Maj. General of Artillery V.I. Khokhlov, associated with the Main Artillery Administration, was arrested (July 1941) and later released.

· Lt. General P.S. Klenov, Chief of Staff of the Baltic Military District/Northwest Front, was shot in 1941.

· Lt. (Maj.?) General R.Iu. Kliavin'sh, pre-war Minister of Defense and Commander of in Chief of the Latvian Army, and later of 24 Territorial Corps in Latvia (September 1940), was arrested in early 1941. His fate is unknown.

· Lt. General of Artillery N.A. Klich, Commander Artillery, West Front, was courtmartialed and shot in September 1941. He was rehabilitated November 5, 1956.

· Maj. General V.E. Klimovskikh, Chief of Staff West Front, was court-martialed and shot in July 1941. He was rehabilitated November 5, 1956.

· Maj. General A.A. Korobkov, Commander 4 Army West Front, was court-martialed and shot in July 1941. He was rehabilitated November 5, 1956.

· Maj. General I.S. Kosobutskii, Commander 41 Rifle Corps, Leningrad Front, was courtmartialed on July 26, 1941, and sentenced to 10 years. Released (October 21, 1942), he was cleared of charges (October 30, 1943), and became Commander of 34 Rifle Corps.

· Maj. General of Tank Troops P.V. Kotov, Official in the Main Artillery Administration, was arrested (July 1941) and later released.

· Maj. General A.N. Krustyn'sh, Commander 183 Rifle Division, 24 Territorial Corps, Baltic Military District, was arrested in early 1941. His fate is unknown.

· Maj. General Ia.Ia. Kruus, Commander 182 Rifle Division, 22 Territorial Corps, was arrested in the beginning of the war. He was condemned to death by an NKVD court (April 1942).

· Maj. General F.K. Kuz'min, Head of Operations-Tactics Frunze Academy, was arrested December 29, 1941. Accused by Abakumov of advocating contact with the enemy and belonging to a conspiracy in the academy, he was sentenced to 25 years (October 19, 1951) and released after Stalin's death. He died in 1955.

· Maj. General I.A. Laskin (also incorrectly listed as Lt. General), former Chief of Staff of 15 Rifle Division, was captured in August 1941, escaped in September 1941, and fought in the defense of Sevastopol (Commander of 172 Rifle Division) and Stalingrad (Chief of Staff, 64 Army). Arrested on December 20, 1943, after having served as Chief of Staff of North Caucasus Front for over six months, he was accused by Abakumov of cooperation with German intelligence. Sent to prison without trial, he was released and wrote his memoirs (1986).

· Maj. General of Aviation N.A. Laskin, Chief of Staff Southwest Front Air Force, was arrested (July 12, 1941)on a charge of membership in a "counterrevolutionary conspiracy" during 1936–1937. Shot in 1942, he was rehabilitated in 1956.

· Maj. General I.S. Lazarenko, Commander of 42 Rifle Division 4 Army, West Front, was court-martialed on September 17, 1942, and sentenced to death but freed in 1942 or 1943.

· Maj. General of Tank Troops I.G. Lazarev, Official in the Main Artillery Administration, was arrested (July 1941) and later released.

· Maj. General I.L. Leonovich, Chief of Staff 18 Army South Front, was arrested on April 28, 1942. He was released in December 1945.

· Admiral G.I. Levchenko, Commander Crimea, was sentenced to 10 years in December 1941 but was later released and restored to command.

· Maj. General of Aviation A.A. Levin, Deputy Commander Leningrad Military District Air Force, was arrested July 7, 1941.

· Maj. General Ia.P. Liepin'sh, Commander 181 Rifle Division, 24 Territorial Corps (September 1940), in Latvia and then attached to General Staff Academy, was arrested in 1941–1942. He was sentenced to death by the military tribunal of the Baltic Military District (January 20, 1941 or 1942).

· Col. General and member of Central Committee A.D. Loktionov, former Commander of the Baltic Special Military District, was shot October 28, 1941.

· Komkor M.P. Mager, former Chief of Staff, Leningrad Military District, was arrested September 10, 1938, released February 29, 1939, and re-arrested April 8, 1941. Sentenced to death July 20, 1941, he was executed October 16, 1941 and rehabilitated October 15, 1955.

· Maj. General V.A. Melikov, Head of the Department of Military History in General Staff Academy, was arrested January 18, 1942. Accused by Abakumov of making comments critical of Soviet political and military leadership, he died in prison.

· Army General (future Marshal of the Soviet Union) K.A. Meretskov, Deputy Commissar of Defense, was arrested during the first week of the war and was later released.

· Maj. General S.M. Mishchenko, instructor in the Frunze Academy, was arrested by the Special Department (April 21, 1941) and accused of anti-Soviet activities. Sentenced to death (September 17, 1941), he was shot (October 10, 1941) and later rehabilitated (January 5, 1955).

· Maj. General Artillery S.A. Moshenin, Commander of the Artillery in 24 Army, remained behind enemy lines and was arrested on August 31, 1943, after the Soviets returned. He was accused by Abakumov of anti-Soviet agitation during his absence and not trying to return to the Soviet side.

· Maj. General M.A. Moskvin, Chief of Staff 62 Army Stalingrad Front (July 1942), was arrested and demoted to Private.

· Corps. Commissar S.I. Mrochkovskii, formerly with the GRU commercial network, was arrested January 18, 1943. He was accused by Abakumov of Trotskiism, contact with French intelligence, and anti-Soviet statements to cellmates.

· Maj. General V.I. Nichiporovich, Deputy Commander 4 Guard Cavalry Corps, was arrested in May 1943.

· Maj. General of Aviation D.N. Nikishev, Chief of Staff of the Air Force, disappeared.

· Maj. General S.I. Oborin, Commander 14 Mechanized Corps, 4 Army, West Front, was arrested July 6, 1941. Court-martialed and shot in mid-July 1941, he was rehabilitated November 5, 1956.

· Maj. General of Tank Troops V.V. Obukhov, instructor in the Stalin Mechanized and Motorized Academy, was expelled from the Army and arrested March 26, 1942.

· Maj. General I.Kh. Pauka, instructor in the General Staff Academy, was expelled from the Army and arrested July 27, 1941. He died in May 1943.

· Army General D.G. Pavlov, Commander West Front (June 22, 1941–June 30, 1941), was court-martialed and shot July 22, 1941. He was rehabilitated November 5, 1956.

· Maj. General of Artillery E.S. Petrov, former Head of Smolensk Artillery School, was arrested May 22, 1943. Accused by Abakumov of doubting Soviet victory and criticizing the military leadership, he was sentenced to 25 years (March 25, 1952). In prison until August 1953, Petrov served in the reserves from October 1953.

· Maj. General M.I. Petrov, instructor in the Artillery Academy, was arrested June 30, 1941.

· Lt. General K.P. Piadyshev, First Deputy Commander, Leningrad Military District (January 28, 1941) was Commander of Luga Operative Group (fall 1941). He disappeared and was stricken from the ranks June 9, 1943. He was rehabilitated January 28, 1958.

· Maj. General N.I. Pliusnin, former Department Chair in the Frunze Academy, was arrested on November 22, 1941. Accused by Abakumov of being a member of an anti-Soviet conspiracy in the academy, he was sentenced to 25 years on October 19, 1951, and released after Stalin's death.

· Maj. General D.F. Popov, former Chief of Training in the Red Army Formations Department, was arrested, sentenced to two years in 1941, and re-arrested on July 30, 1943. Accused by Abakumov of anti-Soviet thoughts going back to 1914, lack of faith in the Red Army troops, complaints about collective farms, and slander against the government, the Party, and their policies, he was sentenced to 10 years on March 27, 1952. Released after Stalin's death, he died in 1960.

· Maj. General of Tank Troops A.G. Potaturchev, Commander of 4 Tank Division, 6 Mechanized Corps, West Front, he was not, contrary to Russian sources (*VIZH*, October 1992), taken prisoner and did not die in captivity. He was arrested during the war for loss of equipment and died in prison or was shot (September 30, 1945).

· Lt. General of Aviation and Hero of the Soviet Union I.I. Proskurov, former head of GRU, was shot October 28, 1941 and rehabilitated (May 11, 1954).

· Lt. General of Aviation and Hero of the Soviet Union E.S. Ptukhin, former Commander of PVO and Commander Kiev Military District Air Force, was arrested in July 1941, tried, and shot February 23, 1942.

· Lt. General of Aviation and Hero of the Soviet Union P.I. Pumpur, Commander of Air Force in Moscow Military District, was arrested May 31, 1941, shot February 13 or March 23, 1942, and rehabilitated June 25, 1955.

· Maj. General B.S. Rikhter, Chief of Staff 6 Rifle Corps, 6 Army Southwest Front, was captured June 28, 1941. Accused of being a collaborator, he was condemned to death in absentia (June 1943); his fate is unknown.

· Maj. General F.N. Romanov, former Chief of Staff 27 Army (October 11, 1941–December 25, 1941), was arrested January 11, 1942. Accused by Abakumov of blaming the early setbacks on the Soviet leadership and also being a member of a military conspiracy, he was sent to prison without trial.

· Maj. General of Rear Services T.Iu. Rotberg, a former officer of the Estonian Army and Assistant Minister of War in Estonia (1938), joined the Red Army after occupation (1940). At the start of the war, he headed Rear Services of the 22 Estonian Rifle Corps, Northwest Front. Taken prisoner in July 1941, he was arrested November 20, 1944, after the recapture of Tallin. He was accused by Abakumov of having helped the German intelligence. An order of the Ministry of Defense dated January 30, 1958, indicates that Rotberg "died" most probably during 1944–1953, but gives no further details.

· Army Military Jurist N.S. Rozovskii, former Chief Military Prosecutor of the Red Army, was arrested June 6, 1941, and died in prison.

· Maj. General of Aviation I.N. Rukhle, Deputy Chief of Staff Stalingrad Front, was arrested October 5, 1942, but eventually released. Abakumov accused him of a dubious past as well as responsibility for a number of failed operations.

· Lt. General of Aviation and Hero of the Soviet Union P.V. Rychagov, former Commander of the Air Force, was shot October 28, 1941 and rehabilitated July 23, 1954.

· Maj. General M.B. Salikhov, Co. 60 Alpine Division, 12 Army Southwest Front, was court-martialed in mid-July 1941 and sentenced to 10 years. The sentence was later set aside. Demoted and returned to the front, he was captured in August 1941. An alleged collaborator, he was sentenced to death in absentia (1943). His fate is unknown.

· Rear Admiral K.I. Samoilov, former Head of Naval Training and Head of Leningrad Naval Defense, was arrested June 18, 1941. Accused later by Abakumov of having had contact with the French intelligence in Baku in 1922–1924 and later having been a member of a military conspiracy organized by former Commander in Chief of the Navy V.M. Orlov (shot in 1937) and former Deputy Commander in Chief of Navy P.I. Smirnov-Svetlovskii (shot in 1940), he was expelled from the Navy (October 26, 1946). He was shot or died in prison.

· Captain 3 Rank I.I. Santpank, Commander of the merchant ship *Pikker*, was attached to the Baltic Fleet and before 1940 the Commander in Chief of the Estonian Navy. Arrested on June 23, 1941, he was accused by Abakumov of having provided British intelligence with information for using Estonia as a springboard to attack the USSR, of having destroyed secret documents after the occupation of Estonia, and of undermining Soviet rule among other Estonian officers who had joined the Red Army.

· Maj. General of Artillery G.K. Savchenko, Deputy Head Main Artillery Administration, was shot October 28, 1941.

· Lt. General of I.V. Selivanov, Commander of the 30 Rifle Corps, West Front, was shot February 1942. He was later rehabilitated.

· Maj. General V.V. Semashko, Deputy Chief of Staff Leningrad Front, was arrested April 10, 1945. He was released December 1945.

· Maj. General I.I. Semenov, Head of Operations Department West Front, was court-martialed on October 7, 1941, and sentenced to 10 years; he was later freed.

· Komdiv I.P. Sergeev, instructor in the General Staff Academy and former Commissar of Munition (from January 11, 1939) and member of the Central

Committee (1939), was arrested (May 30, 1941) and sentenced to death (February 13, 1942). He was later rehabilitated (November 22, 1955).

· Maj. General of Aviation and Hero of the Soviet Union E.G. Shakht, an immigrant from Switzerland, Head of the Air Force Orel Military District, was shot March 23, 1942.

· Brigade Engineer N.A. Shaposhnikov, former department head in the Voroshilov Naval Academy, was arrested on October 29, 1941 and released in December 1945.

· Maj. General A.G. Shirmakher, former senior instructor in the Frunze Academy, was arrested December 19, 1941 and was accused by Abakumov of unspecified charges and a dubious past. He died in prison in 1953.

· Col. General and Hero of the Soviet Union and member of the Central Committee, G.M. Shtern, former Head of PVO, was arrested in June 1941, shot October 28, 1941, and rehabilitated August 25, 1954).

· S.O. Sklizkov, Head of the Infantry/Artillery Department in the Main Artillery Administration was shot onOctober 28, 1941.

· Lt. General of Aviation, twice Hero of the Soviet Union and candidate member of the Central Committee, Ia.V. Smushkevich, Assistant Chief of General Staff for Aviation, was arrested July 7, 1941, shot October 28, 1941, and rehabilitated May 11, 1954.

· Lt. General P.P. Sobennikov, Commander of the 8 Army (Northwest Front) in the beginning of the war; Commander of the Northwest Front (July 4 or 7, 1941–August 23, 1941); and Commander of the 43 Army West Front (September 1941–October 1941), was arrested and court-martialed (February 6, 1942). Sentenced to 5 years, he was later released but demoted to Deputy Commander of the 3 Army.

· Maj. General A.Ia. Sokolov, former senior instructor, Frunze Academy, was arrested December 29, 1941. He was accused by Abakumov of having organized an anti-Soviet conspiracy in the academy with Maj. General N.I. Pliusnin.

· Maj. General G.I. Sokolov, Chief of Staff 6 Army, Kiev Special Military District, was expelled from the Army and arrested May 26, 1941. He died in prison or was shot (July 1943).

· Lt. General of Aviation N.A. Sokolov-Sokolenok, Head of Zhukovskii Air Force Engineering Academy, was arrested(?), then released.

· Engineer-Captain 1 Rank V.L. Survillo, professor in the Voroshilov Naval Academy, was arrested on January 6, 1942, and released December 1945.

· Maj. General P.V. Sysoev, former Commander of 36 Rifle Corp, was captured, escaped in August 1943, and joined the partisans. Arrested on April 25, 1944, he was released December 1945.

· Maj. General of Aviation A.I. Taiurskii, Deputy Commander Air Force West Front, was shot July 22, 1941. He was rehabilitated November 5, 1956.

· Komdiv A.A. Tal'kovskii, head of course in the Frunze Academy, was first arrested under Ezhov (December 23, 1937). Released on May 16, 1940, he was re-arrested (June 30, 1941), sentenced to death (February 13, 1942), shot (February 23, 1942), and later rehabilitated (April 25, 1956).

· Lt. General of Tank Troops V.S. Tamruchi, Commander of 22 Mechanized Corps 5 Army, Southwest Front (June 25, 1941–July 29, 1941) then Deputy Commander of Southwest Front for Armor, was arrested May 22, 1943. Accused by Abakumov of defeatism, criticism of the Soviet government and military leadership and latent "Trotskiism," he died in prison October 28, 1950 of a heart attack. He was rehabilitated August 5, 1953.

· Maj. General of Aviation B.L. Teplinskii, Chief of Staff Siberia Military District Air Force, was arrested on April 27 or 29, 1943. Accused by Abakumov of being a Trotskiite and plotting terrorist acts against Stalin, he was not released until 1952 or 1953.

· Maj. General A.A. Tiurin, Commander of Army Baltic Military District and Commander of the Orel Military District, was arrested January 20, 1942, and sentenced to 7 years but later released.

· Maj. General R.I. Tomberg, former Deputy Head of Cadres in Frunze Academy and before 1940 Commander of the Estonian Air Force, Commander 180 Rifle Division (September 1940), was arrested on February 26, 1942. Accused by Abakumov of anti-Soviet agitation and contacts with British intelligence, he was in prison until 1952 before being tried. Sentenced to 5 years in prison and loss of property by the USSR Military Collegium (March 28, 1952), and loss of rank by the order of the Council of Ministers (April 12, 1952), he was later rehabilitated (March 4, 1956), freed (June 18, 1956), and had his rank restored (August 1, 1956).

· Military Engineer 1 Rank Treier, Head of the Anti-Aircraft Artillery Branch, Main Artillery Administration, was arrested in 1941.

· Lt. General of Technical Services I.I. Trubetskii, Head of the Red Army Railroad Administration, was arrested and shot.

· Maj. General P.G. Tsyrul'nikov, former Commander of 51 Rifle Division South Front, was captured in October 1941. He escaped and was arrested on February 18, 1942. Accused by Abakumov of having helped the German intelligence, he nevertheless survived. He died in 1985.

· Maj. General of Aviation A.A. Turzhanskii, former senior instructor in the Command/Navigation Academy, was arrested on February 19, 1942. Accused by Abakumov of making critical comments about the Sovietgovernment and the Communist Party and believing in the superiority of German weapons, he was tried (March 25, 1952) and sentenced. He was released after Stalin's death.

· Future Col. General of Artillery/Engineering Service B.L. Vannikov, Commissar of the Defense Industry, was arrested July 4, 1941 and later released.

· Komdiv N.N. Vasil'chenko, Assistant General Inspector of the Air Force, was arrested on June 1, 1941, and sentenced to death on February 13, 1942. On September 17, 1955, he was rehabilitated.

· Maj. General A.A. Veis, former Commander of 6 Reserve Artillery Brigade, was arrested on June 18, 1943.

· Maj. General S.I. Vetoshkin, Official in the Main Artillery Administration, was arrested (July 1941) and later released.

· Maj. General of Aviation P.S. Volodin, appointed Chief of Staff of the Air Force on June 22, 1941, was arrested a week later and executed October 28, 1941.

· Maj. General of Artillery V.I. Zhilis, Commander of Artillery 29 Rifle Corps, Baltic Military District, was arrested on June 24, 1941. Sentenced by an NKVD troika to 10 years (September 5, 1942), he was then exiled. Freed on August 31, 1955, he was rehabilitated July 18, 1956. He died in Kaunaus on October 10, 1972.

· Division Commissar I.I. Zhukov, former Commissar of Staff of the 18 Army South Front, was arrested May 13, 1942 and accused by Abakumov of defeatism, belief in the superiority of the German military, and complaints that the frontline troops were not given adequate supplies.

In December 1940, about 20 former officers of the Baltic Armies were given the rank of General in the Red Army. Most of them, including Generals Iodishus, Zhilis, Kazekamp, Tomberg, Chernius, Krustyn'sh, Kliavin'sh, and Liepin'sh were arrested during 1941–1942. Baltic Generals whose fates are not known include O.Ia. Uden'tin'sh, V.I. Vitkauskas, Ch.A. Chapauskas, V.A. Karvialis, A.Ia. Dannenberg, G.Iu. Ionson, G.F. Brede, A.Ia. Kauler, O.G. Grossbarts, and A.Ia. Dal'bergs. In 1944, a number of senior officers from the Baltics were reportedly shot in camps after engaging in a "conspiracy." Their names have yet to be released and may include some of those already mentioned.

Other commanders whose war-time fate remains mysteries include Maj. General A.E. Trofimov, Deputy Head of Manpower in the Cavalry, who died on August 2, 1944; and Rear Admiral A.V. Trofimov, Head of Cadres in the Naval Academy, who died on March 18, 1943. Officially, all the senior officers still in prison after the war were expelled from the Red Army on October 26, 1945.

Most of the victims were arrested by the Special Department and, later, SMERSH while Abakumov was in charge. Along with these, there were a number of commanders whose positions and careers were jeopardized by Beriia's intrigues. These were men who had the misfortune of serving in the Caucasus, which Beriia considered his private preserve, and where he twice represented the Stavka in August 1942 and March 1943. The second time, according to Shtemenko, was for only ten days (Beriia was to be back in 1944, after the Germans had left to organize the deportations). Among them were Chief of Soviet Artillery, Chief Marshal of Artillery N.N. Voronov; Commander of the South Front, the future Marshal of the Soviet Union R. Ia. Malinovskii; the Commander of the Transcaucasus Front, Army General I.V. Tiulenev; the Commander of the North Caucasus Front, Army General I.E. Petrov; and the Commander of the 46 Army, Maj. General V.F. Segratskov, with whom Beriia had violent disagreements about the defense of mountain passes in the Caucasus in August 1942.[9] Other senior officers who came under suspicion during the war included I. Kh. Bagramian, I.S. Konev, I.R. Apanasenko, P.I. Batov, M.A. Reiter, V.D. Sokolovskii, M.S. Khozin, A.V. Khrulov, P.P. Vechnyi, A.N. Pervushin, F.I. Tolbukhin, and P.V. Dement'ev (Deputy Commissar of the Aviation Industry, and from 1953 to 1977 Minister of Aviation). There were also unsubstantiated charges against such commanders as S.M. Budennyi, G.F. Zakharov, S.M. Timoshenko, V.I. Chuikov, P.A. Rotmistrov, N.F. Vatutin, M.P. Kirponos, F.N. Remizov, and V.A.

Iushkevich. Then there were the cases of 23 captured generals (some members of the Vlasov movement) who were accused of collaboration with the enemy and were arrested by SMERSH at the end of the war. They will be discussed later.

Commanders in the Red Army, as elsewhere, were also removed when their performance proved to be unsatisfactory, but there was also a threat of a greater humiliation—reduction in rank. Among those who thus suffered besides Kulik and Mekhlis were Army General M.M. Popov, Commander of the 2 Baltic Front, demoted to Col. General in April 1944; Army General I.E. Petrov, Commander of the Coastal Army, demoted to Col. General in March 1944; Lt. General D.T. Kozlov, Commander of the Crimea Front Force, in May 1942 demoted to Maj. General; Lt. General S.I. Cherniak, Commander of the 44 Army Crimea Front, in May 1942 reduced to Colonel; Maj. General K.S. Kolganov, Commander of the 47 Army Crimea Front, in May 1942 reduced to Colonel; Division Commissar F.A. Shamanin, Commissar of the Crimea Front, in May 1942 reduced to Brigade Commissar; and Maj. General of Aviation E.M. Nikolaenko, Commander of the Air Force in Crimea Front, reduced to Colonel. The careers of these men never completely recovered. It took M.M. Popov, a potential Marshal of the Soviet Union during the war, nine more years to regain his old rank of Army General, first given to him in October 1943.

Even a worse fate than demotion in rank was assignment to punishment battalions and companies which were virtually a death sentence. They were set up (*Krasnaia Zvezda*, December 12, 1991) under two directives: from Stalin on July 28, 1942, and by Zhukov on September 26, 1942. The battalions of 800 men were made up of middle and senior officers, the companies from junior officers and soldiers. Clearing minefields was one of the less dangerous assignments. The list of senior officers who served in punishment battalions has yet to be released.

Even some who had died a hero's death on the battlefield came under suspicion. The best known is Lt. General V.Ia. Kachalov, whose story is the subject of a detailed study by L.E. Reshin and V.S. Stepanov (*VIZH*, 8/1993). Kachalov, born in 1890, had been an officer in the old Army, but had joined the Red Army in July 1918 and was a Party member from 1927. In the 1920s, he had fought against the Basmachis and twice received the Order of the Red Banner. In the late 1930s, he had been Commander of the North Caucasus and Arkhangel Military Districts. At the beginning of the war, Kachalov was appointed Commander of the 28 Army, which was later surrounded by the enemy. On August 4, 1941, during a breakout attempt, Kachalov's tank was hit by an enemy shell, killing him and the crew. In the confusion, it was reported that he had deserted to the enemy, a charge accepted by Mekhlis. On August 16, 1941, under the infamous Order 270 of the Commissariat of Defense, he was sentenced to death in absentia for desertion along with two others, Generals Ponedelin and Kirillov, who will be discussed later. The order was signed by Stalin, Mekhlis, Molotov, Budennyi, Voroshilov, Timoshenko, Shaposhnikov and Zhukov— some probably under duress. On August 20, 1941, Kachalov's wife, E.N. Khanchin-Kachalova, and her mother, E.I. Khanchina, were arrested, and on December 27, 1941, each was sentenced to 8 years in Siberian camps, where the older woman died in 1944. In 1943, Abakumov had Kachalov's wife taken to Moscow for questioning in regard to her husband's fate. Since she obviously had no such knowledge, she was returned to camp, but returned to Moscow after amnesty in 1949 to be near her son. Meanwhile, after the war, there were rumors that Kachalov actually had survived but died fighting as a partisan, but investigations proved inconclusive. After her release, Khanchin-Kachalova started a campaign to clear her husband's name and wrote in the latter part of 1951 to the Military Prosecutors Nikolaev and to Malenkov, who ordered his Deputy, F.Ia. Lisitsin, to contact the chief Military Prosecutor, A. Vavilov, who professed that they had no new information about Kachalov. On January 23, 1952, Khanchin-Kachalova wrote a moving letter to Stalin, asking for an investigation into the fate of her husband. Soon after this letter, the Central Committee Administrative Organ office received a report from L.F. Tsanava, the recently appointed Deputy Minister MGB. Like a good Chekist, Tsanava, ferret-like, explored all possible angles. His investigation showed that interviews with returning captured Generals such as Dobroserdov, Trukhin, and Snegov had been inconclusive. Captured German intelligence officers as well as senior officers such as Generals Schmidt and de Anglais, Field Marshal Schorner and Admiral Voss also had no knowledge of Kachalov being captured. In his investigation, Tsanava also included one bizarre allegation that the British intelligence had helped Kachalov to escape from German captivity to Turkey and later employed him in Casablanca as head of the anti-Soviet "Tri bogatyr'" an organization even unknown to the MGB! This kind of falsification was second nature in the organs. On September 17, 1950, in response to an inquiry, the MGB informed the family of Maj. General A.N. DeLazari, in prison since June 1941, that he had died of an infection at age 70, when in fact he had been shot eight years earlier.

What followed for Khanchin-Kachalova was a bureaucratic nightmare of Kafkaesque proportions. The case now was being kicked back and forth between MGB's 3 Department (counterintelligence), the Administrative Organ office of the Central Committee and the office of the Military Prosecutor and its investigative branch. The upshot was that she was arrested on August 6, 1952, by the MGB for writing anonymous anti-Soviet letters to various branches of government. Only after Stalin's death in view of overwhelming evidence was the case cleared. Writing on December 7, 1953, to Malenkov and Khrushchev, Prosecutor General Rudenko admitted that Kachalov had not been guilty of treason. The report of Colonel of Judiciary P. Kul'chitskii, head of the Investigation Branch of the Military Prosecutor's Office, finally set the record straight. Khanchin-Kachalova was vindicated. She died in 1957. Her courage and loyalty to her husband, not unusual among the surviving wives of purge victims, were the only bright chapter in this otherwise sordid story. A somewhat similar case which involved Maj. General V.A. Khomenko will be covered later.

Senior officers were, of course, not the only victims. During the war, thousands of soldiers and junior officers were arrested by SMERSH. The historian V.N. Vasil'ev, whose father and brother had been arrested in 1940, was typical. Vasil'ev, who had fought in the Battle of Stalingrad (where he was awarded the Order of Red Star), was arrested on August 16, 1943, by the SMERSH of the 57 Army on trumped-up charges. One member of the three-man court that he faced wanted him shot; another proposed a 10-year sentence. Vasil'ev ended up receiving a 15-year term.[10] Hero of the Soviet Union (May 6, 1965) A.A. Timofeeva (Egorova), a rare woman Shturmovik pilot, was shot down and captured in August 1944 after completing 243 combat sorties. Despite her severe injuries, she was arrested after her return from captivity. The memoirs of Lt. General of Judiciary B.A. Viktorov also cite cases of the highhanded way in which SMERSH treated common soldiers.

Although the Special Department and, later, SMERSH were responsible for investigation, arrest, and indictment, the victims were tried by military tribunals whose cruelty and cavalier attitude toward due process matched those of the worst NKVD troikas. Criticizing Soviet equipment or comparing it unfavorably to that of the enemy was considered a major crime. Documents published in *Skrytaia Pravda Voiny: 1941 god* (Moscow: 1992) show a typical case. Between November 1941 and February 1942, in the 305, 326, and 330 Rifle Divisions, 10 Army, West Front, there were 740 court-martials resulting in 233 death sentences and 507 prison convictions. The Military Tribunal of the South Front under Ul'rikh's old colleague I.O. Matulevich was particularly vicious. Under Matulevich there were only two sentences—outright execution or delayed execution through assignment to "punishment battalions." In 1942, during the Soviet retreat from Voroshilovgrad, Matulevich on his own ordered the mass execution of all prisoners to prevent them from falling into German hands. On July 28, 1942, following the collapse of the Soviet summer campaign, Stalin further strengthened the hands of the military courts by making unauthorized retreat a crime subject to court-martial by issuing his notorious Stavka Order No. 277. The achievements of these tribunals include sending thousands of totally unfit Gypsies to serve in punishment battalions. During the Khrushchev years, Matulevich and his fellow Jurists Detistov and Suslov were expelled from the Party and lost their military rank, but were otherwise untouched. F.D. Sverdlov, in *Evrei-Generaly*, incorrectly lists Matulevich as a victim of the Great Terror, although it is possible that he may have lost a job at the height of the anti-Semitic campaigns in the early 1950s following his presiding over the court which tried the principle victims of the Leningrad Affair. The history of military courts and their granddaddy, the Military Collegium of the USSR Supreme Court, has yet to be written. Also in need of further study is the sinister role played by the office of the Chief Military Prosecutor, particularly under N.S. Rozovskii (the latter part of the 1930s), V.I. Nosov (1941–1945), and N.P. Afanas'ev and F.L. Petrovskii (1945–1950), who closely cooperated with the repressive organs. In fairness, it must be added that P.F. Gavrilov, who held this office during 1939–1941, tried to introduce some sanity and fairness under extremely dangerous conditions, but without success. Another military judge, A.A. Cheptsov, whose career will be discussed later, also seems to have tried to put up some unsuccessful resistance against outright miscarriage of justice.

The recent study by Bobrenev and Riazntsev, *Palachi i Zhertvy*, sheds some light on the sinister career of N.S. Rozovskii, the Chief Military Prosecutor during the Great Purge, who worked closely with Ezhov and Vyshinskii and for whose efforts received both the Orders of Red Star and Red Banner. There is also a discussion of the fate of Military Prosecutors such as M.M. Ishov, N.M. Kuznetsov, V.I. Malkis, E.A. Perfil'ev, R.I. Romanovskii, G.G. Suslov, Pavlovskii, Ol'skii, and others whose lack of enthusiasm, or even resistance to lawless terror, led to their downfall. For all of his efforts, Rozovskii had been too closely associated with Ezhov to suit Beriia, who had him arrested in June 1941.

The military was, of course, not the only segment of the Soviet society that was targeted for punishment. According to the historian S. Kudriashev in *Barbarossa, the Axis and the Allies*, between July 1941 and July 1942, 282,760 individuals were sentenced to prison. In May 1942, however, the need for cannon fodder forced the release of nearly 600,000 prisoners while others were being taken into custody.

Next to the execution wall and prisons, deportation on a mass scale was the main hallmark of the Stalinist terror. The first victims of deportation based on nationality rather than class were the Poles. During 1923–1926, two Polish autonomous districts were established on the frontier regions. The Iu.Iu. Markhlevskii (Marchlewski), named after one of the founders of the Social-Democratic movement in Poland, was established in Ukraine, while the F. Dzerzhinskii district, named after the founder of Cheka, was founded in Belorussia. In the beginning, the two districts enjoyed considerable cultural autonomy, but their resistance to collectivization spelled their doom. The Markhlevskii district was liquidated in 1935 and the Dzerzhinskii district in 1938. The Poles were deported to Central Asia, mostly to the Kokchchetav oblast in Kazakhstan. In 1938 Stalin, through Comintern, dissolved the Polish Communist Party and purged most of its leaders.[11] Further experience during the pre-war period in the newly occupied territories, as well as in the Far East, honed NKVD's considerable skills in this area, first applied to the Kulaks and then the Poles. Massive deportations took place in summer 1937 under the brutal leadership of G.S. Liushkov, Head of NKVD in the Far East, first of the Chinese and then of the Koreans, many of them refugees from Japanese rule, who were deported from the border areas of the Far East. The Koreans numbered an estimated 160,000. They were deported from Buriat-Mongol ASSR, Chita oblast, Khabarovsk, and Maritime territories to Uzbek and Kazakh SSR. On December 20, 1937, the Central Committee expressed its thanks to Liushkov. During a seven-month period (August 1946–March 1947), some of the Koreans tried to return to their old home, causing the MVD to take notice.[12] We have previously touched on deportations carried out after the occupation of Western Ukraine, Belorussia, and the Baltic states from 1939 to 1941.

As Robert Conquest points out, even in the most critical days of the war, Stalin would spare considerable human and material resources to carry out operations in which whole nationalities, in contrast to "classes" (which Marx and Lenin would have approved), were uprooted from their homes and deported to faraway places under unspeakably harsh conditions.

The compilation of documents *Iosif Stalin-Lavrentiiu Berii: "Ikh nado deportirovat"* (Moscow: 1992), collected by N.F. Bugai, is the most comprehensive account of war time deportations. The cold official documents written in bureaucratese and usually signed by People's Commissar of Interior and General Commissar of State Security L.P. Beriia only give a hint of the enormous tragedy that was taking place but provide considerable information about one of the few areas in which the police state operated with a semblance of efficiency. At the start of the war, the NKVD apparently had a complete record of every Soviet citizen of German and Finnish descent. Almost immediately after the start of the war, the local NKVDs from Leningrad to the Far East began to arrest these citizens. In the Volga German Republic and other areas where there were heavy concentrations, the operation would be more complex. Stalin also had made the deportations somewhat easier by his 1938 decision to dissolve all autonomous German administrative units including 16 districts and 550 communities and incorporate them into adjacent administrative units, leaving the German Volga Republic alone. To deport the Germans, Beriia put his Deputy I.E. Serov in charge (in 1943–1944 in the Caucasus, Beriia himself led the operation) and also organized local teams which consisted of a representative from the central apparatus as well as the local NKVD. For instance, in the Volga Republic, the Chief of Gulag Major of State Security V.G. Nasedkin would work with the head of the local NKVD, Major of State Security V.V. Gubin. In Stravropol, Major of State Security L.F. Raikhman, Deputy Head of the Counterintelligence Department, would be with Lt. of State Security V.G. Viktorov, and in Stalingrad oblast the team would consist of A.G. Galkin, Head of the Militia; Major of State Security I.M. Tkachenko, Head of the NKVD Economics Department; and Major of State Security A.I. Voronin, the oblast NKVD leader. In Krasnoiarsk, Major of State Security D.R. Bykov and the local leader, Major of State Security I.P. Semenov, and in Altai, Captain of State Security A.I. Langfang from the NKVD Foreign Department and local leader Major of State Security Voloshenko were in charge. These teams guaranteed central control and also made sure that several individuals were involved in doing the dirty work—a common practice not only in the Soviet Union, but also in Nazi Germany.

In his report to Stalin on March 7, 1944, Beriia stated that 19,000 officials of NKVD, NKGB, and SMERSH (the only time Beriia mentions the latter in his reports) and 100,000 NKVD troops were used during the deportations from the North Caucasus. In another report dating from July 5, 1944, Beriia set forth that the Crimean deportations were accomplished by 9,000 officials of NKVD and NKGB and 23,000 NKVD troops. No mention was made of SMERSH even though the arrested including 998 alleged spies.[13] The first such operation during the war was carried out in August 1941 against the Volga Germans, and it set the pattern for others which occurred in 1943–1944. The Central Committee (Stalin) ordered deportation of all Germans, including members of the Communist Party and Komsomols from the Volga German Republic and Saratov and Stalingrad raions. The released Soviet documents (*Istoriia SSSR*, February 1991) point out that the center provided leadership and expertise through the presence of Deputy Commissars of NKVD I.E. Serov, V.V. Chernyshev and B.P. Obruchnikov; V.G. Nasedkin, Head of Gulag, P.V. Fedotov, Head of NKVD 2nd Department (Counterintelligence [KRU]) and his Deputy, L.F. Raikhman; Major of State Security N.T. Ratushnyi, Deputy Head of NKVD in Ukraine; N.I. Sinegrubov, veteran of the killing of the Polish officers and now a senior Major of State Security and head of the NKVD Transportation Department; and Maj. General A.N. Apollonov, Head of NKVD troops. The local force was composed of V.V. Gubin, Head of NKVD of the Volga German ASSR and V.G. Viktorov, Head of NKVD in Saratov. The Special Department was represented by P.G. Drozdetskii and locally by one Il'in.[14] This involved the deportation of nearly 480,000 people to Central Asia, particularly to Kazakh SSR and Siberia. The Volga Germans were soon to be followed by other Germans from areas still under Soviet rule such as Crimea and the Caucasus (there were nearly 1.5 million Soviet Germans in 1941). For this and similar efforts, in July 1945, Nasedkin, Raikhman and Drozdetskii received the rank of Lt. General and Gubin the rank of Maj. General. In 1942, it was the turn of Soviet Finns. The circumstances of their deportation remain obscure but apparently were organized by V.V. Chernyshev.

The deportation of Volga Germans and Finns, however, was only a prelude to what was going to take place from September 1943 to April 1944 after the Germans were driven out of the Caucasus and the southern part of Russia and involved nearly a million people. It included entire nationalities such as Karachi (October–November 1943), Kalmyks (December 1943), Chechen-Ingush (February–March 1944), Balkars (April 1944), Crimean Tatars (June 1944), Crimean Greeks (1944), and Meskhetians, whose travails in Central Asia continue to the present day. Other victims included Turks and Khemshidis. Some of the deported, for good reason, may have collaborated with the occupying Germans. The deportations were on a massive scale and carried out with unusual brutality. Even some NKVD leaders such as M. Kuznetsov in the Kostomir oblast complained about the conditions. There was very little housing for the deportees in the harsh climate of central Asia. The deportees were also politically suspect and. in fact. Beriia issued an order on December 2, 1945, about subversive political activities among them, which led to a number of arrests. In a 1949 report (*Istoriia SSR* 1/1991), Colonel V.V. Shiian, Head of MVD Special Settlement Department, indicates that the death rate among the deportees was about 20%. The deportation decisions, of course, must have originated with Stalin. Also involved were Voroshilov, Suslov and Beriia, the latter using most of his Georgian mafia in organizing the operation. Only on December 13, 1955, a directive from the Presidium of the Supreme Soviet tried to undo the injustice done to the Soviet Germans, but it was not until 1972 that they could return to their original homes, now in many cases occupied by others.

Two factors need to be considered in the massive deportations that took place in the north Caucasus during 1943–1944. Despite two decades of Soviet rule, unrest and banditry had continued in this area and had been intensified by forced collectivization. According to files of the Georgia NKVD (*Voprosy Istorii*, No. 1, 1990) during February to December 1938, there were 98 "incidents" involving Chechen Ingush in which 49 officials and Party workers were killed. An investigation by I.A. Serov at the beginning of the war resulted in a report that proposed that only "operative-Chekist" methods could be effective in north Caucausus. Further, during the first two years of the war, NKVD claimed to have liquidated 7,161 "bands"

(54,130 individuals), of which 963 (17,563) were in north Caucasus. In addition, as studies by Gerlad Reitlinger and by N.F. Bugai clearly show, subversion of the Caucasus nationalities with dubious loyalty to the Soviet Union was a priority for the Germany military and civilian authorities. This took the form of recruiting anti-Communist émigrés, landing saboteurs behind Soviet lines, and eventually creating national legions. The German attempts at subversion were not without success, and Bugai lists a number of well-known Communist functionaries who fell victim to the enemy agents. As early as February 1942, the Soviets had formed 12 "interceptor battalions" to combat the German effort which reached its height with a number of air drops in the summer of 1942 as the Wehrmacht continued its advance to Caucasus. The *Bugai Collection* (pp. 100–11) includes a number of relevant reports from S.I. Filatov, Head of NKVD (later of NKGB) Kabardo-Balkar ASSR, dated December 12, 1941, and one dated somewhat later; a report from K.P. Bziava, Filatov's successor as head of the NKVD dated June 10, 1943; and one from Sh.O. Tsereteli, head of the Georgia NKVD dated July 16, 1943—all addressed to Beriia and speaking of local unrest which had not abated even with the Germans in retreat. On July 9, 1943, Tserteli actually went to Moscow to discuss with Beriia the measures needed to liquidate the "insurrection" before returning to Nal'chik to carry out the operation.

This unacceptable behavior, as well as past rebelliousness, prompted Stalin and Beriia to launch the ethnic cleansing operation after the German retreat. The Red Army went on the offensive on December 24, 1942, and Malgobek and Mozdok were recaptured on January 3, 1943. By the end of February, the Germans had been pushed out of most of north Caucasus. In November 1943, V.V. Chernyshev, Deputy Commissar of NKVD, met with NKVD chiefs from Altai, Krasnoiarsk, Omsk and Novosibirsk to organize the manpower needed to carry out the operation. Like their Nazi counterparts, such operations required the cooperation of all elements of government.

On January 5, 1944, R.A. Markar'ian (Lt. General, July 1945), Chief of Dagestan NKVD, reported to Beriia about requisitioning from K.V. Il'chenko, head of Ordzhonikidze railroads, 40 trains and 6000 trucks to carry out the deportations. In March 1944, the task of preparing the railroad transport for deportees was handled by D.V. Arkad'ev (Maj. General, July 1945), variously identified as head of NKVD Transportation or Deputy Head of NKGB 3rd Department, who requisitioned 180 trains to carry out the deportations. Along with railroad transport, hundreds of American Lend-Lease trucks, shipped via Iran and badly needed at the front, were assembled in Georgia and put under the control of NKVD Transportation Department to facilitate the operation.

K.S. Karol, who was there, is correct when he writes that Stalin used minimal cooperation between the deported nationalities and the enemy as an excuse to "de-Islamicize" the Caucasus (except for the Greeks, all the deportees were Muslims). The deportations were looked at with indifference if not selfish approval by the Christian nationalities of the Caucasus and the recently revived Orthodox Church in a manner similar to their attitude toward Tsarist pogroms and the nonchalant reaction of the Gentile Poles and the Catholic Church to Hitler's "Final Solution," or for that matter, most Americans to the round up of Japanese following Pearl Harbor. Stalin, of course, did not invent the ethnic tensions in the Caucasus, but his efforts further poisoned the atmosphere for generations yet to come.

On November 2, 1943, the residents of the Karachi Autonomous Oblast (nearly 70,000 people) were deported, and on October 5, 1944, the area now renamed Klukhorskii raion was incorporated into the Georgian SSR. The city of Karachaevsk (until 1944 Mikoian-Shakhar) was renamed Klukhori—a name that lasted until January 1, 1957. At the end of December 1943, 230,000 Kalmyks were deported at the time that 20,000 of their compatriots were fighting at the front. By 1944 only two Kalmyks, Col. General O.I. Govorodnikov, veteran of the 1 Cavalry Army and at the time Chief Inspector of the Red Army Cavalry, and his son remained in the ranks. The Kalmyk deportations were led by I.A. Serov and directed from Elista. The Kalmyk ASSR was divided among Astrakhan, Rostov and Stalingrad oblasts. In one of his reports, Beriia, accusing the Karachis and Kalmyks of treason, indicated that they had helped the Germans massacre the Jewish refugees who had been evacuated to the North Caucasus from Leningrad, Crimea, and Rostov. There may be some basis to this charge. After Karachis and Kalmyks, it was the turn of Chechen and Ingush. On February 20, 1944, Beriia, accompanied by I.A. Serov, B.Z. Kobulov, S.S. Mamulov (Head of NKVD Chancellery) and others, arrived in Georgia to lead the operation. At the other end in Central Asia, I.M. Mal'tsev (later replaced by M.M. Kuznetsov), Head of NKVD Special Settlement Department (OSP), later joined by S.N. Kruglov, formed the reception committee for the deportees.

On February 25, 1944, Kobulov, accompanied by Z.D. Kumekhov, First Party Secretary for Kabaro-Balkar, met in Ordzhonikidze with Beriia, Serov, K.P. Bziava, and S.I. Filatov (the local NKVD and NKGB leaders). Kumekhov was treated rudely by Beriia and was informed that the locals had collaborated with the Germans. Deportations had already begun on February 23 and the population was moved to northeast Kazakhstan and Kirgizia. On March 22, 1944, by order of the Presidium of the Supreme Soviet, Chechen-Ingush ASSR was incorporated as an oblast in Georgia SSR. On February 24, 1944, while he was supervising the deportation of the Chechens, Beriia wrote to Stalin recommending the deportation of the Balkars. On March 8, 1944, nearly 40,000 Balkars were also deported from Nal'chik to Kazakhstan and Kirgizia. Kabardo-Balkar ASSR was renamed Kabar ASSR. On March 14, 1944, Beriia informed the members of the Politburo that the operation had been carried out successfully. On the same day, Malenkov called Kumekhov, informing him that Beriia's recommendation to dismiss him as the Party Secretary had been approved. In a report to Stalin, Molotov and Malenkov dating from July 1944 (*Kommunist*, No. 3, 1990), during February–March 1944, Beriia stated that 602,193 people from the Caucasus were deported, including 496,460 Chechen-Ingush, 68,237 Karachi and 37,406 Balkars. 138,788 Chechen and 43,810 Ingush were relocated in special camps in Kazakh SSR, 39,663 Chechen and 1,389 Ingush to Kirgiz SSR, 102 Chechen and 102 Ingush to Uzbek SSR. The rest were exiled in other regions of the USSR. It took nearly 200 trains to carry out the operation.

During November 15–25, 1944, it was the turn of Turks, Kurds and Khemish residents of the Caucasus, mostly in Georgia, although there was scant evidence of their collaboration with the enemy. *Bugai Collection* documents (p. 152) show this to be primarily a Georgian operation supervised by Beriia and led by Commissars of State Security 3 Rank A.N. Rapava and G.T. Karanadze, respectively head of NKGB and NKVD in Georgia, and their Deputies I.I. Nibladze, S.S. Davlianidze, Tutuzov and Nachkebiia. Troops for the operation were provided by the elite 1 Moscow Dzerzhinskii NKVD Rifle Division (the best known unit in NKVD) commanded by Maj. General I.I. Piiashev and the NKVD Georgia Internal Troops commanded by Maj. General A.E. Bulyga. Support from the center was provided by Deputy Commissars A.N. Apollonov, V.V. Chernyshev, B.Z. Kobulov and B.P. Obruchnikov; Deputy Head of Gulag G.P. Dobrynin; Maj. General M.I. Sladkevich (NKVD Troops) and Maj. General N.N. Potekhin (NKVD Cavalry). The question of transportation, supplies and fuel was handled by Lt. General of Quartermaster A.A. Vurgraft, head of NKVD Supplies; Commissar of State Security 3 Rank S.R. Mil'shtein, Head of NKGB 3 (Transportation Department), and his Deputy A.P. Volkov; D.V. Arkad'ev, head of NKVD Special Transport Branch. Army General A.V. Khrulev, head of the Red Army Supplies, and a man who supposedly had clean hands, provided 900 U.S.-made Studebaker trucks for the operation.

Recent revelations indicate that Khrulev, one of the handful of survivors of the 1930 Military Soviet, was implicated in intrigue which resulted in the arrest and execution of Marshal A.I. Egorov. Despite his proven loyalty, Khrulev's Jewish wife was arrested during the post-war anti-Semitic campaigns. In his report to Stalin dated December 2, 1944, Beriia stated that 91,095 Kurds, Turks and Khemshis had now been settled in Uzbek, Kirgiz and Kazakh SSR and 413 decorations including 18 Orders of Red Star had been awarded. For the deportees this was, however, no picnic as could be seen through the accounts of some of the survivors (*Soiuz*, Nos. 23, 33, and 38, 1990).

At the time the deportations were taking place, thousands of men from deported nationalities were serving in the Red Army. During the war, for instance, 36 Chechen-Ingush received the title of Hero of the Soviet Union. A massive purge now began to rid the Red Army of members of the deported nationalities with V.V. Chernyshev playing the central part and with no objection from the Red Army. Most of the troops from north Caucasus nationalities were deployed on the southern part of the front. In February 1944, I. Pavlov, Commander of NKVD Troops attached to the 3 Ukraine Front, reported that all Karachi, Chechen-Ingush and Balkar troops were now under the jurisdiction of Kazakh SSR NKVD. According to I.M. Mal'tsev, 5,943 officers, 20,209 sergeants, and 130,691 troops were eventually exiled, many directly from the front lines.[15] Other Soviet documents (*Bugai Collection*, p. 250) dating from March 1949 give a total of 209,545 veterans, including 8,343 officers and 28,001 sergeants, who were exiled. These included nationalities from the Caucasus and Crimea as well as Soviet Germans.

On May 29, 1944, Beriia wrote to Stalin (*Kommunist*, No. 3, 1990) that in addition to the Tatars, the Crimean Greeks (who had engaged in "private enterprise" during the German occupation) as well as the Crimean Bulgars andArmenians should also be deported. According to a report dating from January 7, 1949, from Kruglov and G.N. Safonov, USSR Prosecutor General (*Bugai Collection*) during May 1944, 228,392 Crimean Tatars, Greeks, Armenians, and Bulgarians were removed from Crimea. The population of Crimean ASSR on April 1, 1940, was 1,126,800, of which 218,000 were Tatars. All who had survived the German occupation or did not retreat with them were deported. In addition, during 1947–1948 a further 2,012 returning veterans were deported by the local MVD. Most of the original deportees were Crimean Tatars, but the number included 10,231 Greeks, 8,605 Bulgarians and 5,514 Armenians. The collection, *Nashe Otechestvo*, however, gives slightly different figures for the 1943–1944 deportations which include 93,139 Kalmyks (October 1943), 68,327 Karachis (early November 1943), 496,460 Chechen-Ingush (February 1944), 37,406 Balkars (March 1944), 183,155 Crimean Tatars (May 1944), 12,422 Bulgarians (May 1944), 15,040 Greeks (May 1944), 9,621 Armenians (May 1944), 1,119 German Crimeans (May 1944), 3,652 other Crimeans (May 1944), and 91,095 Turks, Kurds, and Khemshis from Georgia (November 1944). These joined more than one million Volga Germans who had been deported in August/September 1941. Similar figures are also given in the unpublished memoirs of N.P. Dudorov, Head of MVD (January 1956–January 1960) in *Sovetskaia Militsiia* (June 1990), which shows that by October 1, 1945, there had been a 15% loss among the deported Karachis, Kalmyks, Chechen-Ingush, and those deported from Crimea. From 872,835 deportees, now remained 741,500. There were, of course, further losses during 1945–1956. The survivors were only allowed to return in March 1956.

The Crimean deportations were organized by Beriia and the usual cast of characters, his Deputies B.Z. Kobulov, I.A. Serov, B.P. Obruchnikov, M.G. Svinelupov, and A.N. Apollonov. Field operations were led by G.P. Dobrynin (Deputy Head of Gulag), Colonel of State Security G.A. Bezhanov (Order of Red Banner, March 9, 1944; Maj. General, July 1945), Maj. General I.I. Piiashev, Commissar State Security 3 Rank S.A. Klepov (Order of Kutuzov Grade 2; Maj. General, July 1945), Lt. General I.S. Sheredega of NKVD Internal Troops (Order of Suvorov Grade 2), Lt. Colonel of State Security M.N. Shestakov (Order of Red Banner, March 9, 1944), Commissar of State Security B.I. Tekaev (Order of Red Banner, March 9, 1944; Maj. General, July 1945). Besides these, there were two local leaders, P.M. Fokin (Lt. General, July 1945), Head of Crimea NKGB and V.T. Sergienko (Lt. General, July 1945). Sergienko as the acting head of NKVD in Ukraine during the early months of the war had accused Khrushchev of defeatism. Later he was involved in the defense of Kiev and also served as a member of Central Partisan Staff. Khrushchev, in his memoirs, is understandably critical of him, but he gets a better review in Bagramian's memoirs. For the Crimean operation, NKVD provided 3,000 men and NKGB 2,000. Two directives from Stalin dated May 1944 (*Bugai Collection*, pp. 134, 142) show that every facet of Soviet government from finance to transport was involved in carrying out the operation.

Despite the addition of these Christians, the 1943–1944 deportation was primarily aimed at the Muslim populations of the Caucasus, with the exception of the Azeris whose main territory the Germans had failed to reach. The list of awards given out for participation in deportations on March 8, 1944, reads like a *Who's Who* of the Soviet secret police. Beriia, who in 1943 had received Orders of Lenin and Socialist Labor, B.Z. Kobulov, Kruglov (who also had supervised the settling of deportees in Kazakhstan), and Serov received the Order of Suvorov Grade 1; Merkulov, A.N. Apollonov, and I.I. Piiashev received the Order of Kutuzov Grade 1. Abakumov, Goglidze, M.M. Gvishiani, M.I. Sladkevich, S.R. Mil'shtein, S.I. Ogol'tsov, A.N. Rapava, G.P. Dobrynin, Sh.O. Tsetereli and A.I. Voronin received the Order of Suvorov Grade 2. I.M. Tkachenko (NKVD Head in Stavropol), A.M. Leont'ev (Head of NKVD Office for Security of Front Armies) and R.A. Markar'ian (head of NKVD in Dagestan) received the Order of Kutuzov Grade 2. B.V. Arkad'ev, K.P. Bziava, and S.S. Mamulov received the Order of Red Star; S.S. Davlianidze, A.P. Volkov, S.I. Filatov, A.A. Vurgraft, G.T. Drozdov, and G.T. Karandze received the Order of Red Banner. Most of these awards were rescinded during the Khrushchev years. The fact that Abakumov received the lower citation, and in view of the fact that most of those decorated were affiliated with NKVD and NKGB, indicates that the contributions of SMERSH to these operations must have been considered secondary. It is also possible that the decorations were given to Abakumov and S.I. Ogol'tsov (head of NKVD in Kuibyshev) for reasons unrelated to the deportations. The historians Kh.M. Ibragimbeili, N.F. Bugai, and V.S. Parsadanova, who have done extensive research in this area (*Politicheskoe Obrazovanie*, April 1989; *Voprosy istorii*, July 1990; and *Novaia i NoveishaiaIstoriia*, February 1989), do not mention Abakumov or SMERSH in their writings. Even more conclusive is the previously mentioned collection of documents by N.F. Bugai, which includes most of the important archival material connected with war time deportations and reads like a *Who's Who* of NKVD but nevertheless makes no mention of Abakumov.

One man who did play a significant part in the deportations, even though he was not a part of the police apparatus, was M.A. Suslov, First Party Secretary in Stavropol, and for a brief period, Commissar of the North Group of Transcaucasus Front, whose leadership of the partisan movement in the North Caucasus had been a singular failure. The Karachis and Kalmyks were to pay a heavy price for their lack of enthusiasm for the Soviet cause. Suslov, however, gained valuable experience in the art of deportation, which, as related by V. Oskotskii (*Sovershenno Sekretno*, No. 5, 1991), helped him later in his role as the Soviet proconsul in re-occupied Lithuania.

During the war, Beriia, as a member of GKO (State Defense Committee), twice visited the Caucasus, in August 1942 and in March 1943. Beriia's visits have given rise to claims that he was actually appointed Commissar of the Transcaucasus Front, but documents so far released do not confirm this. More likely, he was the Stavka representative. In his visits, Beriia was accompanied by Karanadze, B.Z. Kobulov, Mamulov, Mil'shtein, Piiashev, Rukhadze, Tsanava and Vlodzimirskii, but not by Abakumov.[16]

Beriia's son, on the other hand, denies this in his conversations with R.Sh. Chilachava and claims that during his visits to the Caucasus during the war, his father was accompanied by military men such as Colonel S.M. Shtemenko of the

General Staff, rather than by his NKVD colleagues. S.L. Beriia also complains, with justification, that such commanders as Zhukov, Vasilevskii, Grechko, Shtemenko, and Admiral Kuznetsov, with whom his father had close and cordial relations (particularly with Shtemenko and Kuznetsov), fail to give credit to Beriia's contribution to the war effort. Grechko's official history of the Battle of Caucasus (1967) and Shtemenko's memoirs (1968) understandably fail to mention Beriia. S.G. Beriia further denies that his father tried to compromise Army General I.V. Tiulenev, Commander of the Transcaucasus Front, but admits that he recommended the removal of S.M. Budennyi, Commander of the North Caucasus Front, on September 3, 1942, because of proven incompetence and desertion. Budennyi's less-than-stellar performance at the front, and perhaps even Mikheev's report in the first month of the war questioning his loyalty, finally caused the downfall of the veteran cavalrist. Budennyi was put to pasture in charge of the Soviet Cavalry, but Stalin ordered Kobulov to tap his phone.

Beriia also managed to get rid of Kaganovich. Although the Soviet histories are silent, the fact remains that Kaganovich served as the Political Commissar of the North Caucasus Front (July–August 1942) and in the first formation of the Transcaucasus Front (November 1942–February 1943). According to his son, Beriia not only promoted the career of General K.N. Leselidze, which is already known, but also that of A.A. Grechko, the future Minister of Defense.

Writing during the Glasnost years, Army General P.I. Ivashutin, who during the war had served as the head of SMERSH in the 47 Army of the North Caucasus Front, claimed that Abakumov had built a massive intelligence-counterintelligence apparatus which was more successful than the NKVD and NKGB in frustrating the German attempts to disunite the Soviet people.[17] The deportations may have been a belated effort of NKVD/NKGB to save face. On May 9, 1945, K.N. Charkviani, First Party Secretary in Georgia, called Beriia the architect of the German defeat in the Caucasus. On March 8, 1944, the Presidium of the Supreme Soviet, following Beriia's recommendations, awarded 714 individuals associated with NKVD and NKGB with various decorations including Orders of Suvorov, Kutuzov and Red Banner. On April 4, 1964, the same organization rescinded all these awards.

The triumphant march of the Red Army and the occupation of East Europe brought a new wave of arrests and deportations. Many in those territories that had been previously occupied by the Soviet Union during 1939–1941 did not wait for the Red Army to return. They decided to take their chances with the fleeing Germans. This contributed to the massive refugee problem of the post-war years. Others, particularly in the Baltic, had even more urgent reasons not to want to be under Soviet rule, since they had actively collaborated with the Nazis. Himmler had affectionately called the Balts the "savage people" and used thousands of them in the ranks of Waffen SS to which they contributed three Divisions (20 Estonian, 15 and 19 Latvian), as well as in police and auxiliary units used in the dirty war against partisans, as concentration camp guards, and most importantly as active participants in carrying out Hitler's No. 1 priority, the "Final Solution" of the Jewish problem. In that area the Balts had some expertise, having provided, along with the Cossacks, the necessary foot soldiers for the Tsarist pogroms. The 19 Latvian Division was commanded by S.S. Gruppenführer Bruno Streckenbach, Heydrich's former Deputy at RSHA, who in 1941 had been in charge of selecting the personnel for the "Einsatzgruppen" which had murdered nearly a million East European Jews. Needless to say, some of the local participants found their way to the West and found refuge and employment under new masters who were also engaged in games of intelligence and whose indifference to checkered pasts matched that of their Soviet counterparts. Occasionally during the Cold War years, some of these men were exposed, outraging their ethnic brethren and millions of Americans for whom anti-Communism was something next to godliness. The men were branded as innocent victims of a conspiracy among the KGB, the U.S. Justice Department, and the Mossad, and their arrest created strains among the various factions that formed the anti-evil empire coalition. We can rest assured that the role played by the Baltic people in exterminating the Jews either by helping the Nazis or through local "self-defense" organizations is not a top priority for historical research in the newly independent Baltic countries.

During the post-war years even before Glasnost, we know that there was at least one major deportation in which the MGB played a significant part. In 1949, unhappy over the turn of events in the Greek Civil War, Stalin deported the Soviet Greeks, who unlike their brothers in Crimea, had been spared during the war. In 1953, the population of the Gulag included nearly 15,000 Greeks. Those who organized this operation included Lt. General A.S. Blinov, Deputy Minister of MGB; Lt. General P.V. Burmak, Head MGB Internal Troops; Maj. General M.G. Svinelupov, yet still another Deputy Minister, in this case for Cadres; Maj. General A.S. Golovko from MVD, who in 1942 was head of Rear Security, Northwest Front; and Maj. General E.P. Pitovarnov (living in 1989), who at this time was Head of the MGB Foreign Department or a Deputy Minister MVD. The MGB was also represented by V.I. Komarov, Deputy Head of the Department for the Investigation of Especially Important Cases.[18] Along with Crimean Greeks, there were over 11,000 Greek émigré Communists, remnants of the defeated guerrilla army that left Albania and arrived in the USSR during September 10–30, 1949, to a decidedly frigid reception. Contemporary documents reproduced in *The Bugai Collection* and in *Soiuz* (No. 33, 1990), and *Novaia i Noveishaia Istoriia* (February 1989) show that the newly arrived were soon put to work in Uzbek SSR as slave labor under conditions that would have been imposed in Greece had they been on the winning side. Kruglov duly reported to Stalin about the new "settlers." In 1949, pretending a resurgence of Dashnaks, Stalin ordered a massive deportation of Armenians from Armenia, Georgia and Azerbaidzhan. On June 14, 1949, nearly 100,000 Armenians, many of them post-war repatriates from diaspora, were deported to the Altai region.

A 1949 report (*Kommunist*, March 1991; *Sotsiologicheskie Issledovaniia*, No. 2, 1990) from Colonel V. V. Shiian, head of the MVD Department for Special Settlements (deportees), indicates that during the war 3,332,589 individuals were deported, including 1,235,322 Germans (210,600 of them in January 1945); 606,749 Chechen, Ingush, Karachi and Balkar; 228,392 Crimean Tatars, Bulgarians,

Armenians, and Greeks; 94,955 Turks, Kurds and Khemshils; 91,919 Kalmyks; 100,310 Ukrainian nationalists; 148,079 Vlasovites; 49,331 Lithuanians; 41,722 Poles, and 962,251 former Kulaks (810,614 were released during the war, only to be re-arrested in 1948). At the time of the report, 2,275,900 remained in exile. The death rate given for several groups ranges from over 14% for the Turks to nearly 24% for the Chechen-Ingush, Karachi, and Balkar. The statistics of the Gulag population from January 1953 show that prisoners represented over 100 nationalities, including nearly 140,000 deported from the Baltic region during 1945–1949, 35,000 from Moldavia in 1949, 18,000 Kulaks from Lithuania in 1951, 11,600 Georgians from 1951–1952, over 1,100 Kulaks from the Izmail'sk oblast in 1950, 1,300 "bandits" (mostly Baltic nationalist partisans) from the Pskov oblast in 1950, 4,500 Poles who had served under General Anders and were arrested in the late 1940s, and nearly 6,000 Kulaks from Ukraine and Belorussia in 1951–1952. How the latter had survived nearly 20 years of collectivization was not explained. There were 4,700 surviving Iranians arrested in 1950 in Georgia, most of them Communist refugees from Azerbaidzhan, embarrassing witnesses to Stalin's sellout of their rump "Republic" in May 1946. Stalin had agreed to withdraw from Northwest Iran without informing his proxies, allowing most of them to fall into the Shah's hands. This "victory" started the Shah (a "wimpish tyrant" in the words of his CIA controller, Kermit Roosevelt) on the road to becoming the local bully and developing Stalin-like megalomania. In 1989, his vast Army of modern "Prussians" (in the words of no less than Maxwell Taylor) melted before the Islamic mobs, forcing the Shah to flee to his Swiss bank accounts, leaving behind some of his followers to face Khomeini—a man for whom mercy was as alien a concept as it was for Stalin. The Armenians in camps included many who had returned from diaspora after the war in the soon-to-be dashed hopes of finding a better life in the Soviet Union. Their story, as well as those of the returning Georgian émigrés, deserves further study.

There was also an unspecified number of prisoners rounded up in the summer of 1947 by the MVD (mostly in Ukraine) as scapegoats for grain shortages. In 1953, over 28,000 prisoners remained from two "anti-parasite" campaigns dating from June 2, 1948 and July 23, 1951. These were of course the surviving prisoners and do not include those who had died in the deportations and the rough regime of the camps. Although the Gulag was the responsibility of MVD, there is little doubt that the MGB and Abakumov (the latter until his arrest) were involved in most of the operations whose details have yet to be revealed.[19] MVD documents include a report from Abakumov on March 18, 1948 about the poor conditions of Korean slave laborers employed by the MVD Dal'stroi industries in the far east.

A poignant footnote to the deportations was the heroic deeds of individual members of the victimized nationalities. Captain, later Major, Sultan Amet-Khan, a Crimean Tatar, shot down 30 enemy planes and twice (August 24, 1943 and June 29, 19445) received the title of Hero of the Soviet Union. Amet-Khan, whose brother was also an ace, was killed on a test flight on February 1, 1971. Another Tatar, poet M.M. Dzhalil', taken prisoner while serving as a political officer in Vlasov's 2 Assault Army was executed on August 15, 1944 by the Gestapo for resistance. Author of the widely read *Moabit Notebook*, he became a posthumous Hero of the Soviet Union in 1956.

NOTES

1. The most detailed account of this massacre is in *Izvestiia TSK KPSS* (11/1990).

2. Arkady Vaksberg, *Stalin's Prosecutor*, p. 202.

3. *Beriia: Konets Kar'erv*, p. 102.

4. For the massacre of senior officers see *Literaturnaia Gazeta* (April 20, 1988); *VIZH* (10/1988); and D.A. Volkogonov, *Triumf i Tragediia*. For Loktionov, see *Istoriia SSSR*; *VIZH* (8/1993 and 6/1989), *Istoriia Pribaltiiskogo Voenno Okruqa*, and *Krsanoznamennyi Turkestanskii*. For Shtern, see *Sozvezdie Polkovodtsev, Soviet Jewish Affairs* (1/1975), N.G. Kuznetsov, *Nakanune, Krasnaia Zvezdva* (August 6, 1988), *Geroi Khalkhin Gola, Folksshtimme* (May 8, 1971), and P.G. Grigorenko, *Memoirs*. For Arzhenukhin, see S.I. Shingarev, *"Chatos" Idut v Ataku*. For Proskurov, see *My Internatsionalisty, Pod Znamennem Ispanskoi Respubliki, Izvestiia TSK KPSS* (3/1990), *VIZH* (12/1991), Viktor Suvorov, *Inside Soviet Military Intelligence*, and Pierre de Villemarest, *GRU*. For Rychagor, see B.A. Smirnov, *Nebo Moei Molodosti, V Nebe Kitaia 1937–1940*, and M.N. Kozhevnikov, *Komandivanie i Shtab VVS Sovetskoi Armii v Velikoi Otechestvennoi Voine 1941–1945 gg*. For Smushkevich, see Antonio Arias, *V Ognennom Nebe, Vmeste s Patroitami IsDanii*, A.I. Gusev, *Gnevnoe Nebo Ispanii, Liudi Bessmertnoqo Podviga*, D.Ia. Zil'manovich, *Na Orbite Bol'shoi Zhizni*, Ilya Ehrenburg, *Memoirs: 1921-1941, Beriia: Konets Kar'ery*, and *AiersDace Historian* (Fall, 1979). For Meretskov, see K.A. Meretskov, *Nekolebimo kak Rossiia*, and *Na Sluzhbe Narodu, Polkovodtsy I Voenachal'niki Velikoi Otechestvennoi*, P.Ia. Egorov, *Marshal Meretskov, Karel'skii front Vel. Otech. Voine, Khrushchev Remembers*, and *VIZH* (7/1967, 6/1977 and 10/1988). For Vannikov, see A.I. Shakhurin, *Krvl'ia Pobedy*, D.F. Ustinov, *Vo Imia Pobedy*, V.N. Novikov, *Nakanune i.v. Dni Ispytanii*, *VIZH* (2/1962), *Voprosy Istorii* (10/1968, 1/1969), and *Izvestiia TsK KPSS* (2/1991).

5. Peter Deriabin and Frank Gibney, *The Secret World*, p. 187.

6. For purges in the defense industry, see V.N. Novikov, *Nakanune i.v. Dni Ispytanii*; and A.K. Sul'ianov, *Arestovat' v Kremle*.

7. *Beriia: Konets Kar'ery*, pp. 102–03.

8. For arrest of the leadership of the West Front, see A.M. Samsonov, *Znat'i Pomnit'*; D.A. Volkogonov, *Triumf*; I.F. Stadniuk, *Voina*; and *Journal of Soviet Military Studies* (6/1991).

9. For Generals victimized during the war, see *Beriia: Konets Kar'ery*; *VIZH* (10/1988); Volkogonov, *Triumf*; and the forthcoming Michael Parrish, *Sacrifice of the Generals. Senior Soviet Officer 1939-1953*.

10. *Knizhnoe obozrenie* (August 11, 1989), p. 3.

11. V.K. Abarinov, *Katynskii Labirint*, pp. 75–77.

12. *Acta Slavica Iaponica*, p. 47 and *Istoriia SSSR* (2/1991),

13. *Beriia: Konets Kar'ery*, p. 399.

14. *VIZH* (9/1990) pp. 28-38; and *Time* (July 22, 1992), p. 67.

15. *Politicheskoe Obrazovanie* (4/1989), pp. 58–63; K.S. Karol, *Between the Two Worlds*, p. 145; *Voprosy Istorii* (No. 7, 1990), p. 41.

16. Volkogonov, *Triumf*, book 1: part 2, p. 288.

17. Stoliarov, *Golgofa*, p. 73.

19. *Istoriia SSSR* (5/1991), p. 155.

Chapter 4

SMERSH and Abakumov

As mentioned previously, on February 3, 1941, Stalin divided the NKVD into two different Commissariats (NKVD under Beriia and NKGB under Merkulov). On February 8, 1941, he also transferred the GUGB/NKVD 3 (Special) Branch to the Red Army, which was now designated as the 3 Department of Commissariat of Defense (Counterintelligence). A similar department was also set up in the Commissariat of the Navy. The duties of the 3 Department were to struggle with counterrevolutionaries, spies, diversionists and all those engaged in anti-Soviet activities in the Red Army. In view of such a broad mandate, it was obvious that no one in the military could be safe from the 3 Department, whose creation had followed two other ominous steps. On July 13, 1940, the Council of People's Commissars approved the re-establishment of penal companies and battalions in the Red Army, which had been dissolved after the Civil War and were later to become a feature of the Soviet operations during the Great Patriotic War, particularly after the summer defeats of 1942, when Stalin issued an order on July 28, 1942, making retreat a crime. On December 13, 1940, the Supreme Soviet also vastly increased the power of military tribunals.[1] These changes were brought about since fear was now the most prominent feature of the Soviet state. Stalin was not indifferent to what was happening elsewhere in Europe and, while preparing for the worst, was hoping against hope that his policy of appeasement would divert Hitler's attention from the USSR at least until the decapitated Red Army could be revived.

On July 30, 1941, the two Commissariats of NKVD and NKGB were once again combined in NKVD under Beriia with Merkulov, who had been the head of NKGB, serving as his First Deputy. It also seems that the 3 Department was transferred back to NKVD (the date for this transfer is usually given as July 24, 1941), but there are still some doubts. In an obscure article written in 1967, the future Army General and Chairman of KGB V.I. Fedorchuk (at this time head of counterintelligence with Soviet forces in Germany), however, spoke of the existence in November 1941 of the NKVD Special Department in the 6 Army of the Southwest

Front.[2] A number of documents published in *Skrytaia Pravda Voiny: 1941 God* indicate that in late 1941 the 3 Department was part of NKVD. A Soviet document dated July 11, 1941, refers to the Special Department as the NKVD 3 Department.[3] Other sources from the fall of 1941, however, refer to Abakumov as the head of the 3 Department (Counterintelligence) of the *Red Army*.[4] Information provided to the author by the Russian Federation Counterintelligence Service in 1994 indicate that Abakumov, Deputy Commissar of NKVD from February 26, 1941, was appointed as Head of NKVD Special Department on July 31, 1941, a date that seems logical, since around this time his predecessor, A.N. Mikheev, was transferred to Ukraine. Abakumov also seems to have remained as Deputy Commissar of NKVD, as well as Deputy Commissar of Defense during the war under Stalin, surely an unusual position for a mere head of counterintelligence.

Abakumov's rank is also not known at the time of his appointment in 1941, but a document dated August 6, 1942, from Senior Major of State Security (N.D.?) Mel'nikov, Head of the Volkhov Front Special Department, about the operations of 2 Assault Army addresses Abakumov as "Commissar of State Security 1 Rank" and Deputy Commissar of NKVD. (There is no mention of SMERSH yet.) Considering that in April 1940, Abakumov had been a mere Senior Major, this is a jump of three ranks in slightly over two years—a remarkable rise by any standard. Only two other men in the Red Army could even come close to such rapid rise: Army General I.D. Cherniakhovskii, a bonafide hero (twice Hero of the Soviet Union), killed in action on January 13, 1945, as Commander of the 3 Belorussian Front; and Chief Marshal of Aviation A.E. Golovanov, Commander of the nonexistent Long Range Aviation, but a special favorite of Stalin since the 1930s when as the chief pilot of NKVD, he had flown the doomed officers from the Far East to an uncertain fate in Moscow.

Recently released information (*VIZH*, September 1994) indicates that Abakumov's first important assignment as Head of the Special Department was to the Northwest Front in late August and early September 1941. The Front had collapsed before the German onslaught, and the counterattacks, particularly in the direction of Staraia Russa where the embattled 34 Army had lost more than 80% of its personnel and all of its artillery, had failed dismally. The Commissar of the Army, Maj. General (an unusual rank since Political Commissars were not given the rank of General until December 20, 1942) Voinov wrote to Stalin on August 20, 1941 and as a result, Beriia sent Abakumov to investigate. Upon arrival, Abakumov worked closely with Captain of State Security M.I. Belkin, Head of the Special Department in the 34 Army (after the war, Deputy Head of MGB Counterintelligence), who provided the necessary incriminating material for L.Z. Mekhlis, who had arrived as a part of commission on September 9, 1941, along with N.A. Bulganin and K.A. Meretskov as representatives of the Supreme Command to the Northwest Front. Bulganin shortly returned to Moscow and Meretskov, who had just been released from prison, was appointed to the command of Volkhov Front on September 17, 1941. Mekhlis alone stayed until October 2 waging a reign of terror. On September 12, 1941, he had Maj. General of Artillery V.S. Goncharov shot in front of the staff officers. The commander of the 34 Army, Maj. General K.M. Kachanov was arrested on September 11, 1941 and was sentenced to death on September 26, 1941 by a military court that took its orders from Mekhlis, who also demoted the Commanders of 33 and 262 Rifle Divisions, Maj. Generals K.A. Zheleznikov and M.N. Kleshnin. For all of his troubles, Voinov was also sacked on September 15, 1941.

On July 3, 1941, Abakumov joined the Evacuation Commission when Shvernik replaced Kaganovich as chairman. On October 5, 1941, Soviet reconnaissance flights reported the approach of enemy columns in the vicinity of Iukhov, almost a Moscow suburb, which was then duly reported by Col. (later, Lt. General of Aviation) N.A. Sybtov, Commander of the Moscow Defense Zone Air Force. Abakumov contacted him and called him and his pilots panic-mongers, a capital crime in Stalin's Russia. Only further flights which confirmed Sbytov's report and an interview by K.F. Telegin, Commissar of the Moscow Defense Zone, resulted in Soviet countermeasures thus also saving Sbytov from arrest.[5]   Earlier Telegin also had reported a similar breakthrough to an equally skeptical Stalin. Catching panic-mongers did not take up all of Abakumov's time. In his letter of February 2, 1948, to Stalin (*Voennye arkhivy Rossiia*) in response to Abakumov's intrigues, I.A. Serov claimed that during the Battle of Moscow, Abakumov spent time with his mistress in the comfort of Hotel "Moskva." The hotel with its deep air shelter served as the home for many Soviet dignitaries during the war, among them A.A. Fadeev, singer L.O. Utesov, and publisher A.N. Tikhonov (not the future politician, N.A. Tikhonov, as stated in *Staliniada*). When Stalin found out that Tikhonov was involved in an extramarital affair, he had Tikhonov's wife flown out of the besieged Leningrad. One can well understand Stalin's comments, after a performance of Othello, that Iago was an "excellent organizer."

Late in 1941 and early in 1942, Abakumov discovered a major "conspiracy" in the Frunze Academy, which had been evacuated to Tashkent. Abakumov was aware that in April 1941 his predecessors in the Special Department had arrested Maj. General S.M. Mishchenko, an instructor in the academy, for "anti-Soviet" activities who was duly executed in Moscow on October 10, 1941, so the Frunze Academy obviously had possibilities. Those arrested by Abakumov included Maj. Generals G.A. Armaderov, F.S. Burlachko, G.S. D'iakov, A.G. Shirmakher, F.K. Kuz'min, N.I. Pliusin, and G.A. Sokolov. They were accused of "defeatism," "anti-Soviet" activities and joining up with the enemy in view of the inevitable Soviet defeat. According to the latest revelations (*VIZH*, 6/1994), the officers had met and discussed the reasons for the massive failures of the Red Army during the first months of the war and possible measures to remedy the situation. This is, after all, the role supposedly to be played by military academies, but not under Stalin. Strangely enough, Abakumov did not associate them with the already convicted Tishchenko. The two official Soviet histories of the Frunze Academy *Akademiia Imeni M.V.Frunze* (1973) and *Voennaia Akademiia imeni M.V. Frunze* (1980) not only are silent about this episode, but fail to mention the arrested officers as faculty members.

There is some dispute about the exact date that SMERSH was actually formed. Most sources indicate late 1942, although Romanov, ever the contrarian, gives an earlier date (summer 1942). The name, SMERSH (Death to Spies), of course, was coined by none other than Stalin, who had a lifelong obsession with espionage. The official date for the creation of SMERSH is April 14, 1943, when the pretext was the existence on the German side of the eastern front of 130 organizations and 60,000 operatives engaged in intelligence and subversion against the Soviet Union. A recent article by Col. V.V. Korovin (*VIZH*, 1/1995) discusses how SMERSH infiltrated and subverted the attempts by German intelligence agencies to infiltrate the Soviet Union, including by a group headed by the poet Sedov. Actually, SMERSH was less concerned about this activity than about the loyalty of the Red Army and itsCommanders. SMERSH was officially in existence until March or April 1946 when its duties were transferred to NKGB. Besides a SMERSH that watched over the Red Army, there was also one for the Navy headed by P.A. Gladkov. Sh.M. Spektor (Sudoplatov confuses him with M.B. Spektor, another Chekist), former head of Merkulov's Secretariat, was appointed Gladkov's Deputy. Spektor received the Order of Patriotic War Grade I on March 9, 1944. SMERSH reported directly to the Commissar of Defense, and, in fact, at times Abakumov has been identified as a Deputy Commissar of Defense.[6] Regardless of the debate about the exact date of its formation, SMERSH was fully operative by spring 1943. In April 1943, with the stabilization of the military situation, Stalin repeated the reorganization of February 1941. Beriia's once unified empire was divided officially into three branches. Beriia held on to the NKVD portfolio, the NKGB was under Merkulov, and SMERSH was under Abakumov. As had been the case with the Special Department back in February 1941, SMERSH was part of the Commissariat of Defense, which meant that Abakumov reported directly to Stalin, although he was also supposed to coordinate SMERSH's activities with NKVD and NKGB. There are also mentions in passing, usually in defector literature, that during the war Kruglov was also First Deputy Head of SMERSH under Abakumov. This does not seem likely since it would have subordinated a First Deputy Minister (Kruglov in NKVD) to a mere Deputy Minister (Abakumov). Documents have yet to be produced to connect Kruglov directly with SMERSH. As proved to be the case after the war, both Abakumov and Kruglov were the up and coming men in the security and police apparatus.[7] The name of B.Z. Kobulov is mentioned as the deputy head of SMERSH, but this must be a confusion with his position as deputy Commissar of NKGB under Merkulov. Kobulov was older and more senior than Abakumov (as was Kruglov) and, in fact, had been identified as Abakumov's mentor and former boss in the Secret Political Department (in 1947, Abakumov managed to ease out Kobulov from MGB). A more likely candidate as Deputy Head of SMERSH during the war is L.F. Tsanava, another favorite of Beriia. N.N. Selivanovskii, P.Ia. Meshik, and M.I. Belkin may have also served as Deputy Heads of SMERSH.

What were the exact duties of SMERSH? The literature on SMERSH is not substantial. *Voennyi Entsiklopedicheskii Slovar'* and *Sovetskia Veonnaia Entsiklopediia* do not mention it at all, while *Velikaia Otechestvennaia Voina 1941– 1945, Entsikloediia* devotes only three lines. Memoir writers rarely mention SMERSH, and even detailed orders of battle do not list the local SMERSH Commanders. In the vast Soviet literature on the Battle of Kursk, I have yet to come across a single reference to L.F. Tsanava, the local SMERSH Commander. Other studies are mere propaganda. The Western studies are based on secondary materials, while defector literature, with the exception of Romanov's *The Nights Are Longest Here*, are usually either written by officers too junior in rank or laced with the writer's various grinding axes. SMERSH was represented at Front, Corps, and Division levels, but there were also agents in smaller units. There was undoubtedly tension between SMERSH and the military Commanders as well as the political Commissars who were competing watchdogs. A hint of this, for instance, can be seen in difficulties between V. Zarelua, Head of Counterintelligence of the Black Sea Group of North Caucasus Front, and Head of the Political Department of the 18 Army L.I. Brezhnev.[8]

At times it seems that Stalin, who also liked to encourage rivalries among his satraps, played SMERSH against NKVD and NKGB. In 1945, SMERSH found inconvertible evidence of Hitler's remains and the circumstances surrounding his death only to see Stalin order a new investigation a year later—this time under the auspices of MVD. The name SMERSH on the surface indicates an organization designed for counter-intelligence purposes, but SMERSH was more than that. With the weakening of the Institute of Political Commissars, Stalin, ever suspicious of the military, needed additional watchdogs and SMERSH filled this role. Espionage was, however, such a common crime under Stalin that we can only speculate on the lines of demarcation between SMERSH, NKGB, NKVD, the Military Courts, and the weakened, but still active, Political Commissars. It was a wonder that with so many eyes watching them the Red Army Commanders somehow also managed to run a war. For Stalin, as well as spy agencies everywhere, the perfect intelligence system was one that had been devised by the former Emir of Bokhara, an early opponent of Soviet intrusion in Central Asia. Operating from Afghan sanctuaries, the Emir (an early Mujaheddin) continued to harass the occupying Bolsheviks. According to Sir Fitzroy MacLean, under the Emir whose unorthodox guerrilla tactics included dropping one favorite dancing boy after another to delay the pursuing Red Cavalry, to whom he attributed his deplorable habits, *every* citizen was required to be a part-time spy.[9] This also seems to have been the system put to use by the late Nicolas Ceausescu. Under Stalin, enormous progress was made in creating such a system. Mikoian stated (*Pravda*, December 21, 1937) that every citizen of the USSR must be an employee of NKVD, and by 1952 Minister of State Security S.D. Igant'ev claimed that there were ten million informers in the USSR, both paid and voluntary. Besides its watchdog and counterintelligence activities, SMERSH was also involved in fighting the economic crimes which plagued the Red Army during the war—"socialist morality" notwithstanding. Oleg Pen'kovskii relates the story of a Major Loshak arrested in 1944 by SMERSH for black market activities and shot even though he happened to be the son-in-law of Col. General of Artillery S.S. Varentsov, Commander of Artillery in the 1 Ukraine Front.[10]

For the present, we can also wonder about the exact respective duties of SMERSH vis-à-vis the NKGB counter-intelligence and the "executive action" (also called "Special Tasks" and "Special Services") departments, the latter responsible for individual acts of terror under the redoubtable P.A. Sudoplatov (more about him later), who must have had an impressive empire of his own. At least three of the men who received the rank of Lieutenant General in 1945, N.D. Gorlinskii, L.F. Raikhman and I.G. Shevelv, as well as two who were made Major Generals, L.I. Eitingon and G.B. Ovakimian, were associated with this department.

The returning Soviet POWs and deportees were at times interrogated by SMERSH, but also frequently by the functionaries of NKGB's 4th Department. In a report to Stalin, Beriia stated that in 1943 in recaptured areas the security organs had questioned nearly 950,000 people, including nearly 600,000 servicemen, and as a result, over 80,000 individuals were arrested.

According to retired Colonel of Judiciary A. Liskin (*Shchit i Mech*, 3/1993), during 1941–1945 the security organs questioned nearly seven million individuals and over two million were put under arrest. During 1943–1945, the Army could have fielded 250 Rifle Divisions of spies. Since the number of the arrested was the measure by which the various components of security organs were judged, there was breakneck competition in this area resulting in the detention of thousands of innocent victims. Even after the war, anyone who had lived in the occupied areas was a suspect regardless of subsequent behavior. In February 1942, Senior Lieutenant P.E. Broiko had managed to escape after being left behind the enemy lines and joined Kovpak's partisans in which he showed outstanding leadership. In August 1944, he received the coveted title of Hero of the Soviet Union. After the war, while studying in the Frunze Academy, he was arrested by MGB since he had not been forthcoming about his capture by the enemy.

In one respect, however, SMERSH remained a junior partner to the other organs. In May 1945, of the nearly 270,000 inmates in Soviet prisons (outside the Gulag) only slightly over 2,000 had been arrested by SMERSH as against over 57,000 by NKVD and over 18,000 by NKGB.

The similarities between the Nazi and Soviet instruments of security and intelligence are indeed striking; the one major difference is the complete lack of any conspiracies against Stalin on the Soviet side. Under Hitler, organizations such as Abwehr, SD, Gestapo, SIPO, SD, and Feldgendarmerie were all involved in promoting the Nazis' military and political goals, but this was not done by systematic cooperation, and in fact, rivalry and suspicion bordering on sabotage characterized the modus operandi. Such competition must have also existed under Stalin, but to what extent we have yet to find out. We do know of tensions between the GRU and NKGB intelligence services, and although the final blame must lie on Stalin, the fact is that the Soviet use of intelligence during the war was marred by error and missed opportunities including the disastrous misreading of Hitler's aggressive intentions in the spring and summer 1941. An example of rivalry was the arrest of the leaders of the Home Army in February 1945, not by SMERSH, but by NKGB's Department of Investigation of Especially Important Cases under L.E. Vlodzimirskii. On February 28, 1945, 16 leaders of the Polish underground, including Leopold Obulicki (1898–1946), Jan Stanislaw Jankowski (1882–1953), the Commander of Polish Armed Forces, Kazimierz Puzak (1883–1950), Adam Bien (1899–?), Antoni Pajdak (1894–1988), Stanislaw Jasiukowicz (1882–1950), Kazimierz Baginski

(1890–1966), Aleksander Zwierzynski (1880–1958), Jozef Chacinski (1889–1954), Eugeniusz Czarnowski (1904–1947), Stanislaw Mierzwa (1905–1985), Franciszek Urbanski (1891–1955), Zbigniew Stypulkowski (1904–1979), Stanislaw Michalowski (1903–1984), Kazimierz Kobylanski (1892–1978), and Jozef Stemler (1888–1965) were kidnapped in Pruszkow while waiting to meet with I.A. Serov (masquerading under the name of General S.P. Ivanov) and his assistant—one Col. Pimenov. They were taken byNKGB to Moscow where they were interrogated. The investigators were headed by L.E. Vlodzimirskii and included Kruglov (on a busman's holiday) and V.M. Tikhonov, whose career went back to 1937, and who had also been implicated in the execution of the senior military officers and Lt. Colonel Gusev and Majors Galkin, Gromov, and Konopolev in Kuibyshev in October 1941. Their show trial of 15 took place in Moscow on June 17, 1945. The Military Collegium was chaired by Ul'rikh. The prosecution was led by R.A. Rudenko, Chief Soviet Prosecutor, who was assisted by Maj. General (later promoted for his efforts to Lt. General) of Judiciary N.P. Afanas'ev, who during the post-war years was to serve as the Chief Military Prosecutor.

Ul'rikh and Afans'ev had previous experience with matters Polish. On January 28, 1940, they had agreed that the jurisdiction over Polish POW officers should be transferred from the Red Army to NKVD, thus providing the legal framework for mass murder. The charges against the leaders of the Home Army included "preparation of an armed uprising against the USSR in league with the Germans," "espionage for the Polish government in London," "provocative distortions about the behavior of Soviet troops in Poland," "creation of military units and terrorist groups against the Red Army," and "sabotage." Okulicki was sentenced to 10 years (and was probably murdered in prison in 1946), Jankowski to 8, Bien and Jasiukowicz to 5. Only Bien returned to Poland from prison. Others received lighter sentences or were acquitted. All in all, the punishments were light in view of Stalinist standards—notwithstanding the temporary abolition of the death penalty.[11] Abarinov, who is usually careful, also makes the reckless charge that Kim Philby, ordered by Moscow, organized the sabotage of the plane carrying General Sikorski which crashed into the sea near Gibraltar. The meticulous investigation by a Royal Air Force team and the testimony of the surviving co-pilot contradict this, and Philby, who was not shy about his accomplishments, made no claim in this regard.[12] Blaming NKVD for Sikorski's death has as much basis as the spurious claims that the KGB was involved in Kennedy's assassination or the attempt on the Pope's life. Nothing was, of course, past Stalin, but even under him there were accidents and people died natural deaths.

Equally complicated must have been the relations between SMERSH and the NKVD Troops. As early as June 25, 1941, the Council of People's Commissars assigned the responsibility for security of Fronts and Armies to NKVD Border and Internal Troops. In April 1942, the Department of NKVD Troops for the Security of Operations Armies was formed, and in May 1943, the Main Department of NKVD Troops. Under its various names, this department was responsible for rear security, counterintelligence, communication security, and guarding of POWs. It was also responsible for disposal of the equipment left on the battlefield by the enemy and the Red Army which provided the NKVD troops with a private arsenal. On January 4, 1942, the GKO gave the NKVD troops the additional responsibility of working with the regular NKVD in recaptured areas. Many of these duties paralleled what SMERSH was also doing. Both organizations were also helped by a GKO State Defense Committee directive issued on November 17, 1941, strengthening the power of NKVD troikas.[13]

The troikas were founded by an order of the Council of People's Commissars on November 5, 1934, to be used against "socially dangerous" individuals. Under the new GKO directive, the troikas were given the right to move against "counter-revolutionary crimes and those aimed against the administrative order of the USSR" and determine the punishment, which included the "highest measure." Most of the cases investigated by NKVD, NKGB and SMERSH ended up in these courts, which remained in existence until their dissolution in September 1, 1953, by a decree of the Supreme Soviet. The legal framework for sentencing those brought to these courts was the all-purpose Article 58 of the RFSFR Criminal Code, which covered crimes ranging from treason and sabotage to praising enemies' weapons and telling jokes about Stalin.

Besides police duties, the NKVD Troops also took part in combat and constituted independent brigades and rifle divisions. Finally, in 1943 they were formed into a complete army (70). More than 150 of the soldiers and officers received the title of Hero of the Soviet Union. The NKVD rear security had a well-deserved unsavory reputation, perhaps even more savage than that of SMERSH. The Polish officers on their way to Katyn were escorted by the NKVD Cavalry commanded by V.M. Sharapov, who later served as Chief of Staff of 29 and 70 Armies. During the war, the NKVD Cavalry was commanded by M.S. Krivenko, who may have served as a Deputy to V.M. Blokhin at the execution squads and was deeply implicated in the slaughter of Polish POWs from the Oshtakov camp. The NKVD troops played a major part in the deportations of 1943–1944, and for this their Deputy Commander, A.N.Apollonov, received the Order of Kutuzov 1 Grade. There is some question about who commanded the NKVD Troops (not to be confused with Border Troops, who were also part of NKVD and were commanded by N.P. Stekhanov); Apollonov has been identified as both Commander and Deputy Commander. Two other men, I.N. Kiriushin and M.I. Sladkevich, have also been identified as Deputy Commanders.[14]

It would make sense that for bureaucratic efficiency (perhaps a contradiction in terms), SMERSH's duties should have been confined to areas near the front and newly occupied territories, but this was not the case. This conflict between bureaucracies of terror gave rise to the Teplinskii-Il'in affair which proved to be a watershed in Abakumov's relationship with Beriia and Merkulov. On April 28, 1943, Abakumov personally arrested Maj. General of Aviation, B.L. Teplinskii (identified by Abakumov as Russian, Jewish by others), head of operation section in the air forces attached to the Siberian Military District far from the front. Teplinskii, who had been condemned to death in 1938 as a member of military conspiracy but was spared, was now accused of plotting against the Soviet rule and harboring traitorous thoughts. Abakumov tore out Teplinskii's shoulderboards after accusing him of holding Trotskiist views. Also arrested in this affair was Commissar of State Security 3 Rank, V.N. Il'in, Head of the NKGB secret political department.

What had caused Abakumov's action was Teplinskii's telephone inquiry to Il'in, an old friend from the Civil War days about reasons for a delay in promotions apparently blocked by Abakumov as head of SMERSH. Informed about this contact, Abakumov arrested Teplinskii and had little trouble exacting a confession, not only in regard to his own activities, but also implicating Il'in, whose arrest was now sanctioned by Stalin. Il'in, however, proved to be a hard nut to crack refusing to confess even when confronted by Teplinskii. Abakumov could not prove his case, but even though both Teplinskii and Il'in spent many years in prison without trial with Il'in ending up in the same cells with A.A. Novikov and A.I. Shakhurin. After Abakumov's arrest, the prosecutors approached Il'in in prison for testimony against him, but Il'in had trouble beliving that his old enemy was now in a nearby cell. Sudoplatov, in his memoirs (pp. 162–67), discusses this fascinating affair, and Abakumov's breach of etiquette by arresting the veteran Il'in, since 1942 head of the Secret Political Department replacing N.D. Gorlinskii and before that deputy head for four years, without the approval from his bosses Merkulov and Beriia. Sudoplatov is correct when he states that Abakumov went from being a former subordinate to a rival. In the 1960s, Il'in served as the Secretary of the Moscow Union of Writers, a most unusual position for an ex-policeman, and was involved with writer V.S. Grossman, who had his share of troubles with the Soviet establishment. Il'in died in 1990, and one hopes that he has left some memoirs.

In 1943, Abakumov also tried to take over the radio deception games that was the private preserve of NKGB's 4 Department under Sudoplatov, but only had partial success when Stalin excluded the "Monastery" and "Couriers" operations, the two plums. According to Sudoplatov (p. 162), a peeved Abakumov told him, "I will not forget this, I've made my decision not to cooperate with you." Merkulov also could not have been too happy about the invasion of his turf. In late 1944 or early 1945, the SMERSH arrested Prince Janus Radziwill, a long time NKVD agent (the right hand perhaps did not know what the left hand was doing) and transferred him from Poland to Lubianka. According to Sudoplatov (p. 224), Beriia had to intervene to save Radziwill, who among his other duties, had served as the interpreter during meetings with Averell Harriman—both men having had business interests in pre-war Poland.

Usually a hint from Stalin was all Abakumov needed to track down a victim. In an August 1942 telegram to Malenkov and Vasilevskii, Stalin complained about Eremenko's leadership of Stalingrad Front comparing it with his command of Briansk Front in 1941. In passing he mentioned that in both cases Maj. General of Aviation I.N. Rukhle had been Eremenko's assistant. Abakumov immediately went to work. He accused Rukhle of having made contact during April–October 1918 (!) in some Godforsaken corner of the Ukraine near Molodechno with the occupying Germans and having been expelled in 1938 from the Red Army for knowing one Andrianov chief of staff of Special Task Aviation Army (sentenced to death) and one Tarnonskii-

Tepletskii, commander of the 21 Air Brigade (sentenced to 8 years). Rukhle, however, had been cleared and was appointed as an instructor in the Voroshilov Academy. Abakumov arrested Rukhle on October 5, 1942, but he was eventually released.[15]

A more serious case, however, involved attempts to compromise the future Marshal G.K. Zhukov. If we are tobelieve Zhukov, his problems dated back to the purge years when the command of the Belorussian Military District was being decimated. His enemies there included Division Commissar N.A. Iung, commissar of 4 Cavalry and Division 3 and Cavalry Corps commanded by Zhukov, and F.I. Golikov, who in 1938 served as the commissar of the District and whose stormy relations with Zhukov was going to last a lifetime. Iung, however, was soon transferred to the Siberia Military District where he served as the Military Commissar. He was arrested on January 30, 1938 and condemned to death on July 2, 1938. Despite his intrigues against Zhukov, he was rehabilitated on April 25, 1956. Notwithstanding Zhukov's performance against the Japanese in Khalkhin-Gol in 1939, and his leadership during the early days of the war, the security organs were aware of Zhukov's past and his association with such purged commanders as I.P. Uberovich and E.I. Goriachev. In spring 1942, Maj. General V.S. Golushkevish, former Chief of Operations Section of West Front (commanded at that time by Zhukov), was transferred to Southwest Front only to be arrested, perhaps by Abakumov in person. The effect of this arrest on Zhukov must have been obvious, and it is a testimony to the paranoia and terror that dominated the Stalinist state even during the critical days of the war. The interests of "security" took precedence over urgent military needs.[16] The details of the campaign to "get" Zhukov will be covered in Chapter 6.

Whatever the exact duties performed by SMERSH, Stalin must have been pleased. During the war, Abakumov, who had already been awarded the Order of Red Banner on April 27, 1940, received the Orders of Suvorov 2 and 1 Grade (March 8, 1944 and July 31, 1944) and Kutuzov 1 Grade (April 21, 1945). On July 27, 1945, he was one of nine police officers to receive the rank of Col. General. There are claims that SMERSH foiled a German attempt to assassinate Stalin during the war. The details are murky, but apparently it involved Maj. General I.M. Shepetov, former commander of the 96 Alpine Division, 18 Army, South Front, who had been awarded the title of Hero of the Soviet Union on September 11, 1941 for breaking out of enemy encirclement. Shepetov was captured near Izium during the 1942 summer campaign and was murdered on May 21, 1943 in Flussenberg concentration camp after attempting to escape. A Soviet POW officer who had changed sides was given Shepetov's medal by the German intelligence and was parachuted near Moscow to assassinate Stalin during a military parade, but the SMERSH apparently arrested him before the plan could be carried out.[17]

In *Moi Otets*, Beriia's son dates the attempt coded "Operation Zeppelin" from September 6, 1944, when a German transport landed a group of agents in Belorussia. SMERSH and PVO apparently foiled this attempt and arrested the saboteurs. The man designated to assassinate Stalin was one P.I. Shilo, a 33-year-old native of Chernigov oblast from a kulak family, who was masquerading as a Hero of the

Soviet Union, Major Tavrin, from SMERSH. Also on November 6, 1942, a Red Army deserter, S. Dmitriev, fired his weapon in the Red Square in the direction of Mikoian's car. No one was hurt, and Dmitriev was not shot until August 25, 1950. There are also rumors about an attempt by German agents to assassinate the Allied leaders during the 1943 meeting in Tehran, which was also foiled.

Abakumov's record, however, was not without blemish. The existence of Vlasov and his movement was testimony that the Special Department, SMERSH, as well as the whole NKGB/NKVD apparatus, had not done its job in unmasking the potential traitors in the military ranks. Stalin, ever suspicious, continued to view the military with jaundiced eyes. The fate of Lt. General V.A. Khomenko, an NKVD man of long standing, and next to Maslennikov, the most successful of the Border Troop generals, is a case in point. Between 1935–1941, Khomenko had been Deputy Commander and Commander of Border Troops in Leningrad, Moldavia and Ukraine. During the war, he commanded the 30, 24, 58, and 44 Armies attached to various fronts. The future Marshal of the Soviet Union S.S. Biriuzov claimed in his memoirs that on September 11, 1943, while traveling behind the enemy lines, Khomenko was killed in ambush. The German intelligence, however, tried a cheap propaganda trick by trying to pass him off as a defector. Stalin was perfectly willing to believe that a man who had spent his professional life in NKVD had gone over to the enemy at a time when ultimate victory seemed certain.[18]

The previous account is not, however, completely accurate. The Ukrainian historian A.A. Maslov (personal correspondence with the author in January 1994), using archival materials, states that Khomenko, Commander of the 44 Army South (from October 20, 1943, 4 Ukraine Front), and his Artillery Commander Maj. General of Artillery S.A. Bobkov disappeared on October 28 or 29, 1943, during a reconnaissance operation and no trace of them could be found. On November 15, 1943, NKGB found out through their Rumanian contacts that both Commanders had been ambushed and killed as they approached the enemy lines. On November 19 the document was sent to Stalin, who thought that this was a German disinformation campaign using the Rumanians and that Khomenko had actually deserted to the enemy. Since Khomenko was out of reach, Stalin ordered that the 44 Army, veterans of the Kerch, Caucasus and Rostov campaigns, be deactivated in November 1943 and, in fact, this number has never been used again by the Red Army. On May 16, 1944, in the recapture of Crimea, the 4 Ukraine Front SMERSH, interrogating captured German intelligence officers, established the actual fate of Khomenko and Bobkov. SMERSH exhumed the bodies that had been buried in early November 1943 near Vel. Lepetikhi. At least the two men will not be branded as traitors, as had been V.Ia. Kachalov.

The Chekists also felt at home in the partisan war with its aura of secretiveness, illegality, and brutality. According to Soviet documents (*Izvestiia TsK KPSS* 2, 1990), as early as August 8, 1941, Beriia proposed to Stalin forming three partisan detachments in Ukraine and 14 in Belorussia made up of 1,000 to 1,200 Chekists. In addition to these, nearly 9,000 members of "interceptor" batallions would be left behind the enemy lines. These units would work in cooperation with the Red Army.

Later in the war, many partisan units were led by men such as S.A. Kovpak, A.N. Saburov, and T.A. Strokach, who had NKVD connections. In Karelia, the partisan movement was organized by the Chekist M.I. Baskakov, assisted by the future head of KGB, Iu. V. Andropov, who was at this time only a Party functionary. K.F. Firsanov, Head of NKVD in Orel, who had participated in the massacres of September 1941, was an important leader of the partisan movement in Orel oblast. Ponomarenko, Head of the Main Partisan Staff, was primarily a Party man from Belorussia, where the partisans were most active, but he had as his Deputies S.S. Bel'chenko and, at least from 1943, L.F. Tsanava. These two were veteran Chekists. At the same time, Tsanava may have also served as one of Abakumov's Deputies at SMERSH. Whether the Soviet efforts at partisan war were worth the cost and contributed in any significant way to the final victory remains debatable. They served, however, as a powerful psychological force reminding the population in occupied territories of the Stalinist presence. Assassination of German overlords such as Gauleiter Wilhelm Kube on September 22, 1943, in Minsk reinforced this point. Kube, disillusioned and homesick for Germany, was less brutal than the average Nazi colonial satrap and thus even more dangerous in the eyes of the Soviets. Kube's assassination was planned by a team organized by Sudoplatov and included one N.E. Khokhlov, who in May 1954 balked at carrying out a similar operation in West Germany aimed at G. Okolovich, leader of the anti-Soviet émigré "Popular Labor Union," who had made the KGB hit list. Khokhlov's later defection proved a major embarrassment. The losses suffered by the partisans and civilians who were victimized by both sides were enormous even though the exact numbers are hard to determine despite determined efforts by such Russian historians as V.K. Shomodyi. K. Kudriashov, in *Barbarossa, the Axis and the Allies*, estimated at least a million killed. The organs were also aware of collaboration between the invaders and the local population and blamed it on the "kulak elements" without explaining how so many could have survived the collectivization.

During the last years of the war, SMERSH was highly active in the newly occupied territories, and it was SMERSH officers who on January 17, 1945, arrested Wallenberg. In January 1993, Swedish sources claimed that the order to arrest Wallenberg was issued on January 17, 1945, in a telegram signed by N.A. Bulganin, who was at that time a Deputy Commissar of Defense. Why this order came from Bulganin rather than Abakumov remains a mystery. Stalin, of course, liked to divide responsibility and blame among his lackeys.[19] On July 17, 1947, it was, however, Abakumov as the Minister of State Security who ordered Wallenberg's cremation without autopsy.

Helene Carlöck-Isotalo's research on the Wallenberg case using the Swedish archives (*Scandinavian Journal of History*, No. 3, 1992) shows that in the beginning the Soviets did not consider Wallenberg an important prisoner. In his attempts to save the trapped Jews of Budapest, Wallenberg had made contact with the SS and their Hungarian allies in the Arrow Cross government, and that made him suspect in the eyes of the Soviets. Wallenberg's humanitarian instincts, however, were concepts that were totally alien to the likes of Bulganin and Abakumov. Wallenberg, arrested as a "prisoner of war" on January 14, 1945, by the SMERSH of the 151 Rifle Division (Commander, Maj. General D.P. Podshivailov), 7 Guard Army, 2 Ukraine Front, and was interrogated only six times between February 1945 and July 1947, with each session not lasting more than two hours. This was not the typical manner of interrogation of important prisoners. Meanwhile, the Swedish government started to make inquiries to the Soviet Union. It is a testimony to Abakumov's power as head of SMERSH and later of MGB that he simply ignored the inquiries made by K.V. Novikov, Head of the European Section of the Commissariat/Ministry of Foreign Affairs; Dekanozov and Vyshinskii, Deputy Commissars/Ministers; and various other officials. Abakumov could have easily provided this information through P.V. Fedotov, Deputy Minister of MGB and head of the 2 (Foreign) Department, who at this time also served as a member of the "KI" commission nominally chaired by Molotov. Only in February 1947 did Abakumov finally admit that the MGB was holding Wallenberg, but he refused to provide details, forcing the new Deputy Foreign Minister Vyshinskii to write on May 14, 1947, to Molotov requesting that Abakumov provide additional information. Abakumov's stonewalling in a case not deemed significant at that time is a testimony to the arrogance of a man who would only take orders from Stalin.

From August 18, 1947, when they already knew of Wallenberg's fate, until February 7, 1957, the Soviet government denied any knowledge of Wallenberg. When they finally owned up, Abakumov was blamed. An inquiry after Stalin's death by Molotov and I.E. Serov, then head of KGB, determined that Abakumov, using the dubious testimony of an employee of the Swedish Embassy in Budapest, had ordered the arrest and removal to Moscow of Wallenberg as a suspected German spy. In Moscow, Wallenberg was allegedly interrogated primarily by Lt. Col. D. Koppelianskii, still living, who denies ever meeting Wallenberg. A report by the Head of Medical Services of Lubianka, A.L. Smoltsov, to Abakumov dating from July 17, 1947, reported the sudden death of Wallenberg, presumably of cardiac arrest. Abakumov ordered cremation without an autopsy. Sudoplatov believes through his own intuition and by reading between the lines of a series of articles by E. Maksimova that appeared in *Izvestiia* in June 1993 that Wallenberg was murdered by poison administered by G.M. Maironovskii (more about him later), who received his order from Abakumov, who in turn was carrying out Molotov's directive. The problem here is that as documents indicate, Abakumov did not take his orders from Molotov. If he arranged for the murder of Wallenberg, and this is not unlikely, the approval must have come from Stalin. Incidentally, Beriia's son (*Pravda Ukrainy*, June 10, 1994) heatedly denies that his father had anything to do with Wallenberg's arrest and finds the rumors that the Swedish diplomat was serving as a go-between for Himmler and Beriia as ludicrous.

Wallenberg's case became a cause célèbre during the Cold War. One of the rumors involved his imprisonment in Vladimir prison; it is not confirmed by B.G. Men'shagin, P.A. Sudoplatov, and R.I. Pimenov who spent time there. To my knowledge, no serious attempt has yet to be made to trace the fate of Wallenberg's chauffeur, who was arrested with him. The arrest and tragic fate of Wallenberg must be viewed with the understanding that the humanitarian principles that motivated him were totally alien to Stalin and his henchmen, who, of course, had no trouble identifying with, and in fact were quite familiar with, the kind of operations that Eichmann had been engaged in in Hungary. SMERSH, along with A.A. Zhdanov, was also involved both during and after the war in tracing the fate of Stalin's older son, Lt. of Artillery Ia.I. Dzhugashvili, Battery Commander in the 14 Heavy Artillery Regiment 14 Tank Division, West Front, who fell into enemy hands in mid-July 1941 near Vitebsk and committed suicide in a POW camp on April 14, 1943. The most important documents on this subject released so far have appeared in the collection *Iosif Stalin v Ob'iatiiakh Sem'i*. They include a translation of Dzhugashvili's interrogation from July 18, 1941, and submitted by Merkulov to Stalin on January 31, 1946, and a detailed report on the matter from Serov to Kruglov dating from September 14, 1946.

There were even more grisly tasks such as recovering and identifying the remains of dead Nazi leaders, including Hitler. In case of Hitler, SMERSH was to arrive first, and, despite the solid evidence, Stalin remained suspicious. In May 1946, the NKVD/MVD, which had been left out of the original investigation, was sent to find additional evidence, and according to Commonwealth TV (February 19, 1993) managed to discover some bone fragments missed by the SMERSH. Stalin finally sent Beriia to visit Hitler's bunker and the proceedings were filmed for his viewing. As a result, the remains of Hitler, Eva Braun, and other Nazis were repeatedly moved, with Hitler's skull ending up in Russian archives.

Even civilians who had remained behind to fight the enemy were unsafe. A.P. Petrovskii, First Secretary of the Odessa Underground Party, was arrested by the Rumanians on October 21, 1941, and in 1943, but managed to survive while some of his colleagues were shot, and this was ground for suspicion. On June 29, 1945, he was condemned to death and executed on September 5, 1945, even though captured Rumanian documents showed his innocence. Petrovskii was only rehabilitated in 1966.

According to the memoirs of journalist D.I. Ortenberg, in 1943, Abakumov, with active help from Maj. General of the Judiciary V.I. Nosov, the Chief Military Prosecutor, targeted N.N. Kruzhkov, Deputy Chief Correspondent of *Krasnaia Zvezda*, a well-known journalist. Kruzhkov was arrested in March 1943 for being in possession of copies of *Kuban* and *Aramvisrkaia Zhizn'^*, propaganda newspapers published by the Germans to promote subversion among the people of Caucasus. On April 22, 1944, an NKVD troika sentenced Kruzhkov to 10 years in camps for "anti-Soviet agitation." Krushkov survived his sentence which was spent near Irkutsk in the company of common criminals. He was rehabilitated only on December 24, 1954.

Abakumov, as Minister of State Security, was behind an even more unjustified trial when in January 1947, the "Pannwitz Cossacks" faced the Military Collegium. The defendants included Ataman P.N. Krasnov, Lt. General A.G. Shkuro, Maj. Generals S.N. Krasnov, T.I. Domanov, and Maj. General Count K. Sultan-Gireia.

Also in the dock was Maj. General of Wehrmacht (identified incorrectly in Soviet sources as a member of the SS) Helmuth Von Pannwitz. The Cossack Generals had served with the White Armies during the Russian Civil War and during World War II in Yugoslavia. As the recent events in the former Yugoslavia show, family squabbling among the Slavs could turn extremely nasty. The Cossack Corps had fought in Yugoslavia with a ferocity second only to that of the Ustashi thugs, but not much worse than the other combatants. Their behavior harkened back to the good old days when they led the Tsarist pogroms against Ghettos, with the Yugoslavs now replacing the helpless Jews. Despite their odious record in anti-partisan war, the Corps had never been deployed on Soviet soil, nor had the Generals ever been Soviet citizens, but the niceties of international law had never restrained Stalin. After a perfunctory trial on January 17, 1947, they were all hanged, including Pannwitz, who became a true rarity, an active German officer executed for war crimes and, in this case, without justification.[20] The tragic and unjust fate of the Cossack Generals, romanticized by a number of British writers who are critical of their forced repatriation by the Western allies at the end of the war, should not blind us to their criminal behavior in Yugoslavia where they should have been rightfully tried and probably would have suffered the same fate, but with ample justification. In Yugoslavia, the SMERSH also managed to trace V.V. Shul'gin, once leader of the anti-Semitic "Black Hundred," who as a member of the Duma in 1917 had received the abdication of Nicholas II. Shul'gin was sentenced to prison, which he survived, in Vladimir. Amnestied in 1956, he made his peace with the Communists. Sudoplatov states that Shul'gin died in 1976 at age 98, although a death date of 1965 is also given.[21]

The organs also caught Ataman G.M. Semenov, one of the most ferocious of the early enemies of Bolshevism, who, along with Baron Ungern-Shternberg, had waged a campaign of unparalleled cruelty during the Civil War on the Mongolian border. Living in Korea since September 1921 under Japanese protection, Semenov, through his contacts in the émigré community, was a source of intelligence for his new masters. In March 1940, the Japanese high command was once again pondering a strike against the Soviets. Early in April, Semenov was in Shanghai discussing the formation of a White Army to fight on the Japanese side. The visit, as well as other signs, made the Soviet high command so nervous that in July 1940, the forces in the Far East were put on a war footing with the formation of the Far Eastern Front under the command of G.M. Shtern and were heavily reinforced. Despite the signing of a neutrality pact in February 1941 and Pearl Harbor, the Far Eastern Front continued to exist for the remainder of the war. Semenov's role in anti-Soviet activities was also not, however, forgotten. He was captured after the war and hanged on August 8, 1946. Five other captured collaborators, K.V. Rodzaevskii, A.P. Baksheev, L.P. Vasil'evskii, B.N. Shepunov and I.A. Mikhailov, were shot. Two defendants, Prince N. Ukhtomskii and L.P. Okhotis, were, respectively, sentenced to 20 and 15 years imprisonment.[22] The prize catch, G.S. Liushkov, the first senior NKVD official to defect, was, however, shot by the Japanese before surrender. The murderous Liushkov had entered the Cheka in 1920 and had served as an agent provocateur in Ukraine and later as a spy in Germany. Later as head of NKVD in the Black Sea, Azov, and

Rostov, he organized a reign of terror. During 1934–1936 as the Deputy Head of NKVD Secret Political Department, he had been involved in the Zinov'ev, Evodkimov, Riutin and Kirov cases. In the summer of 1937, he was appointed Head of the NKVD in the Far East, where he later organized the deportation of the Koreans. Liushkov, however, began to see the handwriting on the wall and was also not helped by the fact that his predecessor, Ia.S. Vizel', had managed to commit suicide while kept as a prisoner in Khabarovsk. The imminent arrival of Mekhlis and Frinovskii in the Far East in August 1938 could have spelled doom for Liushkov as it did for many others, and he was not going to wait to find out. On June 13, 1938, he crossed the border and defected to the Japanese and probably provided them with information that proved to be helpful in the imminent hostilities at Lake Khasan. The SMERSH also had a mixed record in capturing the organizers of various anti-Communist national movements who had operated under German sponsorship during the war. Many were protected by the Western intelligence agencies and the Vatican, later to re-surface during the Cold War years as troublesome thorns in the Kremlin's side. Among those who were caught was the Commander of the Armenian units Maj. General (in Wehrmacht) Vardan Sarkisian, who allegedly was executed in the Soviet Union in 1945.[23]

There was also the case of actres O.L. Knipper-Chekhova, as related in some detail by S.L. Beriia in *Moi Otets*. Daughter of a German father and a Russian mother, in 1916 she married actor Mikhail Chekhov (1891–1955), nephew of the playwright. They both emigrated in 1922 and were later divorced. Chekhov eventually ended up in Hollywood where he made a number of movies in the 1940s and 1950s including *The Song of Russia* in 1943, a blatant piece of pro-Soviet propaganda. His former wife, however, ended up in Germany making films and was a favorite of Hitler and Goebbels, who ran the film industry. In 1936, she received the title of distinguished artist. In November 1945, Maj. General Utekhin, Head of the 4 Department of SMERSH persuaded Chekhova to return to the Soviet Union and become a Soviet agent. SMERSH whose main responsibility was counterintelligence, and not recruiting spies, was unaware that Chekhova was already a Soviet agent of long-standing, and the good actress had no trouble going along with the charade. According to Beriia's son, his father kept the truth from Abakumov, and Chekhova eventually returned to the West and continued to provide intelligence to the Soviets, although her memoirs are silent about this facet of her career. In the Soviet Union as well as in Nazi Germany, it was not unusual for the right hand not to know what the left was doing. In her memoirs published in West Germany, Chekhova is silent about her alleged career as a spy and S.L. Beriia's account has yet to be supported by other sources.

One area in which the Soviet government and MGB took little interest was the massive crimes committed by the German occupiers on Soviet soil against civilians, partisans, POWs and, above all, Jews, and this despite the fact that Stalin once suggested to Churchill that after the war, 50,000 German officers should be shot outright in what could have been a bigger Katyn. On November 2, 1942, the Supreme Soviet set up an "Extraordinary State Commission on Establishing and Investigation of the Atrocities of German Invaders and Their Accomplices." The commission was charged by N.M. Shvernik, and its members included A.A. Zhdanov, Metropolitan Nicholas, writer A.N. Tolstoi, jurist I.P. Trainin, military doctor N.N. Burdenko, hydrologist B.E. Vedeneev, historian E.V. Tarle, pseudogeneticist T.D. Lysenko, and V.S. Grizodublova. The presence of so many professors and the absence of anyone from the security organs were clear indications that Stalin's interest in crimes committed by the Germans on Soviet territory was purely academic. In fact, the commission's main contribution was the appointment of Burdenko as head of a commission which in 1943 concocted the Soviet version of Katyn. On April 19, 1943, the Presidium of the Supreme Soviet passed a resolution in regard to the "German-Fascist villains and their henchmen who had committed crimes against Soviet civilians and captured prisoners." According to Maj. General L. Ivashov (*Krasnaia Zvezda*, August 4, 1990) by July 1944, 5,200 sentences had been pronounced, but most of these were against the small fry and their local collaborators. Late in 1943, two war crime trials took place in Krasnodar and Kharkov. In Krasnodar, 10 collaborators were hung, and in Kharkov, four individuals, three small-time SS officers who somehow had been left behind. Later as new territories were captured, elderly German local rear area commanders were publicly hanged after perfunctory trials. These men and those tried in Krasnodar and Kharkov were, however, not major criminals and their trials were held to show the flag as well as to convince the Western allies of Soviet seriousness about war crimes. After the war, however, no serious attempts were made to extradite implicated senior German military commanders such as Hermann Hoth, Erich Manstein, Otto Wöhler, Richard Ruoff, or the SS commanders Kurt Meyer (who once had an entire village wiped out because someone had taken a potshot at his dog) and Sepp Dietrich, or the commanders of the deadly Einsatzgruppen who had been the vanguard of the Final Solution on Soviet soil. Also left in peace were the senior surviving German Rear Area Commander, General of Infantry Franz von Roques (Army Group North), and General of Infantry Erich Friderici (Army Group South), who along with General of Infantry Max von Schenckendorff (Army Group Center), who died in July 1943, had presided over an empire of terror and brutality. When implicated individuals such as Field Marshal Schörner or Einsatzgruppe Commander Bruno Streckenbach actually fell into Russian hands, they were treated as mere POWs. The Russians also managed to capture an enormous amount of documents on the "Final Solution" campaign which they failed to share with the Western Allies. On March 4, 1946, they arrested Gustav Braun, head of development for the Topf Brothers, who had designed the gas chambers at Auschwitz, and the site engineers Fritz Sander, Kurt Prüfer, and Karl Schultze, who were all returned to Germany in 1955. Between 1944 and 1946, a group of writers led by I.G. Erenburg and V.S. Grossman compiled a massive Black Book of German crimes, which fell victim to the post-war anti-Semitic campaigns and was only published in Israel in 1980.

There was, however, one senior German officer in whom the Soviets took a deep interest, Field Marshal Ewald von Kleist, Commander of Army Group B in the Caucasus in 1942, who had played a part in trying to win over the local population to the German side. In 1948, Kleist was extradited from Yugoslavia to the Soviet

Union, where he was tried and sentenced to prison. He died in Vladimir prison on October 10, 1954.[24]

Heinz Pannwitz, Head of Gestapo in Czechoslovakia at the time of Lidice, decided at the end of the war that he would be safer falling into Russian hands. After his arrival in Moscow, he was met personally by Abakumov and, despite serious charges against him, was neither tried nor extradited but eventually returned to Germany with the POWs.[25] The infamous Reich Commissar Erich Koch (another ex-Communist Nazi), who had waged a campaign of terror and exploitation in the Ukraine, was left to the Poles and life in prison until his death in 1986 without the benefit of a trial that would have proved embarrassing to Stalin. Ditto with SS Gruppeenführer Gerret Korsemann, who during 1942–1943 had served as the Higher SS and Police leader (not a job for the faint of heart) for the Caucasus, South Russia, and finally Central Russia. Korseman, who had been cashiered by Himmler, was captured while serving as a junior officer. After spending four years in Polish prisons, he was allowed in 1949 to return to Germany. During 1942–1953, SS Obersturmbannführer Eduard Strauch had commanded the security police in Belorussia where a particularly savage war was being waged against the partisans and their sympathizers. After the war, the Russians stood by while he was extradited to Belgium, on whose territory he had served briefly during the Ardennes counter-offensive. At the end of the war, thousands of troops from the SS Division Totenkopf were captured by the Red Army in Austria after being deserted by the founder of Waffen SS, (as well as Hitler's onetime chauffeur and personal executioner), Sepp Dieterich who was concerned—as it turned out mistakingly—that after the war, the Russians would be bent on revenge for the crimes committed by his units against the civilians and POWs. The Division, originally made up of former concentration camp guards, and, in fact, led until 1943 by SS Oberggruppenführer Theodore Eicke, the first Commandant of Dachau, had a well-deserved reputation for brutality and, like most Waffen SS units, rarely bothered to take prisoners in the East (sometimes in the West also, as in Malmedy during the Battle of the Bulge). A number of officers from Totenkopf were tried in Poltava in 1947 and received prison sentences. The veterans of the Division were all released in the 1950s and returned to West Germany. It is interesting to compare their fate with what happened to SS Obersturmbannführer Fritz Knöchlein, Commander of 3 Company 1 Battalion 2 Regiment of Totenkopf, whose troops on May 27, 1940, near Le Paradis, France, had gunned down 80 English POWs from the 2 Royal Norfolk Regiment. Knöchlein was hanged in January 1949 after being sentenced by a British military court in a trial that was no less perfunctory than that faced by his camrades in Poltava.

The last Commander of Totenkopf, the incorrigible SS Brigadeführer Helmut Becker, the personification of the brutal landknechts who formed the high-ranking officers of the Waffen SS, however, tried his jailers' patience by trying to manufacture explosives in prison, and thus had the misfortune of being re-tried and shot in February 1952.[26] All in all, for war crimes committed, only 20 German Senior Commanders paid the ultimate price. They included Lt. Generals Friedrich Bernhard (Commander Special Corp 532 in the 9 Army), Karl Burkhardt (Commandant Kiev), Albrecht

Digeon von Monteton (Commandant Libau), Helmuth von Pannwitz (Commander Cossack Corps), Fritz Rudolf von Rappard (Commandant Marienburg, Commander 7 Infantry Division), Herrmann Winkler (Commandant Nikoleav), Maj. Generals Gottfried von Erdmannsdorff (Commandant Mogilev), AdolfHamann (Commandant Bobruisk), Emil Just (Commander, Field Group 396 in Kovno), Hans Küpper (Commander Field Group 818 in Frauenburg), Bonislaw Pawel (attached to Army Group Kurland), Johann Georg Tichert (Commander 35 Infantry Division), Eckard von Tschammer und Osten (Commander Field Group 531), Herrmann Werther (Commander Field Group 186 in charge of coastal fortifications in Riga), Siegfrid Ruff (Commandant Riga), Heinrich Remlinger (Commander Field Group 186, Commandant Pleskau), SS and Police Generals Fridrich Jeckeln (Higher SS and Police Leader Army Groups South and North), Helmut Becker (Commander SS Division "Totenkopf"), Schmausser (Higher SS and Police Leader Silesia), and Eberhard Herf (Commander Order Police in Ukraine).

There were some exceptional cases in which major Nazi war criminals, more by accident than by design, were punished at Russian hands. A case in point happened on February 3, 1946, when six German officers were tried and hanged on the same day in Riga. Five of them were sundry Rear Area Commanders, but SS Obergruppenführer Fridrich Jeckeln, the former Higher SS and Higher Police Leader for the Army Groups South and North, had at least a quarter-of-a-million Jewish victims on his conscience. Jeckeln's routine trial, however, was based on crimes that had been committed against the local pro-Soviet partisans. Theodore von Rientel, from 1941 the General Commissar in Lithuania, was also executed in 1946. There was also the strange case of Friedrich Panzinger, once the number two man in Gestapo and, from September 1943, Head of Security Police and SD in Ostland, who was repatriated to the Soviets in November 1946, but was not tried until March 1952, when he was sentenced to 25 years only to be let go and return to Germany in September 1955. He committed suicide in August 1959 when the West German authorities started investigating his part in the mass murder of Soviet POWs. Stalin's indifference also extended to the war criminals who managed to escape through a network which at times included officials of the Roman Catholic Church. The latter were particularly active in helping such criminals as the functionaries of the Croatian Ustashi, devout Christians who also practiced genocide with gusto that even made the SS gasp. During the post-war years, a number of German war criminals found refuge in Arab countries where virulent anti-Semitism which was supposed to have died with Auschwitz found fertile ground. For instance, after the war SS Standardenführer Walter Rauff, who had pioneered the use of mobile gas chambers, managed to escape to Syria with the help of "Opera San Raffaelle," the Vatican refugee aid organization, and the Geneva branch of the OSS. Rauff was employed by the Syrian military until 1949 before moving to South America, where he died in Chile in 1984. Historian Ia.Ia. Etinger (*Kuranty*, May 22, 1992) claims that in the 1950s nearly 8,000 former Nazi military and security personnel including 2,000 associated with the SS found new homes in Egypt, Syria, and Iraq. Some of the better known were former General of Artillery Wilhelm Fahrmbacher, Commander of the 25 Corps and "Army Group Normandie"; well-known commando Otto Skorzeny; and Eugen Demling, former head of Gestapo in Ruhr. Etinger also claims that the notorious Oskar Dirlewanger, who had commanded convict units in Warsaw during the Home Army rebellion (and was supposedly killed in June 1945), spent the summer of 1952 in Egypt training saboteurs for Nasser. Etinger further adds that the Soviet government was aware of these events, but preferred to remain silent—at the same time accusing the West and the Federal Republic of Germany of harboring the Nazi war criminals. The lackadaisical attitude toward crimes committed by the German occupiers contrasts sharply with the Soviet attempts to ferret out and bring to justice her own citizens who may have collaborated with the enemy. Stalin's behavior with regard to German crimes made perfect sense. Mass trials would have shown the magnitude of Soviet defeat as well as the collapse of the Stalinist state in occupied areas. Stalin also approved of the German occupation policies since they mirrored his own. As the architect of collectivization, the Gulag, and Katyn, he would have been the last person to have moral objections to Lidice, Babii Iar, and Auschwitz.

For nearly 50 years, the official Soviet views on German war crimes were colored by indifference, deception, and outright lies. German crimes were discussed as if all groups had been equally victimized. From the very beginning, every attempt was made to conceal the special fate reserved for the Jews. The words "Final Solution" rarely appear in Soviet writings of the Second World War. It is true that the Germans victimized, starved, and enslaved many of their vassals in East Europe, but at least during the war, no group except the Jews and the Gypsies had been singled out for outright physical extermination. Stalin's successors continued the policy of deception. The extent of the German crimes in the occupied territories has yet to be completely revealed and would require the release of Soviet documents. Recent studies by Omer Bartov and others provide evidence that the SS and police were not alone in waging terror and were actively aided by the Wehrmacht, long claimed by its apologists to have been a mere bystander.

According to Soviet documents (*Istoriia SSSR*, 4/1990) and the records of the Nuremberg trials, during the war nearly five million citizens left Soviet territory, mostly as forced laborers, but undoubtedly some of their own free will. Many of these deportees were women, the majority from Ukraine, and used primarily as slave labor, but also subjects of medical experiments in camps and forced abortions, the latter a felony under Nazi law. There is no evidence that the Roman Catholic Church, which managed with little difficulty to put a stop to the Nazis' euthanasia program but showed no concern over the Jewish persecutions, ever objected to these mass abortions. The relationship between the Roman Catholic Church and the Nazis was no different than the war-time relation between the Russian Orthodox Church and Stalin.

A report dated October 20, 1945, speaks of nearly seven million former Soviet citizens including over two million POWs under German rule at the end of the war. For Stalin, their return, by force if necessary, was a top priority, a process that incidentally necessitated the cooperation of the Western powers which, regardless of moral issues, was forthcoming in view of war-time politics. On October 4, 1944, the Council of People's Commissars set up a commission for repatriation affairs and two days later appointed Col. General F.I. Golikov, Deputy Commissar of Defense, as its head. From that point on, this was Golikov's main responsibility. He and his Deputy Lt. General K.D. Golubev worked closely in this area with NKVD/NKGB and SMERSH, and many of the deportees were to end up in the Gulag. Beriia's Deputy V.V. Chernyshev was NKVD's contact with this commission, while Abakumov's main responsibility entailed returning military officers.

The problem of returning Soviet POWs was another subject of deep interest to Stalin, whose feeling about POWs and their rights was best expressed in the Katyn woods. He certainly would have been baffled over the 20-year uproar in the United States over the fate of a handful of MIAs from the Vietnam War. Stalin was at best indifferent to the fate of Soviet POWs (the second largest group of victims of Nazism), but deeply concerned about the subversive tendencies of the returning survivors. This fear also extended to those citizens of the USSR, mostly women, who had been used as slave labor by the Nazis.

According to A.K. Sul'ianov in *Arestovat' v Kremle*, in May 1945 Stalin issued a directive to Marshals G.K. Zhukov, K.K. Rokossovskii, I.S. Konev, R.Ia. Malinovskii, F.I. Tolbukhin and Army General A.I.Eremenko (respectively Commanders of 1 and 2 Belorussian and 1, 2, 3, and 4 Ukraine Fronts); Army General A.V. Khrulev (Head of Red Army Supplies); L.P. Beriia (Head of NKVD); V.N. Merkulov (Head of NKGB); V.S. Abakumov (Head of SMERSH); Army General F.I. Golikov (Chairman of the Repatriation Commission) and his Deputy, Col. General K.D. Golubev, to prepare 95 camps, each with a capacity of 10,000, to receive the former citizens of the USSR who had come under enemy control. The civilians would be interrogated by NKVD and NKGB commissions. Those who had been with the military would fall under the jurisdiction of SMERSH.

During the war, the Germans captured at least 5.7 million Russian prisoners, although a figure as high as 6.2 million is also given (*Nezavismaia Gazeta*, October 29, 1991), of which between 100,000 and 200,000 managed to escape. According to the higher estimate, 3.8 million prisoners fell into enemy hands in 1941, 1.6 in 1942, over one-half million in 1943, about 50,000 in 1944, and 34,000 in the first four months of 1945. At the end of the war, 1,836,000 were repatriated. Even if we include those who somehow managed to stay in the West, between 3.3 and 4.2 million (60% to nearly 70%) of Soviet POWs were to die in captivity under the tender care of the Wehrmacht, the more chivalrous branch of the Nazi state, a loss rate comparable to that of the Jews under Hitler. This compared with a less than 2% death rate of Western Allied prisoners who were held by the Germans (1.58% for the French, 1.15% for the British, and 0.3% for the Americans). Incidentally, the death rate of Russian POWs in German captivity was much higher than that of Allied prisoners in Japanese captivity and Axis prisoners in the Gulag, where nearly 40% survived a much longer period of imprisonment.

For the Soviet POWS who made it to camps, and many did not, the options were limited to death of hunger, disease, and execution, or joining the enemy. A typical example was S.T. Bychkov, former Deputy Commander of the 482 Air Interceptor Regiment, 322 Interceptor Division, who had won the coveted Hero of the Soviet Union award on September 9, 1943 (the post-war official list, however, omits his name) before being shot down and captured. According to his testimony on March 8, 1946 (*Novaia i Noveishaia Istoriia*, 2/1993), he was given the option of death or joining the ROA by the Vlasovite Col. V.I. Mal'tsev. In February 1944, Bychkov jointed the ROA. What is extraordinary is not the number of those who joined up with Vlasov, but those who refused under circumstances that were tantamount to suicide. Even escape to the Soviet side was not viable since this meant arrest or worse. According to the historians A.N. Mertsalov and L.A. Mertsalova in their study *Dovol'no o Voine?*, by October 1, 1944, 354,592 former members (including 50,441 officers) of the Red Army who had spent time in German-occupied territory had been arrested and 18,382 (including 16,200 officers) had been forced to serve in penal battalions. According to the collection *Nashe Otechestvo*, by October 1944, there existed 20 penal battalions made up of 920 individuals. Four more formed in NKVD special camps after this date. The fate of writer V.A. Rubin was typical of those who had managed to avoid captivity. Captured in October 1941 during the Battle of Smolensk, he managed to escape after three days to serve in combat for three more months, suffering frostbite. It was discovered that in June 1942, when serving in the military school in Tomsk, that he had been captured, which meant collaboration even though he was Jewish. The punishment was swift: he was expelled and forced to work in mines. Then there was the case of Battalion Commissar I.Ia. Kernes. The archives (*Novaia i Noveishaia Istorria*, 2/1993) show that he managed to escape and provided the Soviets with detailed reports on the Vlasov movement. On December 4, 1946, he was sentenced to 20 years under Article 58 and was not released until September 1955 and later rehabilitated. He died in 1969.

Then there is the case of Guard Senior Lieutenant M.V. Deviataev, later subject of two books, *Polet k Solntse* (Moscow: 1972) and *Pobeg iz Ada* (Saransk: 1985). Deviataev, a Mordov, was attached to the 104 Guard Interceptor Regiment, 9 Air Division, 2 Air Army, 1 Ukraine Front, and credited with nine aerial victories when he was shot down behind enemy lines on July 13, 1944. His captors sent him to camp on the Baltic coast where rockets and new weapons were being tested. On February 8, 1945, Deviataev and nine other Soviet POWs managed to highjack an experimental Heinkel-III bomber and flew back to Soviet territory where they were arrested by the SMERSH. For his efforts, Deviataev ended up in the Gulag. On August 15, 1957, 12 years after his heroic act, he was awarded the title of Hero of the Soviet Union.

There is no doubt that Stalin, who had refused to sign the Geneva Convention and, in fact, in 1941 was behind the doctrine "Whoever surrenders is a traitor," usually attributed to L.Z. Mekhlis, Head of the Political Administration of the Red Army, contributed to this holocaust.[27] Hitler's extermination of Soviet POWs played right into Stalin's hands. The returning prisoners were considered a security risk since they had been exposed to non-Soviet rule, as well as being embarrassing witnesses of the collapse of the supposedly invincible Red Army. Their sheer numbers would have also taxed the resources of the Gulag. During the Nuremberg trials, there was one solitary witness representing the Soviet POWs, Lt. of Medical Services E. Kivelisha, whose testimony made it clear that the treatment accorded to the Russian prisoners was similar to that meted out to the Jews. In fact, the Auschwitz gas chambers were first tested on Soviet POWs. The Soviets made no attempt to extradite the architect of this holocaust, General of Infantry Hermann Reinecke, who headed the Prisoner of War Department of the OKW and was a man with as many lives on his conscience as Adolph Eichmann. In 1944, Reinecke served as a member of the People's Court which tried the July 20 conspirators, sitting next to the raving chief judge, Roland Freisler, Hitler's Ul'rikh and an ex-Communist, no less.

The Soviets made no attempt to extradite Reinecke nor the smaller fry who were guilty of crimes against the Soviet POWs. A case in point was the massacre of nearly 2,000 Soviet prisoners in Passau (hometown of Julius Streicher and where Eichmann had been married). The chief organizer of this affair was Maj. General Erich Hasenstein, a regular Wehrmacht officer and a former commander of an infantry school who at this time commanded a rag-tag infantry division. He later committed suicide in a Götterdämmerung fashion, but the Soviets made no attempt to bring to justice the other culprits and showed no interest when the U.S. occupying forces launched an investigation into the matter. Incidentally, today Hassenstein lies in a hero's grave in the same cemetery in which the names of local Jewish victims of the Nazis have been defaced. Maj. General of Artillery V.N. Sotenskii, former Commander of the Artillery of 5 Army who had been taken prisoner in September 1941, was active in the resistance movement during captivity in various camps. He was murdered on April 21, 1945, by the SS at the Wültzberg Fortress an hour before the arrival of the American troops. The Soviets showed no interest in him or other Soviet Generals who had been murdered during captivity for resisting the Nazis. Only in 1992 did the Russians began to translate and serialize Christian Streit's *Keine Kamaredan*, the masterly study of the tragedy of Soviet prisoners first published in 1978 and incidentally still awaiting an English translation.[28]

The Soviet prisoners who managed to escape were also in for a rude reception. On December 27, 1941, GKO Order 1069 directed the formation of NKVD Special (later renamed "counter infiltration") camps for former POWs and escapees from the enemy-occupied areas. From 1942 to October 1944, nearly half-a-million prisoners were kept in these camps, including 350,000 former members of the Red Army, among them 50,000 officers. Both NKVD and SMERSH were involved in rounding up the prisoners. In January 1946, the camps became part of the Gulag. As was revealed by *Moscow News* in June 1993, the Soviets had kept open in Germany two prisons and nine former Nazi concentration camps including Buchenwald and Sachsenhausen. These special camps were formed under NKVD Order No. 00315 on April 15, 1945; were incorporated in the Gulag in 1948; and were finally transferred to GDR authorities in 1950. Col. General I.A. Serov was in charge, and his staff was made up mostly of SMERSH officers attached to the 1 Belorussian Front. Besides former Soviet citizens, the camps housed junior-level Nazi functionaries as well as thousands of Hitler Youth teenagers suspected of belonging to the Wehrwolf, the much heralded but actually mythical Nazi guerrilla organization. There were also other prisoners, including the old Communist Ewald Pieck, whose brother, Wilhelm, was to become President of GDR. All and all, 155,000 prisoners went through these camps, including 33,000 former Soviet citizens. About 42,000 of the prisoners died of cold, hunger, and disease, and 756 were executed. As bad as these camps were, after the war even worse things were happening in Poland, where the Polish Security Service (UB), organized by the Russians, set up concentration camps run by the understandably vengeful survivors of the Holocaust in which thousands of German civilians died. Jack Sack's study, of this subject, *An Eye for an Eye*, does not mention any Soviet officials, but the operation seems to be something inspired, if not actually led, by I.A. Serov.

After liberation, the POWs who had survived captivity and "liberation," even those who had remained loyal to the Soviet Union, received less than a hearty welcome when they returned to the motherland. Most were packed off to the camps. An example is the case of Maj. P.M. Gavrilov, Commander of the Brest Fortress, overrun in the early days of the war. The fortress held out until July 23, 1941, and Gavrilov, wounded, was captured. In 1946 after returning to the Soviet Union, he, a Tatar, was arrested and ended up spending more time in the Gulag than in German captivity. On January 30, 1957, he received a belated title of "Hero of the Soviet Union."

Documents finally released in Russia in 1993 show that only 15% of the Generals who were captured collaborated with the enemy and that the evidence against some of the secondary figures is circumstantial. Most of the Generals who were captured, even in the dark days of 1941–1942, when an ultimate Soviet victory seemed remote, remained loyal to the Soviet state, and, in fact, a number paid the ultimate penalty by resisting in captivity an enemy as merciless as the man under whose banner they had fought. The refusal to join the Vlasov movement seems even more remarkable in that the Generals remained loyal to the Soviet Union knowing the fate of returning Soviet POWs after the Winter War. The depth of Russian patriotism, even of the misguided variety, to say nothing of the capacity for suffering and self-deception, should never be underestimated.[29]

During the war, about 85 Generals, Komdivs, and Kombrigs were taken prisoner. Among those captured, six Generals managed to escape, and 24 or 25 died or were murdered in captivity. Only 12 (15% of those captured) collaborated to some extent with the enemy, a fact which along with Vlasov's service in military tribunals of Leningrad and Kiev Military Districts in 1937–1938 is not mentioned by his apologists.

The Generals taken prisoner included Lt. Generals A.A. Vlasov, F.A. Ershakov, M.F. Lukin, L.A. Mazanov (Artillery), I.N. Muzychenko and D.M. Karbyshev (Engineering Troops), and Maj. Generals P.I. Abramidze, Kh.N. Alaverdov (Alaverdian), I.I. Alekseev, I.M. Antiufeev, P.D. Artemenko, S.V. Baranov (Technical Services), M.A. Beleshev (Aviation), I.P. Bikzhanov, I.A. Blagoveshchenskii (Coastal Artillery), P.V. Bogdanov, A.V. Bondovskii(?), M.D. Borisov, A.E. Budykho, S.E.

Danilov, K.L. Dobroserdov, E.A. Egorov, G.I. Fedorov (Artillery), I.M. Gerasimov, N.K. Kirilov, V.V. Kirpichnikov, I.A. Kornilov, V.A. Koptsov(?), I.P. Kruppenikov, A.D. Kuleshev, K.E. Kulikov, I.M. Liubovtsev, P.G. Makarov, V.F. Malyshkin, I.I. Mel'nikov, N.F. Mikhailov(Tank Troops), S.A. Moshenin, A.Z. Naumov, I.S. Nikitin, P.G. Novikov, T.Ia. Novikov, A.A. Noskov, S.Ia. Ogurtsov, P.P. Pavlov, M.O. Petrov (Artillery), P.G. Ponedelin, M.I. Potapov (Tank Troops), I.A. Presniakov, P.F. Privalov, I.P. Prokhorov (Artillery), V.I. Prokhorov, N.I. Proshkin, B.S. Rikhter, M.T. Romanov, T.Iu. Rotberg (Rear Services), F.D. Rubtsov, M.B. Salikhov, A.G. Samokhin, M.M. Shaimuratov, I.M. Shepetov, N.M. Shestopalov, M.N. Sivaev (Technical Services), I.M. Skugarev, M.G. Snegov, V.N. Sotenskii (Artillery), N.M. Starostin (Artillery), P.V. Sysoev, S.A. Tkachenko, G.I. Tkhor (Aviation), Ia.I. Tonkonogov, F.I. Trukhin, P.G. Tsyrul'nikov, S.V. Vishnevskii, G.M. Zaitsev, D.E. Zakutnyi, A.S. Zotov, G.M. Zusmanovich (Rear Services), and E.S. Zybin. Also taken prisoner or remaining behind the enemy lines were Kombrigs I.G. Bessonov, M.V. Bogdanov, N.G. Lazutin, M.A. Romanov, A.N. Ryzhkov, and A.N. Sevast'ianov (temporary Kombrig), Brigade Surgeon I.A. Naumov, Corps Commissar F.A. Semenovskii, Division Commissar E.P. Rykov, and Brigade Commissar G.N. Zhilenkov. There are also rumors about the capture of Maj. General S.M. Chestokhvalov and Maj. General of Medical Services P.Ia. Novikov. Some sources also add I.A. Laskin, even though at the time of capture, he was probably only a Colonel. Also, two Soviet Generals, Kombrig A.S. Chichkanov and Maj. General of Artillery S.A. Moshenin, who were trapped behind the enemy lines chose to remain even though they had no contact with the enemy. At least one captured General, a Komdiv Kalinin, has yet to be traced. Not all those taken prisoner spent much time in captivity. N.M. Shestopalov died of wounds a few days after capture. M.O. Petrov, F.D. Rubtsov, and M.M. Shaimuratov were almost immediately murdered by their captors. There are also rumors that Hero of the Soviet Union Maj. General of Aviation I.S. Polbin, shot down over Breslau on Feb. 11, 1945, survived the crash and was actually killed after capture. In addition, the previous claims that Maj. General of Tank Troops A.G. Potaturchev was taken prisoner have now been refuted.

Nearly 30 generals did not return from German captivity. Murdered while in prison were Lt. General D.I. Karbyshev, Maj. Generals G.I. Tkhor, S.A. Tkachenko, P.G. Novikov, V.N. Sotenskii, Kh.N. Alaverdov, V.I. Prokhorov, M.P. Romanov, P.S. Mishutin, I.S. Nikitin, I.A. Presniakov, V.I. Prokhorov, S.A. Shepchuk, I.M. Shepetov, and Corps Commissar F.A. Semenovskii. Those who died in captivity of wounds, hunger, disease, and exhaustion were Maj. Generals N.I. Proshkin, S.V. Baranov, K.E. Kulikov, G.M. Zusmanovich, S.E. Dailov, A.D. Kuleshov, P.G. Makarov, K.E. Kulikov, M.O. Petrov, N.M. Shestopalov, and I.M. Starostin, and Division Commissar E.P. Rykov, who died of wounds that he may have suffered after being captured. Another was Lt. General F.A. Ershakov, who died either in camps or shortly after liberation. It is also possible that some among the ten or so high-ranking political Commissars such as Corps Commissar A.S. Nikolaev and Division Commissars A.M. Shustin and I.O. Sheklanov (Shcheklanov) who lost their lives during the war were in fact captured and then were executed under Hitler's

"Commissar Order." Most of these individuals are still listed as "missing in action" and proof only exists for Corps Commissar F.A. Semenovskii, who was murdered after capture, and Brigade Commissar G.N. Zhilenkov, who managed to conceal his rank and position before joining the Vlasov movement in 1942.

The captured Generals all had information about a regime in which secrecy was an article of faith. Their fate and behavior in captivity were of deep concern to SMERSH. Until Glasnost, except for Vlasov and his colleagues, little had appeared in print about Soviet Generals captured by the Germans. By 1982 only two, Maj. General P.I. Abramidze (born 1901), former Commander of the 26 Alpine Division, Southwest Front, captured in August 1941, and possibly Maj. General I.P. Bikzhanov (born 1895), Commander of the 29 Motorized Division, West Front, captured in July 1941, were still living. One hopes that some of the captured Generals left memoirs or personal archives that have yet to be discovered.

Besides Vlasov, Trukhin, Malyshkin, Zakutnyi, Blagoveshenskii, and Zhilenkov, as already mentioned, there is some evidence of collaboration by the following: Maj. Generals P.V. Bogdanov, A.E. Budykho, A.Z. Naumov, B.S. Rikhter, and M.B. Salikhov and Kombrigs I.G. Bessonov, A.N. Sevast'ianov, and M.V. Bogdanov, whose careers will be discussed in the next chapter. None of them was tried with the Vlasov group.

Of the 37 Generals returned from captivity, 26 eventually were exonerated, but Abakumov and SMERSH were to take an unhealthy interest in the rest. Already during the war, SMERSH had shown its hand by its treatment of a number of Generals who had managed to escape. These included Maj. General I.I. Alekseev, former Commander of the 6 Rifle Corps, Southwest Front, captured on September 1941, who had managed to escape on October 11, 1941. Alekseev was arrested on December 14, 1941. Colonel or Kombrig I.A. Laskin, Chief of Staff of 15 Sivash Rifle Division, was captured in August 1941 but managed to escape a month later. Next, Laskin fought as Commander of the 106 Rifle Division in defense of Crimea and Sevastopol. After being evacuated on September 7, 1942, at the height of the Battle of Stalingrad, he was appointed Chief of Staff of the embattled 64 Army which, with the neighboring 62 Army, provided the last line of defense in the city. Laskin performed well, since on October 14, 1942, he was promoted to Maj. General. On May 13, 1943, he became the Chief of Staff of the North Caucasus Front (2 Formation), serving with I.E. Petrov, who on the same day had replaced the NKVD man Col. General I.I. Maslennikov. The Political Commissar was none other than A.Ia. Fominykh, already mentioned in these pages. On December 20, 1943, Laskin was arrested by SMERSH, accused of having cooperated with the enemy during his brief captivity. Maj. General V.V. Kirpichnikov, former Commander of the 43 Rifle Division, was captured by the Finns in September 1941 near Vyborg. After Finland's surrender, he was repatriated but was arrested on October 20, 1944. Maj. General P.V. Sysoev, former Commander of the 36 Rifle Corps Southwest Front, was captured in July 1941 and was posing as a common soldier before he managed to escape and join the partisan units commanded by the twice Hero of the Soviet Union A.F. Fedorov. After the return of the Red Army, Sysoev was arrested on October 24, 1944. Maj. General

P.G. Tsirul'nikov, former Commander of the 51 Rifle Division, was captured on October 9, 1941, but escaped and rejoined the Red Army on November 11, 1941, and was arrested on Feb. 18, 1942. Kombrig A.S. Chichkanov, Commander of the 189 Rifle Division, was left behind in August 1941 after his unit was surrounded by the enemy and chose to remain behind the enemy lines. He was arrested on March 17, 1943, after the Soviet forces returned. Also Maj. General of Artillery S.A. Moshenin, Commander of Artillery 24 Army, West Front, was left behind and was arrested when the Red Army captured El'nia.

The fate of these men did not bode well for those Generals who had survived German captivity. On May 27, 1945, Abakumov wrote to Stalin stating that on the previous day, two planeloads of captured senior officers had arrived from Paris carrying 29 Soviet Generals, three Kombrigs (a pre-war and early-war rank discontinued in 1942), and one Brigade Surgeon. The list included Lt. Generals M.F. Lukin and I.N. Muzychenko; Lt. General of Artillery L.A. Mazanov; Maj. Generals P.I. Abramidze, P.D. Artemenko, I.M. Antiufeev, I.P. Beleshev, M.A. Beleshev, I.P. Biiuzhanov, M.D. Borisov, S.V. Vishnevskii, I.M. Gerasimov, K.L.Dobroserdov, E.A. Egorov, G.M. Zaitsev, E.S. Zybin, N.K. Kirillov, I.A. Kornilov, I.P. Krupennikov, I.M. Liubovtsev, I.I. Mel'nikov, N.F. Mikhailov, A.A. Noskov, P.P. Pavlov, P.G. Ponedelin, M.I. Potapov, I.P. Prokhorov, A.G. Samokhin, M.N. Sivaev, M.G. Snegov, Kombrigs N.G. Lazutin, M.A. Romanov, A.N. Ryzhkov; and Brigade Surgeon I.A. Naumov. Sometime later the names of Maj. General A.S. Zotov, P.F. Privalov, I.M. Skugarev, and Ia. I. Tonkogonov were added. To this list, we must also add two more names of Generals who were liberated before the end of the war. The Estonian Maj. General of Rear Services T.Iu. Rotberg was taken prisoner in August 1941 and was freed after Tallinn fell into Russian hands in 1944. He was arrested on November 20, 1944. Maj. General V.V. Kirpichnikov was captured by the Finns in September 1941 and repatriated after the armistice and was arrested on October 20, 1944. Abakumov indicated that each individual would be carefully investigated and the results reported to Stalin.

On August 31, 1945, Abakumov reported to Stalin, again listing 17 Generals and Kombrigs who were under investigation. At this time, he named only one, Kombrig N.G. Lazutin, former Chief of Staff of 61 Rifle Corps, as a candidate for arrest and listed others such as Lukin, Liubovtsev, and Mikhailov who had suffered amputations or were ill still under investigation. He also proposed freeing Dobroserdov, Zotov, Kornilov, Liubovtsev, Mel'nikov, Mikhailov, Pavlov, and Skugarev, a decision that was rejected by Stalin. In fact, by December 1945, the fate of only one General (M.F. Lukin) had been resolved. Instead, Stalin formed a committee made up of N.A. Bulganin, Deputy Commissar of Defense; Army General A.I. Antonov, Chief of Staff, and Abakumov. Helping the committee was Army General F.I. Golikov, Deputy Commissar of Defense (April 1943), Head of the Red Army Cadres (May 1943) and Head of the Repatriation Commission (October 1944). During the Khrushchev years, Bulganin was passed off as a grandfatherly oaf with a goatee. In point of fact, as his involvement here shows, he was no less than a former Chekist (1918–1921), whose excessive drinking had done little to dampen his enthusiasm for Stalinist policies. Golikov was also another hardened Stalinist who had no trouble making the necessary accommodations with the new rulers after Stalin's death. Unlike their counterparts in democracies, committees under Stalin, except when he used them for public relations, were not places for idle chat and employment of those with nothing to do and were expected to produce results. With Stalin giving the signal that he was after blood, Abakumov went to work and the committee's report on December 21, 1945, singled out 11 Generals as potential candidates for court-martial. To make the charges stick, Abakumov had searched the files for any damaging material about those who, after several years in German captivity, were now about to face another ordeal.

The sacrificial lambs included Maj. General (June 1940) P.G. Ponedelin. Born in 1893, he had attended the Moscow school for Warrant Officers in 1916 and risen to command a Battalion in World War I. He entered the Red Army in 1917 and joined the Party in August 1918. During the Civil War, he commanded Regiments and Brigades while fighting against Kolchak, Denikin, Angel, Marusi and Bulak-Bulakhovich. In fighting against Kolchak, he commanded the 29 Rifle Regiment, suffered a leg wound, and received the Order of Red Banner. Against Denikin, he commanded the 56 Regiment and during the Polish campaign the 19 and 21 Rifle Brigades—all in all a most impressive record. In 1926, Ponedelin graduated from the Frunze Academy and continued to rise in ranks, in 1938 becoming Commander of the 1 Rifle Corps in the Leningrad Military District. During the Winter War, he was Chief of Staff of the 8 Army. In March 1941, he was appointed Commander of the 12 Army in Kiev Special Military District. During his career, he had won the Orders of Lenin and Red Banner. In late July 1941, the remainders of the 12 Army and "Battlegroup Ponedelin" were caught in the Uman Pocket and forced to surrender. The Commander and the Political Commissar of the South Front, Army General I.V. Tiulenev, and Corps Commissar A.I. Zaporozhete (former head of the Political Administration of the Red Army just before the war) used Ponedelin and Maj. General N.K. Kirillov, Commander of the 13 Rifle Corps, as scapegoats for the failure of the South Front by accusing them of "panic" (in the lexicon of crimes under Stalin, only espionage and subversion ranked higher).

On August 17, 1941, ten days after Ponedelin was captured, Stavka Directive No. 270, signed by G.K. Zhukov, among others, addressed to Party leaders down to the local level, accused the two men as well as Lt. General V.Ia. Kachalov, Commander of the 28 Army, who actually died a hero's death on the battlefield, of desertion. Ponedelin and Kirillov's cause was not helped by the posed photographs that were dropped by their captors over the Russian lines and convinced Stalin and Budennyi of their perfidy. On October 13, 1941, the Military Collegium of the USSR Supreme Court sentenced Ponedelin and Kirillov to death. A day earlier, an NKVD troika had sentenced Ponedelin's wife and father to 5 years in camps as relatives of a traitor. Whether Ponedelin was aware of these events is doubtful. As a prisoner in the Wolfheide camp, Ponedelin categorically rejected the overtures from Vlasovites. After his liberation by U.S. forces in 1945, Ponedelin contacted the Soviet mission in Paris and was repatriated. Besides the charges already made against Ponedelin, the committee's report indicated that he had been disciplined by the Leningrad Party Organization in 1937, and he had also made critical remarks about the Soviet Union and Stalin in his prison diary. Other charges included the testimony of fellow prisoners Muzychenko, Skugarev, and Kirillov, as well as an alleged confession by Ponedelin of anti-Soviet sentiments going back to 1929. Fellow prisoner Ia.I. Tonkogonov, who had shared a room with Ponedelin, claimed that Ponedelin stood at attention in the presence of German officers. Abakumov's investigators also discovered that in 1925, Ponedelin had married the daughter of a former Tsarist Colonel and that two of her brothers had served with Denikin. Ponedelin was left to rot in Lefortovo. According to Colonel of Judiciary A. Liskin (*Shchit i Mech*, No. 13, 1993), the Chief Military Prosecutor N.P. Afanas'ev approached Beriia about a decision in regard to Ponedelin and N.K. Kirillov, who were kept in Sukhanov prison, since the war—after all—had been a long time ago. Beriia approached Stalin, who ordered that both men be court-martialed and shot on August 25, 1950. The two men had spent more time in Russian prisons than in German captivity.

Charges against Maj. General P.D. Artemenko (born 1896, in the Red Army from 1917, Party member from 1925), former Commander of the 27 Rifle Crops, 5 Army, Southwest Front, included failing to resist the enemy and voluntarily surrendering on September 27, 1941. As a result, he was condemned to death on April 10, 1942, by the Military Tribunal of the Southwest Front. Abakumov also claimed that after his capture, Artemenko had given valuable information to the enemy. His cooperative attitude during captivity was confirmed by the testimony of fellow prisoners Budykho, Dobroserdov, Kirillov, and Abramidze. Artemenko was eventually shot in April 1950.

Maj. General E.A. Egorov (born 1891, in the Red Army from 1918, Party member from 1925), former Commander 4 Rifle Corps, 3 Army, West Front, was taken prisoner on June 29, 1941. The text of Egorov's interrogation by the intelligence officers of the Army Group Center (*VIZH*, 10, 1993) does not indicate a potential collaborator. In December 1941, Egorov became involved with the German-sponsored "Russian Working People's Party" and was appointed Head of the Military Branch. In April 1943, he was sent to the Nuremberg camp and in September to the Würtsberg Fortress. He stayed there until April 1945, when the captured Generals were transferred to Marburg when they were freed by U.S. forces and returned home via Paris. Abakumov, in his letter of December 28, 1945, claimed that Egorov had surrendered to the enemy without a fight, and in Hammelsburg camp (Bavaria) had met with two Vlasovite Generals, F.I. Trukhin and I.A. Blagoveshchenskii, and was active in the anti-Soviet "Russian People Workers Party." Besides the two Vlasovite Generals, other captured Generals M.I. Potapov, P.I. Abramidze, M.K. Kirillov, and I.M. Skugarev provided testimony against Egorov. Egorov was arrested on September 3, 1946, and was kept in prison until 1950, when the case against him was reopened. The indictment was prepared by Lt. General S.I. Ogol'tsov, Abakumov's First Deputy, and on April 19, 1950, the USSR Military Collegium under A.A. Cheptsov sentenced Egorov to death despite his claim that he had joined the Todt Labor organization only to escape to the Soviet side.

Maj. General E.S. Zybin (born 1894, in the Red Army from 1918, Party member from 1927), former Commander of 36 Cavalry Division (incorrectly listed as Southwest) West Front, was first arrested by NKVD in 1938 for taking part in a military conspiracy. He surrendered on August 28, 1941, and was accused by Abakumov of divulging military secrets and with meeting with Trukhin and Blagoveshchenskii in captivity, and involvement in the "Russian People Workers Party." Besides the two Vlasovites, other captured Generals including A.G. Samokhin, I.M. Gerasimov, P.D. Artemenko and E.A. Egorov also testified against him. Zybin had already been condemned to death in absentia on October 13, 1942, by the Military Collegium, and his wife was sentenced to 5 years in exile in Omsk by an NKVD troika on June 26, 1943.

Maj. General I.P. Krupennikov (born 1896, in the Red Army from 1918, candidate member of the Party from 1942), was the former Chief of Staff of 3 Guard Army Southwest Front. The report does not indicate the date of his capture, but German records indicate this happened on December 20, 1942, when he lost his way. The charges against him included giving the enemy vital information about the 3 Guard Army and engaging in enemy- and ROA-inspired propaganda in early 1943 among Soviet prisoners in Lettsenk camp. According to Sven Steenberg, Vlasov's biographer, Krupennikov was interrogated by Maj. Heniz Herre of the "Foreign Armies East" and expressed conditional interest in joining the fight against Stalin, but Vlasov refused to meet Krupennikov and apparently nothing came out of these efforts. To reinforce his case against Krupennikov, Abakumov managed to find in prison Komdiv S.V. Nikitin, former Commander of the 11 Rifle Corps, who on July 20, 1939, had been sentenced to ten years in prison for membership in a "military conspiracy." Nikitin was willing to name Krupennikov as a fellow conspirator. Fellow prisoners Lt. General of Artillery L.A. Mazanov, Maj. General M.D. Borisov, and Lt. Colonels I.M. Tkachev (Chief of Staff) and Vol'vachyi (Head of Training 47 Army) had also provided evidence against Krupennikov. The case against him was particularly flimsy, and Abakumov even resorted to seeking evidence from one D.E. Kalimbeta, who had served as the librarian in the Lettsenk camp. Post-war Soviet histories of the Battle of Stalingrad, however, list Krupennikov as an officer in good standing.

Kombrig N.G. Lazutin (born 1901, in the Red Army from 1919, Party member from 1920, but expelled in 1933 for non-Socialist background), former Head of Artillery in 61 Rifle Corps, 13 Army, West Front, captured at the end of June 1941, was accused of having collaborated with the Germans in late 1941 and serving as block leader in the Zamost camp. The charges against him included working with the Gestapo and beating other prisoners in Zamost and Hammelsburg camps. Charges were supported by fellow prisoners Maj. Generals A.A. Noskov, I.M. Gerasimov, K.L. Dobroserdov and I.M. Skugarev. The case was somewhat unusual since several junior officers had also testified against him.

Maj. General A.G. Samokhin (born 1902, in the Red Army from 1919, Party member from 1920) had been the military attaché to Yugoslavia in 1940–1941 and then head of the 2 Department in GRU. On April 21, 1942, on his way to assume the command of the 48 Army, Briansk Front, his PR–5 courier plane lost its way and was forced to land in the enemy-held Mtsensk instead of at the headquarters of the 48 Army at El'ts. Whether Samokhin managed to destroy the Stavka's orders before his capture is debatable. The future Marshal of the Soviet Union, S.I. Biriuzov, at that time Chief of Staff of the 48 Army and the future Col. General, L.M. Sandalov, Chief of Staff of the Briansk Front, claim that Samokhin's capture compromised the Soviet plans for 1942 and contributed to the failure of the summer offensive at Kharkov. According to Abakumov, Samokhin gave the enemy information about the structure of GRU and the real names of the senior officers in the General Staff such as Panfilov, Bodin, and Shevchenko. It was further stated that Samokhin seemed "insincere" during his interrogation, a characterization which probably meant a refusal to confess. Samokhin was in a particularly delicate position because of his previous employment with GRU.

Maj. General P.F. Privalov (born 1898, in the Red Army from 1918, Party member from 1919), former Commander of 15 Rifle Corps Southwest Front, was ambushed on December 22, 1942, near Kantemirovka. In March 1943, while held in prison in Kiev, Privalov volunteered to help the Germans, but in June 1943, he attempted to escape and was sent to prison in Berlin. Privalov claimed that during his interrogation his attempts to ingratiate himself were motivated by a desire to escape.

Maj. General of Aviation M.A. Beleshev (born 1900, in the Red Army from 1919, Party member from 1919), former Commander of Air Forces of the 2 Assault Army, Volkhov Front, was captured in September 1942, apparently on the ground after being surrounded and not as a result of air action. According to charges, he tried, while in prison in Vinnitsa, to join the Vlasovites but was rejected for unknown reasons. It was alleged that after giving information to the enemy about captured Soviet pilots, he was sent as an informer to Marienfeld, where Air Force prisoners were kept. According to his fellow prisoner Kombrig I.G. Bessonov in 1943, Beleshev agreed to help the Germans with the air drops behind the Soviet lines, a charge Beleshev denied. In May 1943, after attempting to escape, Beleshev was removed from his prison command and was kept in Würtsberg Fortress until liberation. Beleshev's fate remains unknown.

Maj. General (June 1940) N.K. Kirillov, born 1897, entered the old Army in 1917 and graduated from a warrant officer school. During World War I, he rose to command a Battalion. He entered the Red Army in 1920 and took part in the Civil War as a Company Commander. He joined the Party in 1930 or 1931 and then graduated from the "Vystrel" course in the Air Force Academy and rose to command a Regiment and a Division. On February 13, 1938, he became Commander of the 13 Rifle Corps, which, as a part of the 12 Army, took part in the Polish campaign. During his career, he received the Order of Red Banner and was elected to the Ukraine Supreme Soviet. Charges against him as the former Commander of the 13 Rifle Corps South Front (incorrectly listed as Southwest Front) were similar to those against Ponedelin. He was accused of having surrendered on August 7, 1941, in the Uman Pocket without offering resistance. It was claimed that he had been interviewed by the victorious German Commander Ewald von Kleist, who tried to persuade him to join the ROA; he refused. The problem with this charge is that in August 1941 there was no ROA and Vlasov was fighting in the ranks of the Red Army. Fellow prisoners Maj. Generals P.I. Abramidze, I.M. Gerasimov, I.M. Skugarev, K.L. Dobroserdov, and M.I. Potapov stated that Kirillov had not collaborated with the enemy. On October 13, 1941, the USSR Military Collegium sentenced Kirillov to death in absentia and on October 19, 1941, the Military Tribunal of the Volga Military District, instead of the usual NKVD troika, sentenced Kirillov's wife to 5 years exile in Krasnoiarsk.

Maj. General of Technical Services M.N. Sivaev (born 1891, in the Red Army and the Party from 1918), Head of Communications 24 Army, Reserve Front, was captured on November 2, 1941, and, according to Abakumov, gave the enemy secret information about Soviet railroads. Fellow prisoner Maj. General K.L. Dobroserdov also testified that in the Wolfheide camp, Sivaev was enrolled in anti-Soviet propaganda courses offered by the Germans.

Maj. General (June 1940) V.V. Kirpichnikov (born 1903), in the Red Army (1922) and Party member (1930), in August 1941, was Commander of the 43 Rifle Division, Leningrad Front. Captured by the Finns after being wounded, he was released in 1944 after the armistice. He was arrested on October 20, 1944 (another date given is May 18, 1945). According to Abakumov's charges from his report on December 21, 1945, Kirpichnikov, after his capture, had given information about his Division and other Soviet forces to the enemy. Abakumov, however, admitted that in captivity Kirpichnikov had rejected overtures from anti-Soviet POWs. Despite this, Kirpichnikov was condemned to death on October 10, 1950.

Abakumov's list at this time did not include Maj. Generals A.E. Budykho and P.V. Bogdanov, who may have collaborated during their captivity but had managed to defect to the Soviet side before the end of the war. They, along with Kombrigs I.G. Bessonov and M.V. Bogdanov and others, would also be shot in April 1950. Regardless, all the Generals who were kept in prison were expelled from the Red Army on October 26, 1946.

The case against the returning Generals shows clearly that the inspiration came from Stalin and Abakumov, as a good Chekist would go to any length to make the charges stick. These of course included the time-tried practice of obtaining testimony from one defendant against another as well as searching the pre-war records for incriminating material. Throughout his report, Abakumov refers to Vlasov and his colleagues as traitors and criminals even though these men had yet to be tried.

Abakumov was also busy on other fronts. On August 31, 1945, he wrote to GKO discussing a number of Generals who were arrested during the war, including some from the Frunze Academy who had been arrested in late 1941. This report, followed by another to Stalin on December 21, 1945, was signed by Abakumov, A.I. Antonov, and Bulganin. The trio suggested conditional release, based on future good behavior, of seven Generals: Lt. General F.S. Ivanov, Maj. Generals V.V. Semashko, I.L. Leonovich, P.V. Sysoev, and I.I. Alekseev, as well as Brigade Engineer N.A. Shaposhnikov and Engineering Captain 1 Rank V.L. Survillo. The report, however, proposed that 36 other senior officers, against whom there were more serious charges, be kept in prison and tried. This group included Lt. General of Tank Troops V.S. Tamruchi (an Armenian, misidentified by Abakumov as Russian); Lt. Generals S.A. Kalinin and I.A. Laskin (actually a Maj. General); Maj. Generals of Artillery S.A. Moshenin and E.S. Petrov; Maj. Generals of Aviation I.N. Rukhle, A.A. Turzhanskii and B.L. Teplinskii; Maj. General of Rear Services T.Iu. Rotberg; and Maj. Generals D.F. Popov, N.I. Pliusnin, F.S. Burlachko, G.A. Armaderov, A.Ia. Sokolov, F.K. Kuz'min, A.A. Veis, A.F. Bychkovskii, F.N. Romanov, R.I. Tomberg, V.A. Melikov, A.G. Shirmakher, N.I. Gapich, G.A. Burichenkov, P.G. Tsirul'nikov, I.F. Dashichev, V.S. Golushkevich, V.V. Kirpichnikov, and P.A. Gel'vikh. Also to be kept in prison and tried were Rear Admiral K.I. Samilov, Corps Commissar S.I. Mrochkovskii, Kombrigs N.F. Gus'kov and A.S. Chichkanov, Division Commissar I.I. Zhukov, Captain of 3 Rank I.I. Santpank, and Military Engineer 1 Rank A.A. Giunner. The charges varied including having known Tukhachevskii, membership in military "conspiracies," attempts to contact the enemy, service in foreign (including British) intelligence, defeatism, engaging in "disinformation" and, for a surprisingly large number, opposition to collective farms. Many of them had previous arrest records during the Great Purge. Most of the prisoners were Slavs, but there was an unusually high number of Volga Germans (Shirmakher and Gel'vikh; Veis was half-German), as well as Estonians (Rotberg, Tamberg, and Santpank), and even a Czech (Giunner). The date of arrest ranged from June 18, 1941, to May 18, 1945.

While General S.A. Kalinin was languishing in prison, his son Captain Lieutenant M.S. Kalinin, Commander of Submarine *Shch–307* in the Baltic Fleet, was awarded the title of Hero of the Soviet Union on March 6, 1945. One man, Maj. General of Artillery P.A. Gel'vikh, was 72 years old and had already been arrested in 1919, 1939, 1938, and finally 1944. All in all during the war, an estimated 43,000 members of the Armed Forces were "repressed" by the security apparatus, with SMERSH claiming a major share. At the time, Abakumov's investigation contained factual errors including incorrect listing of nationalities of officers involved, units which they had commanded, and fronts to which they were attached. The striking fact about the charges against the senior officers is not the basing of many of the alleged crimes on rumor, innuendo, and hearsay, but the almost legalistic tone used by Abakumov. His language is a far cry from the wild ludicrous charges hurled during the Great Purge against those singled out as "enemies of the people". Despite his subservience and opportunism, Abakumov was no Ezhov, and his "professionalism" in the long run proved to be a handicap in the eyes of Stalin. In psychobabble parlance, Abakumov was not "proactive" enough for Stalin. A.I. Romanov in his memoirs, *Nights Are Longest Here*, quotes various comments made more than 20 years earlier in 1945 by Abakumov about "lulling the West to sleep, corrupting them from within and driving them into dead ends, etc." These speeches (if made at all) were, however, made to rouse the troops. In his official reports, Abakumov was a bureaucrat par excellence.

In February 1945 in East Prussia the SMERSH also arrested a young officer attached to Artillery Units of the 46 Army, 2 Belorussian Front, one A.I. Solzhenitsyn, who allegedly had made remarks critical of Stalin. Solzhenitsyn's experiences as related by him and in Michael Scammell's biography were similar to those of thousands who ran afoul of SMERSH. On July 7, 1945, Solzhenitsyn was sentenced to 8 years.

In May 1946, SMERSH became part of MGB, but the name disappeared in February 1947 and its duties were taken over by the MGB/KGB 3 Department, which was responsible for counter—intelligence in the Soviet Armed Forces.

NOTES

1. *VIZH* (8/1992), p. 15.

2. *VIZH* (12/1967), p. 113.

3. V.K. Abarinov, *Katynskii Labirint,* p. 44.

4. Amy Knight, "The KGB's Special Department in the Soviet Armed Forces," *Orbis* (Summer 1984); O.F. Suvenirov, "Narkomat Oborony i NKVD v Predvoennye Gody," *Yoprosy istorii* (6/1991), p. 34.

5. *Leninaradskoe Delo*, pp. 401–02; A.M. Samsonov, *Mogkva* 1941, p. 82; Abarinov, *Katynskiia*, p. 44; A.K. and Sul'ianov, *Arestovat' v Kremle*, pp. 182–93.

6. For SMERSH, see Ia. Aizenshtat, *Zapiski Sekretaria Voennogo Tribunala*; Robert Stephan, *Death to Spies*; S.Z. Ostrlakov, *Voennye Chekisty*; *Voenny Kontarazvedchiki, SMERSH*; A.I. Romanov, *Nights Are Longest Here*; *VIZH* (1/1969), etc.

7. K. Kostliarov, *Golaofa*, p. 64.

8. Knight, *KGB's Special Department*, pp. 266–67.

9. Fitzroy MacLean, *A Person from England*, p. 63.

10. *The Penkovsky Papers*, p. 62.

11. Krystyna Kersten, *The Establishment of Communist Rule in Poland*, pp. 134–35, 154; *International Affairs* (5/1991), pp. 114–126; and Eugeniusz Eugeniusz, *General Iwanow Zaprasza*, p. 167.

12. For the circumstances of Sikorski's death, see *Sikorski: Soldier and Statesman*, pp. 167–207, and V.K. Abarinov, *Murderers of Katyn*, p. 379.

13. *Izvestiia TsK KPSS* (1/1991), p. 153 and *Kommunist* (3/1991).

14. For NKVD troops and their commanders, see *Sovestkaia voennaia entsiklopediia* and *Vnutrennie voiska v Vel. Otech. Voine 1941–1945*

15. *Leningradskoe delo*, pp. 402–03, Volkogonov (op. cit.), Book 2, Part 1, pp. 199–200, *YIZH* (12/1992), p. 19.

16. For attempts to compromise Zhukov, see K.M. Simonov, *Glazami cheloveka moeqo pokoleniia* (Moscow: 1990); *Marshal Zhukov. kakim my ego pomnim* (Moscow: 1988); G.K. Zhukov, *Vospominanii razmyshleniia* (Moscow: 1990); N.N. Iakovlev, *Stranits zhizni marshala G.K. Zhukova* (Moscow: 1985); *Marshal Zhukov. polkovodets i chelovek* (Moscow: 1988); *VIZH* (6/1987, 10/1988, 12/1988); *Krasnaia zvezda* (January 12, 1989; December 23, 1989; August 6, 1988); *Pravda* (January 20, 1989; August 17, 1991; August 19, 1991); *Kommunist* (9/1988, Issue 14, 1988) and *Voprosy istorii* (11/1990 and 2 and 3/1991).

17. For attempts to assassinate Stalin during the James Lucas, *Kommando. German Special Forces Durina the War*; Gunther Gellermann, *Moskau Ruft Heeres-Gruppe Mitte*; and S.Z. Ostriakov, *Voennye Chekisty*.

18. S.S. Biriuzov, *Surovye Gody*, pp. 237–40.

19. *Beriia: Konets Kar'ery*, p. 23; *Svenska Dagbladet* (January 22, 1993).

20. *Noetvratimoe Vozmezdie*, pp. 122–45. See also Samuel Newland, *Cossacks in the German Army. 1941–1945*, an apologia for the Cossacks.

21. Michael Glenny and Robert Stone, *The Other Russia*, p. 181.

22. *Knizhnoe Obozrenie* (October 26, 1990); Jonathan Haslam, *The Soviet Union and the Threat from the East. 1933-1941*, p. 143.

23. Joachim Hoffmann, *Kaukasien 1942-1943*, p. 98.

24. Samuel Mitcham, *Hitler's Field Marshals and Their Battles*, pp. 75–104; *Die Deutschen General-Feldmarshälle und Grossadmirale*, pp. 60–4.

25. Giles Perraut, *The Red Orchestra*, p. 467.

26. *Sovetskaia Prokuratura*, p. 125; Jost Schneider, *Verleihung Genehmigt*, p. 31.

27. *VIZH* (7/1987), p. 53.

28. Christian Streit, *Keine Kameraden: Der Wehrmacht und die Sowjetischen Kriegsgefangen 1941–1945*.

29. For captured Soviet generals, see Michael Parrish, "Soviet Generals in German Captivity," *Survey* (6/1989); E.G. Dolmatovskii, *Zelenaia Brama*; and *VIZH* (10/1992, 9/1993).

Chapter 5

The Vlasov Movement and Other Collaborators

Hitler's invasion of the Soviet Union, like most modern wars, was more than a massive movement of arms and men. It also involved attempts to subvert the enemy's economy, communications, and political will to fight. From the first day of the war, there were attempts, at least by the Wehrmacht, to recruit from masses of captured Soviet prisoners, informers, and auxiliary troops even when such policies ran contrary to Hitler's edicts. A particular target were captured senior officers, who presumably were in possession of intelligence useful to the Wehrmacht. As the Glasnost documents show, long before Vlasov was captured, there had been attempts (at times, successful) to seduce the captured officers to the German cause. The movement gained momentum once the prospect of victory began to dim, and in Vlasov it found a charismatic leader. By 1944, the need for cannon fodder even persuaded the Nazi racialists to modify their views toward the once-untermensch Slavs, and by the latter part of 1944, when it was already too late, Himmler became the main sponsor of Vlasov and his movement.[1] Himmler's desperate and opportunistic conversion, however, made more sense than the pathetic attempts by the pro-Vlasov "pragmatists" in the Wehrmacht who for years had tried to pass off a thoroughly predatory war as a campaign of liberation. A case has yet to be made that Vlasov's troops were ever engaged in serious fighting with their former comrades, and in any case, this was not their designated role. What Hitler and Himmler had in mind was using them for the messy work that their type of war demanded—mainly terror and anti-partisan fighting, preferably against fellow Slavs such as the Home Army. This was a war that was fought with utmost savagery. It is interesting to note that the Polish Home Army, which at times even took SS prisoners, would show no mercy to former Russian troops fighting in the German ranks. It is egregious nonsense to suggest that in case of Stalin's defeat, Vlasov and his ragtag army sponsored by the victorious Nazis, would have presided over a free Russia. There is little doubt that the Russians were aware of the German attempts in an area which, in fact, they later tried to imitate by setting up the Free German Committee, made up mostly of captured

senior officers and Communist emigres. There has been considerable literature about
the Vlasov movement in the West, but little other than propaganda (and even little of
that) in the Soviet Union until the Glasnost period. In recent years, there have been
a number of significant Russian publications, particularly a series of articles by L.E.
Reshin and V.S. Stepanov which appeared in various issues of *VIZH* in 1992 and
1993. The articles, based mainly on the archives of the Military Collegium of the
USSR, exemplify solid historical research and are free of the sins of omission,
commission, and obligatory propaganda which marred so much of pre-Glasnost
Soviet historical writing. The recent Russian research provides a wealth of information
about the movement as well as Vlasov's colleagues. There are also such tantalizing
vignettes as Vlasov's service in the Military Courts of the Leningrad Military District
at the height of the Great Purge and his 1938 Party report in which he was praised
for vigilance in liquidating the remnants of sabotage in his units, a fact not known or
omitted by his apologists in the West, who had presented him as a closet democrat.

One of the more interesting documents (*VIZH*, 3/1993) is a text of a report
written July 26 and 28, 1943, for SMERSH by Valsov's second wife, A. Pavlova,
the former Medical Officer in the Signals Regiment of the 37 Army commanded by
Vlasov. The Army was surrounded on September 26, 1941, during the Battle of
Kiev, but Vlasov, his wife, and a small group of companions managed to reach the
Soviet line, although not until November 1. Their desperate attempts to evade captivity
show that Vlasov was not a congenital traitor as portrayed in Soviet propaganda but
must have been deeply affected by the defeat of the Second Assault Army in May
1942. The most detailed report about the circumstances surrounding the destruction
of the 2 Assault Army and Vlasov can be found in a report dating from August 6,
1942, from Senior Major of State Security Mel'nikov, head of the Volkhov Front
Special Department, to Abakumov. The tragedy of the 2 Assault Army, which must
have played a part in Vlasov's decision to join the enemy, however, was not unique.
During the war, particularly in the first two years, many regular armies (3, 5, 10, 16,
19, 21, 22, 24, 33, and 50) and many others (some twice), all of the five Tank Armies
in their first formations (the 4 Tank, according to General P.I. Batov, was named
after the number of its tanks), the 25-odd Mechanized Corps deployed in the early
days of the war, and dozens of Rifle Divisions were decimated as part of theSoviet
strategy to trade blood for time. The new documents also provide considerable
information about Vlasov's colleagues, their various routes to collaboration, and
their attempts at the end of the war to avoid repatriation. Even more important is the
revelation for the first time that not all the collaborationist officers were tried with
Vlasov. A number were kept in the cooler and not tried until April 1950. Not only
during the war, but also after the victory, SMERSH took a deep interest in the activities
of Vlasov and his movement.

The arrest and trial of Vlasov and his colleagues were orchestrated by Abakumov,
and the interrogations were led by Maj. General A.G. Leonov, head of the SMERSH
Investigation Department, the future head of MGB's Department of Investigation of
Especially Important Cases, and finally Abakumov's co-defendant in 1954. Among
Vlasov's colleagues, Trukhin was captured on May 7, 1945, Buniachenko on May

13, Zakutnyi on June 15, and Zverev in August. Vlasov himself was captured on May 11, 1945. Three days later, he was already in Lubianka and met with Abakumov for 40 minutes. The minutes of this meeting are not available, but it apparently resulted in Leonov's ordering Mironov, head of the internal prison, to provide extra rations for prisoner no. 31 (Vlasov). This humane gesture, however, belies the fact that during their trial, Vlasov and his colleagues looked utterly worn and almost zombie-like. Vlasov was interrogated between May 16 and May 25 and on May 26, 1945, and Abakumov reported the results to Stalin, Molotov, and Beriia. On January 4, 1946, Abakumov wrote to Stalin that groundwork was being prepared to try Vlasov, Trukhin, Zakutnyi, Blagoveschenskii, Mal'tsev, Buniachenko, Zverev, Korbukov, and Shatov. Also on the list was one Kombrig M.V. Bogdanov, whom Abakumov identified as head of the ROA Artillery. Abakumov added that efforts were also being made to extradite V.F. Malyshkin and G.N. Zhilenkov from the American zone. Abakumov suggested that a trial for 12 men could start as early as January 25, 1946, and the defendants should be sentenced to death by hanging under the order issued on April 19, 1943, by the Presidium of the Supreme Soviet. There were, however, delays, and on March 27, 1946, Abakumov wrote to Stalin and Molotov that thanks to the efforts of F.I. Golikov, who was in charge of repatriation matters, Malyshkin and Zhilenkov had been returned by the Americans. On March 28, 1946, Abakumov wrote to Stalin via Zhdanov, listing the 12 men to be tried by the Military Collegium, but for some unknown reason replaced M.V. Bogdanov with Col. M.A. Meandrov (Bogdanov was not shot until April 1950). Abakumov proposed a court chaired by Ul'rikh or Maj. General of Judiciary Ievlev and also including Maj. General of Judiciary Dmitriev and Colonel (future Maj. General) of Judiciary V.V. Siul'din. Abakumov's candidate to lead the prosecution was Lt. General of Judiciary A.P. Vavilov, Deputy Chief USSR Prosecutor, who was to cooperate closely with Abakumov four years later during the "Leningrad Affair." Abakumov's selection of Siul'din was ironic since he ended up being a member of the court that sentenced Abakumov to death in December 1954. Abakumov followed his March 28 missive with another report to Stalin on April 26, this time with Ul'rikh and Vavilov proposing that the trial start on May 10, 1946, with Maj. General of Judiciary F.F. Karavaikov as Chairman of the Court. The trio also agreed to the charges against the defendant and the sentences, another example of the cooperation among investigators, prosecutors, and judges which was the hallmark of Stalinist justice. As Reshin and Stepanov point out (*VIZH*, 6/1993), Ul'rikh's reluctance to chair the court remains a mystery and was in vain since Stalin put him in charge anyway. There were, however, further delays and on July 23, 1946, the Politburo approved the indictments and sentences. The actual indictments were approved under Articles 58–1(b), 58–8, 58–9, and 59–11 of the RSFSR Code and signed by Abakumov, now as the Minister of MGB, and the Chief Military Prosecutor, Maj. General of Judiciary F.L. Petrovskii, who during the war had waged a campaign of terror as head of the Military Courts in North Caucasus. The 38-page document prepared by Leonov was presented by a court whose members were not Abakumov's original candidates. Ul'rikh was the Chairman and was assisted by Maj. General of Judiciary F.F. Karavaikov, who had originally been proposed as a Chairman, and Colonel of Judiciary G.N. Danilov. Colonels M.S. Pochitalin and A.S. Mazur were the secretaries. The trial began at 12:05 on the afternoon of July 30, 1946, and sentences were pronounced at 7:00 p.m. on July 31. The trial was held in secret and the defendants, who were denied legal assistance, confessed to their crimes against the Soviet state and asked for severe punishment. The hangings began at 2:00 a.m. on August 1, 1946, along the prison wall, and were over within a half-hour. The next day there was a brief announcement in *Pravda*. To carry out these executions, Blokhin and his men had to learn a new skill since the Supreme Soviet on April 14, 1943, had decreed hanging the appropriate measure of punishment for the "German Fascist Monsters," their Soviet assistants, as well as those guilty of espionage. Over the years, there have been rumors that the defendants were hanged by piano wire in the same manner as some of the July 20 conspirators against Hitler. Pictures reproduced in *VIZH* disprove this. Considering that several of the defendants had already been condemned to death in absentia and that the trial was going to be held in secret, the elaborate charade played by Abakumov and his colleagues makes little sense. Also, unlike the defendants in the 1930s show trials, the Vlasov group had some serious charges against them and there were grains of truth in their confessions. Under Stalin only the truly innocent confessed to preposterous charges. Regardless, the trial of Vlasov was another feather in Abakumov's cap. There is little substance to rumors that Beriia met with Vlasov in prison which are also strongly denied by S.L. Beriia in *Moi Etets*. Iu.B. Borev, in *Staliniada*, however, claims that Stalin actually met with Vlasov, and after personal interrogation, ordered him to be hanged. Borev also adds that the Vlasov movement was infiltrated by Soviet agents which included Vlasov's own chauffeur.

Who were the men who faced the court for betraying the Soviet state and collaborating with the enemy? Were they saints, disillusioned idealists, or mere opportunists who guessed wrong? We now have considerable new information about them, much of it ferreted out by Abakumov, Leonov, and their bloodhounds. These former officers of the Red Army included Lt. General A.A. Vlasov; Maj. Generals V.F. Malyshkin, F.I. Trukhin, and D.E. Zakutnyi; Maj. General of Coastal Artillery I.A. Blagoveshchenskii; and Corps Commissar G.N. Zhilenkov, whose careers will be covered in some detail. Also in the docks were former Air Force Reserve Colonel V.I. Mal'tsev, born in 1895, former head of Aerofleet Sanatorium in Yalta; Colonel (ROA Maj. General) S.K. Buniachenko, born in 1902, former Commander of the 59 Rifle Brigade and 389 Rifle Division; Colonel G.A. Zverev, born in 1900, former Commander of the 350 Rifle Division, West Front (the only senior officer from Vlasov's old command); Colonel M.A. Meandrov, born in 1894, former Deputy Chief of Staff 6 Army, Southwest Front; Lt. Colonel V.D. Korbukov, born in 1900, former Assistant Head of Signals in the 2 Assault Army, Volkhov Front; and Lt. Colonel N.S. Shatov, former Head of Artillery Supplies in the North Caucasus Military District. Their apologists to the contrary, none of these men except Vlasov had held a truly high position in the Red Army.

One member of Vlasov's entourage who did not have to face trial was the former Colonel V.I. Boiarskii (also known as V.G. Baerskii), who had been Chief of Staff of the 31 Rifle Corps from March 1941 to January 1942, and then until June 1942 was Commander of the 42 Rifle Division in the Southwest Front. He was captured during the abortive summer campaign to recapture Kharkov. Shortly after his capture on August 3, 1942, he had helped Vlasov to prepare the memorandum which provided the framework for ROA. Boiarskii was hanged on May 7, 1945, by the Czech partisans. The fate of another senior Vlasovite, the former Soviet Colonel M.M. Shapovalov, who served as a Division Commander in ROA, needs clarification.

Soviet documents indicate that former Lt. General (December 1941) A.A. Vlasov, born in 1901, in the Red Army since 1920, Party member since 1930, and winner of Orders of Lenin and Red Banner, was captured on July 12, 1942, near Liuban as Commander of the 2 Assault Army Volkhov Front. During the 1930s, Vlasov had first served in the Leningrad and Kiev Military Districts, rising to command of the 72 Rifle Division. From November 1938, for a year, he was Chief of Staff under A.I. Cherepanov of the Soviet Military Mission to nationalist China. After his return from China, Vlasov was posted to the Kiev Special Military District. His first job was to inspect the 99 Rifle Division. According to the archives (*Novaia i Noveishaia Istoriia*, 2/1993), he reported that the Commander of the Division was guilty of studying German tactics; as a result the latter was arrested and replaced by Vlasov. From December 1939, Vlasov commanded the 99 Rifle Division, one of the better units in the Red Army. In June 1940 when the rank of General was introduced in the Red Army, Vlasov received the rank of Major General. At the start of the war, Vlasov commanded the 4 Mechanized Corps in the Southwest Front, which, like similar units, was decimated by the enemy. In August 1941, Vlasov took over the 37 Army, which was soon trapped in Kiev. Stalin's belated order on September 17, 1941, for partial withdrawal of the 37 Army allowed Vlasov to escape death or captivity, the fate of some of his trapped colleagues. Considering the circumstances, Vlasov's performance as Commander of the Rearguard in Kiev was impressive. Unfortunately, the only eyewitness account by a major figure is that of Colonel (later Col. General) A.I. Rodimtsev, Commander of the 5 Airborne Brigade, who served under Vlasov. His memoirs, *Tvoi, Otechestvo, Synov'a* and *Na Beregakh Mansanaresa i Volgi*, were published inthe mid-1960s. Rodimtsev, a brave man in combat, gave a biased account of Vlasov's performance and, in fact, through what seems psychic powers, recognized in Vlasov a potential traitor. Recently released Russian documents (*Skrytaia Pravda Voiny: 1941 Gody*) show Vlasov as head of Rear Southwest Front on November 15, 1941, with A.Ia. Fominykh, the deposed former Commissar of the West Front, serving as his Political Commissar. By November 18, however, Vlasov had been replaced by Maj. General I.I. Marshalkov. After spending time on sick leave in Voronezh, on November 30, 1941, Vlasov took over the 20 Army of the West Front and fought in the Battle of Moscow. The army was deployed in the Volokolmansk direction and on December 12, 1941, re-captured Solnechnogorsk. Vlasov was promoted to Lt. General and received the Order of Red Banner. His picture, along with those of other commanders, appeared in newspapers. On a report dating from January 24, 1942, G.K. Zhukov, Commander of the West Front, praised Vlasov's leadership of the 20 Army. On March 8, 1942, he was replaced in this position by Lt. General M.A. Reiter. Later in March 1942, he became Deputy Commander of the Volkhov Front and on April 21, 1942, took over the troubled 2 Assault Army, soon to be trapped and destroyed in the abortive attempt to relieve Leningrad. The 2 Assault Army was already in trouble at the time of Vlasov's appointment, and the previous Commander Lt. General N.K. Klykov, suffering from nervous exhaustion, had to be flown out. The subject of a new commander was broached on April 16, 1942, between Commissar of the 2 Assault Army Division Commissar I.V. Zuev and Commander of the Volkhov Front Army General K.A. Meretskov, who agreed that Vlasov would be a suitable candidate. The matter was reported to Stalin, who after consulting Chief of Staff Marshal B.M. Shaposhnikov on April 20, 1942, agreed to Vlasov's appointment, but with the unusual proviso that Valsov continue to remain as Deputy Commander of the Volkhov Front.

The destruction of the 2 Assault Army was not only a military defeat, but a major tragedy. Vlasov, however, was almost alone among the senior commanders of this army in surrendering to the enemy, joined only by Lt. Colonel V.D. Korbukov, Deputy Commander of Signals. His Deputy, Maj. General P.F. Alfer'ev (former Commander of the 34 Army), went missing and presumed killed in action. The Chief of Staff, Col. P.S. Vinogradov, fell in combat. Division Commissar I.V. Zuev, the Political Commissar of the Army, and the badly wounded head of the Special Department, A.G. Shashkov, committed suicide. Division Commanders Colonels S.I. Bulanov and F.E. Chernyi also fell in combat. The Chief of Signals, Maj. General of Signal Troops A.V. Afanas'ev, joined the partisans, and the head of intelligence, A.S. Rogov, managed to break through to the Soviet side. According to Soviet documents (*VIZH*, 11/1993), another member of the Vlasov command who joined the Germans (in 1943) was Battalion Commissar Ia.A. Chugunov, Assistant Head of the Political Section (for Komsomols) of the 2 Assault, who defected back to the Soviet side in 1944, and for his efforts was sentenced to 10 years in prison under Article 58.

After his capture, Vlasov was interrogated at the headquarters of the Army Group North on July 15, 1942, and met with Col. General Georg Lindemann, Commander of the German 18 Army. He allegedly provided information about Soviet forces in Leningrad and Volkhov which may have alerted the Germans that the Soviets did not plan a major offensive in this area, and thus they could transfer forces south to Stalingrad. After spending a short time in the POW camp in Lützen, Vlasov was transferred to Vinnitsa to a camp under the direct control of OKW. Here on August 3, 1942, with the help of the former Colonel V.I. Boiarskii, he authored the memorandum about forming armed units from Soviet POWs to spearhead a "liberation movement." On August 10, Vlasov met with Gustav Hilger, the former Counselor in the German Embassy in Moscow, and in October he was transferred to Berlin and attached to the Wehrmacht's Propaganda Section. Here he also met with Malyshkin and Blagovshchenskii, who were already collaborating with the Germans. In December 1942, he met with his fellow prisoners Lt. General M.F. Lukin and Maj. Generals P.G. Ponedelin and M.G. Snegov, but nothing materialized from these meetings. In December Vlasov, with the help of Malyshkin, Wehrmacht Captain Wilfried Strik-Strikfeldt, and the mysterious figure M. Zykov (murdered probably by the Gestapo in July 1944), was behind the "Smolensk Manifesto" which laid the groundwork for the ROA. In March 16, 1943, Vlasov wrote a tract about why he had chosen to fight the Bolsheviks and in a meeting at Pskov with Field Marshal Busch, Commander of the Army Group North and man with impeccable Nazi credentials, declared that without Russian help the Germans could not defeat Bolshevism. This was not the kind of propaganda that Himmler would like to hear and Vlasov was soon under house arrest. On July 20, 1944, a meeting was scheduled between Himmler and Vlasov, but because of the attempt on Hitler's life, it was postponed to September 18. Himmler, through his Deputy, Gottlieb Berger, now took Vlasov under his wing and this, in turn, led to formation of the "Committee to Liberate the Russian People" (KONR). In November 14, 1944, the first meeting of the committee took place in Prague and Vlasov was surrounded by a motley group of anti-Bolsheviks who ranged from monarchists to crypto-fascists. The meeting, aptly called a "danse macabre" by Gerald Reitliner, was held in the shadow of the Red flood that was engulfing East Europe. It would be 50 years, long after the main actors were gone, that the stated goals of the committee were finally achieved. The committee was also being used for propaganda purposes by the Germans, and, in fact, Vlasov personally met with Geobbels in December 1944 to discuss this matter.

According to Vlasov's own testimony, until 1944 the Wehrmacht was his chief sponsor, but by September 1944 he came under the control of the SS and Himmler agreed to the forming of five Russian Divisions. Already there were a number of such units, as the 600 Russian Infantry Division, later renamed the 29 SS Division (Russian). The 650 Russian Infantry Division was now renamed 2 ROA Division and the 700 Russian Infantry Division as the 3 ROA. In December 1944, the 1 ROA Division, located in Münsingen, had on paper a force of 20,000 troops and 1,000 officers. The 2 ROA Division being formed in Hüberg had a strength of 12,000. Actually these units never came up to strength and were poorly equipped. The KONR Armed Forces Staff was not actually formed until April 28, 1945, a few days before the end of the war. In February 1945, a force of about 120 made up of students in the propaganda school and Vlasov's bodyguards were deployed on the Oder River to create confusion. A few days later, the 1604 Regiment of the 599 "Russian" Brigade, which was not part of Vlasov's forces, was also deployed, only to be taken out later and attached to the 1 ROA Division. On April 14, 1945, two regiments of the ROA 1 Division were used in fighting near Fürstenwald, only to be withdrawn after a few hours of combat, leaving behind weapons and wounded. By the end of the war, the 1 ROA Division was down to 100 heavy weapons and 12 "T–34" tanks. The Commander, S.K. Buniachenko, now usually under an alcoholic haze, moved the Division toward Prague, and here Vlasov in the beginning of May was involved in the fight between the long-dormant Czech partisans and the local last-ditch defenders of Hitler's crumbling empire. Vlasov was arrested on May 11, 1945, by the Motorized Battalion (Commander Captain I.M. Iakushev), attached to the 162 Tank Brigade, 25 Tank Corps, 3 Guard Tank Army 1 Ukraine Front, and handed over to Maj. P.T. Vinogradov, Commander of SMERSH in the 162 Tank Brigade. The place of arrest was the road between Berlin and Pilsen on the Uslav

River. On May 29, 1945, the Commander of the 25 Tank Corps, Maj. General of Tank Troops E.I. Fominykh, received the title of Hero of the Soviet Union. The commendation was for distinction in crossing of the Oder and the Berlin operation, but more likely for capturing Vlasov and personally interrogating him. The Glasnost revelations of Vlasov confirm what we already know about him—at best naive, at worst an opportunist, and at the end less than brave. Vlasov was no DeGaulle, but a tragic and flawed figure whose personal behavior including sexual proclivities, fully exploited by his captors, was not without blemish. With typical Slavic fatalism, Vlasov and his cohorts surrendered to their captors, offering no resistance and even rejecting suicide (except Zverev and Mal'tsev, who made unsuccessful attempts *after* their capture), certainly an honorable alternative to what was awaiting them in the Lubianka cellars. Vlasov told the court that he was guilty of great crimes and expected to be severely punished. The Glasnost documents provide us with detailed pictures of many of the senior officers who joined Vlasov and their torturous paths to fight Stalin under Hitler's banner.

They include Maj. General of Coastal Artillery (May 21, 1941) I.A. Blagoveshchenskii, Russian, born in 1893, who joined the Red Army in 1918 and the Party in 1921. He had been awarded the Order of Red Star and the "20th Anniversary of the Red Army" medal. At the start of the war, he was head of the Naval Anti-Aircraft School in Libau. According to his record of post-war interrogation by the SMERSH of the 2 Ukraine Front, until June 27, 1941, the students of the school were engaged in defending the north section of the city when they were ordered by the Commander of the 657 Rifle Division and the overall Commander of Libau's defense, Maj. General N.A. Dedaev (killed in action in July), to break through the enemy encirclement and join the Red Army unit in Riga. Blagoveshchenskii and a group of 300 military personnel and their families took to the road, but on the night of July 7, he and two companions, hiding in a forest near Sirava (48 miles north of Libau), were captured by the local residents and handed over to the Germans. After being kept in a local camp in Til'zitsk in early August 1941, Blagoveshchenskii was transferred to Hammelsberg. Here he gave the enemy information about the Libau Naval Base, the disposition of Baltic Fleet submarines and the destroyer *Lenin*. He also provided information about the military conditions and fortifications in the Caucasus and the anti-artillery defense of refineries in Batum. Early on, he joined the "Committee for Struggle with Bolshevism" and served in its Presidium. He and the former Maj. General F.I. Trukhin were the guiding spirits behind this organization. The committee was the creation of the 4 Branch of RHSA (Reich Main Security Office), and by February 1942 had recruited 2,000 former Soviet POWs. However, rivalries and denunciations led to its dissolution in June 1942 (Blagoveshchenskii had spoken against Kombrig I.G. Bessonov, a former NKVD functionary who was also active in the organization). In April 1942, Blagoveshchenskii found himself in Wolfheide, where he developed a course and was put in charge of a "youth school" made up of prisoners between 14 and 17 years who were being trained as saboteurs. In December 1942, he became editor of the journal *Zaria*, a propaganda publication for the Soviet POWs, and soon began living in the Star Hotel in Berlin, which also housed Vlasov and Zykov. After the formation of the "Russian Committee" chaired by Vlasov, he had his colleague V.F. Malyshkin on February 4, 1943, swore allegiance to Hitler. In March 1943, Blagoveshchenskii was appointed Head of the ROA propaganda program which enrolled more than 3,000 students. In December 1943, he was given the rank of Maj. General of ROA. Here he was responsible for the arrest of the head of training, Col. N.S. Rumanov (former Chief of Staff of 32 Army), as a Soviet agent. In December 1944, the Russian Committee was renamed the Committee to Liberate the People of Russia (KONR); and Blagoveshchenskii was put in charge of the "ideological group" and was soon awarded the "Medal for Bravery II Class," recommended by the German Liaison Officer Captain Strik-Strikfeldt and approved by Malyshkin. In February 4, 1945, because of the advance of the Red Army, KONR moved from Berlin to Coblenz and after a few days, the propaganda section was transferred to Marienbad. In March, Vlasov ordered Blagovshchenskii to contact the Americans for possible granting of political asylum to the leaders of the KONR. On May 6, 1945, American authorities in Marienbad arrested Blagovshchenskii. On June 3, 1945, Soviet officers arranged for his transfer from a local hotel to a repatriation camp, but on the way out, the SMERSH arrested him. In court, Blagoveshchnskii claimed in vain that he had joined the Vlasov movement to subvert it from within.

Brigade Commissar N.G. Zhilenkov, Russian, born in 1910, had joined the Party in 1929 and the Red Army in 1941 and had won the Order of Labor Red Banner. Before the war, he had served as Party Secretary in the Rostokinskii sector of Moscow and as a member of the city's Party Committee. With the start of the war, he had been appointed the Commissar of the 32 Army, West Front. According to Zhilenkov, on October 7, 1941, he tried to escape through the enemy lines but on October 14 was captured near Volostopiatnits. Perhaps aware of Hitler's "Commissar Order," he passed himself off as one Maksimov, a common soldier, and began to serve as a driver for the German 252 Infantry Division and even organized an underground group made up of other captured Russian drivers which even carried out subversive acts. In May 1942, he was found out after an explosion in the Czatsk ammunition dump; under torture he revealed his real name and agreed to cooperate with the Germans. After interrogation by the officers of the Army Group Center, Zhilenkov was shipped to the camp at Lützen and met with Col. Von Roenne, who assigned him to the propaganda section and made him editor of publications and leaflets that were dropped behind the Russian lines. In August 1942, Zhilenkov was sent to Osintorf (50 miles from Smolensk) and here joined the Russian People National Army Brigade (RHHA) which included many White Russian émigré officers, such as S.N. Ivanov (future Head of ROA Intelligence), I.K. Sakharov (son of the Tsarist General Sakharov who had also been Kolchak's Chief of Staff as well as a participant on the nationalist side during the Spanish Civil War, and finally as a Colonel in ROA and Vlasov's Adjutant), K.G. Kromiadi (former Colonel in the Tsarist Army and future head of Vlasov's personal secretariat). Shortly after, a former Soviet officer, Colonel V.I. Boiarskii, captured as recently as June 1942 as Commander of the 41 Rifle Division, was appointed Head of the RHHA. In October

1942, Zhilenkov and Boiarskii wrote a report advocating combining the People's Liberation Committee and the ROA. Already by the summer of 1943, they were also involved in sending saboteurs behind the Red Army lines.

By December 1942, Field Marshal von Kluge, the Commander of the Army Group Center, had ordered the deployment of two battalions of RHHA troops near Berezino to fight the partisans. Shortly afterward, the entire contingent (1,500 troops) was deployed near Veliki Luki to help break through to the surrounded German forces. The Russian auxiliaries, however, deserted to the partisans. Zhilenkov and Boiarskii blamed this on lack of experience but were put under arrest, only to be released shortly after. Zhilenkov was now transferred from the Wehrmacht to Vlasov's Russian Committee and was engaged in propaganda work including serving as the Chief Editor of the newspaper *Dobrovolets*. In February 1943, Vlasov, Zhilenkov, Malyshkin, and Blagoveshchenskii suggested forming a Russian National Army (RNA) to the Germans. In April 1943, Zhilenkov took part in organizing the ROA Guard Assault Brigade, sponsored by the RSHA, which was then renamed the 1 SS Russian National Brigade and finally the ROA Guard Assault Brigade. It was put under Gil-Rodinov, who will be discussed later in some detail in relation to the career of Maj. General P.V. Bogdanov. The Brigade deserted to the partisans, and Zhilenkov returned to propaganda work. In February 1944, Zhilenkov met with Field Marshal von Rundstedt about the use of two battalions of "Eastern" troops in building the Atlantic Wall. In June 1944, Zhilenkov was in Lvov helping the staff of "Scorpion," a propaganda organization under Himmler. He also organized a new publication, *Za Mir i Svobodu*, which was dropped behind the Red Army lines. Zhilenkov's efforts impressed Himmler, who agreed to Zhilenkov's suggestion to form the Committee to Liberate the People of Russia and meet with Vlasov to discuss the matter. During September and October 1944, Zhilenkov, Vlasov, Malyshkin and Zakutnyi worked to form the "KONR," which was approved by Himmler. The result was the already discussed conference in Prague. Zhilenkov was appointed the Head of KONR's main propaganda administration. In March 1945, Zhilenkov left for the southern part of Germany to an area between Salzburg and Innsbruck, where he tried to contact the U.S. forces. On April 19, 1945, he was in northern Italy trying to join some Cossack troops, who were escaping from Tito's partisans.

On May 3, 1945, the U.S. forces captured the area, and on May 18, Zhilenkov was arrested. On May 26, 1945, Zhilenkov and Malyshkin came into contact with U.S. intelligence. On January 7, 1946, Zhilenkov found himself in a camp for repatriation, and here he was interrogated by one Lt. Maxim, who represented U.S. Intelligence. On May 1, 1946, he was returned to the USSR. On July 31, 1946, Zhilenkov informed his interrogators that he was in possession of information about Germany's atomic energy program, but this did not save him from being sentenced to death. His last words were that if the court spared him, he would be ready to serve the nation.

Maj. General (June 1940) D.E. Zakutnyi was born in 1897; he joined the Red Army in 1918 and the Communist Party a year later. In July 1941, he took over the Command of the 21 Rifle Corps, attached to the 4 and 13 Armies of the West Front, after the Commander, Maj. General V.B. Borisov, was killed. On July 26, 1941, the staff of the Corps was surrounded near Malaia Zimnitsy in Gomel oblast and Zakutunyi was taken prisoner. He was taken to a corps headquarters of the 2 Army (Army Group Center), where he claimed that he was told that other Soviet senior officers, such as Lt. General of Engineering D.M. Karbyshev, had also been taken prisoner. German documents, however, show that he volunteered this information to his captors and identified Karbyshev as one of the prisoners. Zakuntnyi was later transferred to Lodz and in November 1941 to Hammelsberg, where he apparently indicated his disaffection with the Soviet system and interest in an alternative government sponsored by the Germans. Here he also began contact with the German intelligence services. On October 30, 1941, Zakutnyi was transferred to Camp Lichtenfeld, near Berlin, where French POWs were housed. Here he provided the Germans with information about the fortified areas as well as Red Army regulations. In March 1942, he was in Zittenhorst, a camp run by Rosenberg's Ministry, where cadres were being trained to serve in the occupied territories. In January 1943, he was in a new camp in Wüstrau, and a month later he joined the "Vineta" special organization, which prepared propaganda material for the occupied territories. In August 1944, Zakutnyi was transferred to Vlasov's command and soon became the Head of KONR's "Civil Affairs" program. In April 1945, Vlasov put him in charge of political training in KONR, and he moved to Füssen. The city was captured by the U.S. forces and Zakutnyi was arrested by the military police but was soon released. He was re-arrested on May 20 and was repatriated on June 13, 1945. He asked the court to give him another chance to serve the country.

Maj. General (October 7, 1941) V.F. Malyshkin was born in 1896, in the Red Army from 1918, a Party member from 1919, and winner of the Order of Red Banner. He had been arrested in 1938 and spent fourteen months in prison. In October 1941, he was the Chief of Staff of the 19 Army, West Front, that was surrounded. Attempts to break through the encirclement on October 12 failed, and Soviet Commanders, including the badly wounded Commander of the 19 Army Lt General M.F. Lukin, tried to escape in small groups to Mozhaisk. Malyshkin, in civilian clothes, however, tried to escape in the direction of Gzhatsk but was taken prisoner on October 24, 1941. In captivity, he claimed to be one Volodin, a soldier in a construction battalion. He was first taken to a camp near Viazma, but in the beginning of November, he was transferred to the Smolensk camp for POWs. In January 1942, he was in Fürstenberg camp, where he came in contact with the Abwehr. In April, he was in Wolfheide as a student and later as an instructor in a propaganda course. In December 1942, Malyshkin was transferred to Berlin and attached to the Wehrmacht Propaganda Section. He also met with Vlasov and was involved in the formation of the German-sponsored Russian Committee whose members included B.G. Men'shagin, the former Mayor of Smolensk mentioned elsewhere in this book. Men'shagin's presence gave the impression that the committee was a Russian rather than a German creation. In May 1943, Malyshkin organized a conference devoted to the training of anti-Soviet propagandists. The conference was said to have taken place in Smolensk but was actually held in Dabendorf. In July 1943, Captain Strik-Strikfeldt, the German Liaison

Officer, sent Malyshkin to Paris to contact various émigré groups. On July 24, he made a speech in behalf of the liberation movement. In March 1944, he returned to France and spoke to various Eastern legions and construction workers deployed on the Atlantic Wall, urging them to resist the invasion. In KONR, Malyshkin ran the Organization Department and was also the Financial Officer. Through him, the Germans dispersed funds. He was also in control of the Security Branch, which was run by Lt. Colonel Tenzorov (real name, N.V. Vetlugin). In March 1945, KONR moved to Karlsbad and Malyshkin tried to form armed units to be deployed in the Tyrols. On April 20 in Fürst, he made his first contact with American and British forces, and on April 29, he met with General Patch, Commander of the U.S. 10 Army, and explored the possibility of political asylum for members of KONR. Instead, Malyshkin was moved to the U.S. POW camp at Augsberg, where Zhilenkov was already held.

Here the two men volunteered their services and on October 2, 1945, in Obersül camp (12 miles from Frankfurt), along with a number of other Vlasovite Commanders, provided U.S. Intelligence with information about the Red Army command and training system. On March 27, 1946, Abakumov informed Molotov and Stalin that through the efforts of F.I. Golikov, who headed the repatriation teams, Maylshkin was now in Soviet hands, the transfer having taken place the day before near Eisenach. Abakumov added that Zhilenkov had also been returned, and in fact, SMERSH had been trailing the two men since September 1945. Abakumov also informed Stalin that with the entire Vlasov High Command now in Soviet hands, he was proceeding in accordance with Stalin's order. Material about Vlasov and his movement was now also being forwarded to Zhdanov, and steps were also being taken to bring 11 of the ringleaders, including Malyshkin, to justice. In his last words to the court, Malyshkin admitted that he was guilty of major crimes and expected severe punishment. According to Volkogonov, when Beriia informed Stalin that Malyshkin had been arrested in 1938 only to be released, Stalin ordered an investigation of those who had petitioned in Malyshkin's behalf. Maj. General F.I. Trukhin, Head of the Operations Section of the Northwest Front, had joined the Red Army in 1918 but had never been a Party member. He was the winner of the Order of Red Banner. Testimony of his former driver, A.G. Mudrov, on October 31, 1942, indicated that on June 27, 1941, the car in which Trukhin, his adjutant, and another soldier were riding was ambushed by German armor. During the attempt to escape, Trukhin's companions were killed and Mudrov was injured in the leg. The two sought refuge in a forest but were separated. In Trukhin's own words, he chose to surrender to German tanks. After interrogation by the staff of a corps, he arrived on June 30, 1941, in the POW camp in Stahlup, but after a few days he was transferred to Hammelsberg. In September 1941, Trukhin joined the Russian Workers Party formed by one Mal'tsev, who before his capture had served as a prosecutor in the 100 Rifle Division. The Party had about 200 members who were allowed to work outside the camp and received extra rations. Trukhin worked in the Military Branch of this Party and spoke of forming a Russian National Army made of POWs. His appeal was later used by the Germans to encourage desertion among Soviet troops. In

November 1941, Trukhin was in Wahl POW camp where he met with officials of Rosenberg's Ministry for the Eastern Territories. In May 1942, he was appointed Head of Camp in Zintenhorst, where freed Soviet POWs were trained to help the Germans in the occupied territories, but he did not actually take over. Instead, he was appointed as instructor in an intelligence school in Warsaw. In September 1942, he returned to Zintenhorst, first as an instructor and later as a senior teacher. In March 1943, he met with Vlasov and Malyshkin and familiarized Vlasov with the propaganda campaigns of the German Army. Trukhin now formed a special propaganda battalion and shortly afterward was teaching a course and heading the Propaganda Section in Dabenford. He now received the rank of ROA Maj. General, although with a salary of only 280 marks a month, the same amount paid a German Corporal.

In November 1944, Trukhin was in Berlin taking an active part in the formation of KONR. A month later, he was appointed Chief of Staff of the KONR Armed Forces. Actually, the formation of the latter was not announced until January 28, 1944, and Trukhin's appointment was not officially announced until April 28, 1945. In the KONR journal, *Volia Naroda*, on November 18, 1944, Trukhin wrote that soldiers and officers of KONR under the leadership of Lt. General A.A. Vlasov would fight against the Red Army to liberate the Russian people from Bolshevism. As Reshin and Stepanov observe, it is difficult to understand how Trukhin, who in the 1930s had taught higher tactics in the General Staff Academy, failed to notice the desperate military situation of his sponsors at this late date. Besides his duties as Chief of Staff, Trukhin was also involved in organizing KONR's intelligence services. In April 1945, Trukhin came in contact with Anglo-American forces, and on May 4, 1945, he sent two emissaries, Artsezov and Pozdniakov, to explore the possibilities of political asylum for KONR leadership, a request that was rejected by the Allies although they were willing to accept them as prisoners. On May 7, 1945, Trukhin was captured by the Red Army units near Prizhibr. Facing the court, he admitted to all heinous crimes of which he was accused and his readiness for well-deserved punishment. Until recently, it was thought that the Vlasov high command who were tried with him in August 1946 constituted the extent of collaboration between captured senior Soviet officers and the enemy.

There are, however, others, each with his own checkered past. As noted, Abakumov replaced one of them, M.V. Bogdanov, with M.A. Meandrov for the trial. In the case of the senior collaborator, I.G. Bessonov, Abakumov had good reason to keep him in the cooler, since before the war Bessonov had been a senior officer in the Border Troops. Regardless, the other collaborators were kept in prison for nearly 5 years before being dragged to the Military Collegium in April 1950 (a month that proved as deadly for the Red Army senior officers as October 1941) and sentenced to death. The collaborationist Generals were the following: Maj. General P.V. Bogdanov, born in 1900, was in the Red Army since 1918 and a Party member since 1931. Bogdanov had been expelled from the Party in January 1938. At the end of 1938, Bogdanov was appointed Chief of Staff of 67 Rifle Division and in August 1939 Commander of 48 Rifle Division. In June 1940, he received the rank of Maj. General. In the beginning of the war, his unit was attached to the 11 Rifle Corps, 8 Army Northwest Front. He was captured on June 25, 1941. According to charges against him, Bogdanov approached German intelligence as early as July 17, 1941, and nine days later he fingered a number of captured Political Commissars who were duly shot. In Berlin and in the Wolfheide camp, Bogdanov closely cooperated with the enemy, joining various German sponsored organizations. In December 1942, he joined the 2 Russian SS Detachment and in January 1943 was appointed Deputy Chief of Staff. In 1943, after the formation of the 1 SS Russian Regiment (later a brigade of nearly 3,000 men), Bogdanov, now a Major, became the Head of the regiment's counterintelligence. In April 1943, he was promoted to Maj. General, surely an unusually high rank for a man in such a lowly position. Bogdanov, at first, was a close collaborator, ordering the execution of a number of men suspected of attempting to cross over to the Soviet Union. The Brigade was commanded by the Lt. Colonel V.V. Gil-Rodinov, the former Chief of Staff of the 29 Rifle Division. Doublecross was the rule in such units and on August 14 or 16, 1943, the Brigade murdered their German officers and went over to the Soviet partisans. Gil-Rodinov, who was killed later while fighting on the Soviet side, arrested Bogdanov and turned him over to the SMERSH on August 20, 1943. Despite the serious charge against him, Bogdanov was not tried until April 24, 1950, when he was sentenced to death.

Kombrig I.G. Bessonov, born in 1905, in the Red Army from 1920, and a Party member from 1932, had served in the Border Troops from 1930 until April 1941. During 1939–1940, he was the head of training for NKVD Border and Internal Troops. On July 5, 1941, he was appointed Chief of Staff of the 102 Rifle Division, 21 Army, Central Front, where he took part in fighting in the failed attempts to recapture Zhlobin and Rogachev. On August 21, 1941, the Commander of the Division, Col. P.M. Gudz', was arrested (later released) and replaced by Bessonov, who may have been involved inintrigue against his commander. On August 26, 1941, Bessonov became a prisoner. He spent time in camps in Gomel, Bobruisk, and Minsk before ending up in Hammelsberg in November 1941. In January 1942, Bessonov was attached to the Historical Branch of the German Army, and in April of the same year, he became part of the "Zitadel" organization, which was involved in sabotage on the Eastern Front including the dropping of agents near labor camps to liberate and arm the prisoners. In fact, on June 2, 1943, a drop was made in Komi ASSR but was frustrated by the NKVD. There was also an attempt late in 1942 to compromise A.M. Vasilevskii by a forged letter that was to be planted for SMERSH. Bessonov was also approached but refused to join the Vlasov movement, since he felt that he had a higher rank than Vlasov. In May 1943, Bessonov was allegedly responsible for the death of POWs who had tried to escape. Early in June 1943, SD arrested Bessonov and he was placed in the A Block of the Sachsenhausen camp, where he remained until April 1945. In May, he was evacuated to Dachau, Flossenberg, and Innsbruck camps. Freed by U.S. troops on May 15, 1945, Bessonov asked not to be returned to the USSR. For a time, he was held in the same camp as Lt. Ia.I. Dzhugashvili, Stalin's son, and in his secret report to Kruglov dating from

September 14, 1946 (*Iosif Stalin v. Ob'iatiiakh Sem'i*), I.A. Serov discusses Bessonov and his collaboration with the enemy. After spending nearly 5 years in prison, Bessonov was tried and was sentenced to death on April 19, 1950.

Maj. General A.E. Budykho was born in 1893 and joined the Red Army in 1918 and the Party a year later. During his career, he was awarded the Order of the Red Banner. In the beginning of the war, he commanded the 171 Rifle Division on the Southwest Front, which fought with distinction. Budykho was wounded on September 23 and 26, 1941, and was replaced by his Chief of Staff. On October 22, 1941, Budykho was among a small group of men who fell into enemy hands in Belgorod. After spending time in a camp in Poltava, he finally ended up at the end of June 1942 in the Hammelsberg camp, where he met with the aforementioned Bessonov and joined the German-sponsored Political Center for Struggle with Bolshevism. During February to May 1943, he served as head of the counter-intelligence. Later, he volunteered to join the ROA, but nothing came of this, although he spent some time in the Lützen camp from September 13, 1943 where ROA had a training facility. Here Budykho received the rank of Maj. General and was attached to the Russian "Hiwi" (auxiliary) units serving with the German 16 Army. On October 10, 1943, in the Solentskii region of the Leningrad oblast, a major part of these units defected to Soviet partisans. On October 12, 1943, Budykho and other officers captured some weapons, managed to escape, and on October 19, joined the 1 Leningrad partisan brigade. On November 7, 1943, Budykho was arrested and on November 23 was first interrogated by SMERSH. According to Volkogonov, the text of Budykho's interrogation, which included the visit by Vlasov's representative Zhilenkov, was forwarded to Beriia, who passed it on to Stalin. On April 19, 1950, after more than 6 years in prison, he was tried and condemned to death by the Military Collegium despite his pleas that he and Bessonov had cooperated with the enemy so they could get close to the front lines and escape to the Soviet side.

Maj. General A.Z. Naumov, born in 1891, joined the Red Army in 1918 and the Party in 1925. A Maj. General since June 1940, at the start of the war Naumov was Commander of the 13 Rifle Division, 5 Corps, 10 Army, West Front, which was badly smashed in the Battle of Belostok, resulting in the disappearance of the Corps Commander Maj. General A.V. Garnov. The 13 Division, under heavy attack by enemy aviation, was deployed on the left bank of the Narva and on the night of June 26 received the order to withdraw, which turned into a rout. Surrounded by the enemy, the division ceased to exist, but some of the personnel, including Naumov, managed to escape in small groups. Naumov, in civilian clothes, managed to hide in Minsk with his wife but was arrested on October 18, 1941. He spent time in Minsk prison, where he apparently decided to work for the enemy. In April 1942, Naumov was first transferred to a POW camp in Lithuania and then to Hammelsberg, where he was interviewed by Gustav Hilger, the former Counsellor in the German Embassy in Moscow (Hilger's memoirs are silent on this point). On September 24, 1942 Naumov wrote to the camp commander of the existence of Soviet agents among the POWs who were working against those prisoners who wanted to free their country from the Bolsheviks. Among them, he named Maj. Generals I.M. Shepetov and

I. Tonkonogov, Maj. General of Aviation G.I. Tkhor, Col. Prodimov and Lt. Col. Novodarov. The only member of this group to survive was Tonkonogov. In October 1942, Naumov joined the Todt organization and was put in charge of a construction unit near Berlin butwas later transferred to a marshy area near Borisov. In May 1943, a number of workers tried to escape and Naumov was removed from command and was transferred to a camp near Lodz which also housed his wife. In October 1944, they were transferred to Berlin, where they were employed in a Klaus textile factory. On July 23, 1945, Naumov was arrested by SMERSH. After nearly 5 years in prison, on April 19, 1950, Naumov was sentenced to death by the Military Collegium. In his last words to the court, he admitted that he was guilty, but he also claimed to the court that he was not an enemy of Soviet power.

Kombrig M.V. Bogdanov, born in 1897, had joined the Red Army in 1919 but had never been a Party member. In August 1941, he was Commander of the Artillery in 8 Rifle Corps, which was surrounded in the Uman pocket. On August 7, 1941, plans were worked out to break through Soviet lines by tanks in one of which rode Commander of the Corps Maj. General M.G. Snegov. The plan failed and Snegov was captured. In his absence, the Chief of Staff of the Corps, Col. Bobrov, organized small groups who would try to escape. Bogdanov and two others moved in a southeast direction, but on August 8 his companions were captured even though he managed to escape detection. On August 10 while hiding in a forest, Bogdanov was captured and was taken to a German division headquarters where the Commander informed him that his colleagues Maj. Generals Ponedelin and Kirillov had also been captured. Bogdanov was not cooperative during his interrogation and was eventually transferred on April 6, 1942, to Hammelsberg POW camp. Here Bogdanov worked on the history of the 8 Rifle Corps and provided the Germans with information about the operations of the Southwest Front during the Kiev campaign. On November 5, 1942, the Todt organization came to the camp and on November 18, Bogdanov and 120 other POWs were hired and moved to an area near Berlin. Shortly afterward, Bogdanov was put in charge of training in the Higher Russian-German school for specialists which provided skilled Russian labor to work for military construction in the German occupied areas. In June 1943 while serving in this unit, Bogdanov managed to make secret contact with one Maj. of State Security I.G. Pastukhov, who claimed to be a Soviet representative with the local partisans. Pastukhov suggested that Bogdanov join the ROA and assassinate Vlasov. He also asked Bogdanov about Soviet POW officers who were active in the resistance movement in camps, and Bogdanov named Lt. General of Engineering Troops D.M. Karbyshev, who was eventually murdered. Post-war testimony of other returning Soviet POWs who had had similar offers made it clear that the alleged Soviet agent in fact was an "agent provocateur" and apparently Bogdanov was aware of this. On August 30, 1943, Bogdanov met with Vlasov in Berlin. The two men had known each other since Vlasov's 99 Rifle Division had at one time been a part of the 8 Rifle Corps. Bogdanov testified after the war that Vlasov had told him that the war would be over in 1946 with an armistice because of losses suffered on both sides and Vlasov, in command of a powerful Russian liberation army, would be in a position to dictate his own terms. Bogdanov made no attempt to harm Vlasov. In 1943 he became the deputy head of the Russian construction units attached to the Todt organization that were deployed in the rear of the Army Group Center. In October 1943, the unit was disbanded. In October 1943, Bogdanov joined a special propaganda unit of Vlasov's ROA and in November an inspection unit commanded by the Vlasovite Maj. General I.A. Blagoveshchenskii, now receiving the salary of a German junior officer. After this, Bogdanov also met with POW I.V. Evstifeev, who had also been approached by the bogus partisan leader with the suggestion to assassinate Vlasov. On December 1, 1944, Bogdanov became a Maj. General, and at the end of December 1944, Bogdanov was appointed Head of the Artillery in the staff of KONR Heiberg camp, where the 650 Russian Infantry and the 2 ROA Divisions were also located. In May 1945, the units were moved to the Salzburg-Innsbruck area and Bogdanov tried to contact the Czech partisans without success. He was captured on May 10, 1945, and put under arrest on May 18, 1945. As previously stated, for reasons unknown Abakumov decided not to have him tried with the Vlasov group, replacing him with Colonel M.A. Meandrov and thus allowing Bogdanov to survive for nearly four more years. On April 19, 1950, he was sentenced to death by the Military Collegium. He told the court that he had received a task (killing Vlasov) that he could not carry out since the job was too much for one man and he had no help.

In interrogation by SMERSH on February 18, 1946, Kombrig A.N. Sevast'ianov claimed first that he joined the old army as an Artillery officer and studied in the Mikhailov Artillery School and the Artillery Academy. In 1915, he was sent to the front and reached the rank of Staff Captain and was awarded a number of medals. In 1918, he joined the Red Army and at first served as the Head of Artillery in the 2 Rifle Division before serving in the Artillery Administration of the Moscow Military District. Later interrogations and examination of archives proved that Sevast'ianov was actually born in 1887 in a salesman's family, had graduated from a commercial school in 1905 and was employed in a trade firm in Moscow. In 1915, he joined the Army and served as a gunner in the 64 Artillery Brigade. On February 17, 1916, he received a Gregory Cross 4th degree and two months later became a commissioned officer, but the latter claim proved to be incorrect. In 1918, he entered the Red Army and was demobilized in 1922. From 1922, he worked as an accountant. In 1924, speculation with gold led to a two month suspension. In 1927 he received a 7-year sentence for embezzlement. In the beginning of the war, Sevast'ianov managed to pass himself off as an artillery specialist and was appointed Commander of Artillery of the 266 Rifle Division as a Captain, but was promoted to Kombrig by Maj. General of Artillery N.S. Fomin, Commander of the Artillery of the 21 Army. The 266 Rifle Division formerly from the Moscow Military District entered combat on August 18, 1941, and Sevat'ianov was captured on September 18, 1941. In his first interrogation, however, he claimed that when the 21 Army was encircled in September 1941 (at a time when he was already a POW), the Commander Lt. General V.I. Kuznetsov promoted him to Maj. General. After arriving in a POW camp where he passed himself off as a General, Sevast'ianov and a group of officers were sent to Vladimir-Volyneskii camp, then in April 1942 to Stalag "ZA;" in July he was in the Wolfheide camp, where he attended a propaganda course. In August 1942, he was transferred to the Hammelsberg camp where he took an active part in the Historical Study office. In November, Sevat'lianov joined the Todt organization and became the head of the Higher Russian-German School for Specialists (Volga). In June 1943, the other members of Volga were behind the German lines, helping to build fortifications, but soon they were recalled and, with the notorious Kaminskii Brigade formed the nucleus of the 29 SS (Russian) Division, and later the 650 (Russian) Infantry Division, which was eventually re-formed as the 1 ROA Division. After the dissolution of Volga on Oct. 20, 1943, Sevat'lianov joined the ROA as a Maj. General and was appointed head of the officers' propaganda school. From April 1944, he was in an inspection group whose aim was to persuade the Russian POWs to join the ROA. In Oct. 1944, he was attached to the ROA General Staff in charge of "materiale support." At the end of April 1945, the staff of ROA found itself in the village of Rossbach near the Czech border and attached to the 2 ROA Division. On May 3, 1945, contacts were made with U.S. forces and Sevat'lianov managed to make his escape; he was not repatriated until Feburary 15, 1946. He was tried on February 10, 1947, by the Military Collegium and sentenced to death despite his plea of old age; the sentence was carried out on March 10, 1947. As the authors of the *VIZH* series point out, Sevast'ianov was an unusual case—a common criminal who passed himself off as a General in the Red Army and ROA. There were, however, several other senior ROA officers such as the former Brigade Commissar G.N. Zhilenkov and Colonels Boiarskii, Shapovalov and Artsezov who ended up as ROA Generals without having had this rank while serving in the Red Army.

There were also two Generals against whom SMERSH had strong cases who could not be found. Maj. General M.B. Salikhov, a Tatar born in 1896, had served in the Kolchak Army from May to November 1919 before switching sides and joining the Red Army in 1919 and the Party a year later. In 1935, he received the rank of Colonel, and in June 1940 that of Maj. General. In April 1940, he was appointed Commander of the 60 Alpine Division in the Kiev Special Military District. The war started poorly for Salikhov. On July 29, 1941, the Military Tribunal of the South Front sentenced him to ten years in prison, but it was set aside and he was demoted to Colonel and appointed to command the 980 Regiment in the 275 Rifle Division. There is evidence, however, that he may have returned to command the 60 Alpine Division. He took part in fighting near Dnepropetrovsk in the ranks of the 12 Army, South Front, and disappeared in action. He was officially declared missing in January 1942. On June 6, 1942, a captured German agent in the sector of the 3 Assault Army informed SMERSH that Salikhov was working for the enemy under the assumed name "Osmanov." Other enemy agents captured elsewhere confirmed this, and finally one individual interrogated on March 3, 1943, stated that Salikhov had been employed by the Germans in the Vladimir-Volynskii camp near Warsaw since May 5, 1942, training saboteurs to be used against the Soviet Union. Criminal charges against Salikhov were filed on May 12, 1943, and on June 20, 1943, the Military Collegium under Ul'rikh sentenced him to death in absentia and confiscation of property, but Salikhov could not be found after the war.

Maj. General B.S. Rikhter was born in 1898. From the nobility, he had served as a junior officer in the Tsarist Army, taking part in World War I on the Southwest Front. He had joined the Red Army in June 1918 and had fought during the Civil War against Antonov. He had an excellent record in the peacetime army, graduating from both the Frunze and General Staff Academies. He joined the Party in 1928 and was promoted to Colonel in 1935, but his suspect background probably prevented him from receiving more senior commands. At the start of the war, he was Chief of Staff of the 6 Rifle Corps, 6 Army, Southwest Front. Post-war testimony by the army Commander Lt. General I.N. Muzychenko and the Corps Commander I.I. Alekseev, both also POWs, indicated that Rikhter had been reported missing on June 27 or June 28, 1941, near Rava-Russkaia in the vicinity of Lvov. On August 28, 1941, Rikhter was officially declared missing in action. Captured enemy agents in 1942–1943, however, indicated the presence of a former Soviet senior officer who used the name of Rudaev in a German-sponsored school near Warsaw that trained saboteurs against the Soviet Union. The officer was identified as a former Chief of Staff of an Army and a Corps and used the same first and middle name as Rikhter. Further documents found by SMERSH on December 18, 1942, and the correct identification of Rikhter's picture by the captured enemy agents convinced the Soviet authorities that he was a traitor. On June 21, 1943, the Military Collegium condemned him to death in absentia and to confiscation of property, but Rikhter could not be found after the war. In 1965, the USSR Chief Military Prosecutor, Lt. General of Judiciary A.M. Gornyi, found further evidence that Rudaev and Rikhter were the same person, but doubts persist. The captured German documents in the National Archives and the CIA records do not contain material about Salikhov and Rikhter except a reference in the SS documents about Salikhov's capture.

The mass of Vlasovite troops who fell into Soviet hands naturally ended up in the Gulag. What is striking, however, is the fact that on January 1, 1953 of over 2.7 million prisoners held in the Gulag, only 56,000 were classified as "Vlasovites."

NOTES

1. Besides the articles by Reshing and Stepanov, there are recently published books in Russia on the Vlasov movement including: A.N. Kolesnik,*V Roa Vlasvoskaia armii* (Kharkov: 1990) and *General Vlaspv-predatel' ili geroi* (Moscow: 1991). Other books and articles on Vlasov and his movement include: V.V.Pozdniakov, *Andrei Andreevich Vlasov* (Buenos Aires: 1973), *Po dorogam Kitaia, 1937–1945, vospominaniia* (Moscow: 1989), *Bitva pod Moskvoi* (Moscow: 1989), *Leninaradskii Universitet* (No. 21, 1989); Catherine Andreyev, *Vlasov and the Russian Liberation Movement* (New York: 1987); Gerald Reitlinger, *The House Built on Sand* (New York: 1960), *American Intelliaence Journal* (Spring 1990), *New York Review of Books* (November 24, 1988); A.Ia. Kaliagin, *Po neznakomym dorogam* (Moscow: 1969), English translation *Along Alien Roads* (New York: 1983), *Komsomol'skaia pravda* (March 3, 1988), *VIZH* 1/1965, 6/1990, 4/1991, 2/1992, 8/1992), *Literaturnaia aazeta* (No. 37, 1989), *Smena* (August 27, 1989), *Novoe vremia* (No. 43, 1990), *Ogonek* (No. 46, 1990); A.M. Samsonov, *Moskva. 1941 god* (Moscow: 1991); Leopold Trepper, *The Great Game* (New York: 1977); A. Kiselev, *Oblik generala a.a. Vlasova* (New York: 1980), *Radio Liberty*

(December 28, 1990); B.I. Dvinov, *Vlasovskoe dvizhenie* (New York: 1950); G.A. Aronson, *Pravda vlasovstakh problemy novoi emigratsii* (New York: 1950); George Fisher, *Soviet Opposition to Stalin*, (Cambridge, MA: 1952), *Sovetskii voin* (Issue 20, 1989), *Znanie-sila* (4/1989), *Sobesednik* (No. 52, 1987), *Novvyi zhurnal* (No. 129, 1977 and No. 157, 1981), *Sovestkaiia Rossiia* (August 12, 1987), *VIZH* (6/1990); Joachim Hoffmann, *Die Geschichte der Wlassow-Armee* (Freiburg, Germany: 1984), *Verkhovny sud SSSR* (Moscow: 1974); V. Osokin, *Andrei Andreevich Vlasov* (New York: 1966), *Military Affairs* (4/1982); Boris Pliushchov, *General Mal'tsev* (New York: 1982), *Na Volkhovskom fronte. vospominaniia veteranov* (1978), *Na Volkhovskom fronte 1941–1944* (1982), *Vtoraia udarnaia v bitve za Leninarad* (Moscow: 1983); A.I. Rodimtsev, *Na beregakh Mansanaresa i Volgi* (1966), and *Tvoi, Otechestvo, Synov'ia* (1966); D.A. Volkogonov, *Triumf i tragediia* (Moscow: 1989); Sergei Frelikh, *General Vlasov* (Koln: 1990); *Nezavisimaia gazeta* (October 29, 1991), *Novaia i noveishaia istoriia* (2/1993), *Vtoria Udarnaia v bitve za Leninarad* (Moscow, 1983).

Chapter 6

Abakumov as Head of MGB

On February 25, 1946, the once-despised title of "Ministry" replaced the People's Commissariats, and NKGB duly became MGB with Merkulov still at the helm, but not for long. On October 18, 1946, he was officially replaced by Abakumov. In the atmosphere of secrecy and paranoia which permeated Stalin's Russia, the official and actual dates of major appointments were not necessarily the same. In this case, it seems that Abakumov had been put in charge of MGB at an earlier date. Documents from the Vlasov trial show that, although in the beginning of 1946 Abakumov was referred to as head of SMERSH, by late July he was being identified as the Minister of State Security.

Why was Abakumov picked? Since none of the participants in this monumental decision has left any memoirs, we can only repeat the colorful and confused account published by Malenkov's son, A.G. Malenkov.[1] The junior Malenkov's account, which is highly favorable to his father, insists that Beriia and Malenkov had been at loggerheads during their entire careers. According to this account, in 1945, Malenkov tried to expose V.N. Merkulov, Commissar of NKGB and Beriia's close ally. Beriia, however, managed to thwart these attempts and had Merkulov move over to the Commissariat of State Control. This account, also repeated by Kostiliarov, is not completely accurate, since Merkulov actually was appointed for the next four years as Chief of Soviet Repatriation in the occupied areas. It was only in October 1950 that he returned to the USSR and became what was now Minister of State Control, replacing L.Z. Mekhlis, who had held the position in 1946.[2] According to A.G. Malenkov, his father's candidate for the new Minister of State Security was none other than A.A. Kuznetsov, a man closely associated with Malenkov's chief rival, Zhdanov. Beriia, however, prevailed and had his candidate, Abakumov, appointed to the position in March 1946. According to this account, this appointment was a victory for Beriia and a defeat for Malenkov. Nothing is said in this account about the role, if any, played by Stalin in this critical appointment. Kostliarov speculates that Stalin, who liked to "shuffle" cadres, had decided by 1946 that Zhdanov was the man of the hour even though he had once blamed him for the Navy's poor performance during the war. The phlegmatic and laconic Zhdanov, who liked to open meetings with "Comrade Stalin and I have decided" soon had his own men in important positions in government and the Party. These included A.A. Kuznetsov in the Central Committee, Voznesenskii in government, and Bulganin in the military. This was not all, since Zhdanov was probably also involved in Malenkov's exile to Central Asia, Beriia's move to the Committee for Atomic Energy, as well as the demotions and transfers of Marshal Zhukov; Admiral N.G. Kuznetsov, Minister of the Navy; and the appointment of Marshal of Aviation K.A. Vershinin as Commander in Chief of the Air Force. Zhdanov did not feel comfortable with Beriia's toady Merkulov as head of security and pushed for the candidacy of Abakumov, the only high-ranking Chekist who did not owe his position to Beriia, but rather directly to Stalin. Kostliarov adds that Abakumov's persistent campaign to compromise Marshal Zhukov was inspired by Zhdanov, who had long held a grudge against Zhukov dating back to the dark days of October 1941 when Zhukov had commanded the Leningrad Front in his typical high-handed fashion while Zhdanov lay paralyzed in a drunken stupor and the nominal Commander of the Leningrad Front, Lt. General M.S. Khozin, was busy being entertained by his "PPZH" (campaign wife).

Sudoplatov's account, in chapter 8 of his memoir, which seems plausible, claims that after the war Stalin ordered Merkulov to submit a plan for reorganization of the state security. Later in a meeting of the Politburo, Merkulov, and his Deputies, Stalin expressed his dissatisfaction with the proposed plan and Merkulov's hesitant defense. Stalin suggested that now the war was over, SMERSH should be transferred from the Ministry of Defense, which Stalin was about to give up, to the state security and with its head (Abakumov) serving as a Deputy Minister. Merkulov agreed readily, perhaps too readily, with this suggestion, proposing that Abakumov should be made a First Deputy Minister, but Stalin was not finished and suggested that S.I. Ogol'tsev, one of Merkulov's Deputies, be considered as the head of the MGB. The proposal was indefensible since Ogol'tsov, a Party man whose previous experience was confined to heading the MGB in Krasnoirask (this according to Sudoplatov, actually head of NKVD in Kuibyshev), humbly declined the honor, thereby giving Stalin his chance to nominate Abakumov, who was enthusiastically supported by Zhdanov. Molotov and Beriia remained silent and the latter would later curse Merkulov for his poor performance. The whole affair was obviously stage-managed by Stalin, and no one did it better than he. A few days later, a commission of the Central Committee headed by A.A. Kuznetsov arrived in Lubianka to look into "criminal mistakes" made by the previous leadership of MGB including the alleged stopping of the campaign against Trotskiites in 1941, which also meant the release and re-employment of purged Chekists—several of whom were employed by Sudoplatov during the war. Sudoplatov, however, managed to blame the repressions on the discredited Ezhov, and the hearing was closed. Merkulov's career, however, went into eclipse. According to Beriia's son, his father had nothing to do with Abakumov's appointment. He adds in passing that, unlike other senior Chekists, Abakumov was never a guest at their house.

The death of his sponsor Zhdanov on August 31, 1948, however, did not prove fatal for Abakumov as it did for Voznesenskii and A.A. Kuznetsov. Somehow, Abakumov had made his peace with Malenkov and Beriia and had taken an enthusiastic part in the "Leningrad Affair," whose chief beneficiaries were the two satraps.[3] It has been suggested in the West that Zhdanov represented a "moderate" faction in mortal combat against the "radicals"–supposedly Beriia and Malenkov– with an "embattled" Stalin acting as a "mediator." This, of course, flies in the face of all we know about Zhdanov as the Leningrad Party Secretary after Kirov's murder, his record in Karelia and Estonia, his support of Katyn, and later as Stalin's cultural czar, his savage treatment of helpless individuals such as A.A. Akhmatova, to say nothing of the whole manner in which Stalin operated. My own feeling is that Zhadnov and other satraps were mere pawns of Stalin who enjoyed playing the divide-and-conquer games which characterized his style of leadership. Abakumov became head of MGB because he was Stalin's candidate. Even Kostliarov admits that Abakumov took his orders from Stalin and no one else. Beriia could not possibly have been happy to see Merkulov, his closest ally, replaced by Abakumov, but he tried to make the best of a bad bargain and made attempts at a policy of coexistence with Abakumov. Merkulov, however, never forgot his fall, but he could do little since Beriia could offer nothing but sympathy.

Over at NKVD (now MVD), Kruglov had replaced Beriia in Jan. 1946. Abakumov and Kruglov were the new leaders to supervise security and repression operations during the post-war years. Beriia, however, remained on the scene and continued as an adviser to Stalin on security matters. Beriia, a Marshal of the Soviet Union since July 1945, was now a Deputy Chairman of the Council of Ministers. Besides overseeing the defense industry during the war, at least during the early months, Beriia had presided over an industrial empire that, according to Maj. General V.F. Nekrasov (*Komsomol'skaia Pravda*, No. 11, 1990), had produced 315 tons of gold, 14,398 tons of tin, 6,511 tons of nickel, nearly 9,000,000 tons of coal, 407,000 tons of oil, and over 30 million shells, a background which made him eminently qualified for the State Atomic Trust.

The history of the Soviet atomic energy program has been covered by a number of books (e.g., David Holloway, Andreas Heinmann-Grüder, and A.I. Ioirysh), the memoirs of P.A. Sudoplatov, various biographies of I.V. Kurchatov, and the important article by the academician Iu.B. Khariton (*Bulletin of the Atomic Scientists*, May 1993), in which he denies the significance of espionage. Sudoplatov, on the other hand, gives the lion's share of credit to his spies, and here he is supported by those Cold Warriors that have believed all along that on her own, the Soviet Union could accomplish little. This does not explain the success of the equally complex Soviet space program, in which espionage did not play a part. Since 1940, the USSR Academy of Sciences had been involved in atomic energy research led by the academicians V.G. Khlopin, A.I. Ioffe, and the elderly V.I. Vernadskii. The genesis of the program to develop the atomic bomb was a letter written in 1940 by the physicist F.F. Lange (an emigrant from Germany) to the State Defense Committee, which was, however, rejected as "premature." A similar letter from the Soviet physicist N.N. Semenov to the Commissariat of Defense was also left unanswered.

The matter was, however, revived when on March 10, 1942, when Beriia wrote to Stalin about research that was taking place in the West and proposed establishment of a scientific committee to study the matter as well as approval of intelligence operations to collect information. Stalin agreed, but proposed setting up a second committee comprised of non-scientists. This committee was made up of Beriia, Molotov, Malenkov, M.G. Pervukhin, N.A. Voznesenskii, and others. The committee was chaired by Molotov and Pervukhin but was actually run by Beriia. After personally consulting the scientists, Stalin on February 11, 1943, ordered a special committee to develop atomic energy chaired by Molotov with Beriia as his Deputy for Procurement. Beriia, however, soon replaced Molotov and had at his disposal not only the Soviet Union's leading physicists, whom he usually treated cordially, but also his intelligence network (called Department S and headed by Sudoplatov), as well as a number of Party, government, and police functionaries such as V.A. Makhenv, Deputy Commissar of State Control before the war, and A.P. Zaveniagin of the Gulag administration, as well as some of "Caucasian" cronies who became unemployed during the post-war takeover of state security by Abakumov. The reactions of the scientific community who came in contact with Beriia were mixed. P.L. Kapitsa and M. Sadovskii found him insufferable, whereas Khariton and the German Nikolaus Riehl had more favorable impressions. There is little doubt that the scientists were pampered within the limits of post-war Russia ("golden cage" is how life is described by Riehl). Beriia also protected his people during the post-war anti-Semitic campaigns, and on one occasion he discouraged the secret police's interest in the academician L. Al'tshuler, who allegedly had made disparaging remarks about Lysenko. According to Beriia's son, Stalin also had received information that Khariton was a British spy, and his father had to go to great lengths to convince Stalin not to have the physicist arrested.

On August 20, 1945, two weeks after the dropping of the atomic bomb on Hiroshima, the GKO established a committee charged with "coordinating the work on the use of uranium energy" which later was transferred to a special committee under the Council of Ministers. Beriia chaired this committee which lasted until June 26, 1953, and whose members included G.M. Malenkov, N.A. Voznesenskii, B.L. Vannikov, A.P. Zaveniagin, I.V. Kurchatov, P.L. Kapitsa, V.A. Makhnev, M.G. Pervukhin, and possibly S.N. Kruglov at a later date. The administrative arm of this committee was the "First Central (Scientific/Technical) Administration of the Council of Ministers" headed by Vannikov, which under this high-sounding title performed the actual work of producing Soviet nuclear weapons. (On June 26, 1953, this office was put under the Ministry of Medium Machine Industry with Vannikov and Zaveniagin as Deputies under V.A. Malyshev.) The documentary *Red Atom*, telecast in 1994 on the Discovery Channel, gives the impression, supported strangely enough by both Sudoplatov and the former Cold Warriors, that the Soviet bomb was made purely through the efforts of spies and Kurchatov's major problem was the lack of a photocopying machine. Beriia's contributions were also considerable. It is difficult to argue with Kurchatov that without Beriia there would have been no bomb. In retrospect, the Soviet Union may have been better off without nuclear weapons, which only provided a facade of power for a system that was rotting from within.

During the post-war years, Beriia would receive well-deserved credit for the development of nuclear weapons. Beriia also served as Stalin's general troubleshooter since he was a rarity—a Communist bureaucrat who got things done, in his case by hook and by crook. One does not have to admire his methods to be impressed by the accomplishments of the defense industry during the war and the production of nuclear weapons. He would also be involved in other activities. A story, possibly apocryphal, is that he was assigned by the Politburo to supervise the division of the Coal Ministry into two separate ministries covering the western and eastern parts of the USSR and respectively headed by V.V. Vakrushev and D.G. Onika. Beriia ordered the two men to work out an agreement and then asked them to present him with a plan. He then asked them whether there were any complaints. Vakrushev had none, Onika many. Beriia, Solomon-like, approved the plan but switched the assignments, which may have contributed to Vakhrushev's heart attack. On March 29, 1949, when Beriia received his fifth Order of Lenin from the hands of M.I. Kalinin, he was called a "true pupil of Lenin and compatriot of Comrade Stalin." On August 29, 1949, the first Soviet atomic bomb was tested. Despite all of this, Beriia's position was not completely secure—under Stalin, no one's was. In March 1946, Beriia, a candidate member since 1939, became a full member of the Politburo. Malenkov, a candidate member since February 1941, also became a full member. The two joined Stalin, Andreev, Kaganovich, Voroshilov, Kalinin (who died on June 3, 1946), Khrushchev, Mikoian, Molotov, and Zhdanov. The new candidate members were Bulganin and Kosygin, who joined Shvernik (elected in 1939) and Voznesenskii (elected in February 1941). Candidate member A.S. Shcherbakov (elected in February 1941) had died on May 10, 1945. For the first time since July 1938, Beriia was not *directly* involved with security and police matters. Beriia, however, continued to have some influence in the organs, particularly at the MVD, where S.S. Mamulov, a man he had known since the 1920s, served as Deputy Minister and head of Gulag. Over at MGB, provincial leaders such as Goglidze in the Far East and Tsanava in Belorussia also owed their primary loyalty to Beriia, but otherwise the leadership of MGB became increasingly free of Beriia's "Caucasian" cohorts. Only in the last months of Stalin's life did Beriia once again begin to flex his muscles. The war years were not kind to Beriia, nor was he helped by the dissolute life that he had been leading. He began to gain weight, and the once handsome face was now replaced by a puffiness that made him look much older (his pictures from this period are heavily doctored). This, however, did not diminish his capacity for hard work and, of course, for intrigue. At least two senior Soviet government officials, I.F. Tevosian (once also targeted by Ezhov at the end of his career), Minister of the Ferrous Metal Industry (1946) and V.V. Vakhrushev (1902–1947), Commissar/Minister of the Coal Industry (1939–1946) were to suffer in his hands; in Vakhrushev's case this led to a fatal heart attack on Jan. 13, 1947.[4] Beriia's son, however, claims that Tevosian was a friend of his father.

Robert Conquest states that Abakumov was no enemy of Beriia, but he was not a mere stooge as claimed in Khrushchev's memoirs. As late as 1993, in such books as *Stalin's Generals*, experts continued to repeat the myth fabricated by Khrushchev about a Beriia/Abakumov machine and referring to Abakumov as one of Beriia's "foremost henchmen." The fact remains that the relationship between the two men was much more complex and marked by cooperation as well as competition and rivalry and wariness on both sides. For most of the war, Abakumov, as head of SMERSH, and during the post-war years when he replaced Merkulov, Beriia's closest ally as head of MGB, he reported directly to Stalin. Abakumov's arrogant behavior during the Wallenberg case, as already related, is an example of a man who felt subordinate only to Stalin. Marshal Zhukov, one man who dared to oppose Abakumov, barely escaped with his life. There seems little doubt that Abakumov, or for that matter even Vlasik, would have arrested Beriia had he been so ordered by Stalin.

Beriia's reports are almost always addressed to Stalin and sometimes with copies to Molotov and Malenkov, but not to Abakumov. Most of Abakumov's reports also went directly to Stalin with copies to Bulganin, Zhdanov, Malenkov, A.I. Antonov (Chief of Staff), and sometimes Beriia. There is no evidence of Stalin's having frequent meetings with both men at the same time or for that matter with Beriia and Merkulov. That ultimate bureaucrat, Heinrich Himmler, had a policy of never meeting with two subordinates at the same time, which he felt would only encourage "office politics." Stalin, a firm believer in divide-and-conquer tactics, also apparently believed in this, particularly in areas as sensitive as state security. The fact that there were no conspiracies against Stalin or Himmler is proof that inefficiency and confusion were a small price to pay for a sense of security.

Abakumov had his own agenda and, in fact, complained at the time of appointment that his predecessors (who else, but Beriia and Merkulov) had not shown sufficient vigilance in combatting Trotskiites and deviationists.[5] Abakumov was wary of and deferential to Beriia but, as he said truthfully in his interrogation, he took his orders from one man only—and Stalin would not have had it any other way. The complexity of relationship between Beriia and Abakumov is best shown by Beriia's inability or unwillingness to act in Abakumov's behalf when the latter was arrested in July 1951 or to release him after Stalin's death. Although he kept some of the men appointed by his predecessors, Abakumov slowly brought in his own people in the same tradition established by Ezhov and Beriia, except that this time the fallen were not led to the execution wall. First, some time between 1946 and 1948, B.Z. Kobulov was removed from his post as First Deputy Minister. Abakumov's Deputy Ministers included A.S. Blinov, P.V. Fedotov, N.K. Koval'chuk, S.I. Ogol'tsev, N.N. Selivanoskii, and M.G. Svinelupov, who replaced either A.N. Babkin or M.V. Gribov as head of the MGB cadres. Sudoplatov also identifies M.I. Belkin, who had been employed by SMERSH during the war as a Deputy Minister, but he was likely a Deputy Department Head. Sudoplatov also mentions E.P. Pitovranov, until 1944 head of NKVD in Gor'kii as a Deputy Minister, but he was probably Deputy Head of the Foreign Department, where he had been employed since 1944. During the war, next to Moscow, Kuibyshev was the most important center for police and security operations, and two of Abakumov's Deputies, Blinov and Ogol'tsev, had served there as head of NKVD. (Blinov has also been identified as head of the local NKGB when it was a separate commissariat.) On February 25, 1941, Gribov

(Maj. General, July 1945), who had been identified as Deputy Commissar NKGB for Cadres, probably was replaced during the war by Babkin (Lt. General, July 1945), who in 1940 had headed the NKVD in Tula where he received the Order of Red Star on April 27, 1940. He was replaced in this position probably by Major of State Security I.I. Il'iushin-Edelman. At the start of the war, Babkin was head of NKVD in Kazakh SSR and played a significant part in the resettlement of the deported Volga Germans. Babkin then returned to Moscow to take over the NKGB Personnel Department before being replaced and transferred to Novosibirsk. He died in 1950. We will examine the careers of some of these men in some detail later, but they all had one thing in common—they were all Slavs. Abakumov, however, kept or was forced to accept some of Beriia's men in the provinces such as Goglidze in the Far East, Tsanava in Belorussia, and G.A. Bezhanov in Kabard ASSR. In Latvia, A.P. Eglit, who had worked under Beriia in the Transcaucasus Cheka and had been the Head of NKGB in Latvia since 1945, was retained as Head of MGB. In Kazakh SSR the job of Head of the MGB went to Lt. General P.M. Fitin, who had been the Head of the Foreign Department from April 1939 until 1946. In Lithuania, Abakumov kept D.A. Efimov, who had been the Head of the local NKGB since 1945. A survivor of the Ezhov period (Order of the Red Star, December 1937), Efimov stayed in Lithuania until 1949. M.I. Baskakov, Head of NKGB in Gor'kii since 1943, was appointed Head of MGB in Uzbek SSR in 1947. Also retained until 1949 as Head of the MGB in the Ukraine was S.R. Savchenko, who had been the First Head of NKGB following the Soviet return in 1943. In his own bailiwick of Georgia, Beriia had in A.N. Rapava, Head of MGB, and G.T. Karanadze, Head of MVD, two trusted agents, but in 1948 Abakumov managed to replace Rapava with N.M. Rukhadze, another Georgian, but not a fellow Mingrelian of Beriia. Later Rukhadze showed that he was quite willing to doublecross Beriia.

There is some controversy in regard to Svineupov's appointment. Uri Ra'anan, quoting Deriabin, claims that Abakumov's first choice to head the cadres was Deputy Head (and former Head of SMERSH Cadres) I.I. Vradyi, but he was turned down by the CC CPSU Administrative Organs Committee, which was headed by A.A. Kuznetsov, who had veto power over such matters. The reason given was the excessive brutality by Vradyi during fighting against the Basmachi in Central Asia.[6] Kuznetsov may have vetoed Vradyi's appointment, and thus aroused Abakumov's enmity, but the reasoning does not seem convincing. In 1946, brutality against the Basmachi guerrillas (the early Mujahedins), who on their side gave no quarter, would seem an unlikely reason to disqualify someone from serving in MGB. Abakumov also kept P.V. Fedotov as Head of the Foreign Department, a position he had held since July 5, 1946. On September 7, 1946 Fedotov also became a Deputy Minister of MGB. Another former SMERSH officer, Maj. General (later Lt. General) Ia.A. Edunov, also eventually took over the 3 Main Department (counterintelligence). Edunov survived Abakumov's fall. Abakumov kept F.G. Shubniakov (only a Colonel) as the head of the Secret Political Department (in charge of ideology and culture) who had held this position since 1943, after Abakumov's famous run-in with his predecessor, V.N. Il'in. In August 1946, he would organize the investigation of satirist M.M. Zoshchenko and in October 1949 took part in the deportation of Greeks. Shubniakov was also involved in the murder of S.M. Mikhoels. D.N. Shadrin had been identified in 1946 as Head of the 2 Main Department. A.Ia. Gertovskii, formerly Bashtakov's Deputy and a participant in Katyn, was appointed Head of the "A" Department, which dealt with financial and economic matters. Gertovskii, Belkin, and Ia.M. Broverman, Deputy Head of the MGB Chancellery, were the only Jews in Abakumov's immediate entourage. Abakumov also proceeded to put his own men in the Department for Investigation of Especially Important Cases, MGB's main instrument of terror. This department, founded after Beriia's ascendancy, had replaced the old Investigation Department. Under B.Z. Kobulov and later L.E. Vlodzirmirskii, it had done yeoman's work to counter all those deemed hostile to the regime. Here Abakumov had Beriia's man, L.E. Vlodzimirskii, replaced by Maj. General A.G. Leonov, former Head of the SMERSH Investigation Department, who had, among other things, organized the investigation of Vlasov and his colleagues. Leonov, along with M.T. Likhachev, V.I. Komarov, L.L. Shvartsman, and later M.D. Riumin, formed the vanguard of terror. In the case of Riumin, Abakumov's policeman eyes, however, failed to see the treachery and ambition behind the insignificant-looking former accountant who had served the war as a SMERSH officer in the backwaters of Archangel Military District. For his neglect, Abakumov was to pay a heavy price. One action of Abakumov that was somewhat puzzling was his doing away with the NKGB 4 Department responsible for terrorism and sabotage and headed by Sudoplatov. Instead, he set up a "Special Service" with Sudoplatov and Eitingon for such operations. The record of this bureau, as discussed later in this book, was far from impressive, and in 1949 Abakumov liquidated this service, which was revived in 1950 as two bureaus. Abakumov's lack of enthusiasm for such operations could be traced to a number of factors. Sudoplatov and Eitingon were not his men, and like the old Bolsheviks, he may have disdained individual acts of terror (massive acts were, of course, a different matter) as counter-productive. Abakumov had a point. When intelligence agencies engage in individual acts of terror such as the assassination of Ukrainian émigré nationalist leaders in Germany, President Diem in Vietnam, or the killing of environmental terrorists in New Zealand, the truth will out and prove to be embarrassing and even counter-productive.

Abakumov, as the new head of MGB, was handicapped by a number of factors. His rise had been too rapid to allow him to meet a large number of kindred spirits. Unlike Ezhov and Beriia, who had experience in both Party and government, he had been only a Chekist and was also not given the luxury of a thorough housecleaning enjoyed by his predecessors.

In the atmosphere of intrigue that permeated Stalin's court, Abakumov was also hampered by the fact that he did not belong to the inner circle. One would assume that Abakumov, arguably the second most powerful man in the post-war Soviet Union, would belong at least to the Central Committee if not the Politburo. In fact, Abakumov made it only to the rubber stamp Supreme Soviet, representing the Soviet occupation forces in Germany. It would be many years before the head of secret police would sit in the Politburo and, in the case of Andropov, become the Party's

General Secretary. Abakumov's exclusion was, of course, a deliberate policy of Stalin's, since this made the secret police chief directly responsible to him and prevented him from forming alliances with the other satraps. In this climate and with the continuous jockeying for power that went on around Stalin, Abakumov had to step gingerly in treacherous shoals to avoid ending up on the losing side.

Abakumov's main contribution, besides serving as Stalin's mailed fist, was the purge of the ethnics (although he continued to employ some Jews), and thus making MGB along with its successors, MVD and KGB, except for a brief period after Stalin's death, organizations made up almost completely of Slavs. In the final analysis, Iagoda, Ezhov, Beriia, and Abakumov were nothing more than Stalin's personal instruments, ready and willing to go to any length to create his vision of the Brave New World. Abakumov correctly assessed Stalin's post-war leifmotiv, namely anti-Semitism and the ever-present fear of Bonapartism as the main concerns of the security organs. The military and the Jews were in for bad times. In 1946, shortly after his appointment as the head of MGB, Abakumov personally interrogated Leopold Trepper, the organizer of the "Rote Kapelle" spy ring who had been languishing in Lefortovo since 1944. Among his few questions, "Tell me in your network, why did you have so many Jews?"[7] In 1948, Stalin also began to talk about "new enemies" made up of "neo-Trotskiists," "neo-Menshevists" and "neo-SRs." Meanwhile, Zhdanov, Stalin's favorite idealogue, was sounding the alarm against the "cosmopolists." How these could have survived despite relentless repression is a question that Stalin failed to answer, but he believed, as had Dostoevskii, that the idea of "two and two make five" was not without possibilities. Regardless, the resurgence of the "enemies of the people" reflected poorly on the performance of the organs who was more than willing to accommodate Stalin's cry-wolf hallucinations. On February 18, 1948, Abakumov and Kruglov wrote to Stalin about organizing new camps for "particularly dangerous criminals," and by January 1950 two new camps were built to house them.[8]

The MGB was hampered by the fact that the death penalty in peacetime had been abolished on May 26, 1947, and replaced by 25 years in camps. Stalin, however, rectified this situation by re-introducing capital punishment on January 12, 1950.

NOTES

1. *Zhurnalist* (2/1991).
2. Kostliarov, op. Cit., p. 42.
3. Ibid., pp. 74–5.
4. *Izvestiia TsK KPPS* (2/1991), p. 187.
5. Ra'anan, Uri, *Inside the Aparat*, p. 152.
6. Ibid., p.32.
7. Trepper, Leopold, *The Great Game*, p. 366.
8. Volkogonov, op. Cit., book 2, part 2, p. 39.

Prisoner No. 15 (former Minister of State Security Abakumov), 1951.

Chief Marshal of Aviation, A. A. Novikov. Principle victim of the "Aviators' Affair." Commander in Chief of the Air Force (April 1942–April 1946). Picture taken at Lubianka Prison, the day after his arrest (April 23, 1946).

Army General I. I. Maslennikov, highest ranking of NKVD troops officers. Commanded various fronts and armies during the war. Deputy Commissar NKVD (February 1941–July 1943). Deputy Minister MVD (June 1948–April 1954). Suicide (April 1954).

Col. General of Judiciary, V. V. Ul'rikh. Chairman Military Collegium of the USSR Supreme Court (1926–1948). Stalin's hanging judge, world record holder in the number of people sentenced to death.

Army General V. N. Merkulov. Deputy Commissar NKVD (December 1938–February 1941). Commissar NKGB (February 1941–July 1941). Commissar/Minister NKGB/MGB (April 1943–October 1946). Organizer of Katyn. Shot (December 1953).

L. P. Beriia. Commissar General of State Security (future Marshal of the Soviet Union). Commissar NKVD (November 1938–January 1946). Minister MVD (March 1953–June 1953). Shot (December 1953).

Col. General of Aviation-Engineers A. I. Shakhurin. Commissar/Minister Aviation Industry (March 1940–March 1946). Victim of the "Aviators' Affair." Spent seven years in prison. Released in March of 1953. Picture taken in 1970s.

Lt. General K. F. Telegin (1899–1981). Political Commissar of Soviet Forces in Germany. Arrested (January 30, 1948). Sentenced to 25 years (March 20, 1952). Released after Stalin's death. Picture from 1970s.

Chapter 7

Post-War Campaigns Against the Military

A number of changes during the immediate post-war period indicated Stalin's dissatisfaction with the structure and personnel of the High Command. On February 25, 1946, on the base of the People's Commissariat of Defense and the Navy, the Commissariat of the USSR Armed Forces was formed; in March 1946 it was renamed the Ministry (as were other People's Commissariats) of the USSR Armed Forces. Stalin, the Commissar of Defense since July 1941, continued to head the Armed Forces until March 1947, when he was replaced by N.A. Bulganin. Meanwhile, in April 1946, a Higher Military Soviet was formed as a consulting body. In March 1946, Army General A.I. Antonov, Chief of Staff since February 1945, was replaced by A.M. Vasilevskii, a military man whom Stalin found non-threatening—and a younger version of B.M. Shaposhnikov. Vasilevskii, Bulganin (the ultimate jasägar with a special fondness for the bottle), and Shtemenko were Stalin's candidates to run the Armed Forces after the war.

The death of A.S. Shcherbakov on May 10, 1945 had also left vacant the position of Head of the Political Administration of the Red Army. I.V. Shikin, who held a similar position with the Soviet forces in the Far East, took over this position early in 1946. Shikin had served with the Leningrad Military District, the North Fleet, and Leningrad and Volkhov Fronts between August 1939 and May 1942, before being appointed as Shcherbakov's Deputy, a position he held until July 1945. He would play a part in placing people sympathetic to Zhdanov in the military. On February 25, 1946, the Commissariat of Navy was disbanded and the Commissar Admiral N.G. Kuznetsov was appointed as Deputy Minister of the Armed Forces and Commander in Chief of the Navy. Meanwhile, at least two committees were set up, headed by Malenkov, to study the uses of radar and strategic rockets, while the building of nuclear weapons would become the bailiwick of Beriia.

Even before his appointment as head of MGB, Abakumov was in several different campaigns involving the military. Immediately after the war, the SMERSH began to arrest a number of officers attached to Soviet occupation forces in Germany.

Zhukov, at this time at the height of his power, managed to frustrate Abakumov's attempts and thus guarantee the latter's enmity.

The first senior military officer arrested during the post-war period was probably Marshal of Aviation S.A. Khudiakov (Khanferiants), Commander of the Air Force in the Far East. In June 1941, Khudiakov was the Chief of Staff of Air Forces in the Belorussian Military District, whose units were decimated by the Luftwaffe in the early days of the war, leading to the suicide of the Commander, Maj. General of Aviation I.I. Kopets, and the arrest of his Deputy, A.I. Taiurskii. Khudiakov must have acquitted himself since he served as Chief of the Staff of the entire Air Force during the summer 1942 and then again from May 1943 to June 1945. In the process he jumped four ranks, from Colonel to Marshal of Aviation, in a little over three years. In March 1943, Lt. General of Aviation Khudiakov, Commander of the 1 Air Army attached to the West Front, had the unpleasant task of informing N.S. Khrushchev, at this time Political Commissar of the Voronezh Front, that his son Guard Senior Lieutenant L.N. Khrushchev, a fighter pilot attached to the 18 Guard Interceptor Regiment, had crashed behind enemy lines on March 11, 1943 after a dogfight with two enemy Focke-Wolf 190 fighters. The search for him proved fruitless, and no trace of the young Khrushchev was ever found. In his youth, the younger Khrushchev had been a juvenile delinquent, but after joining the Air Force, he completed 134 bomber and 33 interceptor sorties, dying a hero's death. His disappearance later gave rise to unfounded rumors that he had been taken prisoner and became a Vlasovite. Khudiakov was arrested on December 14, 1945, without warrant. On August 22, 1947, he was charged with being recruited by British Intelligence in 1918 when he was 16 years old. He was shot on April 18, 1950, apparently without trial, one of the several prominent military men who were shot during this period, which followed the reintroduction of the death penalty in 1950.[1]

The "Aviator's Affair" was not initiated by Abakumov, but by Stalin's son, Maj. General Aviation V.I. Stalin, who after visiting Germany after the war, complained with reason about the quality of Soviet planes in comparison to those of the Western Allies. This was a subject about which Stalin was sensitive, and there are rumors that similar complaints before the war instead had led to the arrest of the complainer. Of the 80,300 aircraft lost during the war, an incredible 37,200—47% of the total—were destroyed as a result of accidents. In fact, in spring 1941, Timoshenko and Zhukov used this excuse to remove the 29-year-old P.V. Rychagov from his post as Commander of the Air Force who, along with his wife, was duly executed in Oct. 1941.[2] In August 1945, V.I. Stalin wrote a letter to his father about the introduction of the Iak–9 fighters in the Air Force combat units before adequate testing which had led to a number of accidents. His charges were backed by one Col. A.A. Kats, the dismissed Chief of Staff of an interceptor aviation corps. Later, another letter along the same lines surfaced, this time by Lt. General of Aviation N.A. Sbytov, Commander of Aviation in the Moscow Military District, whose troubles with Abakumov during the Battle of Moscow have already been discussed. This letter could have been inspired by Abakumov. In March 1946 a "red ribbon" commission made up of G.M. Malenkov, G.K. Zhukov, A.M. Vasilevskii, S.M.

Shtemenko, I.V. Shikin (Political Commissar of the Air Force, 1946–1949), and senior Air Force officers S.I. Rudenko, K.A. Vershinin and V.A. Sudets and chaired by N.A. Bulganin was formed to look into the matter. Novikov and his Deputies G.A. Vorozheikin and F.Ia. Falaleev were pointedly excluded from the proceedings. On March 4, 1946, Novikov, who in the previous month had been elected to the Supreme Soviet, was dismissed. This was indeed shocking since Novikov was considered a protégé of Stalin. In fact, the dictator thought so highly of him that on November 12, 1942, he had told G.K. Zhukov that the counter-offensive in Stalingrad should not start without Novikov's agreement.

It is doubtful that the junior Stalin's provocation alone led to the arrest of the principal victims, Shakhurin and Novikov, since Stalin had a low opinion of his own children and, in the case of the dissolute and dilettante Vasilii, with good reason. During his military career, V.I. Stalin usually received good evaluations from his superiors, but there were also hints of criticism which would have been unthinkable without orders from above, and, in fact, when he was informed on May 26, 1943, that V.I. Stalin had been drinking on the job, he angrily ordered Novikov to remove him as Commander of an air regiment. Novikov carried out the order even though he was a friend and neighbor of the young Stalin. Stalin was reminding his own son, as well as everyone else, who the boss was. Despite all of this, the junior Stalin had a meteoric rise, becoming a Colonel at the age of 20 (February 19, 1942), and a Major General of Avaiation four years later (March 2, 1946, two weeks before Novikov's arrest), and a Lt. General of Aviation (May 1, 1949). In 1946, he was Commander of the 1 Interceptor Aviation Corps based in Germany. According to Volkogonov, V.I. Stalin flew 27 combat missions and shot down an enemy fighter during the war. It is interesting that Stalin would risk him to capture after what had happened to his older son.

In the "Aviators' Affair", Stalin may have been after even bigger fish—Zhukov and, perhaps, Malenkov. In his detailed writings on this subject in the 1994 issues of *VIZH*, Col. I.N. Kostenko makes a strong case for Stalin's complicity in this matter and for using the "Avaitors' Affair" to get Zhukov. On April 30, 1946, in one of his last reports as Head of SMERSH, Abakumov wrote to Stalin about this matter refering to "your personal orders." Five days later on May 4, 1946, Stalin, obviously pleased with Abakumov's performance, appointed him as Minister of State Security. On April 23, 1946, after the celebration of the first Victory Day parade, the SMERSH had arrested A.I. Shakhurin, Commissar/Minister of Aviation Industry since March 1940 and Chief Marshal of Aviation A.A. Novikov, Commander in Chief of the Air Force from April 1942 until his removal.[3] A full member of the Central Committee, Shakhurin had also been a member of the military mission that had visited England on September 21, 1941, and thus was doubly suspect. Those out of favor, even including Molotov, were considered potential spies if they had ever visited foreign countries during the course of their duties. Also removed, demoted, and later arrested was Marshal of Aviation G.A. Vorozheikin (who also had been arrested in the 1930s, but released before the war), First Deputy Commander in Chief of the Air Force since summer 1942. Others arrested were Col. General A.K. Repin, Chief Engineer of the Air Force during the war; Lt. General of Aviation N.G. Seleznev, Head of Air Force Procurement; Col. General N.S. Shimanov, Political Commissar of the Air Force since March 1943; as well as A.V. Budnikov and G.M. Grigor'ian, two Branch Heads in the Cadre Department of the Central Committee, whose responsibilities included aviation matters. Novikov's other Deputy and Chief of Staff of the Air Force Marshal of Aviation F.Ia. Falaleev was questioned, but was only dismissed and then appointed as Head of the Air Force Academy until his retirement in 1950. The designer of the Iak–9, A.S. Iakovlev, a favorite of Stalin, was left untouched. Shakhurin was replaced with M.V. Khrunichiev, a man with a background in police work who had served in the Militia during 1924–1930 before transferring to economic work. He was a direct beneficiary of the purge, becoming a Deputy Commissar of Defense (May 19, 1938), Deputy Commissar of Aviation Industry (January 28, 1939) and first Deputy Commissar of Munitions (1942). Novikov was replaced by K.A. Vershinin, former Commander of the 4 Air Army. Vershinin served in this position until September 1949, when he was replaced by P.F. Zhigarev. Khrunichiev was replaced in 1953 by P.V. Dement'ev.

According to A.K. Sul'ianov, Abakumov also played another part in the "Aviators' Affair." The immense aerial victories claimed by the Luftwaffe aces and their Western apologists, particularly against the Soviet Air Force, remain a controversial subject which awaits resolution through search in appropriate Soviet archives. Abakumov informed Stalin that 300 German pilots had shot down 24,000 Soviet planes, that 104 were credited with shooting down more than 100 planes each. He specifically mentioned three names: Erich Hartman with 352 (342 against the Russians), Gerhard Barkhorn with 301 (all on the Eastern Front), and Erich Rudorffer with 222 (136 against the Russians). In comparison, the two top Soviet aces I.N. Kozhedub and A.I. Pokryshkin had shot down only 62 and 59 enemy planes, a total which incidentally was higher than that of their Western counterparts, who had even lower scores against the Axis, a fact of which Abakumov failed to inform Stalin. The choice of Rudorffer also seems odd since there were several other German pilots who, along with Hartman and Barkhorn, had even higher scores against the Russians. Abakumov probably did not also tell Stalin that Hartman himself had been shot down several times, and, in fact, had once been captured by the Russians but somehow managed to escape. Stalin at first dismissed the German claims as propaganda and asked Abakumov to investigate the matter; in his report Abakumov blamed inferior Soviet planes and poor training. Stalin was understandably furious at the humiliating defeats and his anger helped seal the fate of Novikov, Shakhurin, and Malenkov.

To build a case against Novikov and Shakhrurin, in March 1946, without a warrant, Abakumov and his assistant, one Kor'kov, arrested Maj. General of Aviation F.I. Zharov, who had spent the war years with the Air Force Rear Services. Abakumov accused him of having sent falsified reports. Khor'kov, who supervised the torture, told Zharov, "We are the Central Committee; we are the government." Abakumov also threatened to arrest all seven Marshals of Aviation and even assigned V.I. Komarov to interrogate Col. General N.S. Shimanov, the Central Committee official in charge of aviation who had served as the Chief Political Commissar of the Air Force during the last two years of the war. During Abakumov's trial in 1954, the prosecution claimed that Komarov, Riumin, Likhachev, Shvartsman, Broverman, and Chernov were all involved in this campaign.[4] According to Sudoplatov, Abakumov suggested that Novikov and Shakhurin be shot, but Stalin spared them so they could provide testimony against Zhukov. By Stalinist standards, the sentences were relatively mild. Shakhurin received 7, Repin 6, Novikov 5, Shimanov 4, Seleznev 3, and Budnikov and Grigor'ian 2 years each. Most, however, were kept longer. Novikov spent an extra 10 months in what he called "Stalin's Academy" and tried to return to service. In 1965, the retired Bulganin claimed that he tried in vain to intercede on Novikov's behalf with Stalin. Molotov, in his conversations with F.I. Chuev, discounts the campaign against Zhukov as the reason for the downfall of Shakhurin and Novikov. Molotov claims that the two men, for economic reasons decided on their own and without informing the Politburo as they were supposed to, dispensed with wingspars on a certain type of aircraft already in service which resulted in fatal accidents which were duly reported to Stalin (probably by Abakumov and V.I. Stalin). Recent research (*Journal of Slavic Military Studies*, September 1994) indicates that there was some basis in the charges against Novikov and Shakhurin, who probably were guilty of "double accounting" and fabrication of statistics during the war, a common practice in centrally planned economies.

According to released documents (*VIZH*, 6/1994), following Stalin's death, Novikov, who had been released on February 1952 after serving 10 months beyond the original sentence, wrote to Beriia on April 2, 1953, requesting rehabilitation. He told Beriia about his treatment by Abakumov and M.T. Likhachev, and how they had forced him to sign statements which contained fabricated accusations against Zhukov, Malenkov, and Serov. On May 26, 1953, Beriia, whose involvement with the "Aviators' Affair" was marginal, wrote a detailed report to Malenkov (*VIZH*, 8/1994) exonerating Novikov and his colleagues who were rehabilitated by the Party Presidium on June 12, 1953. Novikov had had close calls before. In 1937, he had been expelled from the Party and the Red Army only to be re-admitted through the intervention of the Political Commissar of the Belorussian Military District, A.I. Mezis who,in turn, was soon arrested.

In the summer of 1941, as head of the Air Force in the Leningrad Military District, he was scheduled to switch jobs with E.S. Ptukhin, who held a similar position in the Kiev Special Military District. The outbreak of war precluded this exchange. Ptukhin was arrested in July 1941 as one of the scapegoats for the collapse of the Soviet Air Force. According to Solzhenitsyn, when in prison Ptukhin had remarked, "If I had known, I would have first bombed our Dear Father, and then gone off to prison." Ptukhin was shot in February 1942. Novikov, on the other hand, became Commander in Chief of the Air Force and the first man to receive (on February 21, 1944) the rank of Chief Marshal of Aviation. Such were the vagaries of fortune under Stalin.

One of the interesting memoirs (*VIZH*, 11/1993) of this period is by the former Col. General I.S. Glebov, appointed after the war as Deputy Chief of Operations

Section of the General Staff and possibly the last surviving member of the Stalin's High Command. There are, however, problems with Glebov's account. He claims that in 1946, Col. General of M.S. Gromadin, who had been the Head of PVO and Deputy Commissar of Defense since November 9, 1941, was also removed as part of the purge. In fact, Gromadin had been demoted in August 1943 and was sent to command, in succession, the PVO forces of the West, North, and Central Fronts. After the war, he was assigned to a military district, but in 1946 he was actually called back to his old job as Commander of the Anti-Aircraft Forces, a position he held until 1950.

In his letter to the Central Committee on January 19, 1959 (*Iosif Stalin v. Ob'iatiiakh Sem'i*), Stalin's son tries to shift the blame elsewhere. He calls Novikov and Shakhurin nothing more than Malenkov's lackeys who served as fall guys for mistakes that were made by Malenkov. The "Aviators' Affair" also influenced the attempt to compromise Marshal Zhukov, who was viewed by Abakumov as a potential Tukhachevskii. As the first step in this campaign, Abakumov had in the spring of 1942 arrested Maj. General V.S. Golushkevich, Chief of the Operations Section of the West Front, in an unsuccessful attempt to find incriminating material. Golushkevich was arrested on July 19, 1942, after being transferred to the Southwest Front, which was in dire straits after the collapse of the Soviet summer offensive. Abakumov, however, found time and energy to arrest important officers. In his report to Stalin on December 27, 1945 (*VIZH*, 12/1992) he does not mention Zhukov's name, but instead claims that two arrested officers, Maj. General G.S. D'iakov and one Colonel Bukin, had testified about conversations with Golushkevich in which the latter was critical of the Soviet government. Bukin further added that Golushkevich also belonged to the military conspiracy organized by D'iakov and another conspirator, Maj. General F.K. Kuz'min (both members of the faculty in the Frunze Academy), to carry out terroristic acts against the leaders of the Soviet government and the Party. (Bukin later retracted his allegations.) Golushkevich denied thm, but was nonetheless kept in prison until July 1952.

From June 1945 until March 1946, Zhukov was Commander in Chief of Soviet Forces in Germany and Head of the Soviet Military Administration. It was during this time that Abakumov, who incidentally was the elected representative of the Soviet occupying forces to the Supreme Soviet, arrived in Germany and began arresting a number of officers. With his prestige, Zhukov was able to put a stop to this and send Abakumov packing, telling him to go back to where he came from, thus guaranteeing a lifetime of enmity. Novikov's arrest, however, gave Abakumov a new opportunity. Under torture Novikov implicated Zhukov. Abakumov also managed to come up with additional incriminating material through arrest and interrogation of Lt. Colonel Semochkin, a former Adjutant of Zhukov. He also had the Marshal's dacha in Sosnovka searched. Stalin soon convened a meeting of senior military officers to discuss the charges against Zhukov. When Zhukov returned to Moscow there was another meeting attended by Stalin, Beriia, Kaganovich, Molotov, Malenkov, N.A. Bulganin, A.M. Vasilevskii, F.I. Golikov, I.S. Konev, V.D. Sokolovskii, K.K. Rokossovskii, P.S. Rybalko, S.M. Shtemenko, Zhukov, and others, but not Abakumov. Shtemenko read Novikov's testimony, which claimed that Zhukov considered Stalin to be an amateur in military matters, an episode which Shtemenko omits from his memoirs. Beriia, Kaganovich, and Golikov (a long-time enemy of Zhukov) also spoke against the Marshal. Others, however, did not support the allegations, not even Konev, despite his own turbulent relationship with Zhukov. Particularly spirited was the defense of Marshal of Tank Troops P.S. Rybalko, the former Commander of the 3 Guard Tank Army—a man of honor and incidentally the only Soviet official of whom General Anders has anything good to say.

Rybalko's defense of Zhukov is also unusual in view of his run-in with him during the Battle of Berlin, when the latter ordered Rybalko's Army, the spearhead of Konev's 1 Ukraine Front, to stop its advance to Berlin so units of Zhukov's 1 Belorussian Front could capture the city. Iu.B. Borev claims in *Staliniada* that, when Stalin praised the Russian people for winning the war, Rybalko told him that as a Georgian he was not the right person to make this judgement, and as the result, Rybalko was disgraced. This story needs further confirmation. Rybalko died on August 28, 1948 at age 54. His obituary in *Krasnaia Zvezda* does not indicate that he was out of favor. The inconclusive nature of the meeting persuaded Stalin to lay off Zhukov, at least for the present. Zhukov's enemies also included Zhdanov, who was behind Zhukov's removal from the Central Committee, claiming that he was not "mature enough." Zhukov was recalled from Germany in March 1946 and was told by Stalin that Bulganin, the newly appointed Deputy Minister of Defense, did not intend to employ him in a major position in the post-war army. Despite this, Zhukov received an appointment as Commander of Land Forces, which lasted six weeks (in some versions, four months). On June 9, 1946, Stalin, signing as Generalissimo of SSR (a rank created just for him) and Minister of Defense, sent a top-secret message to Bulganin and Vasilevskii stating that on June 3 the Council of Ministers had approved the decisions of the Higher Military Soviet of June 1 in replacing Zhukov as Commander of Land Forces. Zhukov's sins were listed as "personal ambition," claims to have been the sole architect of Soviet victory claiming credit for what should have gone to other military leaders such as Konev, Rokossovskii, and the "Supreme Command," as well as self-admitted mistakes.[5] On a personal level, Zhukov was accused of having awarded the popular singer L.A. Ruslanova, with whom he may have had an affair, the Order of Red Star—a prerogative of the Supreme Soviet. Here there was also the additional embarrassment that Ruslanava at that time was married to the Hero of the Soviet Union Lt. General V.V. Kriukov, soon to be arrested along with his wife. In July 1946, Zhukov was officially appointed Commander of the Odessa Military District where he had been since June 13 expecting momentary arrest. Zhukov knew quite well that many of Stalin's victims in the military, such as Tukhachevskii, had been arrested after appointment to distant military districts. This did not happen to Zhukov, but 1947 was pure hell for him, and his health began to suffer. In January 1948, Zhukov's case was investigated by the Politburo at the time when he was hospitalized. The upshot was that on February 12, 1948, Zhukov was appointed as commander of the Ural Military District.

At an unspecified date during the post-war period, there was a meeting of Stalin and Zhukov, which would have taxed the satirical imagination of a Gogol. The dictator informed the Marshal of the dossier Abakumov and *Beriia* had prepared accusing him of serving in British intelligence and of his doubts about its accuracy. Even more extraordinary than the accusations is Zhukov's claim that the dossier was prepared by Abakumov and Beriia without prodding from Stalin. The fact that the two policemen went unpunished for making such slanderous charges is a good indication that the campaign was inspired, if not actually directed, by Stalin. Zhukov's remarks are inspired less by complete naivete than an attempt to divert the blame from Stalin, his sponsor, and a man with whom he had worked closely during and even before the war. Stalin's remarks implicating Beriia in the case against Zhukov are also subject to question. Beriia's son, in *Moi Otets*, claims that his father enjoyed the most cordial relations with Zhukov during the war and that the Marshal was a frequent visitor to their house. Zhukov, in fact, asked Beriia to have I.A. Serov assigned to him (in his reports to Stalin, Abakumov tried to associate Zhukov with Serov's corrupt activities in occupied Germany). The latter claim is also supported by A.N. Buchin (Zhukov's chauffeur) in his recent memoirs. Zhukov, who admired competence, must have been impressed with Beriia, who had a way of getting things done. It is quite possible that Stalin used Beriia's name merely to reinforce his case and create bad blood between the two men. Regardless of claims made by Beriia's son, it is true that Zhukov was an active participant of the conspiracy against Beriia and personally arrested him during the famous Politburo meeting in 1953. By 1950, Stalin, perhaps suffering from pangs of nostalgia in his old age, ordered a thaw and Zhukov for a second time was elected a candidate member of the Supreme Soviet. In July 1951, Zhukov went to Poland and met with his old commander, colleague, subordinate, and finally rival K.K. Rokossovskii, whom Stalin had forced on the Poles as Minister of Defense. In 1952, Zhukov represented Sverdlovsk in the 19 Party Congress and was elected a candidate member of the Central Committee, from which he had been quietly dropped in 1946. In late February 1953, Zhukov was recalled to Moscow, but without an exact appointment. He was there when Stalin died and was soon involved in the power struggle that led to Beriia's arrest by him and his colleagues during a Politburo meeting.

It is estimated that at least 75 people were arrested in attempts to "get" Zhukov. Abakumov, however, was not finished with him and other serious attempts were made in 1948 to compromise Zhukov through the arrest of Lt. General K.F. Telegin, Commissar of the Soviet Forces in Germany, and Dr. S.S. Iudin, Chief Surgeon in the Sklifosovskii Institute. Arrested on December 23, 1948, Iudin was accused of being a member of a counter-revolutionary conspiracy led by Chief Marshal of Artillery N.N. Voronov, whose goal was to replace Stalin with Marshal Zhukov.[6] In 1945 after the victory parade, Voronov was approached by Vlasik, who had inquired on behalf of Stalin about Zhukov's loyalty. Voronov's refusal to compromise Zhukov contributed to his own dismissal in March 1950 from the post of Commander of the Soviet Artillery, but he was not arrested even though his name was brought up later in Riumin's charges against Abakumov. It is interesting to compare Zhukov's fate with that of Tukhachevskii. Ezhov had provided the smoking gun to implicate Tukhachevskii, but Abakumov failed, despite Herculean efforts, to do the same in the case of Zhukov and convince the "Court of Honor," convened by Stalin, of Zhukov's treasonable activities. This was the kind of failure that Stalin was bound to remember and eventually punish.

The latest batch of documents released from the Soviet period (*Voennye Arkhivy Rossii*, 1993; and *VIZH*, 6/1994) provides fresh insight into the machinations of Stalin and Abakumov. It includes Novikov's confessions dated April 30, 1946, and forwarded by Abakumov to Stalin. Then there is a letter from Bulganin to Stalin dated August 23, 1946, listing seven boxcar loads of "trophies" which may have been earmarked for the personal use of the leadership of the Soviet forces in Germany. The next document from Abakumov to Stalin, dated January 10, 1948, lists the expensive items discovered in Zhukov's apartment after a secret search. Similar action was also taken in Zhukov's residence in Odessa, where he served as Commander of the Military District. In the next document, from February 1948, Abakumov lists a number of MGB officials including Deputy Minister A.S. Blinov and Department Head A.Ia. Gertovskii who were involved in estimating the value of Zhukov's loot. The next document dated February 1948 is the text of the interrogation of Maj. General A.M. Sidnev, during 1945–1947 head of the MVD Operation Section in Berlin, which not only indicates rampant corruption, but also implicates the mighty I.A. Serov and some of his underlings. Then there is a letter dated two days later from Serov to Stalin denying Abakumov's allegations, calling Abakumov a liar and claiming he had embarked on destroying his career and was actually a friend of Zhukov (according to Serov, the two men had sat next to each other during the meeting of the Supreme Soviet). Serov added that Abakumov was also hostile to Meshik, Rapava, Mil'shtein, and even Fedotov (all Beriia's friends but Fedotov were actually serving under Abakumov as head of the Foreign Department. Next there is a letter to the Central Committee dated April 25, 1953, from Guard Lt. General V.V. Kriukov, one of the men arrested to build a case against Zhukov. Abakumov told Kriukov that the MGB no longer used methods associated with "ezhovshchina," but then proceeded along with Likhachev and investigator Captain Samarin (also involved in the questioning of K.F. Telegin) to torture him to prove that he was part of a military conspiracy headed by Zhukov.

These documents reveal pervasive corruption among the Soviet occupying forces in Germany where apparently everyone was helping himself to the loot. This was not without precedent and, in fact, had its historical roots in the Russian entry into Paris following Napoleon's defeat.

The whole affair illustrates Stalin's style of leadership, which encouraged the two Chekists to intrigue against each other (at the time of writing, Serov was the First Deputy Minister of MVD). As it turned out, neither Abakumov nor Serov was punished, even though they were probably both guilty of corruption, but lifetime enmity between the two men was guaranteed. Corruption, particularly when it involved captured trophies, was not a major concern of Stalin, and accusations by rival satraps were music to his ear. What concerned him was cooperation, and perhaps even friendship, among those in his circle, the stuff which would give rise to potential conspiracies.

Abakumov understandably continued to be obsessed with Zhukov, and even after his own arrest, during interrogations continued to refer to the Marshal as a "most dangerous" man. In the final analysis, it seems that Zhukov was saved not so much by the lack of a substantial case against him, but by the fact that despite personal jealousy and fear of Bonapartism, Stalin had an objective admiration for those whose toughness and cruelty matched his own, with Zhukov and Mekhlis being the prime examples. Despite enormous adulation, Zhukov continues to be a controversial figure. His most severe critic, the late dissident P.I. Grigorenko, for instance, credits G.M. Shtern, considered by others including Zhukov as a figurehead, for the victory at Khalkhin Gol. In his memoirs, Col. Army General A.T. Stuchenko, head of the Frunze Academy (April 1968–March 1969), who was also at Khalkhin Gol, also expresses his lack of admiration although in a more guarded fashion. Marshal I.S. Konev, whom Zhukov may have saved from court-martial in October 1941, and Marshal K.K. Rokossovskii, once a superior, also had reservations about Zhukov as a military leader, while Marshal V.I. Chuikov almost calls him an amateur during the Berlin operation. Col. General V.I. Kuznetsov, one of the toughest Commanders of the war, who was in combat from the first to the last day as head of various armies, found Zhukov callous and indifferent to excessive losses, the very factors that may have endeared him to Stalin. The book *Poslednimi Dorogami General Efromova* (Moscow, 1992) is critical of the role played by Zhukov in the tragedy of the 33 Army which suffered a fate similar to that of Vlasov's 2 Assault Army. The study *Dolov'no o Voine?* cites a number of examples of Zhukov's high-handedness and cruelty, including a threat to shoot Maj. General I.V. Panfilov, Commander of the 316 Rifle Division and later a bona fide hero of the Battle of Moscow. A.I. Eremenko in his diary (*VIZH*, 5/1994), perhaps overcome by jealousy, calls Zhukov a terrible and shallow individual, a careerist, and so forth. On further examination, Zhukov's tactics, best exemplified in the Battle of Berlin, seem crude, wasteful, and indifferent to suffering, which made him and Stalin such kindred spirits. Zhukov also put his signature on documents calling those who had surrendered traitors in August 1941 and the creation of punishment battalions in September 1942. No one who worked for Stalin would end up with clean hands and, in fact, Stalin insisted on it.

On the plus side, we must mention Zhukov's loyalty to his colleagues, as shown by his efforts to rehabilitate Generals Telegin and Golushkevich after Stalin's death. Zhukov turned out to be a major player during the power struggle following Stalin's death but could not get along with Khrushchev, who also feared "Bonapartism" among the military. Zhukov was the only purely military man to receive the coveted title of Hero of the Soviet Union four times and only once (on December 1956) for political reasons. On the other hand, Brezhnev, who was also a four-time winner (1966, 1976, 1978, and 1981), received the title for purely non-military reasons. Besides, Brezhnev also received the title Hero of Socialist Labor (1961) and eight Orders of Lenin against Zhukov's six.

An indirect victim of the "Aviators' Affair" was G.M. Malenkov, who had been in charge of the introduction of new aircraft during the war, for which on September 30, 1943, he had received the title Hero of Socialist Labor and an Order of Lenin in November 1945. Malenkov also reportedly had clashes with the younger Stalin during the Battle of Stalingrad.[7] Stalin replaced Malenkov, his Chief Assistant in the Party since the mid-1930s (first as an assistant to Ezhov), as the Secretary of the Central Committee, with S.D. Patolichev (born in 1908), the local Party leader from Cheliabinsk who had been head of the CC CPSU Organization and Instruction Department since February 1946. Besides Patolichev, the Central Committee Secretaries included Stalin, Zhdanov, A.A. Kuznetsov and G.M. Popov (First Party Secretary in Moscow). Several of Malenkov's operatives were also purged. Stalin made sure that Patolichev reported to him and not to Zhdanov and A.A. Kuznetsov. V.M. Andriianov was appointed Patolichev's First Deputy and I.A. Borkov, S.D. Igant'ev and later N.M. Pogov his Deputies. We will come across Igant'ev again. Kostliarov, however, sees the hand of Zhadanov in Malenkov's downfall. Malenkov was removed from the Central Committee on May 4, 1946, and exiled to Tashkent as the First Party Secretary of Uzbek SSR only to make an unprecedented recovery and comeback in July 1948 to be heavily involved in the "Leningrad Affair", for which Abakumov provided the mailed fist. Stalin occasionally would play cat and mouse with potential victims, but he was not in the habit of giving round-trip tickets to those who fell out of grace.

Patolichev, however, lasted in this job only until 1947, when he was sent to the Ukraine to hold a similar position with the Ukraine Party. He held it until 1950 before being demoted to a Party job in Rostov. He was not completely out of favor since in 1950, he became the Party Secretary in Belorussia, a position which he held until 1956. During 1952–1953 he was also a candidate member in the Party Presidium.[8]

Meanwhile, a campaign was being launched against another military man, the disgraced former Marshal of the Soviet Union G.I. Kulik. Kulik, who had known Stalin since 1918 when he had commanded the Artillery during the defense of Tsaritsyn, was, along with Voroshilov, Mekhlis, and Shchadenko, Stalin's closest military henchmanafter the decimation of the High Command, although there are rumors that he did not share his colleague's enthusiasm for bloodletting. The daughter of Army General D.G. Pavlov (shot in 1941 after the collapse of the West Front) claims that her father and Kulik tried to intercede in behalf of the purged officers, a claim which may have some basis since after the Polish campaign, Kulik made the sensible and humane suggestion that Polish POWs who hailed from areas that had been incorporated into the Soviet Union be allowed to return home. Kulik, who had served in the Spanish Civil War, had come back drawing the wrong lessons about the role of tanks in future wars. In June 1940, he became, along with Timoshenko and Shaposhnikov, a Marshal of the Soviet Union, replacing the purged Tukhachevskii, Egorov, and Bliukher, even though even Stalin had reservations about his conservative military views. Despite this, at the time of Barbarossa, he was Head of the Red Army Artillery and a Deputy Commissar of Defense and member of the Main Military Soviet.

As was mentioned in Chapter 1, on July 16, 1941, A.N. Mikheev, Abakumov's predecessor as head of the 3 Department, wrote a highly critical report (*VIZH* 12/ 1993) to Malenkov about Kulik. The report questioned Kulik's professional competence by using the testimony of other arrested officers and, worse, his loyalty. Looking even worse was Kulik's wife, whose father was identified as Count I.K. Simonich, head of Tsarist Counterintelligence in Helsinki, who had been shot by the Cheka in 1919. According to Mikheev, Simonich-Kulik's two brothers were shot as spies by NKVD, one sister was arrested as a spy, and two other sisters had left the USSR with Italian and German husbands, joining their mother, already an émigré in Italy. Simonich-Kulik had also smuggled a son from a previous marriage to Italy and had kept in contact with her sisters, who were engaged in espionage. It may be coincidental, but three days after this report, Kulik was sacked, but was not arrested. At the time of his report, Mikheev probably was not aware that Kulik's wife was already dead. According to the testimony of Vlodzimirskii, in 1939, Beriia ordered Merkulov to kidnap Simonich-Kulik, which was done on May 5, 1939 by a small group, which, besides Vlodzimirskii, also included V.N. Gul'st (Maj. General, July 1945). Beriia told Merkulov that the order had come from "above." The actual killing was carried out by V.M. Blokhin, Head of the Execution Squads, and A.N. Mironov in the presence of Vlodzimirskii. Bochkov and Kobulov showed up later, the former complaining that Blokhin should have waited for them.

In one of the first meetings of the Politburo after the outbreak of the war, Stalin had roundly denounced Kulik even though he had approved of all Kulik's proposals. Beriia, now Supervisor of the Defense Industries, only needed this hint, and in one of his first acts, he ordered the arrest of B.L. Vannikov, the Commissar of Armaments. Under torture, Vannikov, who had had disagreements with Kulik, may have also implicated a number of people associated with Kulik as part of a German spy network, some of them already under arrest. These included Kulik's Adjutant Maj. General of Artillery M.M. Kaiukov, Kulik's Deputy Maj. General of Artillery G.K.. Savchenko, Head of Small Artillery Department S.O. Sklizkov, and Commander of the Air Navigation Academy Lt. General of Aviation F.K. Arzhenukhin. As discussed before, Kulik was spared arrest at this time. Also as discussed previously, the accused officers were executed on October 10, 1941, near Kuibyshev. Among the arrested high-ranking officers, only Vannikov (perhaps for his testimony?) and K.A. Meretskov were spared. On July 19, 1941, Kulik was replaced by N.N. Voronov as head of the Red Army Artillery. Voronov was also going to have his share of troubles with Beriia, and in fact, according to Voronov's son, Beriia was responsible for persuading Stalin to sack Voronov. So, under unpleasant circumstances, Kulik started the war as a representative of Stalin to the collapsing West Front before taking over the command of the 54 Army of the Leningrad Front in August 1941. This was a position far too junior for a man of his rank. Kulik was replaced on September 25, 1941, but Stalin enjoyed humiliating those who had failed him and, in fact, in mid-July, he had briefly appointed another Marshal of the Soviet Union S.M. Budennyi as Commander of the 21 Army. In November 1941, Kulik was the Representative of the Supreme Command in Crimea, where superior Soviet forces were decimated by the enemy. In February 1942, Kulik and the Commander of Crimea, Vice Admiral G.I. Levchenko, were court-martialed by a tribunal headed by the hanging judge V.V. Ul'rikh, whose members included NKVD Lt. General P.A. Artem'ev and Col. General E.A. Shchadenko, Head of the Red Army's Cadres and were cashiered. (Levchenko received 10 years, but was freed in 1942 and actually promoted in 1944.)

The third high-ranking officer to face the Military Collegium as a result of the catastrophe in Crimea was Maj.General I.F. Dashichev, Commander of the 9 Rifle Corps (listed mistakenly by Abakumov as Commander of the 44 Army in his post-war report to Stalin), who was sentenced to 4 years for surrendering Fedosiia. He was also released shortly after, only to be arrested by Abakumov on July 4, 1942, while attached to the Kalinin Front. He was now accused of having made anti-Soviet and anti-Semitic remarks, the only time the latter charge appears in Abakumov's indictments (*VIZH* (12/1992).

Besides being demoted, Kulik also lost his decorations, including the coveted title of Hero of the Soviet Union, received in March 1940. On February 24, 1942, Stalin signed a document (*Istoricheskii Arkhiv*, 1/1992) expelling Kulik from the Central Committee and dismissing him as Deputy Commissar of Defense. Stalin at this time, however, must have had a soft spot in his heart for Kulik since he was restored in March 1942 to the rank of Maj. General, and in April 1943 to Lt. General, and appointed as Commander of the elite 4 Guard Army. His poor performance led to his dismissal, as tersely recorded in Zhukov's memoirs. In January 1944, Kulik was appointed Deputy Head of the Red Army Formation and Staffing Department, but problems continued. In April 1945, he was once again demoted to Maj. General, and this time expelled from the Party. He was appointed as Deputy Commander of the Volga Military District under another turbulent figure, Col. General V.N. Gordov, who during the war had the temerity to suggest that the institution of political commissars be dissolved. Despite his subsequent tragic fate, Gordov was a martinet of the worst kind. His instability prevented him from achieving higher position. A man with a Napoleonic complex, he had been removed as Commander of the Stalingrad Front, where he had disagreements with Khrushchev. Recently released documents (*Novaia i Noveishaia Istoriia*, 1/1994) show him in a poor light. During his command of the ill-fated 33 Army (October 1942–March 1944), West Front, his tactics brought death or injury to four Division Commanders, eight Deputy Division Commanders and Chiefs of Staff, 38 Regimental and 174 Battalion Commanders. He was a believer in execution with or without court-martial and threatened Maj. General Gladyshev, Commander of the 277 Rifle Division, and the Polish General Stanislaw Poplawski, Commander of 45 Rifle Corps, with this fate. On April 12, 1944, during the shake-up of the leadership of the West Front, the High Command warned Gordov that repeating the mistakes that he made as Commander of the 33 Army would be cause for removal from his position and reduction in rank. Nevertheless, in April 1944 Gordov was appointed as Commander of the 3 Guard Army, which he led for the remainder of the war.

Kulik was arrested on January 11, 1947. Also arrested were Gordov and Maj. General Rybal'chenko, Chief of Staff of the District. The grounds for arrest was an alleged treasonous conversation between those arrested and Army General I.E. Petrov (another military leader Stalin did not much care for) and Col. General G.F. Zakharov. Kulik was sentenced to death by the USSR Military Collegium on August 24, 1950, and shot on the same day; Gordov was shot on December 12, 1951, and Rybal'chenko sometime in August 1950. Whether the latter men were actually tried, we don't know.[9]

The Navy's turn was next. Stalin had an objective admiration for the tough Admiral of the Fleet, N.G. Kuznetsov (as he also did for Marshal Zhukov), who had commanded the Navy since April 1939, even though he may not have been fond of him personally. In fact, after the war, Stalin had offered Kuznetsov's job to Admiral I.S. Isakov, who reminded him that loss of a leg in combat in October 1942 made him unfit for such an arduous position. Stalin accepted Isakov's excuse, but remarked that since the Red Army had been commanded by people without heads, a missing leg should not be a major handicap. In 1946, Stalin had complained of Kuznetsov's "rough" talk, which seems odd since Stalin himself was not a stranger to gutter language as well as dirty and practical jokes, but he also had a prudish streak that would be offended by, among other things, Mao Tse-tung's proclivity for scatological jokes. The Soviet Navy did not perform well during the war, bottled up in ports by small forces of an enemy whose naval interests were elsewhere, and it suffered considerable losses, particularly at the hands of the Luftwaffe. When the Navy ventured out as in the case with submarines, the losses were appalling and the results negligible. Except for cursing Zhdanov, Stalin, however, seems not to have complained, and except for Admirals L.G. Levchenko and V.P. Bogolepov (who were arrested and later released) and the execution of Rear Admiral K.I. Samoilov, head of Leningrad Naval Defense in the beginning of the war, senior naval officers seem to have suffered little of his wrath during the war. In February 1946, Stalin decided to divide the Baltic Fleet into the 4th and 8th and the Pacific Fleet into the 5th and 7th Fleets. There was no merit to this lunatic proposal except that Stalin was beginning to believe his own propaganda about being the Greatest Military Leader of All Time. Stalin's own contribution to *Stalin: The Short Biography*, in fact, includes the passage "Stalin's military mastery was displayed in defense and offense. With the judgement of genius, Comrade Stalin divined the enemy's plans and repulsed them," and all of this about a man who had continued to insist until it was too late that Barbarossa was an act of provocation by the German Generals.

Kuznetsov and other Admirals had expressed reservation about this plan. Kuznetsov also had his share of disagreements with his boss, N.A. Bulganin, the Minister of Armed Forces/War. Kuznetsov was replaced in January 1947 by I.S. Iumashev. Soon charges that bore all the earmarks of a fabrication began to surface. An officer-inventor, Captain of 1 Rank V.A. Alferov had written a letter accusing Kuznetsov of having given designs of secret Soviet torpedo plans (based on captured German acoustic torpedoes) and classified maps to the Western Allies. Although documents have yet to be produced to link Alferov with the security organs, the nature of the charges strongly points in that direction. Stalin through Bulganin convened a "Court of Honor" in December 1947 presided over by Marshal L.A.

Govorov, Chief Inspector of the Ministry of Defense, a man with dark secrets in his own past (serving with Kolchak during the Civil War and coming close to being purged in 1940). Stalin had a long record of using former opponents of the Bolsheviks who had later seen the light, for his own purposes. These men, because of their pasts, were open to blackmail and thus were malleable tools. The best known were, of course, the former Mensheviks A.Ia. Vyshinskii and L.Z. Mekhlis. Others included S.I. Kavtaradze (who nevertheless served a term in prison), I.M. Maiskii, and D.I. Zaslavskii. Govorov was later to claim that all the orders came directly from Stalin. Besides Govorov, the members of the court included Army General V.A. Zakharov, Chief of the General Staff Academy; Col. General F.I. Golikov, Head of Cadres in the Ministry of Defense; Admiral G.I. Levchenko, and Vice Admiral P.S. Aban'kin, both Deputy Commanders in Chief of the Navy; Vice Admiral N.M. Kharlamov, Navy Deputy Chief of Staff (who during the war had served as head of the Soviet naval mission to Great Britain); and Vice Admiral N.M. Kulakov, Deputy Commander in Chief for Political Matters and member of the Navy's Military Soviet. The defendants were accused of "anti-government and anti-patriotic activities." The court met on January 11, 1948, and there was testimony against the defendants, particularly against Galler, who had had disagreement with Beriia during the war, by experts as well as by naval colleagues. In his testimony, the chief accuser, V.A. Alferov, even dragged the names of such long-purged "enemies of the people" as V.M. Orlov (former Commander of the Navy until 1937), I.P. Pavlunovskii (possibly the first Head of the Cheka Special Department) and G.L. Piatakov. Also working behind the scenes against Kuznetsov were Vice Admiral N.M. Kulakov and Vice Admiral P.S. Aban'kin, Deputy Commander of the Navy and head of naval construction. The court found the defendants guilty and turned the matter over to the Military Collegium under Ul'rikh for sentencing. The sentences were pronounced on February 10, 1948. Kuznetsov was reduced to Rear Admiral and removed from all command on March 8, 1948, but ended up in the Far East in July 1948 as Deputy Commander for naval matters. In February 1950, he once again took over the Pacific Fleet.

Stalin, a consummate bureaucrat, was a firm believer in committees made up of his satraps which would also prove to be convenient scapegoats. He was not pleased with the performance of I.S. Iumashev, who had replaced Kuznetsov, and so in January 1951, he appointed a committee made up of Malenkov and Beriia and the two Wise Men came up with Kuznetsov's name as the replacement. He was recalled in July 1951 to become once again Minister of Navy and soon also a member of the Central Committee (Stalin's son claimed in 1959 that Beriia was behind Kuznetsov's rehabilitation). Less fortunate were Admiral V.A. Alafuzov, Head of the Naval Academy, and Vice Admiral G.A. Stepanov, Head of Naval Training and former Commander of the White Sea Flotilla, who during the war had worked closely with the British and U.S. Navies. Both were sentenced to 10 years. Even less lucky was Admiral L.M. Galler, who received a 4-year sentence and lost his rank and on March 3, 1948, was expelled from the Navy. The last correspondence from Galler dates from October 23, 1948. Suffering from poor health, Galler died in Kazan prison on

July 12, 1950, and his place of burial is not known. All sentences were set aside on May 13, 1953, and the whole affair was blamed on M.D. Riumin. Galler was one of the two Fleet Commanders and the only Flagman 2 Rank (Vice Admiral) to have survived the Great Purge, but his luck ran out during the post-war years. Even less fortunate was Vice Admiral L.G. Goncharov, department head in the Leningrad Higher Naval School, who had twice before survived arrest and imprisonment. He was arrested on April 8, 1948, and died on April 23, 1948, during interrogation by V.I. Komarov.[10] On January 1, 1947, Admiral I.S. Iumashev took over the Navy and held this position until July 20, 1951, when the demoted Kuznetsov was recalled from the Far East.

The next immediate target of MGB also involved the Navy, but only indirectly. On April 10, 1948, on his 45th birthday, Minister of Merchant Marine A.A. Afanas'ev, who had just replaced P.P. Shirshov in this post, was kidnapped from his car in the middle of Moscow, blindfolded, and taken to a vacant building. The unknown assailants who identified themselves as members of American intelligence, proposed that since Afanas'ev was already working for British intelligence, he might want to consider spying for the Americans as well. Upon his release, Afanas'ev, smelling a provocation, tried unsuccessfully to reach Stalin but managed to contact only Beriia, who told him he deserved a medal for his vigilance. Beriia then upbraided Abakumov about laxity in the MGB. Abakumov, however, managed to find the "American agent" who supposedly had recruited Afanas'ev. He was in due course arrested. After being worked over for 20 days by V.I. Komarov, he confessed and received a 20-year sentence.[11] By 1948, although for all practical purposes, Marshal Zhukov had been neutralized and was consigned to the backwaters of the Volga Military District, another attempt was made to compromise him through a most unlikely candidate, Lt. General K.F. Telegin, a man with impeccable Stalinist credentials and whose career provides a shining example that under Stalin no one was ever safe.

A Chekist since the mid-1920s, Telegin had served as Political Commissar of the NKVD Troops during the Ezhov years. On June 13, 1938, Commissar of State Security 3rd Rank G.S. Liushkov, Head of NKVD in the Far East, who had since the summer of 1937 waged a campaign of terror which led to 25,000 arrests including those of the leaders of the local military, apparently guessing correctly that his patron Ezhov was about to get the axe, became the first senior Soviet Chekist to defect. Telegin was sent to the Far East as head of the Border Troops along with G.F. Gorbach, the new head of NKVD, and must have had an important part in the inevitable bloodbath that followed Liushkov's flight. Gorbach was purged in November 1938 and was replaced by Beriia's man, M.M. Gvishiani, but Telegin survived. After serving in the Lake Khasan campaign, Telegin returned to Moscow and was attached to NKVD Headquarters.

During the Winter War against Finland, after the initial Soviet defeats, 27 NKVD "control groups" each of 100 men were formed to watch over the fighting troops.[12] L.Z. Mekhlis and a number of party and NKVD functionaries were sent to stiffen the Soviet resistance and Telegin was appointed Head of the Rear and Commissar of the 9 Army commanded by V.I. Chuikov, the future hero of Stalingrad. Telegin replaced A.N. Apollonov, who at the time was also Deputy Head of Border Troops. The result was the court-martial and execution of the Commander of the 44 Rifle Division, A. I. Vinogradaov; his Chief of Staff, O.I. Volkov; and the Division's Political Commissar, I.T. Pakhomenko. These were the only Soviet senior officers who were shot in the aftermath of the Winter War, even though many were deserving of such a fate. Stalin, however, at this time could not afford another bloodbath among the military. He sacked Voroshilov, Commissar of Defense, as well as Ia.V. Smushkevich, Commander of the Air Force, whose planes had managed to bomb the Soviet Embassy in their first night attack on Helsinki. The half measures, however, failed to impress Hitler, who was convinced more than ever by the miserable performance of the Red Army in the Winter War, that the Soviet Union was a "rotten corpse" ready to collapse. A year-and-a-half later, the bloody fields of Karelia were to be repeated in Belorussia and Ukraine.

At the start of the war, Telegin was employed once again in the NKVD central apparatus in Moscow. In the dark days of October 1941, the Soviet command formed the Moscow Defense Zone to defend the capital, and NKVD Lt. General P.A. Artem'ev was appointed as Commander. Although a virtual dictator, and ruling with typical Stalinist sturm-und-drang tactics, Arteme'ev was probably the last person in the Soviet Union with Bonapartist ambitions. Just in case, Telegin, even more trustworthy, was appointed Political Commissar of the zone and actually ran the show when Artem'ev was absent. With the danger past, Telegin was assigned as Political Commissar of the Don, Central, Belorussian and 1 Belorussian Fronts, which were all commanded by the once imprisoned K.K. Rokosovsskii, who remained a fervent admirer of Stalin despite his arrest and imprisonment in 1937 and replacement during the war by Zhukov as Commander of the 1 Belorussian Front before the Battle of Berlin. Rokosovsskii had the misfortune of also being watched for a time by L.F. Tsanava, who headed theSMERSH of Central Front. Telegin continued on with Zhukov when the latter replaced Rokosovskii in Nov. 1944 to monopolize the glory that would go with the capture of Berlin. Telegin continued to serve as Commissar of Soviet Forces in Germany after Zhukov's recall, but his position was shaky. After the war, I.A. Serov reporting to Stalin and Beriia had complained about Telegin's bias toward the NKVD. Telegin also did not help his own cause by being too inquisitive about the corrupt practices of the secret police in occupied Germany. As a Chekist, he could not help but notice the trainloads of stolen goods that were being shipped back to Russia, and he informed Zhukov to this effect. Late in 1947, MGB arrested Telegin's brother, D.F. Telegin, an alcoholic who had allegedly made anti-Soviet statements. Through him they managed to gather incriminating material against Telegin, who was arrested on January 30, 1948. A number of books on Zhukov incorrectly claim that Telegin was arrested earlier, at the same time as Novikov and Shakhurin. Maj. General V. Nekrasov (*Sovetkaia Militsia*, 6/1990), for instance, claims that Telegin was arrested in Nov. 1945. In the final analysis, during the post-war year, Soviet occupied Germany was a cesspool of corruption, which led not only to the charges against Telegin and even Zhukov, but also to tension between Serov and another Chekist with less than clean hands—

Abakumov. Also arrested in the same case in Sepember 1948 were Hero of the Soviet Union Guard Lt. General V.V. Kriukov, and his wife, the popular singer L.A. Ruslanova. The accused were charged not only with anti-Soviet activities, but with theft of artworks. It is ironic that the corruption charges against Kriukov and Ruslanova were also true of Abakumov, who was responsible for their arrest and interrogation. Illegal theft in occupied areas of Germany—not to be confused with the official plunder that was government policy—is one of the dirty little secrets of Stalinism that need further study. It went far beyond common Red Army soldiers sporting dozens of "liberated" watches on their wrists.

It was not until November 1951, after Abakumov's own arrest, that Kriukov was sentenced to 25 years. Telegin also received 25 years on March 20, 1952. The prosecution was led by Lt. General of Judiciary N.P. Afanas'ev, Chief Military Prosecutor of the USSR whose aesthetic demeanor hid a committed Stalinist.

In 1951, during interrogations following his own arrest, Abakumov took pride in arresting Telegin and eight others connected to Marshal Zhukov. Telegin was released in July 1953 and died in 1981. His memoirs are silent about his arrest and imprisonment. Telegin and Kriukov were not the only senior officers who were arrested in the campaign against Zhukov. Others were Lt. General F.E. Bobkov, former Commissar of the Group of Soviet Forces in Germany; Lt. General I.S. Varennikov, former Chief of Staff 40 Army; Maj. General A.A. Filatov, former Commander of 12 Guard Rifle Division; and Lt. General L.F. Miniuk, Zhukov's Adjutant. The exact dates of their arrests are not known, and it is possible that they were rounded up in 1946 when the first serious attempts were made to compromise Zhukov. Despite Telegin's and others' testimony against Zhukov, he was left alone at the Ural Military District. Soviet documents show that although Riumin, now a Lt. Colonel, was in charge of the case, it was Stalin who was pulling the strings.[13] What is surprising is that it took so long before the accused were tried and sentenced. During the post-war period, Stalin was simply not energetic enough, and Abakumov's men simply could not match the ferocity and efficiency of their Ezhovite predecessors. In April 1950, a number of Generals who, although not members of the Vlasov movement, had been accused of collaboration with the enemy, were tried and shot. The careers of most of them have already been discussed in Chapters 5 and 6.

NOTES

1. *Bakinskii Rabochii* (October 2, 1968); and A.M. Samsonov, *Znat' i Pomnit'*, p. 283.
2. Volkogonov, *Triumf*, book 2, part 1, p. 73.
3. *Izvestiia TsK KPPS* (1/1991).
4. *Leningradskoe Delo*, pp. 403–95 and Kostliarov, *Golgofa*, pp. 33, 64.
5. For Zhukov, see *VIZH* (6/1987, 10/1988, 12/1988, 2/1993, 5/1993); *Krasnaia Zvezda* (August 6, 1988, January 12, 1989, December 23, 1989); *Pravda* (January 20, 1989, August 17, 1991, August 19, 1991); *Kommunist* (9/1988, Issue 14, 1988); *Voprosy Istorii* (11/1990, 2–3/1991); *Marshal Zhukov. Kakim My Ego Pomnim*; *Marshal Zhukov. Polkovodets i Chelovek*; G.K. Zhukov, *Yospeminaniia i Razmyshleniia*, 4th ed.; and Robert Conquest, *Stalin, Breaker of Nations*.

6. Kostliarov, *Golgofa*, p. 10.

7. *Voprosy Istorii KPSS* (11/1990).

8. N.S. Patoliahev, *Measures of Maturity*, pp. 282–87.

9. For Kulik, see N.N. Voronov, *Na Sluzhbe Voennoi*; D.A. Volkogonov, op. cit.; A.M. Samsonov, op. cit.; *Bitva za Leninarad*; G.K. Zhukov, *Vospominaniia*; *VIZH* (9/1961, 12/1988, 3/1990, 10/1991); *Moscow News* (12/1990); *Krasnaia Zvezda* (August 6, 1988); *Sputnik* (10/1988); *Izvestiia TsK KPSS* (2/1989, 7/1991, 8/1991). For Vannikov and the Commissariat of the Defense Industry in the beginning of the war, see V.N. Novikov, *Nakanune i v Dni Ispytanii*; V.S. Emel'ianov, *Na Poroge Voiny*; A.I. Shakhurin, *Kryl'ia Pobedy*; D.F. Ustinov, *Vo Imia Pobedy*; V.A. Chalmaev, *Malyshev*; I.G. Golovin, *I.V. Kurchatov*; *YIZH* (2/1962); *Voprosy Istorii* (10/1968 and 1/1969), available in English translation JPRS 48371–July 8, 1969; *Literaturnaia Gazeta* (April 20, 1988); and *Izvestiia TsK KPSS* (2/1991).

10. For Kuznetsov and post-war purge in the Navy, see N.G. Kuznetsov, *Nakanune*; V.I. Platonov, *Zapiski Admiral*; *VIZH* (9/1965 and 1/1992); *Oktiabr'* (11/1965); *Izvestiia* (August 28, 1988); *Sovetskaia Rossiia* (July 29, 1988); *Druzhba Narodov* (11/1988); and *Krasnaia Zvezda* (August 6, 1988). For Galler, see S.A. Zonin, *Admiral L.M. Galler*. For Goncharov, see Kostliarov (op. cit.).

11. For Afanas'ev, see *Beriia: Konets Kar'erv*, p. 143; and *Leningradskoe Delo*, p. 406.

12. *Istoriia SSSR* (2/1991).

13. For Telegin, see K.F. Telegin, *Voiny Neschitannye Versty*; Volkogonov, *Triumf*, book 2, part 2, p. 214; Kostliarov, *Golgofa*, p. 14; *Znamia* (12/1986); *and VIZH* (5/1975 and 6/1989).

Chapter 8

The Anti-Semitic Campaigns

Stalin's anti-Semitism went back to his exile days with Ia. M. Sverdlov and his later battles with Trotskii, Kamenev, and Zinov'ev. It has been suggested that Stalin, who remained first and foremost a Georgian throughout his life, somehow became a "Great Russian" and decided that Jews would make a scapegoat for the ills of the Soviet Union. Others, such as the Polish writer Aleksander Wat (a victim himself), claim that Stalin was not an anti-Semite by nature, but the pro-Americanism of Soviet Jews forced him to follow a deliberate policy of anti-Semitism.[1] Wat's views are, however, colored by the fact that Stalin, for obvious reasons, at first had to depend on Jewish Communists to help carry out his post-war policies in Poland. I believe a better explanation was Stalin's sense of envy (an occupational hazard for Marxists), which consumed him throughout his life. He also found in Jews a convenient target. By late 1930, Stalin, as Alliluyeva's memoirs indicate, was suffering from a full-blown case of anti-Semitism. When General Sikorski, the Prime Minister of the Polish Government in Exile, visited the Soviet Union in December 1941, he and Stalin would lighten up the serious negotiations by exchanging anti-semitic jokes, a reminder of Stalin's and the Poles' indifference to the grim fate of Jews in German-occupied Europe. On other occasions, Jews were obstacles to Stalin's plans. In 1939, when he had embarked on a policy of rapprochement with Nazi Germany and had replaced Litvinov with Molotov, he ordered the latter to purge the Foreign Service of Jews. Iu.B. Borev in *Staliniada* states that after the war the task of preparing a new criminal code was assigned to the Deputy Prosecutor General (an unnamed Lt. General) who included anti-Semitism as a crime. Stalin objected to this and ordered the man removed. At times, Stalin's anti-Semitism would take bizarre turns. In the list of Red Army Generals published in May-June 1940, we come across a Maj. General A.S. Zhidov, the future Commander of the 5 Guard Army and a Hero of the Soviet Union. All of these honors, however, came to Zhidov, in reality a Slav, after he was persuaded by Stalin to change his name to Zhadov. Stalin also apparently did not care for Armenian names (Stalin may have also felt that the Armenians had designs on his native Georgia), and Beriia's Armenian colleagues such as Dekanozov, Mamulov, and the Kobulov brothers all had Russified names. Sudoplatov denies that Stalin was anti-Semitic per se, but rather opposed to nationalism in any form, except perhaps the Great Russian variety. In his remarks to F.I. Chuev cited in *Molotov Remembers*, Chief Marshal of Aviation A.E. Golovanov provides some striking examples of the latter sentiment. Stalin's views about the threat of nationalism to Soviet power were colored by his own experiences including service as Commissar of the Nationalities, as well as the events of World War II. The recent collapse of the Soviet Union vindicates Stalin's fears in this area.

The post-war anti-cosmopolitist campaign organized by Zhdanov was launched on August 14, 1946 targeted with a Central Committee resolution critical of journals *Zvezda* and *Leningrad*. The first targets in September 1946 were Jewish drama critics and writers, as well as such nonconformist Slavs as A.A. Akhmatova and M.M. Zoshchenko. Paradoxically, during 1945–1947, numerous Jews were also winners of the Stalin Prize.[2] Regardless, Zhdanov's death in August 1948 did not stop the campaign. The fact that over half-a-million Jews had served in the Red Army during the war and nearly 200,000 had been killed in combat was now forgotten.

The Great Terror claimed many Jewish victims, but it was not per se an anti-Semitic campaign. According to J. Arch Getty and his colleagues (*American Historical Review*, October 1993), by 1940 0.61% of the Jewish population of the USSR was in custody, lower than that of most of the other nationalities. This percentage, however, does not tell the entire story. In some professions, it was undoubtedly higher. For instance, among the 100 or so imprisoned scientists who were employed in the "Tupolev sharaga," 18 were Jewish. This was more than all the other non-Russian nationalities combined.[3]

As a nationality singled out for persecution under the Romanovs, Jews understandably were highly active in various revolutionary movements. They were overwhelmingly represented in the first Soviet Council of Commissars, which included only two Russians (Lenin and Chicherin). The Jews were also well-represented in the Commissariats of War, Internal Affairs, Finance, Justice, Foreign Affairs, and later GOSPLAN. Even in 1936, Jews formed a majority in SOVNARKOM, and 61 members of the Central Committee were Jewish. In the beginning of 1937, the Jews constituted 5.3% of all Party members and here ranked third among the ethnic groups. At the highest level of government and the Party, the representatives became increasingly less significant. Even as early as 1922, only four of the 13 members of Politburo (Kamenev, Zinov'ev, Trotskii, and Sokolnikov) were Jewish, and Stalin soon eased them out. At the apex of his power, Stalin's inner circle included only two Jews: Kaganovich and Mekhlis. Lenin and Stalin, despite their protestations to the contrary, played the politics of ethnicity with as much enthusiasm as the affirmative action bean counters in the contemporary U.S. It was no accident that in such messy affairs as the murder of the Tsar and his family, minorities such as Jews and Latvians were well-represented.

A look at the record of Trotskii and I.M. Sverdlov during the Civil War or the activities of Bela Kun and R.S. Zemliachka in the Crimea in 1920; or F.I.

Goloshchekin in West Siberia and Central Asia; of Kaganovich during the 1930s; and Mekhlis, I.O. Matulevich, and L.R. Sheinin during the Great Purge and the Great Patriotic War; and of G.M. Maironovskii, head of the secret toxicological laboratory, is proof that savagery is not a monopoly of one race or nationality. Also, in the 1930s, many of Stalin's closest henchmen such as Iagoda, Kaganovich, Mekhlis, P.N. Pospelov, E.M. Iaroslavskii, and D.I. Zaslavskii (leading mouthpieces) were Jewish. Ditto Ia.A. Iakovev and M.M. Khataevich, the architect and chief executioner of collectivization. Fourteen of the 20 top officials under Iagoda (Agranov, L.D. Bul', I.L. Ioffe, B.I. Mogilevskii, Firin, Flekser, Pauker, Slutskii, Ostrovskii, Katznel'son, Gai, etc.) were Jewish and, in fact, G.E. Prokof'ev, the Second Deputy Commissar of NKVD, was the only Slav among Iagoda's closest collaborators. Many who served under Ezhov (Frinovskii, Bel'skii, Dagin, Litvin, Kogan, Gerzon, Shapiro, Shpigel'glas, the Berman brothers, Leplevskii, Liushkov, L.I. Reikhman, Zalpeter, etc.) were also Jewish. The first leaders of the Gulag (Abrampol'skii, Belitskii, Fainovich, M. Finkel'shtein, Fridberg, Raiskii, Z.B. Katsnel'son, L.I. Kogan, I.I. Pliner, S.G. Firin, M.D. Berman, N.P. Zeligman, and N.A. Frankel') were all Jewish (all except Frankel' fell victim to the repressions). The writer V.D. Uspenskii claims that 95% of early camp commanders were Jewish. By 1946 the picture, however, had changed drastically. Of 259 general officers in police and security services, no more than a handful were Jewish.

Despite this and the post-war anti-Semitic campaigns, a number of Jews such as L.F. Raikhman, L.L. Shvartsman, and L.R. Sheinin were significant players in the machinery of terror. Stalin, the "breaker of all nations," victimized all, but those who assisted him—the flotsam of the Soviet society, the fanatics, opportunists and sadists—also represented all races and nationalities. Beriia, whose own background was suspect, also tolerated Jews, but usually in mid-level positions. It was only during the post-war years under Abakumov and Kruglov that the process of excluding Jews from high positions began and was continued after Stalin's death.

Although the claims made during the Cold War years about a Kremlin master plan to take over the world are highly exaggerated, the Soviet Union as an alleged superpower embarked on or was sometimes inadvertently drawn into policies which meant wooing and arming the Third World and Arab states, usually with unsatisfactory results. The Soviet policy meant support for the anti-Semitic campaigns of Arab states, including the uprooting and deporting of Jewish communities thousands of years old. It also included propaganda which at times in its crudity matched that of the Nazis. The insensitivity of Soviet leadership to the concerns and feelings of the Jewish citizens not only was morally reprehensible, but proved to be a major policy blunder, in the long run leading, among other things, to mass emigration of some of the Soviet Union's most productive citizens. The Soviet support for international thugs such as Idi Amin, Kaddafi, Megistu, and the PLO terrorists and a domestic policy which smacked of anti-Semitism finally deprived the Soviet Union of any moral authority that she might have enjoyed as a revolutionary state bound to follow a different path in international affairs. It showed her to be a selfish and crude state and one ultimately with feet of clay. In the long run, the adventurist policies of Khrushchev and Brezhnev contributed even more than the Stalinist terror to the collapse of Communism. These anti-Semitic policies of Stalin and his successor, more than any other factor, also gave rise to the neo-conservative movement in the United States, which provided the ideological underpinning of the militant anti-Communism of the Reagan years. In the absence of Stalinist terror, the contradictions of the Soviet system would have caused its eventual collapse, but its chances of survival were not helped by trying to keep up with the Carter/Reagan arms build-up. The genesis of the post-war anti-Semitic campaigns was in the formation of the Jewish Antifascist Committee (JAC) in the early days of the war. The committee, like similar groups, was officially sponsored in 1942 by the Soviet Information Bureau headed officially by A.S. Shcherbakov, who had replaced Mekhlis as Head of the Political Administration of the Red Army in June 1942. Shcherbakov, a crude Stalinist, was also a candidate member of the Politburo. It is quite likely that because of his many responsibilities, the anti-fascist committees were run by his Deputy, the veteran diplomat S.A. Lozovskii.[4] The basis for the JAC organization was a political rally held in August 1941 in Moscow by a number of Jewish residents. The committee was formed in April 1942 in Kuibyshev and was also supported by Beriia, who may have gotten the idea from two refugee Jewish labor leaders, G.G.V.M. Erlikh (Henryk Erlich), born in 1892, and V.I. Alter (Viktor Alter), born in 1890. The two veteran Polish Bund leaders, although anti-Bolshevik, had supported collective security in the 1930s and cooperation with the Soviet Union. Both, according to documents released by the USSR General Prosecutor (*Shchit i Mech*, September 3, 1992; *Dissent*, Spring 1993; *East European Jewish Affairs*, No. 2, 1992; *Forward*, December 11, 1992), were arrested on October 4, 1939, in Brest Litovsk after the Soviet occupation of Eastern Poland. On July 28, 1941, they, along with other prisoners, were transferred to the Saratov prison.

On August 2, 1941, Erlich was sentenced to death by the Military Tribunal of the NKVD Troops of the Saratov oblast; his sentence was later commuted to 10 years in prison, confirmed by the USSR Supreme Court on August 22. On September 11, 1941, Erlich was brought to Moscow and released a day later as part of the Soviet-Polish agreement of July 17, 1941. Alter was sentenced to death by the Military Collegium of the USSR Supreme Court on July 20, 1941, but on July 22 the sentence was reduced by the USSR Supreme Court to 10 years. He was released on September 13, 1941. On October 15, 1941, the two, along with the staff of the Polish Embassy, were evacuated to Kuibyshev. On December 3 or 4, 1941, they were again arrested. Erlich committed suicide on May 14, 1942, in Kuibyshev prison (another date given is May 7, 1942). His suicide caused two NKVD officials to be sentenced to 5 and 10 years in prison for negligence and increased the security for Alter, who reportedly also attempted suicide. On February 17, 1943, Alter was executed in the same prison. The order to execute Alter and Erlich is found in a falsely dated sentence by the Military Collegium chaired by Ul'rikh and joined by D.Ia. Kandybin and V.V. Bukanov. The court allegedly met on December 23, 1941, and found that after receiving amnesty, the two men did not terminate their criminal activities against the Soviet Union and systematically appealed to the troops to stop the bloodshed by concluding peace with Fascist Germany, a course which incidentally was being explored at the same time by Stalin. The two men were found guilty under Articles 58 and 319–320 of the RSFSR Criminal Code and were sentenced to death. It is doubtful that such a court meeting ever took place, but if it did, it must have not been in December 1941, but after Erlich's suicide. Presiding over Alter's execution and burning of his personal effects was Senior Major of State Security S.I. Ogol'tsev, Head of NKVD in Kuibushev. We can speculate that Erlich's suicide may have led to Alter's execution since he would prove to be an embarrassing witness. Three days *before* Alter's execution, Stalin ordered Litvinov, now Ambassador to the United States, to announce that they had been shot in *December 1942* for anti-Soviet, pro-German activities. Two months later, Litvinov amended the date to December 1941. With their American contacts, Erlich and Alter would have been highly valuable in fostering friendly relations between the United States and the USSR. The fate of Erlich and Alter does not make sense at all, and it rightly poisoned the atmosphere between the Western Jews and the USSR just as Katyn had Soviet-Polish relations. Sudoplatov (p. 290) blames the two men's death on their popularity abroad, which made them not completely pliable tools of Stalin. Or perhaps they simply knew too much. Those who had tried to intervene on their behalf included Albert Einstein, Wendell Willkie, Reinhold Niebuhr, Mayor La Guardia, and labor leaders William Green, David Dubinsky, and Philip Murray. Various reasons have been given for Stalin's act of savagery, which on the surface defies logic. The most plausible is that as in the case of Katyn, Stalin was willing to go to any length to destroy all potential opponents with Polish connections.

The released Soviet documents show the importance of the two men. Many of the chief actors in Katyn such as Beriia, Merkulov, L.F. Raikhman, G.S. Zhukov, and P.V. Fedotov were also involved here. Also implicated were Bashtakov of the NKVD 1 Special Section, who was in "operational" charge of the prisoners and to whom Reikhman would send Beriia's instructions, as well as Bashtakov's local representative Major of State Security Butenko and his successor Captain of State Security Timofeev. Local support was provided by the head of NKVD in Kuibyshev, Senior Major of State Security A.S. Blinov, head of NKVD in Kuibyshev in 1942 and his successor Senior Major of State Security S.I. Ogol'tsev. These two were rising stars in the secret police, serving after the war as Deputy Minister and First Deputy Minister MGB under Abakumov, with the latter briefly Acting Minister in July 1951 after Abakumov's arrest. Ul'rikh and his colleagues in the Military Collegium and V.M. Bochkov provided the cover-up. With so many distinguished personalities, there is little doubt that Alter's execution was ordered by Stalin himself. The Alter-Erlich affair claimed only two victims, but in its senseless cruelty and deception, was a mini-Katyn. It would be nearly 50 years before the truth would be known.

The Jewish Anti-Fascist Committee had 70 members, including a number of prominent non-Jewish writers and artists such as the physicist P.L. Kapitsa. The Executive Committee had 19 members and its chairman was S.M. Mikhoel's, Director of the Moscow Yiddish State Theater. The Secretary of the Committee was at first S. Epshtein, editor of the Yiddish newspaper *Einikait*. After his death, the writer I.S.

Fefer, a Party member since 1919, became secretary. Before that he had been a member of the Jewish "Bund." Fefer was considered by many as Beriia's stalking horse in JAC. Other members included S.M. Shpigel'glas, Deputy Secretary of the Committee and a Party member since 1919, and according to Vaksberg, the former Acting Head of NKVD Foreign Department; P.D. Markish, the leading Yiddish poet and winner of the Stalin Award; L.A. Gol'dberg, former editor of *Der Emes*; S.O. Berman and A. Kats of the Stalin Military Academy; B.A. Shimelovich, of the Red Army Medical Services; and of course the best known, the writer Il'ia Erenburg. Besides Fefer, there was to be at least another member with a checkered past. The writer L.R. Sheinin had served as Vyshinskii's Deputy. Since Vyshinskii was a physical coward, Sheinin represented him in many executions. Besides political propaganda, the committee tried to influence Western public opinion and promote the anti-Nazi coalition. A year after its formation, JAC moved to Moscow. After the war, the Soviet Union on the surface was not openly hostile to Jewish interests in Palestine, recognizing the new state of Israel and allowing the shipment of arms to save the day in the First War of Independence. At the same time, Stalin, through A.A. Zhdanov, launched a cultural revolution aimed at, among others, "rootless cosmopolitans," which carried strong anti-Semitic overtones. Besides ideological attacks, there were also more concrete charges such as a Jewish conspiracy to detach Crimea, an area de-populated by Stalin's war-time deportations, as an independent state to resettle the Jews. This idea was first proposed to the Jewish leaders by no less than Molotov and Kagnovich, who may have been acting as Stalin's agents provocateurs.[5] Thus, the post-war anti-Jewish campaigns are also referred to as "Crimean." Sudoplatov's memoirs provide considerable evidence that the whole Crimean scheme was a cynical ploy by Stalin to attract what he considered Jewish capital for the post-war reconstruction of Russia.

The spark for the campaign is usually attributed to the enthusiastic reception given by the local Jewish population when Golda Meier visited Moscow on September 2, 1948. Soviet archives, however, tell a different story. The groundwork for the campaign, however, had been laid at an earlier date. On December 25, 1945, M.F. Shkiriatov, Deputy Chairman (later Chairman) of the Party Control Commission, "the conscience of the Party" and a stalwart Stalinist wrote to Malenkov questioning the necessity of the JAC and suggesting that its activities be severely curtailed. A.I. Vaksberg is not sure whether Malenkov shared Shkiriatov's misgivings with Stalin. A study of Shkiriatov's career, however, provides plenty of evidence that the letter could have only been written on Stalin's insistance. Independent action was not the forte of Shkiriatov, the most faceless of Stalin's toadies. On October 12, 1946, two days after he had officially taken over the Ministry of State Security (MGB), Abakumov wrote to the CC CPSU about the "nationalist tendencies" of several members of the Committee. On November 26, 1946 M.A. Suslov, on behalf of CC CPSU, wrote to Stalin suggesting the dissolution of the committee. On December 19, 1947, the first arrest, of Dr. I.I. Gol'shtein, an economist attached to the Academy of Sciences, was made. This was followed eight days later by the arrest of Z.G. Grinberg, researcher at the Gor'kii Institute of World Literature. Their interrogation implicated several members of the Jewish Anti-Fascist Committee, including S.A.

Lozovskii and I.S. Fefer, duly reported by Abakumov to the CC CPSU on March 1, 1948. Three members of the JAC, I.S. Fefer, B.L. Zuskin, and D.N. Gold'shtein, were soon arrested. Stalin, who was undoubtedly organizing the whole affair, was getting impatient and intervened directly by arranging the murders of the Yiddish actor S.M.Mikhoels (a prominent member of JAC) and the critic V.I. Golubov-Potapov, which were carried out in Minsk on January 13, 1948.[6] Svetlana Alliluyeva claims that she heard her father speaking in Georgian, ordering Mikhoel's murder to L.F. Tsanava, head of the MGB in Belorussia. Sudoplatov, in his memoirs, claims that Golubov-Potapov, whom he identifies as an MGB agent, lured Fefer to a dacha outside Minsk where both men were murdered by poison by one Colonel Lebedev and his assistants. The bodies were then thrown under trucks to fake an accident. All the individuals involved received decorations which were rescinded in 1954.

The vehicles used were borrowed from the Belorussian Military District whose commander, Col. General S.G. Trofimenko, was kept in the dark. According to A.I. Vaksberg in *Stalin Against the Jews*, on February 11, 1948, Bodunov, Deputy Head of the MVD Militia, wrote to I.A. Serov, Deputy Minister MVD, about Mikhoels' death. By reading between the lines, it was obvious that Mikhoels had been eliminated by official sanction. There seems little doubt that Serov shared this information with Beriia who made use of it after Stalin's death. Again according to Vaksberg, Stalin was not sure how to use Mikhoels murder to eliminate the JAC, and, in fact, he sent investigator and novelist L.R. Sheinin to come up with a plausible scenario (the Kirov Affair was being played out again). In March 1948, Sheinin was called back to Moscow and soon lost his job with the Prosecutor's Office. Stalin finally decided to let Abakumov and the MGB come up with the campaign, without using Mikhoels murder as a driving wedge.

Beriia's version of events appears in a letter dating from April 2, 1953, to Malenkov and the Party Presidium (*Argumenty i Fakty*, May 1992; *Novyi Mir*, October 1993). Here Beriia claims that according to the personal testimony of the imprisoned Abakumov, he was ordered by Stalin to organize the murder of Mikhoels, which he arranged through his First Deputy S.I. Ogol'tsov and another MGB functionary, F.G. Shubniakov. This was then carried out in Minsk with the help of L.F. Tsanava (head of MGB in Belorussia). Beriia added that he had ordered the arrest of Ogol'tsov and Tsanava. There are problems with Beriia's letter. The date of Mikhoel's and Golubov-Potapov's killing is given as February rather than January, and what were Beriia's motives for writing this self-serving letter? Surely Malenkov and the members of the Presidium must have known or guessed how Mikhoel's had died, and a sense of justice, belated or otherwise, was not one of Beriia's strong points. Here Beriia wanted to shift the blame of the post-war repressions to Stalin and the MGB, and he was not totally off the mark. He may also have wanted to justify keeping in prison Abakumov, who, after all, had been put there by Stalin at the time when Beriia was releasing other prisoners. So much for the supposed alliance between Beriia and Abakumov.

In his important article, A. Borshchagovskii (*Novyi Mir*, October 1993) shows how Mikhoel's was designated as the fall guy for the anti-Jewish campaigns. Of the first two victims arrested by Abakumov, Grinberg was to die in prison on December

22, 1949, but Gol'dshtein survived, and in a letter dated from October 11, 1953, while still in prison and in other testimony, revealed how Abakumov, Komarov, Likhachev, and Sorokin tried to drag testimony from him implicating Mikhoel's as well as Fefer, E.A. Alliluyeva, and Morozov, Svetlana's Jewish husband. Although Mikhoel's at this time was a free man, Abakumov continued to refer to him as a "scoundrel." Gol'dshtein and Grinberg were arrested without prosecutorial sanctions in violation of Soviet law. Abakumov and his predecessors would dispense with such niceties, particularly in the very beginning when they were building a case and needed the arrest of those whose forced testimonies would then be used to round up others in a more "legal" manner. The report by Colonel of Judiciary N. Zhukov of the Chief Military Prosecutor's Office dating from November 4, 1955, exonerating the victims associated with the JAC is based on Gol'dshtein's testimony. Zhukov's report, however, was nearly a year too late to be used in Abakumov's trial, which already had been held in December 1954 and was based mainly on crimes committed in connection with the "Leningrad Affair."

Besides Abakumov, the organizers of the campaign against the JAC included Lt. General S.I. Ogol'tsov, Maj. Generals A.G. Leonov and E.P. Pitovranov, Colonels Komarov, Likhachev, Romanov, Riumin, Shubniakov, Sorokin, Kholev, and other 30 other more investigators including Grishaev, Gerasimov, Kuz'min, Lebedev, Rassypninskii, Shishkov, Tsvetaev, Pogrebnoi (veteran of Katyn), Zhirukhin, and a Captain Merkulov.

Three recent studies, two by A.I. Vaksberg (*Neraskrytye Tainy*, 1993) and *Stalin Against the Jews*, 1994), and one by A. Borshchagovskii (*Obviniaetsaia Krol'*, 1994) add considerably to our knowledge of the anti-Semitic campaigns. The latter, the most detailed study of persecution of JAC leaders, puts Abakumov in the center stage, but provides little evidence that he was doing anything but Stalin's bidding. It would have been unthinkable for Abakumov and his colleagues to organize the murder of Mikhoels or the arrest of Molotov's wife on their own. Once given carte blanche by Stalin, they would go about this with their typical brutality with all stops pulled.

During 1948, the anti-Jewish campaigns gained momentum and even Ehrenburg was forced to write an article in *Pravda* denouncing Jewish "nationalism." On March 26, 1948, Abakumov sent a report to the Central Committee with copies to Stalin, Molotov, Zhdanov, and A.A. Kuznet'sov, but not to Beriia, implicating the JAC leaders in anti-Soviet activities. On November 20, 1948, the Politburo approved the Council of Ministers' order to dissolve JAC.[7] On January 13, 1949, Lozovskii, a member of CC CPSU, met with Malenkov and M.F. Shkiriatov. Five days later, he was expelled from the Party and on January 26, he was arrested (A.I. Vaksberg gives an earlier date of January 16). Also arrested in January were Shimeliovich, I.S. Iuzefovich, L.M. Kvitko, P.D. Markish (on January 17), D.R. Bergel'son, I.S. Vatenberg, Ch. Vatenberg-Ostrovsakia, and E.I. Teumin. Besides providing the MGB's investigative organs, at times Abakumov took a more personal interest in the campaign. During the last week of December 1948, he showed up at the Moscow Yiddish Theater accompanied by the poet I.S. Fefer to find compromising material about the martyr S.M. Mikhoel's. Fefer's collaboration with Abakumov, however, did not save him from being arrested on December 24, 1948. Early in 1949, Abakumov personally interrogated the academician L.S. Shtern, who had returned to the Soviet Union from the United States in the late 1930s, and called her a Zionist whore and part of a conspiracy to detach Crimea from the USSR.[8]

Despite long imprisonment and typical MGB investigative methods (now organized by Riumin), at first some of the accused such as Lozovskii and Fefer denied the charges before being finally "persuaded." On August 24, 1951, the new Minister of State Security, S.D. Ignat'ev, who had replaced Abakumov, in a letter to Malenkov and Beriia, confirmed the "nationalist and espionage" activities of the accused. On April 3, 1952, Ignat'ev forwarded the indictment to Stalin with copies to Malenkov and Beriia. The accused were all to be shot except academician L.S. Shtern, whose specialty of gerontology was of interest to the aging dictator. The Military Collegium of the USSR Supreme Court, chaired by Lt. General of Judiciary A.A. Cheptsov, met on April 7, 1952, and passed out the sentences. There were no prosecutors or defense lawyers. Thirteen defendants were sentenced to death. These sentences were carried out between May 8 and July 18, 1952. A non-Soviet source gives August 12, 1952, as the execution date for one victim, B.A. Shikhliovich. A Soviet source also states that S.A. Lozovskii was sentenced on July 18, 1952, and was shot in August.[9] Riumin was present at the executions. Testimony against the defendants had been provided under torture by I.I. Gold'shtein and Z.G. Grinberg. B.A. Shimelovich was the only defendant who refused to confess until the end. I.S. Fefer, who had earlier testified against other defendants, reportedly withdrew his confession, claiming that it was based on threats personally made by Abakumov.

Shtern, the Soviet Union's leading gerontologist, was the only defendant not sentenced to death. Stalin had a deep interest in this subject, which had implications for his own rule. With the exception of Lysenko, no "scientist" fared better under him than academician A.A. Bogomolets (Hero of Socialist Labor, Stalin Prize, etc.), who had claimed men could live to 150. When Bogomolets died in 1945 at age 65, a disappointed Stalin called him a swindler and a fraud. It remains a mystery why it took so long to bring this affair to a conclusion. The investigative material in the JAC case ran to 42 volumes and the court proceedings took another ten volumes. We can only speculate about Beriia's feelings about the whole affair since he had, after all, sponsored the JAC during the war. For the record, on November 22, 1955 the Military Collegium of the USSR set aside the sentences that the same court had pronounced on July 18, 1952.

In regard to delays in the trial of Jewish intellectuals, the Soviet sources also give some credit to the change in leadership of the Military Collegium of USSR. In a report submitted on August 15, 1955, by Lt. General of Judiciary A.A. Cheptsov, who chaired the Military Collegium of the USSR during the trial, one finds a detailed account. The report was prepared in response to a request by Marshal G.K. Zhukov, who was Minister of Defense at that time. The highlights of this report as produced by A.I. Vaksberg are probably accurate, but understandably self-serving so far as Cheptsov is concerned. He was no shrinking violet. After all, he had presided over the trial of K.F. Telegin, who had been sentenced (but not to death) on equally falsified grounds. In April 1950, he was also the presiding judge over another miscarriage of justice when a number of captured former Generals accused of collaboration were sentenced to death. According to Cheptsov, the JAC case involved 34 investigators, as well as a number of military prosecutors. On top of this, some of the defendants had also been interrogated by M.F. Shkiriatov, Chairman of the Party Control Commission (after Stalin's death Shkiriatov destroyed all his papers as part of his "Party" duty). Abakumov, Riumin, and Shkiriatov assured the judges of the prisoners' guilt; some had already confessed and implicated others. During the trial, cracks began to appear when some of the defendants began to retract their confessions, and Riumin and his chief assistant, P.I. Grishaev, refused to respond to the court's request for additional evidence. Cheptsov then informed Igant'ev, supposedly Riumin's boss, that Riumin had falsified the case. Igant'ev, knowing that Riumin was working directly with Stalin, refused to interfere. After suspending the trial in July 1952, Cheptsov appealed to G.N. Safonov, former USSR Prosecutor General, and A.A. Volin, former Chairman of the USSR Supreme Court, to join him in an appeal to the Central Committee, but he was turned down. He then contacted Shkiriatov, again to no avail. N.M. Shvernik, then Chairman of the Presidium of the Supreme Council of the USSR, was the next man to whom Cheptsov appealed, and he was told that Malenkov was the man to see. The result was a stormy meeting of Malenkov, Igant'ev, Cheptsov and Riumin. In response to Cheptsov's accusation that Riumin was committing unlawful acts, Riumin responded that the court had been dragging its feet. Malenkov brought the meeting to a close by saying that the sentence against the criminals had been approved by the Politburo. Cheptsov, who claimed he was cursed by Riumin after the meeting, began to prepare a case against him in August-September 1952.

The Military Collegium sentenced the prisoners as instructed by Malenkov, but despite Riumin's insistence, allowed them to appeal. The appeal was denied.[10] Riumin, incidentally, was tried and shot in July 1954, but his chief assistant, Grishaev, survived to become a professor in the Department of Criminal Law in the All-Union Open Institute of Law. Shkiriatov, who died in January 1954, also went unpunished. The courts under Stalin were usually integral parts of the terror. As Gerald Reitlinger had written in a similar context, it must seem incredible that men calling themselves judges worked hand-in-hand with those whose sole mission in life was denial of justice. These events, however, happened in the twentieth century, not an age of exceptional frivolity, but as we are sometimes reminded, the century of the common man.[11] No institution did Stalin's bidding more than the Military Collegium of the USSR Supreme Court chaired by V.V. Ul'rikh since 1926, when he replaced the Old Bolshevik V.A. Trifonov (purged in 1938). Along with his colleagues, A.P. Goriachov, N.M. Rychkov, I.O. Matulevich, M.R. Romanychev, I.T. Goliakov, I.I. Nikitchenko, A.M. Orlov, D.Ia Kandybin, Bukanov, Dmitriev, Solodilov, Zarianov, Suslin, and Detisov (all of whom survived, although Orlov, and possibly even Matulevich, may have been dismissed during the anti-Semitic campaigns), Ul'rikh sentenced thousands of people to death in a career that went back to Boris Savinkov's trial in August

1924. Before serving in the Military Çollegium (from January 1926, as Chairman), Ul'rikh, a crude professional revolutionary born to a Latvian father and Russian mother, had spent his formative years in Siberia and served as the Head of the Main Tribunal of the Internal Security Troops, a position to which he was appointed by Dzerzhinskii. Between October 1, 1936 and September 30, 1938, Ul'rikh personally sentenced 30,514 defendants to death and another 5,000 to various prison terms. Ul'rikh and Vyshinskii also came up with the idea that the NKVD troika, rather than military courts, be given the power of stripping officers from their ranks. In April 1938, Ul'rikh further suggested that the Military Collegium, which he chaired, be removed from the authority of the USSR Supreme Court and become an independent military tribunal. Ul'rikh was not happy with the slowdown of terror in 1939 and wrote to Stalin on June 14, 1939, about the pending cases in various military districts against assorted "enemies of the people." The role played by Ul'rikh and his court in various trials during the war and the cover-up of the Erlich-Alter affair have already been discussed. Ul'rikh's picture dating from the Vlasov trial shows him to be as haggard as the defendants, in his case, probably from excessive drinking. The trial of Admiral Kuznetsov and his colleagues was the last over which Ul'rikh presided. He was removed in 1948 from a job that he had held for 22 years and assigned to the Military Law Academy, where he stayed until his death in 1951. Ul'rikh spent his last years living alone in a drunken stupor in Motropol Hotel in Moscow regaling prostitutes with stories about the old days when he would routinely send former members of the Politburo to death.[12]

There is no evidence that the USSR Supreme Court under I.I. Goliakov (August 17, 1938–1948), a former colleague of Ul'rikh and A.A. Volin (1948–1957) ever interfered on the side of justice. Even their successor, A.F. Gorkin (1957–1972), was a committed Stalinist. The nature of the relationship between Abakumov and G.N. Safonov, who served as the USSR Prosecutor during the post-war years is less clear. Ul'rikh's successor Maj. General (later Lt. General) of Judiciary A.A. Cheptsov was no civil libertarian, but he had the lawyer's knack for procedure and the case against the Jewish intellectuals was so patently false that he was reluctant to move until pressured by Malenkov, who informed him the Politburo had dealt with the matter on three occasions. Cheptsov's reluctance helped him during the post-Stalin years, and in fact he was involved in rehabilitation of the victims of the "Leningrad Affair." In April 1956, he presided over a court in Tbilisi which tried the last group of Beriia's colleagues (M.A.D. Bagirov, etc.). In January 1957, he also presided over the court that rehabilitated Tukhachevskii and his colleagues. Ignat'ev, who played a more sinister part, also survived the Khrushchev years even though he had not opposed the sentences and he had been particularly active in sending to exile the relatives of victims.[13] The Soviet sources claim the total number of Jewish victims as 23 executed and others sentenced to long terms of imprisonment, but these were "official" victims and there undoubtedly must have been those who were died or were without trial, including such men as M.M. Borodin (Gruzenberg), once senior adviser to Sun Yat-sen and Chiang Kai-shek and later the obscure editor of *Moscow News* and Professor I. Nusinov. Two other victims shot on November 23, 1950 were journalist M. Zheleznov and Head of the Moscow Automobile Factory, S. Persov. Two days later, the same sentence was meted out to A. Tokar, a high-ranking official in the Cadres Department of the Red Army. It is estimated that the post-war anti-Jewish campaigns claimed at least 110 victims. As was the accepted practice under Stalin, the families of the arrested were also targeted. In the case of academician Shtern, since she was not married, her sister, A.S. Romendik, was dragged away.

The fact is that few Jews in prominent positions were safe during the post war years, but even ordinary mortals such as Ia. G. Morozov who had the misfortune of being the father of Svetlana Alliluyeva's former Jewish husband was arrested. Keeping the families of suspected individuals hostage was a common Bolshevik practice going back to Lenin and Trotskii. On July 5, 1937, the Politburo approved the arrest of the wives of "spy-traitors" and of Trotskiites being sent to prison for at least 5 to 8 years. Stalin was now extending this to protective custody, involving his colleagues and even his own family. Already arrested was the Jewish widow of Lt. Ia. I. Stalin and the mother of Stalin's first grandchild. Stalin tried to persuade Marshal of Signal Troops I.A. Peresypkin and Army General A.V. Khrulev, who had, respectively, led the Red Army Signals and Rear Services during the war, to abandon their Jewish wives.[14] Their refusal led to the arrest of at least Khrulev's wife. Other military officers which resisted the anti-Semitic campaigns included Col. General and future Marshal of Aviation V.A. Sudets, and Hero of the Soviet Union Col. General S.G. Trofimenko, Commander of the Belorussian Military District at the time of Mikhoel's murder. Trofimenko, who had a distinguished war-time career had been Commander of the district since 1946, but his sins included having a number of Jewish friends, which made him potentially dangerous in view of what had happened to Mikhoel's. In January 1949, he was recalled to Moscow and was appointed as Commander of the North Caucasus Military District. Trofimenko, who died in October 1953, never rose above the rank of Col. General, which he had held since 1944. Stalin still tolerated Kaganovich and Mekhlis, but he had the Jewish wives of Molotov and A.A. Andreev arrested. Only the spineless Voroshilov, for once, showed any moral courage by refusing to part with his wife, who was spared. Voroshilov, who had shown no hesitation in signing the death sentences of thousands of innocent people, threatened to shoot it out with those who would come to arrest his wife, and Stalin, a fan of American movies, decided to forego a potential OK Corral in the middle of Moscow involving the former Commissar of Defense. P.S. Zhemchuzhina (Karpovskaia), Molotov's wife, and former Commissar of Fisheries, was arrested in February 1949 supposedly because she had corresponded with Golda Meir. When Molotov contacted Abakumov, he was told that the decision was made by Stalin. She was sent to Kazakhstan to become the unwelcome guest of Lt. General P.M. Fitin, the local head of MGB. *Kremlevskie Zheny* contains the partial text of her interrogation from February 2 and 9, 1949, in which she was questioned by M.T. Likhachev about her relationship with Mikhoel's, Lozovskii, Golda Meir, and the Jewish Anti-Fascist Committee. Likhachev also interrogated Zhemchuzhina's brother and sister and her secretary, one Mel'nik. While in prison, Zhemchuzhina was known as "prisoner No. 12." According to A.I. Vaksberg, she was brought to Moscow from the Kustanai region of Kazakh SSR in January 1953 to serve as the star witness in the planned trial of the arrested doctors. Five days after Stalin's death, Beriia personally escorted her to Molotov's dacha. Zhemchuzhina, who had reportedly fainted when she heard the news of Stalin's demise remained, like her husband, an unrepentant Stalinist, and, as Dr. Johnson said about re-marriage, an example of triumph of hope over experience. Even less fortunate was B.S. Poskrebysheva, the wife of Stalin's closest confidant, A.I. Poskrebyshev. Poskrebysheva, one of whose sisters was married to one of Trotskii's sons, was kept in prison for 3 years before being shot as a spy. Stalin told Poskrebyshev that Abakumov had a strong case against his wife and assured him, "We'll find you a new wife."[15]

Stalin's campaign against the wives of his confidants went back to the 'thirties, when he ordered the arrest of the wife of Kalinin and the second wife of Marshal S.M. Budennyi, neither Jewish. The Estonian E.I. Kalinina (born in 1882) was arrested on October 25, 1938. On April 22, 1939, she was sentenced to 15 + 5 for membership in a "Trotskiist terror organization." She was not released until December 14, 1946, despite pleas by her husband, who died on June 3, 1946, and whose funeral was attended by Stalin. In camps, the once statuesque woman was reduced to a broken shell. The soprano O.S. Mikhailova, born in 1905, married the future Marshal S.M. Budennyi in 1925, a year after his first wife had committed suicide. In a letter to the Chief Military Prosecutor (*Kremlevskie Zheny*) dated July 23, 1955, Budennyi relates how in the beginning of 1937, Stalin and Ezhov started a campaign against his wife based on her interest in Italy, which seemed natural considering her profession. Mikhailova was arrested in August 1937 and on November 18, 1939, was sentenced to 8 years in camps. On August 15, 1945, she was transferred to the Vladimir prison and was sent to exile in April 1948. Budennyi, meanwhile, had remarried and fathered three children. The kidnapping and murder of Marshal G.I. Kulik's wife has already been discussed. By placing the wives of his close colleagues in prison, Stalin was also indicating to their husbands that they were also under suspicion, and under his system a spouse of an "enemy of the people" was equally guilty. Stalin was not, of course, unique in keeping tabs on the activities of his satraps' wives. On our side, FDR would have the FBI put the wife of Harry Hopkins, his closest advisor, under surveillance.

Even the security services were not exempt from the anti-Semitic campaigns. By 1947, according to Sudoplatov, B.P. Obruchnikov, Deputy Minister MGB for Cadres, had initiated a policy of not recruiting Jews. Following Abakumov's arrest, such old NKVD standbys as Lt. General L.F. Raikhman, head of NKVD's Polish Office in 1940, was arrested in October 1951. Also arrested on July 13, 1951 was the former Deputy Head of the Department for Investigation of Especially Important Cases, the brutal L.I. Shvartsman. Even L.I. Eitington, who in 1940 had been involved in Trotskii's murder, was put under house arrest in October 1951.

Even pure technicians, such as M. Makliarskii and Ia.M. Raites, the latter one of the interrogators of arrested senior officers in October 1941, lost their jobs. L.R. Sheinin, Vyshinskii's former Assistant, was arrested on October 20, 1951 as a result of testimony by L.L. Shvartsman. Sheinin's sinister career and downfall is discussed in considerable detail in various books by A.I. Vaksberg. Sheinin, who survived, died in 1967.

Some Jewish intelligence operatives such as Kheiftez and Serebrianskii were arrested, while others such as S. Semnov (Taubman) and L. Vasilevskii were dismissed without pensions. Even the poisoner G.M. Maironovskii, privy to many dark secrets, was put under arrest. On October 27, 1950, the axe fell on L.Z. Mekhlis, Minister of State Control and, along with L.L. Kaganovich, Stalin's closest Jewish henchman, whose poor health may have contributed to his dismissal.

Incidentally, despite his involvement in the persecution of the Jews, Abakumov was not an innate anti-Semite and, in fact, in July 1942, had arrested Maj. General I.F. Dashichev specifically for making anti-Semitic remarks; he also continued to employ Jews such as Raikhman, Shvartsman, and Broverman in MGB, a policy which cost him dearly after his own arrest. Abakumov, or for that matter Beriia and Himmler, existed merely to carry out the boss' orders and as bureaucrats were not concerned with questions of morality and conscience. They would have just as soon arrested the left-handed people had they so been ordered by Stalin or Hitler.

Stalin, however, spared such leading Jewish artists as set designer I.M. Rabimovich; translator S.Ia. Marshak; film directors R.L. Karmen, S.Ia. Kogan, D.L. Sholomovich, A.G. Krichevskii, I.N. Veinerovich, O.B. Reizman, I.B. Arons, Iu.Ia. Raizman, and I.E. Kheifits; actor S. Khromchenko; poets and writers S. Gorshman, Z. Telesin, S.Roitman, A. Magid, V.V. Vaverin, P.G. Antokolskii, and Ia. Khavinson; critics U. Finkel', M. Notovich, Liubomirskii; linguists E. Falkovich and M. Al'tshuler; and journalists M. Malamud, I.G. Erenburg, D.I. Ortenberg (dismissed, however, from the Army on July 29, 1950), I.L. Sel'vinskii, A.I. Bezymenskii, V.S. Grossman, and D.I. Zaslavskii; as well as Pasternak (who was not a member of JAC), for whom Stalin had a soft spot and whose wife was a profuse admirer of Stalin. Pasternek's mistress, O. Ovinskaia, however, was hauled away. Musicians such as violinists D.F. Oistrakh (whose playing Stalin enjoyed) and L.B. Kogan (who in 1947 was explicity ordered by Stalin to win the first prize in the Queen Elizabeth of Belgium international competition); pianists E.G. Gilel's, A.B. Goldenvizer, Ia.V. Flier, M.V. Iudina and Ia.I. Zaks; composers R.M. Glier (Gliere) and M. Blanter; baritone M.O. Reizen (Stalin's favorite singer); jazz singer L.O. Utesov; conductors S.A. Samsod, A. Pazovskii and Iu.F. Faier; and ballet dancers A. Messerer and M. Gabovich were unharmed even though many of them had belonged to JAC. Most of the writers and artists who were not arrested, nevertheless lost their positions or suffered demotions. Also untouched were the Stalinist historians I.I. Mints, I.M. Razgon, and E.V. Tarle; the painters A.M. Birshtein, R.R. Fal'k, A.M. Gristal', E.A. Katsman, V.N. Perel'man, G.M. Shegal', A.G. Tyshler; sculptor M.G. Manizier; chess champion M. Botvinnik; and the economist E. Varga (immigrant from Hungary) who was, however, prevented from publishing his slightly unorthodox views.

There was also a purge of Jewish officers in the Red Army including Hero of the Soviet Union Ia. N. Kreizer, the only Jewish officer to attain the rank of Army General (1962), and another Hero of the Soviet Union, Col. General of Engineering

Troops L.Z. Kotliar, who had commanded the Engineering Troops during 1941–1942 before serving with distinction in the same capacity with a number of fronts. Other Jewish senior officers who were forced out of the Red Army during the post-war years include Lt. General (MVD) M.I. Belkin; Lt. Generals A.I. Andreev, A.A. Vurgraft, Iu.A. Lianda, M.L. Cherniavskii, M.A. Levin, and A.M. Rafalovich; Rear Admiral A.Ia. Iurovskii; and Maj. Generals S.V. Aginskii, L.A. Baitin, L.I. Berenzon, D.G. Bidinskii, E.M. Borisov (Minkov), A.S. Botvinnik, M.Z. Bravo-Zhivtovskii, A.I. Broval'skii, G.M. Brusser, S.A. Chernetskii, S.G. Frankfurt, M.S. Gannushkin, L.S. Goberman, M.L. Gorikker, B.N. Ibragimov, Kh.R. Karasik, A.D. Kats, A.A. Katsnel'son, Ia.N. Katsnel'son, G.M. Koblents, R.P. Khmel'nitskii (former adjutant of Voroshilov), V.A. Kreichman, A.M. Krivulin, A.V. Kronik, M.N. Kurkovskii, A.M. Khasin, G.A. Leikin, E.Kh. Lipets, Z.G. Lopatin, V.L. Makhlinovskii, M.E. Moskalik, S.A. Nevstruev, B.M. Ol'shanskii, A.M. Orlov (Ul'rikh's assistant at the Military Collegium), N.E. Nosovskii, B.S. Lareev, B.R. Pisarevskii, V.I. Polikovskii, G.E. Preisman, Iu.I. Rabiner, S.S. Raikin, Kh.E. Rubinchik, M.A. Shamashkin, G.S. Shimanovskii, A.E. Shkol'nikov, I.V. Shur, A.E. Shpiller, I.M. Sorkin, L.B. Sosedov, V.L. Tsetlin, Ia.L. Shteinman, K.M. Varshavskii, M.S. Vovsi (arrested in connection with the Doctors' Plot), M.S. Zhezlov, P.Ia. Zalesskii, I.M. Zal'tsman, V.A. Zemlerub, and others. The dismissal of these officers, many with technical and scientific expertise, was a blow to the Red Army, but was insignificant when compared to the losses suffered by the mass immigration of Jewish professionals under Stalin's successors. It seems, though, that the Jews in the critical defense industry were unharmed, among them Maj. General of Engineering Services (twice Hero of Socialist Labor, 1943 and 1950) S.A. Lavochkin, designer of the LAG plane (whose designs were promoted by Beriia); M.I. Gurevich (Hero of Socialist Labor, 1957), the designer of the aircraft engines and the other half of the Mikoian-Gurevich team responsible for the MIG planes; aircraft designer E.S. Fel'sner, a member of the P.O. Sukhoi team, and I.M. Zaks; tank designer I.M. Zal'tsman (Hero of Socialist Labor, 1941); weapons specialist I.M. Rabinovich (Hero of Socialist Labor, 1966); chief designer S.A. Kosberg (Hero of Socialist Labor, 1966); radar specialist A.L. Mints (Hero of Socialist Labor, 1956); test pilot as well as writer and future Hero of the Soviet Union (May 1, 1957) M.L. Gallai; Maj. General of Artillery Engineers L.R. Gonor (head of a research institute and Hero of Socialist Labor, 1942); scientists and winners of the Stalin prize G.A. Fil'tser, Ia.B. Fridman, and A.B. Shapiro; and V.E. Dymshits, Deputy Minister for the Construction of Metallurgical and Chemical Industries, who was, however, sent to India in 1950, where he stayed until 1957.

Those who were involved with atomic energy and weapons were spared. These included the former Commissar of the Defense Industry, Col. General of Artillery Engineering Service, Vannikov, who had come within a hair's breadth of being shot in the early days of the war. Since August 1945, Vannikov had chaired the ad hoc group "First Main Administration," under the Council of Ministers to supervise the technical aspects of the use of atomic energy and production of nuclear weapons. The advisers to this group included academicians A.F. Ioffe (Hero of Socialist Labor, 1955), I.K. Kikoin, and L. Al'tshuler.

Also coming through unscathed were nuclear physicists and scientists E.L. Feinberg, V.L. Ginzburg, M.L. Goldberger, B.L. Ioffe, I.M. Khalatnikov, Iu.B. Khariton, L.D. Landau (who had been imprisoned in the late 1930s as a German spy), I.Ia. Pomeranchuk, I.S. Shapiro, and Ia. B. Zel'dovich. It should be noted that at the height of the anti-Semitic campaigns, a number of Jewish physicists were awarded the title of Hero of Socialist Labor: Kikoin (1951), Zel'dovich (1949, 1951), and Khariton (1949, 1951). Some of the physicists had even been members of JAC. Involvement with military technology, however, was no guarantee against arrest. Maj. General of Engineering/Technical Service G.A. Uger, Deputy Chairman of the Radar Technology Commission headed by Malenkov was arrested. It must also sadly be recorded that a number of Jewish writers and intellectuals, motivated primarily by self-preservation, took part in the campaigns by denouncing colleagues. This would continue even after Stalin's death, when the anti-Semitic campaigns were camouflaged by anti-Zionist and anti-Israel rhetoric.

The anti-Semitic campaigns continued after Abakumov's downfall, culminating in the "Doctors' Plot" of 1952 and early 1953. Arrested were Maj. General of Medical Services M.S. Vovsi (first cousin of Mikhoel's), chief internist of the Red Army during the war; internist B.B. Kogan (whose cousin, M.B. Kogan, also a doctor had died under arrest on November 26, 1951); pathologist Ia. L. Rapoport; as well as Drs. A.I. Fel'dman, A.M. Grinshtein, N.A. Shereshevskii, M.Ia. Sereiskii, Ia.S. Temkin, E.M. Gel'shtein, N.A. Zakusov, I.I. Feigel, N.A. Maiorov, N.L. Vil'k, V.E. Nezlin and B.I. Zbarskii (who had been involved in the cover-up of Mikhoel's murder). Ia.G. Etinger, who had died in prison on March 2, 1951, and M.I. Pevzner, also already dead, were also mentioned as having belonged to this group. Besides these, there are also a number of non-Jewish doctors included: V.N. Vinogradov (Stalin's own doctor), and N.A. Popova, M.I. Egorov, V.Kh. Vasilenko, V.F. Zelenin, and B.S. Preobrazhenskii. The official announcement of the Doctors' Plot (*Pravda*, January 13, 1953), however, listed only nine men, Vovsi, M.B. Kogan, B.B. Kogan, Fel'dman, Grinshtein, Etinger, Vinogradov, Egorov, and Mairov—the first six Jewish—who were accused of belonging to an "international Jewish bourgeois nationalist organization." The Gentile doctors were accused of being old agents of "British intelligence." A note of interest: of the six other arrested doctors whose names *did not* appear in the official announcement, only Shereshevskii was Jewish. This was obviously done to put the weight of responsibility on the Jewish doctors. At least five of those arrested, Vinogradov, Shereshevskii, Vovsi, Zelenin, and B.B. Kogan, had given false testimony in the 1930s during the purge trials in regard to Gor'kii's having been poisoned by the opposition.[16] Whether Abakumov, who had been rotting away in prison for over a year, knew anything about these events is doubtful. Other non-Jewish victims included Anna Redens, Stalin's sister-in-law, widow of S.F. Redens, Head of NKVD in Moscow and Kazakhstan (shot 1941), who had been friendly to Jewish artists, and Evgenia Allilueva, widow of Stalin's brother-in-law, P. Alliluev, who had been remarried to a Jew. They were arrested in 1947–1948 and sentenced to 10 years and were not released until 1954. Stalin thought the two knew too much. Anna Redens came out completely broken.[17] After the war, the MGB tried to track down the children of some of the purge victims who, for some reason, usually their youth (although this was not a guarantee), had escaped arrest. For instance, in 1946, the MGB discovered that M.Ia. Peters, the daughter of Ia.Kh. Peters, one of the most ferocious of the early Cheka leaders, who was shot without trial in 1938 for conspiring to "assassinate" Stalin, somehow had remained free. She was arrested as a member of the family of an "enemy of the people" and was sent to camps. Architect I.Ia. Peters, son of Ia.Kh. Peters from a second marriage, was arrested in 1953 and freed after Stalin's death, only to die shortly after.[18] N.I. Smigla, daughter of veteran Bolshevik N.I. Smigla (shot in 1938), was also arrested in 1949.[19] In 1950, the MGB arrested V.L. Glebov, the surviving illegitimate son of the old Bolshevik L.B. Kamanev. He was sentenced to 10 years for "aesthetic tendencies" and was not released until 1956. On August 18, 1951, V.A. Kravchenko, the 22-old grandson of L.B. Kamenev by his older son, who had been shot in 1938, was also arrested. Kravchenko was not released until November 11, 1955. He committed suicide on August 3, 1966.[20] Iagoda's son, only nine years old when his father was shot on March 15, 1938, was arrested in 1949 and not released until after Stalin's death. After studying engineering, he moved to Ukraine under an assumed name. His mother, I.L. Iagoda, identified perhaps incorrectly as the niece of Ia.M. Sverdlov, perished in camps.

In the late 1940s, a massive campaign, whose genesis remains unclear, targeted released prisoners who were now re-arrested. A typical example was N.A. Ioffe, daughter of the old Bolshevik, A.A. Ioffe (V. Krymskii), who had committed suicide on November 11 1927 to protest Stalin's policies. Twice arrested after her father's death, N.A. Ioffe returned from Kolima in 1946 only to be re-arrested in 1949 and sent to Siberian exile.[21] In 1948–1949, the state security discovered the existence of an anti-Stalinist youth cell in Voronezh, whose leaders V.A. Zhigulin, Iu. Kiselev, B. Batuev, and V. Radkevich matched the bravery and recklessness of Hans and Sophie Scholl, who had started a similar campaign in Germany at the height of Hitler's power with even direr results.[22]

In 1948 in Voronezh, the MGB arrested 24 individuals in Voronezh accused of "Trotskiism." Stalin worked closely with Abakumov in determining their fate. In 1951, the MGB arrested 17 young people as members of an underground conspiracy. The group, organized in 1950, was led by one B. Slutskii. Of the ringleaders, three were shot and the others were sent to camps where two died. Adam Hochschild recently interviewed the only survivor, S.S. Pechuro, who had been personally interrogated by Abakumov.[23] On August 10, 1946, Abakumov wrote a secret report to A.A. Kuznetsov in the Central Committee about the satirist M.M. Zoshchenko including the text of Zoshchenko's interrogation in Leningrad on July 20, 1944. The result was that Zoshchenko had to write letters of explanation to Stalin and Zhdanov to save his neck.[24] Zoshchenko escaped arrest, but was expelled from the Writers Union and his writings were not published until after Stalin's death.

One of the less-known victims of this period was the former Deputy Minister of Public Health, Academician V.V. Parin, who was arrested in 1947 in connection with the Kliueva-Roskin Affair, which involved two Soviet cancer specialists who had allowed their research to be published in the U.S. Recent research by Ia. Rapoport (*Nauka i Zhizn'*, 1/1988), V.D. Eskaov and E. S. Levina (*Kentavr*, 2/1994), and N. Krementsov of the Institute of History of Science and Technology (unpublished) indicate that this was mainly a Party affair inspired by the Cold War tensions and the rising campaign against intellectuals and scientists, organized by Stalin and Zhdanov. In 1952–1953 a savage campaign was launched against the writer V.S. Grossman, which according to his biographer G. Svirskii was inspired by Stalin, who had once referred to the writer as a "menshevik."

Beginning in October, 1949, a number of high-ranking captured German officers were dragged before courts. Most of these were unreconstructed Nazis or had been less than enthusiastic about the Free Germany Committee. The best known was Lt. General Karl Strecker, who was sentenced to 25 years on April 15, 1950 and the top ace Erich Hartman. Regardless, by 1956 all the German POWs were released.

NOTES

1. Aleksander Wat, *My Century*, pp. 344–45.
2. Svetlana Alliluyeva, *Only One Year*, p. 155.
3. A. Sharagin, *Tupolevskaia Shatga*, p. 29.
4. Shimon Redlich, *The Jews Under Soviet Rule During World II*, p. 140.
5. Esther Markish, *The Long Return*, p. 236.
6. Svetlana Alliluyeva, ibid., p. 153.
7. *Izvestiia TsK KPSS* (12/1989).
8. Markish, *Lona Return*, p. 255.
9. *Izvestiia TsK KPSS*, ibid.
10. For the judicial maneuvering and the role played by Cheptsov, see *Izvestiia TsK KPSS*, ibid., and Arkady Vaksberg, *Stalin's Prosecutor*, pp. 262–72.
11. Gerald Reitlinger, *SS an Alibi of a Nation*, p. 82.
12. For Ul'rikh, see *Radianska Ukraina* (February 3–5, 1989), *Mezhdunarodnaia Zhizn'* (5/1990), and A. Vaksberg, *Stalin's Prosecutor*.
13. Markish, ibid., p. 202.
15. Vaksberg, ibid., p. 278.
16. For the "Doctors Plot," see Yakov Rapoport, *The Doctors' Plot of 1953*; Louis Rapoport, *Stalin's War Against the Jews*; and D.A. Volkogonov, (op. cit.).
17. Svetlana Alliluyeva, ibid., p. 146.
18. *Nauka i Zhizn* (6/1989), p. 72.
19. *Nauka I Zhizn* (12/1989), p. 64.
20. L.N. Vasil'eva, *Kremlevskie Zheny*, p. 147.
21. Adam Hochschild, *The Unquiet Ghost*, pp. 143–46.
22. For the Voronezh youth group, see A.V. Zhigulin: *Chernve Kamni* and *Zarok*.
23. Hochschild, ibid., pp. 29–40.
24. *Istoricheskii Arkhiv* (1/1992) pp. 132–43.

Chapter 9

The Leningrad Affair

After the war, Stalin began to make noises about the need for new blood in the Party and made favorable comments about A.A. Kuznetsov and N.A. Voznesenskii as worthy heirs who should, respectively, lead the Party and the government after him. As head of the CC CPSU administrative organs, Kuznetsov was the Central Committee's watchdog of MGB, MVD, and the Judiciary, while Voznesenskii, a full member of the Politburo since 1947 and a Deputy Chairman of the USSR Council of Ministers since March 1946, had considerable influence on economic and government policy. Stalin's praise was an indirect signal to the other satraps in his entourage to plot against the favored two. On May 4, 1946, because of the repercussions of the "Aviators' Affair," Malenkov was removed from the Central Committee and exiled to Tashkent. This allowed his rival, Zhdanov, to get rid of Malenkov's people in the Central Committee apparatus. Between September 1947 and April 1948, A.A. Kuznetsov, with help from M.A. Suslov, organized the first major post-war political purge, against K.S. Kuzakov, M.E. Shcherbakov, K.S. Kuzovkov, and, later, I.V. Kovalev, all obscure officials attached to the CC CPSU and probably associated with Malenkov. The machinery to get rid of these individuals was a Party "Court of Honor" formed in December 1947 and chaired by Suslov, whose members included Stalin, Zhdanov, Poskrebyshev, Shkiriatov, G.M. Popov (First Party Secretary in Moscow), and A.A. Kuznetsov, who also served as the rapporteur. Malenkov, however, was called back in July 1948, a month before Zhdanov's death, bent on revenge. Zhdanov, the alleged patron of Kuznetsov and Voznesenskii, had died under mysterious circumstances on August 31, 1948. This gave additional impetus to the campaign, whose chief beneficiary was to be Malenkov. Besides Malenkov, Beriia, and M.F. Shkiriatov, the latter a total creature of Stalin, were also involved. Abakumov, who could not have been very happy about Kuznetsov's watching over the MGB, provided the mailed fist.

Besides Kuznetsov and Voznesenskii, the principal victims included P.S. Popkov, First Secretary of the Leningrad Party Organization (who had replaced Kuznetsov in 1946); M.I. Rodionov, Chairman of the RFSFR Council of Ministers; G.F. Badaev, Second Party Secretary in Leningrad; P.G. Lazutin, Head of Leningrad Komsomols; Ia. F. Kapustin, Second City Party Secretary in Leningrad; N.V. Solov'ev, First Party Secretary in Crimea, who had served in Leningrad during 1938–1946; I.M. Turko, Deputy Chairman of Executive Committee in Vladimir; T.V. Zakrzhevskaia, Head of Department of Party, Labor Union and Komsomols in the Leningrad Party Organization; I.S. Kharitonov, Chairman of the Executive Committee of the Leningrad Soviet; P.I. Levin, Secretary of the Leningrad City Committee; M.V. Basov, Chairman of the RFSFR Planning Commission; A.D. Verbitskii, Second Regional Party Secretary in Murmansk; A.A. Bubnov, Secretary of the Leningrad Executive Committee; G.N. Kuprianov, Party Secretary in Karelia; and F.E. Mikheev, Head of the Organizations Department in Leningrad Party Organization. A.N. Kosygin and Colonel General T.F. Shtykov, the former Political Commissar of the Volkhov and Karelia Fronts, had narrow escapes.

The campaign started rather innocuously, involving the All-Russia Wholesale Fair held in Leningrad in mid-January 1949. On January 13, 1949, after Rodionov, Chairman of the RSFSR Council of Ministers, had written to Malenkov announcing the opening of the fair, Malenkov wrote to Beriia, Voznesenskii, Mikoian, and A.D. Kruitkov (Deputy Chairman of the USSR Council of Ministers) informing them that the fair was illegal. Malenkov charged that Kuznetsov, Popkov, Rodionov, and Kapustin had organized the fair without approval from the Central Committee even though such an event had the sanction of the USSR Council of Ministers.

Meanwhile, a parallel campaign against the accused was launched via Party channels. Late in December 1948, the Central Committee received an anonymous letter that the leaders of the Party organization in Leningrad had rigged their own election and falsely claimed that they had unanimous support. On February 15, 1949, the Politburo, citing a number of charges, specifically accused Kuznetsov, Rodinov and P.S. Popkov of "anti-state" actions caused by "a sick and non-Bolshevik deviation" and of "separatism": creating a wall between the Leningrad Party Organization and the Central Committee. Finally, the report stated that the long-dead Zionov'ev had resorted to the same anti-Leninist methods. Voznesenskii was reprimanded for not telling the Central Committee about the activities of the Leningrad group even though he had rejected Popkov's invitation to join the cabal. Early in the summer, Abakumov entered the act by writing to Stalin on July 21, 1949, that there was reason to believe that Ia. F. Kapustin was a British agent, and in fact, he had been involved in subversive activities since 1937. Lt. General P.N. Kubatkin, former head of MGB in Leningrad (Abakumov's own man), had covered up for Kapustin by destroying the incriminating material. Two days later Kapustin was arrested without a warrant. According to rumors, Voznesenskii's real crime was insufficient praise for Stalin in his book on the Societ economy during the war. Under torture, he confessed to the existence of an anti-Party group in Leningrad. On August 13, 1949, Kuznetsov, Popkov, Rodinov, P.G. Lazutin, and N.V. Solov'ev were arrested in Malenkov's office, again without a warrant. With Komarov and Riumin working the prisoners over, a case was soon prepared. A tandem case was also being prepared against Voznesenskii, first by a report from M.T. Pomaznev, Deputy Chairman of the USSR State Supply Committee, accusing the USSR State Planning Committee (chaired by Voznesenskii) of having deliberately reduced the national industrial plan for the first quarter of 1949. On March 5, 1949, the USSR Council of Ministers issued a report using Stalin's own words that to fabricate such statistics is a criminal offense.

On March 5, 1949, the USSR Council of Ministers dismissed Voznesenskii as Chairman of the USSR Planning Commission, at the same time one E.E. Andreev, the Central Committee's watchdog at the Planning Commission, reported that some of the documents for the period 1944-1949 had turned up missing. This allowed the Party Control Commission chaired by M.F. Shkiriatv to get into the act by accusing Voznesenskii of "anti-Party behavior." The noose was beginning to close on Voznesenskii's neck. On September 9, 1949, Shkiriatov suggested to Malenkov that Voznesenskii be expelled from the Central Committee. The Politburo put this decision to the Central Committee on September 12 and 13, and it was duly approved. Voznesenskii was arrested on October 27, 1949. At the same time, Malenkov and his crony V.M. Andrianov, the new First Secretary of the Leningrad Party Organization, launched a massive purge which resulted in dismissal of nearly 2,000 government and Party workers. This obsession with the Leningrad Affair was indeed extraordinary. Historian Iu.S. Aksenov (*Voprosy Istorii KPSS*, November 1990) states that all ten meetings of the Politburo in 1949 were devoted to this issue. Beriia's son, in *Moi Otets*, claims that his father had nothing to do with the "Leningrad Affair," which was cooked up by the triumvirate of Melenkov, Khrushchev, and Shkiriatov. The latter's report sealed the fate of the "Leningraders," who were now left at the mercy of Abakumov and his goons.

On January 18, 1950, Abakumov presented Stalin with a list of 44 arrested persons and suggested that they be tried in camera by the Military Collegium of the USSR Supreme Court without benefit of counsel on either side. On September 4, 1950, now working hand in hand with Chief Military Prosecutor, Lt. General of Judiciary A.P. Vavilov, Abakumov submitted a list suggesting the execution of six of the defendants. Stalin approved and on September 30, 1950, a day after the start of the trial, the Politburo endorsed his decision. The formal indictment was written by Colonel of Judiciary N.N. Nikolaev and endorsed by the aforementioned Vavilov. The trial was held on September 29-30, 1950, presided over by I.O. Matulevich, a member of the Military Collegium since the 1930s and a close colleague of Ul'rikh. Matulevich had chaired the Military Collegium in Minsk and Leningrad, where hundreds had been sentenced to death. During 1941-1942, as Chairman of the Military Tribunal of the South Front, Matulevich waged a campaign of terror. To expect mercy in his court would have been inconceivable. At 59 minutes past midnight, on October 1, 1950, the sentences were pronounced. There was, of course, no appeal, and the sentences were carried out an hour later. Shot were N.A.Voznesenskii, A.A. Kuznetsov, P.S. Popkov, Ia. F. Kapustin, and G.P. Lazutin. I.M. Turko was sentenced to 15 years and F.E. Mikheev and T.V. Zakrzhevskaia each to 10 years. There have been rumors that Voznesenskii's execution was delayed, and in fact, A.G. Malenkov, in the biography of his father, states that Stalin inquired whether Voznesenskii had arrived at the Urals for work, only to be told that the latter had been sent in an unheated freight car and without winter clothing and had frozen to death. Malenkov felt that Stalin's concern was genuine, but the fact that no one was punished points to the contrary. The executions of October 1, 1950, were only the tip of the iceberg. Other victims included the aforementioned M.V. Basov, I.S. Kharitonov, N.V. Solov'ev, A.A. Bubnov, P.N. Kubatkin, A.D. Verbitskii, and P.I. Levin (one of the two Jewish victims; the other, Ia. L. Beilinson, received a 25-year sentence). Also shot, possibly without trial, were Voznesenskii's brother and sister, A.A. Voznesenskii, RFSFR Minister of Education and M.A. Voznesenskiia,Second Party Secretary in the Kuibyshev District of Leningrad. Besides Solov'ev, the victims from Crimea included P.A. Chursin and M.I. Petrovskii, as well as the former Political Commissar of the Black Sea Fleet, Rear Admiral P.T. Bondarenko. Also shot was M.I. Safonov, former Party official in Estonia and later First Party Secretary in Novogorod. G.T. Kedrov, First Party Secretary in Estonia, was sentenced to 25 years in prison.[1]

The wives of some of the victims such as M.I. Rodionov were sent to camps in Komi ASSR, while Rodionov's daughter ended up in Kuzbass camps in accordance with the official Stalinist practice. The purge would go to extremes. In the case of G. Kedrov, for instance, not only his wife was arrested, but his brothers. One brother, a Major of State Security, was purged, as was his wife.[2] The Leningrad Affair probably claimed more than 1,300 victims, including over 100 who were shot, nearly 2,000 people who were dismissed, and many arrested. As late as August 15, 1952, the 50 former Leningrad Party officials were arrested and sentenced to prison. Those lucky enough just to lose their jobs included B.M. Kedrov, editor of *Voprosy Filosofii*, Zhdanov's mouthpiece, who was removed in 1949. B.M. Kedrov was the surviving son of the old Chekist M.S. Kedrov, encountered elsewhere in this book. In November 1987, the Politburo appointed a Special Commission to look into the repressions of the Stalin period. The Chief of the Party Control Commission for Leningrad, A.I. Kirsanov, began to look into the "Leningrad Affair."[3] The Commission determined that at least 550 victims from Leningrad alone have yet to be rehabilitated.[4] The major victims were, however, rehabilitated in April 1954 by the USSR Supreme Court chaired by A.A. Volin. Some of those responsible for the Leningrad Affair such as Abakumov were later tried, but to my knowledge, the Judge Matulevich and the Prosecutors Vavilov and Nikolaev, as well as the interrogators, were left untouched.

The victims of the Leningrad Affair were not drawing room revolutionaries. They were hard-nosed Stalinists who had survived and benefitted from the bloodbaths of the 1930s. Admiral Kuznetsov claims that Voznesenskii would not hesitate to denounce General G.M. Shtern, a completely innocent individual, to Stalin. According to his son, Kapustin was afraid of no one including Stalin.[5] Others such as A.A. Kuznetsov and N.V. Solov'ev had spent the entire war in the Leningrad blockade. A.A. Kuznetsov's tragic fate and brave performance during the trial should not blind us to his past deeds. Arriving in Leningrad in 1932, he must have been involved in the massive purges following Kirov's murder which claimed nearly

130,000 Party members during the first four years of Zhdanov's stewardship. In 1938 Kuznetsov became the Second Regional Party Secretary in Leningrad. He spent the entire war in Leningrad and reached the rank of Lt. General. He served at times as Political Commissar of the Leningrad Front and the Baltic Fleet, substituting for the drunk or incapacitated A.A. Zhdanov. Kuznetsov was also well connected in other ways: his daughter was the wife of S.I. Mikoian, the historian son of A.I. Mikoian. Documents recently released show Kuznetsov to be a typical Stalinist operative. In one report, he informs Stalin of the sexual proclivities of comrade Sharapov, Party Secretary in Kurgan. In another, he proposes discontinuation of small pensions to Kirov's sisters, aged 63 and 56, a suggestion which apparently Stalin accepted.[6] Incidentally, Stalin also ordered the secret police to keep a continuous watch over Kirov's widow until her death.

After the war, Stalin brought the tough and ambitious Kuznetsov to Moscow and appointed him the Secretary of the Central Committee of CPSU at age 41. As part of Stalin's leadership style, in which even the watchdogs were being watched, Kuznetsov was appointed the Central Committee's watchdog over security organs and judiciary. It seems that the new Minister of State Security Abakumov must have found this discomforting, but he had no reason to feel overt hostility to Kuznetsov who, after all, was sponsored by Zhdanov, the man who may have also played a part in Abakumov's own appointment as Head of the MGB. Abakumov moved decisively against Kuznetsov and the "Leningraders" because he was ordered to do so by Stalin. Besides his association with war-time Leningrad and with Zhdanov, which put him in the center of the "Leningrad Affair," Kuznetsov at one time had told Stalin that all the secrets of Kirov's murder had yet to be disclosed. These remarks may have been made out of naivete or in attempt to ingratiate himself with Stalin, but in view of what we know today, they could have been potentially fatal.

Kuznetsov's former Secretary, G.V. D'iankov, not an unbiased source, in the collection *Oni ne Molchali* and in *Komsomol'skaia Pravda* (January 15, 1988), draws a more favorable picture of his late boss. He claims that Kuznetsov was an open (in contrast to Malenkov) Party worker who tried to keep in touch with subordinates and attract competent and honest people to the ranks. Above all, he was concerned with the role of the Party vis-à-vis the security organs and felt that the latter should be subordinate to the Party, as it had been under Dzerzhinskii, rather than being a state within a state. His unpleasant experience with Merkulov during the first days of the war must have reinforced this view. Kuznetsov was also privy to a letter written in the summer of 1948 by a Captain Bystrov to Stalin that he had witnessed in 1946–1947 in Germany massive theft of state property for the personal use of Abakumov. Stalin passed the letter on to Zhdanov and Kuznetsov. Zhdanov, however, went on vacation and died before he could follow up. Kuznetsov and his Assistant Nikitin, however, met with Bystrov and then informed Abakumov and invited him to meet with them. Four meetings were held to discuss Bystrov's charges. Abakumov, now alarmed, managed somehow to eliminate Bystrov, but the danger remained. After Zhdanov's death and Malenkov's return, Kuznetsov was on the way out. Malenkov did not return his greeting, and more ominously Poskrebyshev failed to return his calls. He wrote to Stalin twice, but got no answer. A colleague suggested that he contact Suslov, but Kuznetsov refused, knowing full well Suslov's reputation as the Kremlin's top expert on wind direction. After Stalin's death, Suslov would replace Shkiriatov. From February 15, 1949, until August 13, 1949, Kuznetsov was in limbo. Beriia and Malenkov tried to have Stalin approve a Politburo decision to send Kuznetsov to Khabarovsk to head the Party in the Far East, and it seems that he tried to recruit some of his Assistants to help him in his new assignment. In March, the decision was revoked. Kuznetsov, a Lt. General, was assigned to the "Vystrel" military course in Perkhushkovo near Moscow. In mid-August he was called to Malenkov's office and was arrested by a Colonel Zakharov, a member of Malenkov's bodyguard.

Regardless of the respective roles played by Malenkov and Beriia in the Leningrad Affair, the fact remains that it could have been organized only with Stalin's blessing. It would be unthinkable for Abakumov, or for that matter Ezhov, to have arrested anyone of the stature of Kuznetsov and Voznesenskii without Stalin's approval. The most telling remark about Stalin's role involves G.N. Kupriianov, Secretary of the Karelia Party Organization and one of the less significant victims of the affair. During the war, Kupriianov, who had served as Commissar with the Karelia Front, had reached the temporary rank of Maj. General (political). Apparently executions of individuals of such a common rank required the approval of Stalin. Twice Malenkov wrote to Stalin requesting his approval. Stalin for some reason refused and Kupriianov survived.[7] According to the unpublished memoirs of N.P. Dudorov, Head of MVD (1956-1960), in *Sovetskaia Militsiia*, 6/1990), Kuznetsov, Voznesenskii, and perhaps others were kept in the "Special Prison" and were also interrogated by Malenkov, Beriia, Molotov, and Bulganin, who would arrive together incognito and without guard. There is also a report dating from June 26, 1957 in which Dr. Nemchenko writes about examining Kuznetsov, who had suffered from ear damage as a result of interrogations.

The official Soviet accounts published during Glasnost also claim that Malenkov, with the help of his assistant, A.M. Petrokovskii, destroyed considerable amounts of incriminatory materials related to the "Leningrad Affair." The material placed in a safe belonging to Malenkov's Assistant, D.N. Sukhanov, allegedly contained Malenkov's notes during his trips to Leningrad, the text of his speeches, the Politburo resolutions expelling Voznesenskii and material on the role played by V.M. Andrianov, First Secretary of the Leningrad Party Organization following the purge.[8] Sukhanov was arrested on May 14, 1956 (*Sovetskaia Militsiia*, 6/1990) for allegedly having taken 100,000 rubles from Beriia's safe after the latter's arrest. On June 23, 1956, N.P. Dudorov, Head of MVD, presented a report to the Party Presidium about Malenkov's crimes, but the matter was not taken up until the June 1957 Central Committee plenum, which led to Malenkov's disgrace. The previously mentioned article by Malenkov's son, however, strongly disputes the official version. In this account, G.M. Malenkov, if not quite a saint, is portrayed as a committed civil libertarian and a general all-around nice guy.[9] Kostliarov hits the mark when he calls the younger Malenkov "no Pavlik Morozov."

According to A.G. Malenkov, his father was almost a "Leningrader." He had flown to the besieged city in September 1941 to meet a disheveled Zhdanov and a defeatist Voroshilov. Malenkov, with assistance by A.A. Kuznetsov, had managed to shore up the defenses and persuaded Stalin to replace Voroshilov with Zhukov. After the war, Malenkov had proposed that Kuznetsov replace Merkulov as head of the NKGB/MGB. According to this version, Malenkov was a mere bystander during the "Leningrad Affair," which was the work of Beriia, Abakumov, and V.M. Andrianov. In March 1949 when Kuznetsov was dismissed, Malenkov tried to save him by appointing him First Party Secretary in the Maritime region, but Kuznetsov decided to stay in Moscow and fight Beriia and was arrested in October 1949. Everyone except his father, including Khrushchev, who according to him received Kuznetsov's mantle, benefited from the "Leningrad Affair." After Stalin's death, Malenkov tried to improve the living conditions of the people, only to be frustrated by the true Stalinists such as Khrushchev. The younger Malenkov's account has been sharply challenged in the 1991 issues of *Zhurnalist* by journalist V. Demidov and historians D. Kutuzov and K. Kostliarov. The critical comments here, however, pale beside charges made by Stalin's younger son in his rambling letter dated January 19, 1959, to the Central Committee, where Malenkov, at that time rotting away as the head of Ust-Kamenogorsk power station, comes across as the devil incarnate. The executed Beriia fares only slightly better by being merely called "a scoundrel, liar and hypocrite." Khrushchev, understandably, is praised.[10]

NOTES

1. There is considerable literature about the Leningrad Affair. The most important are *Izvestiia TsK KPSS* (2/1989); *Leninaradskoe Delo*; *Beriia: Konets Kar'ery*; D.A. Volkogonov, *Triumf i Tragediia*; and *Sovetskaia Militsia* (4/1991).

2. *Leningradskoe delo* (op. cit.), pp. 210, 231.

3. *Leninaradskaia Pravda* (May 18, 1988).

4. *Leningradskoe Delo*, p. 21.

5. Ibid., p. 46.

6. *Voprosy Istorii KPSS* (November 1990), pp. 102–03. For a fascinating account of Kuznetsov, see *Yozvrashchennye Imena*, Vol. 1, pp. 317–34.

7. *Leningradskoe Delo*, pp. 281–97.

8. *Izvestiia TsK KPSS*.

9. *Zhurnalist* (2/1991), pp. 60–65.

10. *Iosif Stalin v Ob'iatiiakh Sem'i*, pp. 129–35.

Chapter 10

Intelligence, Counterintelligence, and Terror Campaigns in East Europe

Espionage, the second oldest (and in Joseph Brodsky's words, the evilest) profession, with its elements of misplaced trust, betrayal, and soap opera has always enjoyed a ready popular market. As John Le Carré has aptly put it, espionage is the secret theater of our society. Many continue to believe that wars are won by childish games played by twisted minds, rather than by the sacrifice of actual combatants. Soviet intelligence operations have always enjoyed a considerable vogue, and there is a great deal of literature on the subject based mostly on defector revelations as well as the writers' own power of imagination, deduction and speculation. Proof, however, has yet to be produced whether intelligence organizations exist for any reason other than providing employment for an army of bureaucrats with twisted psyches. Stalin, of course, was obsessed with intelligence and espionage even in his declining years. On December 15, 1952, he changed the 1 Department of the MGB to the 1 Main Department and decreed that its head would also be a Deputy Minister of MGB. According to Sudoplatov (p. 332), Malenkov quoted Stalin as saying that the work against our main adversary (U.S.) is impossible without adhering to the principle of a grand intelligence network.

Excluding Sudoplatov's memoirs, one area in which little additional information has become available during the Glasnost period is the MGB's "legitimate" activities in intelligence and counterintelligence during the *immediate post-war* period. In contrast, there is, however, considerable information about the KGB in the post-Stalin period. One wonders about the relationship between MGB's Foreign (1) Department and Beriia's Atomic Trust, which was also engaged in espionage activities in acquiring the West's nuclear secrets.[1]

One of the least-known and most fascinating changes of the post-war period was the creation in mid-1947 of a new Committee on Information (KI) under the Council of Ministers. The Committee, which lasted until late 1952 (some sources give an earlier date of 1951), took over the foreign intelligence functions of MGB (1 Department) and, during 1947–1948, also those of GRU. The Committee was chaired by Molotov until 1949, who was succeeded by A. Ia. Vyshinskii, Ia. A. Malik, and V. Zorin, in that order. All these men had Foreign Service experience and were not directly associated with the organs. The Committee paralleled the formation of the CIA, but unlike its American counterpart, soon went into decline. In the summer of 1948, Bulganin, the Minister of Armed Forces, apparently managed to separate the GRU from the KI. We can only wonder about Beriia and Abakumov's reaction to such intrusion into their legitimate sphere of operations. Christopher Andrew and Oleg Gordievsky also claim that the organs started a campaign to undermine the KI, which was finally dissolved in 1951.

Andrew and Gordievsky also claim that P.V. Fedotov, Head of the NKGB/MGB Foreign Department since July 1945, served as Deputy Chairman of KI during 1947–1949 and was in charge of daily operations. The two authors further claim that Fedotov was replaced in 1949 by S.R. Savchenko, Head of MGB in Ukraine, but Savchenko did not take over the Foreign Department until 1952, when KI had already ceased to exist.[2]

The alleged successes of Soviet intelligence during the Cold War years have to be balanced with its disastrous failure to gauge the depth and intensity of anti-Communism in the United States. In a period of less than five years, the Soviets squandered the goodwill of the war-time period to end up as the evil incarnate for millions of Americans. Part of this failure could be attributed to the Marxist blinders which put the blame on Wall Street rather than on a national consensus which included the working class.

It would also be naive to think that after the start of the Cold War, the West did not embark on campaigns of espionage and subversion against the Soviet Union and its satellites. How successful was MGB in countering these attempts, a legitimate concern, rather than arresting the imaginary enemies of the Stalinist state? The MGB also had its hands full in the annexed areas of West Ukraine and in the Baltic, where they were facing armed opposition requiring extensive use of security, intelligence, and military forces. In L'vov, no less a personage than Lt. General L.F. Raikhman, former Deputy Head of NKGB Counterintelligence, was supervising the elimination of OUN and the Home Army. In his interview with Abarinov, Raikhman admitted to fighting the Ukrainian nationalists, but was more hesitant about attempts to liquidate Polish resistance. As late as 1949, armed bands of Ukranian nationalists were still active. For instance, on October 27, they managed to assassinate the pro-Soviet writer Ia. A. Galan in L'vov.[3]

In Ukraine, as well as in the Baltic, a brutal no-holds-barred war was being waged which would serve as the model for the counter-insurgency campaigns of other countries such as the U.S.-sponsored Phoenix program that tried to eliminate the Vietcong cadres in South Vietnam. As early as December 1944, Soviet units under Kruglov were engaged in fighting the Lithuanian partisans.[4] In July 1945, Tkachenko, with the help of NKVD in Stravropol, had deported the Karachis, and took over the deportations in Lithuania, ably assisted by another man with experience in deportations, M.A. Suslov, who was representing the Party.[5] In his speech to the Central Committee in July 1953, A.Iu. Snechkus, First Secretary of the Lithuanian Party, claimed that 13,000 people had been killed by the "bandits."

The occupation of East Europe also presented the MGB with new problems and opportunities. The first goals were the subversion of non- and anti-Communist groups and the establishment of a pro-Communist government including front groups. These included such endeavors as setting up the PAX Party in Poland organized by I.A. Serov and arresting anti-Communist luminaries such as Cardinal Mindszenty in Hungary. The brutality and effectiveness of Soviet attempts are evident in the writings of those officials who managed to survive and escape. Once Communist governments were set up, each had its own MGB and MVD with Soviet advisers to provide the needed expertise and supervision.

Tito's defection and the anti-Semitic campaigns, however, led to a number of purges which claimed many victims among the triumphant Communists and were particularly vicious in Czechoslovakia and Hungary.

The tone was set when Laslo Rajk and a number of other high-ranking Hungarian Communists were arrested on June 16, 1949, and tried in September 1949. In October, after a typical show trial, Rajk and three others were condemned to death. Several of the victims were Jewish, but in this case so was the chief Stalinist operator in Hungary, Matyas Rakosi. In 1950, Rajk's successor as Minister of the Interior, Janos Kadar, was arrested and spent a year in prison. Christopher Andrew and Oleg Gordievsky claim that the Rajk trial was organized by M.I. Belkin (identified in 1946 as Deputy Head MGB Counterintelligence), who was assisted by MGB "Generals" Likhachev and Makarov.[6] By the latter, they must mean Komarov and neither he nor Likhachev was a general. In December 1949, Traicho Kostov, a close confidant of the recently deceased Georgi Dimitrov, was accused of having plotted the latter's death and was hanged. Likhachev may have also been involved in this case.

In July 1951, Gomulka, former Prime Minister and Secretary of the Polish Party, who had lost his job in January 1949, was arrested but not tried despite Stalin's insistence.[7] The purge campaign in Poland was somewhat different since, with the exception of Boleslaw Bierut (who may at one time have worked for NKVD), Stalin did not trust the native Polish Communists. It turned out that here some of the victimizers were, in fact, Jewish.

Most of the victims in Poland came from the military ranks, including Generals Spychalski and Tatar. After his arrest, Spychalski, the Minister of Defense, was replaced by the Soviet/Pole Marshal K.K. Rokossovskii, who held this position from October 1949 until 1956. There was no open bloodletting in Poland so Gomulka not only survived but managed to return to power after Stalin's death.

Chief victim in Rumania in 1952 was Anna Pauker, who had served as Minister of Foreign Affairs since November 1947. Anna was the widow of K.V. Pauker, who was once Stalin's barber and boon companion. Pauker had served as Head of the NKVD Operation Department until August 1937 before being purged. Anna, however, had remained true to Stalinism.

The bloodiest purge campaign in East Europe with strong anti-Semitic overtones was launched in Czechoslovakia. Shortly after the completion of the show trials in Budapest, two of Abakumov's chief bloodhounds, M.T. Likhachev and V.I. Komarov, showed up in Prague. Likhachev had been transfered to Bulgaria in May 1949, before moving to Czechoslovakia. One of their first victims was Eugene Loebl, Deputy Minister of Foreign Trade, who mistakingly identifies Komarov, a Russian from Leningrad, as a Ukrainian. The Czechoslovak purge, however, made little progress, possibly because of the Czech boss, Klement Gottwald's, lack of enthusiasm.[8] Andrew and Gordievsky claim that Likhachev and "Makarov" (Likhachev and Komarov) were replaced in the summer of 1950 by Colonel V.A. Boiarskii, a brutal investigator employed before the war with NKVD in North Ossetia.[9] A more probable date for this is summer 1951, when Likhachev and Komarov lost their jobs after the arrest of their boss, Abakumov. Boiarskii also proved unsatisfactory to Stalin, who was monitoring the events, so he was replaced in November 1951 by A.D. Beschastanov. At the same time, Stalin also sent Mikoian to Prague to persuade Gottwald to jump on the bandwagon.[10] The preparation for the trial took nearly a year and Besehastanov, according to Andrew and Gordievsky, was assisted by Esikov, Galkin, G. Gromov, G. Morozov, and "J. Chernov." I.A. Chernov, Head of the MGB Secretariat, however, had been arrested after Abakumov's fall so it is unlikely that he would have been in Prague at this date.[11] Unlike Likhachev, Komarov, and Chernov, Beschastanov suffered no consequences. He was elected Deputy to the Supreme Soviet and from 1969 to 1974 was Chairman of the KGB in Uzbek SSR.[12] The Czech trials actually took place in November 1952 and resulted in the execution of 11 prominent Communists (mostly Jewish), including the former Party General Secretary, Rudolf Slansky, and the Foreign Secretary, the Gentile Vladimir Clementis. Besides the main victims, also arrested were Minister of Defense Ludvik Svoboda, Chief of Staff Jaroslav Prochazka (for years, Moscow's most trusted agent in the Czech Armed Forces) and Generals Bocek, Klapalek and Prikryl. Most of these men survived, but Prochazaka's chief operative, Bedrich Reicin, was one of those condemned to death during the Slansky trial.[13] It is estimated that between 1948 and 1954, 50,000 political prisoners were arrested in Czechoslovakia and 10,000 ended up in camps. Between October 1948 and January 1953, 232 individuals were sentenced to death and 178 were actually executed.[14]

There was also a mini-purge in Albania when, in October 1948, Kochi Dzodze, Secretary of the Party and Minister of the Interior, was arrested and shot on June 11, 1949. This may have been the result of a family feud among the local Communists rather than something ordered by Moscow. The GDR was left relatively unscathed during the purge campaigns of the post-war years.

There is little doubt that the MGB was also involved in attempts to subvert Tito, whose break from the Soviet Union was a major defeat for Stalin and a cause for additional paranoia. For Stalin, Tito became the new Trotskii. The details have yet to be revealed, but during 1946–1947, the attempts to kill Tito were allegedly led by Maj. General D.N. Shadrin, Head of MGB 2 Department. Shadrin was appointed Head of the Bodyguards Administration (No. 2), but was dismissed in 1948 as a possible "Titoist" and replaced by A.M. Rozanov. Abakumov's failure, however, did not mean an end to the campaign to destroy Tito. In the fall of 1952, Beriia and the recently appointed head of MGB, S.D. Igant'ev, organized a new attempt. Their candidate to carry out the assassination was the shadowy figure I.R.

Grigulevich (also at times listed as Grigudevich, known under the code name "Max"), who after service in Spain in the 1930s had taken part on May 24, 1940 in the abortive attempt in Mexico City by a group of thugs organized by the Communist muralist David Alfaro Siqueiros to assassinate Trotskii. Grigulevich, now considered a specialist in Latin America, was in Costa Rica in 1948 and a year later in Italy working against the Vatican. It was here that a plan was hatched to assassinate Tito by Grigulevich posing as a Costa Rican diplomat stationed in Italy and spraying the Yugoslav with plague germs while presenting his credentials. The attempt planned for early 1953 did not take place, and if we are to believe Poskrybeshev, the failure to eliminate Tito turned Stalin against Beriia, who, incidentally canceled the operation after Stalin's death. Grigulevich later was awarded a doctorate and served as a corresponding member of the USSR Academy of Science attached to the Institute of Ethnography.

Sudoplatov, in his memoirs (pp. 336–38), claims that the real architect of the plan was E.P. Pitovranov, in prison since October 1951 as an associate of Abakumov, but released after writing to Stalin claiming that he was put in prison because Riumin was intent on wrecking his plans for assassinating Tito and other foreign enemies of the Soviet Union. This caught Stalin's eye, who ordered Pitovranov's release. After a month of recuperation Pitovranov supposedly wrote to Stalin concocting the bizarre plan to use Grigulevich to kill Tito. The upshot was a meeting on about February 20, 1953 of Stalin, Igant'ev, and Sudoplatov—who vehemently opposed the plan since he thought it was half-baked and Grigulevich unqualified for the operation. He instead suggested that Eitingon, who was in prison, be brought into the picture. The next day Sudoplatov and Igant'ev met with I.A. Serov, S.R. Savchenko, V.S. Riasnoyi, A.A. Epishov (all Khrushchev men according, to Sudoplatov, who never misses a chance to blacken the latter's name) and Pitovranov, who, supported by Savchenko, continued to insist that the plan was viable. Sudoplatov continued to oppose the plan on tactical grounds and the Hamlet-like Igant'ev could not resolve the matter. In less than two weeks, Stalin was dead and the plans were dropped. Sudoplatov claims that Epishev was extremely vocal in his support for plans to kill Zhukov. When Khrushchev visited Yugoslavia in the summer of 1955 on his crow-eating mission, he was accompanied by Epishev and, in fact, the latter served as the Soviet Ambassador to Belgrade in 1960–1962. Failing to kill Tito, the MGB found solace by arresting the turbulent actress, T. Okunevskaia (once married to Stalinist journalist B. Gorbatov), who had apparently sent Tito into a romantic freefall during a visit to Yugoslavia followed by an affair with the Yugoslav ambassador in the USSR. After 13 months in solitary confinement, Okunevskaia was sent to camps and did not emerge until after Stalin's death.

Under Igant'ev, the MGB's newly founded 1 Bureau was also involved in a number of terror campaigns against potential enemies of the USSR living abroad. These will be discussed later when we take up the career of Sudoplatov.

The role played by MGB in satellite countries during 1945–1953 has not been extensively discussed in the Glasnost literature. Although I do not claim familiarity with the recent historiography of the former Soviet bloc countries, I have reason to believe that this rather sensitive subject with its potential for showing extensive local collaboration has also been neglected. There is little doubt, however, that the archives will show a deep involvement by the MGB in the internal and external affairs of the satellite countries.

NOTES

1. *Soiuz* (Nos. 21 and 23, 1991); V.M. Zubok, *Soviet Intelligence and the Cold War: The "Small" Committee of Information. 1952–1953.*

2. Christopher Andrew and Oleg Gordievsky: *KGB. The Inside Story*, pp. 382–83.

3. *Izvestiia TsK KPPS* (1/1991), p. 180.

4. *Istoriia SSSR* (1/1991).

5. *Beriia: Konets Kar'ery*, p. 407; and *Nauka I Zhizn'* (No. 1, 1989).

6. Christopher Andrew and Oleg Gordievsky, *KGB*, p. 409.

7. Roy Medvedev, *Let History Judge*, p. 795; and *Zeitschrift für Zeitaeschichte* (August 1992), p. 737.

8. Eugen Loebl, *My Mind on Trial*, p. 32; Artur London, *Confession*, p. 79; and *Novaia Mysl'* (July 10, 1968).

9. Andrew and Gordievsky, *KGB*, p. 412.

10. Conquest, *The Great Terror*, p. 458.

11. Andrew and Gordievsky, ibid., p. 413.

12. *Deputaty Verkhovnogo Soveta* SSSR, p. 543.

13. *On All Fronts: Czechoslovaks in World War II*, p. 239.

14. K. Kaplan, *Nekrava Revoluce*, p. 204. See also *Sachauprozesse und Politische Verfolaung in Mittel und Osteuropa*; G.H. Hodos, *Show Trials: Stalinist Purges in Eastern Europe 1948–1954*; and Jan Foitzik, "Die Stalinistischen Sauberungen," *Zeitschrift für Geschichtwissenschaft* (August 1992).

Chapter 11

Downfall

On July 4, 1951, Abakumov was removed as head of MGB. He had also allegedly been expelled from the Party a month earlier. Abakumov must have suspected that something was amiss since Stalin's calendar indicated no meetings of the two men after November 1950. Documents so far released about the senior military officers (mostly returned POWs who were executed in 1950–1951), which logically should have been handled by Abakumov, instead implicate his First Deputy S.I. Ogol'tsev, but this could have been caused by Abakumov's preoccupation with the "Leningrad Affair." They also indicate that there were forces working behind the scenes against him. Peter Deriabin claims that Abakumov was in trouble in early 1951. He was repeatedly summoned to report to the Central Committee, once four times in one day.[1] On July 12, 1951, Jurist 1 Class G.N. Safonov, USSR Prosecutor General since 1943 who undoubtedly had had close professional relations with Abakumov, issued an arrest warrant under Article 58 of the RSFSR Code. The charge: treason and dereliction of duty. Abakumov was first taken to the MVD Sokol'nicheskii prison (popularly known as "Sailor's Silence") before being transferred to Lefortovo prison, where he was merely listed as "prisoner no. 15." (Listing important prisoners such as Vlasov, Alter, Erlich, and Zhemchuzhina under a number rather than a name was a long-held secret police practice going back to Tsarist times.) The next day Abakumov's second wife, Antonina Nikolaeva, age 31, a former employee of the MGB Central Office, and their two-month-old son were taken into custody and put in the MVD prison (they were not released until March 9, 1954), to be followed by Abakumov's first wife, T. Smirnova, who was, however, released shortly.[2] Also arrested were Maj. General A.G. Leonov, head of the MGB Department for Investigation of Especially Important Cases, and his three deputies, Colonels M.T. Likhachev, V.I. Komarov, and L.L. Shvartsman. Colonel F.G. Shubniakov, head of the MGB 2 Branch, Colonel I.A. Chernov, head of Abakumov's secret chancellory and his Deputy Colonel Ia. M. Broverman were also taken into custody, some as late as October.[3] The complete list of Abakumov's associates who were arrested after his fall has yet to be released, but also included Maj. General G.A. Bezhanov, Head of MGB in Kabard ASSR and veteran of war-time deportations in Crimea. Bezhanov, one of the few men associated with Beriia who continued to serve under Abakumov, was to share a cell with V.L. Zuskin, artistic director of the Moscow State Jewish Theater, a victim of the anti-Semitic campaigns. The arrest of Abakumov and his closest associates was followed in October by the removal and arrest of two Deputy Ministers, Lt. Generals N.N. Selivanovskii and E.P. Pitovarnov of the Foreign Department (Pitovarnov for the second time). The latter, who may have replaced Fedotov as head of counterintelligence, was married to Malenkov's niece, but that did not save him from arrest—although he was eventually released in December 1952. Also arrested were several department and deputy department heads, including Lt. Generals L.F. Raikhman and N. Korolev (former Head of Counterintelligence with the Central Group of Forces), (A.P.?) Palkin, Lt. General M.I. Belkin (identified in 1946 as Deputy Head MGB of counterintelligence, later perhaps a Deputy Minister), and one Maj. General Utekhin, identified in 1945 as Head of the SMERSH 4 Department while serving in Germany. Riumin personally arrested Belkin.[4] Soon all the Jewish senior officers with the rank of Colonel or above (some 50 officers according to Sudoplatov) employed by the organs were removed and in most cases arrested. In December 1951, G.M. Maironovskii, who since December 1938 had been the head of secret police labs, allegedly involved in making poison and in human experiments, was also arrested.

The excuse for the removal and arrest of Abakumov was a letter by M.D. Riumin to the Central Committee denouncing Abakumov for involvement with American intelligence operating under a "Jewish bourgeois conspiracy." Riumin accused Abakumov of suppression of the testimony of one Dr. Ia. G. Etinger, who had been arrested in 1950 and died in prison, as well as personal corruption. Abakumov was also accused of having known Dr. S.S. Iudin (arrested on December 23, 1948), an agent of British intelligence and leader of "SDR" (Union for Revolutionary Struggle), a terrorist youth group. After returning from England, Iudin, a member of Korolovskii Surgical Society, had allegedly joined a military conspiracy directed by the Chief Marshal of Artillery N.N. Voronov (who had been sacked in March 1950), whose aim was to replace Stalin with Marshal Zhukov. Abakumov was further accused of involvement with two double agents, Gavrilov and Lavrent'ev, who worked for both MGB and U.S. intelligence.[5] Although the Soviet archives have yet to reveal any direct links between Stalin and the rather lowly Riumin, the plot carries marks of something inspired by Stalin. After all, it seems that Riumin, a mere Lt. Colonel, could not have organized something of this nature against the mighty Abakumov without sanction from above. On the other hand, it is also possible that Riumin, rebuffed by Abakumov (who had begun to mistrust him after the "Leningrad Affair" and may have put incriminating material into Riumin's personnel file) and seeing no future in MGB as long as Abakumov was in charge, decided to risk everything by writing the letter accusing Abakumov of what amounted to treason. This desperate act was not unprecedented. After all, Ezhov, when on his way out, had faked his own assassination. Riumin's charges dovetailed with Stalin's own plans and his disenchantment with Abakumov. Sudoplatov claims that Riumin approached Malenkov's assistant, D.N. Sukhanov, in the spring of 1951 with his charges against Abakumov. Sukhanov suggested, after confering with Malenkov, that Riumin write his infamous letter to Stalin. The letter allegedly went through ten different re-writes because of Riumin's poor education. Sukhanov, who is still living and incidentally served a prison term for theft of expensive personal effects from Beriia's safe, did not mention this in his television appearance in July 1992.

According to A.G. Malenkov, his father told Stalin that the MGB bodyguards (the younger Malenkov mistakenly identifies this as the 9 Department, yet to be created) were appropriating caviar and other delicacies intended for the higher ranks of the Party and government. This, however, was a red herring and must have happened after Abakumov's arrest, which was based on reasons other than corruption—about which Stalin must have been cognizant at least since 1948 when he received the letters from I.A. Serov and Captain Bystrov already discussed.

Why would Malenkov take such a prominent part in Abakumov's downfall when the latter had so recently been instrumental in getting rid of Malenkov's rivals in Leningrad? Sudoplatov states that Malenkov still held a grudge because of Abakumov's role in the "Aviators' Affair." Abakumov, whose appointment as head of the MGB was probably supported by Zhdanov, Malenkov's rival, had allegedly claimed that Malenkov, who had been the Party's watchdog over the aviation industry during the war, had covered up shortcomings and even corruption, and this had resulted in Malenkov's demotion and exile. I think a better explanation is that Malenkov was doing the bidding of Stalin, who had decided that Abakumov must go. Stalin's daily calendar before Abakumov's dismissal is a clear indication of Stalin's disenchantment with the secret police chief. Malenkov also must have felt more comfortable with S.D. Igant'ev, Abakumov's successor and a fellow Party apparatchik. Malenkov had a similar relationship with Ezhov during the Great Purge, at least until Stalin became disillusioned with the "Iron Commissar."

Abakumov was first interrogated by First Deputy General Prosecutor K.A. Mokichev while Safonov was recovering from the effects of a traffic accident. Questions asked included the nature of the relationship between Abakumov and L.L. Shvartsman, now identified as a part of a"Jewish Nationalist Conspiracy." Abakumov called Shvartsman a competent Chekist whom he had inherited from Merkulov, with whom he had been a close associate. On August 19, 1951, Malenkov and the new Minister of State Security, S.D. Ignat'ev, ordered Mokichev to send to Stalin the text of Abakumov's interrogations. Two days later, State Jurist 3 Class L.N. Smirnov, Senior Assistant to the USSR Prosecutor (former Assistant Soviet Prosecutor in Nuremberg and future Chairman of the USSR Supreme Court under Brezhnev), wrote an 11-page report which was sent along with the text of the interrogation to Beriia and Malenkov. Two decrees from the USSR Council of Ministers, dated from July 26 and 26, 1951, and signed by Stalin, deprived Abakumov of the use of his apartment, his house, and the MGB dacha.[6]

Early in 1993, a series of articles in *Shchit i Mech* by retired Colonel of Judiciary A. Liskin shed further light on Abakumov and the circumstances of his arrest. The investigators, besides Liskin and L.N. Smirnov, included Maj. General of Judiciary I.D. Kitaev, Deputy USSR Military Prosecutor under A.P. Vavilov (who took no part in the proceedings); Deputy Military Prosecutor Lt. Colonel of Judiciary V.A. Uspenskii; Chief of Investigation in the Military Prosecutor's Office, Colonel of Judiciary P.A. Kul'chitskii; and his Deputies Lt. Colonels V.P. Markar'ian and S.M. Gromov. In addition, there were the following officers: A.N. Bzenko, I.A. Ivanov, G.A. Terekhov, N.N. Preobrazhenskii, Captain A.V. Iur'eva (from the Personnel Office), P.A. Tsaregradskii, and K. Koverin representing various branches of the Military Prosecutor's Office. Liskin, a young major at this time, had served during the war as Military Prosecutor of the 120 Guard Rifle Division and 80 Rifle Corps, both attached to the 3 Army, 2 Belorussian Front. He had personal experience with Abakumov and SMERSH. He blamed Abakumov's Assistant M.T. Likhachev for the suicide during the Nuremberg trials of his former boss, Col. N.D. Zoria, the Military Prosecutor of the 3 Army.

At the time of Abakumov's arrest, Stalin had developed an additional paranoia that Chekists could not be trusted to investigate other Chekists, which seems strange in view of what had happened to most of Iagoda and Ezhov's operatives but explains why the task of investigating Abakumov had been given to the Military Prosecutors. Liskin thinks that Stalin's suspicions were justified. When the Military Prosecutors arrived at Abakumov's house, they were met by his Deputies. Liskin also believes that the MGB was behind Safonov's traffic accident, caused by his chauffeur, who turned out to be a man with a long criminal record. The investigative team ("Brigade" in Liskin's words) had an unenviable act, caught in a minefield where any misstep could prove to be fatal. At the end, most of them became sick as a result of continuous tension. The texts of interrogations were sent to Beriia, Malenkov, and Stalin. According to Liskin, Beriia had his own mole in the Prosecutor's Office and did not bother to read the documents sent to him, which were apparently examined by one of his assistants for missing materials. The investigators were faced with a Catch–22 since it was obvious that most of Abakumov's major crimes had been committed with the knowledge and approval of Stalin. Abakumov knew this and, in his meetings with the Prosecutors, whom he referred to as "my friends," he behaved as if he were still the Minister of State Security, claiming that his arrest was a misunderstanding that was soon to be corrected by Stalin, and he would be restored to his old position. (Later this arrogant tone was to change.) In August 1951, Abakumov wrote a letter to Stalin and demanded that the letter be typed—a request which was met. The investigators found Abakumov guilty of numerous minor crimes which filled a number of volumes. These included illegally arresting V.N. Il'in and placing him in Sukhanov prison, and having knowledge of crimes committed by his subordinates. (For example, N.S. Zobov, former head of the Secretariat of SMERSH in the 1 Belorussian Front, had used his position to plunder in Germany.) There was also the question of Abakumov's personal corruption. But try as they did and even with the help of S.D. Igant'ev, the new head of MGB, the investigators could not come up with the smoking gun to verify Riumin's charges that Abakumov had been involved with foreign intelligence agencies and "Jewish bourgeois nationalist" groups, had tried to remove the MGB from Party Control, and had engaged in "terroristic" activities including against the person of Stalin. By late fall, the investigators, to their relief, were dismissed, but Abakumov remained in prison.

In order to collect evidence, Lt. General of Judiciary A.F. Katusev, Deputy Chief USSR Prosecutor, even interviewed the former head of the Secret Political Department, V.N. Il'in, in prison since 1943 after his run-in with Abakumov, but the old Chekist, sensing a trap, refused to cooperate. Katusev, in his interview with Kostliarov, stated that there were serious doubts about the legal justification for Abakumov's arrest. In fact, even Riumin, after his own arrest and interrogation in April 1953, admitted that there was little basis for charges of espionage and "nationalist" activities against Abakumov and his colleagues, although he had been involved with the Jewish doctors.

Abakumov's investigation took a strange twist with the testimony of L.L. Shvartsman. A former investigator, he would confess to anything and even made up stories to avoid torture, and here he was helped by his previous employment as a journalist. He admitted to having been Abakumov's Deputy in the Jewish organization in the MGB which planned terrorist actions against the leaders of the Party and government with help from U.S. intelligence agencies. Shvartsman did not stop with this, however, confessing also to sexual relations with Abakumov, the latter's son, his own son, the British Ambassador, two American agents identified as Gavrilov and Lavrent'ev and his own stepdaughter. This claptrap did not hurt Abakumov's cause and persuaded Lt. Colonel Uspenskii to recommend that Shvartsman be committed to a psychiatric facility. Even Stalin, to whom the reports were being sent, refused to believe Shvartsman's confessions. Though he ordered the arrest of all the senior Jewish Chekists, he began to doubt Riumin, who along with the newly appointed Deputy Minister of MGB, S.A. Goglidze, continued to brief him (at times bypassing S.D. Ignat'ev, the actual Head of MGB) on the progress of Abakumov's investigation as well as on the new Jewish conspiracies that were being continuously discovered. These conspiracies culminated in the "Doctors' Plot" in 1952 and also had the potential of being used against Abakumov. The fact that Goglidze, once one of Beriia's closest allies, was involved in poisoning Stalin's mind against Abakumov is testimony to the tenuous relation between Abakumov and Beriia. The interrogations were conducted with extreme brutality by Riumin, who would beat defendants such as Belkin, behavior that Stalin encouraged.[7] Questioning Chernov, Abakumov's Assistant, in February 1952, Riumin said to him, "You are not a stupid man; just tell us how Abakumov had planned to take over the country."[8] Meanwhile, Abakumov, who was now being kept in shackles (how the mighty had fallen), was being shuffled between Lefortovo, Butyrka, and Lubianka prisons. His now pathetic and servile letters to Stalin, Beriia, and Malenkov (whom he addressed as L.P. and G.M.). reproduced in *Golgofa*, complained about prison conditions while swearing undying fealty to Stalin and the Soviet state. According to Beriia's son, his father merely forwarded Abakumov's letters to Malenkov. On March 24, 1952, Lt. Colonel of Medical Services Ianshin, Head of Lefortovo Infirmary, wrote a report (*Nedelia*, 44, 1990) about various medical problems faced by Abakumov. This was followed by a letter dated April 18, 1952, from Abakumov to Beriia and Malenkov requesting treatment as well as intervention on his behalf to Stalin, release of his wife and child, and return to "Sailor's Silence" prison, where his case could be handled by Prosecutors rather than Riumin and company. The prison pictures reproduced in *Golgofa* show Abakumov a broken man, far from the arrogant peacock of previous years. Despite Riumin's splendid efforts, Abakumov and other prisoners were not brought to trial and all were living at the time of Stalin's death. Riumin's own fall in mid-December 1952 must have provided relief, albeit temporary, for Abakumov. The last report sent to Stalin about Abakumov was on February 20, 1953, just before Stalin's death. Sudoplatov, no friend of Abakumov, has nothing but admiration for Abakumov's refusal to break down under torture, which must have been inflicted after the Military Prosecutors failed to produce the desired results and were replaced by Riumin and his crowd and quite possibly continued by Kobulov (until his own arrest) and later Serov after Stalin's death.

After his removal, Abakumov was replaced temporarily by First Deputy Minister MGB S.I. Ogol'tsev, a man who strangely enough had been associated with A.A. Kuznetsov in 1940 in Leningrad. For a short time, Ogol'tsev was assisted by Deputy Ministers A.S. Blinov and N.N. Selivanovskii. Officially, Ogol'tsev remained in charge of MGB until the end of 1951, although other sources indicate a much earlier date. At least one Soviet document lists S.D. Igant'ev as the new Minister on August 19, 1951.[9] Col. Liskin even gives a date as early as July. Igant'ev, born in 1904, had been identified in 1939 as the Party Secretary in Bashkiria, USSR. Rumors that he had helped Mekhlis in the Far East military purges have yet to be confirmed. In 1946, he was the Second Party Secretary in Belorussia, and in March 1946, he was one of the four Deputies under N.S. Patolichev, who had replaced Malenkov as Secretary of the Central Committee. Later he was also assigned to Party work in Uzbek USSR. Ignat'ev had no experience with the security organs, but neither had Ezhov at the time of his appointment. Stalin, who had replaced the professional policeman Iagoda with the Party functionary Ezhov, now repeated the same pattern with Abakumov and Igant'ev, who, however, turned out to be no Ezhov. Stalin continued to work directly with Riumin—as unprincipled and brutal a thug as ever adorned the secret police leadership. Soviet archives now reveal Ignat'ev to be more sinister than he was portrayed during the Khrushchev years when he managed to survive and served first with the CC CPSU as Secretary until April 5, 1953, and as member until April 28, 1953, before being sent to Bashkiria, later to Tataria, and finally attached to the Supreme Soviet. Ignat'ev died in 1976, the only Stalinist police chief to die a natural death. Although more than just a messenger and, in fact, getting Stalin's final approval for the death sentences for Jewish intellectuals, Ignat'ev shared his power with his Deputy, M.D. Riumin, who now replaced Abakumov's man, A.G. Lenov, as Head of the crucial Department for Investigation of Especially Important Cases. Brought from the Far East and appointed Deputy Minister of MGB was the old Beriia crony S.A. Goglidze, who became, along with Riumin, Stalin's confidant in matters of state security.[10] Meanwhile, Stalin appointed a committee made up of Malenkov, Beriia, Shkiriatov, and Igant'ev to look into the affairs of the MGB and perhaps the fate of Abakumov, who, as Stoliarov claims, may have been in possession of documents which compromised both Beriia and Malenkov.[11]

According to Malenkov's son, Igant'ev was his father's candidate to replace Abakumov. Stalin, however, balanced Igant'ev's appointment by appointing S.A. Goglidze, L.F. Tsanava, and A.A. Epishev as Deputy Ministers. The first two were associated wtih Beriia, and Epishev had served with Khrushchev during the war. Meanwhile, at the 19 Party Congress (October 1952), Igant'ev was elected to the Party Presidium. According to Malenkov's son, the 19 Party Congress, in which an enlarged Party Presidium of 25 replaced the former Politburo of 16 members,was a triumph for his father. Presidium members sympathetic to Malenkov included Igant'ev, M.G. Pervukhin, V.A. Malyshev, A.B. Aristov, V.V. Kuznetsov, O.V. Kuusinen, L.G. Mel'nikov, N.A. Mikhailov, P.K. Ponomarenko, and M.Z. Saburov. Other members, kindred spirits, who were also in the Party Secretariat, were A.N. Kosygin, N.S. Patolichev, N.M. Pegov, A.M. Puzanov, I.F. Tevosian, P.F. Iudin, and D.I. Chesnonkov. The return of Marshal Zhukov and his election as a candidate member of CC CPSU also helped this group. According to A.G. Malenkov, facing them were Beriia, Khrushchev, Bulganin, V.M. Andrianov, M.F. Shkiriatov, A.Ia Vyshinskii, and M.D. Bagirov. Poskrebyshev served as the secretary of this body in his usual role of scribe and Stalin's chief informer.

In July 1951, the future Army General A.A. Epishev, later a fixture of the Brezhnev years as Head of the Political Administration of the Red Army, was appointed Deputy Minister of MGB for Cadres.[12]   In August 1951, L.F. Tsanava was called from Belorussia and was also appointed Deputy Minister of MGB, joining Goglidze.[13]   In October 1951, P.I. Ivashutin, the head of counterintelligence in the Southern Group of Forces, was appointed Head of MGB in Ukraine. This was rather odd since Ivashutin had spent most of the war serving in SMERSH under the fallen Abakumov and, as we have seen elsewhere in this book (as quoted by Kostliarov), is the only high-ranking Soviet official who has anything good to say about Abakumov, even in Glasnost days. The Soviet sources claim that in June 1952, the veteran B.P. Obruchnikov was moved from MVD and was appointed Deputy Minister of MGB in charge of cadres.[14] This thus contradicts Epishev's appointment to the same position. In the Foreign Department, S.R. Savchenko replaced P.V. Fedotov. Savchenko, head of MGB in Ukraine during 1946–1949, was also a Deputy Minister. Ia.A. Edunov, a former SMERSH officer, was in charge of the 3 (counterintelligence) Department. Stalin's behavior had always been characterized by brutal efficiency, but in the last 20 months of his life, the Faustian drive began to decline and his actions became increasingly bizarre, though no less bloodthirsty. The singlemindedness which had characterized Stalin during his entire political career began to waver. Chris Ward's observation in *Stalin's Russia* that this was no self-confident tyrant in charge of a smoothly functioning totalitarian machine, but a sickly old man, unpredictable, dangerous, lied to by terrified subordinates, and raging, like Lear, against failure and mortality, is not far off the mark for this period. There were also other manifestations of odd behavior, such as obsessive listening to Mozart's piano concerto No. 23 in A Major, as reported by Iu.B. Borev in *Staliniada*.

At the 19th Party Congress, Stalin proposed a 21-member Central Committee "Presidium" whose membership included individuals who did not even belong to the Central Committee. Stalin further suggested the creation of a "Bureau" from members of the Presidium to include Bulganin, Beriia, Malenkov, Kaganovich, Saburov, Khrushchev, Pervukhin, and Voroshilov. Notable was the exclusion of Molotov and Mikoian, the two senior members of Stalin's inner circle. The inclusion of Voroshilov, who had been out of favor and under suspicion for alleged espionage, was also a surprise, although he ended up being a member in name only. Actually, only four members of the "Bureau," Beriia, Bulganin, Khrushchev, and Malenkov, regularly met with Stalin, and Beriia was also about to come under suspicion. By now, the Central Committee was merely a cosmetic body, but the removal and demotion of a number of individuals associated with Beriia is also worthy of notice. Regardless, Stalin's word continued to be the law.

In 1952, Stalin gave the green light for the last purge campaign of his career, the "Doctors' Plot," which had been in gestation since the latter half of 1951. At first, he worked directly with Riumin, who organized the affair, which ended only with Stalin's death but not before the death under torture of several of the doctors. When Riumin failed to produce the desired results, he was sacked in November 1952, but the campaign continued. According to Malenkov's son, even his father and Igant'ev had doubts about the "Doctors' Plot" which, according to them, was basically a ruse to get to Beriia.[15]

Ignat'ev, meanwhile, was involved in the "Mingrelian Affair" aimed at Beriia's followers in Georgia. In 1937, with the help of his friend, S.A. Goglidze, head of NKVD in the Transcaucasus, Beriia had managed to frustrate Ezhov's attempts to arrest him; Ignat'ev, serving under an enfeebled Stalin, apparently proved to be no match for the wily Georgian, and he was also hampered by the ineffectual Rukhadze, Head of MGB in Georgia. The outline of the "Mingrelian Affair" can be seen by following *Zaria Vostoka* during the period and by the revelations in Sudoplatov's memoirs.

Beriia's position in his power base Georgia had been weakened during the post-war years when in 1947 Abakumov, undoubtedly with Stalin's approval, appointed N.M. Rukhadze Head of MGB, replacing A.N. Rapava, a compatriot of Beriia who had been the head of the local NKVD/NKGB/MGB for nearly ten years. Rukhadze had started his career under Beriia and once had been the Head of the Investigation Department in Georgia NKVD. During the war, however, he had been the head of SMERSH in various fronts operating in the North Caucasus, engaged in intrigue against, among others, the hapless Lt. General D.T. Kozlov, Commander of the Transcaucasus, Caucasus, and Crimea Fronts, who was sacked and demoted. Technically, Rukhadze was subordinate to Abakumov, but there is strong evidence that here he worked directly with Stalin, corresponding and speaking to him in Georgian, another case of Stalin's micromanaging the terror. Here Abakumov was no more than an interested bystander. There is no evidence that any of Abakumov's professional bloodhounds, Leonov, Komarov, and Likhachev, took part in this campaign. Sudoplatov states that Riumin helped Rukhadze in his investigation, but he is alone in making this claim. Even if Riumin was involved, it must have been after Abakumov's arrest. Abakumov's successor, S.D. Igant'ev, took a more active part, but even he was hesitant. Rukhadze started his campaign by investigating corruption among Beriia's Mingrelian cronies, not a difficult task, and putting wiretaps on a number of people, including Beriia's mother. In April 1948, Rapava and G. Sturua, two Beriia allies, lost their jobs in the Georgia Party Politburo, and a month later P.A. Shariia (more about him later) was deposed as the Party Secretary for Propaganda and Agitation. Despite tensions, there was no further shake-up until 1951. During the summer while vacationing in Abkhazia, Stalin ordered Rukhadze to speed up things. The anti-corruption campaign, in gestation since 1948, now came to a boil when, in 1951, charges regarding theft of cars and state property caused the removal of a number of officials, including the Minister of Justice. For the time being, Beriia's chief operatives, K.N. Charkviani, M.Ia. Baramia, and V.D. Budzhiashvill, respectively the Party's three Secretaries (in the case of Charkviani since 1938); Z.N. Chkhubianishvili, Chairman of the Council of Ministers; and V.P. Gagua (Gogua), Chairman of the Republic's Supreme Court, were left untouched although the latter as soon fired. Stalin also ordered Rukhadze to organize sabotage campaigns against Turkey and Iran. Rukhadze's failure to carry out the task may have contributed to his eventual downfall.

Meanwhile, matters became increasingly serious as charges of nationalism and worse—attempts to break away Mingrelia (western part of Georgia and Beriia's home territory) and join up with Turkey—were made. Officially, in November 1951 and later in March 1952, the Central Committee passed resolutions about the existence of a Mingrelian nationalist organization whose goal was to liquidate Soviet power in Georgia and form a breakaway republic.

In 1951 Stalin, in his Machiavellian fashion, was operating on two separate lines vis-à-vis Beriia. At the same time that he was undermining Beriia's position in Georgia, he was honoring him with awards, granting him the singular honor of addressing the Party on the 34th anniversary of the October Revolution on November 6, 1951, as well as decorating him for the success of the Soviet atomic bomb projects, for which he received another Order of Lenin. All and all, during his illustrious career, Beriia received five Orders of Lenin, two Orders of Red Banner, one of Survorov I Grade, as well as being named Hero of the Socialist Labor. Despite all of this, Stalin forced Beriia to chair a 1951 commission to launch a purge of his own colleagues. Sudoplatov also adds that there was additional tension between the two men over the rumors that Beriia's son was a candidate to marry Svetlana Alliluyeva (about to divorce Zhdanov's son), a proposed union which was opposed by Beriia and his wife. On October 27, 1950, Merkulov, the former Minister of State Security and one of Beriia's closest colleagues, whose career had been in limbo for nearly four years (he had served as head of the Soviet Repatriation Commission in Germany), was appointed Minister of State Control, replacing L.Z. Mekhlis. There were also other signs of Stalin's schizophrenic attitude. In his letter to the Central Committee on January 19, 1959 (*Iosif Stalin v Ob'iatiiakh Sem'i*), Stalin's son relates how in 1950 (actually September 1949) his father, in his typically high-handed way, dismissed K.A. Vershinin as Commander of the Air Force, replacing him with P.F. Zhigarev. The younger Stalin found the decision indefensible since Zhigarev had been sacked as Commander in Chief of the Air Force in April 1942 because of drunkenness (a condition with which the younger Stalin had more than a nodding acquaintance). Zhigarev had been sent to command the Air Force in the Far East where he had become a close friend of Goglidze and Beriia. The young Stalin claims that Zhigarev and Admiral N.G. Kuznetsov, who was restored to command of the Navy in July 1951, owed their revivals to Beriia's influence, and this claim is also partially supported by Beriia's son. The fact that both Zhigarev and Kuznetsov were kept in command after Beriia's arrest, however, casts doubt on the intimacy of their relationships. Also removed in February 1949 was I.V. Shikin, Head of the Political Administration of the Red Army and a man considerd a "Leningrader." He was replaced by F.F. Kuznetsov, who during the war had served as Commissar of the 60 Army and Voronezh Front before taking over the GRU in April 1943. Regardless, the double game with Beriia was to continue until Stalin died, and no one, perhaps not even Stalin, knew the final outcome.

In Georgia, Beriia had no choice but to sacrifice his own men. Charkviani and Chukhubianishvili were, respectively, replaced by A.I. Mgeladze and Z.N. Ketskoveli, who reported directly to Stalin. Karandze, head of MVD, was replaced by V.A. Loladze, deputy head of MGB. Beriia also closed the Mingrelian newspapers but did his best to minimize the damage. Mgeladze and N.M. Rukhadze, head of MGB in Georgia since 1948, were the pointmen in carrying out the purge. Those arrested in the last six months of 1951 included Charkviani, A.I. Mirtskhulava, and A.N. Rapava, as well as thousands of Party and government workers. Also arrested were Chief Prosecutor V.I. Shonia and P.A. Shariia, who had served as Beriia's secretary and ghost writer, a duty he had also performed for Stalin and possibly A.S. Zodelava, who before the war had headed the NKVD Transportation Department in Georgia before taking over the NKVD in North Ossetia and carrying out extensive purges there. Strangely enough, at first K.P. Bziava, a Mingrelian, was left as the Deputy Head of MVD, but his intrigue against Rukhadze (reporting the latter's boorish behavior to S.D. Igant'ev) resulted in Stalin's ordering Bziava's arrest. In the Central Committee meeting in early July 1953 following Beriia's arrest, a cornered Ketskoveli tried to put a new spin on the events, blaming Beriia as the instigator rather than a victim of the Mingrelian Affair. V.M. Bakradze, the Chairman of the Council of Ministers of Georgia, also under fire, supported this false version.

In 1952, Beriia was being pushed on other fronts as well. Stalin, who correctly suspected the existence of close relations between Beriia and the Chief of Staff (since June 1950) S.M. Shtemenko (a man who matched Beriia in his penchant for "intrigue"), claiming that the latter was too young for his job and had him replaced in June 1952 as he had A.I. Antonov back in 1946 with a more "experienced" officer, in this case, Marshal V.D. Sokolovskii. After Beriia's arrest in 1953, Shtemenko was questioned, demoted two ranks to Lt. General and sent to exile as Assistant Commander of the Volga Military District. Shtemenko's letter of July 21, 1953 to Khrushchev, published for the first time in *VIZH* (1/1995) after he had been removed because of his alleged rapport with the fallen Beriia, denies any close relationship between the two men. It defies logic why Minister of Defense Zhukov brought Shtemenko back from exile in 1956, promoted him one rank, and appointed him Head of the GRU. In 1952, he also saw the arrest of V. Mataradze, a former mistress of Beriia, who had served as one of his contacts with the Georgian émigrés in France.

The same year also saw the arrest of T. Shavida, nephew of Beriia's wife. Shavdia had been captured during the war by the Germans and had joined their "Georgian Legion" used for rear guard duties in France. After Shavida surrendered to the Allied troops, Beriia, using the services of his assistant P.A.Shariia, managed to have Shavida repatriated. After Stalin's death, the imprisoned Shavida was sent to Georgia under the care of Dekanozov. A.I. Vaksberg, in *Stalin Against the Jews*, claims that the French leftist writer Yves Farge, who was given the Stalin Prize on March 26, 1953 in Moscow, had in his possession documents incriminating Shavida in atrocities committed during the war against the maquis and French civilians; for this reason he went to Georgia, where on March 28, 1953, he fell victim to an arranged "traffic accident" between Tbilisi and Gori. This contradicts other accounts which claim that Farge was killed because he had expressed an unhealthy interest in the victims of the "Doctors' Plot." It is also possible that Farge was going to Gori to pay respect to the birthplace of the still-deified Stalin and accidents on mountainous roads of Georgia are not that rare.

During 1952 and early 1953, Beriia continued to fight a somewhat successful rearguard action against the "Mingrelian Affair," which was as much due to his cunning as to Stalin's debilitation. In April 1952, he engineered the rehabilitation of Rapava, and returned to his old job as Minister of State Control in Georgia, a position he had held since 1948, and induced Stalin to replace his bête noire N.M. Rukhadze as head of MGB in Georgia in June 1952 with the more pliable A.I. Kochlavashvili, an old crony and his former "gofer" in the atomic energy program. Serving under Kochlavashili was Sh.O. Tsereteli. Sudoplatov, who visited Georgia during this period, blames Igant'ev, Rukhadze, and the amateurish officials for the failure of this campaign. He also credits the arrested Mingrelians for not breaking down under torture and implicating Beriia. In the final analysis, Stalin was not interested in the exposure of garden-variety corruption nor in such desperate gambits by Igant'ev and Rukhadze who claimed that Beriia was a hidden Jew. Stalin wanted to know the existence of plots abetted by foreign powers which could be proved by confessions and the local MGB was simply not"professional" enough to produce such results. Rukhadze's downfall and later arrest preceded that of Riumin, another "agent provocatur" who had failed to produce the desired results. According to Sudoplatov, Stalin was also angered by Rukhadze's boast that he had a direct line to Stalin.

In the final analysis, the campaign to "get" Beriia had only limited scope, as illustrated by the fact that his operatives in Azerbaidzhan—namely Bagirov, Sumbatov-Topuridze, and Emil'ianov, were unharmed, ditto in Armenia with G.A. Arutinov and Kh.L. Grigor'ian. By the time Stalin died, Beriia had managed to contain this particular threat although he could not feel completely safe. No one could as long as Stalin was living.

The Gulag population in January 1, 1953, as listed in *Istoriia SSSR* (May 1991) included over 14,000 prisoners arrested in 1951–1952 in Georgia, undoubtedly in connection with the "Mingrelian Affair." Although he finally managed to defuse the affair, Beriia did not forget the excessive zeal shown by Mgeladze and Rukhadze.[16] The "Mingrelian Affair" was unusual as purge campaigns went. Although there were many arrests, there were no trials and bloodletting, evidence of the decline in Stalin's physical and mental prowess, the possibility that he may have lost interest while he was pursuing the "Doctors' Plot," Beriia's preemptive action, and the fact that S.D. Igant'ev was no Ezhov and not even an Abakumov. At the 20th Party Congress, Khrushchev denounced the "Mingrelian Affair," but no one except Rukhadze was made to pay heavily for the crime since the victims had been mostly cohorts of the now-disgraced Beriia. It was the height of irony that in November 1955, Rukhadze, who had arrested Beriia's people and in turn was later arrested by Beriia, shared the docket with Rapava, one of his victims. Both men were accused of being part of the "Beriia machine."

Simultaneously with the "Mingrelian Affair," Stalin was also busy with the "Doctors' Plot," and the problems in Georgia took a back seat to his new obsession. In his heyday, Stalin's cruelty and cunning were matched by his perseverance. The fact that he left the "Mingrelian Affair" unfinished is testimony to the decline in his health, or, perhaps, as Robert Conquest points out, he may still have had a soft spot for Beriia, the only one of his cronies with whom he could converse in Georgian.

In the first version of his article, the aforementioned V. Kutuzov claims that Stalin ordered Abakumov to launch the "Mingrelian Affair" in 1951 by arresting L.F. Tsanava, Head of MGB in Belorussia, and this version of events is accepted by a number of writers, including Amy Knight. Tsanava was, like Beriia, a Mingrelian, and Stalin supposedly reminded Abakumov not to forget the "Chief Mingrelian" (Beriia). All other Soviet sources, however, agree that Stalin's alleged remarks were made not to Abakumov, but to Ignat'ev in 1952, when Abakumov himself was already in prison, and in fact in the second version of his article Kutuzov omits his original claim.[17] One of the major mysteries of the "Mingrelian Affair" is the role played by L.F. Tsanava (Tsanava-Dzhandzhagava), once one of Beriia's closest associates. Tsanava had worked in the early 'twenties with Cheka/OGPU in small towns while Beriia was first employed as Deputy Chief of Azerbaidzhan Cheka. In 1922, Tsanava's Party application was rejected because of certain allegations, only to be accepted in 1924. This started his close association with Beriia. In 1930, he was appointed Assistant Head of the Georgia GPU and served as Beriia's right-hand man and was decorated a number of times. In 1931 when Beriia was appointed First Secretary of the Party in Georgia and a year later of the entire Transcaucacus, Tsanava was appointed Party Secretary for the city of Poti and later of Tskhaevsk region. In 1937, Tsanava was elected to the Supreme Soviet and also served as the First Deputy Commissar of Agriculture of Georgia. In December 1938, shortly after taking over as Head of NKVD, Beriia appointed Tsanava Head of NKVD in Belorussia.

Under Tsanava's predecessor as head of NKVD, B.D. Berman (brother of M.D. Berman, head of Gulag), who was appointed on February 1937, and his successor from May 1938, A.A. Nasedkin, Belorussia had been engulfed by a virtual bloodbath. After his own appointment on December 17, 1938, Tsanava launched his own purge, which in one year claimed 27,000 victims (900 in one day), who included not only the former NKVD officials, but also Deputy Chairman of the BSSR Council of Commissars A. Zhuravlev, Party Secretaries Anan'ev and V. Potapeiko, Commissar of Education V. Pivovarov, and Chairman of the Central Executive Committee A. Temkin. A.K. Sul'ianov in *Arestovat' v Kremle* devotes a chapter to Tsanava and his stormy relations with A.F. Kovalev, Chairman of the Belorussia Council of Commissars; P.K. Ponomarenko, First Party Secretary, and his successor in 1947, N.I. Gusarov. Kovalev called Tsanava "a completely amoral functionary and capable of every dirty trick." Despite this, Ponomarenko had no trouble working with Tsanava during the war, when they both served in the Central Staff of the Partisan Movement. During the post-war years, S.D. Igant'ev, an obscure Party functionary from Bakshira, was appointed as the Second Party Secretary in Belorussia. Little did anyone suspect that Igant'ev would be Stalin's last secret police chief, and Tasanava would briefly serve in 1952 as one of his deputies.

The Katyn Forest was under Tsanava's jurisdiction when the Polish officers were murdered, and for his contribution, he received the Order of Lenin on April 27, 1940. He had already been a delegate to the 18 Party Congress (1939), where he was elected to the Central Committee Revision Commission. After the "Liberation March" into Poland in September 1939, Tsanava bitterly complained about the Red Army's allowing the Polish soldiers to run free and thus compromise security. Belorussia was overrun by the Germans in the early months of the war, and Tsanava was appointed Head of the Special Department for the West Front. According to Sul'ianov, in the early days of the war, Tsanava was responsible for the killing of prisoners to prevent them from falling into enemy hands but left behind sensitive documents which eventually found their way to Germany and after the war to Western archives. Soviet documents so far released do not mention Tsanava's name in the early days of the war, but his Deputy, one Ptushkin. Tsanava's name is also absent from the memoirs of Zhukov and Konev, two men who commanded the West Front. In the summer of 1943, during the Battle of Kursk, he was the head of SMERSH for the Central Front, commanded by K.K. Rokossovskii, before being attached in Podolsk to the staff of the Partisan Movement. Tsanava was then appointed Deputy Head of the Central Staff of the Partisan Movement under P.K. Ponomarenko while serving under Abakumov as one of the Deputy Heads of SMERSH. The recapture of Belorussia in summer 1944 meant the return of Tsanava as head of the NKGB. Here he, along with S.S. Bel'chenko, head of the local NKVD (formerly with Border Troops and the Partisan Movement and during the Khrushchev years Deputy Chairman of KGB), and B.Z. Kobulov started a campaign of repression against suspected enemies of the Soviet state including Baltic nationalist partisans. On July 11, 1945, Tsanava was one of 50 NKVD officials who received the rank of Lt. General. In 1949, the Gizbel Publishing House in Minsk published his *Vesnarodnaia Partizanskaia Voina v Belorussii* devoted to the bloody history of partisan war in Belorussia. In 1951, an expanded edition was published under a slightly different title by "Gosizdat" in Minsk. Between 1967 and 1982, "Belarus" published a massive three-volume edition of nearly 2,500 pages in which Tsanava's name did not appear. (There are over 100 references to Ponomarenko.) Beriia continued to protect him while Tsanava was engaged in intrigue against other Party and government satraps such as S.O. Pritytskii and Saevich. The latter, Belorussia's Minister of Education and a Party member since 1917, had served as a Soviet representative to Tito during the war and thus was suspect. A case was fabricated against him in 1951 and he was sentenced to 10 years in prison. The archives of the Belorussian Academy of Sciences show the arrest of a number of prominent specialists during the post-war years, which Tsanava must have organized. He was also deeply implicated in the murder of Mikhoel's, perhaps working directly with Stalin. For this, on January 27, 1948, Tsanava received another Order of Lenin. For many years, the conventional wisdom had it that in August 1951, shortly after Abakumov's fall, Tsanava was also arrested and this signaled the first step in Stalin's campaign against Beriia. New sources, however, tell a different story. On October 30, 1951, Tsanava was replaced by M.I. Baskakov, who had served with NKGB in Kareliia and Gor'kii before taking over the MGB in the Uzbek SSR during the post-war period. Tsanava was then called to Moscow to become a Deputy Minister of the MGB (along with Goglidze and Epishev). As discussed before, he was involved in stonewalling the efforts of General V.Ia. Kachalov's widow to clear her husband's name. Tsanava was also involved in building a case against the 80-year-old Maj. General of Artillery P.A. Gel'vikh, who had been in prison since January 27, 1944, and Maj. General of Engineering-Technical Service A.G. El'snits, who had been arrested on September 15, 1949 (*VIZH*, 6/1994). The charges against Gel'vikh, who had first been arrested by the Petrograd Cheka in 1919 and then again in 1938 by NKVD, included espionage for the Germans back in 1923 and criticism of the Soviet system. El'snits' sins included expressing regret that Lenin had not been arrested by the opposition and a liking for the poetry of the "enemy of the people" A.A. Akhmatova, who, incidentally, had never been arrested. Gel'vikh was sentenced to 15 and El'snits to 8 years. Tsanava's involvement in cases against the two Generals, as well as his interest in opposing the rehabilitation of General Kachalov, already discussed, indicate that besides being a Deputy Minister, he was also in charge of the MGB 3rd Department during this period. In less than a year, Stalin, about to embark on the "Mingrelian Affair," dismissed Tsanava, to the latter's deep disappointment. His letters to Stalin requesting service in Georgia were ignored but may have been costly after Stalin's death and Beriia's return to power. In April 1953, Tsanava was arrested by Beriia's order. In 1952, Beriia may have felt doublecrossed by Tsanava, and it also made sense at a time when Stalin's Jewish victims were being released to arrest the man who had been involved in starting the anti-Semitic campaign by arranging for the murder of Mikhoels and Golubov-Potapov. In a letter to Malenkov on April 2, 1953, Beriia claimed that he had ordered Tsanava's arrest because of his involvement in Mikhoel's murder as if he were letting Malenkov in on a deep secret (*Argumenty i Fakty*, May 1992). On April 7, 1953, undoubtedly at Beriia's instigation, Tsanava's decorations were rescinded. Tsanava felt outraged about being arrested for what he considered Beriia's betrayal. He was still apparently living at the time of Beriia's arrest. He was not, however, among those who were tried with Beriia nor with those who were tried in May 1956. His rumored suicide makes sense.[18] Sudoplatov claims, I believe erroneously, that Tsanava was free at the time Beriia wrote his letter to Malenkov and was not arrested until October 1953 after Beriia's own arrest. It seems that Tsanava was the only Mingrelian colleague of Beriia's who betrayed him. It is doubtful that Beriia's enemies would have shown any more mercy to Tsanava than they did to Rukhadze, another former friend who had betrayed Beriia but nevertheless ended up being shot in November 1955. *Kommunist Belorussii* (2–3, 1992) gives the date of Tsanava's death as 1955, which may be just a guess since the same issue also claims incorrectly that Tsanava left Belorussia in 1951 to become Beriia's Deputy. After Beriia's arrest, the Belorussian Party under the First Secretary N.S. Patolichev conducted a postmortem in which Tsanava was painted in black colors similar to Beriia. Patolichev's memoirs published in the mid-1970s are silent about Tsanava. The book *Geroi i Antigeroi Otechestva*, published in 1992, however, cites evidence which must have been given by Tsanava after Beriia's arrest in which he calls his former boss a hard and ambitious man. Although we do not have an exact date, it seems reasonable that Tsanava, already in prison, died after Beriia's arrest.

The last year of Stalin's life is still shrouded in some mystery. If we are to believe Svetlana Alliluyeva, Stalin, at least in the last months of his life, was proof positive for Pascal's axiom, "Condition de l'homme: inconstance, ennui, inequietude." For many years, first in émigré journals and recently in Russia (*Novyi Mir*, February 1991), A. Avtorkhanov had proposed that Beriia was responsible for the death of Stalin, a hypothesis denied by Khrushchev, Malenkov, and Molotov, none of them an apologist for Beriia. Avtorkhanov bases his allegations on the downfall and in some cases arrest of a number of people close to Stalin in 1952. These include N.S. Vlasik, Stalin's chief bodyguard; his secretary N.S. Poskrebyshev; his personal physician V.N. Vinogradov; Dr. R.I. Ryzhikov, Deputy Head of the Kremlin sanitorium; and S.F. Kuz'michev, Vlasik's Deputy. The arrests were allegedly part of Beriia's plans to mount a coup. Newly released documents and research by K. Stoliraov (*Golgofa*) indicate that this was a myth. Vlasik had served the dictator since 1931 and perhaps even earlier. His duties, besides babysitting for Stalin's children, included "special assignments" such as approaching Chief Marshal of Artillery N.N. Voronov (later a target of MGB) after the victory parade in 1945 to ask on behalf of Stalin whether Marshal Zhukov was trustworthy. According to Stalin's daughter, over the years, Vlasik, once a common soldier, began to put on airs, even acting as an art and music critic.[19] He may have also been overly fond of ballet dancers. He lost his job not in December 1952, but in May 1952, on the very legitimate grounds that he failed to follow up the letter he received in 1948 from the radiologist L. Timashuk about the existence of terrorists in the Kremlin Hospital. The letter was later used to launch the "Doctors' Plot" into high gear. Incidentally, during his interrogation, Abakumov was also accused of having known about this letter, but not taking any action.[20] The genesis of this letter went back to August 1948, when Zhdanov suffered a heart attack while on vacation. Timashuk, who was one of the attending physicians, disagreed with the prescribed treatment and when Zhdnaov died, wrote to Abakumov and possibly Vlasik accusing the attending doctors of negligence. Her complaints were ignored when an autopsy proved the doctors right. A.I. Vaksberg claims that Riumin somehow found this letter and used it in the fall of 1952 at the time of the 19 Party Congress to launch the "Doctors' Plot." This seems plausible, but in his letter to Stalin, which led to Abakumov's downfall, Riumin said nothing about Timashuk, nor about medical malpractice being the cause of Zhdanov's demise. It is, however, also possible that Riumin discovered the letter after taking over the MGB Investigation Department. Vlasik was at this time appointed Deputy Commander of a labor camp in Sverdlovsk, something equal to exile. On December 15, 1952, he was expelled from the Party, arrested, and later allegedly interrogated by Beriia, B.Z. Kobulov, and Vlodzimirskii, who accused him of having known V.N. Sternberg, an accused spy. In March 1955, Vlasik, writing to Voroshilov from exile in Krasnodar, claimed that Beriia had arrested him in order to implicate Poskrebyshev. This interrogation probably took place after Stalin's death, and Vlasik's original disgrace was more likely engineered by the Igant'ev-Riumin team as part of the "Doctors' Plot" campaign. It seems highly unlikely that what happened to Vlasik, Poskebryshev, and others in 1952–1953 was done behind Stalin's back by Beriia at the time when he was also under suspicion or, for that matter, by anyone else. Stalin must have been cognizant of what was happening to a man whom he had seen on a daily basis for over a quarter-of-a-century. The claim by I. Fost (*Moskovskie Novosti*, June 10, 1990) that Vlasik showed up after Beriia's arrest requires further confirmation. Regardless, Vlasik remained under a cloud. On January 17, 1955, he was sentenced to 10 years in exile, reduced to 5 years because of the Amnesty Act of March 1953, and loss of military rank and medals. In his conversations with F.I. Chuev, Molotov blames Vlasik's and Poskrebyshev's problems on "women" but gives no details. He is more specific about the fondness of other Bolshevik leaders such as Enukidze and Kalinin for ballet dancers, with Stalin blackmailing the latter for spending government funds on ballerina Tatiana Bakh.

Even more bizarre was the fate of Maj. General S.F. Kuz'michev, Vlasik's Deputy, who had served as one of Stalin's personal bodyguards during 1932–1950. He was attached to MGB and MVD. He was under arrest during the first three months of 1953, but by whom? Between March and June 1953, Kuz'michev has also been identified as Head of the MVD Bodyguards. He was arrested after Beriia's fall and reportedly shot, but the plot further thickens when this Beriia crony was rehabilitated in February 1954. Case Kuz'michev remains a mystery.[21]

In May 1952, Beriia, Malenkov and Bulganin had formed an alleged committee to investigate state security activities. Here Stalin's indifference and lethargy would have been unthinkable in the 1930s and are clear indications of the decline in his health. The most detailed study of Beriia published under Glasnost, *Beriia: Konets Kar'ery* (M. 1991), unfortunately sheds very little light on this period.

Besides involvement with the anti-Jewish plots and the "Mingrelian Affair," Ignat'ev was instrumental in at least one other campaign, and once again the military was the victim. On December 31, 1951, the USSR Council of Ministers took up the matter of the "insufficiency of the S–60 57 millimeter anti-aircraft gun." The result was the arrest in February 1952 of Deputy Minister of Defense Marshal of Artillery N.D. Iakovlev (1898–1972), who had had the misfortune of having visited England in September 1941 as part of the Soviet Military Mission; Head of the Main Artillery Administration, Col. General of Artillery, I.I. Volkotrubenko (1896–1986); and Deputy Minister of Armaments, I.A. Mirzakhanov (also arrested and released in the early days of the war). They were freed only after Stalin's death, on April 17, 1953, after Beriia's report to the Politburo.[22] Iakovlev's wife, however, had suffered a breakdown, and their son had lost his job.

The last major victim of terror under Stalin was probably I.M. Maiskii (né Liakhovetskii) (1884–1975), who had started in the diplomatic service in 1922, serving in Great Britain, Japan, and Finland. In 1932, he became the Soviet representative and Ambassador in Great Britain, where he served until 1943, feeding the West with masses of misinformation and disinformation while managing to avoid being purged. At the Yalta Conference, Stalin was flanked by him (Maiskii, if anything, was even shorter than Stalin) and Gromyko. During 1943–1946, he served as Deputy Commissar/Minister of Foreign Affairs before being assigned to the Institute of USSR Academy of Sciences. He was arrested on February 19, 1953, as a British spy as well as the Minister of Foreign Affairs designate after a coup by Abakumov. Also arrested at this time were two of his former employees, Korzh and Zinchenko, as well as S.N. Rostovskii (also known as Ernst Henry), the war-time editor of the London-based *Soviet War News*, and N. Leonidov. All were accused of espionage. The text of his interrogation (*VIZH*, 3/1990) makes for interesting reading today, but we still don't know the reason and the individuals behind his arrest. Historian A.M. Nekrich, a former student of Maiskii, makes a good case (*Survey*, 5/1976) that Maiskii was arrested in order to implicate Molotov, whom Stalin suspected of having been recruited by U.S. intelligence during his war-time visits. But also, according to Nekrich, the interrogators did not question Maiskii on this account.

According to Sudoplatov, following Stalin's death, Beriia, who thought highly of Maiskii and had been the recipient of copies of his ambassadorial report to Molotov, ordered P.V. Fedotov to arrange for Maiskii's release. Instead, Maiskii, feeling a trap, confessed to Fedotov that he had been a Japanese, British, and American spy. Maiskii was under house arrest when Beriia fell and was soon re-arrested as the potential Minister of Foreign Affairs under Beriia. Apparently there existed a document in which Beriia had indicated that he intended to release Maiskii and make use of his services. Beriia had also mentioned the names of other people who were not arrested. As Nekrich points out, the new leadership was reluctant to release Maiskii because of Beriia's favorable remarks and also because of Maiskii's own partial "confession" while under arrest. Regardless, after two-and-a-half years (Sudoplatov incorrectly states four), which Maiskii spent writing children's stories, he was brought to trial. He was accused of "anti-Soviet" activities. The chief witness against him was the military historian G.A. Deborin, a former friend, whose testimony Maiskii managed to demolish without the help of a lawyer, which he had refused.

The charge of treason was dropped, but he was sentenced to 6 years (not 10, as Sudoplatov states) for minor errors while serving as Ambassador and perhaps being overly fond of Western mores, and so on. Maiskii's appeal for pardon was accepted immediately by the Presidium of the Supreme Soviet. As Nekrich points out, even more bizarre was the fact that he was readmitted to the Communist Party even before he received his pardon. Maiskii was fully rehabilitated in 1970. During 1968–1975, he was attached to the Institute of World History, USSR Academy of Science as a research fellow. He died in 1975 at age 91. His memoirs, published in 1965, are completely silent about his ordeal.

There are two mutually exclusive hypotheses about the downfall of Abakumov. It has been claimed that Stalin sacked Abakumov because Abakumov was reluctant to move against Beriia, who had fallen out of favor. The other theory blames Beriia for plotting Abakumov's demise because of the latter's independence. There are problems with both theories. From what we know about Abakumov, it seems likely that he would have moved forcefully against Beriia, or for that matter anyone else, had he been so ordered by Stalin. Although Stalin during 1951–1952 was engaged in intrigue against Beriia, he may have been reluctant to destroy him. After all, he had also spared Zhukov after cutting him down to size. Incidentally, following Abakumov's arrest, S.A. Goglidze and L.F. Tsanava, two of Beriia's closest associates, became Deputy Ministers of MGB, appointments that must have been approved by Stalin. It could, however, also be argued that since loyalty was an alien concept to Stalin's Machiavellian mind, Goglidze and Tsanava were the logical candidates to knife their benefactor. Stalin, afterall, was the man who was supposed to have said that gratitude is a sickness suffered by dogs. The second theory claims that Beriia organized the campaign against Abakumov. There is no doubt that Abakumov had his own agenda, had placed his own men in MGB, and had at times clashed with Beriia, but it is also true that he was also deferential to the Georgian. Abakumov's willingness to pursue the "Leningrad Affair," whose beneficiaries included Malenkov as well as Beriia, shows that he was more than willing to do Beriia's bidding, at least as long as it had Stalin's support. There is also no evidence that Beriia had any close connections with Riumin and, in fact, following Stalin's death, one of Beriia's first acts was to arrest Riumin, who had engineered Abakumov's downfall. Also, there is evidence that Riumin had taken part in the "Mingrelian Affair" aimed at Beriia and had told Stalin that Beriia was a hidden Jew. The fact that Abakumov was replaced by S.D. Igant'ev and not by one of Beriia's henchmen also puts a hole in this theory. It has also been suggested that Stalin was getting ready to organize another massive purge involving his old lackeys and did not think that Abakumov was the right man for the job.

A variation on this theme appears in the article about Army General A.A. Epishev by A. Sulla (*VIZH*, 3/1993) which makes heavy use of secondary *Western* sources, including the highly speculative claims of writers such as A. Avtorkhanov. According to Sulla, Stalin had decided to purge his old comrades, mainly Beriia and Malenkov, and had put Poskebryshev, who had some experience in this area, in charge of the security organs to carry this out. Poskrebyshev felt that Abakumov was too close to

Beriia and so Abakumov was replaced with the more malleable S.D. Igant'ev who mounted such campaigns as the "Mingrelian Affair" and the "Doctors' Plot" aimed against the old guard while hedging his bets by also informing Beriia and Malenkov of Stalin's plans. Sulla's speculations are not new and suffer from his claim that Abakumov was sacked in July 1952, a year after the actual event. There is also the question of the removal of Poskrebyshev and Vlasik at the end of 1952. Were these sanctioned by Stalin or was he so enfeebled at this time that he would stand by helplessly while Beriia carried out what amounted to a palace coup? Solzhenitsyn claims in *The Gulag Archipelago* that *late in 1952* Riumin approached Abakumov with the news that Etinger had confessed to poisoning Zhdanov and Shcherbakov. Abakumov's own interrogation of Etinger led him to conclude that this was a provocation which led to Riumin's contacting Stalin, who believed him and in turn ordered Abakumov's arrest. Meanwhile, Etinger had died or was murdered in prison by Riumin, so there was no way of confirming the charges. This version of events is not without merit except that late in 1952 Etinger had been dead for nearly two years and Abakumov had been in prison for nearly 18 months, and Riumin himself had been sacked by December 1952. Anton Antonov-Ovseenko also claims that Abakumov's lack of enthusiasm for the "Doctors' Plot" cost him his job.[23] Abakumov, of course, would have had no scruples in organizing a campaign along the lines of what transpired as the"Doctors' Plot" had he been so ordered by Stalin. He, after all, had spearheaded the earlier persecution of Jewish intellectuals. His reluctance to follow up on Riumin's provocations may have been inspired by a feeling that he was being set up. In his recent book, *Neraskrytye Tainy*, A.I. Vaksberg speculates that Abakumov's arrest may have also been influenced by the fate of M.M. Borodin, formerly the Soviet military advisor in China. Borodin, working in an obscure position as the editor of the *Moscow News*, was arrested in late January 1949 and died in prison on May 29, 1951 shortly before Abakumov's arrest. Vaksberg, however, admits that he has no proof of such a connection.

In 1989–1990, a series of articles about the "Doctors' Plot" appeared in the journal, *Nauka i Zhizn'*. The article in issue 12, 1988, by the former MGB investigator Trubachev is confusing and incorrect. This version names M.B. Kogan, instead of Etinger, as the man arrested and interrogated by Abakumov and Riumin as the key to the "Doctors' Plot" and whose suicide in prison resulted in Riumin's letter. The problem here is that M.B. Kogan died on October 26, 1951, several months after Abakumov's own arrest. Incidentally, M.B. Kogan's brother, B.B. Kogan, was one of the nine Kremlin doctors mentioned in the TASS announcement of January 13, 1953, who were charged with having caused the death of Zhdanov and A.S. Shcherbakov (two notorious drunkards who suffered from poor health) and conspiring to poison Marshals I.S. Konev, A.M. Vasilevskii, and L.A. Govorov, Army General S.M. Shtemenko, and Admiral G.I. Levchenko. M.B. Kogan and Etinger, long dead, were also mentioned in the indictments. The article by Ia.Ia. Etinger (*Nauka i Zhizn'*, No. 1, 1990, reprinted with some changes in the collection *Zven'ia*) is an entirely different matter. Ia.Ia. Etinger, the son of the late Dr. Ia.G. Etinger, gives us the most focused and accurate description of events that led to the "Doctors' Plot" campaign. The older Etinger, besides being a physician, was a man of many interests, including literature and theater. Among his friends were actor N.P. Khmelev, ballerina E.V. Gel'tser, painters N.P. Krymov and S.V. Maliutin, and writers A.S. Iakovlev and S.Ia. Marshak. The latter, who had translated Shakespeare, Burns, and Byron into Russian, had given him an autographed copy of the sonnets which was later used by the investigators to establish a criminal link between him and Marshak. For many years, Etinger had been a consultant to the Kremlin clinic where such important functionaries as Kirov, F.A. Khodzhaev (shot in 1938), Lakoba, G.V. Chicherin, M.M. Litvinov, L.M. Karakhan (shot in 1937), and M.N. Tukhachevskii (shot in 1937), and foreign Communist leaders such as Togliatti, Pieck, Dimitrov, and Kolarov were treated. He also had been Ordzhonikidze's physician, and perhaps knew about the latter's arranged suicide. In addition, he, along with Vinogradov (Stalin's own doctor), treated the sickly A.S. Shcherbakov, Secretary of the CC CPSU, who had died on May 10, 1945. With such a background, Etinger's interest in politics and his nationality made him a potential candidate for arrest in 1950. As a first step, on October 17, 1950, the younger Etinger, a student of history in the Moscow State University, was arrested on the street and taken to Lubianka, where he was interrogated by Abakumov and Prosecutor General G.N. Safonov and later repeatedly by Riumin. The younger Etinger's interrogation continued until spring 1951 and was entirely devoted to domestic and foreign policy questionsincluding relations between Stalin and Tito. Not once was Etinger asked about medical malpractice by his father.

On May 17, 1951, Etinger was sentenced to 10 years in camps and on June 5 was shipped to Kolima; he arrived in Vanino camp in July on a ship from Magadan. Meanwhile, Etinger's father was arrested on November 18, 1950 only to die in prison on March 2, 1951, of what was diagnosed as a ruptured left ventricle of the heart. This could have been caused by rough treatment in prison, but as Ia.Ia. Etinger points out, his father was 64 years old and had had a history of health problems. On July 16, 1951, Dr. Etinger's, wife R.K. Viktorova, also a doctor, was arrested, to be followed shortly by their housekeeper, M.P. Kharetskaia (who in 1941 had helped the younger Etinger to escape from the Jewish Ghetto in Minsk). Dr. Viktorova's questioning was, however, almost entirely about "medical malpractice." She was finally sentenced to 10 years and spent time in Vladimir and Novocherkask prisons until Stalin's death. Early in August, Ia.Ia. Etinger was brought back to Moscow. Whereas in Kolima he had shared a cabin with 20 other prisoners in the MGB internal prison, in Moscow he was kept in total isolation. On September 1, interrogations began in Lefortovo with the statement by the interrogator, "We know that your father along with Drs. Vinogradov, Vovsi, Gel'shtein, and Zelenin had been involved with harmful treatment of Soviet leaders." Soon Riumin took over the interrogation, shouting insults, but no longer about "agitation and propaganda," charges under which Etinger had been originally arrested. This line of "medical" questioning continued until March 1952, when Etinger was shipped to Viatlag camp in Kirov oblast. Etinger is on solid ground when he claims that if the "Doctors' Plot" had been hatched in late 1950 to early 1951, he, as an important material witness, would not have been sent to Kolima. According to Etinger, the "Doctors' Plot," was probably hatched around August 1951 when Abakumov was already in prison.

Sudoplatov's memoirs fill an important gap in the final chapter of this campaign. Even historians with inside information such as Roi Medvedev (in his biography of Khrushchev) had thought that Riumin had continued to run the anti-Jewish campaigns until Stalin's death. Not so, according to Sudoplatov. By late 1952, Stalin apparently was getting tired of Riumin's failure to provide solid evidence (ditto with Rukhadze in Georgia and his handling of the "Mingrelian Affair"). Riumin was sacked on November 12, 1952, for "inadequate performance" and returned to his job as an accountant in the Ministry of State Control, headed now by none other than Beriia's crony Merkulov. According to Borshchagovskii, in October 1955, N.M. Koniakhin reported to the Central Committee about how the case against the JAC was fabricated. According to Sudoplatov, Riumin had made other mistakes, including arresting G.M. Maironovskii, whose alleged poisoning activities in behalf of Stalin must have been a highly sensitive subject in December 1952. Sudoplatov further states that with Riumin gone, the last phase of the anti-Semitic campaigns, the arrest of the Jewish doctors early in 1953, was organized by N. Mesetsov (under Brezhnev, head of the state radio and television service and later Ambassador to Australia) and N.M. Koniakhin, formerly department head in the CC CPSU Administrative organs, Party hacks sent by the Central Committee working under Igant'ev. Dr. Ia. L. Rapoport, the last survivor among the arrested doctors, does not mention Mesetsov or Koniakhin, but the latter is mentioned in Chernov's remarks to the writer Kostilarov. The last chapter in this sordid drama was a letter to the Politburo drafted by D.I. Zaslavskii and Ia. Khavinson and signed by prominent Jews demanding the severest punishment for "killer doctors" and begging for resettlement of Jewish people to remote areas. According to A.I. Vaksburg in *Stalin Against the Jews*, those who signed included B.L. Vannikov, S.A. Lavochkin, S.Ia. Marshak, P. Antokolskii, M. Aliger, M. Blanter, R.M. Glier, twice Hero of the Soviet Union Lt. General D.A. Dragunskii, and, strangely enough, V.S. Grossman. Those who refused to sign included Hero of the Soviet Union Col. General Ia.N. Kreizer, M. Reizen, E. Varga, E. Dolmatovskii, I. Dunaevskii, I. Trakhtenberg, and V. Kaverin. Erenburg's role here remains controversial. The letter was supposed to have served as the first act which would be followed by a show trial of the accused doctors. The signers would be serving as sonderkommandos in Stalin's planned auto-da-fe for the Jews. There are, however, individuals such as the chess champion M. Botvinnik, who deny the existence of such a letter. Sudoplatov's claim in his memoirs that by the end of February 1953, the anti-Semitic campaign was beginning to wane is debatable, but there was actually a lull starting on March 2, 1953, four days before Stalin's death, in *Pravda's* relentless barrage of accusations.

Amy Knight, who apparently was unfamiliar with Ia.Ia. Etinger's memoirs and the testimony of Lt. General of Judiciary A.F. Katusev (as quoted in Kostliarov, *Golgofa*) when she wrote her biography of Beriia, sees the hand of Khrushchev behind the "Doctors' Plot," but this is just a guess. It would be unthinkable that a campaign of such magnitude would have been launched without sanction from Stalin.

The role of Khrushchev in post-war intrigues is a subject that calls for further study, and there is a possibility that materials incriminating him were destroyed during the years that he was in power. Important, however, is Sudoplatov's statement that he, who incidentally was in the center, continued to believe until 1990 that Abakumov was somehow involved in the "Doctors' Plot," but now after seeing the new evidence is convinced that in this particular case Abakumov was the victim rather than the perpetrator. The announcement of the doctors' arrest early in 1953 was accompanied by strong criticism of the MGB, which had singularly failed to carry out itsduties. The usual cheerleaders were also recruited to join the campaign. K.M. Simonov, who was to see the light after Stalin's death, wrote a vicious article on the murderous doctors in the January 13, 1953 issue of *Literaturnaia Gazeta*. At this time, Simonov, an Armenian, was obviously indifferent to the sufferings of another targeted minority. Also, D.I. Chesnokov, editor of *Voprosy Filiosofii*, wrote a pamphlet in 1952 entitled *Why Jews Must be Resettled from the Industrial Regions of the Country*. Beriia's son, in *Moi Otets*, states that in 1970, Bulganin told Ia.Ia. Etinger that the"Doctors' Plot," as well as the earlier anti-Semitic campaigns were mainly the work of three men: Stalin, Malenkov, and Suslov, and he was not proud of the role that he and others had played during this period. It is quite possible that had Stalin not died and had the doctors been brought to trial, Abakumov (shades of Iagoda) would have shared the dock with them. There is, I believe, a simpler and more plausible reason for Abkumov's fall. He was sacked for the same reason as Iagoda and Ezhov: not because they had failed to carry out Stalin's orders, but because they had become dispensable. So far as Stalin was concerned, once they—and this also applied to Abakumov (and later to his nemesis Riumin)—had served their purpose they were jettisoned, and in Abakumov's case, Riumin and Malenkov provided the excuse that he needed. Stalin's whole life turned around using people, and there was no one who was less user-friendly. Under Stalin, no one was indispensable.

Abakumov served continuously as Stalin's secret police chief for at least five years, longer than anyone else. Iagoda and Ezhov each lasted about 27 months; Beriia and Merkulov each for nearly four years and only on two separate occations. Before heading MGB, Abakumov had also served as Deputy Commissar of Defense for at least three years, all in all, a remarkable record in highly dangerous positions. Despite his brutality, Abakumov had proved to be too slow and methodical for the taste of Stalin, who must have yearned for the old days under Ezhov when trials (if held at all) and executions were held on the same day. The case against Kulik and Gordov and against the Jewish intellectuals took years, and, in fact, the latter were not executed until after Abakumov's fall. Abakumov also failed to provide solid evidence to convince Stalin of Zhukov's treasonable activities. The "Leningrad Affair" was organized with dispatch but was marred by the fact that some of the defendants professed their innocence in court. The case against the Czech Communists in late 1949 under Likhachev and Komarov did not make satisfactory progress and the show trials only took place in November 1952, long after Abakumov was gone. The MGB also singularly failed in subverting Tito's Yugoslavia. Abakumov's Achilles heel, exploited fully by Riumin, proved to be that although he had presided over the campaign against the Jewish intellectuals and may have even stopped recruiting new Jewish Chekists, he had failed to purge the MGB of Jewish veterans and in fact had continued to employ Ia.M. Broverman, a Jew, in his personal Chancellery. During the interrogations following his arrest, Abakumov tried to distance himself from L.L. Shvartsman but would not denounce him.[24] Stalin's puritanical zeal may have also been outraged by Abakumov's personal corruption, although he was willing to overlook this where Beriia was concerned.

There are contrasting views about Abakumov as an individual. Pictures in *Golgofa* show him to be a relatively tall thick-set man with Slavic features. Abakumov's height is important since Stalin preferred his satraps to be short or at least shorter than he was. He was also obviously fond of fancy uniforms and, in fact, his short peaked cap made him look more like a Tsarist than a Soviet officer. There are also pictures of him in civilian clothes taken after the war in Berlin and in Vienna at Beethoven's grave. Solzhenitsyn's Abakumov in *The First Circle* borders on ludicrous. Abakumov is portrayed as a whining windbag, who as Romanov correctly points out, would not have lasted five minutes as head of MGB. Next to absolute loyalty, Stalin admired toughness in his subordinates; this also explains why, despite misgivings, he allowed Zhukov and Admiral Kuznetsov to survive.

According to Solzhenitsyn, Abakumov lived in deathly fear of the hapless Minister of Finance, A.G. Zverev, because of his personal corruption.[25] If anything, the reverse of this is true, and Zverev, who incidentally never mentions Abakumov in his memoirs (*Zapiski Ministra*, 1973), had every reason to fear Abakumov. After all, Zverev had served as Deputy to G.F. Grin'ko and V. Ia. Chubar, both executed as "enemies of the people." In fact, Abakumov may have actually had something to do with Zverev's dismissal from February to December 1948 from a job that he had held for ten years.

An added problem with Solzhenitsyn's account is that, in trying to be another Tolstoi and perhaps write the "Great Russian Novel," he mixes real people such as Stalin, Abakumov, Poskrebyshev, and Riumin with fictional characters and events. Chapters 15–20 in *The First Circle* are primarily about Abakumov, introduced first as a Minister (presumably of MGB) with the rank of Commissar of State Security 2nd Rank, not held by Abakumov since 1941. In fact, at the time of his official appointment as head of MGB on October 10, 1946, Abakumov had been a Colonel General since July 1945. Three pages into chapter 15, Solzhenitsyn's Abakumov became a Colonel General surrounded by ten Deputy Ministers (incorrect) including two characters, "Sevastyanov" and "Osolupov," who I assume are modeled after N.N. Selivanovskii and S.I. Ogol'tsev. In the tearful meeting with Stalin that follows, Abakumov claims that Tito and his gang are about to be blown up, and he begs the "vozhd" to reintroduce the death penalty. Here Solzhenitsyn is not writing history, but docudrama worthy of a Hollywood scriptwriter. S.A. Baruzdin, as quoted in *The Oak and the Calf*, calls Solzhenitsyn's portrayal of Abakumov as "feeble, naive and primitive"—an inescapable conclusion. The picture of Abakumov drawn by Colonel Liskin in his articles in *Shchit i Mech* comes closer to reality. Abakumov was proud of his proletarian roots and his achievements. Arrogant and ambitious (prosecutor L.N. Smirnov called him a "zoological careerist"), there was little doubt about his loyalty to Stalin. At times, just like Beriia, he would take part in interrogations. Victoria Fyodorova in her memoirs claims that her mother, actress Z.A. Fedorova, who had an affair with American naval attaché Jackson Rogers Tate, was questioned rather rudely in December 1946 by one "Abumokov," but it is clear that this is none other than Abakumov. O. Ivinskaia, Pasternak's mistress, was also interrogated after her first arrest by Abakumov. Both Fedorova and Ivinskaia were great beauties, and this may have been the reason Abakumov gave them his personal attention.

Despite kidney trouble, he was fond of shashliks and Georgian wines. A bon vivant, he liked driving several captured Fiats, but he also had a sense of noblesse oblige which he showed by passing alms. The investigators found in his house and dacha a magnificent wardrobe, some of it of Western style and most of it acquired illegally, as well as evidence that Abakumov had used official aircraft to fly underwear from Germany. In his dacha there were cameras and film projection equipment. As Liskin points out, corruption in the Soviet Union was not invented by Brezhnev. Incidentally, for those who take "body language" seriously, Abakumov's pictures as head of SMERSH and MGB in Kosliarov's book effuse with arrogance.

It would also be debatable to call Abakumov (or for that matter, Beriia or Stalin) sadists, as Solzhenitsyn implies. SS Grupenführer Von dem Bach-Zeleski, Hitler's top anti-partisan expert, has remarked that only a bureaucrat could have come up with the idea of the death camp, and indeed Abakumov was a consummate bureaucrat in the machinery of terror and repression which was the indispensable component of the Stalinist state.

An area in which Abakumov was particularly adept was public relations. On the occasion of Stalin's 70th birthday, Abakumov was a member of a committee, along with P. Ponomarenko, N. Parfenov, A. Gromyko, N. Shvernik and V. Grigor'ian, which spent over five million rubles to celebrate the dictator's birthday.[26]

Romanov and the Glasnost accounts portray Abakumov as a ruthless professional and, unusual in a Soviet bureaucrat, something of a dandy. Like many top Chekists, he liked to take part in interrogations, as indicated by his role during the anti-Jewish campaigns. He also enjoyed questioning attractive female prisoners, and occasionally he would also show up in cases when a stubborn victim refused to confess. Mountain climber N. Turov, accused of making maps for a foreign power, relates in his memoirs (*Novyi Zhurnal*, 98/1970) how Abakumov tried to persuade him to sign a confession. Abakumov also reportedly possessed a cynical sense of humor. Leopold Trepper, the organizer of the spy network Rote Kapell, was arrested when he returned to the Soviet Union in January 1945. Abakumov, in the habit of holding conversations with Trepper (who was not released until after Stalin's death), told him that he would have fared much better had he worked for NKGB rather than the rival GRU. After the start of the anti-Jewish campaigns, Abakumov's tone changed and Trepper became the subject of his abuse.[27] Malenkov's son calls Abakumov a man with a fourth-rate education. Romanov, however, is wrong when he denies Abakumov's personal corruption. After Abakumov's arrest, the investigators discovered that the furniture in his apartment belonged to the People's Artist of RSFSR, the singer P.K. Pechkovskii, sentenced to 10 years in prison in 1944 on unspecified charges. During Abakumov's trial, architect Verbitskii testified that enormous state funds were spent for Abakumov's personal benefit. A defector source also claims that after Abakumov married, he gave his wife a 70,000 ruble baby carriage and a 30,000 ruble robe from Vienna.[28] Romanov is also incorrect in his claim that Abakumov was given the rank of Col. General in 1942 (rather than in 1946).

NOTES

1. Peter Deriabin and Frank Gibney, *The Secret World*, p. 167.
2. Kostliarov, *Golgofa*, p. 5; Deriabin and Gibney, *Secret World*, p. 234.
3. Kosliarov, *Golgofa*, pp. 5–6.
4. Ibid., pp. 29, 51.
5. Ibid., p. 10.
6. Ibid., pp. 13–15.
7. Ibid., pp. 28, 31.
8. Ibid., p. 22.
9. Ibid., p. 13.
10. Ibid., p. 28.
11. Ibid., p. 40.
12. A.I. Skryl'nik, *General Armii A.A. Epishev*, p. 208.
13. *Sovetskaia Belorusskaia* (March 23, 1988), p. 3.
14. *Izvestiia TsK KPSS* (2/1991); *VIZH* (12/1991).
15. *Zhurnalist* (2/1991), p. 64.
16. Boris Levytsky, *The Uses of Terror*, p. 197; *Izvestiia TsK KPSS* (1/1991); *Caucasian Review* (6/1958), pp. 54–61.
17. *Leningradskoe Delo*, pp. 400–11.
18. For Tsanava's career, see *Sovetskaia Belorusskaia* (March 23, 1988), p. 3.
19. Robert Conquest, *Stalin: Breaker of Nations*, p. 215.
20. Kosliarov, *Golgofa*, p. 50.
21. *Izvestiia TsK KPSS* (1/1991).
22. For the case against Iakovlev, etc., see *Izvestiia TsK* (1/1991); V.N. Novikov, *Nakanune i v Dni Ispytanii*; and *Pennkovskiy Papers*.
23. Kosliarov, *Golaofa*, p. 14.
24. Anton Antonov-Ovseenko, *The Time of Stalin*, p. 301.
25. A. Solzhenitsyn, *Gulag Archipelago*, p. 60; and *First Circle*, pp. 82–83.
26. Volkogonov, *Triumf*, book 2, part 2, p. 75.
27. Giles Perrault, *The Red Orchestra*, pp. 497–98.
28. *Leningradskoe Delo*, p. 408; Deriabin and Gibney, *Secret World*, p. 234.

Chapter 12

The Aftermath

On March 5, 1953, Stalin died, and almost immediately a quiet struggle ensued between his henchmen to inherit his mantle. On one side there were Malenkov and Khrushchev, later assisted by Bulganin and by Marshal G.K. Zhukov, brought over from the Ural Military District in March and appointed First Deputy Minister of Defense. Facing this group was Beriia, who took over the MVD on March 7, 1953, replacing Kruglov. On March 15, 1953, MVD and MGB, separate organs since April 14, 1943, were combined in a new MVD and for the third time in his career (December 12, 1938 and July 30, 1941, were the earlier dates), Beriia was in complete charge of both security and police organizations. As in 1938, the attempt to consolidate power was combined with a "liberalization" campaign in which the surviving victims of the "Doctors' Plot" and the "Mingrelian Affair" were released. Among Stalin's heirs, Beriia was the leading advocate of conciliatory policies both at home and abroad. As early as March 6, 1953, Beriia also moved to free some of the Gulag prisoners by writing first to Kruglov and later to Malenkov and the Council of Ministers, as well as Khrushchev and the Party Presidium. On March 27, 1953, the Supreme Soviet approved amnesty for 1,181,264 out of a population of 2,526,402.[1] By the end of March, even Jewish prisoners in the Far East were being released.[2] An official announcement by the MVD in *Pravda* (April 4, 1953) exonerated 13 doctors that had been arrested in the "Doctors' Plot" whose arrests had been made by the officials of the former USSR Ministry of State Security who had used in their investigation means which are "impermissible and strictly forbidden under the Soviet law." The announcement did not say that two of the cleared doctors, Ia.G. Etinger and M.B. Kogan, had died in prison. Shortly after, Beriia ordered the reopening of the closed Jewish theatres. On March 10, 1953, Beriia personally escorted the freed Zhemchuzhina to her husband, Molotov. On March 16, Beriia ordered the chief provocateur, Riumin, arrested. On May 26, 1953, Beriia forwarded a detailed report to Malenkov prepared by Vlodzimirskii and his assistants, Serikov and Fedotov, and approved by Kobulov, which completely exonerated the victims of the "Aviators'

Affair" and blamed Abakumov for having fabricated the case. The fact that Malenkov had also suffered because of the same Affair should be duly noted. The Party Presidium approved this report on June 12, 1953, two weeks before Beriia's own arrest. By such actions as well as by arresting Riumin and keeping Abakumov in prison, Beriia was trying to disassociate himself from the post—war crimes. During this period, Beriia was on the side of angels on all fronts. Beriia was, of course, the opportunist par excellence, but he was also blessed with ignorance of Marxism-Leninism whereas his rivals at least paid lip service to the doctrine that had provided them with the framework for advancement. This bizarre change of heart or tactics was to be repeated in the 1980s when another Georgian politician, E.A. Shevradnadze, for seven years head of the MVD in Georgia, became a foremost champion of democratization in the Soviet Union.

Consolidation of power by Beriia meant the removal on March 13, 1953 of S.D. Ignat'ev as Minister of MVD, as the secretary of CC CPSU on April 5, 1953, and from the Central Committee and the Presidium on April 28, 1953. This was quite a fall. Igant'ev who had been a member of the enlarged Party Presidium since October 1952, became on March 14, 1953 one of five Central Committee secretaries along with Khrushchev, P.N. Pospelov, N.N. Shatalin, and M.A. Suslov. He was not, however, elected to the once-again reduced Presidium which now had ten full and four candidate members instead of 25. According to Beriia's son, his father wanted to have Ignat'ev arrested and tried. Beriia, however, kept Kruglov (Head of MVD at the time of Stalin's death) as a deputy at MVD. Serov, Kruglov's former Deputy was also left at MVD. Beriia was going to pay a heavy price for trusting the two men. Also kept as a deputy minister and head of Gulag was S.S. Mamulov, but only until April 14, 1953 when he was moved to Georgia to take over the trade unions and Komsomols and work with the local Central Committee. Mamulov's deputy was G.A. Ordyntsev, another veteran Beriia operative who since 1941 had served as head of the chancellery attached to the deputy Chairman of the Council of Commissars/Ministers, a position also held by Beriia. It would have seemed logical that V.N. Merkulov, Minister of State Control since October 1950 and Beriia's closest associate, would serve as his chief operator following Stalin's death, but for a number of reasons that will be discussed later, the honor went to B.Z. Kobulov who, incidently, was nine years younger than Merkulov.

As in the past, Beriia was using Georgia as a powerbase sending down Dekanozov, B.Z. Kobulov, and Mamulov to organize the 15th Congress of the Communist Party of Georgia. On April 14, 1953 in the meeting of the Central Committee of Georgia, Mgeladze, now exposed as a "careerist," was replaced by A.I. Mirtskhulava who may have been in prison. Of the 14 members and candidate members of the Party's Politburo, 11 were let go and one was demoted. Among the members were Baramia and Zodelava, who also received the additional titles of Minister of Agriculture and First Vice Chairman of Council of Ministers. Rapava was Minister of State Control, and Dekanozov was Head of the MVD with the former MGB chief, A.I. Kochavashvili, serving as his Deputy. V.M. Bakradze, an old crony of Beriia, replaced Ketskhoveli as Chairman of the Council of Ministers with the latter being demoted to Minister of Light and Food Industries. Ketskhoveli was also a member of the Georgia Politburo. The tenure of the new people lasted less than three months and came to an end shortly after their sponsor's arrest in June 1953 when there was another massive shake-up in the Georgia Party and government organizations in which the military was to play an important part—the new first Party secretary, V.P. Mzhavandze, and the head of MVD, A.N. Inauri, both being professional military officers. Mzhavanadze had started the war as the political commissar of the 16 Rifle Division in the Baltic Military District and Inauri as commander of a cavalry regiment on the Southwest Front. The Beriia machine in Georgia was finally dismantled. The new crew was to stay in power for many years, in Inauri's case until 1961 surviving even the embarrassing March 1956 riots in Tbilisi. During Beriia's tenure, Tsanava and soon Riumin were also arrested while Abakumov was allowed to linger in jail. On April 4, 1953, Kremlin radiologist L. Timashuk, MGB's "agent provocateur" in the "Doctors' Plot" case, and a Stalinist version of Joan of Arc, lost the Order of Lenin that had been awarded to her only on January 20, 1953. Otherwise, Timashuk was left alone and continued in her medical practice.

In regard to Abakumov, on November 15, 1952 by the order of Igant'ev, "prisoner no. 15" had been transferred to cell 77 in Butyrka Prison. On November 17, 1952, in response to a request by Igant'ev, Riumin's assistant, Lt. Colonel P.I. Grishaev (a future professor of jurisprudence, no less) wrote a report (*Nedelia* 44, 1990) outlining various measures in regard to Abakumov in order to soften him up as well as to foreclose the possibility of suicide. Early in 1953, Stalin sent down Komsomol official V.N. Zaichikov to investigate the "Abakumov Affair." Riumin and Grishaev conducted the investigation which was probably reported to Malenkov through Ignat'ev and through Goglidze to Beriia. The charges indicated involvement with the Tito-Rankovich gang, Jewish nationalists, and various foreign intelligence services. There were also reports on the medical condition of the prisoner in cell 77 which Stoliarov appropriately calls "the man in the iron mask."[3] On January 16, 1953, one Tsvetaev, identified as the Party secretary in the MGB Department for Investigation of Especially Important Cases, wrote a report (*Nedelia* 44, 1990) in which he suggested medical treatment on "humane grounds" for "prisoner No. 15" before applying the third-degree. The prisoner's condition did not allow more than four hours of interrogation at a time. More time was not needed to extract confessions, and a suggestion was made for medical treatment. Stalin, busy with the "Doctors Plot," apparently died without resolving Abakumov's fate and his heirs were faced with the knotty question of what to do with the fallen security chief. On March 11–12, Beriia met with Colonel Koniakhin (a former Party functionary who had taken over Riumin's responsibilities) and inquired about Abakumov's condition.[4] Shortly after this, Abakumov's nemesis Riumin, who had been fired in mid-December 1952, was arrested and in turn was being questioned by Vlodzimirskii who was back in his old job as Beriia's chief investigator. Lubianka was now rife with rumor about Abakumov's release, but this was not part of Beriia's plan, nor for that matter, of Khrushchev's and Malenkov's. Andrew and Gordievsky's claim that Beriia released Abakumov has no substance.[5] According to Sudoplatov, Beriia claimed that although there was no basis for Abakumov's involvement in the Zionist conspiracy, there were other charges involving abuse of power, corruption, the "Aviators' Affair", and the arrest of Molotov's wife that precluded Abakumov's release. The line of questioning now changed. Abakumov was no longer being questioned about imaginary Jewish nationalist plots. Vlodzimirskii and the other bloodhound, B.Z. Kobulov, Abakumov's old boss in the Secret Political Department, now were asking Abakumov about real crimes such as his involvement in the arrest of Molotov's wife and those connected with the "Aviator's affair" which was aimed at none other than Malenkov. In this way, Beriia was using Abakumov to mend fences with the two fellow satraps. The archives were being searched for other crimes that could be blamed solely on Abakumov and the death under interrogation of Vice Admiral L.G. Goncharov in April 1948 provided extra ammunition.[6] Abakumov at times remained defiant, once telling the investigator G.A. Terekev that he was closer to Stalin than Beriia and Shkiriatov.[7] We have already mentioned the letter from Beriia to Politburo and Malenkov stating that in the interrogation of Abakumov, the latter admitted that he had organized Mikhoel's murder with Ogol'tsev and Tsanava. Kostliarov and Liskin, the leading writers on the subject do not mention a meeting between Beriia and Abakumov and the circumstances of Mikhoel's death could not have been a secret to Beriia or, for that matter, Malenkov. The fact remains that Stalin's heirs had nothing to gain from releasing Abakumov who undoubtedly had compromising material about all of them, so he was left to twist slowly in the wind while they were jockeying for power.

Meanwhile, Beriia brought in some of his old "Caucasian" mafia. B.Z. Kobulov was appointed as Deputy Minister of MVD and was in charge of MVD Security Administration and possibly even Head of the Foreign Department, in the latter position at least until May 1953. S.A. Goglidze was another Deputy Minister and was in charge of the Operations Department. Sudoplatov, however, claims that Goglidze was only appointed to head the military counterintelligence—the old Special Department—a demotion since he had played a part, admittedly unwillingly, in the Mingrelian campaign. M.I. Zhuravlev (not to be confused with P.M. Zhuravev), former head of NKVD in Moscow (1941–1946), but later unemployed, was also appointed as deputy Minister MVD. Dekanozov was put in charge of MVD in Georgia and P. Ia. Meshik, after serving as the inspector general of MVD, was sent to Ukraine. Vlodzimisrkii or perhaps G.G. Paramonov also may have been put in charge of the MVD Investigation Department. In Azerbaidzhan, Beriia had little to worry about since Party Secretary, M.D.A. Bagirov, deputy Chairman of Council of Minister, Iu.D. Sumbatov-Topuridze, and head of MGB, S.F. Emel'ianov, and head of MVD, A.S. O.I. Atakshiev, had been in his pocket for years. Ditto in Armenia with Party Secretary G.A. Arutinov and MVD chief Kh.L. Grigor'ian. The question in the Far East was more complicated. Iu. Krutkov (*Novyi zhurnal*, December 1978) claims that Beriia sent M.M. Gvishiani, who had served in the Maritime Territory before the war, to the Far East, but Gvishiani may have been there already. Regardless, Gvishiani, like Serov and Kruglov, played his cards right and did not suffer after

Beriia's fall. V.V. Gubin, head of MGB in Kazakh SSR since 1950, involved in Katyn as head of NKVD in Gor'kii, and later in the deportation of the ethnic Germans as head of NKVD Volga German ASSR, was left in his position by Beriia. Gubin survived Beriia's fall and was the Head of KGB in Kazakhstan until October 1959. P.P. Kondakov, head of NKVD in Vologda at the time of Katyn, became the head of MVD in Lithuania. Heading the Foreign Department, according to Sudoplatov, was V.S. Riasnoyi, although Beriia was openly critical of him. Beriia also kept S.R. Savchenko the last head of the MGB Foreign Department as a deputy to Riasnoyi. The old pro P.V. Fedotov was put in charge of counterintelligence and N.D. Gorlinskii, head of NKVD in Kiev in 1940 before being appointed in 1941 as the head of Secret Political Department, and later during the war as assistant to Fedotov, was appointed as head of the economic and industrial counterintelligence. E.P. Pitovarnov, the last head of MGB Foreign Department under Abakumov who had been released from prison in December 1952 was appointed as Fedodov's deputy. Beriia also appointed P.A. Sudoplatov as deputy head of Foreign Department. Sudoplatov may have also been put in charge of a newly formed MVD Department. On March 16, 1953, Beriia wrote to Khrushchev recommending the appointment of 82 generals and colonels to various positions in MVD. In Leningrad, Beriia tried to replace N.G. Ermolaev with N.K. Bogdanov, a Deputy Minister of MVD since January 1948. Here he was opposed by V.M. Andrianov, a Malenkov protege, and Leningrad's Party boss since Kuznetsov's downfall. Andrianov's letter on March 16, 1953, free from the false comraderies typical of correspondence among Soviet officials, shows that Beriia was not yet omnipotent.[8] In Belorussia, Beriia also did not feel comfortable with M.I. Baskakov who had replaced Tsanava in August 1952 so he had him removed. Beriia also kept B.P. Obruchnikov, a man who had served him as head of the cadres in NKVD back in 1941. Let go before the end of March was A.A. Epishev, another deputy minister at MGB in charge of cadres. Epishev had served during the war as Commissar of 38 and 40 Armies, commanded by K.S. Moskalenko, a man who would arrest Beriia within three months. Beriia also appointed his personal assistant, N.S. Sazykin, once Sudoplatov's deputy, as Head of the MVD 4 Department (secret political) and his chauffeur and bodyguard, R.S. Sarkisov (Sarkis'ian), as deputy head of another department. Beriia also released S.F. Kuz'michev who had served in Stalin's personal security during 1932–1950, but had been arrested and imprisoned for some unspecified reason in January 1953 and appointed him as Head of MVD Bodyguards.[9]

There were also political maneuverings. In Georgia, Beriia's agents tried to purge the Party of those who had come to power after the "Mingrelian Affair." In the Ukraine, P.Ia. Meshik, the least experienced of Beriia's proconsuls, behaved with uncalled-for arrogance antagonizing the local Party and police leaders for which he was thoroughly denounced in the Central Committee after Beriia's fall. Meshik made an enemy of T.A. Strokach, head of MVD in L'vov, and P.I. Ivashutin, head of MGB Ukraine since 1952. Beriia's high-handed tactics included a meeting attended by B.Z. Kobulov, Meshik, Mil'shtein, Kruglov, Ivashutin, and Obruchnikov. As reported by Strokach (*Novaia i noveishaia istoriia* March 1989), Beriia opened the meeting by attacking Ivashutin about deteriorating security in West Ukraine and indicated that the new appointments would be made by MVD without consulting with the local Party officials. Strokach, for one, lost his job on June 12, 1953. In Belorussia, through his agent Kobulov, Beriia tried unsuccessfully to replace N.S. Patolichev who had served since 1950 as the First Party Secretary with M.V. Zimianin, the Second Party Secretary. In April, 1953, Beriia met with P.P. Kondakov, Head of MVD in Lithuania, and questioned him about possible candidates to replace A. Ia. Snechkus, the Party Secretary. Kondakov's reluctance resulted in sending to Vil'nius, Kobulov, and Sozykin (incognito) to facilitate the matters.[10] Beriia's activities must have also caused discomfort for M.A. Suslov, who at this time was in charge of the Lithuanian bureau of CC CPSU. During the meeting of the Central Committee in early July 1953 following Beriia's arrest, Patolichev and Snechkus were vociferous in their criticism of the fallen police leader while Suslov kept quiet befitting of his role as an éminence grise.

The other side was mainly allied with the military. An example of a change that may not have been favorable to Beriia took place in April 1953, when the political administration of the Red Army was taken over by A.S. Zheltov, replacing F.F. Kuznetsov, who had held this position in the 1949 shake-up. Both men, however, were veterans of fighting in the south part of the front. Less clear was the removal of I.F. Tevosian as the Deputy Chairman of the Council of Ministers, a position he had held since 1949. Tevosian, a candidate member of the Party Presidium regained his job in December 1953. Tevosian at one time had been a target of Ezhov and may have also had a strained relationship with Beriia. There were also attempts by Beriia's opponents to recruit individuals in the organs. After playing a waiting game until the last minute, Kruglov and Serov decided to cast their lot with the Anti-Beriia group although neither side completely trusted the other. After Beriia's arrest, he was put in custody of the military and not the MVD. When Kruglov and Serov showed up at the headquarters of General Moskalenko with the expressed purpose of interrogating the prisoner, they were turned away. A crucial position in this drama was being held by NKVD General P.A. Artem'ev mentioned elsewhere in this book. Except for a two-year period (1947–1949) when he was replaced by K.A. Meretskov, he had been commander of the Moscow Miliary District—perhaps a record. This was the position crucial to the success of the plot against Beriia. Not trusting Artem'ev, the plotters decided to base their operations in the headquarters of the Moscow Military District Anti-Aircraft Forces commanded since 1948 by K.S. Moskalenko, who after the success of the coup, replaced Artem'ev as Commander of the District and became a Marshal of the Soviet Union in 1955. The plotters also looked for possible dissidents in Beriia's group. T.A. Strokach, who during the war had served as chief of staff of pro-Communist partisans in Ukraine, had been head of MVD in Ukraine since 1946 before being supplanted by P. Ia. Meshik after Beriia's return to power. Strokach and M.S. Popereka, Deputy Head of NKVD in L'vov, were more than willing to provide incriminating material about Beriia and Meshik to Malenkov who, in turn, used it to compromise the police chief.[11]

The circumstances of Beriia's arrest by Marshal Zhukov and his military colleagues on June 26, 1953, during a meeting of the Politburo are well-known although many details remain in dispute. Adam Ulam remarks that out of all the ironies attending Soviet history, one of the greatest was that Beriia, the most opprobrious of Stalin's henchmen, was purged because in his bid for supreme power, he advocated liberal nationality policies within the USSR and reapproachment with the West, but according to E.P. Pitovranov, Beriia's beliefs were completely apolitical. The only game that mattered to him was power.[12] Beriia's trial was held during December 18–23, 1953, in Moscow. In the dock were also V.N. Merkulov, former First Deputy Commissar of NKVD as well as Commissar/Minister NKGB/MGB and, finally, Minister of State Control, D.G. Dekanozov, former Head Deputy Commissar of Foreign Affairs and Minister NKVD in Georgia; B.Z. Kobulov, former First Deputy Commissar NKGB and Deputy Minister MVD; S.A. Goglidze, former Head of NKVD in Transcaucasus, Leningrad and Far East and Deputy Minister of MGB and later MVD; P.Ia. Meshik, Head of MVD in Ukraine; and L.E. Vlodzimirskii, former Head of the sinister Department for Investigation of Especially Important Cases in Beriia's heyday and alleged Head of MVD Investigation Department (others claim that G.G. Paromonov held this position). What these men had in common was not only their proximity to Beriia, but the fact that they had been called back to duty by Beriia after Stalin's death.

V.N. Merkulov, a Russian, more likely a Russified Armenian, was born in 1895. He had been a fellow student with Beriia in Baku Polytechnic School back in 1918 before joining the Cheka/OGPU in 1920. He held various minor positions in the 1920s and 1930s, including Head of the Industrial Transportation Section in the Georgia Party Organization. He may also have had some contacts with Stalin. As related in the first chapter, Merkulov arrived on the scene first in September 1938 as Deputy Head of GUGB/NKVD, but by mid-December he was the First Deputy Commissar of NKVD and head of the all-powerful GUGB/NKVD, and allegedly had taken part in the interrogation of Marshal Bliukher, along with Beriia, B.Z. Kobulov, and B.V. Rodos. It was a sign of Beriia's confidence that this non-entity was picked for such important positions. As was revealed during Beriia's trial, Merkulov helped Beriia in the cover-up of his questionable past and, in fact, managed to find documents in Baku to disprove that Beriia had been a Mussavat spy. Merkulov's greatest contribution was, of course, organizing the massacre of Polish POW officers in Katyn and elsewhere, for which he received the Order of Lenin on April 27, 1940. Later he also played a major part in stonewalling the Poles as well as in fabricating the Soviet version of events. In 1940, he and Sudoplatov were also involved in subverting the Latvian government in preparation for Soviet invasion. In November 1940, Merkulov accompanied Molotov to Berlin and, although his name does not appear on the official list, secretly met with Himmler and Kurt Daluege, head of Ordnungspolizei and future "protector" of Bohemia-Moravia, and he may even have hinted about Katyn.[13] He, rather than Beriia, also let the cat out of the bag when he told Zygmunt Berling in October 1940 that a "mistake" had been made in regard to the missing Poles. In 1939, Merkulov was one of Beriia's men, who was elected to the Central Committee. He also had been a Deputy to the Supreme Soviet since 1937. On February 3, 1941, when NKVD was divided into NKGB and NKVD, Merkulov became the first Commissar of NKGB (the grandfather of KGB), a position which gave him direct access to Stalin. In March 1941, working directly with Stalin, Merkulov made arrangements so the Orthodox population of the Baltics (nearly a quarter-of-a-million people) would be placed under Archibishop D.N. Voskresenskii, an NKGB agent.

Merkulov was not a bad spymaster. In June 1941, he forwarded a report from P.M. Fitin, Head of the NKGB Foreign Department, in which it was stated that all of Germany's military measures for preparation of an armed advance against the USSR had been fully completed, and a strike could be expected anytime. Along with this, there was a detailed account of the imminent attack. Stalin returned the report on June 16, 1941, with a note to Merkulov that his German sources could go "f . . . themselves."[14] In early June, Stalin had also been warned by G.M. Dimitrov who had been alerted by his Austrian contacts, that the invasion was imminent (*Vestnik*, 10/1989). Stalin's reply was that there was no cause for alarm since A.A. Zhdanov, a member of the Politburo, Commissar of the Baltic Fleet and the Leningrad Military District, who was in a better position to know, would not have gone on vacation had there been a possibility of a German attack. Despite all of this, Stalin met on June 17, 1941, with Merkulov and Fitin, who repeated their claims. The next day, Fitin informed his agent Z. Voskresenskaia about Stalin's reaction that this was all a bluff. (Stalin's calendar also shows a meeting with Beriia on June 21, but the contents are not known.) This clearly indicates that Merkulov was sure about the German intentions since, as Gustav Hilger relates in his memoirs, Merkulov, despite his enormous power, was extremely reluctant to make even minor decisions that might displease his superiors. Documents published in recent years, including in O.A. Gorchakov's *Nakanune*, indicate that as late as June 21, 1941, Beriia continued to tell Stalin to ignore the dire warnings of Ambassador Dekanozov and the military attache Maj. General V.I. Tupikov about the imminent German invasion. Beriia also typically added in passing that the Soviet military intelligence, until recently, was run by the "Berzin gang," the kind of remark that was music to Stalin's ears. In view of all this evidence, Beriia's son still tries to shift the blame to Lt. General F.I. Golikov, the Head of GRU, for not alerting Stalin.

On July 20, 1941, NKGB and NKVD were combined and put under Beriia, but Merkulov continued to run the NKGB as Beriia's First Deputy. During the early months of the war, Merkulov was in Leningrad, and there is even a telegram from Stalin dated September 21, 1941 to Zhukov, Zhdanov, Kuznetsov, and Merkulov showing Stalin at his bloodthirsty worst.[15] Stalin's calender for the first week of the war (*VIZH*, 6/1994) shows that he met with Merkulov five times, with Beriia not always present. In August 1941, according to the account related by S.D. Voinov (A.A. Kuznetsov's assistant) in *Oni ne Molchali*, a grim, laconic Merkulov arrived in Leningrad to organize the mining of the factories and buildings in anticipation of abandoning the city, a plan apparently approved by Stalin and Beriia which Kuznetsov somehow managed to frustrate. Merkulov went back to Moscow empty-handed, a defeat that Beriia was bound to remember.

On April 14, 1943, once again NKGB and NKVD became separate Commissariats and Merkulov headed the NKGB (on March 19, 1946, NKGB, after the introduction of "Ministries," was renamed MGB), until he was replaced by Abakumov on October 10, 1946. Released documents dating from 1944 (*Kommunist*, March 1991) show Merkulov to have been involved in extermination campaigns against Lithuanians suspected of anti-Soviet activities. In July 1945, Merkulov became the first pure police officer (and the only one during Stalin's life) to receive the rank of Army General and his portrait appeared in *Pravda* (disproving Romanov's claim to the contrary). He was also present at the reviewing stand on May Day celebration in 1946, an honor denied Abakumov. Officially, Merkulov was replaced as head of MGB by Abakumov in October 1946, which was announced without Abakumov's picture. Erudite, but nevertheless a cold-blooded killer, Merkulov, who helped Beriia with the latter's less-than-exemplary Russian, never forgave or forgot his replacement by Abakumov, whom he considered a corrupt lout. Between 1946 and 1950, Merkulov was Chairman of the Soviet Repatriation Commission and spent time in East Germany. The work of this commission, which deserves study, was basically to provide a front for official plunder. He may also have been with Beriia's Atomic Trust. On October 1950, he replaced Mekhlis as Minister of State Control. The Ministry of State Control was not part of the security apparatus, but it did have watchdog functions and, at one time or the other, had been occupied by such pillars of tyranny as A.A. Andreev, L.Z. Mekhlis, and even Molotov and Stalin. This job provided Merkulov with a sinecure and Beriia with a listening post. In 1952, Merkulov, a member of the CC CPSU since 1939, was, however, dropped to a candidate member. It would have been logical that after Stalin's death, Merkulov would become Beriia's foremost operator, but this was not the case. Merkulov was too obvious a toady and also had been away from the security apparatus since his replacement by Abakumov in 1946. He may have also suffered from poor health, and, in fact, his arrest after Beriia's fall took place in the Kremlin hospital where he was recovering from a serious infection. In his memoirs, Khrushchev claims that after Beriia's arrest, he approached Merkulov and asked him to write a report about Beriia and his crimes. This may have been a trap, and Khrushchev received a self-serving document which, according to Amy Knight, contains accusations against the fallen Abakumov, who is called "dishonest." Even in mortal danger, Merkulov could not forget the humiliation that he had suffered back in 1946. After speaking to Prosecutor Rudenko, Khrushchev ordered Merkulov's arrest. In the postmortem meeting of the Central Committee in July 1953 devoted to Beriia's perfidies, Merkulov was not mentioned. After his own arrest, Beriia claimed that Merkulov must have acted on his own when he committed illegal acts. In *Moi Otets*, Beriia's son refers to Merkulov as an intelligent and refined man with an interest in the arts, photography, and film, whose plays—written under the pseudonym Vsevolod Rok—were performed in the famous Small Theater.

The Georgian S.A. Goglidze was the ultimate survivor, having been perhaps the only real senior officer to have served under Iagoda, Ezhov, Beriia, and Abakumov. In the early 1930s, he had been the head of Border Troops in Transcaucasus. A detailed, but undocumented, account in *Geroi i Antigeroi Otechestva* and other books relates how in this position he helped Beriia's schemes to ingratiate himself with Stalin when the dictator visited Abkhazia in September 1933. The alleged harebrained scheme involved a fake assassination attempt against Stalin and Beriia in which the latter would come through as a hero and cast doubt on the competence and loyalty of N. Lakoba, the Communist boss of Abkhazia and a rival for Stalin's affections. The details of this affair in which Iagoda also became involved remain murky despite, or perhaps because of, Goglidze's self-serving confessions after his own arrest following Beriia's fall. Lakoba's case was further complicated when the daughter of A.P. Rozengol'ts, former Commissar of Trade and Candidate member of CC CPSU, committed suicide in his house. Lakoba's own death in a Tbilisi hospital in November 1936 looks decidedly suspicious and was probably arranged by Beriia, B.Z. Kobulov, and M.L. Michurin-Raver. In November 1934, Goglidze became the NKVD Chief for Transcaucasus, a position he held until November 1938. In the 1930s, Goglidze and B.Z. Kobulov were Beriia's leading foot soldiers. Nothing was beyond these men, who at times provided also moral support. On February 11, 1939, during the meeting of the Transcaucasus Military District chaired by the recently appointed Marshal A.E. Egorov, Beriia showed up accompanied by Goglidze, a bad omen for the doomed Egorov. Another case in point was the relentless persecution of the Ordzhonikidze family, which contributed to the February 18, 1937 suicide of Commissar of Heavy Industry and Politburo member G.K. Ordzhonikidze, once one of Stalin's closest henchmen. In 1937, with help from Rapava, Goglidze arranged for the arrest of one brother, P.K. Ordzinikidze, who was charged on November 9, 1937, and subsequently shot. A sister, N.D. Ordzhonikidze, was arrested by Kobulov and sentenced to 8 years in camps on March 29, 1938. On July 14, 1938, a second NKVD troika chaired by Goglidze sentenced her to death. The surviving brother K.K. Ordzhonikidze, who worked in Moscow, was not arrested until May 5, 1941, but refused to confess. Nevertheless, he was sentenced on August 24, 1944 to 5 years by an NKGB troika. In November 1946 instead of being released, he once again faced a troika, which returned him to prison, where he stayed until after Stalin's death and Beriia's own downfall.

The claim that Goglidze was serving in the Far East in 1938 when Mekhlis and M.P. Frinovskii decimated the local Soviet military leadership is not correct. From November 1938 until July 1941, Goglidze was Head of NKVD/NKGB in Leningrad before taking over as Head of NKVD in the Far East, covering Khabarovsk and Maritime krais, Chita oblast and Buriat-Mongol ASSR. During the war, he met with the visiting U.S. Vice President, Henry Wallace (the granddaddy of modern American liberalism), who spoke Russian, and Professor Owen Lattimore, and on them Goglidze made a favorable impression. The spirit of the dead Indian chief which the mystic and woolly-headed Wallace frequently consulted apparently failed to warn him on this occasion that the charming Goglidze was at this time presiding over a slave empire extending from the Arctic to the Pacific. Wallace and Lattimore also met with I.F. Nikishov, the head of the Dalstroyi labor organization which actually supervised the murderous camps, and his corrupt and brutal wife and were equally impressed. During the post-war years, Goglidze continued to serve in the Far East, but may have been removed in 1950. In 1951, with the deterioration of Abakumov's position, Goglidze was appointed Deputy Minister MGB, where he worked closely with Riumin and Stalin. After Stalin's death, Goglidze received an appointment in MVD under Beriia, but Beriia did not feel comfortable with him or with what Goglidze had been forced to do in the last two years of Stalin's life. Goglidze received the rank of Col. General in July 1945 and during his long career also received Orders of Lenin, Red Banner (twice), and Kutuzov. Like Merkulov, he was also elected to the Central Committee (1939) and was a Deputy to the Supreme Soviet, representing the Birbidzhan Autonomous Jewish Region. Goglidze's service in the Far East was going to have tragic consequences for his family. On October 29, 1984, thieves in the village of Malakhovka murdered Goglidze's widow, E.F. Goglidze, and their daughter, G.S. Goglidze. The understandable motive was that during his service in the Far East, Goglidze must have kept some of the gold dug in Kolima by prisoners under his jurisdiction, which was then left to his heirs. The crime remains unsolved.

V.G. Dekanozov, an Armenian from Georgia, was born in 1898. He had worked in the early 1920s with Bagirov and Beriia in the Azerbaidzhan Cheka, where he was attached to the Secret Political Department. In the 1930s he was in government Party work, serving during 1936–1938 as Deputy Chairman of the Georgia Council of Commissars. He was one of Beriia's first appointments in NKVD when he took over the decimated Foreign Department. In April 1939, he was appointed Deputy Commissar of Foreign Affairs, first under Litvinov, and later Molotov. As part of Stalin's rapprochement with Germany, he helped organize a major purge in the Foreign Service. He was the Soviet proconsul in Lithuania and Ambassador Extraordinary to Berlin (November 1940) until the start of the war. There is a good bit of literature about Dekanozov as a diplomat, and his tenure in Lithuania is subject of research by A.G. Dongarov and G.N. Peskova *(Voprosy Istorii*, 1/1991). On July 7, 1940, Dekanozov suggested to Stalin and Molotov that Soviet artists and a ballet company be sent to entertain the restless Lithuanians. DuringDekanozov's stay in Germany, the Nazis took malicious pleasure in taking pictures of the diminutive Dekanozov surrounded by tall Germans. Dekanozov was not a bad Ambassador, continuously warning Moscow of Hitler's malevolent intentions. On December 7, 1940, he reported that Hitler planned to attack the USSR, a warning which went unheeded. On June 20, 1941, he wired Beriia informing him that the Germans planned to attack the next day. Beriia forwarded the message to Stalin, calling it "disinformation," and added that he and his people agreed with "Stalin's wise prediction that in 1941 Hitler will not attack us."[16] In 1939, Dekanozov became a candidate member of CC CPSU and in 1941 a full member. In 1942, Dekanozov, who was in charge of diplomatic relations with the Near East, and L.R. Sheinin, Vyshinskii's erstwhile assistant, were involved in extraditing two Soviet agent provocateurs, Pavlov and Kornilov, who on February 24, 1942, had planted a bomb in the German Embassy in Ankara. The two terrorists were released in August 1944 as Turkey began to shift from neutrality. Otherwise, Dekanozov's career went into decline, and he was finally dismissed in 1947 by Molotov for moral turpitude. In conversations between F.I. Chuev and Molotov, Dekanozov is mentioned three times in passing, but no opinion is expressed. According to V.M. Berezhkov, Stalin's interpreter, although Dekanozov was the Second Deputy Commissar, he behaved like he was only second to Molotov, treating the First Deputy Commissar Vyshinskii with disdain and referring to him as the "Menshevik." Malenkov has also been credited with the sacking of Dekanozov, who ended up in an administrative position in the All-State Radio Committee. Beriia advised patience until the right time.[17] Incidentally, on January 16, 1945, Dekazonov informed the Swedes that Wallenberg was in Soviet hands, a statement that was totally contradicted on August 18, 1947 by Vyshinskii, who denied the existence of Wallenberg.[18] Until Beriia's return to power, Dekanozov held minor positions such as Deputy Chairman of All-State Radio Committee and Merkulov's Deputy in the Main Office of Soviet Property Abroad. He may have also been employed in Beriia's Atomic Trust. At the 19th Party Congress (1952), Dekanozov was removed from the Central Committee. After Stalin's death with Beriia as Head of MVD, he was sent to Georgia to settle the score with those who had organized the "Mingrelian Affair" and also consolidate Beriia's power.

B.Z. Kobulov, born in 1904, another Armenian, along with his brother, A.Z. Kobluv, had long been fixtures of the Beriia machine, although the latter at first had held more important positions. In 1938 B.Z. Kobulov was the Head of NKVD Special Department in Georgia and later Deputy Head NKVD Georgia under Goglidze. As related in chapter 1, Kobulov arrived on the national scene in mid-September 1938 as Head of the Secret-Political Branch of the NKVD 1 Department.[19] In mid-December, he was Deputy Head of the GUGB/NKVD under Merkulov and Head of the NKVD Investigation Department (where Abakumov was also employed) before also taking over the NKVD Economics Department in early April 1939. This must have been a short appointment since he did not hold this position at the start of the war. In December 1938, when A.M. Larina (Bukharin's widow) was transferred to Moscow from Astrakhan, she was first met by Kobulov, who took her to Beriia's office. Larina found Kobulov, whom she incorrectly identifies as Head of the Special Department, no more than a doorkeeper, a non-entity who deferred to Beriia.

In 1939, Kobulov became a candidate member of the Central Committee. In spring 1940, he was a member of a troika, replacing Beriia, that approved the death sentences of the Polish POW officers. As Deputy Commissar of the combined NKVD, he played an important part in the already mentioned Orel massacres of August 1941. He was also involved in one of the most despicable acts of the Stalin regime, the arrest of children of purged officials such as A. Ikramov, former First Secretary of the Uzbek Party. Kobulov was Stalin's favorite wiretapper and, according to Sudoplatov, in 1942 installed listening devices in the homes of Marshals Voroshilov and Budennyi, and Army General G.K. Zhukov. In 1950, Molotov and Mikoian were also wiretapped. The details of Stalin's wiretapping program, which probably targeted all members of the Politburo and the cabinet, had yet to be completely revealed. Kobulov was also something of a clown, entertaining Stalin with imitations of accents of various nationalities and individuals, particularly that of Comrade Bagirov. In 1943, he was the First Deputy Commissar of NKGB under Merkulov and took part in the deportation campaigns of 1943–1944. In 1945, he was active in re-occupied Belorussia, but probably lost his job as First Deputy Commissar when Abakumov took over. He had been identified in Germany in 1948 and was probably a member of Beriia's Atomic Trust. Otherwise, his post-war career remains obscure. In March 1953, he became Deputy Minister of MVD under Beriia and possibly Head of theForeign Department. B.Z. Kobulov was Beriia's closest associate during the period after Stalin's death and was arrested on the same day as his boss. His brother, A.Z. Kobulov, served during the war as NKVD Chief in Uzbek SSR, and after the war as Deputy Head of the Administration of Soviet Property Abroad, before returning to USSR and working as Deputy Head of Gulag and Head of the Department for POWs in the 1950s. In Kruglov's report dating from August 8, 1953, to Malenkov (*Iosif Stalin v Ob'iatiiakh Sem'i*), following the arrest of Stalin's son, B.Z. Kobulov was accused of having provided him camera equipment as well as a Packard automobile from government stores in Germany in 1952. It seems likely that Kruglov is wrong here and the party in question was actually A.Z. Kobulov. After Stalin's death, A.Z. Kobulov became Head of the MVD Control and Inspection Section. He was also arrested, but not tried with this group.

The next defendant, L.E. Vlodzimirskii, was born in 1902 or 1903. On May 8, 1937, he was Deputy Head of the GUGB/NKVD 4 (Secret-Political) Department. He survived Ezhov's fall and on March 4, 1940, was Head of the Investigation Section of the NKVD Economic Department; after Beriia's appointment, he became Kobulov's Deputy in the NKVD Investigations Department. On February 26, 1941, he took over NKGB Investigation (soon to be renamed Department for Investigation of Especially Important Cases). He remained until 1946, when Abakumov replaced him with his own man, A.S. Leonov. Vlodzimirskii received the Order of Red Star on July 22, 1937, and the rank of Major of State Security on March 14, 1940. In 1939, he helped eliminate some of Beriia's personal enemies such as one Bobkun-Luganisa and his wife. Vlodzimirskii was involved in most of the major secret police operations during the war, assisted by such brutal underlings as B.V. Rodos and L.L. Shvartsman. His role vis-à-vis SMERSH merits further study. In the summer of 1945, he helped organize the kidnapping of 16 leaders of the Home Army who were brought to Moscow for trial. Vlodzimirskii was probably employed during the post-war years in Beriia's Atomic Trust before taking over the MVD's Investigation Department under Beriia in spring 1953. One of Vlodzimirskii's last acts before his own arrest was the interrogation of Stalin's son, arrested in April 1953, which took place during May 9–11, 1953, and provides fascinating reading in the collection *Iosif Stalin v Ob'iatiiakh Sem'i*.

The least-known member of the group was P.Ia. Meshik, born in 1910, the son of an alleged agent of Okhrana who had been condemned to death by the Bolsheviks, and opted to join up with Denikin. In the early 1930s Meshik was a Komsomol worker in Samar before attending the OGPU School in 1933. He was then assigned to NKVD's Economic Department. In 1940, he was B.Z. Kobulov's Assistant in the Department for Investigation of Especially Important Cases and may have been an interrogator of R.I. Eikhe during the war. According to Sudoplatov, he was selected to remain in Moscow and organize sabotage in case the city was captured by the Germans. He then served as deputy head of SMERSH. During the post-war period, he seems to have been with the Atomic Trust. In *Palachi i zherty*, Meshik is also identified as a one-time Head of the NKVD Economics Department. Regardless, he formed with Merkulov, B.Z. Kobulov, Vlodzimirskii, Rodos, and Shvartsman, Beriia's inner cabinet charged with investigation and extraction of confessions. All were to share their master's fate.

Abakumov was conspicuous by his absence, an indication that the organizers of the trial recognized that he was not a member of Beriia's team. Equally interesting were the men who sat in judgement of this group. As Chairman of the Special Session of the Military Collegium, Marshal I.S. Konev (a man without any judicial experience) was a curious choice. In October 1941, as Commander of the West Front, he had come within a hair's breadth of being court-martialed before being alleged saved by his future rival G.K. Zhukov, who interceded for him to Stalin. Except for this episode, Konev had been above suspicion during the reign of Stalin, who later played him off against Zhukov. As a result, the relationship between the two Marshals soured. It seemed odd that Zhukov, the Minister of Defense, would have agreed to Konev's appointment as Chairman of the Court. There was, however, also a dark secret in Konev's recent past. Late in 1952, Konev had written to Stalin claiming that he had been a victim of the Kremlin doctors who had been arrested in the "Doctors' Plot." Despite this untoward action, or perhaps because of it, Konev was the Chairman. Sitting next to him was N.M. Shvernik, Chairman of the Presidium of the Supreme Soviet since 1946, as well as the Head of the Trade Unions. He was a man with impeccable Stalinist credentials.

Another member was Army General K.S. Moskalenko, who had now replaced P.A. Artem'ev as Commander of the Moscow Military District. Only in the Soviet Union, would Moskalenko, who had arrested the defendant Beriia, also sit in his judgement. N.A. Mikhailov, First Secretary of the Komsomols since 1938 and Stalin's pointman in destroying Kosarev and the previous Komsomol leadership and now Secretary of the Moscow Oblast Party organization, was another member. He was later to become Minister of Culture. Mikhailov's wife had once suggested to Svetlana Alliluyeva the idea of expelling Moscow's Jewish population. The obscure M.I. Kuchava, Head of the Georgia Trade Unions, was the only non-Slav member. Kuchava had replaced S.S. Mamulov in the Georgia Party organization. There were only two members with judicial backgrounds. One was Lt. General of Judiciary E.L. Zeidin, whom we will meet later, and at this time First Deputy Chairman of the USSR Supreme Court. The other was L.A. Gromov, Chairman of the Moscow City Court. The only Chekist on the panel was K.F. Lunev, listed as Deputy (also identified as First Deputy) Minister of MVD. Lunev, however, was a newcomer to the organs, having been an obscure functionary in the Moscow Party Organization under Khrushchev.

It is interesting that a court which, except for one member, was made up entirely of Slavs, was sitting in judgement of defendants who, again with two exceptions, were non-Slavs. "Affirmative Action" was one injustice, perhaps the only one, that had not been tried in the Soviet Union.

Stalin's successors did not feel comfortable with G.N. Safonov, USSR Prosecutor General since November 1943, even though he had recovered from injuries suffered in an auto accident, and replaced him with R.A. Rudenko. Rudenko had been part of the Stalinist justice system for years, having served in the trial of the kidnapped leaders of the Home Army in June 1945 before being appointed the Chief Soviet Prosecutor in Nuremberg and had also been involved in falsifying records in regard to pre-war Soviet aggressive policies in East Europe as well as in blaming the Germans for Katyn. The charges against the defendants did not involve Katyn, mass deportations, and execution and imprisonment of thousands of innocent citizens, but rather isolated cases in which "socialist legality" had been violated. Beriia was accused of using NKVD to even political scores (such as having M.S. Kedrov shot after he had been acquitted), killing personal enemies such as one Bokun-Lugantsa and his wife, for dubious contacts with the enemies of Soviet power in the Caucasus, contact with the émigré groups, and attempts to usurp power, and just to make sure that the Stalin spirit was still dominating the Soviet legal system, of having tried to restore capitalism. Other charges included personal corruption, including keeping a harem of odalisques befitting an Ottoman sultan. Although Beriia's trial took place in December, most of the charges had already been aired in the July 1953 meeting of the Central Committee where Beriia had been described as the devil incarnate by all the comrades including those like Bagirov, who owed most of his career to him. The charges and the proceedings against Beriia and his colleagues filled 50 volumes.

Until now, with the exception of Tsanava and Rukhadze, Beriia had enjoyed stable relations with his henchmen, some of whom, such as Merkulov, he had known for nearly 30 years. Now with the end in sight, the desperate defendants turned on their old master denouncing him not only for ordering them to commit crimes, but as a "careerist, adventurer and Bonapartist" (B.Z. Kobulov) and as "power hungry" (Dekanozov), and so on. Beriia's case was also not helped by the testimony of the old Bolshevik A.V. Snegov (A.V. Fabinzon, 1898–1991), who had somehow survived nearly 18 years in camps despite having in his possession documents incriminating Beriia. The defendants had to be incurable optimists to have expected mercy from the Military Collegium to which they had sent, when in power, thousands of innocent victims. On December 23, 1953, the court found Beriia guilty of, among other things, service in the Mussavat counterintelligence, conspiracy against the Soviet government in order to restore capitalism, encouragement of "bourgeois-nationalist" elements in the Soviet republics, contact with émigré groups and foreign intelligence agencies including the yet-to-be-rehabilitated Tito, and spying on Soviet leaders. There was also a charge that Beriia had suggested deviation from the socialist path in GDR, which gives credence to claims that he had advocated the liberalization of the harsh conditions which led to the Berlin riots of June 17, 1953. Beriia was found guilty of organizing with his henchmen the 1937 decimation of the Party leadership in Georgia and the murders of I.M. Kedrov, M.S. Kedrov, A. Baturiia, V. Golubev, and some members of the Ordzhonikidze family. Beriia was further found guilty of having tried in the fall of 1941 through third parties to make peace with Hitler by giving up Soviet territory and advocated in 1943 giving up the Caucasus Mountains to the enemy. Last but not least, he was found guilty of having raped a 16-year-old schoolgirl on May 7, 1949, and threatening her and her mother with arrest if they spoke up.

Beriia's son, engineer S.L. Beriia, living in Kiev, denies the charges of moral corruption against his father. The archives of the Pamiat Society (*Sovershenno Sekretno*, August 1991), however, relate the tragedy of Lt. Colonel and Hero of the Soviet Union S.S. Shchirov, who was called to Moscow after shooting down 18 enemy planes. Shchirov's wife apparently was kidnapped by R.S. Sarkisov, Beriia's bodyguard, and was forced to become Beriia's mistress for the next five years. Shchirov was shipped to the Central Asia and later the North Caucasus Military Districts. Here he tried to get himself arrested by pretending that he planned to defect to Turkey. He felt illogically that once under arrest, he could expose Beriia's perfidy to the authorities. For this foolishness, he received a 10-year sentence and ended up in Vorkuta. He was released and rehabilitated shortly after Stalin's death but died shortly afterward in a psychiatric hospital in Kazan at age 40. The compilation *Geroi Sovetskogo Soiuza*, published in 1987, fails to list him.

All the defendants were found guilty under the notorious Articles 58–1(b), 58–8, 58–11, and 58–13 of the RSFSR Code which in their day they had used to send thousands of people to the wall and to the Gulag. The sentences of death by shooting were carried out on December 23, 1953. According to Ambassador V.I. Erofeev (*International Affairs*, 10/1991), Beriia's interrogations (more likely the trial) were broadcast to selected government and Party offices. The cause of justice, if not historical truth, was served.[20] Beriia was personally executed (murdered would be a better term) at 7:50 p.m. on December 23, 1953 by Lt. General P.F. Batitskii, First Deputy Commander Moscow District Anti-Aircraft Forces (PVO), who reportedly found the act personally distasteful, but it must have helped him become a Marshal of the Soviet Union in 1968. More significantly, he received the title of Hero of the Soviet Union on July 5, 1965. The granting of this highest of Soviet military awards during peacetime was usually politically motivated (Brezhnev received this decoration four times, matched only by Marshal Zhukov). Batitskii, who had served as the Military Adviser to China with the rank of Major before the war, had an undistinguished career as Division and Corps Commander during the war, and the conclusion that the award was given for putting Beriia out of the way is unescapable. Also present at Beriia's execution were Army General (future Marshal of the Soviet Union) K.S. Moskalenko and the Prosecutor Rudekno, who, unlike Vyshinskii, was not squeamish about such matters (he had been present when the major Nazi war criminals were hanged in Nuremberg). Rudekno ordered Batitskii to stuff a towel into the mouth of the pleading Beriia and carry out the sentence. Thus, Beriia met the same fate that he had handed out to thousands of others. Dekanozov, Goglidze, Kobulov, Merkulov, Meshik, and Vlodzimirskii were killed at the same night at 9:20 p.m. Present and probably carrying out the executions were Col. General A.L. Getman, Lt. General Bakeev, and Maj. General Sopil'nik. Also present representing the Judiciary were K.F. Lunev, Deputy Chairman of the Court and Maj. General of Judiciary D.Iu. Kitaev, who represented the Military Prosecutor's Office. It is more than coincidence that Getman, a slightly more talented Commander than Batitskii, also received the title of Hero of the Soviet Union on exactly the same date. Beriia's wife, N.T. Gegechkori, and his son were also arrested and were kept in solitary confinement in Butyrka prison but were later exiled to Sverdlovsk. Beriia's wife died on July 7, 1991, in Kiev, where her son still lives employed as a military engineer. The ghost of Beriia was useful to Stalin's successors. During his visit to Yugoslavia in 1955, Khrushchev tried to convince his skeptical hosts that Beriia had been behind the anti-Yugoslavia campaigns of Stalin's years.

Riumin's turn came next. His arrest followed the MVD announcement of April 4, 1953 about the release of the arrested doctors and published under the headline, "Soviet Socialist Law is Invincible" that called Riumin...a despicable adventurer...who had forged documents in a frame-up against honorable citizens...guilty of arbitrary acts and abuse of power...who attempted to fan national enmity, which was completely alien to Soviet society.[21]

As stated before, Riumin was arrested on March 16, 1953 and was handed over to the veteran investigator Col. A.G.Khvat (the interrogator of academician N.I. Vavilov, among others), who was soon joined by Vlodzimirskii, Meshik, and Kobulov. Riumin was in for a rough time. According to A.I. Vaksberg, Riumin did not break, as was also the case with Abakumov. It seemed as if the post-Stalin interrogators were beginning to lose their touch. Riumin was particularly defiant when defending his actions against the Jews. On May 15, 1953, Khvat and his Assistant suggested that Riumin be placed in the punishment cell in Lefortovo. Beriia agreed, but before the necessary confessions could be extracted, he and his chief colleagues were also arrested. As was the case with Abakumov, Beriia's arrest did not mean freedom for Riumin. Deriabin's claim that Riumin (whom he incorrectly identifies as V.S. Riumin) was released for a short time after Beriia's arrest is not based on fact.[22] Riumin was tried *alone* on July 2, 1954 by a special session of the Military Collegium of the USSR chaired by Lt. General of Judiciary E.L. Zeidin, with members Maj. Generals of Judiciary V.V. Siul'din and Stepanov (the first would also soon preside over Abakumov's trial). The trial lasted five days and Riumin was sentenced to death. His appeal for clemency rejected, Riumin was shot on July 22, 1954, which was officially announced a day later. The minutes of the trial have yet to be released, but to my knowledge, none of the surviving victims of the "Doctors' Plot" were asked to testify. Riumin was accused in the illegal arrests of Raikhman, Eitingon, and Sheinin on October 19, 1951 with the help of his Assistant P.I. Grishaev and later of the arrest of Drs. Busalov and Vasilenko. The death sentence pronounced on July 7 could not be appealed and Riumin's request for pardon was rejected by Prosecutor Rudenko. A.I. Vaksberg, who had access to some documents, states in *Stalin Against the Jews* that Riumin continued to be unrepentant in prison defending his actions and claiming truthfully that he received his orders from Stalin. He also claimed, as Abakumov had in the beginning of his arrest, that he had contacts with the highest officials of the state and hinted of blackmail. Riumin was probably unaware that those who had originally arrested him, namely Beriia and company, were now also behind bars.

Who was this man Riumin? Born in 1913, he had graduated from eight grades and then trained as an accountant. He was typical of the flotsam and jetsam of the Soviet society who would drift into the organs to become professional Chekists and are praised by Sudoplatov, in contrast to the Party hacks who occasionally were dispatched when things got out of hand. Before the war, Riumin had worked on the Moscow-Volga Canal, which was being built by slave labor. During the war, he somehow ended up with SMERSH in the backwoods of the Arkhangel Military District, where he probably watched over the locals fraternizing with the foreign sailors. He was involved in the torture of photojournalist Ermolin from the journal *Patriot Rodiny*, whom he falsely accused of being a British spy in 1944. Later in the war, he was a Senior Investigator with SMERSH. After the war, he joined the MGB, but his career was not going well. There are rumors he found employment in Stalin's personal secretariat. This does not seem farfetched in view of the role that he was to play in the campaign against Abakumov. As the Assistant Head of the Department for Investigation of Especially Important Cases, Riumin was the pointman in the "Aviators' Affair," in the case against General Telegin, in the anti-Semitic campaigns, and in the "Leningrad Affair." The ambitious Riumin, however, wanted to be more than a glorified torturer, and there is reason to believe that Abakumov began to mistrust him. In 1950, Riumin came under a cloud when on the way from Lubianka to Lefortovo, he left some important documents in an official bus, but somehow managed to overcome this lapse. No one was really safe from Riumin, a born intriguer and somewhat a gambler.

According to Lt. General of Judiciary A.F. Katusev, as quoted in Kostliarov, after being arrested, Riumin was interrogated in April 1953 by L.E. Vlodzimirskii, Head of the Department for Investigation of Especially Important Cases under Beriia and now back in his old job. Riumin admitted that on May 31, 1951, he saw incriminating material in his MGB dossier in which his father had been identified as a livestock merchant, his brother and sister as criminals, and his father-in-law, one Parkachev, as a former officer in Kolchak's Army. He saw Abakumov's hand in this and decided to strike first, and his letter accusing Abakumov of various crimes played right into Stalin's hand.[23]

After Abakumov's downfall, which Riumin engineered, he became head of the Department for Investigation of Especially Important Cases and possibly a Deputy Minister of MGB. He was the chief fabricator of the "Doctors' Plot" campaign. Similar in physical appearance and temperament to Ezhov, he would have been the ideal candidate for launching a new "Ezhovshchina." Like many high-ranking Soviet secret police officials, with the possible exception of Merkulov, Riumin enjoyed taking part in interrogations, which were considered almost recreational sport. In February 1952, his manner of questioning caused permanent deafness of I. Nezhnyi, the pre-war Director of the Moscow Art Theater.[24]

Beriia's arrest and execution, to which Abakumov reportedly showed no reaction, brought another twist to his fate, and perhaps he hoped that he would now be forgotten. That was not to be the case. As early as August 1953, Serov, now Deputy Minister of MVD, taking direct orders from Khrushchev and working closely with USSR Prosecutor R.A. Rudenko, began a new line of attack, raising the question of a close relationship betweenAbakumov and the fallen Beriia as well as Abakumov's complicity in the "Leningrad Affair" and his personal corruption. Abakumov was now being interrogated in the MVD Internal Prison, having been transferred for health reasons from Lefortovo on September 26, 1953.[25] The Chief Interrogator, however, in this period was Colonel (future Maj. General) of Judiciary D.P. Terekhov, Deputy Military Prosecutor (who was also questioning Riumin). Terekhov later shared some of this information with Solzhenitsyn, who used it in his books. The novelist had great admiration for Terekhov, perhaps somewhat misplaced since Terekhov later served for nearly 20 years (1961–1980) as Deputy Chairman of the Military Collegium, which, although not as deadly as under Ul'rikh, continued to be an organ of repression and injustice. The rehabilitation of the principal victims of the "Leningrad Affair" in April 1954 was another bad omen for Abakumov.

There were, however, problems in trying to implicate Abakumov as a member of Beriia's gang, and his name was hardly mentioned during Beriia's trial. A.Z. Kobulov, in his interrogation, was probably right when he stated that the relationship between Beriia and Abakumov was friendly in the beginning, but deteriorated during and after the war. This was caused by Abakumov's refusal to play second fiddle to Beriia and his replacement of Beriia's people with his own men. On occasions there had been harsh words between the two men.[26] Journalist V.K. Abarinov even claims the existence of a deadly feud between Abakumov and Beriia.[27] According to Beriia's bodyguard, R.S. Sarkisov, Beriia immediately disowned Abakumov once it became obvious that he was to be sacked. Abakumov told Rudenko in court that he had never been in Beriia's home and their relationship was purely professional and official.[28] Despite all of this, the myth of an Abakumov/Beriia machine created by Khrushchev and others for their own reasons continued to be perpetuated. Kostliarov is right when he hints that Khruschev's main goal during this period was to cover his own complicity in Stalin's crimes, and there is every reason to believe that he was helped here by Serov. Abakumov's trial and execution also fit into this scenario. By putting the blame for terror on the security apparatus and its chiefs, Khrushchev was perhaps preparing the foundation for the famous speech to the 22 Party Congress. Abakumov's trial and the revelations about the "Leningrad Affair" also provided him with ammunition against his uneasy partner, Malenkov. The speed with which Abakumov's death sentence was carried out (similar to that of victims of the "Leningrad Affair") makes it clear that he was now a proven liability to Khrushchev's plans.

In regard to Khrushchev's involvement with Stalin's crimes and destruction of documents held by MGB that would have implicated him, Kostliarov claims that the long disgraced Malenkov provided Andropov with documents implicating Khrushchev.[29] In 1988, A.N. Shelepin also told Volkogonov that Serov was involved in removing similar documents. Khrushchev's treatment of Abakumov's family and other defendants did him little credit. Abakumov's wife and son were released on March 9, 1954, after spending 32 months in prison, but were treated no better than families of those condemned under Stalin. Defendant Chernov claims that during his own imprisonment, he lost his mother, wife, and older son to disease and privation, but Abakumov's son, although not his wife, is apparently still living. F.M.

Burlatskii, who in the late 1940s was a graduate student in the Institute of the State and Law of the USSR Academy of Sciences, claims that Abakumov's son was a fellow student. The existence of this son from the first marriage has yet to be confirmed. Since Abakumov was born only in 1908, to have fathered a son near in age to Burlatskii, who was born in 1927, would mean that his first marriage took place before he was 20.[30] The hour of reckoning finally arrived for Abakumov in Leningrad on December 14, 1954. There was poetic justice in the setting of Abakumov's trial in the Officer's House where four years before the victims of the "Leningrad Affair" had been tried. Besides Abakumov, the defendants included A.G. Leonov (born in 1905), former head of MGB Department for Investigation of Especially Important Cases; his Deputies V.I. Komarov (born in 1916) and M.T. Likhachev; head of Abakumov's personal secretariat I.A. Chernov (born in 1907); and his Deputy Ia. M. Broverman. L.L. Shvartsman, who was tried and shot in March 1955, served as a material witness. The Military Collegium of USSR was composed of Lt. General of Judiciary E. L. Zeiden (Chairman), Maj. General of Justice V.V. Siuldin, and Colonel V.V. Borisoglebskii. The accused were defended by four lawyers from Moscow, L.I. Grinev, M.V. Stepanov, N.I. Rogov, and L.V. Pavlov. According to Chernov, the defendants met their lawyers for the first time in court. The charges against Abakumov had already been unfolded in a report of the Party Presidium on May 7, 1954, authored by Khrushchev. Abakumov was charged with a litany of Stalinist crimes: for being a "careerist," "criminal adventurer" and "degenerate bourgeois." Khrushchev also hinted that Abakumov had been expelled from the Party and arrested in July 1951 because of his involvement with the "Leningrad Affair," but that charge was not true. Khrushchev also added the dead Beriia and Merkulov as fellow conspirators with Abakumov in the "Leningrad Affair," even though there is no evidence of Merkulov's participation.[31] The central roles played by Stalin and Malenkov were left out.

There is no better illustration of the tenuous nature of the relationship of Beriia and Abakumov than the proceedings of the early July 1953 meeting of the Central Committee after Beriia was arrested. Abakumov is mentioned in passing three times by N.N. Shatalin (Secretary of the Central Committee), Kaganovich and Khrushchev, the latter two coupling Abakumov's name with those of Iagoda, Ezhov, and Beriia as violators of "socialist legality." In contrast, a real Beriia operative such as P.A. Shariia was denounced by various speakers, including Molotov, for crimes that were mild compared to those committeed by Abakumov. Stalin's heirs knew better than anyone else that Abakumov had marched to a different drummer, but to expose him would have implicated Stalin, at this time still treated as a demigod, as well as their own involvement.

The trial of Abakumov was dictated by the political needs of those now in power who were going to use Abakumov as the fall guy, particularly Khrushchev. The prosecution was led by the USSR General Prosecutor R.A. Rudenko, a long-standing member of Stalinist Judiciary, who had served as the Soviet Chief Prosecutor in Nuremberg but now was perfectly willing to serve the new masters. Rudenko's performance in Nuremberg and his persecution of Solzhenitsyn and Andrei Sakharov during the Brezhnev years (Rudenko remained in his job as the USSR Prosecutor General until 1981) showed him to be no friend of justice.

Despite the claims made by Khrushchev about the existence of a Beriia/ Abakumov machine, the fact that the two were tried separately undermined this claim. In fact, during the trial, Beriia's name was mentioned only by Abakumov, and then pejoratively. Rudenko made the feeble claim that Abakumov and his colleagues were running a rogue organization that was behind the "Leningrad Affair." Abakumov, after complaining about his life in prison, repeated his previous contentions that he had been a victim of slander campaigns by Beriia, as well as by Riumin, who had accused him of heading a Jewish counterrevolutionary operation. He claimed, with justification, that he had taken all his orders from the Central Committee (in court, Abakumov said Stalin). He was being blamed for having pressed for the execution of those involved in the "Leningrad Affair" when he was merely carrying out the decisions made by the Central Committee.[32] In his final statement to the court, Abakumov said, "I am an honest man and a victim of character assassination. During the war, I was head of counterintelligence and then for five years a Minister. I was devoted to the Party and Central Committee."[33] Among the defendants, only Chernov accepted some responsibility for the crimes, while Broverman implicated the other defendants, making them and Chernov, in particular, angry. Abakumov, Leonov, Komarov, and Likhachev were condemned to death, Broverman to 25 years, and Chernov to 15 years. According to Chernov, Abakumov, who had behaved with dignity during the trial, accepted the sentence calmly.[34] As was the usual practice, the court also ordered the confiscation of Abakumov's ill-gotten and considerable wealth and, later, his decorations.

Likhachev and Komarov had been in Czechoslovakia late in 1949 organizing the purge campaign against Czechoslovak Communists. Two of the victims, Eugen Loebl and Artur London, have left a highly uncomplimentary picture of Likhachev (listed as "Likhatsev" by Loebl and "Lihache" by London). On February 18, 1953, Komarov, now in prison, wrote a pleading (was there another kind?) letter to Stalin, excerpts of which have recently been published (*Novyi Mir*, October 1993). Komarov, swearing eternal allegiance, claimed that he had mercilessly dealt with the Jewish nationalists, whom he called "most dangerous and malicious" enemies. He had also tried to warn Abakumov about trusting the Jewish officials of MGB such as Shvartsman, Itkin, and Broverman, who had accused him of anti-Semitism and weakened his position in dealing with Abakumov. Whether Stalin saw this letter in the last two weeks of his life is not known. Chernov, released after 14 years (for a while he shared a cell with L.R. Sheinin), was still living in 1990 (age 83) and had written and spoken about the Abakumov era. He remains bitter about his treatment and about fellow defendant Broverman's attempt to desert his colleagues.[35] In view of Komarov's letter, it is difficult to blame Broverman, the only Jew among the defendants, for trying to save his own skin. I have been unable to trace Broverman after the trial.

The report by Lt. Colonel Talanov, Head of KGB Internal prison, dated December 12, 1954, to Lt. General of Judiciary A.A. Cheptsov, Chairman of the Military

Collegium of the USSR Supreme Court, stated that the court's sentence on Viktor Semenovich Abakumov, born in 1908, was carried out at 12:15 a.m. on December 19, 1954. According to Talanov, Abakumov's last words were "I'll report everything to the Politburo," but he was hit by the bullet before he could finish the sentence.[36] The brief announcement in *Pravda* following Abakumov's execution stated that he had fabricated the "Leningrad Affair" under the direction of Beriia, who, even today, continues to serve as an all-purpose villain for Stalin's crimes.

What could be the last chapter in the Abakumov saga occurred in 1991 when Lt. General of Judiciary P. Boriskin and the Office of the Chief Military Prosecutor reviewed the case against Abakumov and his colleagues. It concluded that although Abakumov was guilty of unlawful repressions, he was not guilty of high treason or crimes against the Party. The recommendation was that abuse of power and falsification of evidence were his actual crimes, for which he had received the appropriate sentence. Sudoplatov is correct that this revision implies that Abakumov's superiors (who else but Stalin and the Politburo?) was equally guilty. Thus, Abakumov received partial rehabilitation.

During the Khrushchev years, Abakumov's name, usually coupled with Beriia's, was used as an example of a violator of "socialist legality." Under Brezhnev and his immediate successor, Abakumov became a non-person. During this period, the official Soviet policy about writing history was lying by omission more than by commission. Biographies of purge victims stopped in 1935 and the Kremlin spin doctors began to accentuate Stalin's "positive characters," and descriptions such as "repressed" and "cult of personality" ceased to be used. To my knowledge, the last time Abakumov's name was invoked until Glasnost was on February 7, 1957. Gromyko, for once telling the truth (only partially), acknowledged to the Swedes that Abakumov, while involved in criminal activities, had given incorrect information about Wallenberg to the Soviet Ministry of Foreign Affairs for several years.

Army General P.I. Ivashutin, Head of SMERSH in various fronts and later First Deputy Chairman of KGB and for nearly a quarter-of-a-century head of GRU, who knew Abakumov during the war and the immediate post-war years, states that Beriia and Abakumov have been described as the Russian counterparts of Himmler and Kaltenbrunner, a comparison which he finds unfair to Abakumov, with whom he had enjoyed a cordial relationship during the war.[37] According to Ivashutin, the tragedy of Abakumov's life was that he would stop at nothing in carrying out Stalin's orders, but then again this charge could also be made against just about everyone in the Soviet government and the Communist Party. The fact remains that Abakumov and the other satraps had no option except unquestioning obedience to Stalin and, as it turned out in numerous cases, even this was no guarantee against the tyrant's displeasure.

Two men were conspicuous by their absence at Abakumov's trial. Riumin had already been tried in July 1954 and condemned to death. The other, the principal beneficiary of the "Leningrad Affair" was none other than G.M. Malenkov, Chairman of the Council of Ministers, a position he held until February 1955. One wonders whether Malenkov saw any ominous signs in the trial and foresaw exile, disgrace, and expulsion from the Party. Perhaps as an old-age born-again Christian, he even reflected and felt sorrow over the untold suffering inflicted on millions in order to build paradise on earth under the Greatest Leader of All Time.

In March 1955, L.L. Shvartsman faced trial and execution. It remains a mystery why he was not tried with Abakumov and company. This was possibly because he had cooperated after his original arrest by admitting the existence of a "Jewish nationalist conspiracy" and fingering others including Abakumov and Raikhman. The details of his trial remain murky. Kostliarov divides the Chekists into "thugs" and "intellectuals" and puts Shvartsman in the latter category. Despite perfunctory education, Shvartsman, born in 1907, had started his career as a journalist in such journals as *Kiveskii Proletarii* and *Rabochaia Moskva* while serving as an NKVD secret agent. In 1937, he officially joined the NKVD and served in the Secret Political Department and later as Deputy Head of the Department for Investigation of Especially Important Cases. The military had a long score to settle with Shvartsman since he had served as Chief Interrogator of senior officers who were arrested and later executed in the early days of the war. He was implicated in the "Aviators' Affair." Shvartsman's presence in the MGB High Command had given Riumin the excuse to frame Abakumov in October 1951. Riumin, helped by two other MGB operatives, V. Uspenskii and P.I. Grishaev, prepared the case against Shvartsman as head of a "Jewish nationalist conspiracy."[38] As was discussed already, Shvartsman would confess to anything. B.V. Rodos was another man with a close association with the Department for Investigation of Especially Important Cases who faced trial and execution. Rodos, born in 1905, had been the NKVD Investigator who had interrogated, among others, Kosior, Chubar, Kosarev, and Meyerhold. He had supervised the execution of senior military officers in Kuibyshev in October 1941 and was another on the military's hit list.

The next trial was to take place in Tbilisi on November 22, 1955. A detailed account of it can be found in *SSR Vnutrennie Protivorechaia* (June 1982) and in Suren Gazarian's *Eto ne Dolzhno Povtorit'sia: 1958–1961*. The Military Collegium was chaired by Lt. General of Judiciary D.D. Chertkev, who back in 1947 had served as a Prosecutor in the trial of Commanders of the veterans of SS Division "Totenkopf." He was joined by A.A. Kostremin and A. Golovtsev. Once again R.A. Rudenko served as the Prosecutor. The defendants, all but two Georgians, were all identified as part of the Beriia group. It is interesting that the two enemies Rukhadze and Rapava were both grouped as part of the Beriia machine. A.N. Rapava had been identified with Georgia NKVD in 1937 before serving as Acting Chairman and Chairman of the Abkhazia Council of People's Commissars. In 1938, he was Deputy Head of NKVD in Georgia. In July 1945, he received the rank of Lt. General. From late 1938 until 1948, he was the Head of NKVD/NKGB/MGB in Georgia when he was removed under a cloud. He was arrested by his successor, Rukhadze, in connection with the "Mingrelian Affair." Beriia, however, managed to get him released and appointed Georgia Minister of State Control in April 1952. Lt. General N.M. Rukhadze had served in Georgia OGPU/NKVD during 1927–1937 before working for a year in the Adzharia Party organization. He returned to NKVD in 1938 and may have been head of the NKVD Investigation Department in Georgia. He served with the SMERSH during the war and was involved in intrigues against the military, particularly the hapless Lt. General D.T. Kozlov, Commander of the Caucasus and Transcaucasus Fronts. In 1944, Rukhadze was promoted to Maj. General. As mentioned before, in 1948, he replaced Rapava as head of MGB in Georgia. He was deeply involved in the "Mingrelian Affair" and arrested some of Beriia's minions in Georgia.[39] In December 1952, Beriia, however, managed to replace Rukhadze with A.I. Kochavashvili and had him arrested soon after Stalin's death. The next defendant, A.S. Khazani, also had some impressive credentials. In 1938, under the pseudonym "Aleksandrov," he had authored *The Moral Outlook of a Soviet Man* while serving in the NKVD Georgia Secret Political Department.[39] K.S. Savitskii had served in 1938 in NKVD Georgia Special Department. S.N. Nadaraia was Beriia's Adjutant and his Chief Procurer. G.G. Paramonov, an old NKVD investigator in Georgia and reportedly an illiterate, had once been tricked by a prankster and ordered the arrest of Sakinadze, Georgia's national poet, who had lived in the 17th century. The last defendant, Sh.O. Tsereteli, was another Beriia colleague with less-than-clean hands. He had been a Tsarist officer and winner of the George Cross. He later became a member of the Georgian Legion sponsored by the Germans and Turks to advance their interests in the Caucasus during World War I. Despite and perhaps because of such a checkered past, he had no difficulty in joining Beriia. According to Beriia's son, when his father was temporarily arrested in November 1922, Tsereteli tried to arrange for his escape but was turned down by Beriia. As head of NKVD in Georgia during the war, he took an important part in deportations. His post-war career is not clear. He had been variously identified as Beriia's candidate as head of the bodyguards and also in 1952 as Deputy Minister of MGB in Georgia.[41] According to Beriia's testimony during his trial, he also once considered appointing Tsereteli as a member of Sudoplatov's terror group. The charges in the trial held in Tbilisi in November 1955 mainly involved crimes that had been committed against those who had opposed Beriia in the byzantine politics of Georgia. Savitskii, for instance, was accused of having organized the arrest of E. Bediiu; and Paramonov for the murder of a personal enemy, one G. Zelents, who in 1937 had been the Head of the Cartography Department in NKVD Georgia.[42]

N.A. Krimian's career with the secret police in Georgia went back to 1932, when he had served as an Investigator. In 1939 he had been head of NKVD in West Ukraine and was responsible for the deportations and mass terror that characterized the Soviet occupation. Krimian, a particularly repulsive figure, was instrumental in the execution of nearly 12,000 prisoners in L'vov in the early days of the war by the NKVD rearguard.

Nothing, of course, was said during the trial of the significant roles played by several defendants in the war time deportation, although after conviction they lost their medals. Krimian, Khazani, Rapava, Rukhadze, Savitskii and Tsereteli were sentenced to death. Paranomov was sentenced to 25 years and Nadaraia to 10 years in prison.

The last major trial involving the former secret police officials took place in Baku from April 12 to April 26, 1956. The Military Collegium was chaired by Lt. General of Judiciary A.A. Cheptsov, already discussed in connection with the cases against Jewish intellectuals and General K.F. Telegin. He was joined by A.A.

Kostremin, who had served in the Tbilisi trial and G.E. Kovalenko. The defendants were M.D.A. Bagirov, Head of Cheka/GPU in Azerbaidzhan during 1920-1930, who gave Beriia his start. Later he had served as Chairman of the Azerbaidzhan Council of Commissars. Starting in 1933 he had been the First Secretary of the Azerbaidzhan Party for 20 years (1933-1953), surely a record during Stalin's rule. In May 1939, to ingratiate himself with Stalin, Bagirov suggested in a meeting chaired by Molotov that the private plots, the most productive part of the Soviet agriculture, be nationalized, an idea that Stalin took under advisement. After Stalin's death, Bagirov became Chairman of the Azerbaidzhan Council of Ministers until his removal after Beriia's arrest. He had been a full member of the Central Committee since 1939 and a candidate member of the Party Presidium after Stalin's death. Bagirov had first appeared on the national scene on January 17, 1938, when, as a Deputy to the First Supreme Soviet, he led the assault on V.N. Krylenko, the doomed Commissar of Justice, accusing him of spending time on mountain climbing and playing chess rather than in dispensing Stalinist Justice.[43] Krylenko, as the RSFSR prosecutor, had taken part in the show trials of the 1920s, running roughshod over truth and justice in the Tactical Center, Right SR, Shakhty, Independent Party, Menshevik, and other trials. His epitaph, that execution of the innocent will impress the masses even more than the killing of the guilty, epitomized what passed as justice under Stalin.

Few members of the First Supreme Soviet survived to see another virtuoso performance (most impressive for someone whose native language was not Russian) by Bagirov in early July 1953, this time before the Central Committee after Beriia's fall. Bagirov called Beriia "a chameleon, a most evil enemy of the Party and our People," a Mussavat spy, and so cunning that Bagirov, who pleaded "excessive gullibility," had failed to see through him. Bagirov added that he had been in Beriia's house only once, accompanied by Comrade Stalin. Unfortunately on this occasion, Bagirov was the defendant and his attempts to distance himself from Beriia failed to impress the skeptical comrades who were challenging him from the floor—a most ominous sign. As a man who had jump-started Beriia's career and later served as a loyal henchman, Bagirov's chances of survival was no better than Krylenko's back in 1938.[44] Bagirov, already under arrest, was expelled from the Party on March 13, 1954. Obscure co-defendants were fellow Azeri A.S. O.I. Atakshiev (Head of MVD in Azerbaidzhan 1950-1953); the Armenians Maj. General Kh.L. Grigor'ian (until 1947 a high-ranking NKVD and MGB official in Azerbaidzhan, Minister MVD Armenian SSR, 1947-1953), Lt. General R.A. Markar'ian (in the 1930s a high-ranking official in the Azerbaidzhan NKVD, Commissar/Minister NKVD/MVD Dagestan 1943-1953); and the Slavs Lt. General T.M. Borshchev (Deputy Head NKVD Azerbaidzhan 1937-1938, then Head of NKVD/MGB in Turkmen SSR and Sverdlovsk) and Maj. General S.F. Emel'ianov (Commissar NKVD Azerbaidzhan 1939-1941, Commissar/Minister NKVD/MGB Azerbaidzhan 1943-1953). The charges were mainly about helping Beriia and eliminating his local enemies. Emel'ianov and Atakishev were sentenced to 25 years; the rest were shot on May 7, 1956.

At times, the trials bordered on the absurd, even soap opera. Beriia was accused of having been treated for syphilis during the war and stashing away nearly 300,000 rubles in his son's safe as well as using the royal "we" when giving orders.[45] Beriia, Kobulov, Krimian, and Savitskii were accused of having organized the killing of L.I. Kartvelishvili, Secretary of the Transcaucasus Party Organization in the early 1930s, who had turned down Stalin's suggestion that Beriia serve as the Second Secretary by saying, "I will not work with this charlatan." After this, Kartvelishvili held a number of important Party positions including in the Far East. His arrest took place on February 22, 1937, at the height of Ezhov's power, when Beriia himself was in danger. His execution on August 22, 1938, was again before Beriia became the NKVD Commissar. A man of Kartvelishvili's stature could have only been arrested and executed by Stalin's order.[46] No one can, however, argue that the defendants in these trials did not deserve the harsh sentences, but in a system as politicized as that of the Soviet Union, justice is only an incidental by-product. The main purpose of the trials was to signal that the era of rampant terror was over and those in authority would have to abide by certain rules. In this sense, the trials were successful. There were no more to be forced public confessions and lawless executions of those politically out of favor.

In reality, there was a major difference between Stalin and those who came after him. Swift said that you can take anyone's innocent letter and prove that it conceals a deep political conspiracy. This was the core belief of the Stalinist police state, and its truly evil nature lay not so much in its harsh treatment of dissenters and potential enemies (few in positions of power anywhere are tolerant of those who try to undermine their authority), but the persecution of millions of innocent, law-abiding, and even patriotic citizens.

The post-Stalin change also characterized the operations of security organs. There were few sins committed by the modern KGB, at least in the international arena, such as espionage, sabotage, terror, and disinformation, that were not also practiced by its counterparts elsewhere, including those in democratic countries.

In the 1980s, a new dogma, however, swept over Western thinking about the Soviet Union. The corrupt, inept, comatose, and increasingly irrelevant regimes that had succeeded Khrushchev were now exposed as Stalinist clones and the geriatric apparatchiks as potential Genghis Khans. Even Gorbachev was dismissed as another mailed fist in the velvet glove. The idea that a Disraeli, or Bismarck, or even Alexander II might emerge from the Soviet Union was dismissed out of hand. The Soviet Union was the first regime in history to be immutable. Under this assumption, had Julius Caesar been a Marxist-Leninist, we all still would be living under Pax Romana. The proponents of this theory advocated their own version of "liberation theology" and included the ideologues of the Reagan administration, most of whom had sat out the crusade in Vietnam engaged in graduate seminar firefights, neo-conservatives disillusioned with their leftist past, understandably bitter dissidents such as A.M. Nekrich and V.K. Bukovskii, and defectors who were willing to say anything to please the new masters. In Europe, their foremost spokesman, the French *philosophe* Jean-François Revel, prophesied the imminent collapse of *the West*. Only the plotters of the abortive coup of August 1991 were perhaps more disappointed at the Soviet collapse than those in the anti-evil empire coalition. Fighting the various neuroses that make up what passes as the Left in the West is simply not the same as manning the ideological barricades against the barbarians. They, however, continue to be vociferous in their claims that it was their hard-nosed policies that led to the collapse of Communism, but are less sanguine of what has replaced the evil empire. Equally ironic is the partial recovery of the former Communists assigned not so long ago to the dustbin of history. They have discovered nearly 50 years too late that they did not need terror and the bayonets of the Red Army to take over the machinery of state. The same results could be reached by practicing the politics of envy and by transferring resources from productive to parasitic, and the time-honored formulas that masquerade under such terms as "compassion" and "social justice" continue to revive the Left despite premature predictions of its demise.

Modern states survive by providing bread and circuses for the masses. The Noble Experiment of Communism, despite the Soviet Union's massive resources, failed miserably to accomplish the former, and over the years the circus began to wear thin. Without the heavy hand of Stalin and with the revolution in telecommunications, it became obvious even to the long-suffering Soviet masses that the emperor was naked indeed. The revolutionaries, as Thomas Sowell has so aptly said, have a tendency to become hustlers. Terror under Stalin, mendacity, and demagoguery under his successors tempered by ineptitude could not stave off the death of Communism, and it was only a matter of time for the entire house of cards to collapse. At the end, the Soviet Union was a greater threat to itself than anyone else.

On the opposite side from the crusaders, there were those who were predicting the imminent conversion of the former Soviet Union into a new Switzerland, forgetting that the only constant factor in Russian history had been chaos accompanied by, or followed by, repression. The fact remains that not a single expert, regardless of ideology, predicted any of the events that have rocked Russia in the last several years. The truth is that attempts to predict the future, whether by academic intuition, biblical prophecies, computer models, or the reading of tea leaves, all very much in vogue, are bound to fail because as Trevelyan put it, an event is itself nothing but a set of circumstances, none of which will ever recur. It is the height of folly to predict who and what ideology will rule Russia, but as Count Vitte, taking a page from Dr. Johnson said, the miracle is not that Russia is badly governed, but that she is governed at all. We can be reasonably sure that Russia will continue to be misgoverned, and here she has on her side the historical tradition as well as the company of most of the world. "Sovietology" also proved to be, like other social "sciences," an exercise in academic delusion good only for getting grants and tenure.

NOTES

1. *Beriia: Konets Kar'ery*, p. 405.
2. Emiot, Israel: *The Birobidzhan Affair*, p. 27; Beriia, *Konets Kar'ery* (op. cit.), p. 340.

3. Kosliarov, K.A. (op. cit.), pp. 42–50.

4 Ibid., p. 50.

5. Andrew, Christopher and Oleg Gordievsky (op. cit.), p. 420.

6. Kostliarov, K.A. (op. cit.), pp. 51–52.

7. *Leningradskoe Delo* (op. cit.), p. 404.

8. *Beriia: Konets Kar'ery* (op. cit.), p. 402.

9. *Izvestiia TsK KPSS* (1/1991).

10. *Beriia: Konets Kar'ery* (op. cit.), p. 409.

11. *Izvestiia TsK KPSS* (1/1991).

12. Adam Ulam, *The Communists,* p. 110; *Beriia: Konets Kar'ery*, p. 192.

13. Abarinov, *Katynskii Labirint*, p. 184.

14. *Journal of Soviet Military Studies* (6/1991), pp. 234–35.

15. *VIZH* (6-7/1992), p. 19.

16. *Beriia: Konets Kar'ery*, p. 399.

17. Ibid., p. 256.

18. Danny Smith, *Wallenberg: Lost Hero*, p. 189.

19. Kostliarov, *Golgofa*, p. 56.

20. The most detailed account of Beriia's trial is in a series of articles in 1989, 1990, and 1991 in *VIZH*; *Izvestiia TsK KPSS* (1 and 2/1991); and *Beriia: Konets Kar'ery*.

21. *Pravda* (April 10, 1953).

22. Deriabin and Gibney, *The Secret World*, p. 166.

23. Kostliarov, *Golgofa*, pp. 26–27.

24. Markish, *The Lona Return*, p. 235.

25. Kostliarov, *Golgofa*, p. 25.

26. Ibid., p. 56.

27. Abarinov, *Katynskii Labirinth*, pp. 93–94.

28. Kostliarov, *Golgofa*, p. 28.

29. Ibid., p. 80.

30. Kostliarov, *Golgofa*, pp. 64, 70; F. Burlatsky, *Khrushchev and the First Russian Spring*, p. 12.

31. *Leningradskoe Delo*, p. 9.

32. Kostliarov, *Golgofa*, p. 37.

33. Ibid., p. 69.

34. Ibid., p. 64.

35. *Sovetskaia Militsiia* (4/1991), pp. 54–62.

36. Kostliarov, *Golgofa*, p. 69.

37. Ibid., p. 73.

38. Kostliarov, *Golgofa*, pp. 14–18, 47, 65–66. For Shvartsman, see also *Nedelia* (20 and 44/1990).

39. For Rukhadze, see *Izvestiia TsK KPSS* (1/1991) and *Zvezda* (2/1989).

40. For Khazani, see *VIZH* (7/1989).

41. *Beriia: Konets Kar'ery*, p. 389.

42. For Savitskii, see *VIZH* (7/1989).

43. Vaksberg, p. 135.

44. For Bagirov, see *VIZH* (7/1989).

45. *Beriia: Konets Kar'ery*, pp. 385–90.

46. Ibid., p. 273.

Chapter 13

Legacy

On May 7, 1940, by the order of the Presidium of the USSR Supreme Soviet, the rank of "General" was introduced to the Red Army and on June 4, 1940, the decree of the USSR Council of People's Commissars awarded ranks to 982 Generals and 74 Admirals. The men thus honored were the survivors of the greatest disaster to befall the High Command of any modern Army, the purges of the 1930s. The suspicion of the military ran deep among the Bolsheviks. It is estimated that during 1929–1936, nearly 3,000 military specialists were arrested, mostly under Iagoda, who headed the OGPU/NKVD from May 1934 until August 1936, when he was replaced by Ezhov. Most of the victims were former Tsarist officers who had switched sides and, according to the study by A.G. Kavtaradze, had made major contributions to the Red Army. The better-known include such senior officers as V.S. Mikhailov (who was shot), I.I. Seliverstov, G.N. Leitsikhovich, V.V. Vitkovskii, E.I. Martinov, A.E. Snesarev, N.E. Kakurin, and the best-known of the group, military theoretician A.A. Svechin, whose downfall was to a certain extent engineered by Tukhachevskii. These early purges have yet to be studied in detail. During this holocaust of the Great Purge, nearly 44,000 Commanders were arrested, including 80% of higher Commanders and 50% of senior Commanders. Between February 27, 1937, and November 12, 1938, Stalin, Molotov and Kaganovich sanctioned the execution of 38,679 officers.[1] Three out of five Marshals of the Soviet Union, 13 out of 15 Army Commanders, 57 out of 85 Corps Commanders, 110 out of 195 Division Commanders and 220 out of 406 Brigade Commanders were arrested. During 1935–1939, of 837 officers holding ranks above Colonel (Kombrig, Komdiv, Komkor, Komandarm 1 and 2, and Marshal of the Soviet Union), 720 were purged.[2] From the 85 members of the Main Military Soviet which was formed in February 1936 and which included the best minds of the Red Army, 68 were arrested and two committed suicide. Of 108 members of the new Military Soviet formed in November 1938, only ten were former members. In 1935, 6,198 officers (4.9%); in 1936, 5,677 (4.2%); in 1937, 18,658 (13.1%); in 1938, 16,362 (9.2%); and in 1939, 1878 (0.7%) in the Red Army (not including the Navy and the Air Force) were shot. During the period May 1937–September 1938, more than 35,000 officers were shot and another 95,000 were arrested. According to the latest Russian documents (*VIZH*, 1/1993), in 1937, 20,643 officers holding command positions were expelled and 5,811 of them were arrested; in 1938, the corresponding figures were 16,118 and 5,057. In the first ten months of 1937, seven Military District Commanders, 12 Deputy District Commanders, twenty Commanders of Corps, 36 Commanders of Divisions, and four heads of military academies were arrested. By April 1963, of the 657 Senior Commanders, 553, or 84%, were found innocent by various Soviet government agencies and were rehabilitated. According to the collection *Oni ne Molchali*, during the period 1937–1939, an average of 1,827 letters a day were sent to Voroshilov by arrested officers and their families and during 1937–1940, three-quarters-of-a-million such letters were received. In 1937, there were 782 cases of suicide among the officers in the Soviet Armed Forces. In 1938, there were 832 cases in the Red Army alone. About 27.5% of these officers were Party members. Some of the better-known victims include Army Commissar 1 Rank Ia.B. Gamarnik, Head of the Political Administration of the Red Army; Army Commissar 2 Rank A.S. Grishin; Komkors I.I. Gar'kavyi, E.I. Goriahev, A.Ia. Lapin, and S.A. Mezheninov; Komdiv Levenzon (V.I. Levenson?); Division Commissar G.F. Nevraev; Brigade Commissar S.T. Solomko; and perhaps Komandarm 2 Rank P.E. Dybenko, the first Commander in Chief of the Soviet Navy, and later Commander of Military Districts of Central Asia, Volga, Siberia and Leningrad, who is officially listed as being shot on July 29, 1938. During the purge, all Commanders of Military Districts were replaced, as were their Deputies and Chiefs of Staff. Of corps commanders 88.4% were replaced as well as 100% of their Deputies and Assistants. Also replaced were 98.5% of Division and Brigade Commanders, 79% of Regiment Commanders, 88% of Regimental Chiefs of Staff, and 87% of Battalion Commanders. In 1939, 85% of the officers in the Red Army were under 35. In June 1941, only 7% of the commanding officers had higher military education (12% of the officers had no military education at all) and more than 70% had held their command for less than a year. A study by the author (*Military Affairs*, April, 1983) shows thatt the start of the war, the average age of Soviet mechanized Corps Commanders was 41, 12 years younger than their German counterparts who commanded the smaller Panzer Divisions, and in fact, only 1.4% of the Red Army officers were over 45. It was with these men that Stalin had to face the tough and experienced Wehrmacht.[3] After the Great Purge, with the exception of B.M. Shaposhnikov, the top Command of the Red Army (Voroshilov, Kulik, Budennyi, and Mekhlis) were thoroughly mediocre. As Marshal Budennyi told fellow Cavalryist O.I. Govordnikov, "We needn't worry; they only arrest the smart ones." Budennyi was not completely accurate since he came close to losing his own head on more than one occasion.

In August 1938 with Ezhov on his way out, the Council of People's Commissars set up a commission to look into the fate of 30,000 officers who had been expelled and on May 1, 1939, 12,461 were restored to rank.[4]

With the introduction of the "General" rank, the Red Army, representing a supposedly classless society, was to have the most complicated ranking system of any modern army. The rank of "Army General," which had not even existed in the Tsarist Army, was now added. This should not have been a surprise in view of the maniacal ceremoniousness attached to titles in the Soviet Union. Also compounding the confusion were a number of senior officers who, because of suspect pasts or lack of education, continued to hold on to the pre-General ranks of "Komkor," "Komdiv," and "Kombrig." There were 114 "Lt. Generals" divided among "Combined Arms" (81), Aviation (13), Artillery (8), Tank (2), Signals (2), Engineers (1), and Quartermasters (1). Six men, P.A. Artem'ev, I.A. Bogdanov, I.I. Maslennikov, V.V. Osokin, G.G. Sokolov, and G.A Stepanov, were listed separately but were not otherwise identified. They were, of course, the NKVD Border Troops Commanders. For some reason, Border and Internal Troops Major Generals such as A.N. Apollonov, A.I. Gul'ev, I.S. Liubyi, V.A. Khomenko, M.P. Marchenkov, I. Petrov, and N.P. Nikol'skii were included among the "Combined Arms" Major Generals. This policy continued throughout the war, but some police officials such as Kruglov, who had served on the frontlines continued to have their state security "Commissar" ranks. During the war, the NKVD units, mainly former Border and Internal Troops, were formed, usually in Regiments, Brigades, and Divisions; at times they were commanded by regular Army officers, and fought in the ranks of the Red Army. They were known for their ferocity in combat, having learned shortly after the war that they were specially targeted by Hitler's Commissar Order. Unlike other Soviet units, whose performances were mixed, the NKVD Troops usually put up stiff resistance during the early days of the war. For instance, the 13 Border Troop Detachment of the Western District commanded by Hero of the Soviet Union Lt. A.V. Lopatin continued to resist for 11 days after its position was overrun by the enemy. Besides the NKVD units, Beriia also kept a large number in reserve, and his reluctance to help out the Red Army during the Battle of the Caucasus was one of the charges against him during his trial.

One entire army, the 70th, was formed from the former NKVD Border and Internal Units in October 1942. It first saw combat in mid-February 1943 on the Central Front and was commanded by G.F. Tarasov (October 1942–March 1943), I.V. Galanin (April 1943–September 1943), V.M. Sharapov (September 1943–October 1943), I.F. Nikolaev (January 1944–March 1944), A.I. Ryzhov (March 1944–May 1944), and V.S. Popov (May 1944–May 1945). Not all of them were NKVD Generals. The 70 Army took part in the Battles of Kursk, Belorussia, and East Prussia. During the Battle of Berlin, it was attached to the 2 Belorussian Front. The best-known of NKVD Generals during the war were I.I. Maslennikov, whom we will discuss later, and V.A. Khomenko, who before the war had commanded the Border Troops in Leningrad, Moldavia, and I,n the Ukraine. During the war, Khomenko commanded the 30, 24, 58 and 44 Armies. On October 28 or 29, 1943, he was ambushed near Nikolopol behind the enemy lines. Besides Khomenko, at least four other high-ranking Border Troop Generals were lost during the war. Lt. General I.A. Bogdanov died of wounds on July 19, 1942, while holding the lowly (for a Lt. General) post of

Deputy Commander of 39 Army, Kalinin Front. Bogdanov had the distinction of having commanded from July 14, 1941, to July 29, 1941, something called the "Front Reserve Army," a designation that was used only once during the war. Bogdonov's boss, Lt. General G.G. Sokolov (1904–1973), Head of Border Troops and Deputy Commissar of NKVD from March 1939 and Commander of NKVD Rear Security for the West Front after the first month of the war, briefly (December 25, 1941, to January 10, 1942) served as Commander of the ill-fated 2 Assault Army. Maj. General K.I. Rakutin, who had served in Cheka and Border Troops since 1920, was in 1941 Head of the Border Troops, Baltic District, and then Head of NKVD Rear Security, Northwest Front. In July 1941, he commanded the 31 Army West Front for two weeks before taking over the 24 Reserve Army in the same Front. According to Volkogonov, Rakutin had ordered the execution of hundreds of deserters, driving one observer, the writer V.P. Stavskii (Secretary of the Soviet Writer's Union), to protest to Stalin. On September 4, 1941, Zhukov had a heated conversation with Rakutin in which he accused him of incompetence and lying. Ratukin fell on October 9, 1941, but Stalin suspected him of desertion. Regardless, in 1990, in the middle of glasnost, this butcher became a posthumous Hero of the Soviet Union. Maj. General L.I. Kotel'nikov, Commander of the 1 Moscow Militia Rifle Division, went missing in action in July 1941. Maj. General G.F. Tarasov, another former Commander of the 70 (NKVD) Army (October 1942–March 1943), served as commander of the 53 Army 2 Ukraine Front December 1943–January 1944 but was demoted to Deputy Commander under I.V. Galinin and I.M. Managarov. He was killed in action on October 19, 1944, near Kisui-Sallesh, Hungary. NKVD Maj. General (November 27, 1942) A.A. Onufriev, Commander of 38 Guard Rifle Division, Southwest Front, was killed in action on February 25, 1943.

During 1944–45, the rank of General was given to a number of SMERSH functionaries such as Meshik and Tsanava, and on July 7, 1945, it was approved for all NKVD/NKGB officials regardless of their function. Besides Beriia, who received the rank of Marshal of the Soviet Union, and Merkulov, who received that of Army General, there were 7 Colonel Generals, 51 Lt. Generals, and 143 Major Generals.[5] All in all, along with SMERSH and a few "specialist" Generals (e.g., V.M. Bochkov, who was now a Lt. General of Judiciary) who had been promoted earlier, there were some 250 men who, along with the more junior officials such as Leonov, Komarov, Likhachev, and Riumin, provided the leadership for repression during the post-war years. They were relatively young (Beriia was 46, Merkulov and Kruglov 45, Serov 40, and Abakumov only 37). A handful had held high positions under Ezhov, but somehow had also made it into the Beriia era. They were overwhelmingly Slav. Only the Georgians, for obvious reasons, were overrepresented. Jews, once prominent in the security apparatus, were conspicuous by their near-absence. Only 13 have been definitely identified as Jewish: I.Ia. Babich, N.A. Frenkel', S.R. Mil'shtein, L.F. Raikhman, G.S. Bolotin-Belianyi (Baliasnyi), L.I. Eitingon, V.N. Gul'st, I.I. Il'iushin-Edelman, M.L. Michurin-Raver, A.I. Gertovskii, A.A. Vurgraft, M.I. Sladkevich, and M.I. Belkin.[6] Frankel' and Vurgraft had their ranks in other services (Engineering-Technical Services and Quartermasters), but they were employed for a major part of their careers by NKVD. In *Beriia, Stalin's First Lieutenant*, Amy Knight adds Iu.D. Sumbatov-Topuridze to this group, but this is unlikely because of his high position in the Muslim Azerbaidzhan as well as the fact that he was left untouched by the anti-Semitic campaigns. Most of the Jewish Chekists had risen in rank during the Beriia years although there were also some hard-nosed survivors from the Ezhov era. There are some questions about the nationality of A.I. Langfang, L.E. Vlodzimirskii, S.E. Belolipetskii, and even Beriia.

The secret police Generals owed their ranks and positions to just about every imaginable crime, including genocide, mass deportations, assassinations, use of torture, and indiscriminate use of terror. We have already discussed some of the specific crimes in which this group was involved. One Soviet source *(Argumeny i Fakty*, May 1989) also claims that during 1946–1953 1.5 million people were arrested by the organs, a figure which has yet to be officially confirmed. It is ironic that at the time that the secret police officials were being honored in the Soviet Union, their counterparts on the losing side were being prosecuted for the very same crimes. The wrongdoings of those facing the international tribunal in Nuremberg and catalogued by such Soviet writers as Boris Polevoi are equally represented by Stalin and those who served under him who just happened to be on the winning side.[7]

A.I. Langfang, whose career is covered in Vaksberg's *Neraskrytye Tainy* was typical of these men. Langfang had a third-grade education, and had joined the Party at age 18, and later the Red Army, where he had served in his division's tribunal. Using references from a number of contacts, including the sister of A.I. Rykov, he had entered the GPU. Under Ezhov, he became a specialist on the Comintern and helped decimate its leadership. In the 1940s Lanfang was the head of 4 section MGB 2 Department assigned to Sinkiang. He survived a suicide attempt in June 1946, but was imprisoned under Khrushchev.

Unlike their Ezhovite predecessors, most of the post-war leaders of security and public organizations survived the Stalin years. In fact, there is reason to believe that only one man, P.N. Kubatkin, Head of MGB in Leningrad, was shot during Stalin's life. On July 21, 1949, Abakumov informed Stalin that Ia. F. Kapustin, Second Party Secretary, was a British agent, and Kubatkin, Head of MGB in Leningrad, had destroyed the incriminating evidence. Two days later, Stalin ordered the arrest of Kubatkin.[8] Kubatkin was probably the only senior secret police official to be shot during Abakumov's rule, although there are rumors about the arrest of Maj. General M.A. Andreev in 1947; he was later released.

During the post-war period while Stalin was still living, the arrested generals included Abakumov, Vlasik, Rapava, Rukhadze, and Kuz'michev, as well as a number of senior Jewish Chekists such as L.F. Raikhman, Eitingon, and Shvartsman. All of these men, as well as M.I. Zhuravlev, who was dismissed in 1946, survived the dictator. Service under Beriia, Abakumov, Kruglov, and Ignat'ev was considerably safer than under Iagoda and Ezhov. To study those who survived the post-Beriia shake-up, we should start with S.D. Igant'ev, the only Stalinist secret police chief to die a natural death. His early career seems obscure. Pierre de Villemarest claims that he had been a member of the Mekhlis-Frinovskii team that swept the High

Command in the Far East in 1938, but this is not confirmed elsewhere. In 1939, he was, however, identified as a member of the Party Central Revision Committee and during the war as the Regional Party Secretary in Bashkir ASSR. After the war, he was the Second Party Secretary in Belorussia and later Chairman of the Party Central Committee in Uzbek SSR. In 1948, he received the Order of Lenin. On August 23, 1951, he became the Minister of MGB and in 1952 a member of the CC CPSU and later its secretary. Finally, he became a member of the Party Presidium. He turned out to be the most ineffectual of Stalin's secret police chiefs, although Glasnost documents show that he was not as innocent of crimes as he is portrayed in Khrushchev's self-serving memoirs. Khrushchev also claims that Igant'ev was bullied continuously by Stalin and in fact suffered a near-fatal heart attack. As discussed before, Igant'ev played a role in the "Doctors' Plot" and "Mingrelian Affair," in the persecution of Jews, and in the arrest of Marshal of Artillery N.D. Iakovlev and his colleagues. He also, in contrast to Abakumov, had a more positive attitude toward individual acts of terrorism. He failed in organizing Tito's assassination but had better luck in some other operations. Despite this, Sudoplatov found Igant'ev a polite but insufferable bureaucrat and grossly incompetent, even worse than Ezhov, but then Sudoplatov blamed the terror not on the Stalinist system, but rather on the amateurs and Party hacks who interfered with the work of professional Chekists such as he. Sudoplatov's low opinion of Igant'ev is shared by Beriia's son, who even accuses him, with little justifiction, of having been behind the "Leningrad Affair." Igant'ev, however, played a part in the "Mingrelian Affair" aimed at Beriia's supporters, and this could explain the hostility of Beriia, his family, and supporters. After Stalin's death, Beriia, of course, replaced Igant'ev as Head of the Secret Police, but the latter managed to be elected as a candidate member to the Presidium's Secretariat, along with L.I. Brezhnev.

The Secretariat had been enlarged from five to ten people and now also included A.B. Aristov, N.A. Mikhailov, and P.K. Ponomarenko as full members. The respite for Igant'ev did not last long. On April 14, 1953, when Beriia announced that the "Doctors' Plot" had been a fabrication, Igant'ev was accused of political blindness and negligence. These were serious charges, but not as fatal as being a "criminal adventurer," which was hurled at Riumin, who was now the designated fall guy for Stalin's heirs. In April 1953, Ignat'ev was also removed as the CC CPSU Secretary and later from the Central Committee itself. Beriia's son claims that his father had every intention of having Igant'ev arrested. Beriia's own arrest, however, did not mean Igant'ev's return to favor. He was too tainted for that, but in December 1953, he became once again the Party Secretary in Bakshiria, where he stayed until 1957, when he received a similar post at Tataria. This lasted until October 1960. He was then assigned to the Supreme Soviet and its Mandate Commission. He got away with a mere slap on the wrist because of his relative passivity as head of the MGB and the fact that he was primarily a Party man. The deplorable part that he played during the "Doctors' Plot" must be balanced with the "Mingrelian Affair," which, after all, had been organized against the discredited Beriia. Ignat'ev was also helped by the fact that his deputy, the monster Riumin, provided such a convenient scapegoat.

There is also a good possibility that during his tenure as Head of the MGB, Igant'ev provided information to Malenkov, Khrushchev, Beriia, and others about Stalin's plans. In 1957, Ignat'ev made a mini-comeback and was once again a member of the CC CPSU. He also won a second Order of Lenin. Rumors, probably spread as part of Western disinformation campaigns, portrayed Ignat'ev as a transvestite and bisexual who used the Gulag to satisfy his depraved habits. The problem is that the Gulag was controlled by Kruglov and not Igant'ev. Igant'ev died in 1976. One hopes that he wrote yet-to-be discovered memoirs.

Another man who was to suffer—at first a demotion—was Head of MVD, S.N. Kruglov. Born in 1907, Kruglov joined the Party in 1918. He worked in agriculture before joining the Red Army, which he left in November 1930. In 1931, he was a student in Karl Libknekht Institute for Industrial Training in Moscow, and during 1934–1935 studied in the Japanese sector of the Far East Institute before entering the Red Professors University. At the end of 1937, he began working for the Central Committee. In November 1938, he became the Central Committee's special representative to NKVD, even though he did not became a candidate member of CC CPSU until 1939 and a full member in 1952. He and I.A. Serov may have also belonged to Stalin's personal secretariat. The two were Party men appointed to high positions under Beriia, who were not part of his Caucasus mafia, although according to S.L. Beriia, his father had met Kruglov in the Caucasus during his service with the Central Committee and was highly impressed. When Beriia took over the NKVD, he asked for Kruglov. The latter was soon a member of the Committee chaired by A.A. Andreev to "reform" the NKVD. On February 29, 1939, Kruglov became Deputy Commissar of NKVD for Cadres; in that post he helped Beriia in purging and rebuilding the organs. Kruglov was involved in providing the personnel for Katyn; for this he received the Order of Red Banner on April 27, 1940. On February 25, 1941, he became the First Deputy Commissar of NKVD under Beriia. During August and September 1941, Kruglov, personally a brave man, was appointed Political Commissar of Reserve Front. This was a massive force of seven Armies deployed behind the West Front and fed piecemeal into the Wehrmacht meatgrinder. It was dissolved on October 1941, and its units divided among other fronts. Besides Kruglov, there is a possibility that one other Chekist, V.M. Bochkov, former Head of the Special Department and later Prosecutor General of the USSR, may have served for a few days in July 1941 as Political Commissar of a Front (Northwest). Beriia may have also held such a position in the Caucausus in 1943, but he was more likely the STAVKA representative. Unlike Kruglov, who is listed under his state security rank, Bochkov is listed as a "Maj. General." Only one Soviet document mentions this fact, which is completely omitted from the official histories as well as the biographies of Lt. General N.F. Vatutin, Chief of Staff and perhaps for a few days Acting Commander of the Northwest Front at this time.[9] Bochkov left after a few days. Bochkov's appointment here also has given rise to a claim that he later commanded the SMERSH in Northwest Front, when, in fact, this position was held by I.Ia. Babich, one of the most decorated police officers during the war, and winner of no less than four Orders of the Red Banner. (Babich died in December 9, 1948, and thus escaped the brunt of the anti-Semitic campaigns.)[10] Bochkov later took part in the cover-up of the Erlich-Alter case; however, by 1943 he was in disgrace, having botched the affair of the "Youth Terrorism Organization," a group allegedly formed by the children of purged officials. Bochkov ended his career in 1954 as head of the Kingir labor camps, where according to Solzhenitsyn in *The Gulag Archipelago* he helped put down a revolt by the inmates.

In October 1941, Kruglov took over the 4 Sapper Army engaged in building fortifications and also joined a committee chaired by Kaganovich (soon to be replaced by N.M. Shvernik) to organize the evacuation of threatened industries. It was here that A.N. Kosygin (the Deputy Chairman) made his mark. During the war, Kruglov continued as the First Deputy Commissar of NKVD. He was involved in the deportation of Karachis and possibly of Chechen-Ingush during 1943–1944; for this he received the Order of Suvorov 1 Grade on March 9, 1944. In May 1944, Kruglov was in Kazakh SSR supervising the settling of deportees from the North Caucasus, and he may have later headed a temporary NKVD Department for Deportations which after the war became the MVD Department for Special Settlements, headed by V.V. Shiian. Kruglov was Head of Security at the Tehran, Yalta, and Potsdam Conferences, but it is hard to detect him in pictures and newsreel films. This had as much to do with his height as with security requirements. Stalin preferred the company of short men and, in fact, it seems this was a requirement for membership in the Politburo (Suslov was perhaps the only exception) and would have been distinctly uncomfortable with a 6-foot, 6-inch Kruglov towering over him. For his services in Tehran, he was to become a Knight of the British Empire and the U.S. Legion of Merit, the only Chekist thus honored. In April–May 1945, Kruglov was in the U.S. during the U.N. San Francisco conference.

With the Red Army on the offensive, Kruglov's major responsibility was the pacification of the recaptured areas and with this in mind a new NKVD Department for Struggle against Bandits was formed in 1943–1944, headed by A.M. Leont'ev, veteran of "interceptor battalions" and war-time deportations. On July 3, 1945, Kruglov, B.Z.Kobulov (taking time off from pacification in Belorussia), A.N. Apollonov, I.M. Tkachenko, M.A. Suslov and Lithuanian Party leader A.Ia. Snechkus arrived in Vil'nius to organize the second Soviet takeover of Lithuania. Those who had not taken the precaution of escaping with the retreating Germans would be in for a hard time.

The "anti-bandit" campaigns were bloody affairs, but no worse than the Phoenix Program organized by the CIA to "decapitate" the Vietcong Cadres in South Vietnam. In a report to Stalin from Beriia (*Bugai Collection*, p. 180) dating from August 11, 1945, it was stated that from February 1944 until August 1, 1945, in Ukraine, 94,196 bandits were killed and 98,848 captured. Soviet losses were 2,181 killed, 2,605 wounded, and 330 missing.

In summer 1945, despite his high rank, Kruglov served as a common interrogator, questioning the 16 leaders of the Home Army who had been kidnapped by Vlodzimirskii's bloodhounds in Poland and taken to Moscow for trial. There are claims that in 1946, he gave archives related to former Russian politicians (Savinkov,

Alekseev, Brusilov, etc.) stolen from Prague to four people, including Stalinist historian I.I. Mints (*The Bibliographical Dictionary Of the Former Soviet Union*, p. 343) On January 1, 1946, Kruglov replaced Beriia as Head of NKVD (renamed MVD on March 18, 1946). *The Bugai Collection* (p. 191) contains a strange document dating from *March 26, 1945* addressed to *USSR People's Commissar of Interior* Beriia from *Minister of Interior* S.N. Kruglov, which shows both men basically holding the same job, but with two different titles, perhaps an indication that at least for a period, the titles of "People's Commissar" and "Minister" were both used. It seems that as the Head of MVD, Kruglov continued to have cordial relations with Beriia, occasionally sending reports to him and no one else. Kruglov may have also been a member of the committee that organized the production of the Soviet atomic bomb. In 1950, Kruglov set up a prison for the use of the Party Control Commission to examine the prisoners who had served their terms and prevent the release of those still deemed dangerous. According to N.P. Dudorov, head of MVD 1956–1960 (*Komsomol'skaia Pravda*, 2/1990), in the "special prisons" similar to those used during the Inquisition, political prisoners could also be questioned by members of the Politburo. Dudorov's unpublished memoirs, and further research by Maj. General V. Nekrasov (*Sovetskaia Militsiia*, 6/1990), is based on the interrogation of Malenkov's former secretary, D.N. Sukhanov, arrested on May 14, 1956. Dudorov's report to the Central Committee on June 23, 1956 dates the "special prisons" from March 4, 1950. The organizers included Central Committee officials Zakharov, Shestakov, Nikiforov, and the MVD official Kleimenov. The prisons allegedly were headed by I.A. Serov and those who were kept there included those who had been arrested in connection with the "Leningrad Affair." This obviously could not have been done without Stalin's knowledge.

Also ending up in this prison was the shadowy figure of P. Fedoseev, Vlasik's assistant as head of Stalin's personal security. Fedoseev's name sometimes appeared in official pronouncements (e.g., the obituary of A.S. Shcherbakov in *Pravda*, May 10, 1945) without identification of position or rank. Once when Fedoseev was delivering the mail, Stalin caught him in his inner office, and, suspecting espionage, ordered his arrest. From the "special prison" Fedoseev would write to Stalin expressing his loyalty. Stalin subsequently ordered Malenkov to interrogate Fedoseev. Two days later, he was shot.

Kruglov was a perfect Stalinist bureaucrat and had no trouble in carrying out Stalin's order to increase the size of the Gulag, which had been reduced during the war because of the need for cannon fodder. Under Kruglov, as it had been the case under Beriia, the MVD was the country's biggest economic enterprise employing the largest labor force involved in construction, mining, industrial and energy production, and scientific researh. Russian publications, such as *Noril'skii Memorial* and *Volia* provide evidence of complicity of Kruglov, and to a lesser extent of Abakumov, in providing slave labor for the construction of the Noril'sk industrial combine during the post-war years. In February 1948, Kruglov joined Abakumov in proposing the establishment of new camps for those deemed particularly dangerous to the Stalinist state.

The total population of the Gulag remains a controversial subject and has been studied during the Glasnost years by, among others, the Russian writers A.N. Dugin, V.N. Zemskov, V.F. Nekrasov, Iu.A. Poliakov, I.N. Kiselev, V.B. Zhiromskaia, I. Ivashov, and A. Emelin, whose research has been published in such journals as *Sotsial'no-Politicheskie Nauki, Istoriia SSSR, Rodina, Na Boevom Postu, Sotsiologiskie Issledovaniia,* and *Krasnaia Zvezda.* In the West, Edwin Bacon, Robert Conquest, Alec Nove, and others have contributed to the debate, usually in the journal *Soviet Studies.* Others involved in this debate include Vera Tolz in various issues of *REE/RL Reports* and J.A. Getty, G. Rittesporn and V.N. Zemskov in the October 1993 issue of *American Historical Review.* In 1955, the Gulag archives contained more than 11 million files containing the names of 9.5 million individuals. On January 1, 1948, Kruglov reported to Stalin that there were 2,199,535 prisoners in camps and 27 new camps had been built. In a report to N.P. Dudorov in September 1957 to head of MVD (*Bugai Collection*, p. 279), Colonel V. Novikov, Head of MVD 4 Special Branch, stated that at the start of the war, 977,110 individuals were under custody. This number, however, nearly tripled over the next 12 years to 2,760,471 by January 1, 1954 (1953?). Subsequently, 2,582,108 inmates were released. Incidentally, these relatively low figures are disputed by the Pamiat Society and by Col. N. Grashoven and Major M. Kirillin, officials of the Russian Federation Ministry of Security who claim that between 1935 and 1945 alone 18 million people were repressed and seven million were executed (*RFE/RL Research Reports*, No. 36–1989 and 18–1192). Getty and his colleagues claim that by 1940, among the population of the USSR the following percentages were in custody: Latvians (3.7), Lithuanians (3.2), Finns (1.9), Estonians (1.7), Koreans (1.3), Belorussians (.85), Russians (0.84), Ukrainians (0.65), and Jews (0.61). Latvians had contributed more than the other Balts to the Communist movement; under Stalinist logic that made them candidates for additional suffering.

According to the study by T.A. Sivokhina and M.R. Zezina, 41.2% of the Gulag population in 1947, 54.3% in 1948, and 38% in 1948 had been sent there for "counterrevolutionary activities," a general all-purpose charge that could cover just about everything. In a report to Stalin dated January 23, 1950, Kruglov stated that in the beginning of the year there were 2,550,275 prisoners in camps, 22.7% of them "counter-revolutionaries" and 366,489 serving more than 10 years. In 1949, Lt. General G.P. Dobrynin, head of MVD/Gulag, reported the presence of over half-a-million women in camps. Malenkov suggested (in honor of Stalin's 70th birthday) releasing those with children under seven since the cost of maintaining children in camps ran to 166 million rubles a year (an indication that the camps were certainly an economic burden). Stalin agreed to this, decreeing that those released should be employed as forced labor in their hometowns. He exempted those sentenced for counter-revolutionary activities from this "humanitarian" gesture. In a report to Khrushchev from Kruglov, Prosecutor General Rudenko and Minister of Justice K.P. Gorshenin dating February 1, 1954, it was stated that from 1921 to the present date the Gulag had received 3,777,380 inmates for counter-revolutionary activities. Regardless, during the period 1946–1953 under Kruglov's stewardship, the population increased from 1.7 million to 2.4 million or even 2.7 million. The highest population was reached during 1949–1950. At the end, over 1.2 million of the inmates were German POWs, but nearly every race, nationality and creed was represented.[11] A fellow camp prisoner of K.S. Karol observed correctly that camps were instruments of death and not production. They served only to destroy the inmates. You would have to see a brigade of men, no longer able to hold themselves upright, harried all day long, prodded with bayonets by convict guards of NKVD, who could have performed the same work in an hour. No free community, or even any penal system, however irrational, organizes production in this way.[12] The Rudenko/Kruglov report also stated that of the nearly 3.8 million who were arrested, 642,980 were sentenced to death, 2,369,220 were sentenced to up to 25 years in camps or prisons, and 765,180 were exiled. Only 877,000 were sentenced by courts and military tribunals, the rest, nearly three million, received their sentences in the hands of OGPU and NKVD troikas.

Stalin had every reason to be pleased with Col. General Kruglov. After Stalin's death, Beriia kept Kruglov as the First Deputy Minister MVD, and the latter played a game of wait-and-see during the jockeying for power.

On April 23, 1953, Kruglov arrested the former Lt. General of Aviation V.I. Stalin (March 24, 1920–March 19,1962). In a detailed report to Malenkov (*Iosif Stalin v Ob'iatiiakh Sem'i*) Kruglov accused V.I. Stalin of numerous crimes, mainly theft and corruption. On September 2, 1955, the USSR Military Collegium sentenced the junior Stalin to 8 years in prison.

After Beriia's arrest, for siding with the anti-Beriia conspirators, Kruglov was rewarded by being appointed as the Head of the still-combined MVD. In the early July 1953 meeting of the Central Committee after Beriia's fall, Kruglov called his former boss an inveterate, cunning, and dangerous enemy, a schemer, slanderer, instigator by trade, scoundrel, amoral to the very core, an accumulation of the greatest baseness and the greatest impudence. He further dissociated the old MVD, which he had been in charge of, from MGB and the combined MVD under Beriia, claiming for it a record as pure as driven snow (or at least slush) and led by honorable men such as Serov,Maslennikov, and presumably Kruglov, himself.

During his brief tenure as head of the combined MVD, Kruglov tried to ingratiate himself with those now in power by increasing the number of terror and sabotage operations in the West. On March 3, 1954 (some claim an earlier date), KGB was officially formed and was put under I.A. Serov. On January 31, 1956, Kruglov was replaced by N.P. Dudorov. Shortly before the 20 Party Congress, Kruglov came under the investigation of a Central Committee commission chaired by A.B. Aristov and was appointed as Deputy Minister of Electrical Construction. In August 1957, he was further demoted to Deputy Chairman of the Kirov economic-administration region. In July 1958, he was dismissed, allegedly for health reasons. In January 1960, the Central Committee expelled Kruglov, and his awards, except the KBE, were rescinded on April 4, 1962. Kruglov died in June 1977. In his biography of Khrushchev, Roi Medvedev claims that Kruglov committed suicide, a la Anna Karenina, when an investigation was launched into his war-time role in the deportations of Chechen-Ingush. In 1977, Stalin's crimes, however, were no longer subject of discussion in polite company, and the Brezhnev regime had no reason to remedy old grievances or punish the guilty. In the official version, Kruglov died accidentally when he was hit by a train, but S.L. Beriia, who, despite Kruglov's betrayal of his father, still holds a soft spot for him, suspects foul play. Circumstances surrounding the death of Kruglov, as well as a number of lesser luminaries, have yet to be cleared.

I.A. Serov, who, along with Kruglov, survived Beriia's fall, was born in 1905. According to rumor, his father was a prison official in Vologda, where political prisoners, including Stalin, had once been kept. Serov joined the Party in 1926 and in 1928 attended the artillery school in Leningrad and later the Frunze Academy. How this military man found his way to NKVD is not clear. There are rumors that he may have been a member of Stalin's personal secretariat. A defector document going back to 1964 claims that in May 1935, Stalin organized a "State Security Commission." Besides Stalin, Ezhov, Zhdanov, Shkiriatov, and Malenkov were members of this committee. The commission set up a "Political State-Security Department" made up of Ia. Sh Agranov (First Deputy Chairman, NKVD, shot in 1938), Malenkov, Poskrebyshev, Shkiriatov, Vyshinskii, and Serov. It was Serov's job to reorganize the executive arm of this organization and collect the mass information needed for launching the "Great Purge."[13] The problem with this claim is that Serov at this time was only 30 years old and a Party member for less than ten years. Glasnost documents have yet to shed light on this particular allegation. In 1938 Serov left the Frunze Academy for NKVD. In September 1939, Serov became the first Beriia-sanctioned head of NKVD in Ukraine, replacing the fallen A.I. Uspenskii. He helped Khrushchev in the recently occupied Western Ukraine and worked closely with the Gestapo in matters of mutual interest. Serov played a major, but as yet not completely revealed, part in the liquidation of the Polish POW officers from the Starobel'sk camp near Kharkov, probably providing the manpower for the actual liquidations. He was rewarded with the first of four Orders of Lenin. He was undoubtedly involved in deportations from the occupied areas of Poland and the Baltic, a subject that has yet to receive extensive coverage in Glasnost literature. According to Sudoplatov, during this period Serov became romantically involved with the Polish diva Wanda Bandrovska, whom he claimed he had recruited as an agent. When Bandrovska moved to Rumania and refused further intelligence work, the matter proved embarrassing to Serov and caused Beriia and Khrushchev to reprimand him. According to Beriia's son, in *Moi Otets*, Serov also had other clashes with Khrushchev (to whom according to rumor, he was related) during his service in Ukraine. This involved criminal activity on the part of Khrushchev's older son, Leonid, who was to die a hero's death during the war.

In 1941, Serov was the First Deputy Commissar of NKGB under Merkulov and became a Deputy Commissar of NKVD under Beriia in July 1941 after NKVD and NKGB were combined and held this position until 1947. In April 1941, Serov organized "Operation Windmill" (also called the "false foreign land affair") in the Far East, where Soviet citizens were sent across a false frontier to be arrested and turned in by agents masquerading as Japanese officials, only to be arrested on their return to the Soviet "side" and condemned to death for having joined the Japanese. The purpose of this entrapment campaign is not clear, perhaps to show that the organs were on the alert. According to Beriia's son, Serov was a highly educated man and knew Japanese. This may have partially explained his involvement in this operation. Just before the war, Serov, who was now identified as Commissar of State Security 3 Rank, organized the massive deportations from the Baltics. The text of his top secret order, published in 1954 by the House Select Committee to Investigate Communist Aggression and the Forced Incorporation of the Baltic States into the USSR, shows him as a man for whom the concept of mercy was meaningless. During the war, he also organized the deportations of Volga Germans and Chechen. For the latter he received the Order of Suvorov I Grade, the highest Soviet award for pure generalship. Soviet documents (*Izvestiia TsK KPSS*, 2/1990) show that in the beginning of the war, Serov was Beriia's candidate to coordinate the formation of partisan and sabotage units made up of NKVD personnel, a responsibility which he may have held only a short time. In October 1941, he was a member of a committee charged with destroying Moscow in case of a German breakthrough. In his letter to the Central Committee (*Iosif Stalin v Ob'iatiiakh Sem'i*) on January 19, 1959, Stalin's son refers to Serov as having served as the Political Commissar of the Air Force in 1942, a claim not encountered elsewhere, but not without foundation. M.N. Kozhevnikov, in his detailed study of the command and leadership in the Air Force during the war, fails to list the Political Commissar for the period August 8, 1942 to March 17, 1943. Serov could have easily been the man, at least for a part of this period. According to Beriia's son, Serov spent a considerable time in the Caucasus during the war, and both his father and Marshal Zhukov were much impressed by him; the latter asked for his transfer to his headquarters when he took over the command of the 1 Belorussian Front in November 1944. Serov played a major part in the pacification of areas of Poland liberated from the Nazis, where, according to Volkogonov, 27,010 people were arrested by NKVD between the summer of 1944 and October 1945.

There are gaps in Serov's post-war career. He definitely played a role in setting up a Communist government in Poland (sometimes using the name "S.P. Ivanov" of the 1 Belorussian Front) and had been implicated in setting up the Trojan horse PAX Party. On May 13, 1946, the Council of Ministers approved the formation of a committee to study the military use of rockets. Chaired by Malenkov, committee members included Serov, as well as D.F. Ustinov, I.G. Zubovich, N.D. Iakovlev, P.I. Kirpichnikov, A.I. Berg, P.N. Goremykin, and N.E. Nosovskii. As mentioned before, Serov was involved in the case against General K.F. Telegin and in the kidnapping of German scientists. On June 6, 1945, the Council of People's Commissars appointed Serov Deputy to Marshal Zhukov for Civil Administration in occupied areas of Germany, a position he held until November 1946. Serov's job in occupied Germany covered a myriad of responsibilities and included removing documents that could embarrass Stalin from German archives. There are rumors that he was given additional responsibilities when on June 16, 1945, Col. General N.E. Berzarin, the

First Commandant of Berlin, died in a mysterious car accident. He was involved in the search for Germany's nuclear energy secrets. On June 30, 1945, Beriia forwarded to Stalin a report written by Serov five days earlier in which he reported the results of investigations into the status of senior German officers held by Western allies. The text of this report (*VIZH*, June 1993) shows that Serov had working for him the veteran A.M. Korotkov, who had been involved during the war with the Rote Kapelle spy ring, and one Col. Potashov, identified as head of the Investigation Section of the NKGB Transport Department. Serov apparently was involved in negotiations with people in the Eisenhower headquarters, including Lt. General George Veazey Strong, Head of Intelligence (former Head of G2 in Joint Chiefs of Staff), and Eisenhower's Chief of Staff General Walter Bedell Smith.

As mentioned before, on April 15, 1945, the NKVD established under Serov its "Special Camp" programs located on the sites of former German concentration camps and he held this position until 1948 when the camps were incorporated into the Gulag. Serov may also have been involved with concentration camps set up in postwar Poland in which thousands of German civilians lost their lives. The Soviet occupation policy in Germany amounted to nothing short of looting, and Serov, along with N.A. Osetrov, Deputy Head of the NKVD Economic Department (later transferred to Beriia's Atomic Trust), were deeply involved in the illegal requisition of captured state property, including jewelry and works of art, for their own and Beriia's personal use. As mentioned before, these activities got Serov in trouble with K.F. Telegin, as well as with Abakumov.

We have already discussed in Chapter 7 the role played by Serov vis-à-vis Abakumov in the campaign against Marshal Zhukov, and the fact that the latter did not try to get rid of him after Beriia's fall indicates that he did not consider him an enemy. The 1990 edition of the Marshal's memoirs fails to mention Serov. Besides his activities in Poland and Germany, which included intrigue against both Zhukov and Abakumov, Serov was also called on to perform on sensitive operations. For instance, on September 14, 1946, he wrote a detailed report to Kruglov (*Iosif Stalin v Ob'iatiiakh Sem'i*) about the fate of Lt. Ia.I. Dzhugashvili, Stalin's son, who had died in German captivity. On February 21, 1947, Serov became the First Deputy Minister MVD under Kruglov and after Stalin's death even Deputy Head of GRU. In 1950, he had been identified as Head of the already discussed Special Prisons that were being set up for the use of the Central Committee. In 1952 he was supposed to have presided over the building of the Volga-Don Canal, as usual with slave labor. Serov, as we discussed, along with Kruglov, backed the winning side during the post-Stalin power struggle and on March 13, 1954, became the first Head of the KGB. After Stalin's death, Serov was involved in interrogating Abakumov, his old enemy. Besides joining the anti-Beriia plotters, he was rumored to have been rewarded for destroying documents that would have implicated Khrushchev in the Stalinist terror. Also, he had been given credit for putting down the East Berlin riots on June 17, 1953. In 1955 Serov became the third police official (after Maslennikov and Merkulov) to receive the rank of Army General. In 1954, Serov was also appointed Chairman of a committee to rehabilitate victims of repression, a position for which he should have been the least likely candidate. Khrushchev, who had kind remarks for Serov in his memoirs, made the mistake of sending him to London in spring 1956 to organize the security for his forthcoming visit. This was a public relations disaster since Serov was met by demonstrations organized by émigré groups with help from Western intelligence agencies trying to embarrass Khrushchev. Serov was also the subject of disinformation campaigns by Western intelligence agencies (not that he needed them) accusing him of such crimes as having personally executed Marshal Tukhachevskii. The 1956 Hungarian revolution which Serov helped crush did not add to the stature of KGB. On November 3, 1956, he repeated his performance with the leaders of the Home Army by arresting General Pal Maleter, the Minister of Defense in Imre Nagy's government, during negotiations which preceded the second Soviet invasion. On December 9, 1958, Serov was replaced by A.N. Shelepin. Serov now took over the GRU and remained there until 1962. For many years, Serov lived on Granovskii Street in Moscow, where his neighbors included Rudenko, Suslov, and Marshal Zhukov.[14] According to Maj. General V. Nekrasov (*Sovetskaia Militsia*, 6/1960), who had access to N.P. Dudorov's unpublished memoirs, in 1957 the Head of MVD in Vologoda oblast wrote to Dudorov claiming that A.P. Serov, the father of I.A. Serov, had been a senior official in Kadomsk prison during 1905–1917, where Stalin had once served time. Since Serov had kept this secret, Dudorov reported the matter to Khrushchev, who asked A.F. Zasiad'ko, Minister of the Coal Industry and Deputy Chairman of the Council of Ministers, to look into the matter. Nothing came of this, and in 1959, Dudorov learned that Serov was also related by marriage to Khrushchev. Serov's fate after 1962 is not clear. There are claims that he was sacked in 1962 in connection with the Pen'kovskii affair and was demoted to Maj. General. Despite rumors of suicide, "liquidation," and early death caused by alcoholism, Serov apparently survived. The latest Russian source (*VIZH*, 1/1995) dates his death in 1990 at age 85. It seems as if no one had bothered to contact him during the Glasnost years, since he surely was privy to even more secrets than Sudoplatov. One hopes that somewhere his papers and memoirs are waiting to be discovered. Even though Serov eventually betrayed his father, Beriia's son has nothing but admiration and calls him a brave and talented Commander and a Hero of the Soviet Union, which he was not, although he received many other awards, including four Orders of Lenin.

In 1945, besides Abakumov, Kruglov, Serov, B.Z. Kobulov, and Goglidze, two other men, V.V. Chernyshev and K.A. Pavlov, received the rank of Col. General. Chernyshev, on whose relations with Abakumov I have already touched, was born in 1896 and was old enough to have served in the old Army. He joined the Party in 1917 and was a member of the Riazansk Soviet. He had served in Cheka/OGPU/Border Troops in the Volga District, in Turkestan and in the Far East. In 1936, he was Commander of the Red Banner Division and the Head of Border Troops in the Far East. From July 8, 1937, he was Deputy Commissar of NKVD for Militia and was the only one of Ezhov's Deputies to serve under Beriia. He was involved in providing escort troops for trains going to Katyn. His service during the war, possibly with SMERSH, is not clear. He is listed in April 1946 as a Deputy Minister of

NKVD, but this could not have been for troops since this position was held by A.N. Apollonov. Chernyshov's responsibilities after the war also need to be clarified. He died in 1952. The least-known of the NKVD Col. Generals was K.A. Pavlov, who headed the Dalstroyi labor camps from 1937 to 1940 and, for his effort, was awarded with the Lenin Prize in 1939. Pavlov's career after his return from the Far East is also not clear. Later he was reportedly suffering from paralysis. Besides those who served as Minister of MVD and MGB, perhaps about 15 served as First Deputy and Deputy Ministers. We have already covered the careers of Serov, Goglidze, Chernyshev, B.Z. Kobulov, and Tsanava.

Among the remainder, one of the better-known is A.N. Apollonov, who had joined the NKVD in 1927 and the Party in 1931. In March 1939, he became Deputy Head for Border Troops and during the Winter War, was head of Rear in 9 Army, where drumhead court-martials were the rule of the day. During the war, he was Deputy Commander of NKVD Internal Troops, and on March 9, 1944, he received the Order of Kutuzov 1 Grade for his major contributions to the deportations. He was appointed Deputy Minister of MVD in April 1946.

V.S. Riasnoi, another Deputy Minister NKVD/MVD, had been a mere senior Lieutenant in 1940. Little is known about his war-time career, but he became the head of NKVD in Ukraine after the Soviets returned in 1943. He was identified on January 15, 1946 as, NKVD First Deputy Commissar and on April 22, 1946, as First Deputy Minister of MVD, a position which he held until February 21, 1947, when he was replaced by I.A. Serov. He managed to remain a Deputy Minister with responsibilities in such areas as the Gulag, deportees, and special settlements. He is also variously identified as having held positions with the Gulag and even as head of the Foreign Department in 1953 and finally in 1955 as Head of MVD in Moscow. He remains one of the most obscure of the senior secret police officials. Like most of those associated with Kruglov, he was untouched.

We know considerably more about A.P. Zaveniagin, a Russified Tatar, also identified as Deputy Minister of MVD in April 1946. Between 1933–1941, he had been Director of Magnitogorsk and Noril'sk Industrial Center, those gigantic testimonies to the inefficiency of state economic planning, as well as serving during 1937–1938 as Deputy Commissar of Heavy Industry. In these positions he had more than a nodding acquaintance with slave labor. During 1946–1951 he was head of 9 Department. From 1945, he was also Deputy Head of the First Central (Scientific-Technical) Administration, assigned by the Council of People's Commissars (Ministers) to build the atomic bomb. In July 1953, after Beriia's fall, Zaveniagin, who was too valuable to be sacked, was merely demoted to Deputy Minister of what was now called the Ministry of Medium Industry, headed by V.A. Malyshev, the genius of the tank industry during the war. In the Central Committee meeting of early June 1953, Zaveniagin denounced Beriia, for whom he had worked since 1941, as a "demagogue," a "helpless bureaucrat," and "a very dangerous and harmful man." Malyshev's tenure lasted until May 1955, when the deficiencies in the nuclear weapons program and the decline of his patron, Malenkov, led to his dismissal. Zaveniagin, despite his disreputable past, was back in the saddle in 1953 (from March 1955 as Minister of Medium Industry), only to die of a heart attack in December 1956 and be buried on the Kremlin wall.[15] Twice Hero of Socialist Labor and a member of the Central Committee since 1939, Zaveniagin worked closely not only with Beriia and Kruglov, but also with the leading members of the Soviet scientific community, including academicians I.V. Kurchatov and A.D. Sakharov. It is interesting that Sakharov's memoirs fail to mention Zaveniagin's service as Deputy Commissar/Minister of NKVD/MVD and his connections with the Gulag. The German atomic scientists who were kidnapped in 1946 and taken to Russia to help develop nuclear weapons found Zaveniagin pleasant and energetic, but deathly afraid of Beriia. Others had a less complimentary view of this slave master.

Another Deputy Commissar/Minister in NKVD/MVD was B.P. Obruchnikov. An investigator with the Operations Department, he had received the Order of the Mark of Honor on July 22, 1937 (for contributions to the Tukhachevskii affair), and somehow managed to survive into the Beriia period. In February 1941, he became Deputy Commissar NKVD for Cadres, probably replacing Kruglov. He held this position until June 1952, when he moved over to MGB, but not with the same responsibilities. This position had been held since August 1951 by A.A. Epishev. After Beriia's return, Obruchnikov became Deputy Minister for Cadres in the combined MVD and lasted until Beriia's fall. A close ally of Beriia, he allegedly provided a home for his illegitimate child.[16] He received the Medal for Bravery on April 27, 1940, for unconfirmed contributions to Katyn. His life after July 1953 remains a mystery, but there is no evidence that he was punished. Obruchnikov helped his own case by being a prosecution witness during the trial of Sudoplatov, Raikhman, and Eitingon and here was joined by Pitovranov.

Another Deputy Minister of MVD from January 7, 1948 was N.K. Bogdanov, on whose career we have already touched. Identified with NKVD in Karagand in 1944 and as Head of NKVD in Kazakh SSR in March 1944, he played an important part in "re-settlement" of deported people, for which he received the Order of Labor Red Banner on April 11, 1944. His report on crop failures in 1943 and famine in Kazakh SSR, which had caused incredible hardships, particularly among the exiles, was forwarded to Stalin and was duly ignored.[17] Bogdanov has been also identified as Deputy Minister in charge of the Gulag during the post-war years; the position was also allegedly held by Zaveniagin. His career as Head of MVD in Leningrad during the Beriia interregnum has already been discussed. Bogdanov was expelled from the KGB in 1959, accused of corruption.

A.A. Paniukov was also identified on July 28, 1948, as Deputy Minister MVD, but we know little about him except that he had received the rank of Maj. General in July 1945.

We also know considerably more about the next man, I.I. Maslennikov, who was identified on June 10, 1948, as a Deputy Minister MVD. He was born in 1900 and joined the Red Guards during the October Revolution and later served in the Cavalry during the Civil War. He joined the Party and OGPU in 1928, and he saw service in Central Asia as Commander of the Khorezemskii OGPU Regiment in fighting against the Basmachis. Maslennikov studied in the Central Asia Communist

University (1933) and Frunze Academy (1935). During the 1930s he was head of training in the Caucasus Border Troops, where he may have met Beriia, and later became Head of Border Troops in Belorussia. On February 29, 1939, he became a Deputy Commissar NKVD under Beriia, but his specific duties are not known, although they may have involved serving with the Gulag or, more likely, the Border Troops. He had been implicated in Katyn. Maslennikov was one of six Border Troop officers to receive the rank of Lt. General in June 1940. At the start of the war, like some of his colleagues, he was appointed to frontline command. He commanded the 29 Army (July 1942 to December 11, 1941) and 39 Army (December 22, 1941 to July 1942) attached to the West and Kalinin Fronts. The 39 Army had been led ineffectually by I.A. Bogdanov, a fellow Chekist (who was demoted to Deputy Commander), but Maslennikov turned out to be not much of an improvement. General P.I. Batov, who during this period served as Commander of the 3 Army and Assistant Commander of the Briansk Front, dismissed Maslennikov as someone with pre-war experience with security organs.[18] On August 8, 1942, Maslennikov took over the newly formed North Group of the Transcaucasus Front and from January 24, 1943 until May 13, 1943, the North Caucasus Front (2nd Formation). During this period, the Soviet forces failed to cut off the German retreat when they were caught deep in the Caucasus allowing the German Commander, Marshal Ewald Von Kleist, to execute a brilliant rearguard action and thus avert what could have been a bigger Stalingrad. Regardless, on January 30, 1943, Maslennikov was promoted to Colonel General.

Caucasus was, of course, the fiefdom of Beriia, and during this period he was also assigned by Stalin to participate in defensive operations. He turned out to be no better than Himmler in similar situations, using terror and bluster while appointing NKVD operatives such as one Lt. Colonel Rudovskii as Deputy Commander of 47 Army. With a direct line to Stalin, Beriia tried to subvert Generals I.E. Petrov, I.V. Tiulenev, and V.F. Segratskov, and as a result, the latter two commanders' careers never recovered.[19] Even Maslennikov may have complained despite his special relationship with Beriia. As Commander of the 39 Army, Maslennikov had gone over the head of the Kalinin Front by making direct appeals to Beriia, and during the Caucasus campaign, he would ignore the orders of the Commander of the Transcaucasus Front I.E. Tiulenev, when they contradicted Beriia's instructions.[20] Maslennikov now was appointed as a Deputy Commander of Fronts, usually a sign of disgrace, and on March 7, 1943 (July 3, 1943 in other sources), he also lost his job as deputy Commissar NKVD. During May to August 1943, he was Deputy Commander of the Volkhov Front; from August to November 1943 he was in the same capacity with the Southwest (re-named 3 Ukraine Front). From October to November 1943, Maslennikov also temporarily replaced the ailing V.I. Chiukov as Commander of the 8 Guard Army. During December 1943 to March 1944, he commanded the 42 Army of Leningrad Front and took part in the final lifting of the blockade. For a brief period, he may have also served as Deputy Commander of the Leningrad Front. On April 21, 1944, STAVKA formed the 3 Baltic Front, made up of forces from the left wing of the Leningrad Front, and Maslennikov was appointed

Commander. The progress against the well-entrenched enemy on the "Panther" line was slow, but Tatru was finally captured. During September and October 1944, the Front, in cooperation with the 1 and 2 Baltic Fronts, was engaged in fighting with the remnants of the German 16 and 18 Armies. On October 16, 1944, the 3 Baltic Front was dissolved. Meanwhile, on July 28, 1944, Maslennikov became the first policeman to receive the rank of Army General. In June 1945, he was appointed Deputy Commander of Soviet forces in the Far East under A.M. Vasilevskii and in this capacity took partin the war against Japan. Why, on September 8, 1945, he received the title of "Hero of the Soviet Union" (for his alleged contribution to the defeat of the Kwantung Army) remains a mystery. In May 1946, on the basis of Baku and Tbilisi Military Districts, once again the Transcaucasus Military District was formed, with Maslennikov as Commander. In February 1947, he was, however, replaced by F.I. Tolbukhin and became a student in the General Staff Academy, from which he graduated in 1948. On June 10, 1948, he was appointed Deputy Minister MVD (later First Deputy Minister), a position which he seems to have held until April 1954. On November 24, 1952, Maslennikov wrote a letter to the head of the General Staff War Studies Department criticizing an article on the Battle of Caucasus which had appeared in the August 1952 issue of the journal *Voennaia Mysl'* for not giving enough credit to Beriia's style of "Stalinist leadership" during the campaign.[21] This seems curious since at this time Beriia was under a cloud. After Stalin's death, Beriia kept Maslennikov, and he survived his mentor's fall but got in trouble because of riots in the labor camps such as Noril'sk (once run by Zaveniagin) in 1953 and the brutal way that they were put down. There are claims that he committed suicide during Beriia's trial (*Moscow News*, No. 23, 1990), but this probably happened later on April 16, 1954, which is the official date of his death. Maslennikov was elected as candidate member of the CC CPSU in the 19th Congress (1952) and was a Deputy to the 1 and 2 Sessions of the Supreme Soviet. Besides being a Hero of the Soviet Union, he had won four Orders of Lenin as well as Orders of the Red Banner, Red Star, Suvorov, and Kutuzov. Personally brave, he was wounded four times during the war.

After Abakumov's takeover of the MGB, it seems that B.Z. Kobulov, who had been identified as the First Deputy Commissar of NKGB in 1946, was eventually replaced by S.I. Ogol'tsev, who was promoted from a Deputy Minister. Ogol'tsev's roots were in the Leningrad Party organization, and in 1940 he had been associated with A.A. Kuznetsov. His receiving of the Order of Red Star on April 27, 1940, indicates possible involvement with Katyn. In 1943, Ogol'tsev was head of NKVD in Kuibyshev with the rank of Senior Major of State Security and later, according to Sudoplatov, possibly with NKGB in Krasnoiarsk and received the rank of Lt. General in July 1945. Despite his connections with Kuznetsov, he seems to have been involved in the "Leningrad Affair." As mentioned before, he was also involved in 1950 in preparing the case against the captured Generals who had been accused of collaboration during their captivity and had been imprisoned since their return. In spring 1950, he, rather than Abakumov, was the MGB's pointman in the campaign that resulted in the execution of a number of those Generals.

Promoted to First Deputy Minister MGB, Ogol'tsov replaced Abakumov as Acting Minister on July 1951 after Abakumov's arrest, but for how long? Ignat'ev was officially appointed Minister of MGB in December 1951, but there is evidence that he actually held this position as early as August 1951. Ogol'tsov's career after this remained in limbo. In his letter to Malenkov dated April 2, 1953 (*Argumenty i Fakty*, May 1992), Beriia stated that he had Ogol'tsev arrested for his involvement with Mikhoel's murder. Ogol'tsev apparently survived Abakumov's fall and took part in the "Doctors Plot" campaign. During Abakumov's trial, the prosecution claimed that Ogol'tsev had been involved in destroying sensitive documents.[22] Previous claims that he was shot have now been disproved thanks to E. Al'bats, who discovered that he ended up being employed as deputy director of the Scientific Research Institute No. 1.[23]

Another Deputy Minister was N.N. Selivanovskii. An investigator with the Operations Department in 1937, he had received the Order of the Mark of Honor on July 22, 1937, and survived into the Beriia period. He had served with SMERSH during the war. On December 10, 1962, Selivanovskii testified before the Central Committee about the interrogation of the military leaders V.M. Primakov and V.K. Putna, whose testimony was used to implicate others. Selivanovskii blamed it all on his fellow interrogator A.A. Avseevich, who was later involved in the massacre of the senior military officers in Kuibyshev. Selivanovskii, however, did not explain why he was decorated in July 1937. Selivanovskii also received a medal in April 1940, possibly for involvement in Katyn. During the war, Selivanovskii served as a Deputy Head of SMERSH. In 1946, he and his colleague B.P. Obruchnikov, now at MVD, were two survivors of the Ezhov era who were now Deputy Ministers. Selivanovskii's specific duties during the post-war period are not clear, but he was involved in fighting the Ukrainian nationalists. One source credits him with founding of UB, the counterpart of the MGB in Poland.[24] He was arrested after Abakumov's downfall. His fate is not clear.

A.S. Blinov had served under Ezhov, probably in a provincial post, and received the Order of Red Star on December 19, 1937. He was in the NKVD in Ivanovo during 1939–1941, receiving the Order of Mark of Honor on April 27, 1940. In 1942, he was identified as NKVD Chief in Kuibyshev, an important position in view of the role of that city in Soviet evacuation plans. It seems logical that he had been involved in the mass execution of senior officers which took place in October 1941. In July 1945, Blinov received the rank of Lt. General. As mentioned previously, his major contribution during the Abakumov period was his participation in the deportation of Soviet Greeks outside Crimea which took place in the fall of 1949. Blinov's career after the fall of Abakumov remains unresolved.

Deputy Minister N.K. Koval'chuk received the Order of Red Star on April 27, 1940. During the war, he had been with SMERSH, serving as its head with the 4 Ukraine Front during 1944–1945, probably watching over the Commander, Army General I.E. Petrov, a man with the dangerous habit of irritating Stalin. Petrov was finally sacked but somehow managed to survive.

I have already touched on M.G. Svinelupov, Deputy Minister of MGB for Cadres since 1946 for his participation in the deportation of Greeks in 1949. Before that, he had received the Medal for Labor Heroism on April 27, 1940. At least one defector source claims that he and Abakumov did not get along.[25]

Also identified on May 7, 1946 as Deputy Minister MGB was P.V. Fedotov, a man about whom we know considerably more. In the 1930s he had been in OGPU/NKVD and may have headed the NKVD Secret Political Department in spring 1939. Fedotov had been blamed for the repressions of A.A. Bekzadian, Ambassador to Hungary; N.A. Popok, First Party Secretary in the Volga German ASSR; and M.K. Amosov, First Party Secretary of Kirgizia, all of whom were shot in July 1938, but his exact position has not been revealed. He was also responsible for arresting the Command of the 76 Armenian Rifle Division at some unspecified date. In 1940, as a Commissar of State Security 3 Rank, he was the head of 2 (counterintelligence) Department, which played a part in Katyn and for which he received the Order of Mark of Honor on April 29, 1940. His exact job during the war is not known, but probably was with SMERSH. In 1941, Fedotov had been reportedly involved with "Operation Windmill," already described in connection with Serov, in the Far East.[26] Fedotov received the rank of Lt. General in July 1945 with regular police Generals. Soviet documents also show him reporting to N.M. Shvernik about German atrocities. In 1946, besides being a Deputy Minister, he was also the Head of the MGB 2 (Foreign) Department, replacing the veteran P.M. Fitin. During 1947–1949, he was Deputy Chairman under Molotov of "KI," the Soviet committee organized to coordinate foreign intelligence. In practice, he may have been running the show. In 1949, he may have been replaced in this position by S.R. Savchenko. In 1953, Fedotov has been identified as head of MGB 2 Department, but his career and fate after this date are unknown.[27] The careers of two other Deputy Ministers of MGB, S.A. Goglidze and L.F. Tsanava, have already been discussed in the previous chapter.

The best-known of the post-war Deputy Ministers of MGB, however, was Army General A.A. Epishev, the apparatchik par excellence. Born in 1908, he joined the Party in 1929, and a year later the Red Army. Between 1931 and 1938, he worked as a political officer in various units and also attended the Red Army Mechanized Academy before finding employment in the Party Central Committee. In 1940, he moved to the Ukraine, and in March 1940, he became the First Party Secretary in Kharkov. At the start of the war, he was appointed Political Commissar of the Kharkov Militia, his first direct contact with the police. After the fall of Ukraine, he moved to the Urals and helped in the organization of evacuated factories and was Deputy Commissar of Medium Industry. On May 27, 1943, Epishev was given the rank of Maj. General (political) and appointed a Commissar of 40 Army Voronezh Front under K.S. Moskalenko (a future conspirator against Beriia). In October 1943, both men took similar positions with the 38 Army and served in its ranks during the remainder of the war. During 1943–1944, Epishev was also reacquainted with Khrushchev, the Commissar of the Voronezh (March 1943 to October 1943) and 1 Ukraine (October 1943 to August 1944) Fronts. On July 1946, Epishev became Secretary of the CC CPSU for Cadres. In spring 1947, he worked in the Party organizations of Zhitomir and Odessa before attending a Party school in 1950. He then became the Odessa Party Secretary, a position he officially held until September 4, 1951. His appointment as Deputy Minister MGB in August 1951 seems unusual because of his lack of experience in securityand police matters, also manifestly absent in his boss, S.D. Igant'ev. This was a period after Abakumov's fall when the MGB was in turmoil. Unfortunately, Epishev's official biography devotes less than a half-page to this period of his career, stating that he tried to recruit the best for service in MGB, but his suggestions were not always heeded.[28] The biography is also silent about the claim made by Sudoplatov that Epishev was a member of the committee that met just before Stalin's death to organize the assassination of Tito. After Beriia's comeback, Epishev was almost immediately replaced by the already-discussed B.P. Obruchnikov. On March 29, 1953, Epishev returned to his old job as Party Secretary in Odessa. From now until September 1955, Epishev was the First Party Secretary in Odessa before serving as Ambassador to Rumania and later to Yugoslavia. On September 1955, he became Head of the Political Administration of the Red Army, a position he held for over 20 years, almost making it into the Glasnost period, a record matched perhaps only by one other Soviet official in a high position, Army General P.I. Ivashutin, as Head of the GRU. Epishev, a long-standing fixture of the Soviet scene, was a candidate member of the CC CPSU (1952) and a member (1964). On February 21, 1978, he was even awarded the Title of Hero of the Soviet Union, once reserved for military heroes, which was considerably cheapened during the Brezhnev era. Epishev died in 1985. During the Khrushchev era, other former senior Chekists were destined for different fates, depending on how close they had been to Beriia, particularly during the period following Stalin's death. The Glasnost period shed light on the fate of some, but not all, of them. We have already discussed N.S. Vlasik's demotion, arrest, and interrogation by Beriia and his cohorts. Beriia's own arrest, however, did not mean the release of Vlasik.[29]

Our information about the fate of those in the middle ranks of MGB/MVD is not complete. There were trials and executions (some in secret) during this period, but they have not been publicized. For instance, the brutal investigators B.V. Rodos and L.L. Shvartsman were arrested (Rodos on October 5, 1953) and shot (Shvartsman on April 21, 1955 and Rodos on April 17, 1956) after testifying before the Central Committee. Rodos, identified as Greek-Russian by Conquest and Jewish by A.I. Vaksberg, had been in the NKVD Investigation Department at least since 1938, starting his career in Odessa, later interrogating, among others, Bliukher, Meyerhold, Chubar, Kosarev, Kosior, Kosarev, and Zubov. The latter survived, but only as a cripple. As the Deputy Head of the Department for Investigation of Especially Important Cases under Vlodzimirskii, he had also been involved in the execution of senior military officers in October 1941. Vaksberg finds the idea of Rodos, a graduate of the fourth grade (he somehow managed to finish the Judiciary Academy after the war), interrogating Meyerhold incongruous, but Stalinism, after all, was about the triumph of the Common Man. Rodos, along with Ia.M. Raites, were among the ace investigators that were eased out of the organs in the late 1940s and were replaced with younger individuals, almost all of them Slavs. Rodos ended up working with

Osoaviakhin (the Civil Defense Organization) in Simferopol until his arrest in 1953. Rodos's son lives in Moscow and has been approached by journalists for interviews. Shvartsman, a former journalist with *Rabochaia Moskva* and a possible secret police informer, officially joined the NKVD in 1937 and served in the Secret Political Department. Late in 1937, he had been the Chief Interrogator of V.A. Antonov-Ovseenko. Later, he may have been another of Vlodzimirskii's deputies. He had been the Chief of Interrogation of the senior military officers in October 1941. Shvartsman was arrested on October 19, 1951 as a "Jewish nationalist" and the contact between Abakumov and Western intelligence and promptly confessed, implicating others such as L.F. Raikhman. Shvartsman survived but does not seem to have been restored to leadership after Beriia's return. Rodos and Shvartsman were singled out mainly because their victims were fallen Stalinists as well as military officers. After Beriia's fall, Marshal Zhukov and his colleagues were in a position to demand retribution. Rodos and Shvartsman were, however, relatively low-ranking functionaries.[30] Those who also reportedly suffered during the Khrushchev years included Maj. General S.S. Davlianidze, sentenced to 25 years. He had worked in 1937 with the Special Department of the Georgia NKVD, and during the war as Deputy Head of NKGB in Georgia under Rapava. He received major citations in April 1940 and August 1944, the latter probably for involvement in deportations. A.Z. Kobulov, the brother of B.Z. Kobulov, may have been shot in secret in 1953. A.Z. Kobulov (Lt. General, July 1945) was one of Beriia's first appointments. He headed the NKVD in Ukraine from December 1938 until September 1939, when he was replaced by I.A.. Serov. He then served in the Soviet Embassy in Berlin until the start of the war. In 1943, he was NKVD Head in the Uzbek SSR. In 1945, he was Head of Administration of Soviet Property Abroad, a position which he lost to Merkulov in 1946. During1951–1953, he was deputy head of Gulag and Head of the NKVD Department for POWs. After Stalin's death, Kobulov was Deputy Head of MVD Control/Inspection and must have been arrested after Beriia's fall. Why he was not tried with Beriia's other colleagues remains unanswered.[31]

Another logical candidate to be tried with Beriia was Col. General S.S. Mamulov (né Mamul'ian) who claimed that he Russified his name because Comrade Stalin did not like Armenian names. Beriia's Georgian operatives, however, kept their original names. Born in 1902 in Tbilisi, he joined the Party in 1921 and served in the Red Army (1921–1923) and the Party organization in Abkhazia (1923–1927). During 1927–1931, he was attached to the Central Committee of the Georgian Party before being transferred to Kazakhstan and Dnepropetrovsk for four years, the only time in his career when he was not in close contact with Beriia. In 1934, he was a member of the Transcaucasus Control Commission, in 1936 a member of the Central Committee of the Communist Party of Georgia, and from 1937 Head of its Leadership (personnel) Branch. In 1938 he joined the NKVD, but his exact duties are not clear. On April 26, 1940, when he received the Order of Red Banner, he has been identified in the rank of Senior Major of State Security. During the war, Mamulov was Head of the NKVD Chancellory and was involved in the 1943–1944 deportations. On April 11, 1946, now a Lt. General, he became the Deputy Minister of MVD and possibly responsible for the Gulag. He was Beriia's main mole in MVD. He may have been removed in 1952 as the result of the "Mingrelian Affair." After Stalin's death, Mamulov was one of the strongmen sent by Beriia to Georgia to reclaim the Party organization and was one of the organizers of the 15th Party Congress. Mamulov was arrested in July 1953 and sentenced to 15 years after an unpublicized trial. (It would have made more sense if he had been tried with the Beriia group.) In the Vladimir prison, he shared a cell with Shariia and Liudvigov and worked in the prison library. He was released in 1968 and moved to Sukhum, but by 1974, he could not be traced.

Lt. General S.R. Mil'shtein, another of Beriia's Jewish associates, had worked in the 1920s in the ranks of the Cheka/OGPU. In October 1938, he was appointed Head of NKVD 3 (Transportation) Department. During the war, he was in a similar position with NKGB and provided transport during the deportations of 1943–1944. In March 1941, he was also identified as Deputy Commissar for the Timber Industry. According to Sudoplatov, in March 1941, Mil'shtein was actually the Deputy Head of the GRU and was sent to Belgrade along with two other operatives, V.S. Zarubin and A.M. Alakhverdov, to organize the overthrow of the pro-German government. On April 27, 1940, he received the Order of Red Banner and on March 9, 1944, the Order of Suvorov II Grade. During the war, he accompanied Beriia on inspection trips. Mil'shtein's post-war career is not clear, and he may have even escaped arrest during the anti-Semitic campaigns of the 1940s. After Beriia's return, he was appointed First Deputy Minister MVD in Ukraine, a position which brought him a 10-year sentence in 1953.[32] In the Central Committee meeting in July 1953, Mil'shtein was roundly denounced for having numerous relatives living in the U.S. and for being the brother of an executed spy. G.A. Pachuliia, in 1938, headed the NKVD in Abkhaz ASSR. Otherwise little is known about him except that he was in prison in 1956 and remained there until the 1970s.[33] Ia. A. Serebrianskii is another Jewish survivor of the Ezhov period whose career is worth investigation. In 1938, Ezhov allegedly ordained a "Special Tasks Administration" under Serebrianskii to organize the assassination of defecting agents in the West. He was reportedly sentenced to death in 1939 but was reprieved.[34] What he did under Beriia and why he was arrested during the Khrushchev years seems unclear. Lt. General Iu. D. Sumbatov-Topuridze, born in 1898 or 1899, an old crony of Beriia and a former Menshevik, had joined the Party in 1918 and was employed in the 1920s in the Azerbaidzhan oil industry. In 1938, he was in the Azerbaidzhan Party Organization and in NKVD, possibly as its head. Between 1939 and 1947, he also served as Head of NKVD Economic Department, but the exact times are not clear because this position was also held during that period by B.Z. Kobulov and I.M. Tkachenko. It is more likely that he was in charge of supplies rather than the head of the department. In 1947, Sumbatov-Topuridze was appointed as Deputy Chairman of the Azerbaidzhan Council of Ministers. He was deprived of this post and his medals on July 22, 1953, and was soon arrested. It would have been logical that he be tried with the Bagirov group, whose career his paralleled.[35] Instead, he ended up in the same psychiatric clinic in Leningrad as Sudoplatov, except that his problems were real. According to

Sudoplatov, his fellow patient claimed that part of Beriia's treasures that had not been smuggled abroad were hidden in the Council of Ministers dacha in Zhukovka near Moscow. Sumbatov-Topuridze was also suffering from cancer—from which he died in 1956. M.I. Zhuravlev, a survivor of the Ezhov era, had served as Head of NKVD/MVD in Moscow. In October 1941, he, along with Serov, Lt. General of Engineers L.Z. Kotliar (Head of Red Army Main Engineering Administration), G.M. Popov and B.N. Chernousev, Secretaries of the Moscow Party Organizations, formed a committee to destroy Moscow in case of a German breakthrough. Zhuravlev was dismissed in 1946 and his post-war career is unknown. Beriia brought him back in spring 1953 and appointed him as a Deputy Minister MVD. His fate after Beriia's arrest needs further investigation. Also unclear is the fate of such Beriia stalwarts as G.T. Karanadze, former Head of NKVD in Dagestan and Head of NKVD/MVD in Georgia; K.P. Bziava, former Head of NKVD in Kabardo-Balkar ASSR and Deputy Head of MVD in Georgia; and A.I. Kochavashvili, Head of MGB Georgia in late 1952 and early 1953. Maj. General M.L. Michurin-Raver had been in Party work in Georgia in the 1930s before joining the NKVD Operations Department in Georgia. A colleague of B.Z. Kobulov and involved in intrigue against N. Lakoba, he provided evidence against Beriia after the latter's arrest, but his subsequent fate remains unknown.

Col. General V.P. Pirozhkov, former Deputy Chairman of the KGB has stated (*Nedelia* 26–1989) that 1,342 former senior police officials had been tried and another 2,370 received Party and administrative punishment. Unfortunately, in this number Pirozhkov includes those officials associated with Iagoda who had been purged by Ezhov and those from the latter's regime who had been eliminated by Beriia. Therefore, the list of former officials associated with repressions since 1939 who suffered any consequences is far from complete. Some trials probably were held in secret, usually under the infamous Article 58, a general-purpose tool which covered such crimes as "major terror," "treason," "espionage," "terror," "economic sabotage," and "membership in conspiracies." Besides such individuals as Raikhman, Shariia, Tsanava, Eitingon, Mamulov, and Sudoplatov, and others who are discussed in more detail elsewhere in this book, there is evidence that the following, mostly associated with Beriia, suffered for their crimes:

· A.M. Alemasov, former Commissar NKVD/MVD in Tatariia (winner of the Order of Red Star, July 22, 1937), later First Party Secretary in Tatariia, was accused in December 1962 of torturing prisoners and was reprimanded.

· Lt. General L.F. Bashtakov, served a prison term for his part in the interrogation of R.I. Eikhe and was later released. In 1990 he was under investigation for his part in the murder of M.A. Spiridonova.

· V.A. Boiarskii, an NKVD investigator, was expelled from the Party.

· M.F. Dechko, Head of Mozyrsk NKVD in the 1930s, was Deputy Chairman of the KGB in Belorussia 1958. He was removed from his position and expelled as a candidate member of the Party.

· Maj. General V.V. Ivanov, an investigator, originally with the Secret Political Department, was involved in the case against Marshal Bliukher. He lost his rank for violating the law on January 3, 1955.

· A.G. Khvat, an NKVD investigator, was arrested and expelled from the Party.

· Col. N.F. Kruzhkov, served as an investigator with the local NKVD during the Leningrad Blockade. Although at that time only a Junior Lieutenant of State Security, he managed to label many scientists and specialists as "enemy of the people." From 1951, he was employed with the MGB in Novogorod. He was sentenced to 25 years by military tribunal in October 1956.

· Lt. General A.I. Langfang, an investigator, was formerly Deputy Head of the KGB in Krasnodar. Arrested in 1957, he was sentenced to prison.

· E.M. Libenson, involved in 1939 in the M.S. Kedrov affair, was sentenced to 25 years in the mid-1950s.

· B.A. Liudvigov, Beriia's chief clerk, was arrested in 1953 and served time in Vladimir prison.

· Ia.N. Matusov, an NKVD investigator, was expelled from the Party.

· Col. N.A. Musatov, Assistant to T.M. Borshchov in NKVD Azerbaidzhan, was sentenced to 25 years.

· Col. R.S. Sarkisov, Beriia's bodyguard, was arrested in 1953. He ended up in the psychiatric clinic in Leningrad. According to his fellow patient Sudoplatov (p. 392), Sarkisov, a former textile factory engineer in Tbilisi, complained that false charges of treason prevented the implementation of a speeded-up five-year plan for the textile industry with the machine that he had invented. He asked the doctors' help to expose the prosecutor Rudenko, who was sabotaging his efforts and was preventing him from becoming a Hero of Socialist Labor.

· O.O. Shikhmuradov, a former Department Head in the Turkmen SSR NKVD, was expelled in 1940 for violation of "socialist legality." In the early 1950s, he was Secretary of the Turkmen CC CPSU. Expelled from the Party, he is now attached to Ashkhabad Teachers College.

· Lt. General M.I. Zhuravlev, Head of NKVD in Moscow during the war and Deputy Minister MVD under Beriia in 1953, was arrested. His fate is unknown.

Besides the preceding individuals, former NKVD functionaries I.I. Rodovanskii, Z.G. Genkin, N.A. Kuleshov, and Ia.N. Matusov (who along with A.Ia. Sverdlov had been the Chief Interrogators of A.M. Larina) may have been sentenced to prison in the 1950s or at least expelled from the Party. In the case of Matusov, he had actually been under arrest since Abakumov's fall. Also, to my knowledge, none of the MGB investigators such as Cols. Gerasimov, Nosov, Rodovanskii, and Sedov; Lt. Col. Polianskii; Major Chechurov; and Captain Merkulov who were involved in cases against the "Jewish intellectuals," the "Leningrad Affair," and the "Doctors' Plot" suffered any major consequences. At the present, it seems that A.Z. Kobulov and two former investigators, Cols. B.V. Rodos and L.L. Shvartsman, were the only Chekists other than the main Beriia and Abakumov associates who were shot. (The fates of Abakumov's Deputies Ogol'tsov and Blinov and close associate Belkin remain unclear.) All in all, and also taking into account P.N. Kubatkin, who was shot under Abakumov, about 25 people paid the supreme penalty for the unprecedented crimes that were committed during 1939–1953.

The fates of such senior officers as L.F. Bashtakov, I.M. Tkachenko, and S.E. Egorov were more typical. Before the war, Bashtakov had been an Interrogator of R.I. Eikhe, with the rank of State Security Major. As head of the sinister "1 NKVD Special Section," he had been involved in the "selection" of Polish POW officers to be liquidated in Katyn and elsewhere, a task for which he received the Order of Red Star. In the same capacity, he had played an important part in the mass execution of political prisoners in Orel in August 1941 and of the senior military officers in October 1941 in Kuibyshev. I.M. Tkachenko in 1941 was the Head of NKVD Economics Department; later as NKVD Chief in Stavropol, he organized the deportation of Karachis, for which he received the Order of Kutuzov II Grade. In 1945 as Head of NKGB in Lithuania, he repeated the operation. S.E. Egorov, having survived Ezhov's fall, was a speaker at the NKVD Party conference held on April 12, 1939. On April 27, 1940, he was a recipient of the Order of Mark of Honor, probably in connection with Katyn. In July 1945, he was a Maj. General, and in August 1955, having survived Beriia, he was the Head of MVD Gulag reporting to Khrushchev. During the Khrushchev years, Deputy Military Prosecutor Lt. General of Judiciary B.A. Viktorov and his assistant, Colonel (later Maj. General) of Judiciary D.P. Terekhov, tried to bring to justice some of the high-ranking officials of the security organs, but their attempts were frustrated by the statute of limitations as well as the reluctance of the political leadership to press the matter vigorously considering their own checkered pasts. Regardless, 38 senior officers (the complete list has yet to be published) of the state security lost their ranks and some were expelled from the Party. A few were even tried, for instance, Lt. General A.I. Langfang, who had organized the case against the former leadership of Comintern, including V.G. Knorin, who later served as Deputy Head of the CC CPSU Agitation and Propaganda Section (arrested 1937, executed 1939); I.A. Piatnintskii; Ia.Ia. Anvelt; G.S. Alikhanian (father of E. Bonner, the wife of A.D. Sakharov); V.T. Chemodanov; and Bela Kun. From April 10, 1938 to July 27, 1938, Langfang interrogated Piatnitskii 72 times lasting over 220 hours in Lefortovo prison using torture. Langfang won the Order of Red Star in 1940, but later he must have come under a cloud. In August 1941, he represented the central apparatus in Altai during the deportations of the Volga Germans. In 1955, he was Deputy Head of KGB in Krasnodar, a lowly position for a Lt. General. He was later arrested and sentenced to camps in Mordovia. After the 22 Party Congress, Langfang and 11 other imprisoned Chekists wrote to the Party and asked that they be freed. According to A.I. Vaksberg, in *Neraskrytye Tainy*, this included Beriia stalwarts Maj. Generals V.A. Kakuchaia, S.S. Davlianidze, A.S. Atakashiev, and S.F. Emel'anov, as well as G.G. Paramnov, R. Gangiia, S. Aksenov-Shcherbitskii, F. Mal'kiev, E. Libenson, N. Grushkov, and G.A. Pachuliia. Their appeals, however, went unanswered. Langfang, however, was released in 1972 and returned to his old address where he died. In Iu. Piatnitskaia's *Dnevnik zheny Bol'shevika*, it is mistakenly stated that Langfang was shot after the 20 Party Congress. The former Col. V. Kruzhkov, who had waged a campaign of terror against the Leningrad scientists during the blockade years, was also convicted. Several other inquisitors such as

A.A. Avseevich (later a Lt. General, no less), V.A. Boiraskii, A.G. Khvat, Ia.N. Matusov, Albogachiev, and Lukhovitskii also came under investigation.

Khvat was a typical case. At an early age, he had been a member of the Leningrad and Pskov Komsomols before moving to Moscow and joining the Osoaviakhin (the Civil Defense Society) before being employed by NKVD. He was finally assigned, along with Albogachiev, to work over academician N.I. Vavilov. At the time of his arrest in 1962, Khvat had been employed as a Party Secretary in the Ministry of Medium Industry. V.A. Boiarskii, as the Head of the NKVD Investigation Department in North Ossetia, along with his Assistant, Gorodnichenko, used "Stakhanovite" methods to extract confessions and caused the death of numerous people. In 1939, Boiarskii, as a Lieutenant of State Security and an NKVD Investigator, had falsified charges against 103 people, resulting in 51 executions. He was, however, less successful when sent to Czechoslovakia in 1951 to prepare the case against the Czech Communists. Boiarskii, as a Doctor of Science, was also employed in the Academy of Sciences in the Institute of Mining History. In 1959, charges were brought against Boiarskii and Gorodnichenko, but they could not be brought to trial since the notorious Article 58 had been repealed. As late as 1986, Khvat (who had been expelled from the Party in 1962) and Boiarskii were demanding full rehabilitation. Ia.N. Matusov's career went back to Iagoda. Under Ezhov, whom he survived, he had interrogated Tukhachevskii, Iakir, and M.A. Larina. He received the Order of Red Star in July 1937 and the Order of Mark of Honor in April 1939. In 1955, he was expelled from the Party. One of the most brutal investigators, Z.M. Ushakov (Ushiminskii), who had tortured Marshal Tukhachevskii and Komkor B.M. Fel'dman, among others, apparently went unpunished after testifying to the rehabilitation commission in 1961. Also untouched was A.Ia. Sverdlov. Under Ezhov, he, the only son of Ia.M. Sverdlov, had been involved in the interrogation of P.G. Petrovskii, A.M. Larina, and poet A. Vasil'ev. During the post-war years, his victims included military historian P. Meshcheriakov. He was apparently left untouched, wrote a doctored biography of Ordzhonikidze and helped P.D. Mal'kov, former Commandant of the Kremlin, write his memoirs. He was a pointman in attacking historian A.M. Nekrich, whose book, *1941 22 Iiunia*, published in 1965, was critical of Soviet military strategy on the eve of war. Sverdlov, who died in November 1969, ended his career by writing children's books under the pseudonym A.Ia. Iakovlev, a perfect ending for a man who had once interrogated the children of arrested officials.

During the Khrushchev years, most of the Chekists who had fallen victim to the Ezhov regime, even such brutes as M.I. Latsis (a chief architect of the Red Terror who in 1918 said that in our investigations we don't look at a man's words or deeds, only his class) and Ia.Kh. Peters were rehabilitated. (Iagoda, however, was an exception.) Some of those who had served under Ezhov (but not his entire High Command) who were purged under Beriia were also cleared. For instance, on August 6, 1955, the Military Collegium of the USSR set aside the sentences of 11 high-ranking Gulag officials (including M.D. Berman, the founder of the system), who had been tried in April 1939 and ordered the release of the survivors.

Other Beriia colleagues who were left untouched included Lt. General (July 1945) M.M. Gvishiani, who somehow managed to survive his master's downfall. Gvishiani had been a member of OGPU/NKVD in the Caucasus from 1928 until September 21, 1937. In November 1937, he became Chairman of the Tbilisi City Executive Committee and on September 1, 1938, was the First Deputy Head NKVD Georgia. In March 1939, Beriia sent him to the Far East as Head of NKVD in Maritime Territory. During the war, he was probably with NKGB or SMERSH. During the post-war years, he held the position of NKVD Chief in Kuibyshev, which had lost its importance after the government agencies returned to Moscow. Elected as candidate member of the CC CPSU (1939), he was dropped in 1952. He may have returned to the Far East when Goglidze was appointed Deputy Minister of MGB after Abakumov's fall. He did not suffer after Beriia's fall, but in April 1962 he lost an Order of Suvorov II Grade awarded in March 1944 for his contribution to deportations. It has been suggested that Gvishiani, whose son was married to Kosygin's daughter, saved Kosygin during the "Leningrad Affair."[36] This is unlikely since as a provincial leader and a man closely associated with Beriia, who was not a member of Abakumov's inner circle, Gvishiani was in no position to help Kosygin or, for that matter, anyone else. Stalin spared Kosygin and T.F. Shtykov and stayed the execution of Kupriianov for the same reason that he refused to arrest Pasternak and Akhmatova. Stalin liked to play the part of the omnipotent "vozhd," reminding all that the final decisions in matters of life and death were his and his alone.

Also spared suffering during the Khrushchev years was G.P. Dobrynin, who received an Order of Suvorov II Grade in March 1944 for his contributions to deportations. In 1949, he had been identified as Head of the Gulag (more likely Deputy Head) when he reported to Stalin about the number of prisoners in camps. Dobrynin was a Delegate to the 20th Party Congress (1956), and we can only wonder whether he applauded Khrushchev's secret speech. Lt. General I.I. Dol'gikh had served in the NKVD in Ukraine and during the war was Head of NKVD in Khabarovsk. He has been identified as Head of the slave-built Volga Don Canal project during the post-war years.

Another survivor, E.P. Pitrovranov, had a most fascinating career. In the 1930s he had been an official in the NKVD Foreign Department before being arrested and interrogated by L.R. Sheinin, Vyshinskii's deputy. He, however, managed to send a letter to Stalin suggesting that he had some new ideas instead of professing loyalty and innocence or asking for mercy. Stalin ordered his release. He continued his work in the Foreign Department and during the post-war years may have been a Deputy Minister in MGB or MVD. IN 1949, he was involved in the deportation of Russian Greeks, for which he received a medal. In the late 1950s, he was in service in Germany. He was again arrested after Abakumov's downfall but was released in December 1952 to take part in the last proposed plan to eliminate Tito. In 1980, he was a member of the USSR Chamber of Commerce and the Head of the KGB "Special

Reserve," which used trade and diplomacy as a cover for espionage.[37] He was still living in 1989. Lt. General A.D. Beschastnov, a central figure in organizing the trial of Slansky and other Czech Communist leaders, served as Head of KGZ (the Czech counterpart of KGB) from November 1969 until October 1974.[38] Before this appointment, he served for nearly five years as head of KGB in Uzbek SSR. His memoirs were published in *Novyi Mir* (December 1981). In 1939, Lt. General A.I. Voronin was Head of NKVD in Stalingrad. His later career is not clear. He was a Delegate to the 18, 19, and 20 Party Congresses, but in April 1962, he lost the Order of Suvorov II Grade, which he had received in March 1944 for contribution to deportations.[39]

Most ironic was the fate of Beriia's Jewish colleagues who came back to power with him only to be imprisoned again after his fall. Besides S.R. Mil'shtein, whose career has already been discussed, the most prominent members of this group were L.F. Raikhman and L.I. Eitengon. Raikhman started his career with the NKVD in Leningrad. During the 1930s, he took part in the investigation of the Mensheviks, the so-called Union of Marxist-Leninists, the Moscow Center, the Leningrad Counter-Revolutionary Zinov'ev Group, and the Joint Anti-Soviet Trotskii-Zinov'ev bloc. In her memoirs, the late A.L. Voitolovskaia, who was arrested in April 1936, gave us a detailed account of Raikhman as an interrogator who used threats, lies, and torture to force confessions from innocent people, then used those confessions against other victims. Raikhman survived Ezhov's fall, and in 1940, was attached to the NKVD Operations Department. As Head of the NKVD Polish Office, he was deeply involved in Katyn and once told Count Jozef Czapski that there were no Polish POWs in Poland. His contribution to Katyn was rewarded by a Medal for Bravery in April 1940. Later he helped put together the falsified version of Katyn that the Soviet Prosecution presented at the Nuremberg trial. In August 1941, Raikhman, now identified as Deputy Head of NKGB/NKVD 2 (Counterintelligence) Department was involved in the deportation of Volga Germans from the Saratov oblast. He was also deeply implicated in the Elrich-Alter case, already discussed. From April 1946, Raikhman was in L'vov helping Sudoplatov in fighting the OUN and the Poles. On June 6, 1951, he went to Moscow to attend his father's funeral, and in October 1951 he was arrested after Abakumov's removal and after, having been denounced by Shvartsman, as well as by his own wife, as a member of "Jewish Nationalist Conspiracy."[40] He was released after Stalin's death. In March 1953, Beriia appointed him Head of MVD Control/Inspection. After Beriia's fall, he was arrested and spent time in prison. When living in Moscow, he was at one-time neighbor of the martyred Jewish poet P.D. Markish. Raikhman was also married for a time to the stunning ballerina O.V. Lepeshinskaia, who finally divorced him to marry in 1956 the widowed Army General A.I. Antonov, the former Chief of General Staff. Raikhman was tried secretly in August 1956 and was sentenced to 5 years but was soon released because of the time he had already served. One of the witnesses at his trial was A.L. Voitoloskaia, who had been tortured in the 1930s, along with her husband, by Raikhman. According to Voitolovskaia's testimony (*Report on the USSR*, December 31, 1991), Raikhman, whose education had come to an end in the second grade, could not comprehend why he, a winner of the Order of Lenin, had to face trial. He added, "It seems that you have forgotten that the NKVD was instructed to uncover and annihilate counterrevolutionaries, terrorists, and agents of Nazi intelligence mercilessly. We were not fighting against hares and ducks. We were fulfilling orders from our government. We were completely absorbed in our work." His rank and privileges, however, were not restored. In retirement, Raikhman became interested in cosmology and "futurology," a subject of particular interest to dreamers and charlatans and, in fact, wrote two books on the subject.[41] In 1990, he made a brief appearance in the Russian-produced TV special *Stalin, a Portrait in Blood*, in which he claimed that he had denounced the use of torture as "counterproductive." Raikhman died on March 16, 1990. In his self-serving interview with the Russian journalist V.K. Abarinov, Raikhman comes through as a clever opportunist by splitting hairs, and making impossible denials and outright fabrications. He claimed that G.S. Zhukov, head of NKVD Central and East European Section, now conveniently dead, rather than he, was involved in questions affecting Polish POWs in Poland. He added that he never met the Polish representative, Count Josef Czapski, despite claims to the contrary in Czapski's memoirs. Raikhman denied having been involved in the preparing of the false Soviet version of Katyn which was presented to the international tribunal at Nuremberg. He admitted that during the post-war years he was based in L'vov and fought against the Ukrainian nationalists, but not the Polish Home Army. Raikhman also showed an objective admiration for Ezhov and Abakumov almost claiming that before Beriia torture was unknown in NKVD.[42]

Even more fascinating was the career of L.I. Eitingon. Eitingon was born on December 1, 1899, to a poor family in the town of Skov in the Mogliev district. Like many Jews in radical politics, he joined the Socialist Revolutionary (SR) Party in 1917 and a year later the Red Army before entering the Cheka, where he served as Deputy Head in Gomel and helped crush a rebellion by the White officers who briefly seized the city. Eitingon joined the Bolsheviks in 1919 (1920 according to Sudoplatov) and soon came to the attention of Dzerzhinskii, who remained his hero. In 1921, he returned to Moscow and was assigned to the Cheka Foreign Department. In 1925, he was a student in the Frunze Academy, where his classmates included the future Marshal V.I. Chiukov. Sudoplatov also claims that the future Chief Marshal of Aviation A.E. Golovanov was a fellow student of Eitingon, but there is no record of Golovanov ever attending the Frunze Academy. Since Eitingon knew several languages (French, English, German, and Spanish), he served as an agent in the Far East and in the U.S. In China, he served with the Nationalist Chinese and knew V.K. Bliukher. In the 1920s, he also lived in France and as a Soviet agent recruited singer Nadezhda Plevitskaia to infiltrate the ranks of émigré White Generals. In the 1930s, Eitingon was all over West Europe, working under such assumed names as Kotov, Comrade Pablo, Leont'ev, Rabinovich, Sakhov, Valery, and Liova. He worked with the Soviet Trade Missions in London and Paris and was in charge of Soviet terrorist activities and the kidnapping of White Generals Kutepov, Miller, and Trotskii's grandson. He played an unsavory part in the liquidation of anarchists and supporters of Trotskii during the Spanish Civil War. He was one of the few of Ezhov's foreign operatives who did not become victims of the Great Purge. In 1939, he was appointed Deputy Head of NKVD 2 (later 4) (Executive Action) Department under P.A. Sudoplatov. In Paris, Eitingon recruited the Spanish Communist Caridad Mercader and her dull-witted son, Ramon Mercader. Caridad, a confused Spanish aristocrat, had deserted her husband after bearing four children, finding solace in radical politics. Eitingon, a notorious womanizer who was married several times, sometimes without the benefit of divorce, may have even had an affair with her, although this is denied as "unprofessional" by Sudoplatov. Revolutionaries, being profoundly immoral in public matters, sometimes lead saint like private lives. Here the Bolsheviks were usually an exception and multiple marriages and liaisons were fairly common among them. Ambassador A.M. Kollontai, now lionized as a bonafide feminist heroine, was one of the better-known practitioners. Another famous Bolshevik beauty, L.M. Reisner, went through at least two husbands, F.F. Raskol'nikov (Il'in) and P.E. Dybenko. She died in 1926 and missed seeing both men victimized by Stalin. Except for Beriia's, the sexual proclivities of Stalin's circle are not well-known. Unlike the Nazi leaders, who despite anti-homosexual rhetoric and laws included a good many of joyful persuasion, the Kremlin crowd seems to have been mostly dull heterosexuals. During his wife's imprisonment, Kalinin, for instance, drowned his sorrows by being a stage-door Johnny at the Bolshoi Theater. There were rumors, possibly planted by the Western intelligence agencies, that the last head of MGB, S.D. Igant'ev, was bisexual. Sudoplatov and Beriia's son who held Igant'ev in utter contempt do not, however, repeat this charge. The famous picture of Brezhnev drooling at the actress Jill St. John, a one-time companion of Dr. Henry Kissinger, during his visit to Washington, to say nothing of Marx's own life, is compelling evidence that Marxist-Leninists are not beyond the temptations of the flesh. The curse of strong drink, however, was an even greater bane of existence for those who toiled in the Kremlin, a condition not helped by working under Stalin. Some of the more famous victims included A.I. Rykov, Bulganin, Zhdanov, V.V. Kuibyshev, A.S. Shcherbakov, V.V. Ul'rikh, as well as Zhigarev and Novikov, who commanded the Air Force during the war, and of course Stalin's own younger son. According to Iu.B. Borev in *Staliniada*, Stalin also took a dim view of homosexuality, which he felt was a blight on the army.

In 1940, Eitingon managed with the help of G.B. Ovakimian (Maj. General, 1945), the Soviet Consul in New York, to infiltrate Trotskii's inner circle. On August 20, 1940, Trotskii died from the effects of an icepick sunk into his brain by Ramon Mercader, who was sentenced to 20 years by Mexican authorities. In April or May 1941, in ceremonies held in the Kremlin, Kalinin awarded Caridad Mercader the Order of Lenin. Sudoplatov and Eitingon were also decorated. In 1960, Ramon was released from prison and a year later, the Khrushchev regime made him a Hero of the Soviet Union (he had received the order of Lenin while in prison), the highest award the government can bestow on an individual, and gave him a pension of 400 rubles a month. Trotskii's murder was one crime of the Stalin regime with which Khrushchev had no quarrel. After living in Cuba, Prague, and Moscow, Mercader spent his last years in Havana, where he died of cancer on October 18, 1976.[43] Castro was motivated by pure opportunism when he provided Ramon Mercader with a last refuge. After all, in 1975, he had declared three days of national mourning when Franco had died, and under Franco, Caridad Mercader was subject to a death sentence.

An article in the April 1988 issue of the *New York Review of Books* on Freud's followers raised the question of Eitingon's relationship with one Max Eitingon, a native of Berlin who had performed dirty tricks for the father of psychoanalysis. As a cult leader, Freud was a far cry from the benign grandfatherly figure portrayed by his propagandists. He took strong exception to the writings of satirist Karl Kraus, who mocked psychoanalysis mumbo-jumbo (e.g., a disease it purports to cure). Although Max Eitingon did not go to the same extremes as had his namesake in eliminating Trotskii, he gave his best college try to destroy the career of Kraus.[44] There were now claims (by John Dziak and others and accepted mistakenly by this author) that Max Eitingon and L.I. Eitingon were actually brothers. Sudoplatov, who knew Eitingon better than anyone else, completely denies any relationship between the two men.

After the war, L.I. Eitingon continued as Sudoplatov's Deputy, but because he was a Jew, his career was in decline. During this period, Eitingon also dabbled in "psychic research," a field fraught with fraud and humbug which for some reason has fascinated the hard-nosed intelligence agencies the world over. He was put under arrest in October 1951 and freed only after Stalin's death. In 1954, he was arrested and sentenced to 10 years for unspecified charges and ended up in the Vladimir prison. After his release, he worked in 1966 with "Mezhdunarodnaia kniga" and "Progress" Publishing Houses which, strangely enough, also employed the dissident writer P.I. Iakir, son of the purged Red Army Commander I.E. Iakir. Eitingon died in 1981, unfortunately without leaving memoirs.[45]

Eitingon was not alone in prison in Vladimir. It also housed his former boss, P.A. Sudoplatov, the last senior survivor of Stalin's police apparatus, whose stunning memoirs were published in April 1994. The memoirs (more of an oral history) written by Sudoplatov and his son, a professor of statistics in the Moscow State University, for which they allegedly received $850,000 from the American publisher, caused a storm of controversy, almost all of it about Sudoplatov's claim that certain American atomic scientists provided his agents with useful information. This is, of course, only a small part of the book and has little relevance to the subject of the present study. Although self-serving and containing its share of errors, it is nevertheless a gold mine of information. In his foreword, Robert Conquest calls it the most informative autobiography to emerge from the Stalinist milieu and the most important single contribution to our knowledge since Khrushchev's secret speech. Nevertheless, there are problems of commission (Denmark was freed by the Red Army) and omissions (hardly a mention of Katyn or such important individuals as L.F. Bashtakov), and Sudoplatov's claims need to be carefully examined against other memoirs, reports, and documents. Sudoplatov's memoirs have also been correctly criticized for making unconfirmed accusations against various scientists employed by the Manhattan Project. These assertions, possibly embellished by others to increase the market value of the book, should not blind us to the fact that the rest of the memoirs contain a considerable amount of new information.

Born in Melitopol in 1907, Sudoplatov ran away from home at the age of 12 to fight the Whites. In 1921, he was assigned to a special department of a division fighting the Ukrainian nationalists. Shortly afterward he became a full-time employee of the Cheka in Zhitomir with the task of penetrating the nationalist underground. After the death of his brother, who served in the Border Troops, he moved back to Melitopol and spent three years establishing a network of informers among the local Greek and German communities. In 1927, he was assigned to the Secret Political Department of the Ukraine OGPU and also married a fellow Chekist. In 1933 (the date given by Sudoplatov, although it may have been earlier), V.A. Balitskii, Head of the Ukraine GPU and Commissar of Interior, was appointed as Deputy Commissar of OGPU under Menzhinskii and took Sudoplatov to Moscow with him. There the latter was assigned as a Senior Inspector in charge of promotions in the Foreign Department and came in contact with its Head, A.Kh. Artuzov; his successor, A.A. Slutskii; and the latter's Deputy and temporary successor M.A. Shpigelglas, a veteran agent who influenced him the most.

In the late 1920s, V.R. Menzhinskii, Head of OGPU, formed a special group for special operations to deploy against counter-revolutionary activities at home and abroad, which eventually became part of the GUGB/NKVD Secret Political and Foreign Departments. The duties of the "special group" (also called "special bureau," "special task," "special service," and "executive action") included criminal acts such as sabotage, murder, and kidnapping of those deemed enemies of the Soviet state such as the émigré White Generals in France, Spanish anarchists during the Civil War, and Trotskii and his family. Sudoplatov became part of this organization where his colleagues included L.I. Eitingon, A.A. Slutskii, G.A. Molchanov, Ia. A. Serebrianskii, M.A. Shpigelglas, P. Zubov, and, later, D.P. Kolesnikov (living in 1990), P.M. Fitin, and, after Beriia's appointment, possibly Sh.O. Tsereteli. Under Ezhov, this unit was called "Iasha's Group," named after its head, Ia.A. Serebrianskii, whose duties allegedly included use of poison. According to journalist N. Gevorkian and N. Petrov (*Moscow News*, Nos. 32 and 36, 1992), Sudoplatov's first operational success was the murder, via explosives, of E. Konovalets, a Ukrainian nationalist émigré leader, in Amsterdam on May 23, 1938. The fate of Konovalets had been decided in November 1937 when Sudoplatov met Stalin for the first time, accompanied by Ezhov. For those obsessed with "documentation," Stalin's instructions were no more incriminatory than what President Kennedy told his operatives which resulted in "termination with extreme prejudice" of President Diem of South Vietnam. As Deputy Head of GUGB/NKVD 4 Department, Sudoplatov was also involved in the murder of Trotskii's son and in the theft of documents from Trotskii's Paris headquarters. Sudoplatov was unusual in two respects: he was a Slav in an organization made up mostly of Jews (Sudoplatov's wife, née E. Kaganova, was Jewish) and he survived the holocaust of the 1930s purges in which most of his colleagues perished although even he had a close call in 1939. In fact, when late in 1938 he was called by Beriia and Dekanozov, the new Head of the Foreign Department, to discuss his boss M.A. Shpigelglas, he expected to be arrested. According to Sudoplatov, Shpigelglas had been purged since he had failed to liquidate

Trotskii, a task that was now assigned to Sudoplatov. (Shpigeglas's purge is questioned by A.I. Vaksberg in *Stalin Against the Jews*.) In March 1939, Sudoplatov met with Stalin, who made it abundantly clear that Trotskii had to be eliminated or else. In March 1939, after the 18 Party Congress, the name of the GUGB/NKVD Foreign Department was changed to the NKVD 1 Department, headed by P.M. Fitin with Sudoplatov as his Deputy. Within the Department, there was a "Special Service" (not to be confused with the 1 NKVD "Special Section" headed by L.F. Bashtakov). In the Stalinist lexicon there was no more sinister word than *Special*. The Special Service was headed by Sudoplatov and the recently released from prison Ia.A. Serebrianskii, and in July 1941 it became an independent department which did not report to any People's Commissariats—in other words, this was mainly Stalin's private terror organization. Its main responsibility was to work behind the enemy lines. In the fall of 1941, it made plans to leave subversives behind in case Moscow fell to the enemy. Plans were even made to assassinate Hitler in case he came to visit the occupied Moscow by using the composer L.K. Knipper (1898–1974), whose wife was related to Olga Chekhova (Tschechowa, 1897–1980, previously mentioned in this book), who had followed her German father to Germany to become a major movie star and a favorite of Hitler. Later, Sudoplatov's group became the NKVD 2 Department, and on January 18, 1942, the NKVD 4 Department headed by Sudoplatov with Eitingon as his Deputy. Along with Eitingon and Serebrianskii, P. Zubov, another veteran agent released from prison, worked with this organization. No fewer than 22 men were associated with this organization and its predecessors, including such well-known personalities as D.N. Medvedev, N.A. Prokopiuk, S.A. Vaupshasov, K.P. Orlovskii, N.I. Kuznetsov, V.A. Karasov, A.N. Shikhov, and E.I. Mirkovskii (Commander of the Dzerzhinskii Partisan Brigade in Belorussia and a close associate of Sudoplatov during the post-war years), won the title Hero of the Soviet Union).

In his memoirs, Sudoplatov discusses some of the heroic acts performed by these men, particularly N.I. Kuznetsov (posthumous Hero of the Soviet Union, November 5, 1944), who successfully impersonated a German officer, and denies the charges made by the Pamiat Society that Kuznetsov was involved in the deportation of Volga Germans in 1941. What Sudoplatov does not tell is the effect of his operations on the course of the war and whether they were justified in view of the enormous losses suffered or the savage German reprisals against the civilian population of the occupied territories. There was also the mystery figure A.P. Osipov, who appears in the collection *The OSS-NKVD Relationship 1943–1945*, as the Head of the "NKVD section conducting subversive activities." Osipov met with General John Deane of the OSS and the British Brigadier George Hill to coordinate operations. These documents, in which even the name of the NKVD Foreign Department head P.M. Fitin is frequently misspelled, however, add very little to our knowledge of Osipov or his subsequent activities. No mention is made of Osipov in Sudoplatov's memoirs. In December 1943, Osipov, Beriia, and Molotov were also involved in negotiations with OSS Chief General William "Wild Bill" Donovan, who, without consulting his superiors, worked out an exchange agreement in which the NKVD and OSS would coordinate their activities against Germany, and in fact, establish liaison offices in Moscow and Washington. Because of bureaucratic rivalries, and even though it made no operational sense, Abakumov, the Head of Counter-intelligence, and his American counterpart, J. Edgar Hoover, were excluded from the proceedings. Hoover, Donovan's implacable enemy, however, managed to frustrate the agreement by backdoor maneuvering.

The 4 Department not only carried out acts of terrorism against the enemy such as the assassination of Gauleiter Kube in Belorussia, but equally targeted such groups as the Ukrainian nationalists or for that matter, anyone suspected of disloyalty behind the enemy lines. As Sudoplatov stated truthfully in 1989 in a letter to the USSR Prosecutor General, in carrying out his duties he did not report to Beriia but to the Central Committee (Stalin). It would be interesting to speculate on the relationship between the 4 Department and SMERSH, who also had a major interest in terror behind enemy lines and the General Staff of the Partisan Movement under P.K. Ponomarenko, whose name is not even mentioned in Sudoplatov's memoirs. During 1944–1946, a "Branch C" was formed in the 4 Department which was engaged in atomic espionage. Sudoplatov was also involved in recruiting agents among the Polish POWs in preparation for Katyn and received the Order of Red Star for his contributions. During the war, he may have also been involved with the Rote Kapelle spy network. In 1942, Beriia ordered Sudoplatov and Fitin to check into the activities of A.F. Kerenskii, with a view of silencing him—a fact also not mentioned in Sudoplatov's memoirs. It seems that after the war, Sudoplatov and his new Deputy, L.F. Raikhman, were stationed in L'vov fighting the Ukrainian nationalists and the Polish Home Army.

Besides atomic espionage and fighting the Ukrainian nationalists, there were other operations, including the use of Kurdish refugees to subvert Western interests in the Middle East. Both Abakumov and Igant'ev worked with Sudoplatov in using the Kurdish leader Mustafa Barzani, in exile in the Soviet Union since 1946 after being double-crossed by the Shah. Sudoplatov was sent to Baku in 1947 under cover to negotiate with the Kurds without informing Bagirov, the Party boss in Azerbaidzhan. The upshot was that the Kurds, whose enemies included Iran, Iraq, and Turkey, were moved to Tashkent and became a pawn of bureaucratic rivalries in the last months of Stalin's life. Nothing came of using him as a subversive force or of setting up a Kurdish autonomous region in the Soviet Union. N.F. Bugai's recent study, *Sovetskie Kurdy* (1993) also does not shed much light on this episode.

In his appeal to the 23rd Party Congress in 1966 while still in prison (*Moscow News*, No. 36, 1992), Sudoplatov stated that in 1946, Abakumov dissolved the 4 Department and instead asked him and Eitingon to set up a "special service" attached to the MGB to carry out acts of terror within and outside the Soviet Union against the enemies of the State. Those who were eliminated in 1946–1947 included the Head of the Greek Catholic Church in Ukraine, Romzha, who was assassinated in the town of Mukachev. According to Sudoplatov, Khrushchev, then First Secretary of the Ukraine Party, had recommended the elimination of Romzha. Another victim was one Shumskii, leader of the so-called Shumskist faction of Ukrainian nationalists, whose elimination was recommended by Stalin and Kaganovich and transmitted by Abakumov. Then there was the case of one Isaak Oggins (Higgins?), an American citizen who had ended up in the Gulag after his arrest on February 20, 1939, but had somehow managed to contact the U.S. Embassy in April 1942 requesting an exit visa. Finally, there was the case of the engineer Samet, a former citizen of Poland living in Ul'ianovsk, who was murdered by direct order of Stalin via Bulganin and Abakumov since he had allegedly planned to leave the Soviet Union to give information about Russian submarines to the Americans. For an organization that had organized the Gulag and Katyn, these seem to be children's games and Abakumov showed little enthusiasm for such operations, but they were favored by Stalin, his successors, as well as the CIA, and the Princes of Camelot. Abakumov, who had also had his share of disagreements with Sudoplatov during the war, also correctly assumes that the latter's loyalty was to Beriia. In fact, Abakumov dissolved the Special Service in 1949. On September 9, 1950, the Central Committee approved MGB's proposal to replace the Special Service with two bureaus: No. 1 headed by Sudoplatov for sabotage operations abroad, and No. 2 headed by Maj. General V.A. Drozdov (Deputy Head of MGB in the Ukraine) for similar operations in the USSR. Sudoplatov's original organization allegedly included a 4th section which supported laboratories that would manufacture poison. Sudoplatov in his memoirs heatedly denies this and claims that this department was part of V.M. Blokhin's Kommandatura Department (execution squads), although he availed himself of their services on a number of occasions.

In March 1939, this section was headed by M.P. Filimonov, who on April 27, 1940, was the recipient of the Order of the Mark of Honor for unspecified accomplishments. In his report, Sudoplatov refers to him as a doctor and pharmacist. Two men who actually headed laboratories, G.M. Maironovskii (the uncle of Mrs. Sudoplatov) and S. Muromtsev, testified during the Beriia trial that Sudoplatov and Eitingon insisted that poison be tried on live subjects. *Moscow News* (No. 23, 1990) cites a number of "special folders" in which Beriia, Merkulov, Sudoplatov, Blokhin, Filimonov, Eitingon, and Maironovskii are implicated in human experiments. In his interrogation dating from August 27, 1953, Maironovskii admitted that he had killed several dozen prisoners delivered by Blokhin, head of the execution squads, by administering poison through food, drink, or injection. Maironovskii is not a completely credible witness. A researcher in toxicology and a graduate of the Grokii All Union Institute of Experimental Medicine, which in 1938 was taken over by NKVD, Maironovskii was employed by the 2 Department, where he was allegedly involved in human experiments, which are, however, denied by the surviving members of his family (*Moscow News*, No. 39, 1990). In December 1951, he was arrested by MGB and accused of espionage and interrogated by Riumin. He was sentenced to 10 years and was kept in prison until after Stalin's death. He also testified, a broken man, during the trial of Sudoplatov and his colleagues. He was released in December 1961 and died three years later. Muromtsev was Head of the NKVD/ NKGB/MGB Microbiology Laboratory between 1937 and 1951 (what went on there is anybody's guess). In 1956, he was appointed Director of the Institute of

Epidemiology and Microbiology at the USSR Academy of Medical Sciences. He died in 1960. No official charges had been placed against him or Filimonov. Regardless, in 1946 after the disbanding of the 4 Special Department, the two laboratories were transferred to the MGB Operational Technologies Department (later KGB Operation Department), where they remained until recently. There are also rumors, denied by Sudoplatov, that he ran a "death laboratory" in Karagand labor camps.

Abakumov's lack of enthusiasm for individual terrorist acts was to be somewhat remedied by his replacement Igant'ev. In December 1951, Igant'ev, with help from Rukahdze, Head of MGB in Georgia, possibly in response to instructions from the Central Committee, sent a plan to Stalin to eliminate E. Gegechkori, N. Zhordania, I. Chkhenkeli, and I. Tsereteli, Georgian émigré leaders in France, and S. Mengarishvili and M. Alshibai, who held similar positions in Turkey and West Germany. Nothing came of this, but it is extraordinary that Stalin now would decide to kill some of the very men whom he had tried to woo back in 1946 when Shariia was sent to Paris. On December 28, 1951, Igant'ev and the War Minister, Marshal of the Soviet Union A.M. Vasilevskii, wrote to Stalin about a joint effort to carry out sabotage in Western military bases, lamenting that such acts had stopped after the war. Their elaborate plan involved setting up a special group to train phony defectors as well as agents who would pose as guardians of Soviet military cemeteries abroad. The focus of the operation would be in Austria and Germany. The fact that Vasilevskii was willing to work with the MGB to carry out missions in direct violation of international laws puts him, usually considered an apolitical professional, in a bad light.

The last operation carried out by the 1 Bureau during Stalin's life took place in Munich on February 13, 1953, when Wolfgang Zalus, a former bodyguard of Trotskii, was poisoned by an MGB agent. The slow-acting poison killed Zalus on March 4, 1953, and his symptoms were diagnosed as pneumonia. Later in March, Igant'ev reported about this operation to Beriia, Malenkov, Molotov, Bulganin and Khrushchev. Drozdov, writing to Kruglov on August 6, 1953, described the mission of the 2 Bureau as to "fulfill assignments inside the Soviet Union aimed at cutting short hostile activities with the use of special methods." According to Gevorkian and Petrov (*Moscow News*, No. 36, 1992), the Bureau had 12 regular and 60 secret employees. Bureau No. 2 lasted from October 1950 until April 1953 and was disbanded shortly after Stalin's death when MVD and MGB were merged under Beriia. In a memo to the Central Committee Presidium, Kruglov, and Serov claimed that the 2 Bureau had handled no secret missions, although they added that it had helped other MGB departments in the elimination of nationalists in the North Caucasus and Lithuania in 1951–1952. Regardless, the terroristic activities did not stay in limbo for long and were soon to surface as the KGB 9 Department (Special Operations) under L.A. Studnikov and M.G. Grivanov and was active throughout the Cold War years.

After Beriia's return, Sudoplatov was the Deputy Head MVD 1 Department until May 1953, and then its Head until his arrest in August or September 1953 along with Eitingon and Serebrianskii. In his memoirs, *In the Name of Conscience*, the defector N.E. Khokhlov, describes his refusal to carry out the assassination of NTS leader G.S. Okolovich in Germany (allegedly organized by A.S. Paniushkin, Soviet Ambassador to the U.S., 1947–1952) in February 1954 and the subsequent defection which proved highly embarrassing to the MVD. Khokhlov who also claims that Beriia actually founded the 9 Department and put Sudoplatov in charge and gives a dramatic account of Sudoplatov's arrest after Beriia's fall. After his arrest, Sudoplatov feigned mental illness and spent five years in a Leningrad clinic before being transferred to a hospital in Kazan and finally to the Vladimir prison. He was brought to trial in 1958. The charges mainly involved being part of the "Beriia machine." Sudoplatov was sentenced to 15 years and lost his rank and medals. After his release, he waged a campaign to restore his good name which came to fruition in January 1992 when the Military Collegium of the Russian Supreme Court rehabilitated him, restoring his pension but not his medals. The pension, to say nothing of the advance received for his memoirs, should provide sufficiently for Sudoplatov for the rest of his life, a strange ending for a Stalinist police operative. Eitingon and Serebrianskii (who died in prison) received 12-year sentences. The odd man out here was the shadowy figure of Ia.I. Serebrianskii. A former SR, he had been a member of the "Special Group" in the NKVD Foreign Department and had organized kidnapping and assassinations in Western Europe as well as the stealing of Trotskii's archives through M.G. Zboroskii. Serebianvskii has been identified as the first Head of the "Special Group," also called "Special Task." Apparently, he was first arrested in 1939 and sentenced to death but was reprieved. His career, however, seems not to have recovered, and he is not listed in the ranks of Police Generals in July 1945. Sudoplatov's memoirs contain considerable information about him. According to Pierre de Villemarest and Sudoplatov, in 1962 Rudolf Abel and 23 other agents signed a petition asking Khrushchev to free Eitingon and Sudoplatov but were turned down. Brezhnev was more sympathetic, and Eitingon was released in 1965 and Sudoplatov in 1968.[46]

During the Khrushchev years, the prison in Vladimir (described in some detail in the memoirs of U–2 pilot Francis Gary Powers, who spent time there) was the government's favorite place of incarceration for those with embarrassing secrets from the past. Besides Sudoplatov, Mamulov, and Eitingon, and until March 1955, the former Lt. General of Aviation V.I. Stalin, the prisoners included German Field Marshal Ewald Von Kleist, Wilhelm Munters, the pre-war Minister of Foreign Affairs in Latvia who had once been a candidate to head a pro-Soviet puppet government, and the fascinating figure of P.A. Shariia, ghost writer not only for Beriia, but for Stalin as well. Born in 1902, Shariia was in the Sukhum Seminary during 1919–1920. Religious training in which one learns that the doctrine can be twisted to justify almost anything was as crucial for Shariia as it had been for Stalin. Shariia joined the Party in 1920 and in 1922 was a student in Tbilisi University. From 1924 to 1930, he was in the Krupskaia Academy and in the Party Institute of Philosophy. He may have also attended the Institute of the Red Professors, a Stalinist seminary cum school for scoundrels whose alumni include Mekhlis, Tovstukha, and P.N.

322 The Lesser Terror

Pospelov (another falsifier, author of *Stalin, a Short Biography*). From 1930 until March 1934, Shariia was a university philosophy professor in Georgia, before being attached to the Propaganda Section of the Tbilisi and later the Georgia Party organization. Shariia has been credited with editing at least one volume of Stalin's works as well as writing with E.D. Bedia (who was later purged) and perhaps other contributors, *On the History of the Bolshevik Organization in Transcaucasus* (1935), an early example of Stalinist historiography, published under Beriia's name, a man who reportedly had not read a book published since Gutenberg. In this patently false account, Shariia followed Kingsley Amis' definition of feminist history by making up facts as he went along. As Orwell said, political language is designed to make lies sound truthful and murder respectable and to give an appearance of solidity to pure wind. Reading the Beriia/Shariia opus, one is also reminded of a review once written by Lord Macaulay: "Compared with the labor of reading these volumes, all other labor, the labor of thieves on the treadmill, the labor of children in the mines, the labor of slaves on the plantation, is but a pleasant recreation." In 1939, Shariia was important enough to be appointed to a commission formed by the CPSU Central Committee to study the excesses of the Ezhov regime. Shariia's career during the war is not clear, but in 1943, he has been identified as having the title "Commissar of State Security 3 Rank." However, he was not on the 1945 list of Police Generals nor among those who received citations during the war. According to Beriia's bodyguard, R.S. Sarkisov, at one time, Shariia and Rapava were Beriia's closest confidants, discussing Stalin in Georgian.[47] Regardless, Shariia was far from being a harmless professor; V.M. Maksimilishvili, who served as Beriia's secretary testified that truncheons used to beat the prisoners were kept in Shariia's office.

In the Central Committee meeting of early July 1953, a claim was made that, after leaving Georgia in 1938, Beriia ruled his old fiefdom through Shariia and Rapava, even though Shariia did not have a high position in the Party or government. In 1943, Shariia's son died of tuberculosis, and this tragedy had political consequences. Shariia, who fancied himself an intellectual, wrote some verses to the memory of his son which were labeled as "mystical," a charge which I don't think was ever hurled against any other member of the Party. Shariia, who had been elected in 1945 as the Party Secretary for Agitation and Propaganda, was reassigned in 1948 to teaching philosophy in Tbilisi, and the decision of the Georgia Party was approved by the CC CPSU on May 31, 1948. In 1945, Shariia became involved in attempts by the USSR government to lure back to their homelands various Soviet nationalities in diaspora. The chief targets were the Armenian survivors and their descendants of the first attempt in the 20th century at a "Final Solution" of an ethnic problem, a tragedy whose enormity has yet to be fully comprehended. Many of those who took up Stalin's offer were to end up in the Gulag. Shariia's job was to go to Paris and persuade the Georgian émigrés to return home. He met with a number of Georgian Menshevik leaders such as N. Zhordania, V. Gambashidze, E. Gegechkori, and I. Gobechia. He also met with the nephew of Beriia's wife, one Shavdia, who after being captured during the war, had joined the German-sponsored

Georgian Legion. Shariia's reports were avidly read by Stalin, who may have felt a touch of nostalgia for his old enemies. On May 26, 1947, the Politburo gave 59 Georgian emigrants and their families the right to return to the USSR. Their fate subsequent to their return is not known. After Beriia's arrest, both he and Shariia were denounced for these contacts, even though they could not have been made without Stalin's approval. It is also interesting, as will be related elsewhere, that in 1951, the MGB under Igan'tev mounted an abortive campaign to assassinate several Georgian émigré leaders in France in what must have been a change in policy. In 1947, Shariia also visited England along with M.A. Suslov and V.V. Kuznetsov. In 1952, Shariia was arrested in connection with the "Mingrelian Affair," but was released in mid- March 1953 after Stalin's death and rejoined the Beriia group, only to be re-arrested after Beriia's fall. In the meeting of the Central Committee in early July 1953, no one except Beriia was denounced in stronger terms than Shariia (a mystic windbag, according to Molotov), and it was a miracle that he did not end up in the dock with the Beriia group in December 1953. Instead, it seems that he was tried in secret and received a 10-year sentence. On June 26, 1963, Shariia was released and returned to the Caucasus, where he died in 1983.[48] His memoirs would be most interesting. Also spending 10 years in the Vladimir prison was B.A. Liudvigov, Beriia's chief clerk during 1939–1953, another whose memoirs would be valuable.

B.G. Men'shagin, the quisling mayor of Smolensk during the German occupation, was also in the Vladimir prison during this period. Men'shagin was a man with a checkered past. Before the war, he had practiced law in Minsk and apparently had close connections with the local NKVD. In 1937, he defended one of the three notorious Zhukov brothers, all employed by the secret police, whose outlaw behavior had even embarrassed the NKVD. (One brother, G.S. Zhukov, was later the Head of the NKVD Office for Central and East Europe and played a part in Katyn and in the formation of the Polish units that served with the Red Army.) Men'shagin became an active collaborator and served as the Mayor of Smolensk during the brutal German occupation. As we were to see during the Cold War period, Soviet security and intelligence operatives had no problem in defecting to the other side to be hailed as Pauls who had seen the light on the road to Damascus and then perfectly willing to parrot the lines of their new masters. Men'shagin left Smolensk with the retreating Germans and for a while served as the Mayor of Bobruisk. At the end of the war, he was interned by the U.S. forces in Karlovy Vary. He was arrested on May 28, 1945, while looking for his family and repatriated to the Soviets. In 1951 was sentenced to 25 years in prison, was released after serving 23 years, and died in 1984.[49] History, however, benefitted from Men'shagin's incarceration since he spent some of his sentence in the Vladimir prison in the company of some of Beriia's surviving henchmen, even sharing a cell with S.S. Mamulov. Besides Beriia's former colleagues, the Vladimir prison held a number of other inmates, including M.A. Shteinberg, veteran of the Spanish Civil War and Soviet agent in Switzerland, who had refused to return to the Soviet Union in the late 1930s only to make the always-fatal mistake of trusting Stalin's promise and return after the war only to end up in prison (Shteinberg was not released until 1965), a fate shared by his wife. Also imprisoned were E. Brik, nephew of O. Brik and a friend of the poet Miaskovskii who had spent time in the U.S., and the veteran Georgian Social Democrat S.L. Goriberidze. Other inmates included the already discussed V.V. Shul'gin, Wilhelm Munters, L.I. Eitingon, S.S. Mamulov, P.A. Shariia, the alleged poisoner G.M. Maironovskii, B.A. Liudvigov (Ludvigov), Lt. General of Aviation V.I. Stalin (who entered there on April 28, 1953 under the name V.P. Vasil'ev, a cover name also used by his father during the war), and two women Ukrainian nationalists, Maria Dydik and Daria Gusiak. The memoirs of Sudoplatov and Men'shagin and those of another prisoner, R.I. Pimenov (O. Volin), (*Sovershenno Sekretno*, June 1989), add considerably to our knowledge of these individuals.

One Chekist who deserves a special mention is V.M. Blokhin, quite possibly the greatest executioner in history. In August 1992, the Soviet government reported that during Stalin's rule, the NKVD carried out 828,000 official executions, a figure strongly disputed by the Pamiat Society and by the aforementioned N. Grashoven and M. Kirillin.[50] Blokhin, as head of the execution squads under Iagoda, Ezhov and Beriia must have been responsible for a good percentage of them. Unlike Beriia and Himmler, who were physical cowards and remote-control killers, Blokhin was a hands-on executioner, taking part, for instance, in the shooting of the Polish POW officers from the Oshtakov camp who were killed in April 1940 in the headquarters of the NKVD in Kalinin. Abarinov claims that Blokhin committed suicide but gives no date. If true, this must have happened after 1945, since Blokhin was then listed as one of the NKVD Maj. Generals.[51]

The question now facing us is whether any of the senior officials who ran Stalin's security and intelligence organizations is still living. As of 1991, the senior surviving Chekist was P.A. Sudoplatov. My own efforts to contact him through his son, a professor in the Moscow State University, were not successful. Lord Nicholas Bethell had better luck and met with Sudoplatov in the summer of 1991. Unfortunately, Sudoplatov, who at 85 was still quite alert, was not forthcoming and merely mouthed off Stalinist propaganda.[52]

Also living in the early 1990s was the former Lt. General L.F. Bashtakov, the former Head of the dreaded 1 NKVD Special Section. He was implicated in almost all the important operations of the early 1940s, including Katyn, the killing of political prisoners and senior military officers in the fall of 1941, and the Erlich-Alter affair. We have already touched on his career.[53] Before the coup, he was under investigation by the Office of the Chief Military Prosecutor for the murder of M.A. Spiridonova, one of the political prisoners shot in Orel on September 11, 1941. Born in 1884, Spiridonova was a member of the Socialist Revolutionary Party. In January 1906, she assassinated the Vice Governor of Tambov. She was in prison until the February Revolution. She was a member of the LSR Party Central Committee and opposed the Brest Litovsk Treaty. In July 1918, she was involved in the LSR revolt in Moscow and in November 1918 was sentenced to a year in prison for her part, but she was amnestied and retired from politics. She was dragged to prison in the 1930s, accused of plotting to assassinate Voroshilov, and had the misfortune of being in the Orel prison in the fall of 1941.[54] Bashtakov has yet to be tried for this crime. Under the new Russia, the wheels of justice are as slow and methodical as they were arbitrary under Stalin.

Another important serving functionary is the former Maj. General P.K. Soprunenko. In April 1940, as Head of the NKVD POW Department, he was deeply involved in organizing the "selections" of Polish POW officers destined for massacre in Katyn and elsewhere. His career otherwise is not well-known, and he was probably replaced as Head of the POW Department in 1951 by A.Z. Kobulov. There is considerable literature, mostly by German prisoners, about POW camp life in which despite the hardships, an average prisoner had a better chance of survival than his Russian counterpart in German captivity. In 1991, the USSR Chief Military Prosecutor began to take action against Soprunenko for his part in the massacre of 6,000 Polish POW officers from the Ostashkov camp. At 83, nearly blind and recovering from a cancer operation, Soprunenko was using a Kaltenbrunner Defense" (denying his own signature, etc.) during interrogations.[55] More forthcoming was another senior official, former Maj. General V.S. Tokarev, Head of NKVD in Kalinin from December 1938. Tokarev's testimony finally shed light on the fate of Polish prisoners in the Oshtakov camp near Kalinin. Tokarev, who at age 89 was quite lucid, claimed that he was an innocent bystander while the death squad from Moscow commanded by V.M. Blokhin and (M.S.?) Krivenko, (both conveniently dead; Krivenko in 1962), killed prisoners, some as young as 18, from the Oshtakov camp in the Kalinin prison in April 1940 with German-made weapons. He also implicated Soprunenko.[56] What Tokarev has yet to explain is for what reason he received the Order of Mark of Honor on April 27, 1940. (Blokhin received the Order of Red Banner on the same date, since he had already received the Order of the Mark of Honor back in 1937.) It seems that the abortive coup of August 1991 slowed the investigation of crimes committed during the Stalin period.

Beriia, Abakumov, their predecessors and cohorts were the logical heirs of the Bolshevik Revolution, as was their leader Stalin. They were also practitioners of the game of "intelligence," a form of malevolent infantile game playing whose usefulness, at least in the international arena, has yet to be proved. If there ever was a relationship between massive investment in intelligence and success on the world scene, then the Soviet Union should have been the ultimate superpower. On the opposing side, Harry Truman, the ultimate recipient of information from a similar massive intelligence apparatus, would state in June 24, 1948, "I like old Joe Stalin. He's a good fellow, but he's a *prisoner* of the Politburo. He would make certain agreements, but they won't let him keep them." The CIA also failed to predict the invasion of South Korea or the development of the Soviet nuclear programs. In the late 1980s, the CIA's analysis of the Soviet economy, which provided the framework for U.S. foreign policy towards the Soviet Union, was as phony as the Soviet GNP figures on which it was based, but more importantly, it served the political agenda of the agency, its allies in Congress, the White House, and academia. Aldrich Ames, who was in a position to know and exploit the situation adds that the espionage business was and is a self-serving sham carried out by career bureaucrats who have managed to deceive several generations of American policymakers and the public.

Foche, the father of modern intelligence, used it to serve and, in turn, betray all his masters. Stalin's police chiefs, perhaps to their eternal regret, never entertained the idea of doublecrossing the "vozhd," although Beriia may have been tempted in the last months of Stalin's rule. For practitioners of intelligence the world over, regardless of affiliation and ideology, deception and betrayal are the central facts of life. "Gentlemen," Henry Stimson said, "do not read other people's mail." Stalin's police chiefs were no gentlemen. In his brief conversation in 1946 with Leopold Trepper, Abakumov remarked, There are only two ways to thank those in the intelligence service: either cover their chests with medals, or cut off their heads." Abakumov was destined for both fates. Abakumov was also the product of what Ron Rosenbaum had called the Age of Paranoia, the plague of suspicion, distrust, disinformation, conspiracy, and the pervasive feeling of unfathomable deceit that has emanated from intelligence agencies East and West.

Abakumov and Beriia, and, for that matter, Himmler, were also modern bureaucrats for whom questions of morality and conscience did not enter into the equation. One needs only to look at the ease with which the Weimar bureaucracy and its functionaries such as Gestapo Müller transferred their allegiance to Hitler to note the absence of ethical considerations in large modern organizations.

Eric Hoffer, who had seen the corruption of the civil rights and the feminist movement adds, "When a mass movement begins to attract people who are interested in their individual careers, it is a sign that it has passed its vigorous stage; that it is no longer engaged in molding a new world, but in possessing and preserving the present. It ceases then to be a movement and becomes an enterprise." These remarks equally apply to Stalinism, which ended up being the greatest criminal enterprise of all time. As these last survivors of the Stalinist period fade into history, the central question remains why a regime with the stated goal of creating utopia could cause so much misery. The Stalinist excesses have been sometimes blamed on Russia's "Asian" roots, but the fact remains that more people were put to death during the Paris Commune than were officially executed in the 19th Century in Russia under the Tsars. Richard Pipes has stated, "Revolutionaries may have the most radical ideas of remaking man and society, but they must build the new order with human material molded by the past. For that reason, sooner or later, they succumb to the past themselves...as objects that revolve do return to their starting point." In the words of playwright Ben Hecht, "There comes a time in all revolutions when the masses get a little punch drunk. A mysterious yearning rises in them, a yearning to surrender to some iron-faced leader who'll rid them of thinking and dreaming." That causal, but astute observer Anthony Daniels has also written "that only those steeped in the Marxist-Leninist philosophy, with its utter contempt for the 'unenlightened' past and for men as they are, combined with its boundless optimism about the perfectibility of Man and the gloriousness of his distant future, would engage in social engineering on so vast a scale, at once tragic and comically half-baked. It was never a utopia, of course. The extraordinary deadness of Communist countries, even at their airports, is simply the deadness of Communist prose transferred to life itself. The schemes of Communist leaders to reform the whole of humanity, to eradicate all vestiges of the past, to build a new world with no connection to the old, are not whims of despots made mad by the exercise of arbitrary power, but the natural outcome of too credulous a belief in a philosophy which is simply arrogant, vituperative, and wrong."[57] Also, Paul Johnson has pointed out the religious overtones of the modern state and the replacement of God by secular power which would justify just about any criminal action for a Greater Cause. When the state is credited with godlike power, then genocide is the logical outcome. If there is a lesson to be learned from the Stalinist experiment, it is the malevolent nature of the modern state. The fact also remains that corruption too is the integral part of any ideology or organization that claims to be infallible.

The great observer of modern politics H.L. Mencken once wrote,

I believe that all government is evil and trying to improve it is largely a waste of time...no government, of its own motion, will increase its own weakness, for that would mean to acquiesce in its own destruction. Governments, whatever their pretensions otherwise, try to preserve themselves by holding the individual down...government itself, indeed, may be reasonably defined as a conspiracy against him. Its one permanent aim, whatever its form, is to hobble him sufficiently to maintain itself.

Stalin is dead, but the main tenet of Stalinism, the state as the ultimate social engineer, is very much alive and dominates the agenda of academia and the intellectual and media elites and is the driving force behind most of what passes as "politically correct" and the never-ending quest for the amorphous "social justice." The left, sharing this fundamental tenet could not quite accept Stalinism as truly evil. It obviously does not heed the words of George F. Kennen, a man they admire, perhaps for the wrong reasons:

Humanity divides...between those who, in their political philosophy, place the emphasis on order and those who place it on justice. Human justice is always imperfect. The laws on which it bases itself are always to some extent unjust. These laws have therefore only a relative value; and it is only relative benefits that can be expected from the effort to improve them. But the good order of society is something tangible and solid. There is little that can be done about men's motives; but if men can be restrained in their behavior, something is accomplished. The benefit of the doubt should lie, therefore, with the forces of order, not with the world-improvers.

Sadly the right, which should have known better, took its cue from the ex-Trotskiite James Burnam, justifying anything, including the creation of an all-powerful imperial central state, once an anathema, to fight what turned out to be a highly overrated enemy. As John LeCarré recently wrote, "The fight against Communism diminished us, it left us in a state of false and corrosive orthodoxy and licensed our excesses."

NOTES

1. *Pravda* (June 22, 1989).
2. *Istoriia SSR* (2/1991).
3. *Sputnik* (10/1988).
4. *VIZH* (8/1992); V.V. Karpov, *Marshal Zhukov*, Vol. 1, pp.75–76.
5. *Beriia: Konets Kar'ery*, p. 399.
6. Aron Abramovich, *V Reshaiushchei Voine*, pp. 536–47.
7. B. Polevoi, *The Final Reckoning: Nuremberg Diaries.*
8. *Leningradskoe Delo*, p. 8.
9. *VIZH* (4–5/1992).
10. Robert Conquest, *Stalin: Breaker of Nations*, p. 242.
11. *Sotsiologicheskie Issledvaniia* (6/1991); Volkogonov, *Triumf*, book 2, part 2, p. 68; *Istoriia SSSR* (5/1991).
12. K.S. Karol, *Between Two Worlds*, p. 213.
13. Robert Tucker, *Stalin in Power*, p. 310.
14. *The Penkovsky Papers*, p. 104.
15. *U Kremlevskoi Steny*, p. 280.
16. *Izvestiia TsK KPPS* (2/1991); *VIZH* (12/1991).
17. Volkogonov, *Triumf*, book 2, part 2, p. 201.
18. For Maslennikov's career during the war, see *Poaranichniki*, pp. 63–108 and Volkogonov, *Triumf*, Book 2: Part 1, pp. 364–65, 396. For early days of the war, see P.I. Batov, *V pokhodakh I Boiakh.*
19. For Beriia's military career, see Volkogonov, *Triumf*, and *Beriia: Konets Kar'ery.*
20. Volkogonov, *Triumf*, book 2, part 1, p. 364.
21. Ibid., p. 365.
22. Kostliarov, *Golgofa*, p. 66.
23. Robert Conquest, *Inside Stalin's Secret Police: NKVD 1936–1939*, p. 155.
24. Christopher Andrew, and Oleg Gordievsky, *KGB. the Inside*, p. 347.
25. P. Deriabin, and Frank Gibney, *The Secret World*, p. 108.
26. V.K. Abarinov, *Katynskii Labirint*, pp. 98–101.
27. P. Deriabin, *Watchdogs of Terror*, p. 109; *Izvestiia TsK KPPS* (11/1989).
28. A.I. Skryl'nik, *General Armii A.A. Epishev*, p. 209. For Ephishev's career during the war, see K.S. Moskalenko, *Na Iuao- Zapadnom Napravlenii 1943–1945.*
29. Volkogonov, *Triumf*, book 2, part 2, pp. 189–90.
30. For Rodos, see *Izvestiia TsK KPSS* (3/1989) and Chapter 4, note 4 of this volume. For Shvartsman, see also the same footnote; K.A. Kostliarov, *Golgofa*; and *Nedelia* (Issues 20 and 44/1990).
31. For A.Z. Kobulov, see *Izvestiia TsK KPSS* (1/1991).
32. Ibid. (2/1991).
33. Leonid Plyushch, *History's Carnival*, p. 238.
34. Alexander Orlov, *The Secret Histoxy of Stalin's Crimes*, p. 230; Vladimir Petrov, *Empire of Fear*, p. 81; and Kirill Khenkin, *Okhotnik Vvrekh Noaami*, p. 25.
35. *Novoye Russkoye Slovo* (March 13, 1982).
36. Conquest, Robert: *Inside Stalin's Secret Police.*
37. For Pitrovanov, see *Izvestiia* (October 4, 1949); Volkogonov, *Triumf*, book 2, pp. 287–88, 296–97.
38. Andrew and Gordievsky, *KGB*, pp. 416–17; *Beriia: Konets Kar'ery*, p. 166.
39. For Voronin, see A. Chuinnov, *Na Stremnine Veka.*

40. *Literaturnaia Gazeta* (September 6, 1989); and Abarinov, op. cit., pp. 84–106;*Izvestiia TsK KPSS* (1/1991); *VIZH* (3/1990 and 9/1990); and Jozef Czpapski, *The Inhuman Land.*

41. *Moskovskii Komsomolets* (May 19, 1989).

42. Abarinov, pp. 84–106.

43. *Beriia: Konets Kar'ery*, pp. 170–74; *Literaturnaia Gazeta* (January 14, 1989).

44. For Mark Eitingon, see Thomas Szasz, *Karl Kraus and the Soul Doctors.*

45. *Literaturnaia Gazeta* (January 4, 1989); and *Minuvshe* (7/1989).

46. For Sudoplatov, see B.G. Men'shagin, *Vospominaniia; Mezhdunarodnaia Zhizn'* (5/1990); *Izvestiia TsK KPSS* (9/1990 and 1/1991); *New Times* (Issue 37, 1991).

47. For Shariia, see *Minuvshe* (7/1989); and *Beriia: Konets Kar'ery.*

48. *Beriia: Konets Kar'ery*, p. 357; Pavel Sudoplatov and Anatoli Sudoplatov, *Special Tasks*, p. 417.

49. For Men'shagin, see V.K. Abarinov, op. cit., pp. 155–65, 173–80; Men'shagin, *Vospominaniia; New Times* (Issue 16, 1990), p. 38.

50. V.K. Abarinov, *The Murders of Katyn*, p. 375; and *RFE/RE Reports* (36/1989, 18/1992). See also Hochschild (op. cit.), pp. 155–58.

51. Ibid., p. 374; *Observer* (October 6, 1991).

52. *New Times* (Issue 37, 1991), pp. 46–47; personal correspondence with Nicholas Bethell.

53. For Bashtakov, see *Moscow News* (12/1990); *Izvestiia TsK KPSS* (11/1990); and Abarinov, op. cit.

54. *Nedelia* (Issue 27, 1989), pp. 17–18.

55. *Observer* (October 6, 1991).

56. Ibid.

57. Anthony Daniels, *Wilder Shores of Marx*, p. 198.

Appendix I

General Officers of NKVD/NKGB (MVD/MGB), SMERSH (March 1945, July 9, 1945–July 11, 1945)*

Marshal of the Soviet Union:
Beriia, L.P. (Georgian)

ARMY GENERALS
Maslennikov, I.I. (Slav) (July 28, 1944) (Border Troops Lt. General from June 6, 1940)
Merkulov, V.N. (Armenian)

COLONEL GENERALS
Abakumov, V.S. (Slav)
Apollonov, A.N. (Slav) (NKVD Troops Maj. General from June 6, 1940, Col. General 1944)
Artem'ev, P.A. (Slav) (NKVD Troops Lt. General from June 6, 1940)
Chernyshev, V.V. (Slav)
Goglidze, S.A. (Georgian)
Kobulov, B.Z. (Armenian)
Kruglov, S.N. (Slav)

Pavlov, K.A. (Slav)
Serov, I.A. (Slav)

LT. GENERALS
Babich, I.Ia. (Jewish) (SMERSH, March 27, 1943)
Babkin, A.N. (Slav)
Bel'chenko, S.S. (Slav)
Belkin, M.I. (Jewish) (SMERSH, July 31, 1943)
Blinov, A.S. (Slav)
Bochkov, V.M. (Lt. General of Judiciary, rank given earlier)
Bogdanov, N.K. (Slav)
Borshchev, T.M. (Slav)
Burdakov, S.N. (Slav)
Dol'gikh, I.I. (Slav)
Drozdetskii, P.G. (Slav)
Egnatashvili, A. Ia. (Georgian)
Fedotov, P.V. (Slav)

---

*Unless otherwise indicated, these ranks were all given in 1945, mostly in July of that year. Occasionally an NKVD official would receive a rank in another branch. A prime example was the veteran V.M. Bochkov, who in 1945 received the rank of Lt. General of Judiciary since he had served as the USSR Prosecutor General during 1940–1943. Also, during the war an NKVD official who had distinguished himself in combat would be given a regular General rank. Case in point: Ukraine Partisan leader T.A. Strokach, who received the rank of Maj. General in 1944.

Firsov, P.A. (Slav) (Border Troops)

Fitin, P.M. (Slav)

Fokin, P.M. (Slav)

Frenkel', N.A. (Jewish) (Lt. General of Engineering/Technical Services, October. 29, 1943 or May 25, 1944)

Gladkov, P.A. (Slav)

Iakubov, M.T. (Turkic)

Karandze, G.T. (Georgian)

Kharitonov, I.S. (Slav)

Kobulov, A.Z. (Armenian)

Koval'chuk, N.K. (Slav) (March 1945)

Kubatkin, P.N. (Slav)

Langfang, A.I.

Lapshin, F.G. (Slav)

Leont'ev, A.M. (Slav)

Liubyi, I.S. (Slav) (NKVD Troops Maj. General from June 6, 1940)

Mamulov (Mamul'ian), S.S. (Armenian)

Marchenkov, M.P. (Slav) (NKVD Troops Maj. General from June 6, 1940)

Markar'ian, R.A. (Armenian)

Mel'nik, N.D. (Slav) (SMERSH)

Meshik, P.Ia. (Slav) (SMERSH, March 27, 1943)

Mil'shtein, S.R. (Jewish)

Moskalenko, I.I. (Slav) (SMERSH, March 27, 1943)

Nasedkin, V.G. (Slav)

Nikishov, I.F. (Slav)

Ogol'tsov, S.I. (Slav)

Osokin, V.V. (Slav) (NKVD Troops Lt. General from June 6, 1940)

Petrov, I. (Slav) (NKVD Troops Maj. General from June 6, 1940)

Raikhman, L.F. (Jewish)

Rapava, A.N. (Georgian)

Riasnoyi, V.S. (Slav)

Rodionov, D.G. (Slav)

Rumiantsev, V.I. (Slav)

Safraz'ian, L.B. (Armenian)

Savchenko, S.R. (Slav)

Sazykin, N.S. (Slav)

Selianovskii, M.N. (Slav) (SMERSH, March 27, 1943)

Sergienko, V.T. (Slav)

Sharapov, V.M. (Slav) (NKVD Troops Maj. General from June 6, 1940)

Sheredega, I.S. (Slav) (1944) (NKVD Troops, also listed as Maj. General)

Shevelev, N.G. (Slav)

Shiktorov, I.S. (Slav)

Sladkevich, M.I. (Jewish) (October 17, 1944)

Sokolov, G.G. (Slav) (NKVD Troops Lt. General from June 6, 1940)

Stepanov, G.A. (Slav) (NKVD Troops Lt. General from June 6, 1940)

Sudoplatov, P.A. (Slav)

Sumbatov-Topuridze, Iu.D. (Georgian)

Tkachenko, I.M. (Slav)

Tsanava, L.F. (Georgian)

Tsereteli, Sh.O. (Georgian)

Tutushkin, F. Ia. (Slav) (SMERSH, March 27, 1943)

Vlasik, N.S. (Slav)

Vlodzimirskii, L.E. (Slav)

Voronin, A.I. (Slav)

Vradyi, I.I. (Slav) (SMERSH, March 27, 1943)

Vurgraft, A.A. (Jewish) (Lt. General of Quartermasters, April 8, 1944)

Zaveniagin, A.P. (Slav)

Zhukov, G.S. (Slav)

Zhuravlev, M.I. (Slav)

MAJOR GENERALS

Abakumov, D.L. (Slav) (NKVD Troops)

Abryzov, V.A. (Slav) (NKVD Troops, 1944)

Alekseev, A.A. (Slav) (NKVD Troops)

Allakhverdov, M.A. (Tadzhik)

Andreev, A.M. (Slav)

Anokhin, N.A. (Slav) (SMERSH, February 21, 1944)

Arkad'ev, D.V. (Slav)

Atakshiev, A.S.I.O. (Azeri)

Babazhanov (Babadzhanian), Iu.B. (Armenian)

Babkin, I.A. (Slav)

Bartashunas, I.M. (Lithuanian)

Bashtakov, L.F. (Slav)

Baskakov, M.I. (Slav)

Belolipetskii, S.E.

Bezhanov, G.A. (Slav)

Blokhin, V.M. (Slav)

Boikov, I.P. (Slav)

Bolotin-Belianyi (Baliasnyi), G.S. (Jewish) (SMERSH, May 26, 1943)

Buianov, L.S. (Slav)

Bulyga, A.E. (Georgian) (NKVD Troops)

Byzov, A.P. (Slav)

Bziava, K.P. (Georgian)

Davlianidze, S.S. (Georgian)

Demin, V.I. (Slav)

Dobrynin, G.P. (Slav)

Donskov, S.I. (Slav) (NKVD Troops)

Drozdov, G.P. (Slav)

Drozdov, V.A. (SMERSH)

Edunov, Ia. A. (Slav) (SMERSH, rank given March 27, 1943)

Efimov, D.A. (Slav)

Eglit, A.P. (Latvian)

Egorov, S.E. (Slav)

Eitingon, L.I. (Jewish)

Emel'ianov, S.F. (Slav)

Ermilov, N.D. (Slav) (NKVD Troops)

Ermolin, I.I. (Slav) (SMERSH, March 27, 1943)

Esaulov, A.A. (Slav)

Esipenko, D.I. (Slav)

Filatov, S.I. (Slav)

Filipov, T.F. (Slav) (NKVD Troops)

Firsanov, K.F. (Slav)

Gagua (Gogua), I.A. (Georgian)

Gertovskii, A.Ia. (Jewish)

Golov'ev, I.I. (Slav) (SMERSH, March 27, 1943)

Golovko, A.S. (Slav) (NKVD Troops)

Golubev, N.A. (Slav)

Gorbenko, I.I. (Slav)

Gorbulin, P.N. (Slav)

Gorgonov, I.I. (Slav) (SMERSH, March 27, 1943)

Gorishnyi, V.A. (Slav) (NKVD Troops)

Gribov, M.V. (Slav)

Gridanev, V.V. (Slav) (NKVD Troops)

Grigor'ian, Kh.I. (Armenian)

Grishakin, A.D. (Slav)

Gubin, V.V. (Slav)

Gudkov, I.S. (Slav) (SMERSH, March 27, 1943)

Guguchiia, A.I. (Georgian)

Gul'ev, A.I. (Slav) (NKVD Troops, rank given June 6, 1940)

Gul'st, V.N. (Jewish)

Gusarov, S.I. (Slav) (NKVD Troops)

Gusev, F.I. (Slav) (SMERSH, March 27, 1943)

Guziavichus (Gudaitis-Guziavichus), A.P. (Lithuanian)

Iakovlev, V.T. (Slav)

Iangel', A.K. (Slav) (NKVD Troops)

Il'iushin-Edelman, I.I. (Jewish)

Istomin, V.N. (Slav) (NKVD Troops)

Iukhimovich, S.P. (Slav)

Ivanov, V.V. (Slav)

Kakuchia, V.A. (Georgian)

Kalinskii, M.I. (Slav)

Kapralov, P.M. (Slav)

Karpov, G.G. (Slav)

Kazantsev, V.I. (Slav) (SMERSH, March 27, 1943)

Khannikov, N.G. (Slav) (SMERSH, March 27, 1943)

Kharchenko, A.V. (Slav)

Kiriushin, I.N. (Slav) (Maj. General of Quartermaster Troops attached to NKVD Troops)

Kiselev, A.Ia. (Slav) (NKVD Troops)

Klepov, S.A. (Slav)

Kochavashvili, A.I. (Georgian)

Komarov, G. Ia. (Slav)
Kondakov, P.P. (Slav)
Konovalov, I.P. (Slav) (SMERSH, March 27, 1943)
Konovalov, P.G. (Slav) (NKVD Troops)
Kopytsev, A.I. (Slav)
Korsakov, G.A. (Slav)
Kovshuk-Berman, M.F.
Kozin, N.D. (Slav) (NKVD Troops)
Kravchenko, V.A. (Slav)
Krivenko, M.S. (Slav) (NKVD Troops)
Kumm, B.G. (Estonian)
Kuz'michev, S.F. (Slav)
Kuznetsov, A.K. (Slav)
Leonov, A.G. (SMERSH)
Leoniuk, F.A. (Slav)
Leont'ev, P.A. (Slav) (NKVD Troops)
Lorent, P.P.
Mal'kov, P.M. (Slav)
Malinin, L.A. (Slav)
Malinovskii (Maj. General Medical Services, 1943)
Mal'tsev, M.M. (Slav)
Markeev, M.I. (Slav)
Martirosov, G.I. (Armenian)
Maslovskii, Ia.E. (Slav) (NKVD Troops)
Matevosov, I.I. (Slav)
Mazhirin, F.M. (Slav) (NKVD Troops)
Medvedev, A.R. (Slav)
Meshchanov, P.S. (Slav)
Michurin-Raver, M.L. (Jewish)
Mironenko, P.N. (Slav) (NKVD Troops)
Mordovets, I.L. (Slav)
Moshenskii, A.L. (Slav)
Muklin, A.F. (Slav)
Nibladze, I.I. (Georgian)
Nikitin, D.M. (Slav)
Nikitinskii, I.I. (Slav)
Nikol'skii, M.I. (Slav)
Nikol'skii, N.P. (Slav) (NKVD Troops Maj. General from June 6, 1940)

Novik, A.A. (Latvian)
Novikov, I.I. (Slav), Maj. General of Medical Services
Novobratskii, L.I. (Slav)
Okunev, P.I. (Slav)
Orlov, P.A. (Slav)
Osiun'kin, K.V. (Slav)
Ovakimian, G.B. (Armenian)
Paniukov, A.A. (Slav)
Pavlov, M.F. (Slav)
Pavlov, N.I. (Slav)
Pavlov, S.N. (Slav)
Pavlov, V.P. (Slav)
Pchelkin, A.A. (Slav)
Petrenko, I.G. (Slav)
Petrov, A.V. (Slav)
Petrovskii, F.P. (Slav)
Piiashev, I.I. (Slav) (NKVD Troops)
Pitovarnov, E.P. (Slav)
Plestov, S.N. (Slav)
Podoliako, N.P. (Slav) (NKVD Troops)
Pogudin, V.I. (Slav)
Pokotilo, S.V. (Slav)
Popereka, M.S. (Slav) (SMERSH, rank given March 27, 1943)
Popkov, I.G. (Slav)
Popov, P.P. (Slav) (SMERSH, rank given March 27, 1943)
Portnov, I.B. (Slav)
Potashnik, M.M. (Slav)
Potekhin, N.N. (Slav) (NKVD Troops)
Prishcheno, T.I. (Slav) (NKVD Troops)
Prishepa (Prishchepa?), P.K. (Slav) (SMERSH, March 27, 1943)
Proshin, V.S. (Slav)
Ratushnyi, I.T. (Slav)
Rezev, A.I. (Slav)
Rodovanskii, Ia. F. (Slav)
Rogatin, V.T. (Slav) (NKVD Troops)
Rogov, V.T. (Slav) (SMERSH, March 27, 1943)
Rozanov, N.A. (Slav) (SMERSH, March 27, 1943)
Ruchkin, A.F. (Slav)

Rukhadze, N.M. (Georgian) (SMERSH, 1944)
Rusak, I.T. (Slav) (SMERSH, March 27, 1943)
Sakharov, M.I. (Slav)
Samygin, D.S. (Slav)
Saraev, A.A. (Slav) (NKVD Troops)
Savinov, M.I. (Slav)
Semenov, I.P. (Slav)
Serikov, M.K. (Slav)
Shadrin, D.N. (Slav)
Shamarin, A.V. (Slav)
Shemen, S.I.
Shitikov, N. (or I.), I. (Slav)
Shpiller, A.E. (Jewish) (Veterinary Services, March 3, 1943)
Sidorov, I.K. (Slav)
Sinilov, K.R. (Slav) (NKVD Troops)
Skorodumov, P.A. (Slav) (NKVD Troops)
Smirnov, P.P. (Slav)
Smirnov, V.I. (Slav)
Smorodinskii, V.T. (Slav)
Sokolov, A.G. (Slav)
Solov'ev, V.A. (Border Troops)
Soprunenko, P.K. (Slav)
Spasenko, F.A. (Slav) (NKVD Troops)
Stefanov, A.G. (Slav)
Sukhopol'skii, V.N. (Slav)
Sushchenskii, P.P. (Slav) (NKVD Troops)
Suslov, N.G. (Slav)
Svinelupov, M.G. (Slav)
Tekaev, B.I. (Slav)
Timofeev, M.M. (Slav)
Timofeev, P.P. (Slav) (SMERSH, March 27, 1943)
Tokarev, V.S. (Slav)
Trofimov, B.P. (Slav)
Trubnikov, V.M. (Slav)
Utekhin, ? (SMERSH)
Vetrov, P.M. (Slav) (NKVD Troops)
Zachepa, I.I. (Slav)
Zakharov, A.P. (Slav)

Zakusilo, A.A. (Slav)
Zapevalin, M.A. (Slav)
Zarubin, V.S. (Slav)
Zheleznikov, N.I. (Slav) (SMERSH, March 27, 1943)
Zhuravlev, P.M. (Slav)
Zimin, P.M. (Slav) (NKVD Troops)
Zverev, A.D. (Slav)

This list is nearly complete for regular NKVD and NKGB police generals but may lack a number of SMERSH and NKVD Troops generals.

Biographies of many on this list are included in the author's *Soviet Security and Intelligence Organizations, 1917–1990.*

Appendix II

Principal Victims of Stalinist Repression During the Abakumov Regime (March 1946–July 1951)*

Afanas'ev, A.A. (Slav) October 4, 1903–1948.

Minister of Merchant Marine, 1948. Arrested (April 1948) and sentenced to 20 years.

Agakov, L.Ia. (Chuvash) 1910–1980.

Member Writers Union, end of 1949. Arrested for anti-Soviet activities, tortured by Komarov.

Aizenshtadt.

See Zheleznov.

Akikusa Shun (Japanese) 1894–March 22, 1949

Major General; Head of Japanese Military Counter-Intelligence in Kharbin (1933–1936); arrested by SMERSH (August 15, 1945); interrogated by Lt. General N.D. Mel'nikov, and later (January 1, 1946) by Abakumov; sentenced to 25 years (December 30, 1948); died from illness in Lefortovo prison.

Alafuzov, V.A. (Slav) April 6, 1901–May 30, 1966.

Admiral (September 1944); Chief of Naval Staff July 1944–April 1945; Head of Naval Academy, April 1945–January 1947; removed, arrested, and sentenced to 10 years (February 1948); rehabilitated (May 13, 1953).

Aleksandrovich, A.I. (Slav) January 22, 1906–January 6, 1963.

Poet, member of Belorussia Academy of Sciences (1936); arrested (July 1, 1938); sentenced to 15 years (April 22, 1939); freed (November 29, 1946). Re-arrested and exiled to Krasnoiarsk (June 8, 1949). Rehabilitated (November 25, 1955).

Allilueva (Redens), A.S. (See Redens.)

Allilueva, E.A. 1898–1974.

The widow of Stalin's brother-in-law, P. Alliluev; arrested (December 25, 1947) along with her second husband N. Molochnikov (actually an MGB informer) and sentenced to

---

*The period covered is the time in which Abakumov was officially in charge of the MGB. Those not listed because the dates of conviction or arrest fall outside this period include those listed at the end of this appendix.

prison (May 29, 1948); released after Stalin's death (1954).

Allilueva, K.

Actress in the Moscow Small Theater; daughter of E.A. Allilueva; arrested (January 6, 1948) and sentenced to 5 years of exile in Ivanovo oblast.

Allilueva, K.A.

Wife of the uncle of Stalin's second wife (1947); arrested, r e l e a s e d after Stalin's death (1954).

Andreev, D.L. (Slav)

Son of émigré writer L.N. Andreev; arrested as head of a "terrorist organization" (post-war).

Andreev, M.A. Police Maj.General

Arrested, released, broken.

Aralov, S.I. (Slav) December 18, 1880– May 22, 1969.

Veteran intelligence officer, alleged first head of military intelligence then in diplomatic work (October 1918–July 1920); purged, but survived as Deputy Head of Literature Museum (1938–1941); at the front (1941–1945); arrested, sentenced to 10 years (1946).

Artemenko, P.D. (Slav) 1896–April 1950.

Major General; commander 4 Rifle Corps, 5 Army, Southwest Front (1941); captured (September 27, 1941); condemned to death in absentia (April 10, 1942); returned from captivity; arrested (October 21, 1945); shot.

Badaev, G.F. (Slav).

Second Party Secretary Leningrad (1950); arrested.

Barth, Albert   –1946.

High-ranking Soviet agent, parachuted into Germany (August 5, 1942), captured and "turned" by the Gestapo (1942); captured by the British after the war and returned to the Soviet Union, where he was executed.

Basov, M.V. (Slav) –1950.

Chairman RFSFR Planning Commission (1950); arrested, shot.

Becker, Helmuth August 12, 1900– February 28, 1952.

SS–Brigadeführer and Maj. General of Waffen SS; Commander of 3 SS Panzer Division "Totenkopf" (1944); tried in Poltava and sentenced to 25 years (1946); tried again while in Soviet captivity for sabotage (February1952); shot.

Beilinson, Ia.L. (Jewish).

Regional Party official; arrested, sentenced to 25 years (1950).

Belenkii, M.S. (Jewish).

Director of school attached to the Moscow Jewish Art Theater; arrested (1949); released after 6 years in camps.

Beleshev, M.A. (Slav) 1900–   .

Maj. General of Aviation; commander aviation in 2 Assault Army, Volkhov Front (1942); captured (September 1942); returned from captivity; arrested (October 21, 1945) and accused of collaboration.

Beregovskii, M.Ia. (Jewish) 1892– 1961.

Musicologist and music teacher in Kiev and Leningrad (1915–1936); director of the Center for Jewish Folklore Music in Ukraine Academy of Sciences (1930–1948); arrested (1949); released after Stalin's death.

Bergel'son, D.R. (Jewish) May 1884– June or August 12, 1952.

Native of Kiev; Yiddish writer and poet (1921–1934), resident of

Germany; returned to USSR, active in JAC (1934–1952); arrested (January 24, 1949), shot.

Bessonov, I.G. (Slav) 1905–April 19, 1950.

Kombrig (NKVD Border Troops); in the Red Army (1920); Party member (1932); in the beginning of the war, Chief of Staff and Commander of the 102 Rifle Division, Central Front; captured (August 26, 1941); alleged collaborator; arrested, imprisoned, tried and shot 5 years later.

Bogdanov, M.V. (Slav) 1897–April 19, 1950.

Kombrig; commander of artillery in 8 Rifle Corps, Southwest Front (August, 1941); captured (August 1941); collaborator ; in prison (May 1945–April 1950); tried and shot.

Bogdanov, P.V. (Slav) 1900–April 24, 1950.

Maj. General (June 1940); Commander 48 Rifle Division, 8 Army, Northwest Front; captured (June 1941); collaborated with the enemy, but defected to the Soviet side (August 1943); arrested by SMERSH (August 20, 1943); tried and shot (April 1950).

Bokov, F.E. (Slav) December 26, 1903– .

Lt. General (1943); Commissar of General Staff (August 1941–July 1942); Commissar Northwest and 2 Belorussian Fronts and 5 Assault Army (April 1943–May 1945); Commissar of Group of Soviet Forces in Germany (June or July 1945–1946); Deputy Commander Volga and Voronezh Military Districts (1947–1949); arrested, in prison (1949–1952).

Bondarenko, P.T. (Slav) 1901–October 28, 1950.

Rear Admiral; Commissar Volga Flotilla (August 1942–October 1942); Commissar Black Sea Fleet (1947–1950); arrested in connection with the "Leningrad Affair" (1950); shot.

Borodin (Gruzenberg), M.M. (Jewish) July 9, 1884–May 29, 1951.

Old Bolshevik Party member (1903); lived abroad; member U.S. Socialist Party (1907–1918); after the revolution Comintern agent, adviser in Nationalist China (1923–1927); Deputy Commissar of Labor; editor of *Moscow News* (1941–1949); Deputy Director of TASS; arrested (late January or early February 1949) or died under interrogation or in the Iakutsk labor camps.

Braiko, P.E. (Slav)   September 9, 1918– .

MVD Colonel; escaped from captivity (February 1942); member of Kovpak partisan detachment; Hero of the Soviet Union (August 7, 1944); arrested and imprisoned after the war.

Bregman, S.L. (Jewish) 1895–May/June, 1952.

Native of Briansk; Deputy Minister RSFSR Ministry of State Control; Party member (1912); arrested (January28, 1949), shot or died in prison.

Bubnov, A.A. (Slav) –1950.

Secretary Leningrad Executive Committee (1950); arrested, shot.

Buchin, A.N. (Slav)

Marshal Zhukov's driver and assistant (1948); arrested, released.

Budnikov, A.V. (Slav) 1907– .

Section Manager in the Cadres Department of CC CPSU involved with aviation (1946); arrested in connection with the Aviators' Affair (spring 1946); sentenced to 2 years; released after 2 years and 7 months; rehabilitated (June 12, 1953).

Budykho, A.E. (Slav) 1893–April 19, 1950.

Maj. General; in the Red Army (1918); Party member (1919); during the war, Commander 171 Rifle Division; captured (October 22, 1941); alleged collaborator; defected to the Soviet side (October 19, 1943); put under arrest (November 11, 1943); tried and shot (April 1950).

Chursin, P.A. (Slav) –1950.

Party official in Crimea (1950); arrested, shot.

Dolitskii, E. (Jewish).

Post–war, economist; arrested, released after Stalin's death after spending 7 years in camps.

Domanov, T.I. (Slav) –January 17, 1947.

Maj. General; Civil War White Officer (1918); service with Pannwitz Cossacks in Yugoslavia (1943); arrested, executed.

Dzhanelidze, I. (Georgian)

Lt. General of Medical Service; arrested after a visit to the U.S. for reporting that the U.S. lifespan was longer than that in the Soviet Union (post-war).

Egorov, E.A. (Slav) 1891–April 19, 1950.

Maj. General; Commander 4 Rifle Corps, 3 Army, West Front (1941); captured (June 26, 1941); returned from captivity; arrested (October 21, 1945) and accused of collaboration; tried and shot (April 1950).

El'snits, A.G. (German-Russian) 1894– .

Maj. General of Engineering-Technical Services; Head of Telephone Communications Department in Budennyi Academy (1935–September 15, 1949); arrested, sentenced to 8 years in camps (March 27, 1952); released and rehabilitated (1953).

Emiot, Israel (I.Ia. Gol'dvasser) (Jewish) January 15, 1909–March 7, 1978.

Writer; arrested (1948); released (March 27, 1953); repatriated to Poland (1956).

Etinger, Ia.G. (Jewish) 1887–March 2, 1951.

Student in Berlin University (1908–1913); Professor in the 2 Moscow Medical Institute (1950); arrested (November 1950) and died in prison, possibly of heart trouble; Riumin's candidate for having caused the death of A.S. Shcherbakov, former candidate member of Politburo, a fact allegedly covered up by Abakumov.

Fedoseev, P. (Slav) –1950.

Assistant Head of Stalin's Personal Security (post-war); arrested on suspicion of espionage and interrogated by Malenkov in the Special Prison, shot 2 days later.

Fefer, I.S. (Jewish) 1900–May/June, 1952 or August 12, 1952.

Poet, former member of the BUND; Party member (1919); accused of Trotskyism (1920s); Secretary of JAC, visited U.S. during the war (1940s); deputy editor of *Eynikeyt*; arrested (1949); shot.

Filatov, A.A. (Slav).

Maj. General (June 1940); Commander 12 Guard Rifle Division, 1 Belorussian Front (April 1945); with Soviet forces in Germany (1947); arrested.

Fishman, Ia.M. (Jewish) April 17, 1887–July 12, 1961

Corps Engineer; Head of the Red Army Military Chemical Administration (1926–1937); member Main Military Soviet; arrested and sentenced to 10 years (May 29, 1940); released; re-arrested (April 20, 1949) and sent to Noril'sk; released and rehabilitated (January 5, 1955); given the rank of Maj. General of Technical Troops (September 10, 1955).

Fortushenko, A.D. (Slav).

Deputy Commissar/Minister of Communications (1941); arrested during the post-war years.

Galkin, Sh. (Jewish)

Poet and playwright; arrested and sentenced to 10 years (January 25, 1950).

Galler, L.M. (Slav) November 17, 1883–July 12, 1950.

Admiral (June, 1940); Head of Main Naval Staff (1938–1940);

Deputy Commissar of Navy (1940–September 1945); removed (January 1947); arrested, sentenced to 4 years (February 1948); died in prison in Kazan; rehabilitated (May 13, 1953).

Garkusha-Shirshova, E.A. (Slav) March 1915–August 1948.

Actress, star of *Piatyi Okean* (1939) and *Neulovimyi Ian* (1943); married to Commissar of Merchant Marine (1942–1946) P.P. Shirov; arrested; sentenced a year later to 8 years

exile; died in Magadan.

Gofshtein (Hofshteyn), D.N. (Jewish) 1889–May/June, 1952 or August 12, 1952.

Native of Kiev oblast; Yiddish poet, resident of Germany and Palestine (1920s), returned to USSR (1926); Party member (1940); active in JAC; arrested (September 16, 1948), shot.

Gol'dshtein, I.I. (Jewish).

Doctor of Economic Sciences, senior researcher at the Institute of Economics, USSR Academy of Sciences; arrested (December 17 or 18, 1947); interrogated by Abakumov and others, text of interrogation sent to Abakumov (January 10, 1948); survived.

Golodnyi (Epstein), M.S. (Jewish) December 24, 1903–January 20, 1949.

Stalinist poet, author of verse glorifying heroes of the Civil War, author of propaganda during World War II; killed in a suspicious traffic accident in Moscow during the postwar anti-Semitic campaigns.

Golubov, V.I. (Potapov, V.) (Jewish) –January 1948.

Critic; on the editorial board of *Teatr*.

Goncharik, M.N. (Slav) November 24, 1899–April 11, 1986.

Physiologist; Party member (1927); member Belorussia Academy of Science (1931); arrested (September 14, 1933) and sentenced to 10 years (January 9, 1934); freed (1947); re-arrested (February 15, 1949); sentenced to exile in Krasnoiarsk (May 18, 1949); rehabilitated (April 18, 1956).

Goncharov, L.G. (Slav) 1885–April 23, 1948.

Vice Admiral; Captain 1st Rank in

the Old Navy (1917); arrested by Leningrad Cheka (1920), but released; arrested and sentenced to 10 years (1930), but released through intervention of Naval High Command; arrested twice more before the war; Department Head in the Higher Naval School in Leningrad (1948); arrested (April 8, 1948) and died during interrogation by V.I. Komarov; rehabilitated (1953).

Gordon, Sh. (Jewish)

Writer; arrested and sentenced to 15 years (July 30, 1952).

Gordov, V.N. (Slav) November 3,1896–December 12, 1951.

Col. General (1943); Commander of 21, 33, and 3 Guard Armies, Commander of Stalingrad Front (1941–1945); Commander Volga Military District (1945–March, 1946); arrested; tried (August 1950) and shot.

Grigor'ev, I.F. (Slav) 1890–1949.

Member of Academy of Sciences (1946); Deputy Minister of Geology (1949), involved in production of uranium for the Soviet atomic bomb; arrested, died or was killed in prison.

Grigor'ian, G.M. (Armenian) 1909– .

Section Manager in the Cadres Department of CC CPSU involved with aviation (1946); arrested (spring 1946); in connection with the Aviators' Affair; sentenced to 2 years; released after serving 2 years and 7 months; rehabilitated (June 12, 1953).

Grinberg, Z.G. (Jewish) 1889–December 22, 1949.

Candidate of Historical Sciences, senior researcher in the Gor'kii Institute for World Literature;

arrested (December 28, 1947); text of interrogation received by Abakumov (March 1, 1948); died in prison of a heart attack.

Gumilev, L.N. (Slav) 1911– .

Historian and orientalist (1935–1937); son of N.S. Gumilev and A.A. Akhmatova; arrested, released, re-arrested (1937); service at the front (1941–1945); arrested again (1949); not released until 1956.

Iudin, S.S. (Slav) 1891–1954.

Chief surgeon in Sklifosovskii Institute (1948); member USSR Academy of Sciences; arrested (December 22 or 23, 1948) and accused of membership in military conspiracy led by Chief Marshal of Artillery N.N. Voronov and Marshal Zhukov; exiled to Berdisk (March 1952).

Iuzefovich, I.S. (Jewish) 1890–May/June, 1952.

Native of Warsaw; researcher with the USSR Academy of S c i e n c e Institute of History; Party member (May 1917); arrested (January 13, 1949), shot.

Ivanov.

First Secretary Leningrad Komsomols (1949); Second Secretary All-Union Komsomol Central Committee; arrested, shot.

Ivinskaia, O. (Slav) 1912– .

Writer and translator, Pasternak's paramour and alleged model for Lara in *Dr. Zhivago* (1949); arrested, interrogated by Abakumov; spent time in prison.

Kamenev, V.L. (Jewish).

Grandson of L.B. Kamenev; arrested, exiled (1951).

Kapler, A.Ia. (Jewish) 1904–1979.

Screenwriter, director of "Lenin in

October" and "Lenin in 1918" (1940s); Svetlana Allilueva's paramour; arrested for "depravity" and "contributing to the delinquency of a minor;" sent to camps.

Kapustin, Ia.F. (Slav) 1904–October 1, 1950.

Second Party Secretary Leningrad City Committee (January 1945–February 1949); arrested, shot.

Kedrov, G.T. (Slav) 1907–   .

Resident of Leningrad (1927); in Komsomols (1933) and Party (1935); graduate of engineering school (1942); Party work in factory, Party Secretary for Cadres in Leningrad (1946); First Party Secretary in Estonia (October 1948–August 28, 1949); sentenced to 25 years (January 21, 1952); rehabilitated (May 14, 1954).

Kharitonov, I.S. (Slav)   –1950.

Chairman Executive Committee, Leningrad Soviet (1950); arrested, shot.

Kheifetz, G. (Jewish).

Veteran intelligence agent in Germany, Italy, and U.S. (Soviet Vice Consul in San Francisco during the war), involved in atomic espionage; arrested (1949); survived.

Khudiakov, S.A. (Khanferiants, A.A.) (Armenian), December 25, 1901–April 18, 1950.

Marshal of Aviation (August 1944); Air Force Chief of Staff (April, 1942–July, 1942); Commander Far East Air Force (August 1945–December 1945); arrested (December 12, 1945); indicted (August 22, 1947) as a British spy and later shot.

Khruleva (Gorelik), E. (Jewish)

Wife of Army General A.V. Khrulev (late 1940s); Head of Red Army Rear during the war; arrested.

Kirpichnikov, V.V. (Slav) 1903–October 28, 1950.

Maj. General (June 1940); Commander, 43 Rifle Division, 23 Army ,Leningrad Front (August 1941–October 1944); captured by the Finns; returned after the armistice; arrested; in prison (October1944–October 1950) and finally condemned to death.

Kirrilov, N.K. (Slav) 1897–August 25, 1950.

Maj. General (June, 1940); Commander 13 Rifle Corps, Southwest Front (July, 1941–August 1941); captured; returned; arrested and finally shot (October 1945–August 1950).

Kochin, N.I. (Slav) 1902–   .

Post-war; author of *Devki* and *Nizhegorodskii Otkos*; arrested, sentenced to 10 years in camps in Central Asia.

Kogan, M.B. (Jewish)   –November 26 or 27, 1951.

Doctor in the Kremlin Hospital; arrested; died in prison (1950).

Koppensteiner, Maria (German) –1953.

Hitler's cousin; arrested (May 1945) and later sentenced to 25 years; died in camps.

Korzhavin (Mandel) N.M. (Jewish) 1925 –   .

Poet, arrested (post-war), later released; immigrated to U.S. (1973).

Kovalev, I.V. (Slav).

Party functionary associated with Malenkov; disciplined by Party "Court of Honor" (April 1947–April 1948).

Krasnaov, P.N. (Slav) (Ataman) –January 17, 1947.

Civil War White Cossack leader (1918); service with Pannwitz Cossacks in Yugoslavia (1943); arrested, tried, executed.

Krasnov, S.N. (Slav)   –January 17, 1947.

Maj. General; Civil War White Officer (1918); service with Pannwitz Cossacks in Yugoslavia (1943); arrested, tried, executed.

Krikheli, A.M. (Georgian Jew) 1906–1974.

Director Literature section, Georgia Commissariat of Education (1928–1943); Director of the Jewish History Museum in Tbilisi (1943–1949); arrested.

Kriukov, V.V. (Slav) July 15, 1987–August 16, 1959.

Guard Lt. General (1943); Commander of 2 Guard Rifle Corps., later attached to 1 Belorussian Front (1941–1945); Deputy Commander 36 Rifle Corps (November 1947); with Soviet forces in Germany; Hero of the Soviet Union (April 6, 1945); married to artist, L.A. Ruslanova; arrested with his wife, allegedly for corruption (September 18, 1948); sentenced to 25 years (November 1951); freed and rehabilitated (July 1953).

Krupennikov, I.P. (Slav) 1896–   .

Maj. General; Chief of Staff 3 Guard Army Southwest Front (December 1942); captured; returned from captivity, arrested (October 21, 1945) and accused of collaboration.

Kubatkin, P.N. (Slav)   –1950.

Police Lt. General (July, 1945); Head NKVD Moscow (1939–1940);

Head NKVD Leningrad during the war; Head MGB Leningrad from 1946 until his arrest (July 21, 1949) in connection with the Leningrad Affair; shot.

Kulik, G.I. (Slav) October 28, 1890–August 24, 1950.

Marshal of the Soviet Union (May, 1940 and 1957); Deputy Commissar of Defense, Head Main Artillery Administration (January 1939); various commands during the war (1941–1945); Deputy Commander Volga Military District (April, 1945); arrested (January 1947); tried (August 1950); shot; rehabilitated (1956) and restored to rank (1957).

Kupriianov, G.N. (Slav) 1905–1979.

Maj. General; First Party Secretary in Kuibyshev, then in Karelia (1937–1942); Commissar of 7 Army (until September 1941); with the Karelia Front (until November 1942); later involved with the partisan movement; First Party Secretary in Karelia (1945–1950); arrested in connection with the "Leningrad Affair" (March 17, 1950) and sentenced to death; spared by Stalin.

Kuzakov, K.S. (Slav).

Party functionary associated with Malenkov; disciplined by the Party "Court of Honor" (September 1947–April, 1948).

Kuznetsov, A.A. (Slav) 1905–October 11, 1950.

Lt. General (1943); Second Regional Party Secretary Leningrad, political commissar with Leningrad Front and the Baltic Fleet during the war (September 1937–1946); after the war, First Party Secretary in Leningrad; Secretary Central Committee CPSU (March

1946–February 1949); arrested (October 1949); shot.

Kuzovkov, K.S. (Slav).

Party functionary associated with Malenkov; disciplined by the Party "Court of Honor" (September 1947–April 1948).

Kvitko, L.M. (Jewish) 1890–May/June, 1952.

Native of Odessa oblast; poet and writer of children's books; resident of Germany (1921–1925); Party member (1941); member of JAC; on the editorial board of *Heymland*; arrested (January 25, 1949); shot.

Lazutin, N.G. (Slav) 1901– .

Kombrig; Commander Artillery 61 Rifle Corps, 13 Army, West Front (1941); captured (end of June 1941); returned from captivity; arrested (October 21, 1945) and accused of collaboration.

Lazutin, P.G. (Slav) 1905–October 1, 1950.

First Deputy Chairman, Executive Committee Leningrad Soviet (1944); Chairman, Executive Committee, Leningrad Soviet (1946); arrested, shot.

Levin, N. (Jewish)   –November 22, 1950.

Editor at JAC; sentenced to death.

Levin, P.I. (Jewish)   –1950.

Secretary Leningrad City Party Committee (1950); arrested, shot.

Levina, R. (Jewish)

Economist, corresponding member of USSR Academy of Sciences (late 1940s); arrested.

Libitskii, E.

Stalin's "double" (August 1952); arrested and imprisoned on an island in the White sea; survived, released after Stalin's death.

Liumkis, I. (Jewish).

Yiddish writer, resident of central Asia, Moscow and Birobidzhan (1925–1948); arrested (end of 1948); released after Stalin's death.

Lozovskii (Dridzo), S.A. (Jewish) 1878–August 1952.

Diplomat's former Deputy Head and Head Soviet Information Bureau; Party member (1901); questioned by Malenkov (January 13, 1949); arrested (January 16, 1949), shot.

Lur'e, N. (Jewish).

Jewish writer from Odessa (late 1940s); arrested, sent to camps.

Maari, G. (Armenian).

Leading poet; in camps (1936–1947); released (1948); re-arrested.

Makliarskii, M. (Jewish)

Secret police official; arrested, provided evidence against L.R.Sheinin.

Markish, P.D. (Jewish) 1895–May June, 1952 or August 12, 1952 (?).

Native of Zhitomir oblast; poet; Secretary JAC; Party member (1939 or 1942); arrested (January 17 or 28, 1949); shot; rehabilitated (1954).

Meshcheriakov, P.

Military historian; arrested (1946); interrogated by A.Ia. Sverdlov.

Mikheev, F.E. (Slav) 1902–November 1975.

Head of Organization and Management, Leningrad Regional and City Party organization (1941–1949); arrested (August 1949); sentenced to 10 years.

Mikhoels (Vovsi), S.M. (Jewish) 1890–January 13, 1948.

Director of Moscow Yiddish Theatre; murdered in Minsk by MGB.

Miler, B.I. (Jewish) 1913– .
  Yiddish writer; Party member
  (1941); editor of *Birobidzhaner
  shtern*; arrested (1949); released
  after Stalin's death.

Miniuk, L.F. (Slav).
  Lt. General; Marshal Zhukov's
  former adjutant (1947); arrested.

Naumov, A.Z. (Slav) 1891–April 19,
1950.
  Maj. General (June 1940);
  Commander 13 Rifle Division West
  Front (1941); in captivity,
  collaborator (October 1941–May
  1945); in prison (May 1945–April
  1950); tried, shot.

Novikov, A.A. (Slav) June 19, 1900–
December 3, 1976.
  Chief Marshal of Aviation (February
  21, 1944); Commander in Chief of
  Air Force (April 1942–March 1946);
  arrested (April 23, 1946), tried, and
  sentenced to 5 years; released after
  serving 5 years and 10 months
  (February 1952); rehabilitated (June
  12, 1953); appointed as Head of
  Strategic Aviation (June 29, 1953).

Nusikov, I. (Jewish)   –October 31,
1950.
  Literary critic; arrested, died in
  prison probably from torture, but
  officially listed as heart attack.

Nusinov, I. (Jewish) –1950.
  Professor (post-war); arrested during
  the anti-Semitic campaigns; died in
  Lefortovo prison as a result of
  beating.

Oggins (?), Isaac (Jewish)   –1947.
  U.S. Communist and NKVD agent
  (from 1938); liquidation ordered by
  Stalin and Molotov to Abakumov,
  allegedly carried out by
  Maironovskii in Butryka prison
  (1947).

Ogul'nik, M.T. (Jewish) 1889– .
  Member Belorussia Academy of
  Science; researcher in the Jewish
  branch; Party member (1920);
  arrested (October 10, 1938);
  sentenced to 5 years; re-arrested
  (June 15, 1949); and exiled to
  Krasnoiarsk; rehabilitated(June 20,
  1956) while living in Chuvash
  ASSR.

Okulicki, Leopold (Polish).
  General; member Polish Home
  Council of Ministers; kidnapped by
  NKGB (February 28, 1945);
  sentenced to 10 years (June 21,
  1945); probably murdered in prison
  (December 24, 1946).

Okunevskaia, T. (Slav)
  Actress; married to *Pravda*
  correspondent B. Gorbatov (1948);
  romantically involved with Marshal
  Tito; arrested; released after Stalin's
  death; living (1994).

Parin, V.V. (Slav) 1903–1971.
  Deputy Minister of Public Health
  (1946); Secretary USSR Academy
  of Medical Sciences; arrested
  (February 1947) in connection with
  Kliueva-Roskin (two researchers
  whose book had been published in
  the U.S.); released and rehabilitated
  after Stalin's death.

Persov, S. (Jewish)   –November 23,
1950.
  Writer, head of the Moscow
  automobile factory (1940s); arrested
  (January 18, 1949), sentenced to
  death (November 22, 1950) and shot
  a day later.

Petrovskii, M.I. (Slav)   –1950.
  Party official in Crimea (1950);
  arrested, shot.

Pevzner, M.I. (Jewish).
  Medical doctor (1950); died under
  arrest.

Polianker, G. (Jewish) 1911– .

Yiddish writer (1930–1945); Party member (1930); participant in the war (1945–1949); active in Jewish literary circles; arrested (1949); released after Stalin's death.

Pondelin, P.G. (Slav) 1893–August 25, 1950.

Maj. General (June 1940); Commander 12 Army Southwest Front (June 1941–August 1941); captured; returned; imprisoned (October 1945–August 1950); tried and shot.

Popkov, P.S. (Slav) 1903–October 1, 1950.

First Deputy Chairman, Leningrad Executive Committee (September 1938–1939); Chairman Leningrad Executive Committee (1939–1946); First Secretary, Leningrad Regional and City Committee (March 1946–March 1949); Candidate Member CC CPSU (18th Party Congress); arrested, shot.

Poskrebysheva, B.S. (Jewish).

Wife of A.N. Poskrebyshev and sister of a daughter-in-law of Trotskii; arrested and accused of espionage; shot after 3 years in prison.

Potash, M.A. (Jewish) April 26, 1892– .

Historian, member of Bund (1914–1920); then in Communist Party; Deputy Head Institute of History, Belorussia Academy of Science (1931–1936); arrested (December 10, 1937); sentenced to 8 years (August 15, 1939); freed (December 1945); re-arrested (November 9, 1948); sentenced to exile (March 2, 1949); rehabilitated (December 12, 1955).

Privalov, P.F. (Slav) 1898– .

Commander 15 Rifle Corp, Southwest Front (1942); captured (December 22, 1942); returned from captivity; arrested (October 21, 1945) and accused of collaboration.

Prut, I. (Jewish).

Playwright, employed by NKVD (1949); arrested as an alleged Zionist; released after Stalin's death.

Raubal, Leo (German).

Luftwaffe Lieutenant; son of Hitler's half–sister and brother of Hitler's alleged mistress Angela Raubal; captured in Stalingrad (1943); sentenced to 25 years (1949); released and repatriated (1955).

Redens (Allilueva) A.S. (German-Georgian) 1896-August 1964

Writer, member of writers' union; sister of Stalin's second wife, widow of S.F. Redens; former Head of NKVD in Moscow and Kazakh SSR, who was shot in 1938; arrested (January 28, 1948); sentenced to 10 years (May 29, 1948); released, broken (1954).

Repin, A.K. (Slav). 1903- .

Col. General of Aviation Engineering Service; Deputy Commander in Chief, Air Force, and Chief Engineer (1942-1946); arrested in spring 1946 in connection with the "Aviators' Affair"; sentenced to 6 years.

Rodionov, M.I. (Slav) 1907–October 1, 1950.

First Secretary of Gor'kii Regional Party Committee (1940); Chairman RSFSR Council of Ministers (1946–March 1949); Member CC CPSU Orgburo (March 1946); arrested, shot.

Romendik, A.S. (Jewish).
    Sister of academician L.M. Shtern; arrested, imprisoned
Romzha Archbishov.
    Head Ukrainian United Church (1947); assassinated in Uzhgorod by Sudoplatov team, allegedly at Khrushchev's recommendation.
Ruslanova, L.A. (Slav) 1900–1973.
    Popular singer; People's Artist of RSFSR (1942); entertained troops during the war; married to Lt. General V.V. Kriukov; arrested with her husband (June 1948); released (July 1953).
Rybal'chenko, F.T. (Slav) 1898–August 1950.
    Maj. General; Chief of Staff, Volga Military District (January 1946–July 1946); arrested, shot.
Safonov, M.I. (Slav) –1950.
    Former Party official in Estonia, First City Party Secretary Novogorod (1950); arrested, shot.
Samet. (Jewish) –1947.
    Marine Engineer, submarine specialist, suspected of defection (1947); liquidation allegedly ordered by Bulganin and carried out by the Sudoplatov team (Eitingon and Marionovskii) in Ulianovsk.
Samokhin, A.G. (Slav) 1902– .
    Commander 48 Army, Briansk Front (April, 1942); captured,returned from captivity; arrested (October 21, 1945); accused of collaboration.
Schartow, Werner (German) February 5, 1890– .
    Former police officer; Lt. General (March 1, 1943); Commander 602 Infantry Division (Wehrmacht) (October 1944); tried in Poltava along with veterans of the SS Totenkopf Division (November

1947); sentenced to prison; returned to Germany (1955).
Seleznev,N.G. (Slav) 1906– .
    Lt. General of Aviation (September 13, 1944); Chief of Staff 8 Air Army (August 18, 1942–February 3, 1943); Chief of Staff 17 Air Army (February 1943–July 1943); Chief of staff 5 Air Army (July 1943–May 1945); Chief of Staff 12 Air Army (June 25, 1945–August 1945); after the war, Deputy Commander in Chief of Air Force for Procurement; arrested in connection with the "Aviators' Affair" (April 1946); sentenced to 3 years; released after 5 years and 10 months; rehabilitated (June 12, 1953); living in 1994, last survivor of the victims of the "Aviators' Affair."
Semenov, G.M. Ataman (Slav) September 13, 1890–August 30, 1946.
    Lt. General (1919); Commissar of Transbaikal (November 1917–September 1921); led the counter-revolution against Soviet power in Transbaikal (November 1917–December 1917) during Kolchak's rule in Siberia; served as Commander of Chita Military District; self-appointed with Japanese help as Ataman of Transbaikal before being defeated by the Bolsheviks (November 1920); escaped to Darien, lived in Korea, Japan and north China (September 1921–September 1945); captured by Soviet forces in Manchuria at the end of the war and was later tried, condemned to death, and executed.
Semochkin.
    Lt. Colonel; former Adjutant of Marshal G.K. Zhukov (1946); arrested.

Sevast'ianov, A.N. (Slav) 1887–March 3, 1947.

(Kombrig) Maj. General of Artillery (temporary) (October 1941); Commander Artillery, 226 Rifle Division, 21 Army, West Front (September 1941); in captivity; repatriated (February 15, 1946); arrested and accused of collaboration, tried and sentenced to death (February 10, 1947).

Shakhurin, A.I. (Slav) December 25, 1904–1975.

Col. General of Aviation-Engineers (1944); Commissar/Minister of Aviation Industry (March 1940–1946); arrested and sentenced to 7 years (March 1946); released (March 1953); rehabilitated (June 12, 1953).

Shatunovskaia, L.A.

Art historian; adopted daughter of old Bolshevik, P.A. Krasikov (October 4, 1870–August 20, 1939); member of CC CPSU and Deputy Chairman USSR Supreme Court until September 1938; graduate of State Institute of the Arts and a student of Meyerhold; arrested (December 12, 1947) along with her second husband, physicist L. Tumerman and sentenced to 20 years; eventually released and immigrated to Israel in the 1970s; author of memoirs published in New York (1982).

Shcherbakov, M.E. (Slav).

Party functionary associated with Malenkov; disciplined by Party "Court of Honor" (September 1947–April 1948).

Sheinin, L.R. (Jewish) 1906–1967.

Vyshinskii's Deputy (1936–1940s); member of Soviet Writers Union and JAC; involved in fabrication of records for the Nuremberg trials; dismissed (1948) and arrested (October 20, 1951); later released.

Shimanov, N.S. (Slav) 1901– .

Col. General of Aviation (February 4, 1944); Head of Aviation Section in the CC CPSU; Political Commissar of the Air Force (March 17, 1943); arrested in connection with the Aviators' Affair (spring 1946); sentenced to 4 years; released after serving 5 years and 10 months; rehabilitated (June 12, 1953).

Shimeliovich, B.A. (Jewish) 1892–August 12, 1952.

Native of Riga, Chief Surgeon Botkin Central Clinic; Party member (1920); arrested (January 13, 1949), shot.

Shkuro, A.G. (Slav)   –January 17, 1947.

Lt. General; Civil War White General (1918); service with Pannwitz Cossacks in Yugoslavia (1943); arrested, tried, executed.

Shlosberg, E.P. (Jewish) December 6, 1906–1970.

Historian; Party member (1940); member Institute of History; Belorussia Academy of Science (1937–1941); participant in the war; arrested by MGB (November 6, 1948); sentenced to 10 years; rehabilitated (May 9, 1956).

Shteinberg, L. (Jewish).

Director Aviation Factory No. 339 (1949); arrested, tortured by V.I. Komarov; survived.

Shtern, L.S. (Jewish) 1878–Spring 1968.

Gerontologist, Director Institute of Physiology USSR Academy of Medical Sciences; Party member

(1938); winner of Order of Red Banner and Labor Red Banner; arrested (January 28, 1949) and sentenced to prison.

Shukheevich, R. (Slav) – March 1950.

Ukrainian nationalist leader involved in pogroms in Lvov after the German occupation (1941); active in opposing the Soviet occupation(1950); murdered by the Sudoplatov team.

Shul'gin, V.V. (Slav) 1878–1976(?).

Leader of the Black Hundred anti-semitic organization and member of Duma (1917); fled after the October Revolution; Active in anti-Soviet émigré organization mainly in Yugoslavia (1917–1944); briefly returned to Soviet Union in 1920s; arrested by SMERSH, sentenced to prison (1944–1956); released (1956).

Shul'man, M.B. (Jewish) 1907– .

Official in the Red Army Political Administration (1937–1949); Party secretary in the Meyerhold Theatre; arrested and later sent to Kolima; released and moved to L'vov. Re-arrested, sentenced to eight years; released during the thaw (1950–1955); emigrated to Israel (1973).

Shumskii, A. (Slav).

Ukrainian national leader (1946); assassinated by the MGB Special Service at the recommendation of Stalin and   Kaganovich.

Sidnev, A.M.

Police Maj. General; Deputy Head SMERSH 1 Ukraine Front (1944); Head Operations Section MVD in Berlin (1945–1947);attached to MGB Tatar ASSR (1948); arrested by Abakumov in attempts to compromise Zhukov and Serov.

Sivaev, M.N. (Slav)   –1951.

Maj. General of Technical Services (June 1940); service on West Front (1941–1945); captured (July 1941); returned from 4 years of captivity; arrested and finally shot after 6 years in prison.

Slutskii, B. (Jewish) 1879–1954.

Yiddish translator (1930s); arrested; released before the war; re-arrested in Birobidzhan (1948); sentenced to 10 years.

Solov'ev, N.V. (Slav)   –1950.

With Leningrad Party Organization (1938–1946); Commissar 42 Army Leningrad Front (1941); First Party Secretary, Crimea (1950); arrested, shot.

Sorkin, G. (Jewish)

Head of the photo department of the Soviet Information Bureau; arrested (January 28, 1948); sentenced to 20 years; released (May 1954).

Spivak, E. (Jewish).

Member of Commission to honor Jewish writers who had died in the war (1947); arrested (1949); shot (?).

Stepanov, G.A. (Slav) November 18, 1890–January 3, 1957.

Vice Admiral (June 1940); Commander of White Sea Fleet (October 1941–March 1943); Chief of naval staff (April 1943–July 1944); Head of naval training (July 1944–1947); removed (January 1947); arrested, sentenced to prison; released after Stalin's death; rehabilitated (May 13, 1953).

Suchkov, B.L. (Slav).

Specialist in German literature attached to CC CPSU; arrested (post-war), released after Stalin's death; on the editorial board of *Znamia*, and later Director of

Institute of Foreign Literature USSR Academy of Sciences; worked closely with M.A. Suslov.

Sultan-Gireia, K. (Slav) –January 17, 1947.

Maj. General; Civil War White Officer (1918); service with Pannwitz Cossacks in Yugoslavia (1943); arrested, tried, executed.

Talalaevskii, M. (Jewish) 1908–1978.

Yiddish poet, participant in the war (1914–1945); Party member (1942); active in Jewish literary circles in Ukraine (1945–1949); arrested (1949); released after Stalin's death.

Tal'mi, L. Ia. (Jewish) 1893–May/June 1952.

Native of Baranov oblast, resident of U.S. (1914–1917); journalist attached to Soviet Information Bureau; arrested (July 3, 1949), shot.

Telegin, K.F. (Slav) October 22, 1899–1981.

Lt. General (1943); Commissar of Moscow Military District, Don, Central, Belorussian and 1 Belorussian Fronts (1941–1945); Commissar of Soviet Forces in German (1945–1948); arrested (January 30, 1948), sentenced to 25 years (March 20, 1952); released (July 27, 1953).

Teumin, E.I. (Jewish) 1905–May/June 1952.

Native of Bern, Switzerland; Party member (1927); editor international publications of Soviet information; arrested (January 28, 1949), shot.

Tokar, A. (Jewish).

Official in the Cadres Administration of the Red Army; sentenced to death (November 24, 1950).

Trepper, Leopold (Polish Jew) February 23, 1904– .

Veteran GRU agent, Head of "Rote Kapelle" spy network in West Europe (1941–1943); returned to Soviet Union (November 1944–November 2, 1973); arrested; sentenced to 15 years (June 19, 1947); reduced to 10 years (January 9, 1952); released a year after Stalin's death (May 23, 1954); emigrated to Poland (April 1957) and to England (1973).

Tumerman, L. (Jewish)

Physicist; second husband of L.A. Shatunovsakaia;arrested (December 1947) and sentenced to 20 years, eventually released.

Turko, I.M. (Slav) 1908– .

Secretary Leningrad Party Regional Committee (September 1944); Second Secretary Leningrad Party Regional Committee then in Party and government in Iaroslavl' and Vladimir (January 1945); arrested (July 1949) and sentenced to 15 years (January 10, 1950).

Uger, G.A. (Jewish) May 1, 1905–October 20, 1972.

Maj. General of Engineer/Technical Services (March 1, 1946); Head of Radar Department in GKO (1943); Deputy Chair of Commission on Radar (post-war); arrested, later released.

Varennikov, I.S. (Slav).

Lt. General; Chief of Staff 26 Army Southwest Front (1941); Chief of Staff Stalingrad Front (October 1942–December 1942); Chief of Staff 40 Army (1943); arrested (1947).

Vatenberg, I.S. (Jewish) 1887–May/June 1952.

Native of Stanislav; lived in New York, member U.S. Communist

Party; chief editor of state artistic publications in foreign languages; arrested (January 24, 1949), shot.

Vatenberg-Ostrovskaia, Ch.S. (Jewish) 1901–May/June 1952.

Native of Kiev oblast; resident of New York; translator in JAC; arrested (January 24, 1949), shot.

Vendrov, D. (Jewish) 1877–   .

Poet; arrested (1949); released (1954).

Verbitskii, A.D. (Slav)   –1950.

Second Regional Party Secretary Murmansk (1950); arrested, shot.

Von Pannwitz, Helmuth October 14, 1898–January 17, 1947.

Lt. General (April 1, 1944); Commander Cossack Corps (June 1, 1943); tried with White Cossack Generals and sentenced to death (January 1947).

Vorozheikin, G.A. (Slav) March 17, 1895–January 30, 1974.

Marshal of Aviation (August 1944); Air Force Chief of Staff (August 1941–March 1942); First Deputy Commander in Chief of Air Force (May 1942–July 1946); arrested (1947) and sentenced to prison; released after Stalin's death.

Voznesenskii, A.A. (Slav)   –1950.

RFSFR Minister of Education; brother of N.I. Voznesenskii; arrested, shot.

Voznesenskii, N.I. (Slav) December 1903–October 11, 1950.

Economic and Government Official; Chairman USSR Gosplan (December 1937–1941); member GKO (1942–1946); Deputy Chairman USSR Council of Ministers (1946–1949); Politburo member (1947); arrested, shot.

Voznesenskiia, M.A. (Slav).

Second Party Secretary in Kuibyshev District of Leningrad; brother of N.I. Voznesenskii; arrested, shot.

Vrachev, I.Ia. (Slav).

Veteran revolutionary, active in opposition; rare survivor, exiled to Komi ASSR; participant in the war; arrested by the order of Abakumov and chief Prosecutor G.N. Safonov (Sep-tember 2, 1949); sentenced to 25 years in camps (March 18, 1950); rehabilitated (October 10, 1956); living (1990).

Wallenberg, Raoul (Swedish) August 4, 1912–July 16, 1947.

Diplomat stationed in Budapest, arrested by SMERSH (January 17, 1945); kept in Lubianka, Lefortovo and again Lubianka Prisons; died in Lubianka (July 16, 1947); cremated without an autopsy by order of Abakumov.

Zakrzhevskaia, T.V. (Slav) 1908–February 1986.

Head of the Department of Party, Labor Union, and Komsomols in the Leningrad Regional Party organization (October 1948); arrested (July 1949); sentenced to 10 years (October 1, 1950).

Zbarskii, B. (Jewish).

Pathologist in charge of preserving Lenin's mummy (1949); involved in cover-up of Mikhoel's murder (1949); arrested and accused of espionage (1952) and interrogated by Riumin; released (December 30, 1953).

Zharov, F.I. (Slav).

Maj. General of Aviation; Attached to Air Force Rear (1941–1945); arrested (March 1946).

Zheleznov (Aizenshtadt), M. (Jewish) –November 23, 1950.

Woman journalist (1940s); arrested; sentenced to death (November 20, 1950); shot.

Zhemchuzhina (Karpovskaia), P.S. (Jewish) 1896 (7)–May 1, 1970.

Head of Perfume Trust (1932); Commissar of Fish Industry (January 19, 1939); Candidate Member CC-CPSU (1939); Molotov's wife, whom he was forced to divorce; arrested (February 1949); spent a year in prison and 3 years in exile in Kazakh SSR; released after Stalin's death.

Zhigulin, A.V. (Jewish) January 1, 1930– .

Author, active in Komsomols, founder of anti-Stalinist underground youth cell in Voronezh (1948–1949); arrested, released after Stalin's death (March 14, 1953).

Zil'berman, G. (Jewish) 1907– .

Yiddish writer, participant in the war; arrested (end of 1948); released after Stalin's death.

Zuskin, V.L. (Jewish) 1889–May/June 1952.

Artistic director Moscow Jewish Art Theatre; after Mikhoel's murder, arrested, shot.

Zybin, E.S. (Slav) 1894– .

Maj. General; Commander 36 Cavalry Division, South Front (1941); captured (August 28, 1941); returned from captivity; arrested (October 21, 1945) and accused of collaboration.

NOTE

The period covered is the time in which Abakumov was officially in charge of the MGB. Those not listed because the dates of conviction or arrest fall outside this period include S.S. Obergrüppenfuhrer, Fridrich Jeckeln, Reichs Commissar Theodore Von Rientel, a number of Rear Area German Commanders, and Fridrich Panzinger, former Head of SD and the Security Police in Ostland. Also not listed are the leaders of the Home Army, except General Leopold Okulicki, who died in prison in December 1946; also those arrested after Abakumov's fall including a number of high ranking Chekists (mostly Jewish) and those arrested in connection with the Doctors' Plot. Individuals not listed who are discussed in the text include S.F. Kuz'michev, G.M. Mairanovskii, N.A. Vlasik, A.N. Rapava, L.F. Tsanava, L.I. Eitingon, S.R. Mil'shtein, L.F. Raikhman, as well as Abakumov's close associates, who are not listed for the same reason. Also not listed are three prominent military men: N.D. Iakovlev, I.I. Volkotrubenko, I.A. Mirzakhanov (arrested in February 1952; also briefly under arrest in the early days of the war), and the diplomat I.M. Maiskii (arrested in February 1953). In August 1951 after Abakumov's arrest, MGB brought charges against a number of German POW officers. The most prominent was Maj. Joachim Kuhn, former Head of Operations in 28 Infantry Division, who had provided the Russians with details of the military conspiracy against Hitler. Kuhn, who probably deserted in August 1944, was charged on August 30, 1951, and sentenced on October 17, 1951, to 25 years for "preparing aggressive war against the Soviet Union." He was amnestied in 1955 and returned to West Germany on September 28, 1955. In March 1953, the MGB arranged for the assassination of Wolfgang Zalus, Trotskii's former bodyguard. Vlasov and his colleagues were also arrested when Abakumov was in charge of SMERSH and tried in July-August 1946 when he was *unofficially* Head of MGB.

Also not listed are most of the doctors arrested in connection with the Doctors' Plot, although they are discussed in the text. There are also a number of Jewish victims who were repressed during 1952-1955, including the lawyer V. Lishits, a friend of Arkady Vaksberg, who was shot in February 1953 for plotting to assassinate Stalin.

Appendix III

List of Victims of Mass Execution in the Medvedev Forest near Orel (September 11, 1941)

Adam, I.K. (1886)
Adzhoian, A.G. (1891)
Aikhenval'd, A.Iu. (1904)
Aliev, Kh.V.K.O. (1881)
Amel'ian, A.A. (1904)
Anin, V.G. (1891)
Apresov, G.A. (1890)
Arnol'd (Vasil'ev), V.V. (1894)
Artemov, A.G. (1917)
Beimut, G.G. (1898)
Bel'fort-Birkengauer, E.V. (1903)
Bessonov, S.A. (1892)
Bogdanov, V.A. (188Q)
*Bolkvadze-Mel'charskaia, G.B. (1906)
Bondarev, V.A. (1880)
Bunte, V.A. (1907)
Butkus, I.F. (1896)
Chaikin, V.A. (1886)
Chernov-Marushak-Vievskii Okhramenko, P.P, (1908)
Chernykh, V.V. (1899)
Chin-Mun-Shen (1878)
Chizhikov, O.L. (1891)
Chumburidze, B.S. (1880)

Chzhan-Di-Shiu (1881)
De-Lazar, V.K. (1906)
Dzasokhov, T.B. (1868)
Eikhenval'd, F.M. (1901)
Ekkerts (Gramatskii), T.G. (1899)
Erdman, I.N. (1900)
Erofeev, D.F. (1879)
Ezhov, S.A. (1904)
Faustman, F.S. (1909)
Ferner, V. (1909)
Finkgeizer, Iu.V. (1880)
Fokin, Z.D. (1907)
Geller, T.L. (1899)
*Gernstengaim, E.M. (1896)
Goy-Min-Tsun (1909)
Guzin, Kh.Ja. (1915)
Iachmenev, A.S. (1914)
Iakkonen, T.E. (1909)
*Iakovleva, V.N. (1885)
Imam, V.I.G. (1896)
Iul'skii, V.A. (Buksgorn, P.K.) (1894)
Iung, G.Ia. (1884)
*Izmailovich, A.A. (1878)
*Kameneva, O.D. (1883)
Karpenko, V.V. (1880)

---

*Denotes female

*Kasparova, V.Dzh. (1883)
Kata-Oka-Kentaro (Tanaka, Simaki,
    Ch.K.Dzh.) (1909)
Keller, V.G. (1862)
Kim Den Man (1909)
*Kitnovskaia, N.A. (1901)
Klepfer, I.I. (1875)
Kol'man, A.I. (1902)
Kondrashechkin, V.N. (1904)
Korkhonen, V.A.V.L. (1918)
Koval', I.K. (1878)
Kozlovskii, A.S. (1897)
Kravets, N.N. (1910)
Kriger-Kreitsburg, A.A. (1892)
Krilyk-Vasil'kov, I.V. (1898)
Kriuger, A.A. (1877)
Kumshimbetov, A. (1911)
Larin, A.M. (1916)
Leman-Ionin, O.O. (1897)
Leonov, S.A. (1907)
Li Dzhun (1905)
Li Tsian' In (1896)
Lidtke, F.G. (1896)
Linkvist, Kh.A. (1898)
Liui Kai Lu (1903)
Logvinov, P.T. (Shirokov, M.I.) (1914)
*Lysova-Mukhotdinova, E.A. (1896)
Maak, E.E. (1898)
Maas, G.G. (1890)
Mairov, I.A. (1890)
Mamed, K.S.O. (1904)
Marer, L.I. (1896)
Matikainen, A.S. (1882)
Matskevich, A.S. (1882)
Mikeladze, Sh.A. (1884)
Minkin, V.A. (1879)
Mirdzhon, R.Z. (1914)
Mironchik, M.K. (1878)
Mizin, P.T. (1878)
Mozhin, F.I. (1891)
Musaev, S.M.O. (1915)
*Muzafarova, M.Kh. (1906)
Myl'nikov, A.S. (1922)
Naka, Kaichiro (1913)

Neigebauer, Ia.Ia. (1883)
Nestroev-Tsypin, G.A. (1877)
Neter, F.M. (1884)
Nikerent, G.M. (1900)
Nikiforov, G.I. (1882)
Nikologorodskii, A.E. (1880)
O-Seng-Chin (O-Khoi-Chen) (1896)
Okeus-ogli (Okeuz-ogli), M.O. (1867)
*Okudzhava, O.S. (1888)
*Ortman-Gavatina, R.M. (1886)
Pallonberg, Ia.Ia. (1909)
Parshkov, M.I. (1887)
Perventsev, P.N. (1892)
Petrovskii, P.G. (1898)
Plentev, D.D. (1872)
Plotnikov, S.P. (1882)
Podgurskii, N.S. (1892)
Pomogaev, I.I. (1893)
Ponomarev, I.S. (1890)
Prodan, N.G. (1905)
*Radionovskaia, M.D. (1908)
Rakovskii, Kh.G. (1873)
Rau, E.E. (1880)
Reinbakh, A.A. (1902)
Reiter, V.I. (1887)
Rempel' (Zuderman), Ia.A. (1883)
Ronkomiaki, K.A. (1907)
Rozenbakh, F.K. (1904)
Rudakov, N.E. (1900)
She-Kui-Sian (1908)
Shimshelevich, S.Z. (1883)
Shleider, G.G. (1904)
Shlikhting-Pastukhova, R.P. (1892)
Shneider, G.K. (1893)
Tablash (Bikfol'vi), I.I. (1880)
Tokhtamyshev, R. (1902)
Val'ter, O.V. (1875)
Vezirov, Dzh.I. (1888)
Vilenkin, Iu.I. (1884)
Volkov, N.I. (1916)
Vorovich, B.G. (1894)
Vyn Do Kui (1917)
*Zharskaia-Matsinovskaia, S.P. (1893)
Zibol'd, G.V. (1897)

NOTE:

Four of the condemned, E.P. Semenov, G.K. Shneider, V.L. Korkhonen, and E.A. Lysova-Mukhotdinova, were shot in prison during the period of September 13–18, 1941; the rest in Medvedev forest. The site of burial has yet to be located.

Appendix IV

Organizational Charts

**Ranks in the Security and Police Organizations Excluding Internal
and Border Troops**

Before 1944–1945
Lieutenant of State Security
Senior Lieutenant of State Security
Captain of State Security
Major of State Security
Senior Major of State Security
Commissar of State Security 3 Rank
Commissar of State Security 2 Rank
Commissar of State Security 1 Rank
Commissar General of State Security

After 1944–1945
Lieutenant
Senior Lieutenant
Captain
Major
Lt. Colonel
Colonel
Major General
Lt. General
Col. General
Army General
Marshal of the Soviet Union

Leadership of State Security and Police 1939–1953

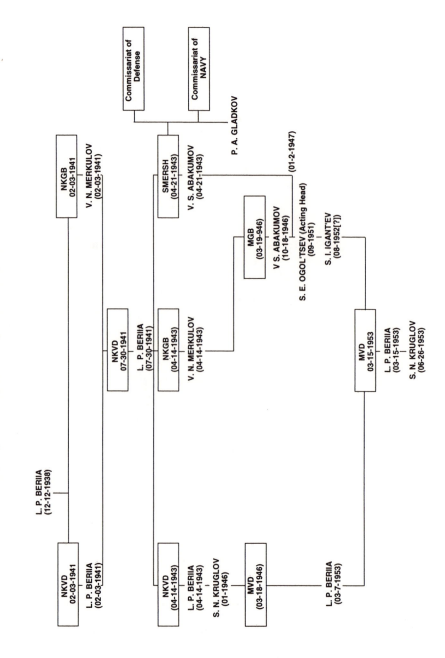

Bibliography

Abarinov, V.K. KATYNSKII LABIRINT. Moscow: Novosti. 1991.

Abarinov, V.K. THE MURDERS OF KATYN. New York: Hippocrene. 1993.

Abramovich, Aron. V RESHAIUSHCHEI VOINE: UCHASTIE I ROL' EVEREEV SSSR V VOINE PROTIV NATSIZMA. Tel Aviv: 1981, 1992. 2 volumes.

Adler, Nancy. VICTIMS OF SOVIET TERROR: THE STORY OF THE MEMORIAL MOVEMENT. Westport, CT: Greenwood. 1993.

Airapetian, G.A. KOMKOR KHAKHAN'IAN. Erevan: Aistan. 1970.

Aizenshtat, Ia. ZAPISKI SEKRETARIA VOENNOCO TRIBUNA. London: Overseas Publications Interchange. 1991.

AKSEL' IVANOVICH BERG. Moscow: Nauka. 1965.

Alaeva, G.S. PODBORKA PISEM SPETSPERESELENTSEV. Moscow: 1991.

Al'bats, E. MINA ZAMEDLENNOGO DEISTVIIA: POLITICHESKII PORTRET KGB SSSR. Moscow: Russlit. 1992.

Albats, Evgeniia. THE STATE WITHIN A STATE. New York: Farrar Straus Giroux. 1994.

Albaz, Jewgeniia (Al'Bats, E.). GEHEIM-IMPERIUM KGB-TOTENGRÄBERDER SOWJETUNION. Munich: Deutscher Taschenbuch Verlag. 1992.

Albrecht, Ulrich. DIE SPEZIALISTEN. Berlin: Dietz. 1992.

_____. THE SOVIET ARMAMENTS INDUSTRY. Langhorne, PA: Harwood Academic. 1993.

ALEKSANDR KOSAREV. Moscow: Politizdat. 1963.

Alexiev, A.R. SOVIET NATIONALITIES IN GERMAN WARTIME STRATEGY. Santa Monica, CA: Rand. 1982.

ALLIANCE FOR MURDER: THE NAZI-UKRAINIAN NATIONALIST PARTNERSHIP IN GENOCIDE. New York: Sarpedon. 1991.

ALLIES AT WAR: THE SOVIET, AMERICAN AND BRITISH EXPERIENCE 1939-1945. New York: St. Martin. 1994.

Alliluyeva, Svetlana. ONLY ONE YEAR. New York: Harper & Row. 1969.

_____. TWENTY LETTERS TO A FRIEND. New York: Harper & Row. 1967.

ANATOMY OF COMMUNIST TAKEOVERS. Munich: Institute for the Study of the Soviet Union. 1971.

ANATOMY OF THE AUSCHWITZ DEATH CAMP. Bloomington: Indiana University Press. 1994.

Anders, Wladsilaw. ARMY IN EXILE. London: Macmillan. 1949.

_____. CRIME OF KATYN. London: Polish Cultural Foundation. 1965.

Andersons, Edgars. LATVIJAS VESTURE, 1920-1940. New York: Daugava. 1984.

Andreev, A.M., Col. General. OT PERVOGO MGNOVENIIA-DO POSLEDNEGO. Moscow: Voenizdat. 1984.

Andrew, Christopher and Oleg Gordievsky. KGB, THE INSIDE STORY. New York: Harper Collins. 1990.

Anfilov, V.A. KRUSHENIE POKHODA GITLERA NA MOSKVY 1941. Moscow: Nauka. 1989.

Annenkov, Iu. DNEVNIK MOIKH VSTRECH: TSIKL TRAGEDII. NY: MLS 1966, Moscow: Khudlit. 1991.

ANTI-SEMITISM IN THE SOVIET UNION: ITS ROOTS AND CONSEQUENCES. New York: Freedom Library Press. 1984.

Antonomov, P. OTCHIZNY VYPPOLNIAIA PRIKAZAN'E. Moscow. 1975.

Antonov-Ovseenko, A. STALIN BEZ MASKI. Moscow: Vsia Moskva. 1989.

_____. THE TIME OF STALIN. New York: Harper & Row. 1981.

Arbatov, Georgi. THE SYSTEM: AN INSIDER'S LIFE IN SOVIET POLITICS. New York: Random House.
1992.

Arzumanian, A.M. IVAN TEVOSIAN. Moscow: Politizdat. 1983.

Astashenkov, P.T. DERZKIE STARTY. Moscow: 1976.

_____. AKADEMIK I.V. KURCHATOV. Moscow: Voenizdat. 1971.

Bacon, Edwin. THE GULAG AT WAR. New York: New York University Press. 1994.

Baidukov, G.F. CHKLAOV. Moscow: Mol.gvardiia. 1975.

Bannykh, S.A. GODY I. LIUDI GRANITSY. Moscow: Pogranichnik. 1972.

BARBAROSSA: THE AXIS AND THE ALLIES. Edinburgh: Edinburgh University Press. 1994.

Barber, John. THE SOVIET HOME FRONT, 1941-1945. London: Longman. 1991.

Barron, John. KGB. New York: Bantam. 1974.

Bartov, Omer. THE EASTERN FRONT: GERMAN TROOPS AND BARBARISATION OF WARFARE. New York: St. Martin. 1986.

_____. HITLER'S ARMY: SOLDIERS, NAZIS AND WAR IN THE THRID REICH. New York: Oxford University Press. 1991.

Barwich, Elfi and Heinz Barwich. DAS ROTE ATOM. Munich: Verlag Scherz. 1967.

Baskakov, V.E. MARSHAL KONEV. Moscow: Patriot. 1992.

Basov, A.V. KRYM V VEL. OTECHESTVENNOI VOINE, 1941--1945. Moscow: Nauka. 1987.

Batov, P.I., Army General. V POKHODAKH I BOIAKH. Moscow: Voenizdat. 1966.

Bauer, Karl. GEDACHTNISPROTOKOLL: EIN PROZESS IN MINSK. Bonn: E.S. Mittler. 1990.

Bazhanov, Boris. BAZHANOV AND THE DAMNATION OF STALIN. Athens, OH: Ohio University Press. 1990.

Bazovskii, V.N. SAMOE DOROGOE: DOKUMENTAL'NOE POVESTVOVANIE OB A.A. KUZNETSOVE. Moscow: Izd-vo polit. lit-ry. 1982.

Bega, F.F. and A.G. Aleksandrov. PETROVSKII. Moscow: Mol.gvardiia. 1963.

Bek, F. RUSSIAN PURGE AND THE EXTRACTION OF CONFESSION. New York: Viking Press. 1951.

Beltov, E. and D. Iurasov. 1937, TOL'KO FAKTY, TOL'KO IMENA. Moscow: Iuridlit. 1990.

Bereschkow (Berezhkov), V.M. ICH WAR STALINS DOLMETSCHER. Munich: Universitas. 1991.

Berezhkov, V. HISTORY IN THE MAKING. Moscow: Progress. 1983.

Berezhkov, V.M. KAK IA STAL PEREVOCHIKOM STALINA. Moscow: DEM. 1993.

Berger, Joseph. SHIPWRECK OF A GENERATION. London: Harvill. 1971.

Bergh, Hendrik van. DIE WARHEIT ÜBER KATYN. Berg am See: Kurt Vowinckel. 1986.

BERIIA AFFAIR: THE SECRET TRANSCRIPTS OF THE MEETINGS SIGNALLING THE END OF STALINISM. New York: Nova Science. 1992.

BERIIA: KONETS KAR'ERY. Moscow: Politizdat. 1991.

Beriia, S.L. (S.A. Gegechkori). MOI OTETS LAVRENTII BERIIA. Moscow: Sovremennik. 1994.

Bertoli, Georges. DEATH OF STALIN. New York: Praeger. 1975.

Bethell, Nicholas. THE LAST SECRET. New York: Basic. 1974.

Bilenko, S.V. ISTREBITEL'NYE BATAL'ONY V VEL. OTECH. VOINE. Moscow: Voenizdat. 1969.

_____. NA OKHRANE TYLA STRANY. Moscow: Nauka. 1988.

Biriuzov, S.S., Marshal of the Soviet Union. SUROVYE GODY. Moscow: Nauka. 1966.

Bliukher, V.V. PO VOENNYM DOROGAM OTTSA. Sverdlovsk: Sred-Ural kn.izd. 1984.

Bloomberg, Marty and Buckley Barrett. STALIN: AN ANNOTATED GUIDE TO BOOKS IN ENGLISH. San Bernadino, CA: Borgo. 1993.

Bobrenev, V.A. and V.B. Riazantsev. PALACHI I ZHERTVY. Moscow: Voenizdat. 1993.

BOEVOI PUT' SOVETSKOGO VOENNO-MORSKOGO FLOTA. Moscow: Voenizdat. 1988.

Boffa, Giuseppe. THE STALIN PHENOMENON. Ithaca, NY: Cornell University Press. 1992.

Bokov, F.E., Lt. General. VESNA POBEDY. Moscow: Voenizdat. 1979.

Bordihn, Peter. BITTERE JAHRE AM POLARKREIS. ALS SOZIALDEMOKRAT IN STALINS LAGER. Berlin: Linksdruck. 1990.

Borev, Iu.B. STALINIADA. Moscow: Pisatel'. 1990.

Bor-Komorovski, Iadeusz. SECRET ARMY. Nashville: Battery Press. 1984.

Borshchagovskii, A. OBVINIAETSIA KROV'. Moscow: Progress. 1994.

Brockdorff, Werner. GEHEIM-KOMMANDOS DES ZWEITEN WELTKRIEGES. Eltville am Rhein, Germany: Rheingauer Verlagsgesellschaft. 1983.

Brodskii, E.A. ZABVENIU NE PODLEZHIT. Moscow: Mysl'. 1993.

_____. ONI NE PROPALI BEZ VESTI. Moscow: Mysl'. 1987.

_____. VO IMIA POBEDY NAD FASHIZMOM. Moscow: Nuaka. 1970.

Buchin, A.N. 170,000 KILOMETROV S.G.K. ZHUKOVYM. Moscow: Mol.gvardiia. 1994.

Buchsweiler, Meir. BIBLIOGRAPHIE DER SOWJETDEUTSCHEN LITERATUR VON DEN ANFANGEN BIS 1941. Köln: Bohlau. 1990.

_____. A COLLECTION OF SOVIET DOCUMENTS CONCERNING GERMANS IN THE USSR. Jerusalem: Hebrew University. 1991.

Bugai, N.F. IOSIF STALIN-LAVRENTIIU BERII: "IKH NADO DEPORTIROVAT.." Moscow: Druzhba narodov. 1992.

Bugai, N.F., T.M. Broev and R.M. Broev. SOVETSKIE KURDY. Moscow: Kap. 1993.

Buianov, M.I. LENIN, STALIN I PSIKHIATRIIA. Moscow: Med-Lit. 1993.

Bullock, Alan. HITLER AND STALIN, PARALLEL LIVES. New York: Knopf. 1991.

Burlatsky, Fedor. KHRUSHCHEV AND THE FIRST RUSSIAN SPRING. London: Weidenfeld and Nicolson. 1988. (NY: Scribner, 1991).

Butkus, Zigmas. MAJOR CRIMES AGAINST THE SOVIET STATE. Washington, DC: Library of Congress. 1985.

Cameron, Kenneth Neill. STALIN, MAN OF CONTRADICTION. Herts, UK: Strong Oak Press. 1987.

Carrere d'Encausse, Helene. THE RUSSIAN SYNDROME. New York: Holmes and Meier. 1992.

_____. STALIN: ORDER THROUGH TERROR. New York: Longman. 1981.

Catroux, Maurice. J'AI VU TOMBER LE RIDEAU DE FER. Paris: Hachette. 1952.

Chalamaev, V.A. MALYSHEV. Moscow: Mol.gvardiia. 1978.

Charaguine, A. EN PRISON AVEC TUPOLEV. Paris: Editions Albin Michel. 1973.

CHASOVYE SOVETSKIKH GRANITS. KRATKII OCHERK POGRANICHNYKH VOIST SSSR. Moscow: Politizdat. 1979.

CHERNAIA KNIGA. Jerusalem: Tarbut. 1980.

Cherniavskii, G.I. V BOR'BE PROTIV SAMOVLASTIIA: KH.G. RAKOVSKII V 1927–1941. Kharkov: In-t kul-tury. 1993.

Chistiakov, N.F. VERKHOVNYI SUD SSSR. Moscow: Nauka. 1991.

CHEKISTY AZERBAIDZHANA. Baku: Azer gosizd. 1981.

CHEKISTY OGNENNYKH LET. Frunze: Kyrguzstan. 1976.

CHEKISTY PETROGRADA NA STRAZHE REVOLIUTSKII. Leningrad: Lenizdat. 1989.

CHEKISTY RASSKAZYVAIUT. Moscow: Sov. Rossiia. various dates.

Chilachava, R.Sh. SYN LAVRENTIIA BERIIA RASSKAZYVAET. Kiev: Inkopress. 1992.

Chubakov, Iu. PALACHI I PRIDURKI. St. Petersburg: Redaktor. 1991.

Chuev, F.I. TAK GOVORIL KAGANOVICH. Moscow: Otechestvo. 1992.

Chugunov, A.I. GRANITSA NAKANUNE VOINY. Moscow: Voenizdat. 1985.

Chuianov, A. NA STREMNINE VEKA: ZAPISKI SEKRETARIA OBKOMA. Moscow: Politizdat. 1976.

Cole, Paul. POW/MIA ISSUES, THE KOREAN WAR. Santa Monica, CA: Rand. 1994.

COMMUNIST PARTIES OF EASTERN EUROPE. New York: Columbia University Press. 1979.

_____. STALIN, BREAKER OF NATIONS. London: Weidenfeld and Nicolson. 1991.

_____. THE GREAT TERROR, A REASSESSMENT. New York: Oxford University Press. 1990.

_____. INSIDE STALIN'S SECRET POLICE, NKVD POLITICS 1936-1939. Stanford, CA: Hoover Institution Press. 1985.

_____. THE GREAT TERROR. New York: Macmillan. 1973.

Conte, Francis. CHRISTIAN RAKOVSKI. New York: Columbia University Press. 1989.

Cookridge, E.H. GEHLEN, SPY OF THE CENTURY. New York: Random House. 1972.

Costello, John and Oleg Tsarev. DEADLY ILLUSIONS. New York: Crown. 1993.

Cotic, Meir. THE PRAGUE TRIAL. New York: Herzl Press. 1987.

Crowe, David. THE BALTIC STATES AND THE GREAT POWER: FOREIGN RELATIONS, 1938-1940. Boulder, CO: Westview. 1993.

Czapski, Joseph. THE INHUMAN LAND. London: Chatto and Windus. 1951.

CZECHOSLOVAK POLITICAL TRIALS 1950-1954. Stanford, CA: Stanford University Press. 1971.

Daniels, Anthony. WILDER SHORES OF MARX. London: Hutchinson. 1991.

Danylenko, V.M., et. al. STALINIZM NA UKRAINI 20-30 TI ROKY. Kiev: Lybid. 1991.

Davies, R.W. SOVIET HISTORY IN THE GORBACHEV REVOLUTION. Bloomington: Indiana University Press. 1989.

Deane, John. STRANGE ALLIANCE. Bloomington, IN: Indiana University Press. 1973.

DER "GENERALPLAN OST". Berlin: Akademie Verlag. 1993.

Deriabin, Peter. KGB MASTERS OF THE SOVIET UNION. New York: Hippocrene. 1989.

_____. WATCHDOGS OF TERROR: RUSSIAN BODYGUARDS FROM TSARS TO THE COMMISSARS. New Rochelle, NY: Arlington House. 1972.

Deriabin, Peter and Frank Gibney. THE SECRET WORLD. Garden City, NY: Doubleday. 1959.

DeVillemarest, P.F. GRU, LE PLUS SECRET DES SERVICES SOVIETIQUES, 1918–1988. Paris: Stock. 1988.

_____. LE NKVD DANS LA GUERRE ET LES GUERILLAS, 1941–1945. Geneva: Ferni. 1978.

_____. LA TERREUR EN URSS DURAN LES ANNEES TRENTE, 1930–1941. Geneva: Ferni. 1978.

D'iakov, Iu.L. and T.S. Bushueva. FASHISTKII MECH KOVALSIA V SSSR: KRASNAIA ARMII I REIKHSVER. Moscow: Sov. Rossiia. 1992.

Dmitriev, P.F. SOLDAT BERII. VOSPOMINANIIA LAGERNOGO OKHRANINKA. Moscow: Chas Pik. 1991.

DOIG I OTVAGA. Moscow: Politizdat. 1988.

DOKUMENTOV ARKHIVA PREZIDENTA ROSSIISKOI FEDERATSII PO KATYN SKOMU DELU. Warsaw: Chancellory of the President. 1992.

DOKUMENTY KATYNIA DECYZJA. Warsaw: Polish Information Agency. 1992.Dolgopolov, Iu.B. VOINA BEZ LINII FRONTA. Moscow: Voenizdat. 1981.

Dolmatovskii, E.A. ZELENAIA BRAMA. Moscow: Politizdat. 1983.

DO POSLEDNEGO PATRONA. Dnepropetrovsk: Promin. 1992.

Dornbach, Alajos. THE SECRET TRIAL OF IMRE NAGY. Westport, CT: Praeger. 1994.

Dowling, Alick. JANEK: A STORY OF SURVIVAL. Letchworth, UK: Ringpress. 1989.

DOZORNYE ZAPADNYKH RUBEZHEI. Kiev: Polizidat Ukrainy. 1972.

Dudko, A.F. and L.G. Liubich. PRAVO NA BESSMERTIE. Kiev: Politizdat Ukrainy. 1988.

Dugin, A.N. NEIZVESTNYI GULAG: DOKUMENTY I FAKTY. Moscow: (unpublished manuscript). 1992.

Duraczynski, Eugeniusz. GENERAL IWANOW ZAPRASA. Warsaw: ALFA. 1989.

Dushen'kin, V.V. OT SOLDATA DO MARSHALA. Moscow: Politizdat. 1964.

Dyadkin, Iosif. UNNATURAL DEATHS IN THE USSR. New Brunswick, NJ: Transaction. 1983.

Dzhugashvili, G.Ia. DED, OTETS, MA I DRUGIE. Moscow: Olimp PP. 1993.

Dziak, John. CHEKISTY. Lexington, MA: Lexington. 1988.

Ebon, Martin. KGB: DEATH AND REBIRTH. Westport, CT: Praeger. 1994.

_____. SVETLANA. New York: New American Library. 1967.

Ehrenburg, I.G. POST-WAR YEARS, 1945–1954. Cleveland: World. 1967.

_____. MEMOIRS, 1921-1941. Cleveland: World. 1963.

Ellis, Frank. VASILIY GROSSMAN. Providence, RI: Berg. 1994.

Emel'ianov, V.S. S CHEGO NACHINALOS'. Moscow: Sov. Rossiia. 1979.

_____. NA POROGE VOINY. Moscow: Sov. Rossiia. 1971.

_____. O VREMENI, O TOVARISHCHAKH, O SEBE. Moscow: Sov. Rossia. 1968.

_____. NAKANUNE VOINY. Moscow: Sov. Rossiia. 1966.

Emiot, Israel. THE BIROBIDZHAN AFFAIR. Philadelphia: Jewish Publications of America. 1981.

Engel, David. IN THE SHADOW OF AUSCHWITZ: THE POLISH GOVERNMENT-IN-EXILE AND THE JEWS 1943–1945. Chapel Hill: University of North Carolina Press. 1993.

Falaleev, F.Ia., Marshal of Aviation. V STROIU KRYLATYKH. Izhevsk: Udmurtiia. 1970.

Favez, Jean-Claude. UNE MISSION IMPOSSIBLE? Lausanne: Payot. 1989.

Feklisov, A.S. ZA OKEANOM I NA OSTROVE. Moscow: DEM. 1994.

Feoktisov, K.P. SEM' SHAGOV V NEBO. Moscow: Mol'gvardiia. 1984.

Finn, Gerhard. DIE POLITISCHE HAFTLINGE IN DER SOWJETZONE 1945–1959. Cologne: Verlag Wissenschaft und Politik. 1989.

FLAGMANY: SBORNIK VOSPOMINANII I OCHERKOV. Moscow: Voenizdat. 1991.

Fleischhauer, Ingeborg. THE SOVIET GERMANS, PAST AND PRESENT. New York: St. Martin. 1986.

FOR HUMAN RIGHTS. Frankfurt: Possev. 1969.

Frish, S.E. SKVOZ' PRIZMU VREMENI. Moscow: Politizdat. 1992.

Fröhlich, Sergej. GENERAL WLASSOW. Cologne: Markus Verlag. 1990.

Fuller, William. THE INTERNAL TROOPS OF MVD. College Station: Texas A&M Center for Strategic Technology. 1983.

Gadourek, I. THE POLITICAL CONTROL OF CZECHOSLOVAKIA. Westport, CT: Greenwood. 1974.

Gaglov, I.I. ARMII GENERAL A.I. ANTONOV. Moscow: Voenizdat. 1978.

Gakaev, Kh.A. V GODY SUROVYKH ISPYTANII GROZNYI. Moscow. 1988.

Gallai, M.L. CHEREZ NEVIDIMUIE BAR'ERY. Moscow: Mol.gvardiia. 1969.

_____. ZAPISKI LETCHIKA-ISPYTATELIA. Moscow: Mol.gvardiia. 1969.

Gamow, George. MY WORLD LINE. New York: Viking. 1970.

Gazarian, Suren. ETO NE DOLZHNO POVTORIT'SIA. 1958–1961 (unpublished manuscript).

Gegechkori, S.A. See Beriia, S.L.

Gellermann, Günther. MOSKAU RUFT HEERES-GRUPPE MITTE. Koblenz: Bernard & Graefe. 1988.

German, A.A. NEMETSKAIA AVTONOMIIA NA VOLGE 1918–1941. Saratov, Russia: Saratov Universiteta. 1992.

GEROI GRAZHDANSKOI VOINY. Moscow: Mol.gvardiia. 1963.

GEROI I ANTIGEROI OTECHESTVA. Moscow: Informekspress. 1992.

GEROI OKTIABRIA. Leningrad: Lenizdat. 1967.

GESCHICHTE DER GRENZTRUPPEN DER UDSSR, HISTORISCHER ABRISS. East Berlin: Militärverlag. 1984.

Getty, J. Arch. ORIGINS OF THE GREAT PURGES. New York: Cambridge University Press. 1985.

Gibian, George. THE MAN IN THE BLACK COAT: RUSSIA'S LITERATURE OF ABSURD. Evanston, IL: Northwestern University Press. 1986.

Gilbert, Martin. ATLAS OF JEWISH HISTORY. New York: William Morrow. 1993.

Gilboa, Yehoshua. THE BLACK YEARS OF SOVIET JEWRY. Boston: Little Brown. 1971.

Ginzburg, Eugenia. JOURNEY INTO THE WHIRLWIND. New York: Harcourt Brace Jovanovich. 1967.

Girenko, Iu.S. STALIN-TITO. Moscow: Politizdat. 1991.

Gladkov, T.K. and N.G. Zaitsev. I IA EMU NE MOGU NE VERIT'. Moscow: Politizdat. 1986.

Glenny, Michael and Norman Stone. THE OTHER RUSSIA. New York: Viking. 1991.

Gnedin, E.A. VYKHOD IZ LABIRINTA. New York: Chalidze. 1982.

_____. IZ ISTORII OSTNOSHENII MEZHDU SSR I FASHISTKOY GERMANII. New York: Khronika. 1977.

_____. KATASROFA I VTOROE ROZHDENIE. Amsterdam: Fond imeni Gertsena. 1977.

Gol'dshtein, Pavel. TOCHKA OPORY. Jerusalem: Graff-Press. 1978, 1982.

Golikov, F.I., Marshal of the Soviet Union. ON A MILITARY MISSION TO GREAT BRITAIN AND THE USA. Moscow: Progress. 1988.

Gologin, I.G. I.V. KURCHATOV. Moscow: Atomizdat. 1978.

Gorbatov, A.V., Army General. GODY I VOINY. Moscow: Voenizdat. 1980.

Gorchakov, O.A. NAKANUNE: ILI TRAGEDIIA KASSANDRY. Moscow: 1991.

Gordon, L.A. and E.V. Kopov. CHTO ETO BYLO? RAZMYSHLENIIA O PREDPOSYLKAKH I ITOGAKH TOGO, CHTO SLUCHILOS' S NAMI V 30-40-E GODY. Moscow: Politizdat. 1989.

Gorshkov, S.G., Admiral of the Fleet of Soviet Union. NA IUZHNOM PRIMORSKOM FLANGE 1941–1944. Moscow: Voenizdat. 1989.

Grabin, V.G., Col. General of Technical Services. ORUZHIE POBEDY. Moscow: Polizdat. 1989.

Granovsky, Anatolii. I WAS AN NKVD AGENT. New York: Devon-Adair. 1962.

Gribanov, S.V. ZALOZHNIKI VREMENI. Moscow: Voenizdat. 1992.

GRIF SEKRETNOSTI SNIAT. POTERI VOORUZHENNYKH SIL SSSR V BOINAKH, BOEVYKH DEISTVIIAKH I VEONNYKH KONFLIKTAKH. Moscow: Voenizdat. 1993.

Grigorenko, P.G. MEMOIRS. New York: Norton. 1982.

Gross, Jan. REVOLUTION FROM ABROAD: THE SOVIET CONQUEST OF POLAND'S WESTERN UKRAINE AND WESTERN BELORUSSIA. Princeton, NJ: Princeton University Press. 1988.

Gubarev, V.S. KONSTRUKTORY. Moscow: Politizdat. 1989.

Gul', R.B. DZERZHINSKY, MENZHINSKY, PETERS, LATSIS, YAGODA. Paris. 1936. (Reprinted Moscow: Mol.gvardiia. 1992).

Gusarov, V.N. MOI PAPA UBIL MIKHOELSA. Frankfurt: Possev. 1978.

Hahn, Werner. POSTWAR SOVIET POLITICS. Ithaca, NY: Cornell University Press. 1982.

Harwarth, Hans von. AGAINST TWO EVILS. London: Collins. 1981.

Haslam, Jonathan. THE SOVIET UNION AND THE THREAT FROM THE EAST, 1933-1941. Pittsburgh: University of Pittsburgh Press. 1992.

Heinmann-Grüder, Andreas. DIE SOWJETISCHE ATOMBOMBE. Munich: Verlag Westfalisches Dampfboot. 1992.

Heller, M.I. and A.M. Nekrich. UTOPIA IN POWER. New York: Summit. 1986.

Henkine, Cyrille (Khenkin, Kirill). L'ESPONAGE SOVIETIQUE: LA CAS RUDOLF ABEL. Paris: Fayard. 1981 (from Russian original OKHOTNIK VVERKH NOGAMI).

Hernandez, Jesus. YO, MINISTRO DE STALIN EN ESPANA. Madrid: Segunda. 1954.

Hilger, Gustav. THE INCOMPATIBLE ALLIES. New York: Hafner. 1971.

Hochschild, Adam. THE UNQUIET GHOST: RUSSIANS REMEMBER STALIN. New York: Viking. 1993.

Hodos, George. SHOW TRIALS: STALINIST PURGES IN EASTERN EUROPE 1948-1954. New York: Praeger. 1987.

Hoffman, Joachim. KAUKASIEN 1942–43: DAS DEUTSCHE HEER UND DIE ORIENTVOLKER DER SOWJETUNIN. Freiburg: Rombach. 1991.

_____. DEUTSCHE UND KALMYKEN 1942 BIS 1945. Freiburg: Verlag Rombach. 1986.

_____. DIE GESCHICHTE DER WLASSOW-ARMEE. Freiburg: Verlag Rombach. 1986.

_____. DIE OSTLEGIONEN 1941–1943. Freiburg, West Germany: Verlag Rombach. 1986.

Holloway, David. STALIN AND THE BOMB. New Haven, CT: Yale University Press. 1994.

_____. SOVIET UNION AND THE ARMS RACE. New Haven, CT: Yale University Press. 1983.

HOLOCUAST IN THE SOVIET UNION. Armonk, NY: M.E. Sharpe. 1993.

Honchalovsky, Andrei and Alexander Lipkov. THE INNER CIRCLE. New York: Newmarket. 1991.

Hughes, Gwyneth. THE RED EMPIRE. London: Weidenfeld and Nicolson. 1990.

Iakovlev, A.S., Col. General of Aviation. TSEL' ZHIZNI. Moscow: Politzidat. 1987.

Iakovlev, N.D. OB ARTILLERII I NEMNOGO O SEBE. Moscow: Vysshaia Shkola. 1984.

Iakupov, N.M. TRAGEDIIA POLKOVODTSEV. Moscow: Mysl'. 1992.

Iakovlev, N.N. ZHUKOV. Moscow: Mol. gvardiia. 1992.

_____. MARSHAL ZHUKOV 19 NOIABRIA 1942-43. SENTIABRIA 1945. g. Moscow: Mysl'. 1990.

Iakovlev, N.N. STRANITSY ZHIZNI MARSHALA G.K. ZHUKOVA. Moscow: Det. lit. 1985.

IAN GAMARNIK, KOMNDARM SHTERN. Vladivostok: Dal'nevost. kn. izd. 1985.

Iarring, Gunnar (Jarring, Gunnar). DO GLASNOSTI I PERESTROIKII. Moscow: Progress. 1992.

Iatsovskis, E.Ia. ZABVENIIU NE PODLEZHIT. Moscow: Voenizdat. 1985.

IMPACT OF WORLD WAR II ON THE SOVIET UNION. Totowa, NJ: Rowman & Allanheld. 1985.

IN DEN FANGEN NKVD: DEUTSCHER OPFER DES STALINISTISCHEN TERROR IN DER USSR. Berlin: Dietz. 1991.

INDUSTRIAL INNOVATION IN THE SOVIET UNION. New Haven, CT: Yale University Press. 1982.

Ioirysk, A.I. O CHEM ZVONIT KOLOKOL. Moscow: Politizdat. 1991.

IOSIF STALIN-LAVRENTIIU BERII: "IKH NADO DEPORTIROVAT." See BUGAI, N.F.

IOSIF STALIN V OB'IATIIAKH SEM'I. Moscow: Rodina. 1993.

IOSIF VISSARIONOVICH STALIN. KRATKAIA BIOGRAFIIA. Moscow: TSOO "Nippur." 1993. (Reprint of the 1950 Politizdat edition.)

ISPYTANIE DOLGOM, VOSPOMINANIIA CHEKISTOV. Donetsk: Donbass. 1989.

ISTORIIA I STALINIZM. Moscow: Politizdat. 1991.

ISTORIIA ROSSIISKIKH NEMETSEV V DOKUMENTAKH, 1763–1992. Moscow: MIGUP. 1993.

ISTORIIA VELKOI OTECHESTVENNOI VOINY SOVETSKOGO SOIUZA. Moscow: Voenizdat. 1960–1965. 6 volumes.

Iuzefovich, L.A. SAMODERZHETS PUSTYNI. Moscow: Ellis Pak. 1993.

Ivinskaia, O. GODY S BORISON PASTERNAKOM. Moscow: Libris. 1992.

_____. A CAPTIVE OF TIME. New York: Doubleday. 1978.

IZ BOIA V. BOI. Leningrad: Lenizdat. 1982.

Jacobs, Dan. BORODIN, STALIN'S MAN IN CHINA. Cambridge, MA: Harvard University Press. 1981.

Jakubowski, Antony A.J. KATYN: A WHISPER IN THE TREES. Santa Monica, CA: Kuma. 1991.

JEWS IN EASTERN POLAND AND THE USSR, 1939–1946. New York: St. Martin. 1991.

Juchneva, Natalja. DER ANTISEMITISMUS IN RUSSLAND HEUTE. Cologne: Bundesinstitut für ostwissenschaftliche und internationale Studien. 1993.

Kadell, Franz-Anton. DIE KATYN LÜGE. GESCHICHTE EINER MANIPULATION. Munich: F.A. Herbig. 1991.

Kalinin, S.A., Lt. General. RAZMYSHLIA O MINUVSHEM. Moscow: Voenizdat. 1963.

Kamenetskii, Iu. GEORGI ZHUKOV. Moscow: Progress. 1991.

KANUN I NACHALO VOINY. Leningrad: Lenizdat. 1991.

Kapitsa, P.L. PIS'MA O NAUKE: 1930-1980. Moscow: Mosk.rabochii. 1989.

Kaplan, Karel. NEKRAVA REVOLUCE. Prague: Mlada Fronta. 1993.

_____. THE SHORT MARCH. London: C. Hurst. 1987.

_____. PROCES POLITIQUES A PRAGUE. Brussels: Complexe. 1980.

Kapusto, Iu.B. POSLEDNIMI DOROGAMI GENERAL EFREMOVA. Moscow: Politizdat. 1992.

Kardashov, V.I. VOROSHILOV. Moscow: Mol.gvardiia. 1976.

Karol, K.S. BETWEEN TWO WORLDS. New York: Holt. 1987.

Karpov, V.V. MARSHAL ZHUKOV. Moscow: Voenizdat. 1992.

Karsten, Heiner. ICH WAR SOWJETSPITZE. Cologne: 1979.

KATYN: DOCUMENTS AND MATERIALS FROM THE SOVIET ARCHIVES. Warsaw: Institute of Political Studies, Polish Academy of Sciences. 1993.

KATYN, LISTA OFIAR I ZAGINIONYCH. Warsaw: ALFA. 1989.

KATYN, STAROBIELSK, OSTASZKOW, KOZIELSK. NAJNOWSZE DOKUMENT NKVD. Paris: Editions Dembinski. 1990.

KATYN WYBOR PUBLICYSTYKI 1943-1988 I "LISTA KATYNSKA." London: Polonia. 1988.

KATYNSKAIA DRAMA. Moscow: Politizdat. 1991.

Kavtaradze, A.G. VOENNYE SPETSIALISTY NA SLUZHBE RESPUBLIKII SOVETOV 1917–1920. Moscow: Nauka. 1988.

Kemp-Welch, Alice. STALIN AND THE LITERARY INTELLIGENTSIA, 1928-1939. New York: St. Martin. 1991.

Kersten, Krystyna. THE ESTABLISHMENT OF COMMUNIST RULE IN POLAND 1943-1948. Berkeley: University of California Press. 1991.

KGB OTKRYVAET TAINY. Moscow: Patriot. 1992.

Khenkin, Kirill. See Henkine, Cyrille.

Khlevniuk, O.V. 1937–I STALIN, NKVD I SOVETSKOE OBSHCHESTVO. Moscow: Respublika. 1992.

_____. 1937 GOD: PROTIVOSTOIANIE. Moscow: Znanie. 1991.

Kholkhov, N.E. IN THE NAME OF CONSCIENCE. New York: David McKay. 1959.

Khorobrykh, A.M. GLAVNYI MARSHAL AVIATSII A.A. NOVIKOV. Moscow: Voenizdat. 1989.

Khrushchev, N.S. KHRUSHCHEV O STALINE. New York: Teleks. 1989.

KHRUSHCHEV REMEMBERS. Boston: Little Brown. 1970.

Khrushchev, Sergei. KHRUSHCHEV ON KHRUSHCHEV. Boston: Little Brown. 1990.

Kiselev, A. OBLIK GENERALA A.A. VLASOVA. New York: Seraphim Foundation. 1976.

Knight, Amy. BERIA, STALIN'S FIRST LIEUTENANT. Princeton: Princeton University Press. 1993.

_____. THE KGB. Boston: Allen and Unwin. 1988.

Kolesnik, A.N.   GENERAL VLASOV: PREDATEL' I GEROI?   Moscow: Tekhinvest. 1991.

_____. MIFY I PRAVDA O SEM'E STALINA. Khar'kov: Prostor. 1991.

Kolesnik, A.N.   ROA-VLASOVSKAIA ARMIIA.   SUDEBNOE DELO A.A. VLASOVA I EGO SPODVIZHNIKOV. Khar'kov: Prostor. 1990.

Kol'tsov, P.S. DIPLOMAT FEDOR RASKOL'NIKOV. Moscow: Politizdat. 1990.

KOMANDARM LUKIN. Moscow: Voenizdat. 1990.

KOMISSARY. SBORNIK. Moscow: Mol.gvardiia. 1988.

KOMMUNISTY: SBORNIK. Moscow: Mol.gvardiia. 1976.

Kondrat'ev, N.D. MARSHAL BLIUKHER. Moscow: Voenizdat. 1965.

Kopelev, Lev. EASE MY SORROWS. New York: Random House. 1983.

_____. THE EDUCATION OF A TRUE BELIEVER. New York: Harper & Row. 1980.

_____. TO BE PRESERVED FOREVER. Philadelphia: Lippincott. 1977.

Korbonski, Stefan. THE JEWS AND THE POLES IN WORLD WAR II. New York: Hippocrene. 1989.

Kosyk, Volodymyr. THE THIRD REICH AND THE UKRAINE. New York: P. Lang. 1993.

Kovpak, S.A., Lt. General. VOSPOMINANIIA, OCHERKI, STAT'I. Kiev: Politizdat Ukrainy. 1987.

Kozhevnikov, M.N. KOMANDOVANIE I SHTAB VVS SOVETSKOI ARMII V VELIKOI OTECHESTVENNOI VOINE 1941–1945 gg. Moscow: Nauka. 1977.

KRASNOZNAMENNYI PRIBALTIISKII POGRANICHNYI. Riga: Avots. 1988.

Kreidlina, L.M. BOL'SHEVIK DRAGOTSENNOI PROBY. Moscow: Politizdat. 1990.

Kreindler, Isabelle. THE SOVIET DEPORTED NATIONALITIES, A SUMMARY AND UPDATE. Jerusalem: Hebrew University. 1985.

Krotkov, Yuri. THE RED MONARCH: SCENES FROM THE LIFE OF STALIN. New York: Norton. 1979.

Kuleshov, G.P. NEZAVISIMO OT ZVANIIA. Moscow: Politizdat. 1989.

Kunetskaia, L.I. and K.A. Mashtakova. KRUPSKAIA. Moscow: Mol.gvardiia. 1973.

Kusnierz, Bronislaw. STALIN AND THE POLES. London: Hollis & Carter. 1949.

Kuznetsov, N.G., Admiral of the Fleet of Soviet Union. NAKANUNE. Moscow: Voenizdat. 1966.

Kwiatkowska-Viatteau, Alexandra.   KATYN, L'ARMÉE POLINAISE ASSASSINEE. Brussels: Editions Complexe. 1989.

Laqueur, Walter. STALIN: THE GLASNOST REVELATIONS. London: Unwin Hyman. 1990.

Larina, Anna. THIS I CANNOT FORGET. New York: Norton. 1993.

Laskin, I.A. Lt. General. U VOLGI I NA KUBANI. Moscow: Voenzidat. 1986.

Laver, John. JOSEPH STALIN. London: Hodder and Stoughton. 1993.

Lazarev, L.L. KOSNUVSHIS' NEBA. Moscow: Profizdat. 1983.

Lebow, Richard and Janice Stein. WE ALL LOST THE COLD WAR. Princeton, NJ: Princeton University Press. 1994.

LENINGRADSKOE DELO. Leningrad: Lenizdat. 1990.

Leonard, Wolfgang. DIE REVOLUTION ENTLASST IHRE KINDER. Cologne: Kiepenheur. 1955.

LETCHIKI: SBORNIK. Moscow: Mol.gvardiia. 1978.

Levin, Nora. JEWS IN THE SOVIET UNION: A HISTORY FROM 1917 TO THE PRESENT. New York: New York University Press. 1988.

Levytsky, Boris. THE USES OF TERROR. New York: Coward. 1972.

LIUDI BESSMERTNOGO PODVIGA. Moscow: Politizdat. 1975.

LIUDI MOLCHALIVOGO PODVIGA. Moscow: Politizdat. 1987.

Low, Alfred. SOVIET JEWRY AND SOVIET POLICY. New York: Columbia University Press. 1990.

Lucas, James. KOMMANDO: GERMAN SPECIAL FORCES IN WORLD WAR II. New York: St. Martin. 1985.

Luckert, Yelena. SOVIET JEWISH HISTORY, 1917–1991: AN ANNOTATED BIBLIOGRAPHY. New York: Garland. 1992.

Lukacs, John. THE END OF THE TWENTIETH CENTURY. New York: Ticknor and Fields. 1993.

Lukas, Richard. FORGOTTEN HOLOCAUST: THE POLES UNDER GERMAN OCCUPATION. Lexington: University of Kentucky Press. 1986.

Lynch, Michael. STALIN AND KHRUSHCHEV. London: Hodder and Stoughton. 1990.

MacLean, Fitzroy. A PERSON FROM ENGLAND. London: Cape. 1958.

_____. ESCAPE TO ADVENTURE. Boston: Little Brown. 1950.

Maiskii, I.M. MEMOIRS OF A SOVIET AMBASSADOR. New York: Scribner. 1968.

Malcher, George. BLANK PAGES: SOVIET GENOCIDE AGAINST THE POLISH PEOPLE. Pyrford, UK: Pyrford Press. 1993.

Malenkov, A.G. O MOEM OTTSE GEORGII MALENKOVE. Moscow: Tekhoekos. 1992.

Malia, Martin. THE SOVIET TRAGEDY. New York: Free Press. 1994.

Mandel'shtam, Nadezhda. HOPE ABANDONED. London: Collins Havrill. 1989.

_____. HOPE AGAINST HOPE. London: Collins Havrill. 1989.

Marialin, G.A. POSTYSHEV. Moscow: Mol.gvardiia. 1965.

Mar'iamov, G.B. KREMLEVSKII TSENZOR. Moscow: Kinotsentr. 1992.

Markish, Esther. THE LONG RETURN. New York: Random House. 1978.

Marples, David. STALINISM IN THE UKRAINE IN THE 1940S. New York: St. Martin. 1993.

_____. UKRAINE IN WORLD WAR II. New York: REF-RL. 1985.

MARSHAL ZHUKOV KAKIM MY EGO POMNIM. Moscow: Politizdat 1988.

MARSHAL ZHUKOV: POLKOVODETS I CHELOVEK. Moscow: Novosti. 1988.

Marton, Kati. WALLENBERG. New York: Random House. 1982.

MASS DEPORTATIONS OF POPULATION FROM THE SOVIET OCCUPIED BALTIC STATES. Stockholm: Latvian National Foundation. 1981.

McCagg, William. STALIN EMBATTLED 1943-1948. Detroit: Wayne State University Press. 1978.

McCauley, Martin. STALIN AND STALINISM. Harlow, UK: Longman. 1983.

McLaughlin, Barry and Walter Szevera. POSTHUM-REHABILITIERT. DATEN ZU 150 ZZ OESTERREICHISCHEN STALIN-OPFERN. Vienna: Zentralkomitee der KPO. 1991.

McNeal, Robert. STALIN: MAN AND RULER. New York: New York University Press. 1988.

Mechetnyi, B. GRUPPA OSOBOGO NAZNACHENIIA. Moscow: Mosk. rabochii. 1987.

Medovoi, B.B. MIKHAIL I MARIIA. Moscow: Politizdat. 1991.

Medvedev, Roy. LET HISTORY JUDGE. New York: Columbia University Press. 1989.

_____. ALL STALIN'S MEN. Oxford: Basil Blackwell. 1983.

_____. ON STALIN AND STALINISM. New York: Oxford University Press. 1979.

Meissner, Boris. RUSSLAND IM UMBRUCH. Frankfort: Verlag für Geschichte und Politik. 1951.

Mel'nikov, S.I. MARSHAL RYBALKO. Kiev: Politizdat Ukariny. 1980.

Men'shagin, B.G. VOSPOMINANIIA. Paris: YMCA. 1988.

Mertsalov, A.N. STALINIZM I VOINA. Moscow: Rodnik. 1994.

Mertsalov, A.N. and L.A. Mertsalova. DOVOL'NO O VOINE? Voronezh: Voronezh. 1992.

Mikel'son, V.I. NAVECHNO V SERDTSE NARODOM. Riga: Avots. 1984.

MIKHAIL KOL'TSOV, KAKIM ON BYL. Moscow: Sov. pisatel'. 1989.

Mikhailov-Konchalovskii, A.S. and A. Lipkov. THE INNER CIRCLE. New York: Newmarket Press. 1991.

Misiunas, Romuald. THE ARCHIVES OF THE LITHUANIAN KGB. Cologne: Bundesinstitut für ostwissenschaftliche und internationale Studien. 1994.

Misiunas, Romuald and Rein Taagepera. THE BALTIC STATES: YEARS OF DEPENDENCE 1940-1990. Berkeley: University of California Press. 1993.

MISSIONARIES OF REVOLUTION: SOVIET ADVISERS AND NATIONALIST CHINA 1920–1927. Cambridge, MA: Harvard University Press. 1989.

Mitcham, Samuel Jr. HITLER'S FIELD MARSHALS AND THEIR BATTLES. Chelsea, MI: Scarborough House. 1985.

Mondich (Sinevirskii), M. SMERSH—GOD V STANE VRAGA. Frankfurt: Possev. 1984.

MORSKOI ENTIKLOPEDICHESKII SLOVAR'. Leningrad: Sudostroenie. 1991.

MOSAIC OF VICTIMS: NON-JEWS PERSECUTED AND MURDERED BY THE NAZIS. New York: New York University Press. 1990.

Moshkin, E.K. RAZVITE OTECHESTVENNOGO RAKETNOGO DVIGATELSTROENIIA. Moscow: Politizdat. 1973.

Moskoff, William. THE BREAD OF AFFLICTION: THE FOOD SUPPLY IN THE USSR DURING WORLD WAR II. New York: Cambridge University Press. 1990.

Moszynski, Adam. LISTA KATYNSKA. Warsaw: Omni Press. 1989.

Müller-Enbergs, H. DER FALL RUDOLF HERRNSTADT. Berlin: Universitas. 1991.

MY INTERNATSIONALISTY. Moscow: Politizdat. 1975.

NA LINII OGNIA. Moscow: Iuridizdat. 1976.

NA STRAZHE SOTSIALISTICHESKOI ZAKONNOSTI. 50 LET VOEN. TRIBUNALLAM. Moscow: Iurizdat. 1968.

NADEZHDA KONSTANTINOVA KRUPSKAIA: BIOGRAFIIA. Moscow: Politizdat. 1988.

NARDONOE OPOLCHENIE ZASHCHISHCHAET RODINU. Moscow: Nauka. 1990.

NASHE OTECHSTVO: OPYT POLITICHESKOI ISTORII. Moscow: Terra. 1991.

NE VYKHODIA IZ BOIA. RASSKAZY O CHEKISTATKH. Kuibyshev: Knizdat. 1984.

NEIZVESTNAIA CHERNAIA KNIGA. Moscow: Gosudarstvennyi arkhiv RF. 1994.

Nekrich, A.M. FORSAKE FEAR. Boston: Unwin Hyman. 1991.

_____. THE PUNISHED PEOPLES. New York: Norton. 1978.

Nenarokov, A.P. VERNOST' DOLGU. Moscow: Politizdat. 1989.

NEOTVRATIMOE VOZMEZDIE. Moscow: Voenizdat. 1973.

NEPRAVEDNYI SUD: POSLEDNII STALINSKII RASSTREL. Moscow: Nauka. 1994.

Neumann, Margarete Buber. UNDER TWO DICTATORS. London: Cape. 1949.

Newland, Samuel. COSSACKS IN THE GERMAN ARMY, 1941–1945. London: Frank Cass. 1991.

NEZRIMYI FRONT. Moscow: Voenizdat. 1961.

Nichol, Jim. STALIN'S CRIME AGAINST THE NON-RUSSIAN NATIONS: THE 1987-1990 REVELATIONS AND DEBATE. Pittsburgh: University of Pittsburgh Center for Russian and East European Studies. 1991.

Nichols, Thomas. THE SACRED CAUSE: CIVIL-MILITARY CONFLICT OVER SOVIET NATIONAL SECURITY 1917–1992. Ithaca, NY: Cornell University Press. 1993.

Niczyporowicz, Janus. BERIA. Wydawn, Poland: Polrus. 1990.

1937, TOL'KO FAKTY, TOL'KO IMENA. Moscow: 1992.

1939, LESSONS OF HISTORY. Moscow: Nauka. 1989.

1941 SAMOE, SAMOE... Moscow: Voenizdat. 1991.

Novikov, A.A., Chief Marshal of Aviation. V NEBE LENINGRADA. Moscow: Nauka. 1970.

Novikov, N.V. VOSPOMINANIIA DIPLOMATA: ZAPISKI 1938–1947. Moscow: Politizdat. 1989.

Novikov, V.N. NAKANUNE I V DNI ISPYTANII. Moscow: Politizdat. 1988.

O GRIGORII PETROVSKOM. Moscow: Politizdat. 1987.

O MIKHAILE KEDROVE. Moscow: Politizdat. 1988.

O NADEZHDE KRUPSKOI. Moscow: Politizdat. 1988.

Obermaier, Ernst. DIE RITTERKREUZTRÄGER DER LUFTWAFFE 1939–1945, JAGDFLIEGER. Mainz: Verlag Dieter Hofmann. 1966.

Obertas, I.L. KOMANDARM FED'KO. Moscow: Voenizdat. 1973.

ODNI POLITICHESKII PROTSESS. Moscow: 1989.

OGLASHENIIU PODLEZHIT. SSSR-GERMANIA 1939–1941. Moscow: Mosk. rabochii. 1991.

ON ALL FRONTS: CZECHOSLOVAKS IN WORLD WAR II. New York: Columbia University Press. 1992.

ONI NE MOLCHALI. Moscow: Politizdat. 1991.

OPERATSIIA "ULUSY." Elista. 1991.

ORGANIZATSIIA SUDA I PROKURATURY V SSSR. Moscow: Iuridizdat. 1961.

Orlov, Alexander. THE SECRET HISTORY OF STALIN'S CRIME. New York: Random House. 1953.

Ortenberg, D.I. SOROK TRETII. Moscow: Politizdat. 1991.

_____. MARSHAL MOSKALENKO. Kiev: Politizdat Ukrainy. 1984.

OSOBOE ZADANIE. Moscow: Mosk.rabochii. 1977.

THE OSS-NKVD RELATIONSHIP, 1943–1945. New York: Garland. 1989.

Ostriakov, S.Z. VOENNYE CHEKISTY. Moscow: Voenizdat. 1979.

Ozerov, G.A. See Sharagin, A.

PALACHI I ZHERTY. Moscow: Voenizdat. 1993.

Panin, D.M. LUBIANKA EKIBASTUZ: LAGERNYE ZAPISKI. Moscow: Skify. 1991.

Parrish, Michael. SOVIET SECURITY AND INTELLIGENCE ORGANIZATIONS 1917–1990. Westport, CT: Greenwood. 1992.

Patolichev, N.S. MEASURES OF MATURITY. Elmsford, NY: Pergamon. 1983.

Paul, Allen. KATYN: THE UNTOLD STORY. New York: Scribner. 1991.

Pegov, N.M. DALEKOE-BLIZKOE. Moscow: Politizda. 1982.

THE PENKOVSKY PAPERS. New York: Avon. 1965.

Pethybridge, Roger. HISTORY OF POSTWAR RUSSIA. London: Allen & Unwin. 1966.

Petroff, Serge. THE RED EMINENCE: A BIOGRAPHY OF MIKAIL A. SUSLOV. Clifton, NJ: Kingston. 1988.

Petrov, M.N. NA STRAZHE ZAKONNOSTI I PRAVOPORIADKA. Norogorod. 1987.

Petrov, Vladimir and Evdokia Petrov. EMPIRE OF FEAR. New York: Praeger. 1956.

Phillips, Hugh. BETWEEN THE REVOLUTION AND THE WEST: A POLITICAL BIOGRAPHY OF MAXIM M. LITVINOV. Boulder, CO: Westview. 1992.

Piatnitskaia, Iu. DNEVNIK ZHENY BOL'SHEVIKA. Benson, VT: Chalidze. 1987.

Pike, David. GERMAN WRITERS IN THE SOVIET UNION 1933–1945. Chapel Hill: University of North Carolina Press. 1982.

Pinkus, Benjamin. THE JEWS OF THE SOVIET UNION. New York: Cambridge University Press. 1988.

_____. THE SOVIET GOVERNMENT AND THE JEWS: 1948–1967. New York: Cambridge University Press. 1984.

Pliushchov, Boris. GENERAL MAL'TSEV. San Francisco: Globus. 1982.

Piotrowski, Tadeusz. VENGEANCE OF THE SWALLOWS. Jefferson, NC: McFarland. 1994.

Plyushch, Leonid. HISTORY'S CARNIVAL. New York: Harcourt Brace Jovanovich. 1979.

POD ZNAMENNES ISPANSKOI RESPUBLIKI, 1936-1939. Moscow: Nauka. 1965.

POEDINOK. Moscow: Mosk. rabochii. 1989.

POGRANICHNIKI. Moscow: Mol.gvardiia. 1973.

Polevoi, Boris. THE FINAL RECKONING: NUREMBERG DIARIES. Moscow: Progress. 1978.

Poliakov, L.E. TSENA VOINY. Moscow: Finansy i statitika. 1985.

POLICIES OF GENOCIDE. JEWS AND SOVIET PRISONERS OF WAR IN NAZI GERMANY. Boston: Allen & Unwin. 1986.

POLKOVODTSY GRAZHDANSKOI VOINY. Moscow: Mol.gvardiia. 1960.

POLKOVODTSY I VOENACHAL'NIKI VELIKOI OTECHESTVENNOI. Moscow: Mol. gvardiia. 1970, 1979, 1985.

Popov, Blagoi. OT PROTSEA V LAIPTSIG DO LAGERITE V SIBIR. Sofia: Khristo Botev. 1991.

Popovskii, M.A. DELO AKADEMIKA VAVILOVA. Ann Arbor, MI: Hermitage. 1983.

Poretsky, Elizabeth. OUR OWN FRIENDS. Ann Arbor: University of Michigan Press. 1970.

Pozdniakov, V.V. ANDREI ANDREEVICH VLASOV. Buenos Aires: Sembrador. 1979.

Pronin, Alexander. BIBLIOGRAPHY OF GUERRILLA ACTION IN THE USSR DURING WORLD WAR II. Springfield, VA: NTIS (AD 464 907). 1965.

Ra'anan, G.D. INTERNATIONAL POLICY FORMATION IN THE USSR. Hamden, CT: Archon. 1983.

Ra'anan, Uri. INSIDE THE APPARAT. Lexington, MA: Lexington. 1990.

Rachlin, Rachel. SIXTEEN YEARS IN SIBERIA. New York: Robert Speller. 1988.

Rapoport, Louis. STALIN'S WAR AGAINST THE JEWS. New York: Free Press. 1990.

Rapoport, Vitaly and Yuri Alexeev. HIGH TREASON. Durham, NC: Duke University Press. 1985.

Rapoport, Yakov. THE DOCTORS' PLOT OF 1953. Cambridge, MA: Harvard University Press. 1991.

Razgon, L.E. TRUE STORIES. Ann Arbor, MI: Ardis. 1994.

_____. NEPRIDUMANNOE. Moscow: Kniga. 1989.

RAZVEDCHIKI V BOIAKH ZA RODINU. Moscow: Politizdat. 1967.

REABILITIROVAN POSMERTNO. Moscow: Iuridlit. 1988.

Read, Anthony. THE DEADLY EMBRACE: HITLER, STALIN, AND THE NAZI-SOVIET PACT 1939-1941. New York: Norton. 1988.

Ready, J. Lee. THE FORGOTTEN AXIS, GERMANY'S PARTNERS AND FOREIGN VOLUNTEERS IN WORLD WAR II. Jefferson, NC: McFarland. 1987.

REAL TRUTH: PROFILES OF SOVIET JEWS. Moscow: Raduga. 1986.

Redlich, Simon. THE JEWS UNDER SOVIET RULE DURING WORLD WAR II. Ann Arbor, MI: University Microfilms. 1986.

_____. PROPAGANDA AND NATIONALISM IN WARTIME RUSSIA, THE JEWISH ANTIFASCIST COMMITTEE IN THE USSR, 1941–1948. Boulder, CO: East European Quarterly. 1982.

Rees, E.A. STALINISM AND SOVIET RAIL TRANSPORT, 1928–1941. New York: St. Martin. 1995.

REHABILITATSIIA. POLITICHESKIE PROTSESSY 30–50–X GODOV. Moscow: Politizdat. 1991.

Reitlinger, Gerald. HOUSE BUILT ON SAND. London: Weidenfeld and Nicolson. 1960.

Remnick, David. LENIN'S TOMB: THE LAST DAYS OF THE SOVIET EMPIRE. New York: Random House. 1993.

Resis, Albert. STALIN, THE POLITBURO, AND THE ONSET OF THE COLD WAR. Pittsburgh: University of Pittsburgh Center for Russian and East European Studies. 1988.

RESISTANCE IN THE GULAG. Moscow. 1992.

Richardson, Rosamond. STALIN'S SHADOW: INSIDE THE FAMILY OF ONE OF THE WORLD'S GREAT TYRANTS. New York: St. Martin. 1994.

Richter, James. RE-EXAMINING SOVIET POLICY TOWARDS GERMANY DURING BERIIA INTERREGNUM. Bonn: Bundeswehr Cold War International History Project. 1992.

Richter, Karel. PRIPAD GENERALS VLASOVA. Prague: Panorama. 1991.

Riehl, Nikolaus. ZEHN JAHRE IM GOLDENEN KÄFIG. Stuttgart: Dr. Rieder Verlag. 1988.

Rittersporn, Gabor Tamas. STALINIST SIMPLIFICATIONS AND SOVIET COMPLICATIONS: SOCIAL TENSIONS AND POLITICAL CONFLICTS IN THE USSR 1933–1953. New York: Harwood Academic. 1992.

Rohrwasser, Michael. DER STALINISMUS UND DIE RENEGATEN. Stuttgart: J.B. Metzler. 1991.

Romano-Petrova, N. STALIN'S DOCTOR, STALIN'S NURSE: A MEMOIR. Princeton, NJ: Kingston. 1984.

Romanov, A.I. NIGHTS ARE LONGEST HERE. Boston, MA: Little Brown. 1972.

Romanov, A.P. KOROLEV. Moscow: Mol.gvardiia. 1990.

Romanov, A.P. and V.S. Gubarev. KONSTRUKTORY. Moscow: Politizdat. 1989.

Rorlich, A.A. THE VOLGA TATARS. Stanford, CA: Hoover Institution Press. 1986.

Rosliakov, M.V. UBIISTVO KIROVA. Leningrad: Lenizdat. 1991.

Rosmus, Anna. WINTERGRUN: VERDRÄNGTE MORDE. Konstanz, Germany: Labhard. 1993.

Rubin, V.A. DNEVNIKI, PIS'MA. Tel Aviv: Biblioteka Aliia. 1988.

Ruge, Wolfgang. STALINISMMUS-EINE SACKGASSE IM LABYRINTH DER GESCHICHTE. Berlin: Deutcher Verlag der Wissenschaften. 1991.

RUKOVODIASHCHIY SOSTAV NKVD-NKGB-MVD-MGB 1936–1953. Samizdat. N.D.

Rumiantsev, N.M. GEROI KHALKHIN-GOLA. Moscow: Voenizdat. 1989.

Rummel, R.J. DEMICIDE, NAZI GENOCIDE AND MASS MURDER. New Brunswick, NJ: Transaction. 1991.

_____. LETHAL POLITICS. SOVIET GENOCIDE AND MASS MURDER SINCE 1917. New Brunswick, NJ: Transaction. 1990.

Ruthven, Malise. TORTURE, THE GRAND CONSPIRACY. London: Weidenfeld. 1978.

Rytov, A.G., Col. General of Aviation. RYTSARI PIATOGO OKEANA. Moscow: Voenizdat. 1968.

Sack, John. AN EYE FOR AN EYE. New York: Basic. 1993.

Safonov, N.S. ZAPISKI ADVOKATA: KRYMSKIE TATARY. Moscow: Vsia Moskva. 1990.

Sagajllo, Witold. MAN IN THE MIDDLE: A STORY OF THE POLISH RESISTANCE. New York: Hippocrene. 1985.

Sagdeev, R.Z. THE MAKING OF A SOVIET SCIENTIST. New York: Wiley. 1994.

Sakharov, A.D. MEMOIRS. New York: Knopf. 1990.

Samsonov, A.M. MOSKVA 1941. Moscow: Mosk. rabochii. 1991.

_____. ZNAT' I POMNIT'. Moscow: Politizdat. 1988.

Samsonov, V.A. PARUS PODNIMAIU. Petrozavodsk: Kareliia. 1993.

Sboichakov, M.I. MIKHAIL SERGEEVICH KEDROV. Moscow: Voenizdat. 1969.

SBZ-HANDBUCH. Munich: R. Oldenbourg. 1990.

Scammell, Michael. SOLZHENITSYN, A BIOGRAPHY. New York: W.W. Norton. 1984.

Schafranek, Hans. DIE BETROGENEN. OESTERREICHER ALS OPFER STALINISTISCHEN TERRORS IN DER SOWJETUNION. Vienna: Picus. 1991.

_____. ZWISCHEN NKVD UND GESTAPO: DIE AUSLIEFERUNG DEUTSCHER UND OSTERREICHISCHER ANTIFASCHISTEN AUS DER SOWJETUNION AN NAZIDEUTSCHLAND 1937–1941. Frankfort: ISP. 1990.

SCHAUPROZESSE UND POLITISCHE VERFOLGUNG IN MITTEL UND OSTEUROPA. Vienna: Mittler. 1991.

Schinke, Georg. RED CAGE. Lawrenceville, VA: Brunswick. 1994.

Schneider, Jost. VERLEIHUNG GENEHMIGT. San Jose, CA: R. James Bender. 1977.

Schulte, Theo. THE GERMAN ARMY AND NAZI POLICIES IN OCCUPIED RUSSIA. New York: St. Martin. 1989.

Schwendemann, Heinrich. DIE WIRTSCHAFTLICHE ZUSAMMENARBEIT ZWISCHEN DEM DEUTSCHEN REICH AND DER SOWJETUNION VON 1939 BIS 1941. Berlin: Akademie Verlag. 1993.

DIE SCHULZE-BOYSEN/HARNACK-ORGANISATION IM ANTI-FASCHISTISCHEN KAMPF. East Berlin: Dietz. 1970.

Sella, Amnon. THE VALUE OF HUMAN LIFE IN SOVIET WARFARE. New York: Routledge. 1992.

Semenov, Iu.I. KOMISSAR GOSBEZOPASNOSTI. Moscow: Politizdat. 1979.

Shainberg, Maurice. KGB SOLUTION AT KATYN. Franklin Lakes, NJ: Lincoln Springs Press. 1989.

_____. BREAKING FROM THE KGB. New York: Shapolsky. 1986.

Shakhurin, A.I., Col. General Aviation-Engineers. KRYL'IA POBEDY. Moscow: Voenizdat. 1990.

Shapiro, Gershon. EVREI-GEROI SOVETSKOGO SOIUZA. Tel Aviv. 1982.

Shapkin, N.I. ONI VOEVALI V RAZVEDKE. Petrozavodsk: Kareliia. 1992.

Sharagin, A. (Ozerov, G.A.) TUPOLEVSKAIA SHARAGA. Frankfort: Possev. 1971.

Shatunovkaia, L.A. ZHIZN' V KREMLE. New York: Chalidze. 1982.

Shchetinov, Iu.A. and B.A. Starkov. KRASNYI MARSHAL. Moscow: Mol. gvardiia. 1990.

Sheinis, Z.S. MAKSIM MAKSIMOVICH LITVINOV. Moscow: Politizdat. 1989.

Shomodyi, V.K. MARSHRUTAMI NARODNOI SLAVY. Moscow: Voenizdat. 1989.

Shtein, Eduard. KATYN, 1940. Warsaw: Glos. 1983.

Shtemenko, S.M. Army General. GENERAL'NYI SHTAB V GODY VOINY. Moscow: Voenizdat. 1985.

Shul'man, M.B. VOSPOMINANIIA, VSTRECHI, PORTRETY. Tel Aviv: 1984.

_____. BUTYRSKII DEKAMERON. Tel Aviv: 1979.

Shumukhin, V.S. SOVETSKAIA VOENNAIA AVIATSIIA, 1917-1941. Moscow: 1986.

SIKORSKI: SOLDIER AND STATESMAN. London: Orbis. 1990.

Simmons, P.J. ARCHIVAL RESEARCH ON THE COLD WAR ERA: A REPORT FROM BUDAPEST, PRAGUE AND WARSAW. Washington, DC: Cold War International History Project. 1992.

Simonian, M.N. EGO PROFESSIIA-REVOLIUTSIIA (N.V. KRYLENKO) Moscow: Znanie. 1975.

Simonov, K.M. GLAZAMI CHELOVEKA MOEGO POKOLENIIA: RAZMYSHLENIIA O I.V. STALINE. Moscow: Kniga. 1990.

Simpson, Christopher. THE SPLENDID BLONDE BEAST: MONEY, LAW AND GENOCIDE IN THE TWENTIETH CENTURY. New York: Grove Press. 1993.
_____. BLOWBACK: AMERICA'S RECRUITMENT OF NAZIS AND ITS EFFECT ON THE COLD WAR. London: Weidenfeld and Nicolson. 1988.
Sinevirskii, N. See Mondich, M.
Sinko, Ervin. ROMAN EINES ROMANS: MOSKAUER TAGEBUGH 1935–1937. Berlin: Das Arsenal. 1990.
Sivokhina, T.A. and M.P. Zezina. APOGEI REZHIMA LICHNOI VLASTI. Moscow: Mosk, Universiteta. 1993.
Skatov, N.N. KOL'TSOV. Moscow: Mol'gvardiia. 1983.
Skryl'nik, A.I. GENERAL ARMII A.A. EPISHEV. Moscow: Voenizdat. 1989.
SKRYTAIA PRAVDA VOINY: 1941 GODA. Moscow: Russkaia kniga. 1992.
Slowes, Salomon. THE ROAD TO KATYN: A SOLDIER'S STORY. Cambridge, MA: Blackwell. 1992.
Smith, Danny. WALLENBERG: LOST HERO. Springfield, IL: Templegate. 1987.
Soifer, Valerii. VLAST' I NAUKA: ISTORIIA RAZGROMA GENETIKI V SSSR. Tenafly, NJ: Ermitazh. 1989.
SOLDATY DZERZHINSKOGO SOIUZ BEREGUT, REKOMENDATEL'NYI UKAZATEL' LITERATURY. Moscow: Kniga. 1972.
Solzhenitsyn, A.I. THE GULAG ARCHIPELAGO. New York: Harper & Row. 1974.
_____. THE FIRST CIRCLE. New York: Harper & Row. 1968.
SOPROTIVLENIE V GULAGE. Moscow: Vozvrashchenie. 1992.
SOVETSKAIA MILITSIIA, 1917-1987. Moscow: Planeta. 1987.
SOVETSKAIA MILITSIIA: ISTORIIA I SOVREMENNOST' 1917–1987. Moscow: Iuridizdat. 1987.
SOVETSKAIA PROKURATURA. Moscow: Iuridizdat. 1982.
SOVETSKIE EVREI PISHUT IL'E ERENBURG 1943-1966. Jerusalem: Prisma. 1993.
SOVETSKIE INZHENERY. Moscow: Mol.gvardiia. 1985.
SOVETSKIE POLKOVODTSY I VOENACHAL'NIKI. Moscow: Mol. gvardiia. 1988.
SOVIET EMPIRE: PRISON HOUSE OF NATIONS AND RACES. Washington, DC: U.S. Senate Committee on the Judiciary. 1958.
SOVIET ENCYCLOPEDIA OF SPACE FLIGHT. Moscow: Mir. 1969.
SOVIET UNION IN EASTERN EUROPE, 1945-1989. New York: St. Martin's Press. 1994.
SOWJEISCHE FORSCHUNGEN (1917 bis 1991 ZUR GESCHICHTE DER DEUTSCH-RUSSIESCHEN BEZIEHUNGEN VON DEN ANFANGEN BIS 1941. BIBLIOGRAPHIE. Berlin: Akademie Verlag. 1992.
SOZVEZDIE POLKOVODTSEV. Khabarovsk: Kn.izd. 1972.
Spahr, William. ZHUKOV. Novato, CA: Presidio. 1993.

SSSR. CHEREZVYCHAINAIA GOS. KOMMISSIA PO USTANOVLENIIU I RASSLEDOVANIIU ZLODEIANII NEMETFASHIST ZAKVATCHIKOV. Moscow: Gospolitizdat. 1945.

Stadniuk, I.F. VOINA. Moscow: Sov. pisatel'. 1974, 1985.

Stajner, Karlo. 7000 DAYS IN SIBERIA. London: Corgi. 1989.

STALIN PHENOMENON.Moscow: Novosti Press Agency. 1988. London: Weidenfeld & Nicolson. 1993.

STALINIST TERROR: NEW PERSPECTIVES. New York: Cambridge University Press. 1993.

STALIN'S GENERALS. New York: Grove Press. 1993.

Steenbeck, Max. IMPULSE UND WIRKUNGEN. East Berlin: Verlag der Nation. 1983.

Stephan, Robert. DEATH TO SPIES: THE STORY OF SMERSH. (M.A. thesis) Washington, DC: American University. 1984.

STO SOROK BESED S MOLTOVYM. Moscow: Terra. 1991.

Stoliarov, K.A. GOLGOFA: DOKUMENTAL'NYE POVEST. Moscow: Goskompechati SSSR. 1991.

STRANITSY ISTORII KPSS. Moscow: Vysshaia shkola. 1988.

Streit, Christian. KEINE KAMERADEN: DER WEHRMACHT UND DIE SOWJETISCHEN KRIEGSGEFANGEN 1941–1945. Stuttgart: Deutsche Verlags-Anstalt. 1978.

Ströbinger, Rudolf. STALIN ENTHAPTET DIE ROTE ARMEE. Stuttgart: Deutsche Verlags-Anstalt. 1990.

Stuchenko, A.T., Army General. ZAVIDNAIA NASHA SUD'BA. Moscow: Voenizdat. 1968.

Stypulowski, Zbigniew. INVITATION TO MOSCOW. London: 1951.

SUD V SSSR. Moscow: Iuridizdat. 1977.

Sudoplatov, Pavel and Anatoli Sudoplatov. SPECIAL TASKS. New York: Little Brown. 1994.

Sul'ianov, A.K. ARESTOVAT' V KREMLE. O ZHIZNI I SMERTI MARSHAL BERIIA. Minsk: Mast. Lit. 1991.

SUROVAIA DRAMA NARODA. Moscow: Politizdat. 1989.

Suvorov, Viktor. ICEBREAKER. London: Hamish Hamilton. 1990.

_____. SOVIET MILITARY INTELLIGENCE. London: Grafton. 1986.

_____. INSIDE SOVIET MILITARY INTELLIGENCE. New York: Macmillan. 1984.

Sverdlov, F.D. EVREI-GENERALY VOORUZHENNYKH SIL SSSR. Moscow: Kniga i Biznes. 1992.

_____. V STROIU OTVAZHNYKH. OCHERKI O EVREIAKH-GEROIAKH SOVETSKOGO SOIUZA. Moscow: Kniga i Biznes. 1992.

Svianevich, Stanislav. V TENI KATYNI. London: Overseas Publications. 1989.

Svistunov, I.I. SKAZANIE O ROKOSSOVSKOM. Moscow: Voenizdat. 1976.

Swiatek, Romuald. THE KATYN FOREST. London: Panda. 1988.

Szasz, Thomas. KARL KRAUS AND THE SOUL-DOCTORS. Baton Rouge: Louisiana State University Press. 1976.

Szczesniak, Andrzej Leszek. KATYN TLO HISTORYCZNE, FAKTY DOKUMENT. Warsaw: Alfa. 1989.

Sztafrowski, Marcel. DIRECTION STALINO. UN POLONAIS DANS LES CAMPS SOVIETIQUE. Paris: Payot. 1987.

Tabachnik, G.D. SLAVA NE MERKET. Moscow: Politizdat. 1967.

Tarianov, N.V. NEVIDIMYE BOI. Moscow: Politizdat. 1964.

TARTARS OF THE CRIMEA, THEIR STRUGGLE FOR SURVIVAL. Durham, NC: Duke University Press. 1988.

TEHERAN, JALTA, POTSDAM: KONFERENZDOKUMENTE DER SOWJETUNION (3 volumes). Cologne: Pahl. 1986.

Telegin, K.F., Lt. General. VOINY NESCHITANNYE VERSTY. Moscow: Voenizdat. 1988.

Tolmachev, E.P. SOVREMENNYI VZLIAD NA ISTORIIU KOMINTERNA, 1924–1943. Moscow: Mosk Universiteta. 1992.

Tolstoy, Nikolai. STALIN'S SECRET WAR. London: Jonathan Cape. 1981.

_____. SECRET BETRAYAL. New York: Scribner. 1978.

Toranska, Teresa. "THEM": STALIN'S POLISH PUPPETS. New York: Harper & Row. 1987.

TRAGEDIA KOMUNISTYCZNEJ PARTII POLSKI. Warsaw: Ksiazka i Wiedza. 1989.

Trepper, Leopold. THE GREAT GAME. New York: McGraw-Hill. 1977.

Trukan, G.A. IAN RUDZUTAK. Moscow: Gospolitizdat. 1963.

Trushchenko, N.V. KOSAREV. Moscow: Mol.gvardiia. 1988.

Tsanava, L.F. VSENARODNAIA PARTIZANSKAIA VOINA V BELORUSSII. Minsk: Gizbel. 1949.

TSENA POBEDY. Moscow: Voenizdat. 1992.

Tsipko. Aleksandr. IS STALINISM REALLY DEAD? New York: Harper & Row. 1990.

Tucholski, Jedrzej. MORD W KATYNIU. Warsaw: PAX. 1991.

Tucker, Robert. STALIN IN POWER. New York: W.W. Norton. 1990.

Tumarkin, Nina. THE LIVING AND THE DEAD. New York: Basic. 1994.

Tuominen, Arvo. THE BELLS OF THE KREMLIN. Hanover, CT: University Press of New England. 1983.

U KREMLEVSKOI STENY. Moscow: Politizdat. 1980.

Ulam, Adam. THE COMMUNISTS. New York: Scribner. 1992.

_____. STALIN: THE MAN AND HIS ERA. Boston: Beacon Press. 1973.

_____. EXPANSION AND CO-EXISTENCE: THE HISTORY OF SOVIET FOREIGN POLICY 1917-1967. New York: Praeger. 1968.

Ulanonvskaia, N. and M. Ulanovskaia. ISTORIIA ODNOI SEM'I. New York: Chalidze. 1982.

UNICHTOZHENIE EVREEV V SSSR V GODY NEMETSKOI OKKUPATSII 1941-1944. Jerusalem: Iad-Va-Shem. 1992.

"UNPERSONEN"—WER WAREN SIE WILKLICH? BUCHARIN, RYKOW, TROTZKI, SINOWJEW,KAMENEW. Berlin: Dietz. 1990.

UPDATE ON RAOUL WALLENBERG. Washington, DC: House Committee on Foreign Affairs. 1983.

Usherovich, S. SMERTNYE KAZANI V TSARSKOI ROSSII. Kha'rkov: Kn.izd. 1933.

Uspenskii, V.D. TAINYI SOVETNIK VOZHDIA. Moscow: Voenizdat. 1992.

Ustinov, D.F., Marshal of the Soviet Union. VO IMIA POBEDY. Moscow: Voenizdat. 1988.

V.P. CHKALOV. Moscow: Planeta. 1984.

V POEDINKE S ABVEROM. Moscow: Voenizdat. 1968.

Vaksberg, A.I. STALIN AGAINST THE JEWS. New York: Knopf. 1994.

_____. NERASKRYTYE TAINY. Moscow: Novosti. 1993.

_____. STALIN'S PROSECUTOR. New York: Grove Weidenfeld. 1991.

_____. THE PROSECUTOR AND THE PREY: VYSHINSKY AND THE 1930s MOSCOW TRIALS. London: Weidenfeld and Nicolson. 1990.

Vasetskii, N. LIKVIDATSIIA. Moscow: Mosk.rabochii. 1989.

Vasil'ev, A.N. V CHAS DNIA VASHE PREVOSKHODITEL'STVO. Moscow: Sov. pisatel'. 1984.

Vasil'eva, L.N. KREMLEVSKIE ZHENY. Moscow: VAGRIUS. 1994.

VELIKIA OTECHESTVENNAIA VOINA SOVETSKOGO NARODA. Moscow: Voenizdat. 1991.

VERKHOVNYI SUD SSSR. Moscow: Iuridizdat. 1977.

VERNOST' DOLGU. OCHERKI O RAZVEDCHIKAKH. Moscow: Politizdat. 1984.

Viktorov, B.A., Lt. General of Judiciary. BEZ GRIFA "SEKRETNO." ZAPISKI VOENNOGO PROKURORA. Moscow: Iuridizdat. 1990.

Viktorov, I.V. PODPOL'SHCHIK, VOIN, CHEKIST. Moscow: Politizdat. 1963.

Vishniakova-Akimova, V.V. TWO YEARS IN REVOLUTIONARY CHINA. Cambridge, MA: Harvard University Press. 1971.

Vizulis, I. Joseph. THE MOLOTOV-RIBBENTROP PACT OF 1939: THE BALTIC CASE. New York: Praeger. 1989.

_____. NATIONS UNDER DURESS: THE BALTIC STATES. Port Washington, NY: Associated Faculty Press. 1985.

VMESTE S PATRIOTAMI ISPANII. Kiev: Politizdat. Ukrainy. 1978.

VNUTRENNIE VOISKA V VELIKOI OTECHESTVENNOI VOINE. 1941–1945. DOKUMENTY I MATERIALY. Moscow: Iurizdat. 1975.

VOENNYE KONTRRAZVEDCHIKI. OSOBYM OTEDELAM VCHK-KGB 60 LET. Moscow: Voenizdat. 1978.

VOINA GERMANII PROTIV SOVETSKOGO SOIUZA 1941–1945. Berlin: Argon. 1992.

Voitoloskaia, A.L. PO SLEDOM SUD'BY MOEGO POKOLENIIA. Moscow: 1990.

Vol'f, Markus. PO SOBSTVENNOMY ZADANIIU: PRIZNANIIA I RAZUM'IA. Moscow: Mezhdunarod. otnos. 1992.

Volkogonov, D.A., Col. General. TROTSKII. Moscow: Novosti. 1992. (2 volumes).

_____. TRIUMF I TRAGEDIIA. Moscow: Novosti. 1989.

Volkov, F.D. VZLET I PAPEDNIE STALINA. Moscow: Spektr. 1992.

Von Bergh, Hendrik. DIE WARRHEIT UBER KATYN. Berg am See: Kurt Vowinckel. 1986.

Von Herwarth, Johnnie. AGAINST TWO EVILS. London: Collins. 1981.

Von Heuer, Gerd. DIE DEUTSCHEN GENERAL-FLEDMARSCHALLE UND GROSSADMIRALE. Rastatt/Baden: Erich Pabel Verlag. 1978.

Voronov, N.N., Chief Marshal of Artillery. NA SLUZHBE VOENNOI. Moscow: Voenizdat. 1963.

Voskresenskaia (Rybkina), Z. TEPER' IA MOGU SKAZAT' PRAVDU. Moscow: Respublika. 1993.

VOSPOMINAMIIA OB I.V. KURCHATOVE. Moscow: Nauka. 1988.

Vovsi-Mikhoels, Nataliia. MOI OTETS SOLOMON MIKHOELS. Tel Aviv: 1984.

VOZHD, KHOZIAN DIKTATOR. Moscow: Patriot. 1990.

VOZVRASHCHENNYE IMENA. Moscow: APN. 1989.

VOZVRASHCHENNYE IMENA: SOTRUDNIKI AN BELARUSI POSTRADAVSHIE V PERIOD STALIN REPRESSII. Minsk: Nauka i technika. 1992.

VTORIA UDARNAIA V BITVE ZA LENINGRAD. Leningrad: Lenizdat. 1983.

VYSSHII SUDEBNYI ORGAN SSSR. Moscow: Iuridizdat. 1984.

Walichnowski, Tadeusz. DEPORTACJE I PRZEMIESZCZENIA LUDNOSCI POLSKIEJ W GLAB ZSRR, 1939–1945. Warsaw: PWN. 1989.

Ward, Chris. STALIN'S RUSSIA. New York: Edward Arnold. 1993.

Wat, Aleksander. MY CENTURY: THE ODYSSEY OF A POLISH INTELLECTUAL. Berkeley: University of California Press. 1988.

Weber, Hermann. "WEISSE FLECKEN" IN DER GESCHICHTE, DIE KPDOPFER DER STALINSCHEN SAUBERUNGEN UND IHRE REHABILITIERUNG. Frankfurt: ISP Verlag. 1990.

Weber, Hermann and Dietrich Staritz. KOMMUNISTEN VERFOLGEN KOMMUNISTEN. STALINISCHER TERROR UND "SABERUNGEN" IN DEN KOMMUNISTISCHEN PARTEIEN EUROPAS SEIT DREISSIGER JAHREN. Berlin: Akademie Verlag. 1993.

Weissberg, Alexander. THE ACCUSED. New York: Simon and Schuster. 1951.

Werbell, Frederick and Thurston Clarke. LOST HERO: THE MYSTERY OF RAOUL WALLENBERG. New York: McGraw-Hill. 1982.

Werblan, Andrzej. STALINIZM W POLSCE. Warsaw: Fakt. 1991.

_____. WLADYSLAW GOMULKA. Warsaw: Ksiazka i Wiedza. 1988.

Werth, Nicolas. LES PROCES DE MOSCOU. Brussels: Editions Complexe. 1987.

Wieczorek, Mieczyslaw. ARMIA LUDOWA. Warsaw: Ministry of Defense. 1979, 1984.

Williams, Eugene. GULAG TO INDEPENDENCE: PERSONAL ACCOUNTS OF LATVIAN DEPORTEES SENT TO SIBERIA UNDER THE STALIN REGIME, 1941–1953. Decatur, MI: Johnson Graphics. 1992.

Wingate-Pike, David. IN THE SERVICE OF STALIN: THE SPANISH COMMUNISTS IN EXILE. New York: Oxford University Press. 1993.

WITNESS: WRITINGS FROM THE ORDEAL OF COMMUNISM. New York: Freedom House. 1993.

Wittlin, Thaddeaus. COMMISSAR. New York: Macmillan. 1972.

Wolin, Simon and Robert Slusser. THE SOVIET SECRET POLICE. New York: Praeger. 1957.

Wolton, Thierry. LE KGB EN FRANCE. Paris: B. Grasset. 1986.

WORLD WAR II AND THE SOVIET PEOPLE. New York: St. Martin. 1993.

Yost, Graham. KGB. New York: Facts on File. 1989.

Zaitsev, A.D. ZACHISLEN NAVECHNO. Moscow: Polizdat. 1990.

Zarod, Kazimierz. INSIDE STALIN'S GULAG. Sussex: The Book Guild. 1990.

ZAROK: POVEST', RASSKAZY, VOSPOMINANIIA. Moscow: Mol.gvardiia. 1989.

Zawodny, J.K. DEATH IN THE FOREST. Notre Dame, IN: University of Notre Dame Press. 1962.

Zhigulin, A.V. CHERNYE KAMNI. Moscow: Kh.palata. 1989.

_____. ZAROK. Moscow: Mol.gvardiia. 1989.

Zhukov, G.K., Marshal of the Soviet Union. VOSPOMINANIIA I RAZMYSHLENIIA. Moscow: Novosti. 1990.

Zil'manovich, D.Ia. NA ORBITE BOLSHOI ZHIZNI. Vil'nius: Mintis. 1971.

Zonin, S.A. ADMIRAL L.M. GALLER. Moscow: Voenizdat. 1991.

Zorin, L.I. OSOBOE ZADANIE. Moscow: Politizdat. 1987.

Zubok, V.M. SOVIET INTELLIGENCE AND THE COLD WAR: THE "SMALL" COMMITTEE OF INFORMATION 1952-1953. Washington, DC: Woodrow Wilson International Center for Scholars. 1992.

ZVEN'IA: ISTORICHESKII AL'MANAKH. Paris: Atheneum. 1990.

Zverev, A.G. ZAPISKI MINISTRA. Moscow: Politizdat. 1973.

SELECTED LIST OF REFERENCE SOURCES

5000 SOWJETKOPFE
BELARUSKAIA SAVESKAIA ENCYKLAPEDIIA
BIOGRAPHIC DIRECTORY OF 100 LEADING SOVIET OFFICIALS
BIOGRAPHICAL DICTIONARY OF THE SOVIET UNION
BIOGRAPHICAL DICTIONARY OF THE FORMER SOVIET UNION
BOEVOI PUT' SOVETSKIKH POGRANICHNYKH VOISK
BOLSHAIA SOVETSKAIA ENTSIKLOPEDIIA
BOL'SHOI ENTSIKLOPEDICHESKII SLOVAR'
CHEKISTY AZERBAIDZHANA

DEPUTATY VERKHOVNOGO SOVETA SSSR
DIPLOMATICHESKII SLOVAR'
ENCYCLOPEDIA OF RUSSIAN HISTORY
ENTSIKLOPEDICHESKII SLOVAR'
EZHEGODNIK BOLSHAIA SOVETSKAIA ENTSIKLOPEDIA
GEROI OKTIABRIA
GEROI SOVETSKOGO SOIUZA. KRATKII BIOGRAFICHESKII SLOVAR'
ISTORIIA URAL'SKOGO VOENNOGO OKRUGA
ISTORIIA PRIBALTIISKOGO VOENNOGO OKRUGA 1940–1967
KIESVKII KRASNOZNAMENNYI
KRASNOZNAMENNYI BELORUSKII VOENNYI OKRUG
KRASNOZNAMENNYI DAL'NEVOSTOCHNYI
KRASNOZNAMENNYI ODESSKII
KRASNOZNAMENNYI PRIBALTIISKII POGRANICHNYI
KRASNOZNAMENNYI SEVERO-KAVKAZSKII
KRASNOZNAMENNYI SEVERO-ZAPADNYI POGRANICHNYI OKRUG
KRASNOZNAMENNYI TURKESTANSKII
KRASNOZNAMENNYI ZAKAVKAZKII
KSIEGA POLAKOW UCZESTNIKOW REWOLUCJI PAZDZIERNIKOWEJ
    1917–1920 BIOGRAFIE
LATVJU ENCIKLOPEDIJA 1962–1982
LEADERSHIP OF THE CENTRAL COMMITTEE OF THE CPSU
MALAIA SOVETSKAIA ENTSIKLOPEDIIA
MILITARY-NAVAL ENCYCLOPEDIA OF RUSSIA AND THE SOVIET UNION
MODERN ENCYCLOPEDIA OF RUSSIAN AND SOVIET HISTORY
MOLODYE DOZORNYI RODINY. KRATKII OCHERK ISTORII
    KOMSOMOL'SKIKH ORGANIZATSII POGRANICHNYKH VOISK, 1918–
    1987
NAVECHNO V SERDTSE NARODOM
ODESSKII KRASNOZNAMENNYI
ORDENA LENINA ZABAIKAL'SKII
ORDENA LENINA LENINGRADSKII VOENNYI OKRUG
ORDENA LENINA MOSKOVSKII VOENNYI OKRUG
POGRANICHNYE VOISKA...all volumes
POLSKI SLOWNIK BIOGRAFICZNY
PROMINENT PERSONALITIES IN THE USSR
RADIO LIBERTY—RADIO FREE EUROPE REPORTS
SOBRANIE POSTANOVELNII I RASPORIAZHENII...
SOBRANIE ZAKONOV I RASPORIAZHENII...
SOVETSKAIA ISTORICHESKAIA ENTSIKLOPEDIIA
SOVETSKAIA VOENNAIA ENTSIKLOPEDIIA
SOVETSKII ENTSIKLOPEDICHESKII SLOVAR'
SOVETSKOE GOSUDARSTVO I PRAVO
SOVIET ARMED FORCES REVIEW ANNUAL

SOVIET BIOGRAPHICAL SERVICE
SOVIET GOVERNMENT OFFICIALS, 1922–1941
UKRAINSKA RAD'IANS'KA ENTSIKLOPEDIIA
UKRAINSKAIA SOVETSKAIA ENTSIKLOPEDIIA
UKRAINSKAIA SSR V VELIKOI OTECHESTVENNOI VOINE SOVETSKOGO
   SOIUZA, 1941–1945
USSR FACTS AND FIGURES
V PLAMENI I SLAVE. OCHERKI ISTORII SIBIRSKOGO VOENNOGO
   OKRUGA
V.I. LENIN I VCHK
VEDOMOSTI S'EZDA NARODNYKH DEPUTATOV I VERKHONOGO
   SOVETA SSSR 1954—VEDOMOSTI VERKHOVNOGO SOVETA SSSR,
   1938–1962
VELIKAIA OTECHESTVENNAIA VOINA 1941–1945. DLOVAR'-
   SPRAVOCHNIK.
VELIKAIA OTECHESTVENNAIA VOINA 1941–1945. SOBYTIIA, LIUDI,
   DOKUMENTY. KRATKII ISTORICHESKII SPRAVOCHNIK
VNUTRENNIE VOISKA...all volumes
VOENNYE ARKHIVY ROSSII
VOENNYE KONTRRAZVEDCHIKI
VOENNYI ENTSIKLOPEDICHESKII SLOVAR'
WHO WAS WHO IN THE SOVIET UNION
ZABAIKAL'SKII VOENNYI OKRUG

SELECTED LIST OF RUSSIAN JOURNALS AND NEWSPAPERS

AGITATOR
ARGUMENTY I FAKTY
BAKUNSKII RABOCHII
CHAS PIK
DAUGAVA
DNI
DONISH
DRUZHBA NARODOV
EKHO PLANETY
ENISEI
GOLOS KURDA
GOLOS RODINY
GORIZONT
GRANITSA
GROZNENSKII RABOCHII
NOSTRANNAIA LITERATURA
INTERNATIONAL AFFAIRS (MOSCOW)

ISTORICHESKII ARKHIV
ISTORICHESKII ZHURNAL
ISTORIIA VELKOI OTECHESTVENNOI VOINY SOVETSKOGO SOIUZA
ISTORIIA SSR
IUNOST'
IZVESTIIA
IZVESTIIA TSK KPSS
KAVKAZSKII RABOCHII
KENTAVR
KHRONIKA TEKUSHCHIKH SOBYTII
KIEVSKIE NOVOSTI
KNIZHNOE OBOZRENIE
KOMMUNIST
KOMMUNIST BELORUSSII
KOMMUNIST GRUZII
KOMMUNIST VOORUZHENNYKH SIL
KOMSOMOL'SKAIA PRAVDA
KOMSOMOL'SKOE ZNAMIA
KRASNAIA ZVEZDA
KURANTY
LENINGRASKAIA PRAVDA
LITERATURNAIA ARMENIIA
LITERATURNAIA GAZETA
LITERATURNAIA GRUZIIA
LITERATURNAIA ROSSIIA
LITERATURNOE OBOZRENIE
LITERATURNY KIRGIZSTAN
LITERATURULI SAKARTVELO
MEZHDUNARODNAIA ZHIZN
MOLODOI KOMMUNIST
MOSCOW NEWS
MOSKOVSKAIA PRAVDA
MOSKOVSKII KOMSOMOLETS
MOSKOVSKIKH NOVOSTEI
NA BOEVOM POSTU
NA RUBEZHE (Paris)
NASH SOVREMENNIK
NAUKA I ZHIZN'
NEDELIA
NEMAN
NEVA
NEW TIMES INTERNATIONAL
NEZAVISIMAIA BALTISKAIA GAZETA
NEZAVISIMAIA GAZETA

NORIL'SKII MEMORIAL
NOVAIA I NOVEISHAIA ISTORIIA
NOVO VREMIA
NOVOE RUSSKOE SLOVO
NOVYI MIR
NOVYI ZHURNAL (New York)
OBSHCHAIA GAZETA
OGONEK
ORLOVSKII PRAVDA
OTECHESTVENNAIA ISTORIIA
POGRANICHNIK
POISK
POLITICHESKOE OBRAZOVANIE
POLITICHESKII DNEVNIK
POLITICHESKII DNEVNIK (Amsterdam)
POLITICHSKII SOBESEDNIK (Minsk)
POZYVNYE ISTORII
PRAVDA
PRAVDA GRUZII
PRAVDA UKRAINY
RABOCHAIA TRIBUNA
RABOCHII KLASS I SOVREMENNYI MIR
RAZDANSKA UKRAINA
RODINA
ROSSIIA
ROSSIISKAIA GAZETA
RUKHOVODIASHCHII SOSTAV
RUSSKAIA MYSL'
RUSSKAIA REKLAMA
SEGODNIA
SEL'SKAIA MOLODEZH
SEVER (Petrozavodsk)
SHCHIT I MECH
SOIUZ
SLAVA I CHEST'
SLOVO
SMENA
SOBESEDNIK
SOBRANIE POSTANOVLENII
SOIUZ
SOTSIALISTICHESKAIA INDUSTRIIA
SOTIAL'NO—POLITICHESKIE NAUKI
SOTSIOLOGICHESKIE ISSLEDOVANIIA
SOVERSHENNO SEKRETNO

SOVETSKAIA BELORUSIIA
SOVETSKAIA ESTONIIA
SOVETSKAIA ETNOGRAFIIA
SOVETSKAIA KUL'TURA
SOVETSKAIA LITVA
SOVETSKAIA MILITSIA
SOVETSKAIA ROSSIIA
SOVETSKAIA TATARIIA
SOVETSKIE ARKHIVY
SOVETSKOE GOSUDARSTVO I PRAVO
SOVETSKOI ROSSII
SOVIET WEEKLY
SPUTNIK
SSSR. VNUTRENNIE PROTIVORECHIA (New York)
STOLITSA
TEATR
TEEGIN GERIA (Elista)
TRIBUNA
TIKHOOKEANSKAIA ZVEZOA
TRUD
UKRANINSKII ISTORICHESKII ZHURNAL
VECHERNIIA MOSKVA
VECHERNII MINSK
VESTNIK AKADEMII NAUK SSSR
VISTI Z UKRAINI
VOENNO ISTORICHESKII ZHURNAL (VIZH)
VOENNYE ARKHIVY ROSSII
VOENNYI VESTNIK
VOLIA
VOPROSY FILOSOFII
VOPROSY ISTORII
VOPROSY ISTORII KPSS
VOPROSY LITERATURY
VZGLIAD
ZARIA VOSTOKA
ZASHCHITNIK RODINY
ZNAMAIA
ZVEZDA

Index

About the Author

MICHAEL PARRISH is Associate Professor, School of Public and Environmental Affairs, Indiana University. He is a recognized authority on Soviet history during the Stalin period. Among his earlier publications are *Soviet Armed Forces, USSR in World War II*, *The Battle for Moscow*, and *Soviet Security and Intelligence Organizations* (Greenwood Press, 1992).

ISBN 0-275-95113-8

90000>

HARDCOVER BAR CODE